Theorizing Rituals: Annotated Bibliography of Ritual Theory, 1966–2005

Numen Book Series

Studies in the History of Religions

VOLUME 114–2

Theorizing Rituals: Annotated Bibliography of Ritual Theory, 1966–2005

Jens Kreinath
Jan Snoek
Michael Stausberg

BRILL

LEIDEN • BOSTON
2007

Cover photo by Jerry Martin

This book is printed on acid-free paper.

Library of Congress Cataloging-in-Publication Data

A C.I.P. record is available from the Library of Congress

ISSN 0169-8834
ISBN 978 90 04 15343 1

PRINTED IN THE NETHERLANDS

CONTENTS

Preface and Acknowledgment (M. Stausberg) vii
Introduction (M. Stausberg) ix

THE BIBLIOGRAPHY

Part A: Primary Literature (442 items) 3
Part B: Secondary Literature (82 items) 487
Part C: Lexicon Articles (96 items) 501
Part D: Readers (8 items) 513
Part E: Bibliographies (5 items) 521

APPENDICES

A: Chronological Listing of Items in the Bibliography (all 620 items) 527
B: Items in the Bibliography of Primary Literature (= Part A) Related to Key-words 538
C: Abbreviations of Titles of Periodicals, Used in the References to the Reviews of Monographs and Edited Volumes (in Parts A, D & E) 559
D: List of Authors Whose Work is Discussed in the Secondary Literature (in Part B) 566
E: Addresses of Contributors to *Theorizing Rituals* 568

PREFACE AND ACKNOWLEDGMENTS

The genesis of this work has been explained in the Preface to Volume I. At this point, for reasons spelled out in the subsequent Introduction, I wish to emphasize that the authors consider Volume II to be more than a mere appendix to Volume I.

This volume is an attempt to map four decades of ritual theory and to make the fruits of this rich collective and interdisciplinary intellectual endeavor conveniently accessible to the scholars and scholarly communities currently engaged in the study of rituals. The annotated bibliography lists a total of 620 carefully selected titles out of which 455 are annotated. It aims to help students and beginners alike to find their way into the rich field of ritual theory; by condensing past theoretical efforts of this field of inquiry it hopes to stimulate future theorizing. In a way, this bibliography attempts to establish ritual theory as a more coherent branch of scholarship in the first place.

Once more, it is my pleasant duty to express our gratitude to a number of institutions and individuals. To begin with, the authors wish to thank the German Research Foundation (*Deutsche Forschungsgemeinschaft*) for enabling our work as part of an Emmy Noether research group in the period 2000 to 2003/4. Moreover, we wish to express our gratitude to the collaborative research center on Ritual Dynamics (*Ritualdynamik*) at the University of Heidelberg (started in 2002) and the Institute for Religious Studies (*Institut für Religionswissenschaft*) directed by Gregor Ahn at the same university.

The format of the bibliography was initially devised by Jan Snoek (based on his two prior published annotated bibliographies on canonization/de-canonization and religious polemics). It was refined after Jens Kreinath became part of the group (in 2001) and started to work on the bibliography. Jens initially wrote most of the abstracts and provided crucial input on the selection of titles to be included in the first place. Moreover, he came up with many creative suggestions that we have adopted when jointly devising a system of refining the format of the bibliography in order to enhance its utility. The technical details will be explained in the Introduction. Throughout the years Jan took care of the database. Moreover, he coordinated the preparation of the final typescript, seeing it through a final round of proofs. Without his prudent and vigilant, but extremely time-consuming management of the database and the typescript the present work would never have been completed.

A number of people have shared part of our work with this bibliography. We gratefully acknowledge the various efforts of Marcus Brainard, Thorsten Gieser, Florian Jeserich, Dorothea Lüddeckens, and Thorsten Storck who all for briefer or longer periods of time were part of our research group. Moreover, Jan Snoek wishes to thank his student assistants Jürgen Kaufmann, Alexandra Heidle, Florian Schaurer and Mariana Pinzón for their help in completing the information in the database in the course of these years. Last but not least, some of the authors of Volume I have come with some valuable advice and contributions to the bibliography.

Composing this bibliography has forced us to do extensive reading of a vast amount of literature which we otherwise probably would never have looked at, and only part of the works we have read has been selected for inclusion in the bibliography. Reading and discussing the literature (and the resulting abstracts) have been at the same time tiring and stimulating processes and we hope that reading the bibliography will in turn be rewarding for the readers and encourage them to theorize.

Bergen, October 2006/February 2007 Michael Stausberg

INTRODUCTION

Michael Stausberg

This introduction tries to argue why the authors consider Volume II to be more than a mere appendix to Volume I. Furthermore, it will comment on the composition of the bibliography and will introduce some of its main features and tools.

Constructing and Reviewing Ritual Theories

Constructing a theory of ritual is a comparatively simple task. Here are some operating guidelines. One may try out any of the following strategies:

- The prototype strategy: Take the ritual you are mostly familiar with, and elaborate on whatever you may regard as theoretically noteworthy characteristics of this ritual (and hence: ritual in general). Theoretically noteworthy are these features that may strike you as constituting the character of the respective action, behavior, or event as ritual (in contradistinction to non-ritual actions, behaviors, or events).
- The application strategy: Take a theory that works for classes of phenomena that in significant ways are analogous or homologous with rituals, and try to transfer the insights from that theory. Make sure not to forget the differences!
- The deviance strategy: Let's assume that ritual is clearly distinct from non-ritual, i.e. from 'ordinary' or 'everyday' reality; hence take a theory of any aspect of 'the real world' and look for where ritual deviates from the 'ordinary' order of things.
- The functional strategy: Wherever the order of things is at an impasse, ritual may well be the way out. Or else ritual may well be the mechanism ultimately holding the ordinary order of things together.
- The history strategy: Let's take it that rituals once originated in the history of mankind, or that they are a thing of the past; wouldn't that what was respectively new or outdated about rituals give us a clue about the origin and function of ritual?

Of course, one may combine these strategies—in fact, this is how it often happens—and there are other promising strategies as well. The point with that caricature (according to the *Oxford English Dictionary* a "[g]rotesque or ludicrous representation of persons or things by exaggeration of their most characteristic and striking features"), is not to debase or to map extant theories of rituals. Quite to the contrary! But if ritual theory needs to be taken seriously, then past attempts in that direction should not be ignored.

The second volume of this work aims to counteract the prevailing idea that theorizing rituals[1] primarily means constructing new theories of rituals. While new theories are obviously welcome and important,[2] there is a danger of forgetting the insights created by earlier scholars (apart from the few standard authors such as V.W. Turner, A. van Gennep, C. Geertz or É. Durkheim,[3] whose work moreover is in the available literature often referred to in a rhetorical and selective if not altogether distorted manner). If one does not as a matter of principle (or for the sake of convenience or as a result of professional egomania and laziness) reject all prior theoretical efforts as sheer nonsense, ignoring earlier theoretical approaches may seriously impede the progress of ritual theory as a sustained and coherent field of study. Moreover, it is only by engaging in critical dialogue with past or present theorists that the field can seriously hope for progress. Sadly, there is little dialogue of that kind available in the extant literature.[4] The present volume will hopefully facilitate such critical theoretical engagement for the future development of the field.

In part, the absence of a sustained critical debate may result from the fact that ritual theories have been developed within a wide range

---

[1] For the authors' understanding of the project of 'theorizing' see the "Introductory Essay" to Volume I, [xiii]–xxv. A similar approach is now sketched by J. Beckford, "'A Minimalist Sociology of Religion'?", J.A. Beckford and J. Walliss (eds), *Theorising Religion. Classical and Contemporary Debates* (Aldershot, Burlington, 2006), 182–196, who briefly refers to "this spirit of instrumental and open-ended theorising" (182).

[2] It has recently been pointed out that "putting forth succesfull 'theories'" is a powerful means for scholars/scientists to gain status within their profession and that "theory-building has more status than theory testing", J.V. Spickard, "Narrative Versus Theory in the Sociology of Religion. Five Stories of Religion's Place in the Late Modern World", Beckford and Walliss (eds), *Theorising Religion*, 169–181, here 179.

[3] See also Jeserich in Volume I, 688–690.

[4] In an essay critically discussing Jonathan Smith's theory of ritual, Ronald Grimes has deplored the general "tendency in ritual studies for theorists to talk past one another, or worse, never to engage one another's ideas either in public or in print" (Grimes 1999, 271).

of scholarly disciplines and intellectual traditions that sometimes may appear quite remote from the close neighborhoods in which most scholars are navigating most of the time in the current age of academic specialization. While it is very well possible that we have missed out on some ritual theories, our ambition has been to present an as complete and various theoretical scenario as possible.

However, our aim with the present volume is not to engage in a theoretical discussion of past theories, but, more modestly, to outline the theoretical arguments of a vast number of theoreticians as a means of laying the ground for future theoretical debates. Therefore we made it a policy to keep our presentation of the content of the titles as unbiased and neutral as possible. This policy finds its stylistic expression in phrasings such as "according to the author" or "the author argues". This is meant to indicate that we tried our best to focus on the authors' arguments and to provide an as neutral presentation as possible, even where the author's argument failed to convince us. We tried hard not to be judgmental and to conceal positive as well as negative attitudes to the content that we summarize. That has not always been as easy as it might appear at first sight. While we did our best to provide fair summaries, not all content is equally easy to summarize.[5] Moreover, not all of us are having the same way of summarizing contents. Some summaries are more abstract, while others go more into detail. While we initially tried to harmonize modes of procedure by mutually reviewing our abstracts—a process we called "controlling"—restrictions in available resources eventually forced us to abandon this procedure.

Selection

The literature on ritual studies has witnessed a massive upsurge in recent decades. In 1985, in his pioneering bibliography of ritual studies Ronald Grimes listed 1633 titles.[6] Some two decades later, after the performative turn has affected the humanities in full force, the literature on ritual

[5] As we soon came to find out, published summaries were not always helpful. In general, we even wrote abstracts when published summaries (mostly provided by the author[s]) are available. Whenever we have used published summaries, this is indicated in the abstracts.

[6] See Grimes 1986 [for bibliographical details and an abstract see section E of this bibliography]).

has obviously increased disproportionally and seems unmanageable for any individual scholar. In order to manage our task, we therefore had to take some crucial decisions.

In the course of the work we decided to adopt two main criteria for the selection of titles to be included in our bibliography: Given our focus on ritual theory (a) the work (book, book-section, article, or edited volume) should principally be theoretical in orientation, and (b) it should be primarily focused on rituals. Both criteria sadly entailed that we would miss out a good number of important works such as—to give just two examples—ethnographies that *en passant* formulate important theoretical insights on the nature of rituals and general works in the humanities that have important implications for the study of ritual.[7] We are well aware that not all the titles that are included are theoretically satisfying, and we are also aware that important titles may be missing. Indeed, we would amongst ourselves not always agree on which titles to include and which to reject (and each of us, individually, is unhappy about some omissions). For all these reasons, this bibliography is not intended as a canon of ritual theory.

The extent of this bibliography went well beyond what we had originally envisaged. It was not initially planned to see the light of the day in the present format.

Chronology

Another crucial decision we had to take pertained to the time-frame of the titles to be included in the bibliography. Where should we start? In the modern Western academia the scientific and theoretical study of ritual started in the second half of the 19th Century. From the scholars whose names are listed in the Index of Names in Volume I, one may (among others) recall P.D. Chantepie de la Saussaye, C.P. Tiele, J.G. Frazer, W. Robertson Smith, and E.B. Tylor from the 19th Century as well as J. Harrison, É. Durkheim, M. Mauss, and A. van Gennep from the early 20th Century. While attempts at constructing theories of ritual would not slacken throughout the 20th Century—witness S. Freud, B. Malinowski, and M. Gluckman—in the Anglo-American academia

[7] While we tried to be consistent with these criteria, the bibliography includes numerous exceptions and borderline cases.

the study of ritual seems to have gained momentum subsequent to the publication of the English translation of Van Gennep's *Les rites de passage* in 1960 (French Original: 1909).

The stage for the contemporary theoretical study of religion was set with a number of influential publications that were published in the eventful years of 1966 to 1968. Most of these works originated in anthropology, with some important contributions from biology and sociology. These key-publications would give rise to several main theoretical approaches in the study of ritual. Suffice it to mention the following titles (summaries of which can of course be found in the bibliography):

- John Beattie: "Ritual and Social Change" (1966)
- Mary Douglas: *Purity and Danger* (1966)
- Clifford Geertz: "Religion as a Cultural System" (1966)
- Julian Huxley (ed.): *A Discussion on Ritualization of Behavior in Animals and Man* (1966)
- Edmund Leach: "Ritualization in Man in Relation to Conceptual and Social Development" (1966)
- Konrad Lorenz: "Evolution of Ritualization in the Biological and Cultural Spheres" (1966)
- Richard Schechner: "Approaches to Theory/Criticism" (1966)
- Anthony Wallace: *Religion. An Anthropological View* (1966)
- Erving Goffman: *Interaction Ritual* (1967)
- Rodney Needham: "Percussion and Transition" (1967)
- Victor W. Turner: *The Forest of Symbols* (1967)
- Paul Hockings: "On Giving Salt to Buffaloes. Ritual as Communication" (1968)
- Anthony Jackson: "Sound and Ritual" (1968)
- Edmund Leach: "Ritual" (1968)
- Roy A. Rappaport: *Pigs for the Ancestors* (1968)
- Stanley J. Tambiah: "The Magical Power of Words" (1968)

This list vividly illustrates that it was in these years (1966–1968) that many of the leading voices that would set the tone for ritual theory made themselves first heard.[8] Investigating the reasons for and mechanisms of the formation of (and subsequent changes within) this new

[8] Appendix A provides a chronological list of all entries in the bibliography.

field of study could well be a rewarding task for a discursive or/and cultural historian.

Groups of Entries, Cross-References, Key-words

The bibliography is made up of five parts. The second part [B] lists secondary literature on relevant authors (i.e. literature that in itself is not committed to produce new theories but rather to present and discuss the work of previous theoreticians). The third part [C] surveys relevant entries in reference works as these sometimes summarize extant ritual theories and sometimes themselves put forward theoretical claims.[9] The fourth part [D] lists relevant readers. The last part [E] specifies relevant bibliographies.

The bulk of the entries, however, can be found in the first part [A] on "Primary Literature". This section includes those titles selected according to the two criteria mentioned above. It numbers 442 items.

Almost all of these titles are provided with an abstract that summarizes its main contents.[10] It also includes summaries of the chapters published in Volume I of the present work. In the case of edited volumes, the abstract lists those chapters of the respective volume that are of particular relevance for ritual theory. In many cases these chapters are also listed separately. In that case, the bibliographical information is provided with an asterisk. In other words: Whenever an asterisk (*) is given, this is to indicate that additional information is to be found in a separate entry in the bibliography. For example, the edited volume:

> **Andresen, Jensine (ed.), 2001, *Religion in Mind. Cognitive Perspectives on Religious Belief, Ritual, and Experience*; Cambridge etc.: Cambridge University Press (ISBN 0–521–80152–4) (xi + 294) (with index and bibliographical references).**
> The index notes the occurrence of the term 'ritual' for the following contributions: Jensine Andresen: "Introduction. Towards a Cognitive Science of Religion" (1–44); Robert N. McCauley: "Ritual, Memory, and Emotion. Comparing two Cognitive Hypotheses" (115–140) (*); E. Thomas Lawson: "Psychological Perspectives on Agency" (141–172); Jensine

[9] The items contained in this section have for the most part been compiled by Florian Jeserich.

[10] Parts B (Secondary Literature) and C (Lexicon Articles) of the bibliography are not provided with abstracts. All translations from languages other than English contained in the abstracts are made by the author of the abstract in question.

Andresen: "Conclusion. Religion in the Flesh. Forging new Methodologies for the Study of Religion" (257–287). [MS]
Key-words: COG, agn, emo.

refers to the article:

McCauley, Robert N., 2001, 'Ritual, Memory, and Emotion. Comparing Two Cognitive Hypotheses', in: Jensine Andresen (ed.), *Religion in Mind. Cognitive Perspectives on Religious Belief, Ritual, and Experience*, Cambridge etc.: Cambridge University Press (ISBN 0–521–80152–4) (*) 115–140 (with index).
This article is a discussion about the ritual frequency hypothesis and the ritual form hypothesis, both of which deal with emotional stimulation in rituals.... [JK]
References: J.W. Fernandez, E.Th. Lawson, D. Sperber, F. Staal, A. van Gennep.
Key-words: cog, EMO, psy, str.

and vice versa.

The entries are indexed with codes referring to key-words. These indicate that we have deemed the respective title relevant for specific issues, topics, approaches, or concepts in ritual theory. To a large extent, these key-words overlap with the issues, topics, approaches, and concepts discussed in Volume I. In that way, Volumes I and II ideally complement each other. However, the list of codes/key-words also covers terms that are not discussed in separate chapters of Volume I. The key-words are underlined in the index of subjects in Volume I. Whenever a title is of special relevance for the discussion of a specific issue, topic, approach, or concept the respective code is written in CAPITALS.
This is the list of codes utilized in Part A of the bibliography:

aes	aesthetics
agn	agency
aut	authenticity
cmp	competence
cog	cognition
com	communication
cpl	complexity, redundancy
cpr	comparison
def	definition and classification
dfr	deference
dnc	dance

dyn	dynamics
ecl	ecology
ecn	economics
eff	efficacy
emb	embodiment
emo	emotion, experience
eth	ethology
exp	explanation
frm	framing
gdr	gender
gen	general and introductory
gst	gesture
hab	habitus
hsc	history of scholarship
idn	identity
int	intentionality
lan	language
med	media
mim	mimesis
mng	meaning/meaninglessness
mus	music
myt	myth/mythology
par	participation
pmc	performance/theatre/play
pmt	performativity
pow	power, violence, hierarchy
prl	praxis (in the sense of action)
pr2	praxis (in the sense of mimesis, embodiment, competence)
psy	psyche/psychology
ref	reference, denotation, expression & exemplification
rel	relationality
rep	representation
rfl	reflexivity
rht	rhetorics
sec	secular (vs. religious) ritual
sem	semiotics
soc	society/sociology
spc	space
str	structure, process, form (& syntax, sequence, repetition)
sym	symbol(ism)

ter	history of the term 'ritual'
tha	theatre and the theatrical
tim	time
tra	transmission
vir	virtuality

A survey assembling all the titles that were deemed relevant for the respective subjective areas (issues, topics, approaches, and concepts) can be found in Appendix B. When looking for literature on any of the subject areas of ritual theory listed above, this survey will therefore present a good starting point.[11] Readers wishing to make themselves familiar with the field as such may start by reading (apart from Volume I) those items listed under GEN.

References, Examples and Reviews

Obviously, ritual theorists do not operate *ex nihilo*. As elsewhere, there are some well-established theoretical genealogies at work that to some extent determine the development of new theories, theoretical approaches and agendas. In order to help the readers in contextualizing (and making sense of) the titles that are included in the bibliography, the abstracts are followed by a field entitled "references" listing the main theoreticians whom the author of the respective title explicitly refers to in his/her text.[12] In many cases, the mode of reception is specified in parenthesis, where (+) stands for a positive and (–) for a negative reception; (+/–) indicates that the author adopts some key-elements while rejecting others. In some cases, when the name is given in **bold** style, the respective theoretician is crucial for the argument.[13] For example:

> **Houseman, Michael & Carlo Severi, 1994, *Naven, ou le donner à voir. Essai d'interpretation de l'action rituelle* (Editions de la Maison des sciences de l'homme. Chemins de l'ethnologie); Paris: CNRS-Editions (ISBN 2-271-05171-1 / 2-7351-0543-1) (224) (with index and bibliography).**

---

[11] The literature given under the keywords often focuses on other aspects of issues or problems than these highlighted by the authors of the relevant chapters in Volume I.

[12] Implicit references are omitted.

[13] The list of references includes theoreticians (of ritual) only. Authors of ethnographies etc. are not listed.

English translation and revision: *Naven or the Other Self. A Relational Approach to Ritual Action* (Studies in the History of Religions 79); Leiden: E.J. Brill 1998 (ISBN 90–04–11220–0) (xvi + 325). Abstract based on this edition.
This book is a structural re-study of the naven-ceremony among the Iatmul of Papua New Guinea.... In considering a series of increasingly different types of other ritual situations, the authors try "to indicate how the relational approach to the analysis of ritual action developed in this book in connection with a detailed analysis of the naven ceremony, may be progressively generalised to other instances of ritual behaviour" (xiv). [JK]
References: F. Barth, **G. Bateson** (+), M.E.F. Bloch (–), J.W. Fernandez, A. van Gennep (–), M. Gluckman, D. Handelman (+/–), B. Kapferer (–), E.R. Leach, C. Lévi-Strauss (+), Th. Reik, D. Sperber (+), F. Staal (–), T.S. Turner, V.W. Turner (–).
Examples: *Naven* and initiation rituals among the Iatmul of Papua New Guinea.
Reviews: P.-J. Stewart *BTTV* 155.4 (1999) 732 f; S. Harrison *JRAI* 6.1 (2000) 139; J. Robbins *Pai* 47 (2001) 254 f.
Key-words: gdr, gst, idn, pmc, pr1, REL, sem, str.

Apart from drawing on prior theoretical attempts, the construction of theories of ritual often departs from specific rituals—be it the Ndembu initiation, Vedic liturgies, the Jain puja, the Zoroastrian Yasna, the naven-ceremony among the Iatmul of Papua New Guinea, or the circumcision ceremonies for boys among the Merina of Madagascar—as explicit (or implicit) prototypes for 'ritual' in the process of theorizing. Compared to constructing theories on a more amorphous basis of data proceeding from specific prototypes has both advantages and disadvantages. Grounding a theory in the analysis of a specific ritual often makes the theory richer, but at the same time runs the risk of unduly emphasizing aspects that may be less important or even absent in many other cases, or taking aspects that are possibly more characteristic for a certain class of rituals such as initiations or liturgies as characteristic for 'ritual' as such. In order to give the readers an idea as to the primary empirical material, or the range of prototypes, engaged in the different contributions to ritual theory that are summarized in Part A of this volume, the abstract and the list of references is (in many cases) followed by indicating the 'examples' engaged by the respective author(s).

Furthermore, as the example above illustrates, we have made an attempt to list reviews of the books or edited volumes which we decided to include in the bibliography. In some cases, the authors have added some reviews which had escaped our attention. However, these lists do not pretend completeness. Extensive reviews (5 pages or more) are indicated by bold style. The abbreviations of titles of periodicals in which the mentioned reviews were published are given in Appendix C.

List of Contributors

As can be seen in the examples above, for each abstract the initials of the contributor who made it are given in square brackets. The initials used are as follows:

JK Jens Kreinath (177 annotations)
JS Jan Snoek (105 annotations)
MS Michael Stausberg (118 annotations)

Most of the authors of the chapters of Volume I have kindly provided abstracts of their chapters. Moreover, some colleagues have provided some further abstracts. Their names are given in full, also between square brackets.

THE BIBLIOGRAPHY

PART A

PRIMARY LITERATURE
(442 items)

Ahearn, Laura M., 2001, 'Language and Agency', *Annual Review of Anthropology* 30:109–137.

"This review describes and critiques some of the many ways agency has been conceptualized in the academy over the past few decades, focusing in particular on practice theorists such as Giddens, Bourdieu, de Certeau, Sahlins, and Ortner.... It demonstrates the importance of looking closely at language and argues that the issues surrounding linguistic form and agency are relevant to anthropologists with widely divergent research agendas. Linguistic anthropologists have made significant contributions to the understanding of agency as it emerges in discourse, and the final sections of this essay describe some of the most promising research in the study of language and gender, literacy practices, and the dialog construction of meaning and agency" (109). The author argues that "in most scholarly endeavors, defining terms is half the battle" (110), and consequently she defines agency as "the socioculturally mediated capacity to act" (112), "while praxis (or practice) can be considered the action itself" (118). It is no wonder, then, that after the sections on "Definitional Starting Points" (110–113) and "Problems in Defining Agency" (113–117), we find a section on "Practice Theory" (117–120). Then follow sections on language ("Grammatical Agents", 120–124, and "Agency in Linguistic Anthropology", 124–130). The article closes with "Conclusions" (130–131). Ritual is treated not as a special context for agency but as one among others. The issues discussed are, however, often directly relevant to ritual theory. And the critical overview of the theories about agency gives a clear introduction to the actual use of the concept, including in the context of ritual theories. [JS]

References: D. Davidson, R.A. Segal, M. Foucault, A. Giddens, P. Bourdieu, M. de Certeau, M. Sahlins, S.B. Ortner, etc.
Key-words: AGN, PR1, gdr, lan, mng, def.

Ahern, Emily M., 1979, 'The Problem of Efficacy. Strong and Weak Illocutionary Acts', ***Man*** **14:1–17.**

This article problematizes the concept of efficacy. The author summarizes her argument as follows: "The problem of efficacy arises when people intend to produce certain effects and, in actuality, their acts produce other effects" (1). A main point of her argument is that the analysis of "different combinations of intended and actual effects allow different ways out of the problem of efficacy. The problem is most acute with respect to 'strong' illocutionary acts like requesting, in which the speaker's or actor's intent to produce an effect is necessarily involved. It need not arise with respect to 'weak' illocutionary acts like wishing, in which effects are not necessarily intended at all" (1). The author starts with the observation that anthropologists address in one way or another the question of whether or not "those who perform rituals intend them to have an effect on the world" (1). In doing so, they comment on the issue of intentionality: "what effect do those who perform rituals intend them to have?" (2). According to the author, this question entails a number of separate issues that give rise to further questions: "(1) Do those who perform ritual acts sometimes explicitly intend them to have an effect on the exterior world (outside themselves)? (2) Do those who perform ritual acts sometimes explicitly intend them to affect their own experience? (3) a) What effects does the performance of ritual acts actually have? b) How does the answer to (3a) relate to the answers to (1) and (2)? (4) Do those who perform ritual acts sometimes not intend them to have *any* effects, either on the world or on themselves, at all? How does the answer to this question relate to the answers to (1) and (2), and (3a)?" (2). Following this line of questioning, the author presents various examples of Chinese rituals and problematizes the concept of efficacy as addressed by Tambiah and Malinowski, as well as Lienhardt and Durkheim. The author concludes by stating that the problem of efficacy is much more complex than the various approaches indicate: "For a case where the intentions described in (1) are present, where strong illocutionary acts intended to affect the world are involved, we must deal with the tensions between intended and actual effects ('apparent' and 'real' efficacy). Along the way we must specify what sort of actual effects the ritual produces. In a case where the intentions described in (2) are present, the intentions to produce precisely the effects a ritual does have, there is no tension between 'apparent' and 'real' efficacy and no puzzle about people's adherence to such action. And in a case where the description in (4) applies, where no effects—whether on performers or on the world—are intended at all, there is again no tension between intended and actual effects" (16). [JK]

References: J.L. Austin, M. Douglas, É. Durkheim, J.G. Frazer, C. Geertz, M. Gluckman, G. Lienhardt, B. Malinowski, R. Otto, J. Piaget, G. Ryle, S.J. Tambiah, L. Wittgenstein.
Examples: Chinese rituals.
Key-words: com, PMT, EFF.

Ahlbäck, Tore (ed.), 1993, *The Problem of Ritual. Based on Papers Read at the Symposium on Religious Rites Held at Åbo, Finland on the 13th–16th of August 1991* (Scripta Instituti Donneriani Aboensis 15); Åbo: The Donner Institute for Research in Religious and Cultural History (ISBN 951-650-196-6) (367) (with bibliography).

Selected contents: Jørgen Podemann Sørensen: "Ritualistics. A New Discipline in the History of Religions" (9–25) (*); Tove Tybjerg: "Wilhelm Mannhardt—A Pioneer in the Study of Rituals" (27–37) (*); Antoon Geels: "A Note on the Psychology of Dhikr. The Halveti-Jerrahi Order of Dervishes in Istanbul" (53–82); Owe Wikström: "Liturgy as Experience—the Psychology of Worship. A Theoretical and Empirical Lacuna" (83–100); René Gothóni: "Pilgrimage = Transformation Journey" (101–115); Nora Ahlberg: "Forced Migration and Muslim Rituals. An Area of Cultural Psychology?" (117–130); Thomas McElwain: "Ritual Change in a Turkish Alevi Village" (131–168); Lilian Portefaix: "Ancient Ephesus. Processions as Media of Religious and Secular Propaganda" (195–210); Jens Peter Schjødt: "The Relation between the two Phenomenological Categories Initiation and Sacrifice as Exemplified by the Norse Myth of Odinn on the Tree" (261–273). [JS]

Key-words: myt, psy, dyn, spc.

Alcorta, Candace & Richard Sosis, 2005, 'Ritual, Emotion, and Sacred Symbols. The Evolution of Religion as an Adaptive Complex', *Human Nature* 16:323–359.

The authors summarize some of their main findings as follows: "Religion is an important and unique human adaptation defined by four recurrent traits: beliefs systems incorporating supernatural agents and counterintuitive concepts, communal ritual, separation of the sacred and the profane, and adolescence as a preferred developmental period for religious transmission. Although the specific expression of each of these traits varies across cultures in socio-ecologically patterned ways, the belief systems and communal rituals of all religions share common structural elements that maximize retention, transmission, and affective engagement. The roots of these structural elements can be found in nonhuman ritual where they serve to neurophysiologically prime participants and ensure reliable communication. Religion's incorporation of music, chanting, and dance intensifies such priming and extends the impacts of ritual beyond dyadic interactions. Music constitutes an abstract representation of ritual that can be recreated across time and space to evoke the emotions elicited by ritual. Human use of ritual to conditionally associate emotion and abstractions creates the sacred; it also lies at the heart of symbolic thought. The brain plasticity of human adolescence offers a unique developmental window for the creation of sacred symbols. Such symbols represent powerful tools for motivating behaviors and promoting in-group cooperation" (348–349). The authors derive some "empirically testable hypotheses" (349) from their theory, including the following: "...religious ritual should be most pronounced within groups of individuals who are not genetically related and are pursuing high-cost cooperative endeavors, and least pronounced among kin groups pursuing individualistic subsistence strategies. Significant associations between ritual intensity, positive and negative symbolic valence, and age of initiation should also exist among these variables" (349). Some further hypotheses (in part based on emotion theory) are advanced. [MS]

References: S. Atran, J. Bering, M.E.F. Bloch, P. Boyer, M. Douglas, É. Durkheim, M. Eliade, L.A. Kirkpatrick, J.E. LeDoux, K.Z. Lorenz, B. Malinowski, P. McNamara, B.G. Myerhoff, R.A. Rappaport, V.W. Turner.
Key-words: COG, COM, cpl, dnc, dyn, eff, EMO, exp, mus, par, pow, sym, tra.

Alexander, Bobby Chris, 1997, 'Ritual and Current Studies on Ritual. Overview', in: Stephen D. Glazier (ed.), *Anthropology of Religion. A Handbook*, Westport (CT), London: Greenwood Press (ISBN 0–313–28351–6) 139–160.

"*Ritual* defined in the most general and basic terms is a performance, planned or improvised, that affects a transition from everyday life to an alternative context within which the everyday is transformed" (139). "This chapter surveys some of the major developments that have taken place in the study of religion over the past twenty-five or thirty years" (139). One of these developments is the insight into "[r]itual's capacity to shape and shape anew" that "is rooted in its capacity to create experiences of self, society, the world, and cosmos that reinforce tradition or generate new views and ways of living" (140). Moreover, "[m]ore recent studies have called attention to less formalized forms of ritual, to ritual experimentation and newly emerging forms of ritual" (141). Furthermore, the new 'ritual studies' approach "focuses, among other interests, on the experimental and performative dimensions of ritual, on the physical, bodily, and gestural features of ritual" (142). "There is a growing interest among newer studies in the convergence of religious and secular interests in ritual" (143). "Newer studies have increasingly shown the dynamic nature of ritual... There is a new emphasis in ritual as flowing and changing activity and greater attention to ritual's improvisatory and indeterminate or open-ended dimensions" (145). Then follows a more extensive discussion of the approaches of Geertz and V.W. Turner (146–151). Moreover, the author observes that "[n]ewer studies of ritual have shied away from the grand theory making that characterized earlier studies.... Newer studies... emphasize the flexible, fluid, and open-ended qualities of ritual. Newer studies are interested in the immediacy and particularities of ritual" (151–152). The final section of the paper introduces the subsequent chapters of the book (on rituals in different parts of the world). [MS]

Key-word: gen.

Alexander, Jeffrey C., 2004, 'Cultural Pragmatics. Social Performance between Ritual and Strategy', *Sociological Theory* 22:527–573.

The author defines 'ritual' as follows: "Rituals are episodes of repeated and simplified cultural communication in which the direct partners to a social interaction, and those observing it, share a mutual belief in the descriptive and prescriptive validity of the communication's symbolic contents and accept the authenticity of one another's intentions. It is because of this shared understanding of intention and content, and in the intrinsic validity of the interaction, that rituals have their effect and affect" (527). While rituals were central to the social organization of earlier forms of society in "more contemporary, large-scale, and complex social organizations" (527), "the centrality of ritual processes has been displaced" (528). Nevertheless, "our societies still seem to be permeated by symbolic, ritual-like activities" (528), and this is the 'puzzle' addressed by this article. The author bases his argument on "a systematic, macro-sociological model of social action as cultural performance" (529). "Cultural performance is the social process by which actors, individually or in concert, display for others the meaning of their social situation" (529). In the following section the author presents a number of distinct elements of cultural performance (background symbols/foreground scripts; actors; observers/audience; means of symbolic production; *mise-en-scène*; social power) (530–533). The author holds "that all ritual has as its core a performative act" (534), but rituals are only one form of cultural performances. In ritual performances the elements of cultural performances are 'fused'. This fusion of the various components of performance typically occurs in less complex societies. However, "as social structure and culture have become more complex and segmented, so the elements that compose performance have become... concretely differentiated, separated, and de-fused in an empirical way" (566) as the author tries to show in his second section (533–547). "The goal of secular performances, whether on stage or in society, remains the same as the ambition of sacred ritual. They stand or fall on their ability to produce psychological identification and cultural extension. The aim is to create, via skillful and affecting performance, the emotional connection of audience with actor and text and thereby to create the conditions for projecting cultural meaning from performance to audience. To the extent these two conditions have been achieved, one can say that the elements of performance have become fused" (547). The third section of the article (547–549) discusses some criteria for success or failure of performances. The fourth and final section (549–565) turns "to a more detailed discussion of the elements and relations that sustain" performance (547). Drawing on insights from drama theory, the author tries "to decompose the basic elements of performance into their more complex component parts" (549–550) and to explore "the challenge of modern performance by investigating the complex nature of the demands that each of its different elements implies" (566). [MS]

References: J. Butler (+), É. Durkheim (–), C. Geertz, E. Goffman, J. Goody, J. Huizinga, C. Lévi-Strauss, S. Lukes, R. Schechner (+/–), V.W. Turner (+/–).
Examples: Various.
Key-words: SOC, sec, com, PMC, pr1, EFF, med, par, aut.

Andresen, Jensine (ed.), 2001, *Religion in Mind. Cognitive Perspectives on Religious Belief, Ritual, and Experience*; Cambridge etc.: Cambridge University Press (ISBN 0–521–80152–4) (xi + 294) (with index and bibliographical references).

The index notes the occurrence of the term 'ritual' for the following contributions: Jensine Andresen: "Introduction. Towards a Cognitive Science of Religion" (1–44); Robert N. McCauley: "Ritual, Memory, and Emotion. Comparing two Cognitive Hypotheses" (115–140) (*); E. Thomas Lawson: "Psychological Perspectives on Agency" (141–172); Jensine Andresen: "Conclusion. Religion in the Flesh. Forging New Methodologies for the Study of Religion" (257–287). [MS]
Key-words: COG, agn, emo.

Anttonen, Pertti J., 1992, 'The Rites of Passage Revisited. A New Look at Van Gennep's Theory of the Ritual Process and Its Application in the Study of Finnish-Karelian Wedding Rituals', *Temenos* 28:15–52.

Although the author regards Van Gennep's rites of passage theory not merely as a ritual theory in the strict sense but rather as an all-inclusive social theory (cf. esp. 20 and 22), he makes some points that seem to be of theoretical importance for the study of rituals in the narrower sense. For precisely because of his wider sociological perspective, the author is able to argue in the first part of his article that the basic processual pattern (separation—liminality—incorporation) that Van Gennep described in his *Les rites de passage* (1909) must not be "understood and read as a rather rigid structure" (18), as, e.g., Honko had done (cf. 19), but in fact as a social dynamic or a 'living organism'. This view he exemplifies by interpreting Van Gennep's terms of *schéma* and *catégorie*: The first, according to Solon Kimball (in his introduction to the English translation of *Les rites de passage* [1960]), inclines one towards dynamics and includes both process and structure. The second "[i]ndicates how the idea of passage applies to any kind of transformation in the cultural and social categories of meaning—not only roles and statuses of individuals as Honko would have it. Time and space as well as human social organization are socially constructed into units, for which the term 'category' is perfectly suitable" (23). The author then points to the "core concept" (23) of Van Gennep's theory, "that movement in social space is accompanied and identified with movement in territorial space" (15, cf. also 23–24). In the second thematic part, the author criticizes

Honko's three-type classification of rites (rites of passage, calendrical rites, crisis rites) as an exercise in nominalistic taxonomy, a mere "convention that can only be legitimated with authority" (26). In addition, he questions the usefulness of the criteria of 'orientation', 'recurrence', and 'anticipation' as distinguishing factors among the three categories. In the third and final part, the author discusses "Applications of the Rites of Passage Theory in Wedding Rituals" (31–49). He re-analyzes the structural descriptions of wedding rituals by Sarmela, Pentikäinen, and Nenola-Kallio, trying to solve thereby (1) terminological and (2) theoretical problems. First, he clarifies the meaning of Van Gennep's basic terms *passage* and *marge*: "Passage and transition are synonymous: passage is transition and transition is passage. In order to avoid confusion, *marge* should not be translated as 'transition' but, for example, as 'limen' or liminality, as Victor Turner chose to do" (32–33). Then the author points out that "[t]he biggest problem is the rigid application of the Van Gennepian scheme, and the attempt to squeeze the ritual movement into it" (35): "Interpreted as an ideal pattern with a fixed structure of three succeeding stages, beginning, midpoint, and end, the theory has made the wedding ritual an object of classificatory exercises, in which the significations of rites are determined by their assumed place in the ideal pattern, rather than by an analysis of meaning" (33). He therefore emphasizes "the multivalent and polysemous character of rites, the multiple meanings of social acts, and the multiplicity of transitional levels" (48). He especially elaborates on the last point, differentiating five levels of liminality: (1) limina or thresholds, (2) the whole transition process, (3) liminal statuses, (4) liminal periods, and (5) liminality as an experience/feeling. Finally, going beyond the scope of Van Gennep, Gluckman, and V.W. Turner, the author concludes: "The rites of passage theory, in its untrivialized form, does, however, offer unused potential for studying the processual character of social life in modern just as well as in non-modern or postmodern societies" (49). [Florian Jeserich]

References: **L. Honko (–)**, G. Kligman (+/–), J. Pentikäinen (–), A. Nenola-Kallio (–), T.S. Turner (+), V.W. Turner (+/–), **A. van Gennep (+)**.
Examples: Viena Karelian and Ingrian weddings.
Key-words: DEF, STR, mng, cpl, dyn, emo, spc, tim.

Argyle, Michael, 2002, 'The Effects of Ritual', *Archive for the Psychology of Religion / Archiv für Religionspsychologie* 24:167–179 (with bibliography).

This article reviews almost 40 (mainly sociological) publications about effects of (mainly Christian) ritual on their participants, summarizing their results. It thus in fact tests the theory, that rituals would not have survived in basically all societies if they would not have some benefit for their members. The author summarizes his findings thus: "rituals enhance the cohesion of groups, and this is one of the reasons for other benefits. The benefits of healing services are largely subjective; there is more effect on mental health. Religious experiences are generated by religious rituals, especially via music and prayer. There is some effect on well-being, and marriages are helped by shared ritual. Religious beliefs are enhanced by religious rituals. Rites of passage may help those undergoing changes of status, but there is little evidence. There are benefits for others too, for example through enhanced charitable giving and social work, but there is one negative effect, in that there may be divisions between different churches. The explanation of these effects is partly in terms of changes of social identity, partly in the power of symbolic non-verbal communication and partly in the effects of music" (178). [JS]

References: L. Festinger, R. Girard, J.D. Laird, V.W. Turner, A. van Gennep, F.W. Young.
Examples: Mainly Christian liturgy.
Key-words: soc, psy, idn, exp, com, EFF, EMO, par, mus.

Asad, Talal, 1988, 'Towards a Genealogy of the Concept of Ritual', in: Wendy James & Douglas H. Johnson (eds), *Vernacular Christianity. Essays in the Social Anthropology of Religion. Presented to Godfrey Lienhardt*, New York: Lilian Barber (ISBN 0–936508–23–x) 73–87.
A revised version was published in: Talal Asad: *Genealogies of Religion. Discipline and Reasons of Power in Christianity and Islam*; Baltimore (MD): John Hopkins University Press 1993 (ISBN 0–8018–4631–5 / 0–8018–4632–3 (p)) 55–79.

In this paper the author first traces the historical development of the meaning of the term 'ritual'. In the first edition of the *Encyclopaedia Britannica* of 1771, 'ritual' is defined as "a book directing the order and manner to be observed in celebrating religious ceremonies, and performing divine service in a particular church, diocese, order, or the like", while "Rite, among divines, denotes the particular manner of celebrating divine service, in this or that country" (74). The third edition (1797) gives: "Ritual, a book directing the order and manner to be observed in performing divine service in a particular church, diocese, or the like. The ancient heathens had also their rituals, which contained their rites and ceremonies to be observed in building a city, consecrating a temple or altar, in sacrificing, and deifying, in dividing the curiae, tribes, centuries, and in general, in all their religious ceremonies" (74). "Both entries are repeated in successive editions up to the seventh (1852). After that, there is no entry at all for 'rite' or 'ritual' until the eleventh edition (1910), when a completely new entry appears under the latter for the first time. It is now five columns long" (74). The author discusses this entry at length. There are two new issues: (1) 'ritual' is regarded as symbolic behavior, and (2) the term "as meaning the prescribed ceremonial routine, is also extended to observances not strictly religious in character" (75). At the same time, "the conception of ritual as a book" (75) has disappeared, although "Rituals appeared as separate books as early as the ninth century, though only in monasteries" (75). Indeed, "[a]ccording to the *Oxford English Dictionary*, 'ritual' entered English as a substantive in the middle of the seventeenth century, when it conveyed the sense either of the prescribed order of performing religious services or of the book containing such prescriptions.... It is only in the latter part of the nineteenth century that 'ritual' comes to signify the actual performance of certain kinds of acts" (76). The author now points out that the older notion implies the notion "that there exists the requirement *to master the performance of services properly*" (78) and "apt performance involves *abilities* to be acquired, not symbols to be interpreted: it presupposes not special meanings or rules, nor even particular kinds of experience, but the formation of bodily and linguistic abilities" (78–79). In the rest of the paper, the author contrasts the two concepts by comparing the meaning that performing the liturgy had for monks in the Middle Ages, with the meaning that anthropologists try to read in rituals today. For the monks, learning to master the correct performance of the liturgy was supposed to evoke virtue in them. Outer action and inner virtue were supposed to be directly related. This view is only disturbed in the Renaissance, when keeping things secret, as well as dissimulation and simulation, come to be seen as part of—at least sometimes—proper behavior. [JS]

Example: Medieval monastic liturgy.
Key-words: TER, def, sec, mng, sym, pr1, pr2, cmp.

Auffarth, Christoph, 1999, 'Feste als Medium antiker Religionen. Methodische Konzeptionen zur Erforschung komplexer Rituale', in: Christophe Batsch, Ulrike Engelhaaf-Gaiser & Ruth Stepper (eds), *Zwischen Krise und Alltag. Antike Religionen im Mittelmeerraum / Conflit et normalité. Religions anciennes dans l'espace méditerranéen*, (Potsdamer altertumswissenschaftliche Beiträge 1), Stuttgart: Franz Steiner Verlag (ISBN 3-515-07513-5) 31-42.
[Festivals as Media of Ancient Religions. Methodic Conceptualizations for the Study of Complex Rituals]

The author mentions some theories of festivals (Durkheim, Eliade, Huizinga, Kerényi) and discusses general methodological issues in the history of religions (*Religionswissenschaft*). He argues against the quest for the 'essence' of festivals in order to highlight their multiple, complex, ambiguous, meaningless, heterogeneous, and inconsistent structure growing out of different (and sometimes competing) traditions and contexts. On his view, *Religionswissenschaft* should aim at describing complexity rather than at reducing it to simple categories. In ancient religions, festivals were an important way to communicate (about) religion. [MS]

References: É. Durkheim, M. Eliade, J. Huizinga, K. Kerényi.
Key-words: mng, cpl, com.

Babcock, Barbara A., 1978, 'Too Many, Too Few. Ritual Modes of Signification', *Semiotica* 23:291-302.

Based on the common identification of art and ritual in terms of order and the disregard of disorder, the author states that in recent studies there has been a tendency "to regard ritual symbols as multivalent and overdetermined, i.e., as having multiple meanings and referents" (292). In contrast to this view of ritual signification, she argues that "this surplus of signifieds is only one mode of ritual signification, that ritual symbolism may also involve a 'surplus of the signifier' and a 'bracketing of signification', and that every ritual process involves at least these three modes of signification in differing degrees of emphasis and combination" (292). One of the main assumptions underlying her approach is that "any ritual, and culture in general, may be regarded as a system of communication, a form of discourse, and analyzed as such. On the one hand, this means seeing and analyzing ritual *as* language... On the other hand, regarding ritual as a system of communication also means paying closer attention to the languages *of* ritual—verbal and non-verbal—and to the specific ways in which signs signify" (292). The author argues that the prevailing concept to "describe and analyze ritual symbols as multivocal or polysemic" (292–293) tends "to eschew or misread other possible modes of signification. The relation between signifier and signified may be one to several; it may also be several to one, or one to one, or signification may be suspended altogether. Describing ritual symbols as multivalent is also distorting insofar as it entails a rather narrow conception of the nature and function of ritual as a serious, ordering, and synthesizing phenomenon" (293–294). According to the author, "in every ritual there is...a dialogue between structure and anti-structure, order and disorder. Liminality and other anti-structural aspects and types of ritual are different modes of discourse characterized by a bracketing of, or a free play with, ordinary and serious modes of signification" (294). The author then retraces the history of the concept of a surplus of signifiers (Lévi-Strauss; Lacan; Derrida). This "surplus of signifiers...creates a self-transgressive discourse which mocks and subverts the monological arrogance of 'official' systems of signification. The bantering *anti*-signified of carnivalesque discourse is an insult both to the complementarity of ordinary speech and to the multi-signified of serious ritual communication...Rather than 'representing' something, discourse by means of a surplus of signifiers designates and celebrates itself" (296). "By playing with the ways in which words and objects and actions signify in normal and ceremonial discourse, discourse by means of a surplus of signifiers paradoxically both questions and reaffirms social, cultural, and cosmological orders of things. While a superfluity of signifiers is predominant and self-evident in ludic or carnevalesque ritual, I would suggest that *all* rituals involve a dialogue or alternation between these two modes of signification—multi-signifier and multi-signified—both of which differ from our daily, ordinary use of signs. In contrast to the complementarity between signifier and signified characteristic of normal discourse, ritual communication involves *both* an extremely economical *and* extremely inflated relation of signifiers to signified" (296). Moreover, rituals differ from the everyday usage of signs because they are especially framed modes of signification: "Ritual events as well as distinct phases or sequences within a given event are initially marked or framed by a bracketing of ordinary signification" (297). Furthermore, the author distinguishes two contrasting forms of ritual: "Whatever the initial frame, ritual sequences that are essentially serious and iterative of structure are ordering and orderly. This means that the majority of signs—verbal and non-verbal—are polysemic or multisignified and that they are hierarchically arranged, the dominant or central symbols marked by extreme multivocality.... In contrast, those rituals or phases of ritual which focus on the ambiguous and inhibited aspects of the social order, or which invert, contradict, or otherwise challenge structure, are disorderly and disordering. Antistructural sequences are likely to be ungrammatical and indeterminate, and this indeterminacy is expressed primarily, though not exclusively, through an excess of 'floating signifiers'" (297). In a certain way, this distinction corresponds to the "marked difference between Anglo-American interpretations of ritual and art emphasizing order, unity, and coherence, and those of the deconstructive French stressing disorder, freeplay, and floating signifiers" (298). She concludes "that ritual communication is always a paradoxical *alliage* of both types of 'set apart' signifying" (299). [JK/MS]

References: F. Barth, J. Derrida, C. Geertz, **C. Lévi-Strauss** (+), N.D. Munn, R.A. Rappaport (+), A.I. Richards, A. Southall, S.J. Tambiah (+), **V.W. Turner** (+/–).
Key-words: com, SEM, STR, SYM, rel, eff, frm.

Baranowski, Ann, 1998, 'A Psychological Comparison of Ritual and Musical Meaning', *Method & Theory in the Study of Religion* 10:3–29.

The topic of this essay "is not simply ritual but ritual experience" (3). It "involves a comparison of ritual cognition and meaning with musical cognition and meaning" (4). After setting out some underlying assumptions of her approach, such as the claim to "analyze ritual as particular cognitive processes and not as particular cognitive products (e.g., beliefs, ideas, concepts,...)" (6), the author reviews some prominent studies of ritual meaning (Boyer, Staal, Sperber, Lawson/McCauley) (7–14). In the next section (14–18), she discusses "three important similarities" between ritual and music "that support the claim that at one level of cognition they are identical. First,..., both are highly patterned" (15), i.e., just as music is not mere sound but consists of recognizable "tonal rhythmic patterns" (16), "all ritual involves some sort of activity, but it is hard to perceive it as *mere* activity, it is hard not to see that the activity is highly patterned and therefore different from ordinary activity" (17). The second similarity is temporality, i.e., both music and ritual have a beginning, middle, and end. In the case of ritual, this "is to say not only that it occurs in time, but also that it is a closed system,...it can be understood without reference to anything outside itself" (17), i.e., it is non-referential. The third similarity consists of certain constraints: "Just as in tonal music, where patterns are perceptible and significant because the tones are organized hierarchically in terms of their position in relation to the position of the tonic, so also patterns in religious rituals are perceivable to the extent that their elements are organized hierarchically in terms of their position in relation to the position of the superhuman agents" (17–18). In the subsequent section, the author discusses eight problems involved in finding representational or expressionist meanings in music and ritual (18–20). In the following section (20–24), the author looks at recent attempts to understand the "complex of processes involved in the cognition and meaning of music" (20). She suggests that music, ritual, and some other practices may ultimately be part of one human faculty ("input system") dealing with activity patterned in time. The next section (24–26) seeks to formulate the hypothesis that the meaning of music and ritual results from this very same process of pattern construction and comparison, which is to say that this form of meaning is "not propositional" (26). The concluding section (26–28) ends with the (admittedly speculative) idea that this "seems to be a level of meaning that is necessary to human life", as "one important way humans meet their need to have a world" (28). [MS]

References: F. Barth, C.M. Bell, P. Boyer, R. Firth, S.K. Langer, E.Th. Lawson & R.N. McCauley, D. Sperber, F. Staal, V.W. Turner.
Key-words: MNG, COG, str, tim, exp, emo, mus.

Barrett, Justin L., 2002, 'Smart Gods, Dumb Gods, and the Role of Social Cognition in Structuring Ritual Intuitions', *Journal of Cognition and Culture* 2:183–193.

Religious activity of the Pomio Kivung people of Melanesia challenges a specific claim of Lawson & McCauley's (1990) theory of religious ritual, but does it challenge the general claim that religious rituals are underpinned by ordinary cognitive capacities? To test further the hypothesis that ordinary social cognition informs judgments of religious ritual efficacy, 64 American Protestant college students rated the likelihood of success of a number of fictitious rituals. The within-subjects manipulation was the manner in which a successful ritual was modified, either by negating the intentions of the ritual actor or by altering the ritual action. The between-subjects manipulation was the sort of religious system in which the rituals were to be performed: one with an all-knowing god ("Smart god") vs. one with a fallible god ("Dumb god").

Participants judged performing the correct action as significantly more important for the success of rituals in the Dumb god condition than in the Smart god condition. In the Smart god condition, performing the correct action was rated as significantly less important for the success of the rituals than having appropriate intentions while performing the ritual. [MS]

Key-word: COG.

Barrett, Justin L. & E. Thomas Lawson, 2001, 'Ritual Intuitions. Cognitive Contributions to Judgments of Ritual Efficacy', *Journal of Cognition and Culture* 1:183–201.

Lawson and McCauley (1990) have argued that non-cultural regularities in how actions are conceptualized inform and constrain participants' understandings of religious rituals. This theory of ritual competence generates three predictions: 1) People with little or no knowledge of any given ritual system will have intuitions about the potential effectiveness of a ritual given minimal information about the structure of the ritual. 2) The representation of superhuman agency in the action structure will be considered to be the most important factor contributing to effectiveness. 3) Having an appropriate intentional agent initiate the action will be considered to be relatively more important than any specific action to be performed. These three predictions were tested in two experiments with 128 North American Protestant college students who rated the probability of various fictitious rituals as effective in bringing about a specified consequence. Results support Lawson and McCauley's predictions and suggest that expectations regarding ordinary social actions apply to religious rituals. [MS]

Reference: E.Th. Lawson & R.N. McCauley.
Examples: Fictitious rituals.
Key-words: EFF, agn, cmp, cog.

Barthelmes, Barbara & Helga de la Motte-Haber (eds), 1999, *Musik und Ritual* (Veröffentlichungen des Instituts für Neue Musik und Musikerziehungen Darmstadt 39); Mainz etc.: Schott (ISBN 3-7957-1779-5) (112).
[Music and Ritual]

Selected contents: Barbara Barthelmes and Helga de la Motte-Haber: "Vorwort" (7); Dieter Schnebel: "Ritual—Musik" (9–17); Heinz-Klaus Metzger: "Rituelle Aspekte des bürgerlichen Musiklebens" (18–30);

Rudolf Frisius: "Musik als Ritual. Karlheinz Stockhausens Komposition INORI" (63–77); Hans Neuhoff: "Musik im Besessenheitsritual" (78–88); Martha Brech: "Im Spannungsfeld zwischen Archaik und Moderne. Riten im Electronic Listening und der Elektroakustischen Musik" (89–109). [JS]

Key-words: gen, psy, aes, pmc, med, mus.

Bateson, Mary Catherine, 1974, 'Ritualization. A Study in Texture and Texture Change', in: Irving I. Zaretsky & Mark P. Leone (eds), *Religious Movements in Contemporary America*, Princeton, Oxford: Princeton University Press (ISBN 0–691–07186–1) 150–165.

In this paper, the author presents "a linguistically derived model to characterize those religious phenomena called rituals in terms of textual rather than *structural* differences from other types of interaction" (150). For this purpose, she derives "a heuristic unit of texture, the *praxon*, from a description of the emerging rituals of a charismatic (tongues-speaking) prayer group. The praxonic analysis of texture is explicitly formulated to apply to the development of rituals (or the process of ritualization) through textual changes to be described as *fusion*" (150). One principal assumption of this model is that "it is possible to describe language without describing content, meaning being invoked only contrastively" (150). In this way, the author attempts "to describe ritual behavior and the distribution of meaning over different units in that behavior, without, however, explaining the content or nature of symbolic meaning" (150). To this end, ritual is defined heuristically as "repeated, customary procedure, associated with religion and involving at least two human participants" (150). The author argues that "ritual cannot be delimited, that ritualization is a more-or-less phenomenon which may be accounted for in terms of texture, and that ritual is not necessarily associated with religion but that there is a wide overlap between ritualization, the social institution of religion, and the phenomenological experience variously referred to as 'cosmic consciousness' or the 'idea of the holy'" (150–151). In order to address the structure of behavior, two central insights of descriptive linguistics are applied to human behavior, that is, 'the notion of *emic* units' and 'the notion of *levels*', and it is assumed that "every stretch of human behavior...is segmentable into emic units at a number of levels" (151). To extend this model "to include all behavior which is culturally patterned and relevant to communication, it needs to be considerably expanded...for including body motion and other vocalization with speech...but ultimately a full analysis of interpersonal codes of culturally patterned communication cannot rest on a sharp separation of modalities" (151). Although the author admits that "*no* segmentary/sequential model is adequate for describing human behavior", she argues that "all human behavior has a segmentary/sequential aspect which presents itself for description" and this multilevel model of human interaction has "a considerable utility for description" (152). After presenting a detailed description of prayer meetings of a group of middle-class, white Christians as an example for ritualization in progress (153–160), the author distinguishes between the structural, textual, and praxonic segmentation of a stretch of human behavior and concludes that "one sequence is, in general, more fused than another" and "that ritualization consists in a high degree of fusion, that rituals typically consist of high-level praxons" (160). Considering the conditions of fusion related to ritual, the author argues that "[f]usion comes about through (a) addition of meaning, (b) atrophy of components, (c) blurring of boundaries, or (d) hyper-regular surface structure" (160). Moreover, "[t]hese four conditions of fusion are interrelated in a number of ways, and all relate to traditionally recognized characteristics of ritual in various societies. The addition of meaning is related to the heightened sense of significance and arousal that often attends religious ceremonial; atrophy of components is related to the common antiquity of rites; blurring of boundaries is related to repetition, group performance, and mixed modalities; and hyperregularity is related to the aesthetic elaboration of religious ceremonial. In ritual, we must see repetition and heightened arousal as gradually producing a measure of the other characteristics" (162). The author continues: "Another way of considering the phenomenon of fusion would be to note that a praxon is a minimal structural segment whose meaning is not deducible from its structure, but that different kinds of meaning are appropriate to different degrees of fusion.... I would argue that the bulkier the praxons of an interaction, the less they are understandable in referential terms.... Thus, the language of highly-fused messages...is only in a minor degree referential, and their truth value should not be judged in terms of reference" (162). In concluding, the author states: "The heuristic use of the concept praxon may provide a bridge between the structural and the phenomenological analysis of behavior that will allow a new understanding of the role of ritual, seen as part of a continuum" (165). [JK]

References: N. Chomsky (–), E.H. Erikson (+), C. Lévi-Strauss (–), R. Otto, K. Pike (+), W. Robertson Smith (–), E.B. Tylor (–).
Example: Charismatic prayer meetings.
Key-words: mng, sec, str, com, eth, sem, ref, dyn, gst.

Baudy, Dorothea, 1998, *Römische Umgangsriten. Eine ethologische Untersuchung der Funktion von Wiederholung für religiöses Verhalten* (Religionsgeschichtliche Versuche und Vorarbeiten 43); Berlin, New York: W. de Gruyter (ISBN 3–11–016077–3) (xi + 299).
[Roman Circumambulation Rites. An Ethologic Study of the Function of Repetition for Religious Behavior]

This dissertation gives a new interpretation of actions that were known as *lustratio* or *lustrum* in Latin antiquity. These mainly consisted of circular processions around a territory, a group of people, or objects, accompanied by animals that were later sacrificed. The author bases her new interpretation of those rituals on an ethological approach to ritual theory that is unfolded in the first chapters of the study. Ritual action is seen here as a special case of the more general category of 'repetition' in *Religionswissenschaft*. Repetitive action provides patterns of action that can be applied in recurrent situations, and parts of the ritual process are performed repeatedly. Moreover, participants see their action as a repetition of a mythical example (Chapter 1). The author distinguishes three types of ritual repetition: regular repetition in calendar-cycles, the ritual introduction of a new period of an individual's life, and the application of repeatable ritual patterns in order to come to terms with extraordinary situations of crisis (Chapter 2). Furthermore, the notion of repetition is analyzed from an ethological perspective (Chapter 3). The formal character of ritual behavior is a prerequisite of its repeatability. A characteristic feature of its formal character is that some of its elements are repeated in a particular rhythm. Ritual action is a kind of repetitive action in the social and communicative sphere. To achieve a communicative dimension, animal behavior changes some of its forms and functions that then continue to exist independently of its original contexts. While these forms of ritualization are genetically transmitted, ritualization can also be observed at the ontogenetic level. Here, it designates the construction of strong communicative structures within a single living being. This entails the emergence of rites that are not genetically determined. Finally, rituals are also transmitted in culture. However, the author argues that there exists a continuum leading from the phylogenetic and ontogenetic to the cultural emergence of rituals (90). While these aspects of ritualization are mainly formal, the author suggests that ethological approaches can also contribute insights into the contents of rituals. This she attempts to demonstrate with the example of territoritality and the construction of space (92–99). [MS]

Example: Roman circumambulations.
Reviews: J. Rüpke *ARG* 2 (2000) 285; W. Liebeschuetz *JRomS* 90 (2000) 209; W. Braun *MTSR* 12 (2000) 549 f; V. Rosenberger *Kl* 83 (2001) 251 f; A. López *StM* 43 (2001) 412 f.; M. Josuttis *VF* 47 (2002) 71.
Key-words: ETH, str, com, emo, gst, spc, myt.

Baudy, Dorothea, 2006, 'Ethology', in: Jens Kreinath, Jan A.M. Snoek & Michael Stausberg (eds), *Theorizing Rituals. Vol. I: Issues, Topics, Approaches, Concepts*, (Numen Book Series 114–1), Leiden, Boston: Brill (ISBN-10: 90–04–15342–x, ISBN-13: 978–90–04–15342–4) 345–359.

All over the world human beings give a ritually defined structure to their habitat, be that their village or the cosmos as a whole. They are creating time insofar as they mark ruptures (and get along with them) by annual calendarical festivities or life-time rituals. Cultic structures constitute social organizations. One single academic discipline will never be able to analyze the fact that and the manner how human beings do this. To proceed with ritualistics means to do it in a combined way, historically as well as systematically, which is impossible without theorizing. An ethological base could contribute to some clearing and help to achieve an integration of the different perspectives. In a biological context the term 'ritualization' has a clear-cut definition: it denotes the evolution of behavioral patterns and accompanying physical features which do not serve any immediate purpose but exist for the sake of communication. The ethological ritualization theory deals with the development of signals and symbolic actions. The primary concern of biological research initially was to explain the phylogenetic development of rites, but from the beginning there was a parallel interest in individually acquired behavior which was combined with the innate patterns. On a long-term basis, out of this area of interest resulted a theory of cultural ritualization. [Dorothea Baudy]

Key-word: ETH.

Bauman, Richard, 1975, 'Verbal Art as Performance', *American Anthropologist* 77:290–311.

Since most conceptions of verbal art are text-centered, the purpose of this essay is to develop a conception of 'verbal art as performance' that expands it to the mode of spoken verbal communication. For the author's approach, "to conceptualize verbal art in communicative terms" means that "performance becomes *constitutive* of the domain of verbal art as spoken communication" (293). Going through a variety of ethnological studies about speaking traditions, the author analyzes the culture-specific nature of performance and verbal art and "the specific conventionalized means that key performance in a particular community" (296). In presenting patterning factors for performance in exemplary ceremonies and rituals, he shows the interactions and interdependence of performance genres, acts, events, and roles. Thus, the author studies the emergent quality of performance underlying the social structure in addition to the text and event structure: "The consideration of the power inherent in performance to transform social structures opens the way to a range of additional considerations concerning the role of the performer in society" (305). He suggests that "[p]erformance ... constitutes ... a point of departure, the nexus of tradition, practice, and emergence in verbal art" (306). [JK]

References: G. Bateson (+), R.H. Finnegan, R. Firth, J. Fox, E. Goffman (+), J. Huizinga, **D. Hymes** (+).
Key-words: com, frm, PMC, pow, pr1, soc, str.

Bauman, Richard & Charles L. Briggs, 1990, 'Poetics and Performance as Critical Perspectives on Language and Social Life', *Annual Review of Anthropology* 19:59–88.

This review article addresses the study of poetics in anthropological research and how its role changed due to a new interest in issues of performance. The authors observe "two opposing assessments of the role of poetics in social life", that is, "verbal art provides a central dynamic force in shaping linguistic structure and linguistic study" and "aesthetic uses of language are merely parasitic upon such 'core' areas of linguistics as phonology, syntax and semantics" (59). "The balance between these two views shifted in favor of poetics ... as a new emphasis on performance directed attention away from study of the formal patterning and symbolic content of texts to the emergence of verbal art in the social interaction between performers and audiences" (59–60).

The authors particularly pay attention to "several basic theoretical issues that have shaped both the way scholars have studied performance and its rejection by other practitioners" (60). They "attempt to provide a framework that will displace reified, object-centered notions of performativity, text, context—notions that presuppose the encompassment of each performance by a single, bounded social interaction" (61). In the first section "From Performativity to the Social Construction of Reality" (62–66), the authors give a critical overview of the discussion of approaches emphasizing language as social action. They write that: "Performance-oriented scholars no longer think of performativity primarily as the use of specific features in signaling particular illocutionary effects within a fixed set of conventions and a given social context. Instead, they view it as the interaction of complex and heterogeneous formal patterns in the social construction of reality" (64–65). In the second section "From Context to Contextualization" (66–72), the authors discuss the recent shift in performance studies, which "are in the midst of a radical reformulation wherein 'text', 'context', and the distinction between them are being redefined" (67). This shift from product to process and from conventional structures to agency "represents a major step towards achieving an agent-centered view of performance. Contextualization involves an active process of negotiation in which participants reflexively examine the discourse as it is emerging, embedding assessments of its structure and significance in the speech itself" (69). In the third section "Entextualization and Decontextualization" (72–78), an alternative perspective is proposed that "has begun to emerge from performance studies and other areas that approaches some of the basic problems in linguistic anthropology from a contrary set of assumptions" (72). Based on the distinction between discourse and text, the authors conceive entextualization as "the process of rendering discourse extractable, of making a stretch of linguistic production into a unit—a *text*—that can be lifted out of its interactional setting. A text, then, from this vantage point, is discourse rendered decontextualizable" (73). Moreover, they consider "the decontexualization and recontextualization of texts to be two aspects of the same process, though time and other factors may mediate between the two phases" (75). In order to account for the transformational process involved, the authors distinguish between six dimensions of transformation: "1. *Framing*—that is, the metacommunicative management of the recontextualized text.... 2. *Form*—including formal means and structures from phonology, to grammar, to speech style, to larger structures of discourse such as generic packing principles.... 3. *Function*—manifest, latent, and performative...4. *Indexical grounding*, including deictic markers of person, spatial location, time, etc.... 5. *Translation*, including both interlingual and intersemiotic translation.... 6. The *emergent structure* of the new context, as shaped by the process of recontextualization" (75–76). In applying these culturally constructed and socially constituted elements to the scholarly discourse the authors argue that "the investigation of decontextualization and recontextualization continues the program of the ethnography of speaking, adding a conceptual framework, centered on discursive practice itself, that links separate situational contexts in terms of the pragmatics of textuality" (77). In line of this argument, they conclude: "The poetics and politics of ethnography are illuminated by the poetics and politics of discourse within the communities about which and within which we write" (80). [JK]

References: **R.D. Abrahams**, J.L. Austin, B.A. Babcock, G. Bateson, D. Ben-Amos, S.H. Blackburn, M.E.F. Bloch, P. Bourdieu, R.H. Finnegan, S.J. Fox, C. Geertz, E. Goffman, D. **Hymes**, R. Jakobson, B. Malinowski, M. Silverstein, B. Stoeltje, D. Tedlock, V.W. Turner.
Key-words: agn, com, dyn, frm, lan, PMC, pmt, rfl.

Baumann, Gerd, 1992, 'Ritual Implicates "Others". Rereading Durkheim in a Plural Society', in: Daniel de Coppet (ed.), *Understanding Rituals*, (European Association of Social Anthropologists), London, New York: Routledge (ISBN 0–415–06120–2 / 0–415–06121–0 (p)) (*) 97–116.

From the author's conclusion: "Narrow readings of Durkheim view rituals as crystallizations of basic values uniformly endorsed by communities that perform them with a view to themselves ultimately to create and confirm their cohesion as communities. In plural societies, this position is complicated by the presence of 'Others', be it as 'visible' participants or as 'invisible' categorical referents. There it appears more useful to replace the idea of a ritual community with that of ritual constituencies, to widen the values celebrated from perpetuation to assimilation and cultural change, and to distinguish participation according to a variety of possible modes. All three propositions arise from the thesis that rituals, in plural societies, are concerned with 'them' as much as with the quasi-Durkheimian 'us'. Since 'us' and 'them' are always contextual and relative terms, it may be useful to trace the concern with 'Others' also in the ritual of 'non-plural' societies...This may allow us to do more ethnographic justice to the differing influences, interests, values, and modes of participation and different participants in any ritual. These participants may include women alongside men, juniors alongside elders, recent participants alongside long-standing ones, converts alongside traditional adherents, guests alongside sponsors, clients alongside patrons, and one or more 'publics' alongside any 'community'. Ritual performances, symbols, and meanings may be directed at these as much as, if not sometimes more than, at the ritual core 'community' itself. There are 'Others' addressed through, or within, a ritual even when they all share the same ethnic denomination" (113–114). [MS]

References: É. Durkheim (–), E.R. Leach (–).
Examples: Christmas and children's birthday among Punjabi families in London.
Key-words: cmp, par, rfl.

Beattie, John H.M., 1966, 'Ritual and Social Change', *Man* 1:60–74.

The author uses the word 'ritual' to refer to "myth, magic and religion" (60). This is then opposed to 'science'. Science is defined as analytical and explanatory, whereas ritual is symbolic and expressive. Accordingly, time and again the author stresses that these are the true characteristics in which they differ from one another, e.g.: "I ally myself squarely, then, with those who assert that ritual is essentially expressive and symbolic, and that it is this that distinguishes it from other aspects of human behaviour" (65), and "I suggest, therefore,... that it is reasonable to regard ritual, whether myth, magic or religion, as essentially expressive and symbolic, and that it is primarily this aspect of it that we indicate when we call it ritual" (68). With respect to the question of why rituals are performed, he asserts that "in so far as magical and religious rites contain an essentially expressive element, they may, so far, be satisfying and rewarding in themselves.... But that is not all. For of course ritual is often, indeed generally, held by its practitioners to be effective as well as expressive" (68). The author thinks that this is because of the power ascribed to words (69). "I would suggest that all [rituals] exhibit...a conviction...that a ritual, dramatic performance will somehow bring about a desired end...it seems, it is the ritual dance or other performance itself, and the symbolic behaviour associated with it, that is believed or hoped will be effective" (70). [JS]

Key-words: com, def, pmc, pmt, sym, EFF, rep, myt, dnc.

Beattie, John H.M., 1970, 'On Understanding Ritual', in: Brian R. Wilson (ed.), *Rationality*, (Key Concepts in the Social Sciences), Evanston (IL), New York: Harper & Row (ISBN 0-631-09900-X) 240–268.

In the same volume as this article three other articles were published, viz. by Robin Horton, I.C. Jarvie & Joseph Agassi, and Steven Lukes. As the present author notes, these essays "are at least in some part responses to some of my arguments" (241, n. 4). The paper to which these authors responded was: John H.M. Beattie: "Ritual and Social Change", *Man* 1 (1966) 60–74 (*). In the present article, the author first summarizes his previous article (240–242) and then responds to Jarvie & Agassi (243–255), Lukes (256–259), and Horton (259–268). However, his arguments are the same as in his previous one (see there). [JS/MB]

References: R. Horton, I.C. Jarvie, J. Agassi, S. Lukes.
Key-words: com, pmc, pmt, sym, eff, rep, myt.

Beeman, William O., 1993, 'The Anthropology of Theater and Spectacle', *Annual Review of Anthropology* 22:369–393.

In this article, the author reviews "studies of theater and spectacle as distinct cultural institutions... to elucidate the specifically theatrical aspect of human life" (369). The article is divided in four sections. In the first, "The Study of Performance in Anthropology" (370–377), the author gives the historical and theoretical background of what he—following Hymes—calls the 'breakthrough into performance'. Here he gives an overview of the development of 'performance theory', mentioning the work of G. Bateson, V.W. Turner, Geertz, Schechner, Goffman, and others. In the following subsection, "The Study of Performance Traditions in Specific Cultures", the author gives an overview of the current research in different areas. In the second section, "The Institutions of Theater and Spectacle" (378–381), he refers to the work of Singer, Schechner, and Turner to specify "the unique qualities of theater and spectacle" by using ritual activity as distinct from theatrical activity. The 'efficacy/entertainment distinction' is here of crucial importance as "a way of separating ritual from theater" (379). According to the author, it is "[t]he use of three descriptive dimensions" as introduced by Schechner and Turner (that is, "efficacy vs. entertainment in intent, participation vs. observation in the audience's role, and symbolic representation vs. literal self-presentation in the performers' role") which "permits a rough distinction between theater and spectacle, on the one hand, and other performance forms, on the other" (379). In the third section, "Genres of Theater and Spectacle" (381–384), the author discusses theater genres in terms of four genre variables, that is, "the media used in presentation, the nature of the performer, the nature of the content of presentation, and the role of the audience", which also can be differentiated "according to the degree to which they are codified" (381). In the fourth section, "Cultural Meaning in Theater and Spectacle" (385–386), the author admits that "[d]espite a great deal of study of theater and spectacle genres, the ultimate meaning of this form of activity for human society remains elusive" (385). After briefly discussing the interrelationship of social drama and stage drama as conceptualized by Turner and Schechner, the author concludes that theater "evokes and solidifies a network of social and cognitive relationships existing in a triangular relationship between performer, spectator, and the world at large" and "no single experience of theater or spectacle is ever exactly like any other. This indeterminacy is part of what makes theater and spectacle forever intriguing" (386). [JK]

References: G. Bateson, R. Bauman, M.Th. Drewal, J. Emigh, J.W. Fernandez, C. Geertz, E. Goffman, D. Handelman, D. Hymes, B. Kapferer, J.J. MacAloon, R. Schechner, M. Singer, V.W. Turner.
Key-word: pmc, THA.

Bell, Catherine M., 1990, 'The Ritual Body and the Dynamics of Ritual Power', *Journal of Ritual Studies* 4.2 (= Holdrege (ed.) 1990 (*)): 299–313.

This article is part of a journal issue on 'ritual and power', which, as the author states, "provides an excellent opportunity to gain analytical clarity through refining our concepts and to articulate tentative theories for practical testing" (299). In this article, the author addresses "the distinctive qualities of ritual power so as to explore both ritual and power" and focuses on "the construction and deployment of 'ritual body'" (300). She notes that "[i]t is striking but not altogether surprising that the emergence of the conception of the social body has entailed a close consideration of ritual" (300). In the first section, "The Ritual Body" (301–305), the author discusses "how the ritually constructed body, as the means and end of ritual practices, involves the mastery of specific strategies of power" (301). She starts with the observation that Bourdieu, Foucault, and Comaroff not only address "the conception of the body within the context of larger analyses of social practices" (301) but also that they "glide neatly from a discussion of social practices into a discussion of ritual ones with little, if any, explication of the implied relation of ritual practices to social practices in general" (302). The assumption "that ritual is a form of social practice" is conceived of as "a corrective to the tendency to isolate ritual from all other forms of social activity" (302). The author addresses ritual in terms of social practice: "Ritual practices certainly appear to be distinctive social practices simply insofar as they deliberately work to contrast themselves with other forms of practice. In this perspective ritual is not a set of distinct acts, but a *way of acting* that draws a privileged contrast between what is being done and other activities aped or mimed by the contrast. It is thus probably more appropriate to speak of 'ritualization' when referring to a way of doing certain activities that differentiates those activities from other more conventional ones" (302). Addressing Bourdieu's notions of the 'logic of practice' and the 'ritualized body', the author argues that "the distinctiveness or ritualization as a type of social practice involves schemes of privileged contrasting as well as the process of internalization and objectification that occurs mutely in the interaction of a body and a ritually structured environment" (305). In the second section, "Ritual Power" (305–310), the author discusses Foucault and Comaroff. She states that Foucault contributes "a provocative reformulation of ritual in terms of the construction of the body and the delineation of power" (307), whereas Comaroff "draws attention to an important feature of ritual practice that is characteristic of its power and the limits of its power" (308). For both, "ritual practices are those social practices that localize power relations within the social body, creating an economy or hierarchy of power relations inscribed as a whole within each person" (309). Common to all three theories is the idea "that ritualization is concerned with contradictions", because they explore "how ritual practices express fundamental experiences of contradiction by setting up a pragmatic set of terms that cast the contradiction as a basic dichotomy underlying the rite" (309). In addition, they assume that "ritual practices produce their historical milieu each moment. The social or cultural context of ritual does not exist separately from the act; the context is created in the act. In other words, ritualization is *historical* practice—historically structured, historically effective, and history-producing" (310). In conclusion, the author states: "The distinctiveness of ritualization as a form of social practice lies in its particular strategy of power. Similarly, the distinctiveness of the power of ritualization lies in its particular strategy as a form of social practice. Ritualization addresses a situation, namely, the experience of a contradiction between the cultural order and the conditions of the historical moment. It does not see what it does to this situation, which is to redefine it. This redefinition is the production of a ritualized body with instinctive schemes for perception and evaluation that can dominate the contradiction.... By virtue of the interaction of a body and a structured environment, ritual works to dispense with conceptualizations or articulations of the relation between its means and ends" (310). Furthermore, the author suggests that "[r]itualization may be a particularly effective strategy for the social construction of a limited form of empowerment when explicit discourse is impossible or counterproductive", "when the power to be localized is understood to derive from beyond individuals and the group as a whole" or "when the contradictions to be domesticated...threaten the very possibility of beliefs, values and personal identity" (311). [JK]

References: L. Althusser, G. Bateson, P. Bourdieu, J. Comaroff, M. Foucault, F. Jameson, M. Johnson, G. Lakoff, J.Z. Smith, T.S. Turner.
Key-words: POW, str, prl, DYN, eff, EMB, idn.

Bell, Catherine M., 1992, *Ritual Theory, Ritual Practice*; Oxford, New York: Oxford University Press (ISBN 0–19–506923–4 / 0–19–507613–3 (p)) (xi + 270) (with index and bibliography).

This book is a critical reexamination of theoretical discourse on ritual in anthropology, ritual studies, and the history of religions. Not meant as an attempt to introduce a new theory of ritual, it is "designed to be something of a lightning rod for the dilemmas of theory, analysis, and practice" (vii). Arguing for a fundamental and critical rethinking of what ritual studies does, the author aims to introduce a new critical framework, "an analytical exploration of the social existence of the concept of ritual, the values ascribed to it, and the ramifications of these perspectives for scholarship" (ix). In the "Introduction" (3–9), she outlines the framework for critically "rethinking ritual" (5). Asking "what we have been doing with the category of ritual, why we have ended up where we are, and how we might formulate an analytical direction better able to grasp how such activities compare to other forms of social action" (4), the author emphasizes that her discussion "remains focused on an explicitly theoretical level of reflection about ritual rather than one more linked to ethnographic data" (4). The argument comprises three levels. Her starting point is "an exploration of what makes us identify some acts as ritual" (4), that is "the construction of ritual as an object of analysis" (5). On a second level—using such notions as 'practice', 'ritualization', 'embodiment', and 'empowerment'—she proposes another framework for assessing ritual activity more adequately "that is less encumbered by assumptions about thinking and acting and more disclosing of the strategies by which ritualized activities do what they do" (4). On a third, meta-theoretical level, the author questions "how categories of ritual practice have been used to define objects and methods of theoretical practice" and thereby raises "questions about the dynamics of theoretical practice as such" (5). These three levels are mirrored in the structure of the book. In the first section, "The Practice of Ritual Theory" (13–66), the author outlines the emergence and construction of the discourse on ritual. The aim of this section is to "show theoretical discourse on ritual to be highly structured by the differentiation and subsequent reintegration of two particular categories of human experience: thought and action" (16). Analyzing the discourse structure with its underlying opposition between thought and action, the author delineates a series of three structural patterns: "In the first, ritual as activity is differentiated from conceptual categories. In the second, ritual is the cultural medium by which thoughts and acts (or concepts and dispositions, beliefs and behaviors, etc.) are reintegrated. In the third, the activities of the object (the actors) and the concepts of the subject (the theorist) are also integrated by means of a discursive focus on the integrative function of ritual" (47–48). In the second section, "The Sense of Ritual" (67–168), the author first outlines two ways in which ritual can be defined as action, namely as an autonomous phenomenon or as an aspect of all human activity. In relating different notions of ritual action, the author introduces the term 'ritualization' as "a way of acting that is designed and orchestrated to distinguish and privilege what is being done in comparison to other, usually quotidian, activities" (74). Focusing on the act itself, she takes 'practice' as "a nonsynthetic and irreducible term for human activity" (81) and uses the term to specify features of human activity: "Practice is (1) situational; (2) strategic; (3) embedded in a misrecognition of what it is in fact doing; and (4) able to reproduce or reconfigure a version of the order of power in the world, or what I will call 'redemptive hegemony'" (81). The notion of 'redemptive hegemony' is defined as "a strategic and practical orientation for acting, a framework possible only insofar as it is embedded in the act itself. As such, of course, the redemptive hegemony of practice does not reflect reality more or less effectively; it creates it more or less effectively" (85). Introducing a theory of practice as a conceptual framework for the study of ritualization as an alternative to the concept of ritual, she concludes: "Yet if ritual is interpreted in terms of practice, it becomes clear that formality, fixity, and repetition are not intrinsic qualities of ritual so much as they are a frequent, but not universal strategy for producing ritualized acts" (92). In the chapter on "The Ritual Body" (94–117), the author discusses the construction of the ritualized body as "a body invested with a 'sense' of ritual" (98). It is the ritualization that "produces this ritualized body through the interaction of the body with a structured and structuring environment" (98); it is seen as "the strategic manipulation of 'context' in the very act of reproducing it" (100). Moreover, the author continues, the main strategies of ritualization are the construction of binary oppositions and their orchestrated hierarchization in asymmetrical relations of dominance and subordination. According to her, it is characteristic of ritualization that it "sees its end, the rectification of a problematic. It does not see what it does in the process of realizing this end, its transformation of the problematic itself" (109). For this reason, the author looks at ritualization and its dynamics in the context of ritual traditions and systems, as well as the problem of continuity and change. Ritualization as a strategic way of acting, the author argues, empowers or disempowers the social agents by way of ritual mastery. In the third section, "Ritual and Power" (169–223), she is concerned with ritual control as a strategic device in power relations. Her aim is to "build upon some alternative understandings of social dynamics to delineate a relationship between the strategies of ritualization and the construction of particular types of power relations" (170). Here the author uses the notion of 'embodiment' in order to discuss the relation between ritual and social control in terms of belief, ideology, and legitimization. She argues that "the projection and embodiment of schemes in ritualization is more effectively viewed as a 'mastering' of relationships of power relations within an arena that affords a negotiated appropriation of the dominant values embedded in the symbolic schemes" (182). In the final chapter, "The Power of Ritualization" (197–223), the author again emphasizes that "ritualization is first and foremost a strategy for the construction of certain types of power relationships effective within particular social organizations" (197). Discussing theories of power and the effects and limits of ritual empowerment, she concludes: "Ritualization is not a matter of transmitting shared beliefs, instilling a dominant ideology as an internal subjectivity, or even providing participants with the concepts to think with. The particular construction and interplay of power relations effected by ritualization defines, empowers, and constrains" (221). [JK]

References: E.M. Ahern, L. Althusser, M.C. Bateson, **M.E.F. Bloch**, **P. Bourdieu** (+), A. Cohen, **J. Comaroff & J. Comaroff**, R.A. Delattre, M. Douglas, **É. Durkheim**, J.W. Fernandez, **M. Foucault** (+), **C. Geertz** (–), **M. Gluckman**, E. Goffman, **J. Goody** (+), R.L. Grimes (+), D. Hymes, **F. Jameson** (+), D.I. Kertzer, E.R. Leach, C. Lévi-Strauss, G.A. Lewis, **S. Lukes**, M. Mauss, N.D. Munn, S.B. Ortner, **R.A. Rappaport**, J.Z. Smith (+), F. Staal, **S.J. Tambiah**, T.S. Turner, **V.W. Turner**, **V. Valeri**.

Reviews: P. Smith *AJS* 98.2 (1992) 420; F.W. Clothey *JRS* 6.2 (1992) 139; J.V. Spickard *SocR* 54.3 (1993) 321; K. Flanagan *Sociol* 26.4 (1992) 744; J. Oosten *CA* 34.1 (1993) 106–108; R. Gardner *JJRS* 21.1 (1994) 118–120; S.Y. Chin *RA* 24.3 (1995) 177–185.

Key-words: agn, def, dyn, eff, EMB, emo, eth, hsc, mim, mng, par, pmc, POW, prl.

Bell, Catherine M., 1993, 'The Authority of Ritual Experts', *Studia Liturgica* 23:98–120.

This text was presented at a conference, where the author had been asked to address three questions. In the first section ("Questions and Issues", 98–100), she mentions these questions, viz. I: Is it "not possible to generate a theoretical model of ritual that simultaneously respects the rites, the participants in those rites, and the social scientists analyzing them"? (98). II: How does one go "about analyzing both the internal dynamics intrinsic to ritual and the external pressures to which rituals respond"? (99). III: This question "concerned evaluation of post-Vatican II liturgical reforms, especially in terms of the power of ritual to shape modern Catholic identity", etc. (99). The author refuses to commit herself to answers, but wants "to show that they are questions that emerge in a particular social and historical situation *vis-à-vis* ritual. They are, that is, the questions of a specific class of ritual experts. I want to explore various types of ritual experts and their roles in defining, shaping, and sometimes magnifying ritual, in establishing the authority of ritual and diagnosing its problems, and in orchestrating specific relationships between liturgical and social change" (99–100). In the second section, "Alternative Model of the Ritual Expert" (100–102), she asks: "What are ritual experts?" As an answer, she first points to the informants of the ethnographers. However, the "role of ritual experts in devising and decreeing rites is in fact much more widespread, dynamic, and complicated than most current models would lead us to suppose" (100). This she illustrates with the example of the Taoist Master Lu Hsiu-ching, who reformed Taoist religion. In the third section, "Experts and Ritual Change" (102–104), she gives a number of examples that "demonstrate that various types of 'so-called ritual experts'...have routinely 'devised and decreed' ritual practices. These examples also illustrate...that ritual is not intrinsically rigid and unchanging; that effective ritual need not spontaneously well up from grassroots communities; nor need it develop smoothly...Why are we so drawn to the opposite, highly romanticized view of ritual—that of authentic ritual as unchanging, spontaneous, and harmonious? Part of the answer may lie in styles of ritualization, but part of it may also lie in the various ways ritual experts shape the practice and understanding of ritual" (104). This brings her to the fourth section, "Oral and Literate Forms of Ritual Expertise" (104–109), in which she discusses the differences of ritual traditions in oral and literate societies. She argues that in oral societies, rituals are more easily adapted to changing circumstances, while the fiction is maintained that they remained unchanged: "Ritual must have both a convincing continuity with remembered rites and a convincing coherence with community life" (106). However, in literate societies, ritual is no longer "a matter of doing what it seems people have always done; it becomes the correct performance or enactment of the textual script. The audience has little right or opportunity to approve or disapprove, since only those who have access to the texts know whether it is being done correctly or not" (107–108). In section five, "Secular Experts and Ritual" (109–113), she looks at "a new type of ritual expert, the secular scholar" (109). She recalls the stories of Frank Cushing, William Robertson Smith, and Frits Staal who, each in his own way, created an image of certain rituals that (as we can see now) differed significantly from the view of the participants. "Here I want simply to make the point that the perspective of social scientific theories of ritual is as socio-historically determined and self-legitimating as the interpretations of ritual given by experts like Ogotemmeli, Master Lu, and the Nambudiri Brahmins" (113). In the sixth section, "Liturgical Experts" (113–118), she admits that "[w]hat had been historically made, of course, could be legitimately re-made. So this scholarship [liturgical studies] directly facilitated ways to think about major liturgical reform" (113). But then she gives an example where it failed, concluding that if a community is too heterogeneous, there is no 'right' ritual that can solve their problems. "[M]any liturgical problems are community problems" (118). In the final section, "Conclusion" (118–120), she summarizes her argumentation, paying special attention to the social scientific and liturgical experts. "Ritual, defined as a type of universal category subsuming activities that participants would never lump together, comes to be seen in terms of social functions and cultural meanings unknown to participants themselves but elucidated by the secular expert" (119). And "[r]itual alone cannot do all the things liturgists want it to do. I also doubt it can do all things social scientists are wont to see it do" (120). [JS]

Key-words: pmc, emb, cmp, eff, POW, DYN, def, soc, rfl.

Bell, Catherine M., 1997, *Ritual. Perspectives and Dimensions*; Oxford, New York: Oxford University Press (ISBN 0-19-511051-x / 0-19-511052-8 (p)) (xv + 351) (with index and bibliography).

At the end of her book, the author writes: "The central concern of this study has been to introduce systematically all of the issues, debates, and areas of inquiry that comprise the modern study of ritual" (267). Indeed, it gives a survey of the whole domain of ritual studies, discussing in Part II, "Rites: The Spectrum of Ritual Activities" (91–169), and in Part III, "Contexts: The Fabric of Ritual Life" (171–267). In the present context, however, esp. Part I, "Theories: The History of Interpretation" (1–89), is significant. Its three chapters deal respectively with "Myth or Ritual: Questions of Origin and Essence" (3–22), "Ritual and Society: Questions of Social Function and Structure" (23–60), and "Ritual Symbols, Syntax, and Praxis: Questions of Cultural Meaning and Interpretation" (61–89). Together they attempt to give an overview of the whole range of ritual theories generated so far. True to her own theoretical position, however, the author also states—in the conclusions of the very last chapter of her book—that ultimately the position of the scholar should be part of the study and theorizing of rituals, because: "Just as modern theories of ritual have had a powerful effect on how people ritualize, how people ritualize profoundly affects what theorists set about to describe and explain. There is no 'scientific' detachment here: ritual theorists, experts, and participants are pulled into a complex circle of interdependence.... If scholarship on ritual as a universal construct has succeeded in creating the beginnings of a shared sense of ritual in many religious and civic practices of Euro-American culture, then we cannot dismiss the concern that such a construct can reach out to restructure practice elsewhere. We may well be in the very process of actually creating ritual as the universal phenomenon we have long taken it to be. Yet creating it has not been our intention, and does not appear to further our more self-conscious goals of understanding" (265).

"A global discourse on ritual, understood as a transcultural language of the human spirit, is more likely to promote a sense of common humanity and cross-cultural respect than the view that one set of religious rites are the revealed truth itself and the idols worshiped by all other peoples must be destroyed. Yet it is clear that this discourse is being constructed not without violence, loss, and deeply rooted assumptions of cultural hegemony. In a purely methodological vein, such concerns suggest the need for revised methodologies" (266). As the author states in her introduction, "this book is meant to a more holistic and pragmatic orientation to multiple dimensions of the phenomenon of ritual" ([ix]). However, "instead of approaching ritual as a clear-cut and timeless object of scrutiny, the following chapters focus on how a variety of definitions and constructed understandings of ritual have emerged and shaped our world. As such, this presentation recognizes that any discussion of ritual is essentially an exercise in reflective historical and comparative analysis" (x). Accordingly, the thesis "that talk about ritual may reveal more about the speakers than about the bespoken" (xi) will apply to this author/book as well. [JS/MS]

Reviews: **D.E. Owen *RSR* 24.1 (1998) 23–30**; M. Collins *ThSt* 59.4 (1998) 755–757; D. Kertzer *AA* 101.4 (1999) 873 f; F. Bird *JSSR* 38.4 (1999) 566–568; A.P. Lyons *MTSR* 11 (1999) 421–426; R. Kirkland *RSR* 25.1 (1999) 54; R. Parmentier *HR* 39.4 (2000) 386–388; J. Carter *JR* 79.2 (1999) 344; N.D. Mitchell *Wor* 73.2 (1999) 95–96.
Key-words: GEN, hsc.

Bell, Catherine M., 1998, 'Performance', in: Mark C. Taylor (ed.), *Critical Terms for Religious Studies*, Chicago, London: University of Chicago Press (ISBN 0–226–79156–4 / 0–226–79157–2 (p)) 205–224.

In this paper on the terminology of performance theory, the author gives an overview of the approaches to performance theory that have become popular since the 1960s. Some quotations illustrate what the author suggests these approaches are about: "Performance approaches seek to explore how activities *create* culture, authority, transcendence, and whatever forms of holistic ordering are required for people to act in meaningful and effective ways. Hence, by virtue of this underlying concern, performance terminology analyzes both religious and secular rituals as orchestrated events that construct people's perceptions and interpretations" (208). "Performance theory does not analyze the phenomenal data by shepherding it into preliminary categories; rather, it tries to ask questions that disclose the holistic dynamics of the phenomenon in its own terms as much as possible. Most radically, it does not start out assuming what religion and ritual are; it attempts to let the activities under scrutiny have ontological and analytic priority, while the scholar deploys tools to untangle those activities in ways that can inform and modify his or her notions of religion and ritual and not simply attest to them" (211). From an analysis of a daily Chinese ritual, the author concludes that "a performative approach does not usually offer a definitive interpretation of a set of ritual actions. Indeed, it is better at conveying the multiple ways in which such activities are meant and experienced, as well as how such multiplicity is integral to the efficacy of ritual performances" (218). The author draws attention to the problem of terminological inflation: "However, when performance theory becomes a dominant metaphor that is systematically developed and applied, its insights may begin to cost more in terms of systematic oversights. Perhaps the greatest challenge to current performance theory lies in its tendency to flirt with universalism, that is, to substitute performance for older notions of ritual in order to create a new general model of action" (218). [JK]

References: T. Asad (+), P. Bourdieu, C. Geertz, E. Goffman, J. Goody (+), **R.L. Grimes**, D. Handelman, D. Hymes, Th.W. Jennings, B. Kapferer, B. Lincoln, **J.J. MacAloon**, **S.F. Moore**, **B.G. Myerhoff**, **R. Schechner**, E.L. Schieffelin, **L.E. Sullivan**, S.J. Tambiah, **V.W. Turner**.
Example: Chinese domestic offerings.
Key-words: PMC, pr1, eff.

Bell, Catherine M., 2005, 'Ritual [Further Considerations]', in: Lindsay Jones (ed.), *The Encyclopedia of Religion. Second Edition* (11), Detroit etc.: Thomson Gale (ISBN 0–02–865980–5) 7848–7856 (with bibliography).

At the outset, the author comments on the notorious difficulties of defining the term 'ritual', and she sketches some of the advantages of the term 'ritualization' (7848). Moreover, she comments on "the ability of ritual to pull together scholars of different subjects, approaches, and disciplines" (7849). "As a 'rough guide' to the current scene [of ritual theory], a first-order distinction can be made between theories that remain heavily rooted in cultural explanation and those that are recreating naturalistic (or scientific) models of explanation. Yet even within these two general positions, no two theories are alike. In addition, several popular theories resist categorization even within a sorting this broad" (7849). Under the heading "Communication and a New

Naturalism", the author then presents and discusses the theories of Rappaport (1999 (*)) and Lawson & McCauley (1990 (*) and 2002 (*)) (7849–7851). Under the heading "Practice and Performance", she presents her own theory and briefly discusses Humphrey & Laidlaw (1994 (*)) (7852–7853). She then proceeds to outline some theoretical implications and versions of performance theories. Furthermore, she briefly presents the popular theories of sacrifice by Bataille and Girard and offers some comments on why they are perceived as provocative (7854). In the final section ("New Directions"), the author comments on the merits of cultural-practice theories and cognitive theories, respectively (7854–7855). Furthermore, she states: "Future theories of ritual may address some of the evidence for how people are actually ritualizing today" (7855). The author concludes by stating: "So, within the field of religion, ritual studies inevitably struggles to identify its peculiar contribution, which is less likely to be a special position or method as a stubborn refusal to reduce…so-called religious phenomenon [sic] into fully other (that is, non-religious, un-holy) components or conclusions" (7855). [MS]
Key-word: GEN.

Bell, Catherine M., 2006, 'Embodiment', in: Jens Kreinath, Jan A.M. Snoek & Michael Stausberg (eds), *Theorizing Rituals. Vol. I: Issues, Topics, Approaches, Concepts*, (Numen Book Series 114–1), Leiden, Boston: Brill (ISBN-10: 90–04–15342–x, ISBN-13: 978–90–04–15342–4) 533–543.

After briefly reviewing major contributions from a variety of sources to the study of the 'body' in the last two decades, this piece offers an assessment of their fruitfulness for the main concerns of scholarship about ritual and embodiment. Two general approaches, how ritual shapes the body and how the body shapes ritual, have generated several insightful versions of a third approach to social constructionism among postmodern theorists. Yet it is questionable how much these theorists really know about ritual in modern and postmodern societies, and so it is questionable how readily their theories can be usefully applied. The piece concludes with some attention to the concerns with bodies within a few examples of ritual practice. [Catherine Bell]
Key-word: EMB.

Bellah, Robert N., 2003, 'The Ritual Roots of Society and Culture', in: Michele Dillon (ed.), *Handbook of the Sociology of Religion*, Cambridge etc.: Cambridge University Press (ISBN 0–521–80624–0 / 0–521–00078–5 (p)) 31–44.

In this chapter the author argues "that ritual is not only real, but, in agreement with Rappaport, that it is 'humanity's basic social act', a position that...has a great deal of evidence in its favor" (44). Starting with a review of Durkheim's position, some of this 'evidence' the author traces from recent theories on the origin of language (32–35) and the origins of music (35–37), all of which, in different ways, refer to ritual. This leads to a discussion of the nature, or basic features, of ritual (37–39), in which the author mainly follows Rappaport. Since rational action theory raises questions as to the "future of ritual in our kind of society" (39), the author goes on to discuss the presence of ritual in various spheres of life focusing on synchronizing, periodicity, keeping together in time, and unisonance (39–43). In a concluding paragraph, the author advocates the necessity of general terms such as 'ritual' in the social science. At the same time "[h]ealthy skepticism about them is always in order" (44). [MS]

References: T. Asad, C.M. Bell (+/–), T. Deacon, **É. Durkheim** (+), E. Goffman (+), **R.A. Rappaport** (+).
Examples: Three days of ritual following the death of J.F. Kennedy, United States federal election of 2000.
Key-words: gen, SOC, tim, mus.

Bird, Frederick B., 1980, 'The Nature and Function of Ritual Forms. A Sociological Discussion', *Studies in Religion* 9:387–402.

In the first part of this article, "Phenomenological and functional characteristics of ritual forms" (387–393), the author has "attempted to develop generalizations which are valid for primitive, historic, and contemporary religions and which are fitting as well for activities associated with etiquette, magic, therapy, and public ceremonies. In the process I have attempted to set forth as broad a view of ritual as possible while still making these generalizations specific enough to distinguish ritual codes from habituated and stylized behaviour and from moral codes" (387–388). He then defines rituals as "culturally transmitted symbolic codes which are stylized, regularly repeated, dramatically structured, authoritatively designated, and intrinsically valued" (388). A discussion of the five components of this definition follows. In the discussion of the first characteristic ("rituals are culturally transmitted codes"), he distinguishes explicitly "between rituals as symbolic codes and ritual actions or ritual processes as forms of behaviour, enacted in keeping with these codes" (388) and stresses that "rituals [such as the celebration of weddings] are not merely habituated behaviour" (388). With respect to the second ("ritual codes are like scripts for dramas"), he remarks that "acting in conformity with the scripts is considered to be intrinsically rewarding" (388). While presenting the third ("rituals are stylized, highly symbolic codes"), he argues that "the dramatic character of rituals is evident in three ways. First, ritual scripts must be acted out and not just spoken. In particular, rituals call for bodily action... Second, by virtue of the ritual enactment, participants expect something to happen. Ritual action is believed at some levels to have an immediate efficacy.... Third, as in theatrical drama, participants assume particular valued positions or characters by virtue of the ritual.... It is more fitting to argue that ritual participants assume a position/character rather than a special social role because within the ritual the focus of attention is on their sense of identity and on their relation to what counts as reality and not on specific tasks and functions" (389–390). The fourth characteristic is that "ritual actions are repeated", and the fifth that they "are authoritatively designated" (390). "For this very reason it is often difficult to construct new rituals, not only because the new rituals may seem arbitrary and unfamiliar but because they lack the authority of tradition itself. Rituals gain authority in part through the very process of their being repeated. However, rituals may gain authority by other means than tradition" (390). Then religious rituals are defined as those rituals that are "means by which persons establish and maintain their relation to what they consider to be sacred" (390). A definition of 'sacred realities' is then given. But "the distinction between religious and non-religious rituals is fluid" (391). After a definition of 'magical rituals', the author continues with an analysis of the functions of rituals: "(1) Ritual codes are often utilized to regulate social behaviour at times and places of transition between existing forms of social organization" (391). That is, "ritual codes reduce the sense of uncertainty and conflict... Groups of persons re-affirm their collective identity... [and] individuals may re-affirm their sense of personal identity" through specific rituals (391). "(2) Dramatic changes in social status and personal identity are often marked, occasioned, and brought about by the utilization of ritual codes, which symbolically set forth these changes" (392). "(3) Ritual codes serve also as a means for communicating a wide range of affections and sentiments" (392). And "(4) Rituals also function as a means for bringing into play intra-personal and inter-personal energies and imaginations which otherwise frequently remain suppressed or dormant" (392). In the second part, "Rituals, ritualisms, and liturgies" (393–395), the author distinguishes "rituals which are alive and powerful from dead ritualism" (393). He links this to ritual dynamics: "Ritual forms which resist change...may thereby in the process lose touch with the evolving forms of social organization, becoming ritualism unattuned to contemporary emotions and life-situations. However innovative, ritual codes are also in danger of becoming ritualisms because they seem unfamiliar and arbitrary" (394). He now moves to the term 'liturgy': "If the word ritual is used to describe the overall symbolic form, then the word liturgy may be used to identify the number and richness of symbolic elements within a given ritual. Rituals are liturgically full, when they involve the use of many different actions and symbols" (394). In the third part, "Types of rituals and their characteristic functions" (395–396), the author classifies rituals into seven "types of ritual forms": 1. Taboos; 2. Purification rites; 3. Spiritual exercises; 4. Rites of passage; 5. Worship; 6. Shamanic rituals; and 7. Etiquettes. These are further refined and commented upon in a table that follows the article (400–402). The fourth and final part, "Changing ritual patterns in contemporary society" (396–399) opens: "As I now briefly depict current development in the utilization of rituals within contemporary North American societies, I will draw upon the preceding observations concerning the nature and function of ritual codes, the differences between rituals and ritualisms, and the typical ritual forms and their functions" (396). Four such developments are then presented. [JS]

References: E.R. Leach, E.H. Erikson, M. Douglas.
Key-words: pmc, tha, sym, str, idn, eff, sec, DYN, DEF.

Bird, Frederick B., 1995, 'Ritual as Communicative Action', in: Jack N. Lightstone & Frederick B. Bird (eds), *Ritual and Ethnic Identity. A Comparative Study of the Social Meaning of Liturgical Ritual in Synagogues*, Waterloo (ON): Wilfried Laurier University Press (ISBN 0–88920–247–8) 23–53.

This article deals with the questions "how do ritual acts differ from non-ritual ones" and "how do variations in the performance of these affect their meaning and impact" (23), by focusing on the communicative character of ritual behavior. In the first part of the article, the author discusses the characteristic features of ritual. He defines "rituals as symbolic acts that are intrinsically valued and usually repeated, ritual actors trying to behave in keeping with expected characters and roles by using stylized gestures and words" (23). Furthermore, he differentiates ritual from non-ritual behavior, stating that non-ritual behavior is strategic, customary, and expressive. Although there are some differences, ritual performances are similar to theatrical ones. In the second part of his article, the author discusses ritual as a medium of communication. For him, ritual as "a unique medium of communication... is both compact and multidimensional" (28). He elaborates on five forms of communication related to ritual, namely constitutive, self-representative, expressive, regulative, and invocative aspects, of which the first four are typical of all rituals, whereas the invocative aspect is to be found only in religious rituals. After analyzing the relation between ritual and food in feasts as a communicative activity, the author illustrates the five forms of communication in order to show the multidimensional character of ritual communication. In the third part, besides stating some possibilities of variation in ritual performance regarding the level of expertise, the author considers the five forms of communication in terms of evaluation and comparison of actual ritual performances. [JK]

References: M. Douglas, É. Durkheim, E.H. Erikson, C. Geertz, E. Goffman, R.L. Grimes, E. Leach, S.J. Tambiah, V.W. Turner.
Key-words: com, eth, mng, pmc, tha, pmt, pr1, rfl, sym, def.

Blackburn, Stuart H., 1988, *Singing of Birth and Death. Texts in Performance*; Philadelphia: University of Pennsylvania Press (ISBN 0–8122–8097–0) (xxiv + 263) (with index and bibliography).

"This is a book about texts and oral performance in a Tamil tradition called the bow song" (xvii). Nevertheless, especially the "Introduction" (xvii–xxiv) and the last chapter, "Conclusions" (214–221), are highly concerned with theoretical issues. In the introduction, the author points out that previous research on rituals since the shift of attention towards performance in the 1970s downplayed the role of textual issues: "Narratives in performance were process not products, events not texts" (xvii). But we "have reached a point from which an advance in the study of oral performance can only be made by first reclaiming its narrative base" (xviii). The author advocates the return to a "text-centered approach to performance" that "starts with the narrative outside its enactment.

It consciously rejects the claim that the meaning of the text lies only in performance, that the text is inseparable from its telling" (xviii). "When bow songs enter performance, they become ritual acts, and in this process lies the key to understanding how these narratives structure their performance. First, there is a degree of reciprocity: narrative and ritual help shape each other. On the one hand, as the event-centered approach predicts, the ritual setting of performance alters story content...On the other hand, as a text-centered approach reveals, the ritual function of a bow song performance itself is dependent on its narrative content" (xix). Bow songs, then, "are ritual language" (xix), and the author puts forward some thoughts about the study of ritual language that, he feels, has hitherto mainly focused on 'religious genres', such as prayer and invocation, or on myth. Starting from the analysis of the bow song, however, the author draws attention to "the essential property of ritual language: not the ability to repeat, but to name" (220). According to the author, the scholarly literature so far has distinguished two types of oral traditions: those in which the actual text is improvised (simultaneous composition or oral formulaic) and those in which the fixed text is memorized before it is performed (prior composition). The first method would dominate in cases of long texts, the second where short texts are concerned. The bow song tradition, however, has long fixed texts (many hours), which are rehearsed and tailored to the actual situation before they are performed (prior preparation). The stories are available in written form, of which only the temple manuscripts are regarded as ritual objects; these have the status of a standard text. In the end, the author concludes: "It is not...the magical power of words that summons gods to a [bow song festival. The gods] come because they are called when their stories are correctly sung on the bow. This is why the lines of a bow song performance are relatively fixed. Fixity, however, is more than the repetition and invariance said to be characteristic of ritual language. In the bow song tradition, fixity is a form of veracity. There is only one true version of the Tampimar story and that version must be faithfully learned, copied, and then sung, even read, in performance. Most important is the singing. It must be precise, for only narrative accuracy ensures ritual efficacy" (221). This efficacy in summoning the gods is crucial, since the ritual deals with the subject of death. "When men and women, the victims of murder and suicide, return as gods and goddesses to dance and speak through their mediums, then death has been beaten back, its finality denied.... In the bow song tradition, worshiping the deified dead signals not a grim resignation to the powerful grip of death, but a partial victory over it" (219). The author only hints at the possibility of generalizing his findings beyond the tradition he studied. [JS/MS]

References: R. Bauman (+), B. Kapferer, P. Seitel (+), J. Sherzer (+), R. Huntington & P. Metcalf, J. Parry & M.E.F. Bloch, G. Obeyesekere, S.J. Tambiah.
Example: The Tamil Bow Song festival.
Reviews: H.L. Seneviratne *AA* 91 (1989) 228; M. Trawick *AE* 16.3 (1989) 573 f; P.S. Richman *AFS* 49.1 (1990) 172–174; J.D. Smith *BSOAS* 53.1 (1990) 160; S. Venugopal *JAF* 103.408 (1990) 229; W.P. Harman *JR* 70.1 (1990) 131.
Key-words: pmc, pmt, pr2, cmp, idn, EFF, rht, med, dyn, dnc.

Blanchard, Kendall, 1980, 'The Ritual Dimensions of Play. Structure and Perspective. Introduction', in: Helen B. Schwartzman (ed.), *Play and Culture. 1978 Proceedings of the Association for the Anthropological Study of Play*, West Point (NY): Leisure Press (ISBN 0–918–4385–27) 49–51.

In his introduction, the author underlines the importance of the analysis of the relationship between ritual and play. The analysis enables, in general, the understanding of the cultural experience and, in particular, the understanding of play through ritual and ritual through play. Before presenting the papers by Steven J. Fox and Don Handelman, the author sums up the theoretical issues that those papers address as follows: "(1) the meaning of the play-ritual interrelationship, (2) the structure and function of play as ritual, (3) the structure and function of ritual as play, (4) the social play context as a setting for the analysis of ritual behavior, (5) play and ritual in the change process, and (6) the possible application of play-as-ritual conceptualizations" (50). [JK]

Reference: E. Norbeck, V.W. Turner.
Key-words: dyn, pmc, str.

Blasi, Anthony J., 1985, 'Ritual as a Form of the Religious Mentality', *Sociological Analysis* 46:59–71.

The author deals with ritual "as a *social scientific* category. That is to say, the designation ritual needs to be used in a way that allows for a coherent and adequate discussion of that which makes an action as well as the experience of that action ritual", in other words, "an understanding of ritual *per se*" (60). At the outset, the author adopts Monica Wilson's (1971) definition of ritual ("ritual is limited to the symbolic enactment of relationships between man and what is conceived of as a transcendental reality") and elucidates what he perceives as this definition's theoretical and methodological implications (60–61). These prohibit (micro- as well as macro-) functionalist and theological approaches to ritual, for they "miss making an analysis of ritual *as ritual*" (62). As an alternative, the author proposes a phenomenological approach based on the following insight: "in the human sciences, the appropriate point of departure for characterizing an object of inquiry obtains in the perspective of the typical social actor who is involved in it. Thus, in ritual, one takes up for consideration the case of the typical social actor who is involved in it. The form of consciousness which the person would have in this kind of institution is the first theoretical datum" (63). Hence, according to the author, "it is essential to speak of the *participant's typified orientation* toward the sacred" (63). "The critical terms in a serious discussion of ritual must therefore refer to this *focusing*, this enacted *orientation*, not merely on the specifics of the enactments or on the sacred *per se*.... In participating in ritual, the person is neither being profane nor being sacred, but is rather being religious. That is, the person's action is embodying a stance" (63). In the subsequent part of the paper, the author introduces some "[c]ategories for description and discussion" (63–69), based on phenomenology and the philosophy of G.H. Mead. He addresses "the consciousness process which is typical of ritual" (65). As a matter of fact, the author finds "that the ritual participants do some of the things that the phenomenologists do" (65). "The present suggestion is that ritual has the *epoché* [which he describes as "the suspension of the belief in or consideration of some aspect of consciousness for purposes of looking at some other aspect" (64–65)] in an unspectacular, taken-for-granted fashion as a presupposition of its very enactment" (65). Then the author discusses some aspects of this continuous *epoché*. "Those who are involved in the ritual 'understand' that 'of course' what they are doing is ceremonial, cultic, set-apart, and in some cases forbidden and sacred" (66). "Within its conventional framework, within its *epoché*, ritual can dwell upon what cannot be mentally addressed elsewhere" (66). "Furthermore, within its *epoché*, ritual can allow for the emergence of attitudes...which would be unthinkable in the everyday world" (67). The author tries to link his ideas to V.W. Turner's theory, and "[f]inally, ritual enacts an *epoché* by suspending the pragmatic efficacy of ordinary actions" (69). "Because of the irrelevance of the means-ends-scheme in ritual, it is analytically meaningless to speak of ritual as either rational or non-rational; it is simply outside of the co-ordinates of the pragmatically rational world" (69). [MS]

References: R. Bocock, R.L. Grimes, S.K. Langer, G.H. Mead, R.A. Rappaport, V.W. Turner, A.F.C. Wallace, M. Wilson.
Examples: Roman Catholic Sacraments.
Key-words: def, com, sec, eff, int, gst.

Bloch, Maurice E.F., 1974, 'Symbols, Song, Dance and Features of Articulation. Is Religion an Extreme Form of Traditional Authority?' ***Archives Européennes de Sociologie*** **15:55–81.**

Through the analysis of their features of articulation, the author compares the linguistic aspect of rituals with traditional forms of authority. Based on his assumption that communication in ritual can be analyzed linguistically, the author criticizes recent studies of ritual symbols because they isolate symbols from the ritual process and interpret them as specific units containing a distinct symbolic meaning. He argues that "symbols in ritual cannot be understood without a prior study of the nature of the communication medium of ritual in which they are embedded" (55). In support of his argument, the author applies modern linguistic theories to the data of a circumcision ceremony of the Merina in Madagascar, but he also uses semantic studies in linguistics that emphasize the identity of syntax and semantics. Assuming this identity, he connects the "creativity of syntax" with the "logical potency of language" in order to specify the linguistic and communicative aspects of ritual, because, for him, ritual makes special use of language: it is "an occasion where syntactic and other linguistic freedoms are reduced" (56). He points out that ritual is "a place where, because the ordinary forms of linguistic communication are changed, we cannot assume the semantic processes of more ordinary communication" (56). He aims to show how this formalization of language is significant in distinct uses of language as traditional authority. Based on a comparison of formalized and everyday speech acts, he distinguishes two kinds of meaning, the propositional force of language and its performative force. After proposing that formalized language diminishes its propositional force, the author states that religion and ritual use forms of communication that do not have a propositional force: "If words in ritual have little explanatory power but much socially useful ambiguity and are little separated from their context, they begin to perform less as parts of a language and more as *things*, in the same way as material symbols" (75). Thus the formalization of language in ritual results in one's only having, in ritual, to follow the sequential order it directs to, because: "Units in ritual do not follow each other logically, but sequentially, since there is no power in the articulation which links them. The sequence of concepts is given and not accepted; it has no 'truth' conditions" (76). The author claims that it is the business of semantics to study the rules of how lexical units can be combined in utterances and that meaning is primarily transmitted by the way these units can be combined. In analyzing songs and dances as different modes of communication used in ritual, the author concludes that symbols cannot be understood as units of meaning on the basis of a signifier/signified model, because it is more important what rituals do: "The experience of the ritual is an experience fused with its context and therefore only an attempt to explain what this event as a whole is for is an explanation of the content" (77). [JK]

References: B. Bettelheim (−), É. Durkheim, E.E. Evans-Pritchard, E. Leach (−), C. Lévi-Strauss, R.A. Rappaport (+), F. de Saussure, S.J. Tambiah (+), V.W. Turner (−).
Example: Circumcision ceremonies of the Merina of Madagascar.
Key-words: com, dnc, eff, med, pmc, pmt, pow, sem, sym.

Bloch, Maurice E.F., 1986, *From Blessing to Violence. History and Ideology in the Circumcision Ritual of the Merina of Madagascar* (Cambridge Studies in Social Anthropology 61); Cambridge etc.: Cambridge University Press (ISBN 0–521–30639–6 / 0–521–31404–6) (x + 210) (with index and bibliography).

In the first chapter ("The Social Determination of Ritual", 1–11), the author finds "the study of ritual endlessly bouncing between two walls—a functionalist wall…and an intellectualist or symbolist wall" (9). His aim is to overcome that dilemma. He argues: "if rituals are a special kind of phenomena, it follows that they will be manifested in history in a special way. If this is so, it is also reasonable to assume that the special way rituals are manifested in history will reveal what kind of phenomena they are" (11). "The aim of this book is therefore to show that the meaning and nature of a ritual can be understood in the process of its historical formation and that by this means the recurring problems of the study of ritual can be overcome" (11). This approach is developed by "an analysis of a particularly rich ritual practised by the Merina of Madagascar: that surrounding the circumcision of young boys" (2). Chapters 2 and 3 provide background information about the politico-religious history of the Merina from 1770–1970 (12–33) and their social organization and religion (34–47), respectively. The following chapters (4: "Description and Preliminary Analysis of a Circumcision Ritual", 48–83; 5: "The Symbolism of Circumcision", 84–104; 6: "The Myth of the Origin of Circumcision", 105–112) attempt a symbolic analysis of the ritual in terms of its social and cultural contexts, while Chapter 7 (113–156) traces "The History of the Circumcision" over a period of almost 200 years. The final and longest chapter is entitled: "The Circumcision Ritual in History: Towards a Theory of the Transformation of Ideology" (157–195). Here, the author spells out his own theory of ritual by critically distancing his own approach from previous ones. "Neither the intellectualist nor the functionalist approach is wrong yet neither is right, and for the same reason some Marxist theories fail. The problem lies in the fact that rituals are neither an exposition of the knowledge of the people studied; nor are they actions whose meaning lies simply in their performance. Rituals are events that combine the properties of statements and actions" (181). According to the author, there is "a way of coming to grips with the nature of statement-actions.... It is to look at ritual...historically" (183). Discussing the "historical implications" of different studies of ritual communication, the author detects a "basic agreement" (183): "The common elements particularly relevant for understanding the historical potential of ritual are (1) repetition, (2) formalisation and (3) the construction of a particular image of time" (184). According to the author, "rituals represent events as though they were general occurrences.... The same ritual procedures, the same gestures, the same songs and so forth are used" (184). Thus repetition and formalization reveal ritual "as an area of human activity very low indeed in creativity" (186). This is connected with a specific vision of time: "Rituals reduce the unique occurrence so that they become a part of a greater fixed and ordered unchanging whole; this whole is constructed identically by every ritual performed in a hazy, weakly propositional manner; it appears to have always existed, and will always exist. Because of this, ritual makes the passage of time, the change in personnel, and the change in situation, inexpressible and therefore irrelevant" (184). According to the author, "ritual can create a world of hazy timelessness in antithesis to another world" (185). In the final section of the book, the author describes "The Circumcision Ritual as Ideology in History" (187–195). "The ritual is a matter of transforming knowledge of the world obtained outside the framework of the ritual" (188) by saying that the world one knows outside the ritual, where sex and birth lead to life, where labour leads to production, where time is irreversible and potentially productive, will not ultimately be the basis of the transcendental existence" (188–189). The suggestion of the existence of a "transcendental world, just over the horizon, after death", is the explanation of "the emotional power of ritual" (189). As the ritual "appears to establish the authority of everybody, in so far as it brings blessings to everybody, and by this transforms everybody...into descent beings" (189). According to the author, "one cannot imagine a person so devoid of all status that he or she would not derive some satisfaction from having a place in an ordered whole that stands against immorality, unpredictability and death" (189). Ritual contains "two key propositions...(1): Creativity is not the product of human action but is due to transcendental force that is mediated by authority, and (2) this fact legitimates, even demands, the violent conquest of inferiors by superiors who are closer to the transcendental ancestors" (189). "Because the ritual can legitimate any authority, it actually legitimates the authority of those who have the coercive potential to insist on being considered as elders or kings. It is not the ritual itself that determines who will be legitimated. Legitimation of violence is only possible for those who already dominate by violence" (191). Moreover, in spite of changing context, the ritual itself does not need to change very much, "because ritual is a vague, weak propositional, construction of timelessness built in an antithesis that will do for any domination" (191). Therefore, "the stability of ritual tells us something about the nature of ideology. The reason the ritual does its ideological job is that it carries at its core a simple and general message.... It is that life is of little value, that it must be rejected...and exchanged for the still transcendence where time has been vanquished by order and where therefore the relevance of birth, death and action has disappeared" (195). The author concludes: "The central contradiction of the ritual, that death is the best sort of life, can largely be forgotten because it is expressed in something that is not fully a statement and not fully an action: a ritual" (195). [JS/MS]

References: W. Robertson Smith (+/–), R.A. Rappaport (–), M. Godelier (–), N.D. Fustel de Coulanges (–), É. Durkheim (–), V.W. Turner (+), C. Lévi-Strauss (+), D. Sperber (+), G.A. Lewis (+), S.J. Tambiah (+).

Example: The circumcision ritual for boys of the Merina of Madagascar.

Reviews: Anon. *CA* 27.4 (1986) 349; V.Y. Mudimbe *AA* 89 (1987) 742–744; S. Ellis *JAfrH* 28.3 (1987) 465; M. Lambek *Man* 22.3 (1987) 573; G. Feeley-Harnik *AE* 15.3

(1988) 593–595; R.K. Kent *AHR* 93.1 (1988) 206; P. v.d. Grijp *BTLV* 144 (1988) 186; G. Aijmer *Ethn* 53.1/2 (1988) 141; D. Casajus *Homme* 29.109 (1989) 152; D.-H. Johnson *JSAS* 16.3 (1990) 594.
Key-words: COM, pmt, sem, mng, pow, med, TIM, DYN, soc, emo, rep, gst, gdr.

Bloch, Maurice E.F., 1987, 'The Ritual of the Royal Bath in Madagascar. The Dissolution of Death, Birth and Fertility into Authority', in: David Cannadine & Simon Price (eds), *Rituals of Royalty. Power and Ceremonial in Traditional Societies*, Cambridge etc.: Cambridge University Press (ISBN 0-521-33513-2 / 0-521-42891-2 (p)) (*) 271–297.

This article is on the royal bath ritual in Madagascar, as well as on ritual theory. In this middle ground between theory and analysis, the author questions a purely interpretative approach to ritual as favored by C. Geertz, while criticizing functional analysis. In other words, he calls into question the bifurcation of contextual particularism and functional generalization in the anthropological study of rituals. In analyzing the symbolic construction of authority out of non-royal symbolism, the author attempts to elaborate the particular meaning and general significance of royal rituals of the Merina state of eighteenth- and nineteenth-century Madagascar, because these rituals "share universal characteristics of the symbolical construction of authority and also gain specific meaning through their adoption and adaptation of symbolic forms which organised non-royal life in Merina culture" (272–274). In the first section, the author describes the ritual of the royal bath in its various temporal sequences and cosmic and social dimensions (274–283). Then he analyzes the role of the royal protagonists in the ritual bath for the creation of a ritual order that transcends mere human experience by devaluing human mutability (283–294). At the very moment of the turn of a year, the ritual bath aligns the society, royalty, and astrology. Therefore, this ritual can represent the royal authority that is beyond challenge: "The ritual of the royal bath presents at its highest point an image of the world where everything is in its place: the heavenly bodies, the kingdom, the kinship system" (283). In this second section, the author investigates the main features of the construction of the ritual of the royal bath against the background of contemporary non-royal rituals of death, birth, and fertility. He points out that the ritual links the cosmic order with emotions which are aroused by death and rebirth. By ordering and synchronizing these emotions, the internal and external order are made to go together. By the analysis of the symbolic construction of the bath ritual, the author shows that the overall pattern of this ritual follows a movement from a funeral sequence to a blessing sequence and up to a resolution sequence. He assumes a unity of meaning and function in royal rituals. The first point he makes in his "Conclusions" (294–297) is a functionalist one, namely that the ritual "clearly demonstrates the legitimation of authority, making royal power an essential aspect of a cosmic social and emotional order which is unitary and unquestionable" (294). But he also argues that this function does not really explain the ritual, because it is necessary to consider, e.g., the specific Merina formulations for the symbolic construction of authority. Therefore, one has to view rituals as organic wholes and understand them in terms of the succession of sequences by means of a detailed analysis of the actual ritual. Then it becomes clear that the ritual of the royal bath is based on other symbolism, which it repeats and advances. "When we follow the various acts of the ritual through we see not only how the ritual parallels others but also how it uses the symbolism of other rituals to create the uniqueness of the royal construction" (294). [JK]

References: Th.O. Beidelman, **C. Geertz** (–), M. Gluckman, P. Smith.
Examples: Rituals of royalty.
Key-words: eff, emo, mng, pow, ref, sem, soc, str, sym, tim.

Bloch, Maurice E.F., 1989, *Ritual, History and Power. Selected Papers in Anthropology* (London School of Economics. Monographs on Social Anthropology 58); London: The Athlone Press (ISBN 0–485–19558–5 / 0–485–19658–1 (p)) (xii + 237) (with index and bibliography).

In this volume of selected papers, the author has reprinted some virtually classical and widely discussed essays. Ethnographically and theoretically, they have many features in common. Although these articles focus on the peoples of Madagascar, esp. the Merina, they are mainly guided by four theoretical tenets which are relevant for ritual theory, namely that: (1) "everyday knowledge is determined, in part by universal psychological characteristics of the genus Homo Sapiens, and in part by the process of intellectual construction which results from the practical interaction of people with their environment, human or otherwise", (2) "the images constructed in ritual are systematic transformations of more implicit forms of non-ritual and non-ideological knowledge", (3) "ideological images cannot be understood outside the experience of political domination", and (4) "although the means of communication through which knowledge is constructed and transmitted cannot determine the content of this knowledge, neither should the means of communication be seen as inert media" (vii–xi).

Selected contents: "The Past and the Present in the Present" (1–18), "Symbols, Song, Dance, and Features of Articulation" (19–45) (*), "The Disconnection Between Power and Rank as a Process" (46–88), "From Cognition to Ideology" (106–136), "The Ritual of the Royal Bath in Madagascar" (187–211) (*). [JK]

Reviews: R. Parkin *Soc* 39.2 (1989) 187–189; M. Lambek *AE* 17.3 (1990) 558 f; Anon. *JRS* 5.1 (1991) 133–135; P. Fluegel *Periph* 11.41 (1991) 96.
Key-words: cog, com, dnc, pow, sem, soc, sym.

Bloch, Maurice E.F., 1992, *Prey into Hunter. The Politics of Religious Experience* (The Lewis Henry Morgan Lectures 1984); Cambridge etc.: Cambridge University Press (ISBN 0–521–41154–8 / 0–521–42312–0 (p)) (xiii + 117) (with index and bibliography).

The central theme of this book is what the author calls "rebounding violence", which he illustrates in chapters on initiation (i.e. puberty rituals) (8–23), sacrifice (24–45), cosmogony and the state (dealing, e.g., with death rituals) (46–64), marriage (65–84), millenarianism (85–98), and myth (99–105). Thus, his theory does not focus exclusively on rituals, nor does it claim to pertain to all rituals. Yet rituals are the main phenomena where the pattern is found. The phrase 'rebounding violence' refers to the fact that in many rituals two stages of violence may be recognized that are related and opposed to one another in a number of ways. In the first step, in such rituals the natural, internal vitality of (part of) the community is destroyed (i.e. the candidates are 'killed'): this is the first, symbolic violence. This act moves the community—not only the candidate(s)—into the spiritual world (i.e. the realm of the dead/spirits/gods). In a later, second step, some external source of vitality (killed animals) is absorbed (eaten): this is the second, real violence. This moves the community, transformed, back into the natural world (i.e. the realm of the living). Also, the first violence is oriented against the own, internal vitality, which is given with natural birth, whereas the second violence is oriented against external vitality, which is acquired by cultural action. Furthermore, in the first step, the natural world is left behind as if it were devoid of value: the 'other' world alone is regarded as valuable. In the second step, this 'other' world is not left behind; the 'natural' world is conquered by it. Those who have gone this path 'really' belong to the 'other' world, and remain part of it; hence their authority over this one. Finally, in the first step, the temporary, unstable, natural world is left behind in order to share in the permanent, eternal, transcendental world. In the second step, this status of immortality is retained, and from now on allows the movement back and forth between the two worlds (such as in the case of priests, who can move into the transcendental world and come back again), even after death (the spirits of the dead periodically return to the world of the living and are more or less part of it). [JS]

References: A. van Gennep (+), M. Eliade (+), V.W. Turner (+), R. Girard (+), W. Burkert (+).

Examples: puberty rituals (among the Orokaiva of Papua New Guinea), sacrifice (with the Dinka of the Sudan, and with the Buid of the Philippines), death rituals (in Hinduism, and in Japanese Shintoism and Buddhism), marriage rituals (in Ladakh in North India), millenarianism (with the Merina of Madagascar).

Reviews: E. Ohnuki-Tierney *AT* 8.5 (1992) 17–20; K. Pedersen *TA* 25 (1992) 129; G. Aijmer *Ethn* 58.1/2 (1993) 126; B. Lincoln *JRS* 7.2 (1993) 125 f; T.O. Beidelmann *JIH* 24.4 (1994) 774; E. McHugh *AE* 22.4 (1995) 1004; D. Gellner *JASO* XXVII.1 (1996) 78–80.

Key-words: sem, mng, STR, pow, rep, exp, soc.

Bloch, Maurice E.F., 2006, 'Deference', in: Jens Kreinath, Jan A.M. Snoek & Michael Stausberg (eds), *Theorizing Rituals. Vol. I: Issues, Topics, Approaches, Concepts*, (Numen Book Series 114–1), Leiden, Boston: Brill (ISBN-10: 90–04–15342–x, ISBN-13: 978–90–04–15342–4) 495–506.

The problem of the attribution of meaning to ritual acts has always been central. It is suggested that the difficulty comes from the fact that actors defer to others in ritual, that is, they repeat the actions of others who they trust to know the reason for these actions. In many cases this leads to an endless regress. If that is what characterizes ritual it can be seen as an extreme form of what is a characteristic of human sociality, that is relying on knowledge of others or making use of what has been called distributed cognition. [Maurice Bloch]

Key-words: pow, str, mng, cog, DFR, TRA.

Blondeau, Anne-Marie & Kristofer Schipper (eds), 1990 / [1990] / 1995, *Essais sur le rituel* (Bibliothèque de l'École des Hautes Études; Section des Sciences Religieuses 92 / 95 / 102); Louvain, Paris: Peters (ISBN 90-6831-122-0 / 90-6831-302-9 / 90-6831-808-x) (xiii + 210 / xvii + 236 / xv + 156) (with contributions in English and French).
[Essays on Ritual]

Selected contents: Vol. I: Mary Douglas: "The Woman-Priest Problem. A Cultural Analysis" (173–194); Annie Comolli: "La description filmique des rites et ses problèmes" (195–203). Vol. II: Jao Tsung-i: "Le Canon des Rites et quelques théories majeures du ritualisme suivant le Commentaire de Zuo des Annales des Printemps et Automnes" (27–44); Jacques Galinier: "Règles, contexte et signification des rituels. Notes américanistes sur deux propositions de Wittgenstein" (201–205); Nicole Belmont: "Rite de passage, passage matériel. Les rituels de la naissance" (229–236). Vol. III: Frits Staal: "Ritual Order" (1–6). [JS]
Key-words: gdr, med, str.

Bocock, Robert, 1970, 'Ritual. Civic and Religious', *The British Journal of Sociology* 21:285–297.

The author's primary motivation for writing this paper is that "at the moment a series of changes are being introduced in the churches' liturgy" (285). As becomes clear from the article, the church he refers to is the Church of England (Anglican), and his own position is in accord with the Anglo-Catholic congregations of this church. To explain his disagreement with the changes taking place, he first reflects on previous theories about ritual. He argues against the usual strict distinction between 'ritual' and 'beliefs', because the two "are intimately interwoven" (285). Referring to Susanne K. Langer, he reminds us that "ritual evokes faith", and stresses that "some things can only be evoked and expressed through ritual action" (286). He argues against functionalist theories, because "ritual may be said to be the cause of the integration of social systems...but the ritual itself is not thereby explained because it has these effects" (286). A section follows on "Action Theory" (286–287), in which he argues, against such authors as J.A. Rex and P. Cohen, that only in some cases do people perform rituals in order to reach a super-empirical end. Rather, the "worship of God is an activity *sui generis*; it is not a means to salvation" (287). "An examination of the rules governing decisions of liturgical change would provide some understanding of the 'logic of religious action'. Action theory revised in the way suggested above gives some explanation of why ritual (liturgy) exists and continues, and begins to suggest how sociologists might account for liturgical change. Ritual action should not be looked at in terms of a means-end scheme and need not be seen as non-rational action" (287). This then leads us to the section on "Religious Ritual and Civic Ritual" (287–293), which opens thus: "It is necessary to distinguish between two major forms of ritual activity when trying to understand the highly differentiated societies of Europe and America. There is on the one hand what will be termed 'civic ritual', and on the other 'religious ritual'. All ritual action is distinguished from other types of action on the basis of the action being oriented to sacred or charismatic objects (material things, persons, or animals), that is objects which are set apart from the profane world, the everyday world of routine and utilitarian action.... In religious ritual the charismatic objects which actors relate to are 'holy', or sacred, in R. Otto's sense of this term...In civic ritual the charismatic objects related to are not connected with the Holy sphere, even though they are set apart from the profane world" (287–288). He then argues that Durkheim, because he worked in societies less differentiated "than modern England", in which also "civic and religious ritual were undifferentiated empirically", wrongly interpreted "the Holy as being an experience of 'society'" (289). According to the author, participating in a civic ritual evokes a very different experience than participating in a religious one, and therefore sociologists should distinguish between the two, even though the distinction is analytical and "empirically some rituals will be a mixture of the two" (289). In churches, some of the rituals are "creating a consciousness of membership of the group...and renewing commitment to its norms and values.... Analytically this is partly 'civic ritual' even though it takes place in a church" (289). Referring to Evelyn Underhill, however, he stresses that religious ritual also evokes another kind of experience: "the main methodological point is that the experiences which worshippers have of a Reality beyond themselves must be treated as a basic datum; this is the meaning which they give to their activities, and to understand religious ritual this subjective meaning must be treated as fundamental to the action" (290). He then shows clearly where he stands: "The Durkheimian and Freudian accounts of religion are best seen as contributions to our understanding of distorted forms of religion. These may, empirically, be the most common forms of religious experience, nevertheless they are best treated theoretically as deviant types of experience, retaining the possibility of a purer type of religious experience, of 'true' worship as this would be understood by the members of a highly developed religion. These deviant types of religious experience are to be understood in the light of the concept of the ideal of religious worship as developed by a particular religious group. Only in the light of such a concept of 'true' worship can deviant forms be seen in a proper perspective" (290). He then proceeds to describe three variables that distinguish civic from religious ritual: "the nature of the symbolism involved, the nature and degree of involvement on the part of the participants which is expected by the culture, and the culturally defined implications for other areas of life of participation in the ritual" (290). "Symbols in religious ritual have a reference to the Holy; those of civic ritual to the group and the secular world" (290). "Participants in religious ritual are expected to be highly involved in the meaning of the ritual... In civic ritual neither the principal participants nor the onlookers need cultivate deep understanding of the inner meaning of the ritual actions and symbols involved... [T]he cultural expectations on participants are not as great in civic ritual as in religious, nor are the rituals supposed to be experienced as deeply meaningful. People are culturally allowed to watch a civic ritual, but should participate in a religious ritual" (291–292). "The implications of a religious ritual, such as the liturgy of churches, are wide ranging in their impact on the rest of the participants' lives; worshippers are to carry over into their whole lives the attitudes of praise, thanksgiving, adoration for the Holy, and, in Christianity, they are to love God and their neighbours. Civic rituals carry very few implications for other areas of life" (292). The author can now turn to his critique of the changes that, in 1970, had taken place recently in the liturgy of the Church of England, basically arguing that these mark a shift from religious to civic ritual. [JS]

References: S.K. Langer (+), J.A. Rex (−), P. Cohen (−), R. Otto (+), **É. Durkheim** (+/−), S. Freud (−), E. Underhill (+), T. Parsons (+).
Example: The liturgy of the Anglican Church.
Key-words: soc, SEC, pr1, emo, par.

Bocock, Robert, 1974, *Ritual in Industrial Society. A Sociological Analysis of Ritualism in Modern England*; London: George Allen & Unwin (ISBN 0–04–300044–4) (209) (with index and bibliography).

The book presents one of the few sociological theories of ritual in modern societies. The author's main interest is in the persistence of ritual in modern industrial society. Due to his focus on the sociological analysis of rituals, he points out that "[r]itual is concerned with the process of either binding people's feelings into the existing organisation of society, or with aiding them to become critical and independent of it" (9). His analysis concentrates on how ritual action prevents or promotes social changes at the political and personal levels. The author rejects the sociological assumption that secularization increases under industrial conditions and that industrial societies should be seen as secular. By contrast, he focuses on ritual action in industrial societies because he assumes that they are more important than has been assumed. Although the author moves towards a positive approach to ritual, he still analyzes ritual actions by referring to them primarily as religious: "If it is said religion means to bind together, then much of the civic and political ritual action could be called religious" (24). Moreover, in the first chapter (19–34), he raises the methodological and philosophical question of how to approach ritual in modern societies. To develop his approach to the sociology of ritual action, he shows in the second chapter (35–59) that members of a modern industrial society participate in a very large number of rituals. Although the category of ritual action was not well established in theories on modern industrial societies, the author defines ritual as "*the symbolic use of bodily movement and gesture in a social situation to express and articulate meaning*" (37). With this notion of ritual action, he introduces a category that can include religious rituals and types of ritual action such as artistic performances, entertainment, sports, life-cycle rituals, and civic-political rituals. On his view, ritual action is rational as well as non-rational and still "continues in modern industrial society" because of "the importance of the non-rational elements in human beings" (41). However, the author is interested more in what the performers of ritual action say they are doing than in the validity of religious beliefs. His hypothesis is that the rituals change due to the degree of how far social relations are differentiated. To understand such changes of ritual in modern societies, the author distinguishes between various types of rituals. He discusses religious and civic rituals (60–72) in general and the religious rituals in the Church of England (73–97) and civic rituals of nationalism (98–117) in particular, life cycle rituals (118–146) and aesthetic ritual (147–170). A comparison of religious and civic rituals leads him in his last chapter "Ritual, Social Change and Counter-Culture" (171–188) to the conclusion that there is a complex process underlying the increasing differentiation of ritual action.

Due to the main institutional areas of industrial society, so the author claims, there is increasing pressure to differentiate religious and political rituals, and because of the emergence of modern countercultures and the interdependence between ritual action and social change, he understands rituals as a way of changing the mode of social relations. Thus he stresses that rituals are "social, co-operative activities which express a kind of creativity, and which relate men to one another and to nature in a way which can provide a glimpse of non-alienated living" (178). By way of conclusion he writes that "Modern industrial societies have been developing specialised roles and organizations for more and more specific tasks and social activities. It is this process of differentiation which has led to the specialised ritual systems of religious organizations, artistic entertainment organizations and political parties and movements" (180). [JK]

References: M. Douglas (+), É. Durkheim (+/–), M. Eliade (+), A. van Gennep (+), M. Gluckman, S.K. Langer (+), C. Lévi-Strauss, R. Otto (+), T. Parsons, J. Piaget, M. Weber (+).
Examples: *Rites de passage*, Christmas, football, Olympic games.
Reviews: K.M. Devlin *AALR* 3.3 (1974) 417; J.A. Beckford *Man* 9.3 (1974) 512; Anon. *JTS* 26 (1975) 262.
Key-words: dyn, emo, idn, mng, pmc, pr1, sec, soc, sym.

Boudewijnse, H. Barbara, 1995, 'The Conceptualisation of Ritual. A History of its Problematic Aspects', *Jaarboek voor Liturgieonderzoek* 11:31–56.

This essay is the result of the author's "struggle to comprehend current debates on ritual" (32). The paper critically discusses the contributions by Zuesse (1987) (*), Gerholm (1988) (*), and Goody (1977) (*). According to the author, much of the recent debate on ritual "comes down to an age-old discussion: Is there really something 'out there', that can be recognized as 'ritual', or is ritual whatever we designate as such?" (43). The author tries to demonstrate that "the elusiveness of ritual phenomena and the nature of scholarly inquiries into ritual are fundamentally intertwined" (43). Furthermore, following Asad (1988, revised 1993) (*), she investigates the history of the concept of 'ritual'. The birth of 'ritual' in the modern sense happened in the nineteenth century when ritual behaviour came to be seen as a distinct category of social action. Since views on ritual (and religious) behavior at that time diverged, "their joining into the concept of ritual has proved an uneasy marriage. As such, the question, for example, whether ritual is expressive of (social) ideas or is basically meaningless, or whether it is psychologically engendered or socially generated, will surface time and again" (53). [MS]

References: T. Asad, J. Goody, Th. Gerholm, E.M. Zuesse.
Key-words: TER, mng, prl.

Boudewijnse, H. Barbara, 1998, 'British Roots of the Concept of Ritual', in: Arie L. Molendijk & Peter Pels (eds), *Religion in the Making. The Emergence of the Science of Religion*, (Studies in the History of Religions 80), Leiden, Boston, Köln: E.J. Brill (ISBN 90-04-11239-1) 277-295.

The author notes that "[m]aking use of old dictionaries and encyclopedias, Talal Asad was the first to more or less systematically explore the etymological history of the word 'ritual' in relation to its genesis as a concept. Taking Asad's findings as my point of departure, I will go on to show that there is a hiatus in his depiction of the etymological history of the term 'ritual'. Because of this hiatus, the when and how of the birth of 'ritual' as a scholarly concept cannot be determined. I intend to bridge this gap and will argue that the genesis of the concept of ritual was a gradual, unintended process and initially a British development" (277–278). The hiatus referred to is the period 1852 to 1910. The authors analyzed for that period include Tylor, Lang, Robertson Smith, Van Gennep, Durkheim, and Chantepie de la Saussaye. [JS]

Key-words: def, TER, sec, mng.

Boudewijnse, H. Barbara, 2006, 'Ritual and Psyche', in: Jens Kreinath, Jan A.M. Snoek & Michael Stausberg (eds), *Theorizing Rituals. Vol. I: Issues, Topics, Approaches, Concepts*, (Numen Book Series 114-1), Leiden, Boston: Brill (ISBN-10: 90-04-15342-x, ISBN-13: 978-90-04-15342-4) 123-141.

In this contribution, it is shown how studies in the social sciences and the sciences of religions tend to explain ritual as an essentially social phenomenon that is ultimately based, implicitly or explicitly, on psychological conditions. These psychological explanations often are little more than very general notions—such as 'the human need to symbolize'—functioning as *a priori* assumptions, which, as such, are not questioned or clarified. When psychological theory serves as an explicit frame of reference—for instance psychoanalytic theory or cognitive psychology—it is used to portray the universal psychological conditions which structure the variable social processes of which ritual is said to be part. Once the psychological constants are established, they themselves are no further discussed but are used to lay bare the supposed universal principles of ritual structure. Ritual itself is invariably seen as a social mechanism. Considering that 'the psyche' has been attributed such a basic role by social scientists and scholars of religions, it is then asked how ritual has been dealt with by psychologists. First, the existing studies are discussed. Within psychology, 'ritual' appears useful only as an instrument for the analysis of behavior concerned with interpersonal relationships. The number of notable psychological studies on ritual being small, the apparent lack of interest in ritual within mainstream psychology is then explained. [H. Barbara Boudewijnse]

Key-words: cog, com, emo, PSY, soc, sym.

Bourdieu, Pierre, 1975, 'Le langage autorisé. Note sur les conditions sociales de l'efficacité du discours rituel', *Actes de la recherche en sciences sociales* 1:183–190.

[Authorized Language. Notes on the Social Conditions of the Efficacy of Ritual Discourse]

Reprinted in P. Bourdieu: *Ce que parler veut dire*, Paris 1982, 103–120. Eng. transl. by Gino Raymond and Matthew Adamson (edited and introduced by John B. Thompson): *Language and Symbolic Power*, Cambridge (MA): Harvard University Press 1991 (ix + 302) (ISBN 0–674–51041–0).

The present article is a critique of a purely linguistic approach to understanding the power and efficacy of linguistic manifestations. Over and over again, the author returns to the following point: For authoritative discourse (such as a course taught by a professor, or a sermon) it is not sufficient that the messages are understood; rather, its power resides in the fact that it is recognized as such. This recognition, however, is achieved only when certain preconditions are fulfilled: (1) In order to be recognized, the authoritative discourse has to be pronounced by the person who has a legitimate right to pronounce it; (2) it has to be pronounced in a legitimate situation; (3) it has to be pronounced in legitimate (syntactic, phonetic, etc.) form (187). Applied to the problem of the efficacy of ritual, this observation leads to the following assumption: "The exclusive attention [that is drawn] towards the formal conditions for the efficacy of ritual tends to forget that the ritual conditions which need to be fulfilled in order for the ritual to function and in order for the sacrament to be at the same time valid and efficacious are never sufficient in as much as the conditions which produce the recognition of that ritual are joined [with them]: the language of authority (*la langage d'autorité*) is unable to govern without the collaboration of those governed by it, i.e. thanks to the social mechanisms which are capable to produce that complicity which is based on misapprehension (*méconnaissance*) and which is at the very origin of all sorts of authority (*au principe de toute autorité*)" (187). [MS]

Reference: J.L. Austin (–).
Example: Ritual changes in the Catholic church.
Key-words: EFF, PMT, com, agn, pow, par, rep, rht, soc, dyn.

Bourdieu, Pierre, 1982, 'Les rites comme actes d'institution', *Actes de la recherche en sciences sociales* 43:58–63.
[Rites as Acts of Institution]
Reprinted in P. Bourdieu: *Ce que parler veut dire*, Paris 1982, 121–134. Eng. transl. by Gino Raymond and Matthew Adamson (edited and introduced by John B. Thompson): *Language and Symbolic Power*, Cambridge (MA): Harvard University Press 1991 (ix + 302) (ISBN 0–674–51041–0).

The author suspects that the concept of *rites de passage* tends to hide the essential effects of those rites commonly classified under that category. Instead, he suggests that they be called 'rites of consecration', 'rites of legitimation', or simply 'rites of institution' (*rites d'institution*). This is because these rites "institute a durable difference" between those who this rite concerns and those who are not concerned by it (58). The notion of 'rite of institution' serves to indicate that "every rite tends to consecrate or to legitimate" by stipulating 'an arbitrary limit' (58). "The symbolic efficacy of rites of institution" (59) consists in their power to affect reality by modifying the representation of reality. "The institution is an act of social magic which can create the difference *ex nihilo* or rather—and this is the case more often than not—by exploiting in some way preexisting differences such as the biological differences between the sexes" (59). "Social magic always succeeds to produce discontinuity out of continuity" (60). To institute an identity is "the imposition of a social essence" (60). This entails a dialectical process: "The social essence is the whole of those social attributes and attributions produced by the act of institution as a solemn act of categorization that tends to produce what it designates" (60). 'To become what you are' is supposed to serve as the formula underlying the performative magic (*la magie performative*) of the 'acts of institution' (61). These acts create "magic borders" (61) that serve the same purpose as the 'acts of institution', namely "to durably discourage the temptation of passage, of transgression, of desertion, and of resignation" (61). The universally employed strategy to avoid that temptation "consists of naturalizing the difference, of making it a second nature through impressing (inculcation) and embodiment (incorporation) in the form of habitus" (61). On the one hand, the power of those attributions that are realized by the acts of institution is such that it is capable of resisting all "practical denials" (62). On the other hand, "one of the privileges of consecration lies in the fact that by awarding an undisputable and indelible essence to the consecrated [people] it authorizes transgressions that are otherwise prohibited" (62). Ultimately, however, these 'acts of social magic' presuppose the 'institution' of another kind, i.e. the guarantee or belief of the group. "The belief of everybody that exists before the ritual (*La croyance de tous, qui préexiste au rituel*) is the condition of its efficacy" (63). In an almost metaphysical sense, the "real miracle produced by the acts of institution without doubt lies in the fact that they succeed in making the consecrated individuals believe that they are justified to exist, that their existence serves something" (63). [MS]

References: É. Durkheim (+), V.W. Turner (–), A. van Gennep (–).
Key-words: pmt, pr2, idn, eff, emb, hab.

Boyer, Pascal, 1994, *The Naturalness of Religious Ideas. A Cognitive Theory of Religion*; Berkeley, Los Angeles, London: University of California Press (ISBN 0-520-07559-5) (xv + 324).

This is one of the founding texts of the new paradigm of the cognitive approach to the study of religion. In Chapter 7 ("Ritual Episodes and Religious Assumption", 185–223), the author does "not propose to give a new 'theory of religious ritual'; indeed, one of the main points of the argument is that there is no unified set of phenomena that could be the object of such a theory" (185). "The starting point of any investigation into ritual is an *intuitive discrimination* of behavior", i.e., "that certain acts, gestures, utterances, and so on seem to be of a particular mode, which sets them off from acts performed in other contexts or situations" (188). "Ritual situations do not seem to display any universals beyond the use of the ritual behavorial mode. There may well be, however, recurrent properties of ritual situations that a cognitive approach to religious ritual should describe and explain. That no satisfactory description or explanation of these recurrent properties can be found in anthropological theory may be a consequence of the preference for *generative* models, as opposed to *selective* ones" (191). The latter models operate with the "assumption... that the ritual mode probably has properties that make it likely that its use will be recurrent in certain types of interaction situations and will be associated with certain recurrent types of mental representations. There is no deterministic link here, only a probabilistic one" (192). Having discussed some ritual theories, the author proceeds "to describe the representation of ritual episodes" (198). He comments on the fact that there are "specific names for ritual actions" (199); the actions are "*categorized*" (199). Hence, in order to highlight what is specific to ritual, one can compare ritual actions not to 'everyday actions' as such, but to "*categorized* non-ritual actions" (203), in particular to so-called 'scripts' (like 'going to the doctor' or 'traveling by train'). While the latter are characterized by "a hierarchy of actions and subactions" and "a corresponding hierarchy of goals and subgoals" (204), this is not the case with ritual actions. According to the author, "it is in most cases impossible to specify the goals or intentions fulfilled by ritual performance" (205). Moreover, the "representation of the background conditions are underspecified" (209); that is exemplified by the 'explanation' that one or the other condition was not present in the case of ritual failure (207–209). According to the author, these features may also explain why rituals are generally perceived as 'rigid' and 'noninstrumental' action (209–211). People who perform a ritual, the author argues, "start from a representation of the components, the ritual 'script' with its complex observable features" (216). During the ritual, various religious assumptions are being activated that "provide conjectures that if true enrich the representation of the episode and provide abductive explanation for the presence of certain features of the sequence" (216). The author refers to this process as abductive inferences (or "tags") (216). These tags are conjectural and "make a certain aspect of the situation observed explainable, given a certain condition" (217). Hence, there is no necessary connection between ritual performance and religious assumptions. As the conceptual structure of rituals is underspecified, "they can always be the object of enrichment provided by new conjectures" (219). [MS]

References: M.E.F. Bloch, J. Goody, B. Kapferer, R. Needham, E.Th. Lawson & R.N. McCauley, R.A. Rappaport, D. Sperber, F. Staal.
Examples: Tikopia rituals (Firth), Fang ancestor cult, initiation.
Key-words: def, str, sec, MNG, sym, exp, COG, eth, tra.

Brandon, Samuel G.F., 1975, *Man and God in Art and Ritual. A Study of Iconography, Architecture and Ritual Action as Primary Evidence of Religious Belief and Practice*; New York: Charles Scribner's Sons (ISBN 0–684–13657–0) (xiv + 514).

This book is written as an iconographic art history of religion. In the first part ("The Priority of Art and Ritual") (1–14), the author considers art and ritual as particular forms of religious expression primary to literature and written documents. Thus he claims that "art was one of the earliest forms in which man expressed himself, and that it long antedated writing, is incontestable" (4). As in the case of ritual, he is interested in "the manner in which art reflects ideas and emotions that may be described as religious" (4). But before 'man' could draw, the author argues, he "doubtless expressed his emotions and ideas in ritual action" (8). In keeping with this expressive notion of ritual, the author defines ritual action "in its original and essential nature" (10). According to him, ritual action is "not just a decorous way of doing things on solemn occasions", but it is "essentially a *dromenon*, a 'thing done'" (10). Or, as he also puts it, "the ritual transaction is held to generate a spiritual potency by the very fact of its being performed or 'done' (*dromenon*)" (10). In the second part of this book, the author reviews the art history of 'religion' and compares various documents of "Ritual and Art as Primary Evidence of Religion" (15–336). Here, he touches upon such issues as the relation of ritual to myth and doctrine, the magical efficacy of ritual action, symbolism, ritual drama, ritual dance, etc. In the third and final part, he gives an interpretation of the relation of "Man and God in Art and Ritual" (337–399). He starts from "The Adumbrations of Palaeolithic Art and Ritual" (341–356) up to "Christian Art and Ritual" (383–394) and "The Paradoxes of Aniconic Faiths" (394–399). [JK]

Reviews: J.N. Tylenda *ThSt* 37.1 (1976) 176; S. Laeuchli *TTo* 33.2 (1976) 215.
Key-words: aes, cpr, emo, myt, rep, sym.

Braungart, Wolfgang, 1996, *Ritual und Literatur* (Konzepte der Sprach- und Literaturwissenschaft 53); Tübingen: Max Niemeyer (ISBN 3–484–22053–8) (xiii + 322) (with index and bibliography).
[Ritual and Literature]

This book explores the interrelation between ritual and literature. In the first part (1–39), the author elaborates some aspects and examples of literature from a ritual point of view. Based on his findings in the poetry of R.M. Rilke and E. Mörike, the author discusses issues of text and textual sense and conceives ritual and literature as forms of symbolic action. He further uses works of F. Hölderlin and G. Keller to compare ritual and aesthetic functions. In the second part (41–118), the author determines the concept of elements of ritual. For heuristic reasons, he proposes a relatively broad concept of ritual in order to indicate the continua between the various forms of ritual and the social and cultural contexts within which this concept should be applicable; this shall one further allow to account for the "dynamics of social processes" (41). He argues that "[r]ituals are not only social actions but also cultural utterances insofar as they are staged, aesthetically elaborated and so intensified. Because there exist differentiated cultural utterances, the concept of ritual has also to be differentiated, if it should be useable for the description of cultural phenomena such as literature and art" (41). After defining ritual, the author relates ritual in various subsections to other concepts like ritualization and convention (41–48), habitus and style (48–57), rite, cult, custom, and ceremony (57–67), and myth (67–73). He summarizes his findings in the following way: "Rituals are aesthetically notably distinguished acts of repetition" (72). In order to delineate and differentiate this definition, he introduces the following characteristics: Rituals are neither mere conventions nor biologically determined patterns of behavior; they are distinguishable in religious-cultic and profane rituals, which can, but do not need to be institutionalized; they exist in a continuum between 'strongly fixed and binding' and 'playful reflexive', between 'controlled and serious' and 'excessive and ecstatic', as well as between 'elaborated and differentiated' and 'schematized and reduced' (73). In order to specify what a ritual is, the author discusses the elements of ritual, while he emphasizes those elements which are relevant within the context of ritual and literature. In the following sections, he examines the repetitive aspect of ritual (74–84), which becomes explicit in its staging up to a special festivity and solemnity (84–91), and considers ritual as self-referential actions (91–101) as well as social functional and communicative actions (101–106). He further addresses the actors and observers of ritual (106–107) and how rituals are conceived as aesthetically organized, symbolic-expressive actions (108–118). The third part is on the hermeneutics of ritual (119–138). Before the author addresses the issues of hermeneutics, he distinguishes between two tendencies in the study of ritual: social communicative and presentational symbolic. As inherently related to one another, the author conceives ritual as an artwork that has a special social function. He contends that "[t]he ritual can only fulfill its specific communicative function because it is staged, expressive and symbolic" (119). He emphasizes the aesthetics of linguistic rituals and focuses upon how rituals are analyzed in linguistic terms. According to him, it is problematic to describe rituals semiotically as texts, in which a particular code is used, as if one could say what is said by ritual in recourse to another code. He argues that "[r]ituals are not replaceable by other codes, because their aesthetical staging and realization are not replaceable.... Understanding is basically more than 'decoding', namely structures of meaning via the understanding of the subject" (122). The fourth and last part of this volume, entitled "Literature and Ritual" (139–254), is divided in seven chapters. The specific affinity to ritual in various literary genres (148–165), repetition and rhythm (166–186), festival and celebration (187–199), cult (200–215), play (216–233) and mimesis (234–253) are discussed. Here again, the author elaborates those concepts and studies central features of literal artwork and its aesthetical and social staging in order to show how ritual and literature are interrelated. In his final remarks, he concludes "that the defining characteristics of ritual—repetition of action, staging, aesthetic elaboration, self-referentiality, expressivity and symbolicity—are also constitutive for literature, although one has to differentiate between genres and various situations and interests of reception. But this is not different from ritual. Also there, the various aspects and functions vary with the ritual. The meaning of literature is for us explainable from its closeness to ritual as well—on most various levels and under most various viewpoints. Among them, the mimesis is the most principal and far-reaching one, but at the same time the most difficult one, because it opens up the present considerations towards a general theory of literature as symbolic action" (254). [JK]

References: K. Burke, M. Douglas, H.-G. Gadamer, C. Geertz, E. Goffman, E.R. Leach, R. Schechner, H.-G. Soeffner, V.W. Turner, Chr. Wulf.
Review: J.-D. Krebs *EG* 52.3 (1997) 475.
Key-words: AES, com, cpl, eth, hab, MIM, pmc, pr1, sec, sem, str.

Bremmer, Jan N., 1998, '"Religion", "Ritual" and the Opposition "Sacred vs. Profane". Notes towards a Terminological "Genealogy"', in: Fritz Graf (ed.), *Ansichten griechischer Rituale. Geburtstags-Symposium für Walter Burkert. Castelen bei Basel 15. bis 18. März 1996*, Stuttgart, Leipzig: B.G. Teubner (ISBN 3-519-07433-8) 9-32.

From a terminological genealogy of the terms 'religion', 'ritual', and the opposition 'sacred vs. profane', the author draws four conclusions (31–32): "First, the terms 'religion', 'ritual' and the opposition 'sacred vs. profane' originated or became redefined around 1900. This development coincided with and can partially be explained by the contemporary rise of the history and sociology of religion as a separate academic discipline, which started to construct its subject. Secondly, . . . we . . . have to be beware of the fact that scholarly terms developed differently in different countries. Thirdly, the fact that we can locate the moment of the birth of the terms discussed with a fair amount of accuracy suggests that contemporary users should remain conscious of their 'invention'. The terms are not faithful reflections of reality but scholarly constructs of which the definitions remain up for negotiation and adaptation. Fourthly, . . . a terminological 'genealogy' of religious key terms is not the same as the study of religion, but the awareness of their ideological origin may lead us to ask new questions in the never-ending quest for insight into the religious lives of our fellow humans . . .". [MS]
Key-word: TER.

Brown, Gavin, 2003, 'Theorizing Ritual as Performance. Explorations of Ritual Indeterminacy', *Journal of Ritual Studies* 17.1:3–18.

"The concern of Part I is to define the difficult term 'performance'" (4). However, further on the author admits: "In discussing the meaning of the concept 'performance' I have consciously avoided making a short, neat definition . . . any attempt to do so would defeat the underlying heuristic value of the term as a conceptual space. Rather, I have sought to identify a range of notions that are built into the meaning and value of the concept. Performance is . . . fundamentally about the *execution* of a series of actions that together constitute the performance. To speak of performance is to explore what is achieved in the very act of performing...Performance is scripted action; it is never spontaneous or accidental, it is reliant on *a priori* cultural imagination. As scripted action it is usually carefully framed to distinguish it from other modes of activity; it is often a heightened sensory and aesthetic mode of activity. Even so...there is a significant unscripted dimension in all performances. It is...susceptible to contingency and indeterminacy...Performance is always 'action for'; it is a dialogic mode of action...it is also a site of cultural production because it reshapes and reconstitutes the scripts. Performance is, therefore, fundamentally about transformation; it is a dynamic cultural activity" (6). In the subsequent section of Part I (7–10), the author explores how ritual can be re-conceptualized as performance (following R. Schechner and V.W. Turner). This leads him to two conclusions: "First, to understand ritual as performance is to approach it as one genre within a wider constellation of cultural performances...Secondly, and perhaps most importantly, to speak of ritual as performance is to be concerned primarily with a sense of ritual action, that is, what ritual achieves in performance. To speak of ritual performance is to shift our concerns away from the 'tyranny of form' associated with ritual and explore instead the cultural dynamism, efficacy and transformations that emerge when ritual is recast, following Turner's thesis, as a processual mode of cultural activity...what ritual achieves...can only be apprehended in performance" (10). "In the second part of this paper, I make the argument that the logical end-point in any scholarly effort to recast ritual as performance opens up conceptual possibilities for exploring the centrality of indeterminacy in ritual form" (10–11). Here, the author is first concerned with what he calls "Privileging the Moment" (11–13). On the one hand, this refers to understanding "ritual performance as a site of meaning construction" (12). On the other hand, though, the "indeterminacy of meaning in ritual performances does...suggest...its fragmentation into a diversity of receptions as ritual participants read and appropriate ritual symbols and actions differently" (12). "Ritual performances manifest indeterminacy...because, like any sign system, the production of meaning emerges in performance and so is yoked to the contingency and multiplicity of the performative moment" (13). In a second section of this part, the author elaborates on Turner's concepts of 'anti-structure' and 'reflexivity' (13–15). In his conclusion (15–16), the author reiterates his main thesis "that the very condition of indeterminacy lies at the heart of ritual form. It is only in performance...that such a paradox becomes apparent, and it is only by recognizing this paradox that the real dynamism and transformative potential of ritual can truly be grasped and appreciated" (16). [MS]

References: R. Barthes (+), R. Bauman, C.M. Bell (+), M. Carlson, J. Goody (+/–), S.F. Moore (+), R. Schechner (+), E.L. Schieffelin (+), V.W. Turner (+).
Key-words: def, pr1, PMC, eff, rfl, mng, dyn.

Bruner, Edward M. (ed.), 1984, *Text, Play, and Story. The Construction and Reconstruction of Self and Society*; Prospect Heights (IL): Waveland (ISBN 0–88133–365–4) (viii + 364).

Selected Contents: Renato I. Rosaldo: "Grief and a Headhunter's Rage. On the Cultural Force of Emotions" (178–195); James W. Fernandez: "Convivial Attitudes. The Ironic Play of Tropes in an International Kayak Festival in Northern Spain" (199–229); Roberto DaMatta: "On Carnaval, Informality, and Magic. A Point of View from Brazil" (230–246); Don Handelman: "Inside-Out. Outside-In. Concealment and Revelation in Newfoundland Christmas Mumming" (247–277); Emiko Ohnuki-Tierney: "Monkey Performances. A Multiple Structure of Meaning and Reflexivity in Japanese Culture" (278–314); John J. MacAloon: "La Pitada Olímpica. Puerto Rico, International Sport, and the Constitution of Politics" (315–355); Edmund Leach: "Further Thoughts on the Realm of Folly" (356–364). [JK]

Reviews: F.E. Manning *AE* 12.2 (1985) 375–377; V. Cobb-Stevens *JAF* 99.392 (1986) 223; E.L.B. Turner *LS* 15 (1986) 95; A. Shuman *WF* 46.1 (1987) 49.
Key-words: com, dyn, emo, frm, idn, PMC, rfl, rht, sec, soc, sym.

Buc, Philippe, 2001, *The Dangers of Ritual. Between Early Medieval Texts and Social Scientific Theory*; Princeton, Oxford: Princeton University Press (ISBN 0–691–01604–6) (xi + 272) (with index).

The aim of this book is not to put forward a new theory of ritual (viii). It is rather a critique of social scientific theories. The author questions the usefulness of the concept of ritual for the study of late antique and medieval texts. In the introduction he states: "This book is an essay. Its surface object is political ritual in the early Middle Ages. By necessity, this object must be vague, because historians have, collectively at least, piled a vast array of motley practices into the category" (1). Questioning the concept of 'ritual', the author continues: "Yet from the start, it should be said that the present essay ends up cautioning against the use of the concept of ritual for the historiography of the Middle Ages. It joins those voices that have underscored how social-scientific models should be employed with extreme caution, without eclecticism, and with full and constant awareness of their intellectual genealogies. In the pages that follow, then, the use of the term 'ritual' is provisional and heuristic (the ultimate aim being to suggest other modes of interpretation more fitted to the documents). Consequently, in the first part of this book, the word 'ritual' will be shorthand for 'a practice twentieth-century historians have identified as ritual'. Throughout, the term stands implicitly between quotation marks. More than medieval political ritual, thus, the essay's final object is the relationship between medieval documents and twentieth-century theories of ritual" (1–2). With this essay, the author aims at three things: "First, it seeks to explicate what late antique and early medieval authors thought happened when events that historians have identified as ritual occurred" (3). "The second aim, consequently, is to understand why authors wrote about these rituals, and how" (4). "The third and final agenda takes us into an analysis of concepts. For the essay's ultimate aim is to examine the fit between, on the one hand, medieval narratives and their implicit anthropology, and, on the other hand, the theories of ritual that twentieth-century historians have employed" (5). "Given the essay's agendas, it is pointless to attempt to survey all the practices that historians have labeled 'ritual'.... More important for this study are early medieval categories and vocabulary" (5). The book is divided in two parts: I. "Late Antique and Early Medieval Narratives" (13–157); and II. "From Theology to the Social Sciences, ca. 1500–ca. 1970" (159–261). The first part "will explore fairly coherent documentary bodies, that is, either whole works or clusters of texts produced in an identifiable milieu" (7). It consists of four chapters: 1. "Writing Ottonian Hegemony. Good Rituals and Bad Rituals in Liudprand of Cremona" (15–50); 2. "Ritual Consensus and Ritual Violence. Texts and Events in Ninth-Century Carolingian Political Culture" (51–87); 3. "Rites of Saints and Rites of Kings. Consensus and Transgression in the Works of Gregory of Tours" (88–122); 4. "The Late Antique Matrix. Martyrdom and Ritual" (123–157). The second part "will *not* consider every anthropological theory that a historian might use to explain the Middle Ages, but focus on the social scientific traditions that twentieth-century historians have most commonly employed" (7). It consists of three more chapters: 5. "Rites, Rituals, and Other, ca. 1500–ca. 1800" (164–202); 6. "Medieval History and the Social Sciences, ca. 1800–ca. 1970" (203–247); 7. "Epilogue"

(248–261). The second part gives an overview of the development of the study of rituals and the development of ritual theories, from ca. 1500 onwards. Ultimately, the author reaches the conclusion: "Yet a scholar should not confuse the intensity of his or her interest in an object (here 'ritual') and the degree of centrality of this object for a past society.... If this essay has focused on 'ritual', as defined by historiography, it is because only this focus could bring out its place in medieval political culture and invalidate some of the claims of this historiography. Another book, by another historian, may well build on this secure sense of limits. Humble, I close mine here" (261). [JK/JS]

References: C.M. Bell, M.E.F. Bloch, J.W. Fernandez, M. Douglas, É. Durkheim, C. Geertz, M. Gluckman, R.I. Rosaldo.
Examples: Medieval political rituals.
Key-words: gen, def.

Burkert, Walter, 1972, *Homo Necans. Interpretationen altgriechischer Opferriten und Mythen* (Religionsgeschichtliche Versuche und Vorarbeiten 32); Berlin: Walter de Gruyter (ISBN 3–11–003875–7) (xii + 356) (with indexes and bibliography). 2nd edition, enlarged with a "Nachwort 1996" [Afterword 1996] (333–352): 1997 (xii + 378) (ISBN 3–11–015098–0 (p)). Eng. transl. by Peter Bing: *Homo Necans. The Anthropology of Ancient Greek Sacrificial Ritual and Myth*, Berkeley, London: University of California Press 1983 (xxv + 334) (ISBN 0–520–03650–6).

[Abstract based on the 2nd German edition.] Although this whole book centers around rituals, the larger part describes and analyses examples from the classical Greek religion. Only the first chapter is more theoretical, and it is here that the author describes his theoretical position towards rituals in two sections: "3. Ritualization" (31–38) and "4. Rite and Myth" (39–45). His concept of "Ritualization" is directly based on that used by Huxley and Lorenz. He summarizes the theory of Lorenz (1966 (*)) and basically adopts its position: Man inherited an inclination for ritual from pre-human primates; upon this inherited basis, culture has built the human forms of ritual; the function of ritual is a strong communication of a stereotype message, which succeeds because ritual is repeated and theatrically exaggerated; ritual hereby creates and confirms social contact between the participants. The author recommends to restrict the word 'rite' (*Ritus*) to "single, possibly inherited schemes" and use the word 'ritual' (*Ritual*) for "the encompassing complexes, which are definitely transmitted culturally"

(33). Since all societies have religions and rituals, these must bring an evolutionary advantage (35). Thus: rituals survive only when they are advantageous to the people who perform them, when their cultural forms are transmitted (which takes place by learning through mimesis), and when individuals who do not comply are eliminated (35–36). Since rituals date from before the existence of the human race, and language is restricted to humans, rituals must be older than myths. Rituals cause emotions and interpretations, not the other way round (36–38). The last point is then still elaborated upon in section 4. The book further concentrates on what the author sees as the most fundamental type of ritual: sacrifices and other killing rituals (*Tötungsrituale*). These must, in his opinion, have originated in hunting societies, and since the killing is always followed by the eating of the killed animal, they form the starting point for further developments of rituals celebrating death and rebirth, be it of individuals or of the society as a whole. As the author summarizes at the end of the book (326–327): "The sacrifice as confrontation with death, as act of killing (*Tötungshandlung*), which yet guarantees the continuation of life and its food, has developed from the form of subsistence of the Paleolithic hunters, and remained the characteristic center of the 'sacred' rituals..." (326). [JS]

References: H. Hubert & M. Mauss, J.S. Huxley (+), **K.Z. Lorenz (+)**, É. Durkheim (+), A.R. Radcliffe-Brown (+), S. Freud (+).
Examples: Rituals from Greek antiquity.
Reviews: R. Crahay *AC* 42 (1973) 338; W. Pötscher *AAW* 27 (1974) 181–184; R. Wagner *AA* 77.2 (1975) 349; Z. Stewart *AJP* 98 (1977) 321; B. Centrone *El* 3 (1982) 387; C. Pignato *Uomo* 6.2 (1982) 307; J.N. Bremmer *CR* 35.2 (1985) 312; D.A. Miller *JSH* 19.3 (1986) 531; S. Humphreys *Man* 21.3 (1986) 557.
Key-words: MYT, soc, pow, psy, str, exp, com, ETH, mim, dyn, emo, rfl, tra.

Burkert, Walter, 1987, 'The Problem of Ritual Killing', in: Robert G. Hamerton-Kelly (ed.), *Violent Origins. Walter Burkert, René Girard, and Jonathan Z. Smith on Ritual Killing and Cultural Formation*, Stanford: Stanford University Press (ISBN 0–8047–1370–7) (*) 149–176.

In this article, the author begins with a discussion of ritual in general (150–162). Starting from "the framework for a definition of ritual" as "action patterns used as signs, in other words, stereotyped demonstrative action" (150), he reminds us that "[i]nteraction in any society may be both pragmatic and communicative; we speak of ritual if the communicative function is dominant" (150). But we "should still distinguish 'ritual' in a strict sense, a stereotype prescribed and predictable in detail, from a looser sense" (150–151). He then introduces the socio-biological approach, which leads him to the definition: "rituals are communicative forms of behavior combining innate elements with imprinting and learning; they are transmitted through the generations in the context of successful strategies of interaction. Religious rituals are highly integrated and complex forms that, with the character of absolute seriousness, shape and replicate societal groups and thus perpetuate themselves" (158). In the second section, he presents his (evolutionary) view of sacrifice rituals, and compares that with the views of others, esp. Girard. [JS]

References: J.S. Huxley (+), K.Z. Lorenz (+).
Key-words: COM, eth, cpl, dyn, soc, def.

Burkert, Walter, 1996, *The Creation of the Sacred. Tracks of Biology in Early Religions*; Cambridge (MA): Harvard University Press (ISBN 0-674-17569-7) (xii + 255) (with index and bibliography).

The aim of this book, which grew out of the 1989 Gifford Lectures in St. Andrews, is to uncover and explain the origins of religion and man's religiosity, as the author considers religion to be a universal feature of human society and thus also to be very resilient. He seeks to extract the common reason for religion as a social and cultural phenomenon in the very core of human biology, not concentrating on studying each religion as an autonomous system but getting the big picture by showing the interactions and mutual influences of different signifying systems and their links from the past to the present. A range of cultures have developed nearly identical attitudes and practices in coping with the mysteries of life. Speaking of biology, religion is not to be understood as some sort of genetic code but as an efficient system that has to be taught and that performs a biological function insofar as it provides direction, meaning, and balance in a complex and hostile world and in the face of the ineluctable fact of death. "By a process of reduction, religion provides orientation within a meaningful cosmos for those who feel helpless vis-à-vis infinite complexity" (26). Religion consoles and fortifies an anxiety-ridden mankind. One preverbal means of communicating distinct strategies of survival and fixed patterns of behavior can be found in rituals that express a close link between the evolution of genes and culture through constant repetition. Sacrifices of substitution, such as finger sacrifice, the phenomenon of scapegoats, or mechanisms of escape and submission, e.g., are both an evolutionary advantage, as well as of cultural significance. Still, there is no reciprocity in rituals since ceremonial giving never reaches its addressee. Although the author considers rituals to be primarily non-verbal, myths play an eminent role especially in initiation rituals. By separating rituals from their actual historical background and developing them mainly as a symbolic procedure—Greek rites of aversion and human sacrifice are mentioned in this context—social and cultural order is adjusted. It is "an exemplary way how the performance of ritual grows out of anxiety and is designed to control it" (36). The author paints a picture of religion as a tradition, transmitted partly by verbal teaching, partly by ritual and certainly by distinct biological aspects, to communicate with unseen powers and thus offering people a sense of coherence and stability in the world. Tracing the parallels between animal behavior and human religious activity, he suggests that there are natural foundations for sacrifices and rituals of escape, for the concept of guilt and punishment, for the practice of gift exchange and the notion of a cosmic hierarchy, and for the development of a system of signs for negotiating with an uncertain environment. In short, he demonstrates the universality of human approaches to the unknown and provides evidence for the roots and persistence of religion and rituals. [Florian Schaurer/JS]

References: E.G. d'Aquili (+/–), C.M. Bell (+/–), M.E.F. Bloch (+), G. Furlani (+), G. Herman (+/–), G.C. Homans (+), B. Lincoln (+), N. Marinatos (+/–), W. Schrank (+), F. Thureau-Dangin (+/–).
Examples: Greek rites of aversion, circumcision rituals and rituals of submission.
Reviews: A. Billault *REG* 109 (1996) 734 f; T. Köves-Zulauf *Gym* 104.6 (1997) 551–553; E.C. Polomé *JIES* 25.3/4 (1997) 465; G. Benavides *JSSR* 36.3 (1997) 468 f; T. Murphy *RSR* 23.4 (1997) 369; **R. Oswald *AAW* 51.3/4 (1998) 238–245**; H. Bowden *CR* 48.1 (1998) 94 f; **D. Baudy *GB* 22 (1998) 289–298**; D.J. Middleton *SHR* 32.2 (1998) 188–190; W. Baun, P. Boyer, C.R. Phillips III, T. Masuzawa & D.C. Dennett, and the reply by W. Burkert *MTSR* 10.1 (1998) 84–132.
Key-words: POW, eth, MYT, cpl, soc, com.

Burkert, Walter, 2002, '"Mythos und Ritual" im Wechselwind der Moderne', in: H.F.J. Horstmanshoff, *et al.* (eds), *Kykeon. Studies in Honour of H.S. Versnel*, (Religions in the Graeco-Roman World 142), Leiden, Boston, Köln: Brill (ISBN 90-04-11983-3) 1-22 (with bibliography after the article and indexes in the volume).
["Myth and Ritual" in the Changing Winds of Modernity]

In this essay, the author approaches the theme of 'myth and ritual' from both a personal and a historical point of view. He starts with an overview of the historical development of this approach to understanding 'ritual' (1–5), and continues by recounting the story of his own involvement with it, which resulted in the publication of his book *Homo Necans* in 1972 (*) (5–7). The author goes on to discuss some problems that can now be detected in that book (7–11). While he acknowledges that some "right-wing relics of Christian acculturation" (11) can be perceived in the book, he gives an account of his debate with structuralism, an approach that was perceived as progressive and leftist at the time (11–13). In the final section, the author attempts to assess some developments in the intervening years since 1971—postmodernism, deconstruction, the rise of the information society, developments in biology, such newly developed theories as 'memes' (R. Dawkins) and sociobiology (E.O. Wilson), newly found texts, etc.—and the problems that these pose to the historian of religions (13–20). At one point of his argument, he remarks: "The dream of the all encompassing anthropological theory of religion is likely to be renounced. To have a theory means making predictions; it puts restrictions on what can be experienced. Rather, I would like to remain prepared for something new and surprising" (17). [JS/MS]
Key-words: MYT, eth, str.

Caduff, Corina & Joanna Pfaff-Czarnecka (eds), 1999, *Rituale heute. Theorien—Kontroversen—Entwürfe*; Berlin: Dietrich Reimer (ISBN 3-496-02666-9) (230).
[Rituals Today. Theories—Controversies—Outlines]

Selected contents: Axel Michaels: "'Le rituel pour le rituel' oder wie sinnlos sind Rituale?" (23–47) (*); David N. Gellner: "Religion, Politik und Ritual. Betrachtungen zu Geertz und Bloch" (49–72) (*); Michael Oppitz: "Montageplan von Ritualen" (73–95). [JK]
Key-words: cpl, mng, pow, str.

Cannadine, David & Simon Price (eds), 1987, *Rituals of Royalty. Power and Ceremonial in Traditional Societies*; Cambridge etc.: Cambridge University Press (ISBN 0–521–33513–2 / 0–521–42891–2 (p)) (xi + 351) (with index and bibliographical notes).

In his introduction, David Cannadine writes: "the broader conclusions to be drawn from these case-studies seem clear: the relationship between pomp and power is much more complex and varied than any simple formulation might suggest; the whole notion of power as a narrow, separate and discreet category seems inappropriate and unsatisfactory; and the idea that splendour and spectacle is but superficial and cosmetic window-dressing appears equally ill-conceived" (15). "What these essays try to show is that no approach which defines power narrowly and ignores spectacle and pageantry can possibly claim to be comprehensive. Politics and ceremonial are not separate subjects, the one serious, the other superficial. Ritual is not the mask of force, but is itself a type of power…if the workings of any society are to be fully unravelled, then the barriers dividing the study of power from the study of pomp need to be broken down. As these essays make plain, different disciplines approach this endeavour in different ways; different societies need different treatment; and at best, the results are often incomplete, speculative and open to disagreement. But even so, it is only by such means that we can begin to probe more deeply into those structures of power and structures of meaning without which no society—past or present, traditional or modern—can ever properly be understood. These essays are offered as a tentative step in that direction" (19).

Contents: David Cannadine: "Introduction. Divine Rites of Kings" (1–19); Amélie Kuhrt: "Usurpation, Conquest and Ceremonial. From Babylon to Persia" (20–55); Simon Price: "From Noble Funerals to Divine Cult. The Consecration of Roman Emperors" (56–105); Averil Cameron: "The Construction of Court Ritual. The Byzantine *Book of Ceremonies*" (106–136); Janet L. Nelson: "The Lord's Anointed and the People's Choice. Carolingian Royal Ritual" (137–180); David McMullen: "Bureaucrats and Cosmology. The Ritual Code of T'ang China" (181–236); Richard Burghart: "Gifts to the Gods. Power, Property and Ceremonial in Nepal" (237–270); Maurice Bloch: "The Ritual of the Royal Bath in Madagascar. The Dissolution of Death, Birth and Fertility into Authority" (271–297) (*); Michelle Gilbert: "The Person of the King. Ritual and Power in a Ghanaian State" (298–330). [JS]

Review: **D.I. Kertzer *JRS* 4.2 (1990) 349–355**.
Key-words: soc, pow.

Cartry, Michel, 1992, 'From One Rite to Another. The Memory of Ritual and the Ethnologist's Recollection', in: Daniel de Coppet (ed.), *Understanding Rituals*, (European Association of Social Anthropologists), London, New York: Routledge (ISBN 0–415–06120–2 / 0–415–06121–0 (p)) (*) 26–36.

Inspired by Wittgenstein's remark that there "is a multiplicity of faces with common features reappearing here and there" in rites, the author focuses on "the question of the multiplicity of reappearances of common features from one rite to another" (26). He tries to discover "the 'lines' that can be drawn from one rite to another in a society's ritual" (26), or ritual system. This entails a criss-cross quest on the part of the ethnologist. Observing that one and the same song may occur in two ritual settings, the author attempts different analogies or metaphors. E.g., the "interdependence of the elements in a ritual" may be "analogous to the form that links the parts, or voices, of a musical score" (29). He tries to employ the musical metaphor of human or instrumental voices 'entering into imitation' with each other in order to describe "two distinct ceremonies 'entering in imitation'" (32). Ultimately, the question seems to be one of two forms of 'displacement', one pertaining to the ritual system and one pertaining to the observing ethnologist: "In the guise of a role change, a new space appears in which actors occupy many places, and this is a perception which immediately induces in the observing ethnologist a shift from one rite to another that allows the recognition of one of the lines it contains. It is this place change which, by doing away with the apparent discontinuity of ritual life, enables the observer, so long as he allows himself to be shifted by this movement, to give 'consistency' to the line he has identified in this occasion" (36). [MS]

References: P. Smith (+), L. Wittgenstein (+).
Key-words: cmp, mus, par, rep, rfl, rht, STR.

Cazeneuve, Jean, 1971, *Sociologie du rite. Tabou, magie, sacré* (Collection SUP—Le Sociologue 23); Paris: Presses Universitaires de France (No ISBN) (334) (with bibliography).
[Sociology of Ritual. Taboo, Magic, Sacred]

According to the author, a rite (*le rite*) is characterized by both its presumed efficacy (*sa prétendue efficacité*) and stereotyped repetition (13). Thus, "a rite is an act that is repeated and whose efficacy is, at least in part, of a meta-empirical order" (17). As all human societies have rites, these must fulfill a necessary function. This is based on the tension between desire for freedom on the one hand and order on the other, a tension that is particular to human nature (*condition humaine*). Since (primitive) man is a mystery to himself, he is divided by the desire to define his human nature through order and rules, and the temptation to remain more powerful than these very rules and to transgress all borders. According to the author, ritual (*le rituel*) provides three types of solution to this problem (36): impurity, magic, and the sacred. Impurity is a rejection of everything that is perceived as terrifying. Magic, on the contrary, is an attempt to appropriate what is otherwise rejected as impurity. The sacred is a synthesis of the numinous force and the human condition (*la force numineuse et la condition humaine*) (315). Through its rites (*rites*), "religion at the same time affirms this transcendence and the possibility for man to participate in its sacred archetypes. Thesis, antithesis, and synthesis, this seems to be the general dialectics of primitive ritual (*rituel primitif*)" (315). The religious rites of primitive man are thus explained by the need to realize a synthesis between his desire to live within the limits of a well-defined "*condition humaine*", and his tendency to secure that power and that true being which is beyond all limits (316). [MS/JS]

References: É. Durkheim, A. van Gennep, J.G. Frazer, R. Otto, C. Lévi-Strauss.
Reviews: C. Patte *RFS* 12.4 (1971) 597 f; J. Bancal *GM* 27 (1972) 237–240; M. Palau Marti *RHR* 184 (1973) 110; G.L. Gold *AJS* 79.1–6 (1973/74) 239; M. Chastaing a.o. *JPNP* 71.3 (1974) 353.
Key-words: exp, myt, eff.

Chambers, Tod S., 2004, 'Performing Religion. Toward a Theory of Participation for Comparative Religion', in: Thomas Ryba (ed.), *Comity and Grace of Method. Essays in Honor of Edmund F. Perry*, Evanston (IL): Northwestern University Press (ISBN: 0–8101–1891–2) 280–303.

Referring to the "radical shift in the academic study of religion" (280) as indicated by W.C. Smith, the author problematizes the emic/etic distinction in comparative religion by way of addressing the scholarly participation in religious practices of the people being studied. He asks: "How can the comparative religionist participate in the ritual activities of another community without losing his or her status as an outsider? If the outside investigator does not wish to deceive the insiders of his or her desire to 'temporarily' participate in their religious activities, how can this even be accomplished?" (281). He contends that "conceiving of an outsider's participation in ritual events as a *performance* permits a conceptual framework for understanding how 'temporary' conversion is workable as a methodological tool" (281–282). In order to address these issues, the author indicates in the first section on "Society in the Subjunctive Mode" (282–286) "the rise of interest in performance in the social sciences and specifically the recognition of subjunctivity in social process" (282) by discussing R. Grimes, V.W. Turner, R. Schechner, and B. Myerhoff. The second section deals with "Subjunctivity in Thai Buddhist Ordinations" (286–291). In the third section, "Subjunctive Insidership" (291–296), the author explores his own participation in a Thai Buddhist ordination and reflects upon the performative nature of his 'temporary' insidership. Based on his observations, he concludes: "All fieldwork can be understood as a form of performance, fieldworker and community performing for one another and, at times, with one another.... I believe that participation in cultural performances, like Buddhist ordination ceremonies, is a particularly good entrance point for actively constructing a subjunctive identity within a community" (297). [JK]

References: C. Geertz, E. Goffman, R.L. Grimes, B.G. Myerhoff, R. Schechner, V.W Turner.
Example: Thai Buddhist Ordinations.
Key-words: frm, par, pmc, rfl.

Cheal, David, 1988, 'The Postmodern Origin of Ritual', *Journal for the Theory of Social Behaviour* 18:269–290 (with bibliography).

The larger part of this article consists of a critical discussion of the universal theories of society as propounded by a number of scholars, notably Rappaport, Durkheim, Parsons, Goffman, Alexander, and Luhmann (269–279). In the remaining part (279–285), the author develops his own alternative. The final section, "Conclusion" (285–286), gives the following summary: "In recent years sociological theories of ritual have fallen behind developments both in social theory and in social life. I have attempted to show here that in both respects a new theory of ritual is required, which rejects concepts of totality and replaces them with concepts of transformation and temporality. It has been argued here that the key to understanding our present difficulties lies in the work of Talcott Parsons, who simultaneously absorbed and enunciated many of the most important influences in sociology in this century. The distorting influence of Parsons's work upon the sociology of ritual has been shown to affect even those who, like Goffman, reacted against it, only to fail to overcome the limitations of its least visible presuppositions. The most fateful presupposition of all was that which equated the theory of action with the concept of the unit act. The account of ritual presented here is based on a theory of action that is Weberian rather than Parsonian. Setting aside Parsons's reduction of action to the monolithic model of the unit act, social life has been analysed as consisting of three distinct types of action. They are reification, resource management and reproduction. The description of these three types of action has been worked out within a general theory of time, considered as the social construction of temporality. According to this theory, all action (that is, all behaviour to which individuals attach a subjective meaning) is conducted with reference to one or more of three possible origins from which meaning may be derived. Those origins are the beginning, the now, and the end. Rituals of reification are derived from representations of the beginning, rituals of resource management are derived from representations of the now, and rituals of reproduction are derived from representations of the end. Of particular importance is the last of these three processes, which is identified here as the postmodern origin of ritual" (285). The author adds a note here: "Rituals of reification, rituals of resource management and rituals of reproduction are present in all societies, but with differences in emphasis. It is suggested here that rituals of reproduction are especially characteristic of those societies which we call postmodern" (287). Two further points should be noted: (1) the author writes explicitly against the background of the threat of a nuclear war (cf., e.g. p. 287 n. 9), which explains his concern with the end of time, and (2) as the term "rituals of reproduction" implies, these are not so much "derived from representations of the end" (as it was formulated above), but rather "[t]he defining characteristic of rituals of reproduction is that in them means are not employed to bring about ends, but they are employed to avoid the end" (284). [JS]

References: R.A. Rappaport, É. Durkheim, **T. Parsons**, E. Goffman, J. Alexander, N. Luhmann, M. Weber.
Key-words: def, SOC, sec, mng, exp, pr1, agn, dyn, emo, frm, int, tra, tim.

Chwe, Michael Suk-Young, 2001, *Rational Ritual. Culture, Coordination, and Common Knowledge*; Princeton, Oxford: Princeton University Press (ISBN 0–691–00949–X) (xi + 130) (with index and bibliography).

This book builds on a seemingly simple and obvious observation from everyday life: "In some situations, called 'coordination problems', each person wants to participate in a joint action only if others participate also" (8). In order to solve this 'coordination problem', 'common knowledge' is required. "We say that an event or fact is common knowledge among a group of people if everyone knows it, everyone knows that everyone knows it, everyone knows that everyone knows that everyone knows it, and so on" (10–11). "[T]his book tries to demonstrate three things. First, the concept of common knowledge has broad explanatory power. Second, common knowledge generation is an essential part of what a public ritual 'does'. Third, the classic dichotomy between rationality and culture should be questioned" (8). According to the author, public rituals are the "best examples" for "social processes that generate common knowledge" and in that way help "people solve coordination problems" (3). In two sections of the book ("Ceremonies and Authority", 19–25; "How Do Rituals Work?", 25–30), the author reinterprets some extant ritual theories on the basis of his theory of common knowledge. "Interpreted in terms of common knowledge generation", repetition, for example, "is about not just making sure that each person gets a message, but also making sure that each person can recognize the repetition and thus know that everyone else gets the message" (28). Modifying Geertz' interpretation of royal progresses, the author "focuses on publicity, how progresses create common knowledge" (22). Challenging Bloch's approach, he finds that "[t]he certainty of the ritual sequence generates authority not by enforcing responses but by helping generate common knowledge" (29), and he argues that "group dancing 'as a body' is an ideal way of creating common knowledge because if any person loses interest, this becomes immediately evident to everyone because the pattern of movement is disrupted" (30). [MS]

References: M.E.F. Bloch (+/–), C. Geertz (+/–), C. Lévi-Strauss, F. Staal (–), S.J. Tambiah (–), V.W. Turner (+/–).
Key-words: soc, pow, str, MNG, COM, cpl, eff, med, par, rfl, tra, aut, gst, dnc.

Clothey, Fred W., 1998, 'Toward a Comprehensive Interpretation of Ritual', *Journal of Ritual Studies* 2.2:147–161.

This essay discusses some methodological questions concerning the comprehensive interpretation of ritual as a religious phenomenon. The author uses phenomenological, anthropological, historical, and morphological approaches to develop a method for the interpretation of the multiple meanings of a ritual: "It is a method concerned for the phenomenon's placement in its appropriate contemporary context, its cultural history, and its universe of morphological significance" (147). According to the author, a phenomenological interpretation of rituals has to do with a plurality of meanings: "Meaning is inevitably plural and, like ritual itself, is dynamically processual—a verbal in constant flux rather than a frozen and finite noun" (148). In terms of meaningfulness as a "mosaic of meanings ascribable to the phenomenon in its total cultural setting" (148), the interpretation "seeks to organize and systematically present these meanings as embodiments of the religion and culture at hand" (150). At the level of theoretical significance of a phenomenological interpretation of ritual, the author argues that "no single theory will exhaust the meaningfulness of any ritual" (151). Secondly, the author also uses the anthropological approach to interpret rituals with regard to different frames. Because "the ritual reflects, to varying degrees, the 'microhistoric whole' which is its contemporary time and place", he argues that an interpretation of ritual is "placing it in its appropriate contemporary frame" (151). Since the microhistoric whole is itself plural and fluid, a comprehensive interpretation should apply all such frames as contextuality, religious, and ideological forms and contemporaneous human situations. The third major concern of the author is that "no religious phenomenon can be adequately understood apart from its 'history'" (154). To study and interpret rituals as a historical embodiment of its cultural history "requires consideration of its past, both recent and ancient" (154). This also means that "even the contemporary itself is not a frozen moment, but rather a moment very much in process" (155). The author's fourth consideration in understanding rituals is concerned with the indigenous structures within the "morphological whole" of which the ritual is a part. This means that one is "obliged to discover those organizing principles or categories of coherence which are operating in the community of the observed" (156). [JK]

References: C. Geertz (+), M. Eliade (+), R.L. Grimes (+), J.Z. Smith (+).
Key-words: mng, emb, cmp, rfl.

Cohen, Abner, 1979, 'Political Symbolism', *Annual Review of Anthropology* 8:87–113.

This article deals with cultural symbols and their political implications in the study of social anthropology and Marxian literature. The main argument is that politics cannot be thought of without power relations, which in turn are interrelated with, and inseparable from, economic relations. Hence, the author asserts that "[p]ower relations and symbolism are present in all social relationships" (91). The author shows how the symbolism of life crises, which seem to refer only to psychological and existential problems, have to do with politics. In analyzing the crisis of death and the related ceremonies, he points out that "the intensity of the ceremonialization of this motif is closely related to fundamental politico-economic factors" (92). Other life crises also have important political significances in many societies, so that the ritual and the secular hierarchies overlap and are used for the power holders' own interests. The universal politicization of symbolism of life crises depends on the fact both that these problems cannot be solved scientifically and that they potentially become an obligation for all group members. The author criticizes the tendency of social anthropological analyses that seem to be contented with sociocultural correlations without showing the mediation between the social and the cultural. According to him, "[o]ne way of doing this is to explore the dramatic process underlying the rituals, ceremonials, and other types of symbolic activities in social life" (105). Although many anthropologists have attempted to develop a science of symbols and meanings, this has yet to lead to the formation of a discipline. However, "[p]ower and symbolism are the two major variables that pervade all social life, and social anthropology already has the possibilities for developing the study of the relations between them into a promisingly cumulative discipline with a working paradigm to guide a fairly open-ended research. What it needs further as a discipline is to be truly comparative" (110). [JK]

References: L. Althusser, E.E. Evans-Pritchard, M. Gluckman, V.W. Turner.
Key-words: sym, pow, cpr, ecn, soc, psy.

Cole, Jennifer, 2004, 'Painful Memories. Ritual and the Transformation of Community Trauma', *Culture, Medicine and Psychiatry* 28:87–105.

Arguing that pain is social, political and historically constituted and expressed, the author "draws together assumptions about the profoundly ideological nature of healing, with a focus on mechanisms of ritual efficacy through a discussion of a dramatic example of how people on the east coast of Madagascar used cattle sacrifice to heal their community after a war" (88). In relating community pain and trauma to memory she argues "that particularly in cases of social violence and healing, the ability of ritual to assuage pain lies in its ability to draw pain into the process of producing...people's memories" (88). She emphasizes that "by focusing more specifically on *memory* as a mechanism that links individual bodies with wider social narratives and *commits* people to a particular narrative by rooting it within their subjective senses of themselves, we gain a powerful way to think about both how ritual efficacy might be achieved and how healing is intrinsically linked to broader ideological projects" (88–89). The main part of this paper is concerned with the ethnographic case at issue and its historical background, which is presented in the following sections: "The Rebellion" (89–91), "After the War. Ritual Healing" (91–94), "Memory and Amnesia, Sickness and Health. Ancestors and Cattle Sacrifices in Betsimisaraka Social Practice" (94–98), and "Affect and Narrative. The Ritual Construction of Memory" (98–100). Summarizing her findings the author writes: "Taken together, the different levels of affect, both the pain of the sponsor and the affect produced collectively during the rite, merge with the narrative constructed in sacrifice to powerfully scaffold people's memories. Through this process, the inchoate sensation of pain becomes articulated with a wider semantic network of meanings, so that individual pain and suffering become constitutive of particular, strategically negotiated interpretations of ongoing social relations, as well as socially negotiated constructions of self" (100). She concludes: "In contrast to those who argue that ritual efficacy is achieved through either the imposition of meaning or the persuasiveness of practice, I have offered an alternative account: that ritual efficacy works by scaffolding individuals' memories, through the fusion of pain, a form of affect, with a strategically produced narrative" (101). [JK]

References: M.E.F. Bloch, Th.J. Csordas, É. Durkheim, C. Geertz, C. Lévi-Strauss, E.L. Schieffelin, S.J. Tambiah, V.W. Turner.
Example: Cattle sacrifice on the East coast of Madagascar.
Key-words: EFF, EMO, idn, mng, pow, soc.

Collins, Elizabeth, 1998, 'Reflections on Ritual and on Theorizing about Ritual', *Journal of Ritual Studies* 12.1:1–7.

In her introductory essay to the subsequent four papers of this volume of the *Journal of Ritual Studies*, the author mentions some general features of a number of well known theoretical works on rituals and tries to link them to the four case studies. The topics that the author briefly addresses include the problem of defining ritual (Wittgenstein), emic terms for ritual "because the word translated as ritual and the ceremony tell one a good deal about the place of ritual in a society" (1), the use of the body in rituals (Asad), the distinction between orthodox traditions, heterodox movements, and *doxa* (Bourdieu), contesting cultural traditions (Clifford & Marcus), and the resulting need to "be aware of the multiple perspectives of participants in a ritual" (2), on the side of the scholar, the question of meaning (Geertz; Ortner; Obeyesekere), the paradox of structure and agency (Bourdieu, Bell)—"What do rituals do to people and what do people do with rituals"? (3)—and the theoretical model of text and performance (Tambiah). "This theoretical perspective shows us that agency and structure are opposite sides of one coin. Rituals do structure human behavior. However, precisely because social relations are ritualized and therefore relatively predictable, people can be effective agents" (4). It is suggested that "the interpreter of ritual needs to employ both the hermeneutics of suspicion and the hermeneutics of agency. Taken together, these opposed perspectives alert one to the contradictions that are often at the heart of the symbolic acts that constitute ritual.... Although ritual forms are frequently embedded in structures of authority that are oppressive...they may be reinterpreted in a way that is empowering to the individual" (4). Moreover, theoretical "models of text and performance have brought a new complexity to ritual studies in emphasizing the different kinds of agency that are involved in the enactment of a ritual (text)" (4). In the final paragraph, the author discusses Tambiah's concept of 'participatory rationality'. As her conclusion, the author posits: "as we begin to see what it would be to take ritual seriously, to think about how rituals construct our own world and to take the responsibility for our rituals, we become agents in the collective creation of a world" (6). [MS]

References: T. Asad (+), C.M. Bell (+), P. Bourdieu (+), C. Geertz (+), G. Obeyesekere (+), S.B. Ortner (+), S.J. Tambiah (+).
Key-words: GEN, pmc, pmt, pr2, cpl, pow, agn, def, ter.

Comaroff, Jean & John Comaroff, 1993, 'Introduction', in: Jean Comaroff & John Comaroff (eds), *Modernity and its Malcontents. Ritual and Power in Postcolonial Africa*, Chicago: University of Chicago Press (ISBN 0–226–11439–2 / 0–226–11440–6 (p)) xi–xxxvii.

In the introduction to a collection of essays on ritual and power in postcolonial Africa, the editors raise some crucial issues in theorizing rituals. They articulate "two general propositions. First, *pace* the long, persistent tradition that sees ritual as conservative and conservationist, as a (indeed, the) prime mechanism of social reproduction, cultural continuity, and political authority, we presume differently: that it may as well be, and frequently is, a site and a means of experimental practice, of subversive poetics, of creative tension and transformative action; that, under its authorship and its authority, individual and collective aspirations weave a thread of imaginative possibilities from which may emerge, wittingly or not, new signs and meanings, conventions and intentions. It is in this sense that ritual is always a vehicle of history-in-the making: at times it conduces to sustain and legitimize the world in place; at times it has the effect of changing more-or-less pervasive features of that world; at times it does both simultaneously" (xxix). The second general thesis "may be phrased as follows: ritual, as an experimental technology intended to affect the flow of power in the universe, is an especially likely response to contradictions created and (literally) engendered by processes of social, material, and cultural transformation, processes re-presented, rationalized, and authorized in the name of modernity and its various alibis" (xxx). [MS]

Examples: postcolonial Africa.
Key-word: pow.

Crapanzano, Vincent, 2000, 'Fragmentarische Überlegungen zu Körper, Schmerz und Gedächtnis', in: Klaus-Peter Köpping & Ursula Rao (eds), *Im Rausch des Rituals. Gestaltung und Transformation der Wirklichkeit in körperlicher Performanz*, (Performanzen. Interkulturelle Studien zu Ritual, Spiel und Theater 1), Münster, Hamburg, London: Lit (ISBN 3–8258–3988–5) (*) 218–239.
[Fragmentary Reflections on Body, Pain, and Memory]

This article aims to uncover intellectual orientations and traces of argumentation on which the thinking of body, pain, memory, trauma, and identity is based. On the example of the trance ritual by a Moslem brotherhood in Morocco, the author elaborates the notion of agency. After discussing the notion of body as found in J. Lacan, J. Genet, and S. Freud, he asserts that the body is considered with and through remembrance, but that it cannot be thought of without pain and without the pain of perception. If the pain is very intense, it can even terminate the remembrance, which can evoke in turn the illusion that one can escape from the remembrance. According to the author, the body is constructed through complex social, cultural, and linguistic processes. These processes influence its biological character, as well as its symbolization and its rhetorical potential. Furthermore, to speak about the body means to perform it, and the body exists for spectators, even if one is the spectator of one's own body. Just as the body is a medium between signifier and signified, and word and thing, so bodily pain can play the same role. The body is a place of inscription that is related to remembrance, such that bodily pain is frequently a part of psychotic rituals. [JK]

Reference: S. Freud, J. Lacan, T.S. Turner.
Example: Trance ritual by a Moslem brotherhood in Morocco.
Key-words: agn, emb, emo, idn, psy, sem.

Crocker, Jon Christopher, 1973, 'Ritual and the Development of Social Structure. Liminality and Inversion', in: James D. Shaughnessy (ed.), *The Roots of Ritual*, Grand Rapids (MI): William B. Eerdman's (ISBN 0-8028-1509-X) (*) 47–86.

"Ritual is a statement in metaphoric terms about the paradoxes of human existence. In this paper I wish to consider the theoretical background and the two prevailing schools of anthropological interpretation of this definition: the view that regards ritual as a type of political action, and that which sees it as an expression of belief. In both cases the particular content of action and belief is interpreted as a related characteristic of a given social structure, but the nature of this relationship is precisely the disputed element.... My tactic in this paper shall be that traditional scholastic device, a combination of the two interpretations that attempts to show them as mutually complementary rather than antithetically opposed. The possible virtues of this synthesis will be illustrated by reference to various ceremonies of the Bororo" (47–48). Thus this paper starts. The first section further presents the positions of the "ritual-as-action theorists" and the "ritual-as-belief theorists", and then defines 'ritual': "For most of my colleagues, ritual expresses those fundamental categories by which men attempt to apprehend and to control their social existence—categories that refer both to social positions and to mystical entities.... Symbolic action affirms something: it makes a statement about the conditions of existence in terms of the relations of persons and groups. Ritual, then, is essentially communication, a language in which societies discuss a variety of matters. It deals with the relationships a man has to other men, to institutions, spirits, and nature... Our immediate problem thus becomes, exactly what is ritual communicating" (49). The following three sections review several older ritual theories, especially those by W. Robertson Smith, É. Durkheim, E.R. Leach, A.R. Radcliffe-Brown, M. Gluckman, C. Lévi-Strauss, and V.W. Turner. The fifth section starts with the summary: "I have attempted to show how the action and belief approaches may be combined through focusing on the common quality that the mystically potent, whether this be a conceptual category, a substance, or a role, all share. To demonstrate that this sharing is also an association, it is necessary to utilize a recent article [by Th.O. Beidelman] that shows the intimate connection between the conceptual entities of religious creed and the particular forces in social life" (71). Then there follows an Appendix of 14 pages with the promised example from the Bororo. Here the author concludes: "Thus two types of liminality might be distinguished, the one resulting from the transformation of one category into its antithesis,... and the other deriving from the total absence of category... Thus, the totality of Bororo ritual is a transition in each dyad from one term to the other through the intermediary of the second dyad as a totality. It is therefore neither opposition nor synthesis but the transformation through inversion of each term into the other that establishes order and controls the organic process of change" (86). [JS]

References: W. Robertson Smith, É. Durkheim, E.R. Leach, A.R. Radcliffe-Brown, M. Gluckman, C. Lévi-Strauss, V.W. Turner, Th.O. Beidelman.
Example: The Bororo from Brasil.
Key-words: COM, pr1, str, rel, def, soc.

Crumrine, N. Ross, 1970, 'Ritual Drama and Culture Change', *Comparative Studies in Society and History* 12:361–372.

The author examines different kinds of relationships between culture change and ritual dramas or ceremonials, which symbolically mediate the structural conflicts within a society or between societies. By referring to the rituals of rebellion and the functions of rituals for social integration, the author examines an Easter ceremonial of the Mayo Indian in the Sonora River Valley, Mexico. After an analysis of the charter represented in this ceremonial, the author concludes "ritual drama is an important element in the adjustment between dominant and subordinate societies or social groups. The ceremonial and the drama can both 1) reinforce traditional values through extremely complex symbolization by mediating structural oppositions either within the society or between the dominant and subordinate societies and 2) can symbolically incorporate individuals into the dominant social structure by providing rites of separation from traditional social structure" (372). [JK]

References: C. Geertz, M. Gluckman, H. Kuper, J.L. Peacock.
Examples: Easter ceremonial of the Mayo Indian in the Sonora River Valley (Mexico), rites of rebellion.
Key-word: dyn.

Crumrine, N. Ross, 1983, 'Introduction. Masks, Participants, and Audience', in: N. Ross Crumrine & Majorie M. Halpin (eds), *The Power of Symbols. Masks and Masquerade in the Americas*, (International Congress of Americanists. Symposium 43), Vancouver (BC): University of British Columbia Press (ISBN 0-7748-0166-2) 1–11.

This article introduces a volume of contributions to a conference on theories and processes of masks and masquerade. The author aims to develop elements of "a general theory of the mask" and defines masking "as the ritual transformation of the human actor into a being of another order" (1). This conceptualization is supposed to be broad enough to include "ritual drama, carnival, clowns, face-painting, and various kinds of transforming costume elements in a general domain of symbolic transformation" (1). The articles on which this volume is based, "treat the question of the power of masks and masquerade to transform participants, audience, and social situations and/or to become idols or power-objects in themselves". The general aim is to show that masking itself involves "the use of power-objects that have either transformed themselves into idols and/or produced a ritual transformation of the human actor into a being of another order" (2). Although the articles examine the transformations given by the power of masks and vary in data and analysis, the author indicates that these differences in their mode of analysis are necessary to set up a more general theoretical analysis: "Such a theory will emerge from sets of relationships and the objects or units of relationships as developed in the articles" (2). Because "these relationships involve the exchange and/or transformation of power as mediated by the objects or units" (2), the author holds the view that "masks might be defined as power-generating, -concentrating, -transforming, and -exchanging objects" (2–3). He argues: "In some rituals, the audience provides the focus of power and is transformed, in others, the masker is possessed by the power of the mask, or of a name, and is transformed. In the remaining cases, the mask supported by a bearer becomes the focus of power and is transformed into an idol" (3). Referring to the contributions in this volume, the author says in summary that even though the articles prove to be diverse, "nevertheless all focus upon certain aspects of a holistic approach that interrelates the mask as material apparatus with the roles of masker and audience, with mythology and ritual symbolism, and with broader ritual and social organization. Not remaining static, however, this holistic approach also examines these interrelations as evolving dynamic historical patterns in adaptation to broader ecological processes.... Focusing upon the individual, the group, and the metaphoric and symbolic structure, the articles in this volume demonstrate how masks achieve such results" (11). [JK/MS]

References: E.R. Leach, C. Lévi-Strauss, V.W. Turner.
Key-words: dyn, pmc, rel, idn, pow, aut, par, rfl.

Csaszi, Lajos, 2001, 'A ritualis kommunikacio neodurkheimi elmelete es a media', *Szociologiai Szemle* 2:3–15.
[A Neo-Durkheimian Theory of Ritual Communication]

Until recently, the Durkheimian perspective has been underestimated in communication research. This work explores how a rediscovered Durkheimian sociology is capable of providing a solution to numerous unsolved problems raised by media researchers. In the course of discussion, the paper compares the neo-Durkheimian moral philosophy with Michel Foucault's social theory. Reviewing the English language literature on rituals, the article seeks an answer as to whether it is possible to use the category of ritual in modern societies. The answer is positive, since media rituals can be regarded as symbolic moral dramas, which provide a public performance of the conflicts of the community. [Adapted from the source document. Source: Illumina.]

Key-words: soc, com, med.

Csikszentmihalyi, Mihaly & Stith Bennett, 1971, 'An Exploratory Model of Play', *American Anthropologist* 73:45–58.

In this paper, the authors aim to develop "a conceptual model for play" (45). They describe and define play as follows: "Play is going. It is what happens after all the decisions are made—when 'let's go' is the last thing one remembers. Play is action generating action: a unified experience flowing from one moment to the next in contradiction to our otherwise disjoint 'everyday' experiences" (45). They argue that "[p]lay is grounded in the concept of possibility" (45) and place emphasis on such 'everyday actions' that are imbued with experiences of 'worry' and 'boredom' in relation to 'voluntary fiat', which contradicts play. Therefore, the experience of play depends on conditions "[w]hen there is a 'balanced' state of affairs, when we can make each action by voluntary fiat, but still do not exhaust possible actions" (46). Moreover, "*[p]lay is experienced when it is impossible for the actor to differentiate projects available by voluntary fiat from assessed situational possibilities*" (46). Because the experience of play is predetermined in most cultures by games, the authors elaborate on three traditional categories of games, namely 'games of chance', 'games of strategy' and 'games of physical skill'. They analyze especially the 'self' that is forgotten in a game situation when "self becomes superfluous, and the player can merge with the process in a state of monistic awareness" (56). Unlike in everyday life, in play situation the traditional theoretical conflict between individual and society is abolished. [JK]

References: P.L. Berger (+), E. Goffman, **J. Huizinga** (+), Th. Luckman (+), G.H. Mead, T. Parsons (+), **J. Piaget** (+), A. Schutz (+).
Key-words: emo, frm, pmc, psy, soc, tim.

Csordas, Thomas J., 1983, 'The Rhetoric of Transformation in Ritual Healing', *Culture, Medicine and Psychiatry* 7:333–375.

From the author's abstract: "The problem of reconciling accounts of religious healing from the points of view of comparative religion and medicine suggests the necessity of an interpretive or hermeneutic approach to the analysis of therapeutic process. This paper, in the context of examining psychotherapeutic ritual among Catholic Pentecostals, formulates an interpretative approach in which healing is conceived as a form of discourse that is both religious and psychiatric. This discourse embodies a cultural rhetoric capable of performing three essential persuasive tasks: to create a *predisposition* to be healed, to create the experience of spiritual *empowerment*, and to create the concrete perception of personal *transformation*. It is shown that this threefold process activates and controls healing processes endogenous to the supplicant in healing, and either redirects the supplicant's attention toward new aspects of his actions and experiences, or alters the manner in which he attends to accustomed aspects of those actions and experiences. The result is the creation of both a new phenomenological world, and new self-meaning for the supplicant as a whole and holy person" (333). [Thorsten Gieser]

References: J.W. Fernandez, B. Kapferer, M. Mauss, S.J. Tambiah.
Example: Catholic Pentecostals' healing rituals.
Key-words: PSY, emo, rfl, RHT.

Dahm, Ulrike, 2003, *Opfer und Ritus. Kommunikationstheoretische Untersuchungen* (Religionswissenschaftliche Reihe 20); Marburg: Diagonal (ISBN 3-927165-84-0) (203).
[Sacrifice and Rite. Communication Theoretical Investigations]

This dissertation presents a systematic discussion of some principal features and contexts of sacrifice, such as food, food-avoidance (23–37), meat food (38–40), the so-called cattle complex (41–58), and the gift-based economy (59–65). The subsequent chapters contain the book's core argument. Here, sacrifice is discussed as just one, albeit universally attested, type of ritual, and hence the argument is of importance for ritual theory in general; for, inspired by her supervisor Hermann Schulz, the author attempts to sketch a generative, four-dimensional syntax of ritual (*Ritus*) as a sort of blueprint for the construction of rites (*Riten-Bauplan*) (66–92). This approach is intended to account for the great variety of ritual practice and its creative formation. In the next chapter (93–132), the author attempts to describe ritual as an action-centered medium of communication (*handlungsorientiertes Kommunikationsmedium*). According to the author, what the word is for language, the action is for ritual. Hence, action is the most important characteristic of ritual communication (177). An action can be translated in turn to become a sign, a symbol, and in human communication it can also be represented by media (a ritual transfer of gifts is not an economic act, but a ritually mediated act carrying a message). Single acts as such are devoid of inherent meaning; rather, they attain different meaning by being inserted into discrete units or programs, which, in turn, may become vehicles for different statements or propositions, i.e., they are operating as media. Hence, contrary to the idea that rituals serve specific purposes (such as the construction of power or identity, or the redistribution of goods), rituals may be considered as general media of communication permitting to make virtually every sort of statement (178–179). Contrary to law or military action, however, ritual does not directly intervene in the behavior or acting of a group (181). Finally, the author tries to provide some reasons why sacrifice is a particularly attractive instrument or medium of communication within ritual practice. While the argument in the first part (15–132) is based on a broad range of source materials, the second part (135–168) discusses the economy of temple ritual and sacrifice in Mesopotamia. [MS]

References: G. Baudy (–), W. Burkert (–), B. Gladigow (+/–), E.Th. Lawson & R.N. McCauley (+), E. Leach, C. Lévi-Strauss, A. Michaels, J.G. Platvoet, R.A. Rappaport (+/–), **H. Schulz (+)**, S.J. Tambiah (–), V.W. Turner.
Example: Sacrifice.
Key-words: COM, AES, pr1, sem, mng, SYM, STR, eth, pow, MED.

D'Aquili, Eugene G., 1983, 'The Myth-Ritual Complex. A Biogenetic Structural Analysis', *Zygon* 18:247–269.

The author summarizes: "The structuring and transformation of myth is presented as a function of a number of brain 'operators'. Each operator is understood to represent specifically evolved neural tissue primarily of the neocortex of the brain. Mythmaking as well as other cognitive processes is seen as a behavior arising from the evolution and integration of certain parts of the brain. Human ceremonial ritual is likewise understood as the culmination of a long phylogenetic evolutionary process, and a neural model is presented to explain its properties. Finally, the mechanism by which ritual is used to resolve the antinomies of myth structure is explored" (247). [JS]

Key-words: COG, ETH, myt.

D'Aquili, Eugene G., 1985, 'Human Ceremonial Ritual and the Modulation of Aggression', *Zygon* 20:21–30.

The author defines "ritual behavior as a sequence of behavior which is structured or patterned; which is rhythmic and repetitive (to some degree at least)...; which acts to synchronize affective, perceptual-cognitive, and motor processes within the central nervous system of individual participants; and which, most particularly, synchronizes these among the various individual participants tending to eliminate aggression and to facilitate cohesion among the participants" (22). The paper is primarily concerned with the last-mentioned aspect. It draws on a number of relevant observations from neurobiology and ethology. The paper is divided into four sections. In the first, "Facilitation of Social Cohesion by Rhythmic Repetitive Behavior" (22–24), the author refers to "increasing evidence that rhythmic or repetitive behavior synchronizes the limbic discharges (i.e., the affective states) of a group of conspecifics. It can generate a level of arousal which is both pleasurable and reasonably uniform among the individuals so that necessary group action is facilitated" (24). In the second section, "Differential Hemispheric Function and Ritual Union" (24–27), the author discusses how "recent discoveries of differential hemispheric functioning fit into our system of thought" (24). This discussion leads the author to the conclusion "that the core central experience of human religious ritual, when it works for an individual, is a marked attenuation of intragroup aggression and the experience of union or oneness" (26). In the third section, "Structural and Anti-Structural Uses of Ritual" (27–28), the author refers to Turner's notion of communitas and states: "This sense of oneness with other participants in a religious ritual and, by extension, with all the members of the social group is a function of ceremonial ritual much closer to the biological basis of a ritual" (27) than its structural use. The final section, "Ritual and Myth Promote Aggression and Cooperation" (28–29), draws attention to the frequent paradoxical effect of ritual's promoting extragroup aggression at the same time that it diminishes intragroup aggression. [MS]

References: K.Z. Lorenz (+), V.W. Turner (+).
Key-words: str, eth, emo, exp, def, soc.

D'Aquili, Eugene G. & Charles D. Laughlin, 1975, 'Biopsychological Determinants of Religious Ritual Behavior', *Zygon* 10:32–58.

The purpose of this article is to apply the method of biogenetic structuralism to an analysis of a 'universal' cultural institution, here human religious ritual. Data from ethology, neurophysiology, cognitive psychology, and hominid evolution are integrated in a theoretical explanation of the origin and maintenance of religious ritual in human societies. The article concludes with a consideration of the limitations of the method, as well as with some ontological and epistemological considerations. The point is made that a materialistic methodology does not necessarily lead to a materialistic worldview, though it may do so. [JS]

Key-words: eth, psy.

D'Aquili, Eugene G., Charles D. Laughlin Jr. & John McManus (eds), 1979, *The Spectrum of Ritual. A Biogenetic Structural Analysis*; New York: Columbia University Press (ISBN 0–231–04514–x) (xiv + 375) (with index and bibliography).

Selected Contents: Ch.D. Laughlin Jr., J. McManus & E.G. d'Aquili: "Introduction" (1–50); Ch.D. Laughlin Jr. & J. McManus: "Mammalian Ritual" (80–116); E.G. d'Aquili & Ch.D. Laughlin Jr.: "The Neurobiology of Myth and Ritual" (152–182); J. McManus: "Ritual and Ontogenetic Development" (183–215); J. McManus: "Ritual and Human Social Cognition" (216–248); T. Burns & Ch.D. Laughlin Jr.: "Ritual and Social Power" (249–279); Ch.D. Laughlin Jr., & E.G. d'Aquili: "Ritual and Stress" (280–317); J. McManus, Ch.D. Laughlin Jr. & E.G. d'Aquili: "Concepts, Methods, and Conclusions" (342–362). [JS]

Reviews: D. Buchdahl *AA* 81.1 (1979) 180 f; L.H. Hicks *CP* 24.10 (1979) 874; V.P. Gay *JSSR* 19.2 (1980) 224; R.J. Miller *SB* 27.4 (1980) 323; E. Pressel *AA* 84.1 (1982) 205; T.H. Lewis *An* 77.3/4 (1982) 604; H.S. Straight *ISP* 14.2 (1982) 91; F.D. Goodman *Zygon* 18.3 (1983) 336 f.
Key-words: myt, soc, pow, psy, COG, ETH.

D'Aquili, Eugene G. & Andrew B. Newberg, 1999, *The Mystical Mind. Probing the Biology of Religious Experience* (Theology and the Science); Minneapolis (MN): Fortress Press (ISBN 0–8006–3163–3) (ix + 228) (with index).

This volume represents the intellectual legacy of Eugene d'Aquili, who passed away prior to its publication. The book is intended as a contribution to "neurotheology", i.e. "the study of theology from a neuropsychological perspective" (15), examining "how the mind/brain functions in terms of humankind's relation to God or ultimate reality" (18). Part one of the book ("Prelude to the Mystical Mind", 1–76) tries to provide an understanding of the function of the brain and explores "how the mind functions in a mystical way" (16). Part two ("The Mystical Mind", 77–143) discusses myth, ritual/liturgy, meditation/mysticism, and near-death experiences. [Part three ("Neurotheology and the Paradox of Phenomenology", 145–211) will be neglected in this abstract, since it does not discuss ritual as such.] The authors assume that "myths form the basis of religions" (79). This is because "[h]uman beings have no choice but to construct myths to explain their worlds" (86). Myths are structured in a dyadic way, and these mythic antinomies, the authors argue, can be resolved either in a mythic or a ritual fashion. "Religious ritual aims at existentially uniting opposites in an effort to achieve some form of control over what appears to be an essentially unpredictable universe. The ultimate union of opposites is that of a vulnerable humanity with a powerful, possibly omnipotent form...we propose that humanity and some 'superhuman' power are the ultimate poles of mythic structure. Furthermore, it is this polarity that is the fundamental problem ritual must resolve existentially" (87–88). "Ritual allows individual humans to become incorporated into myth, and conversely, allows for the very incarnation of myth" (93). The authors argue that myths need to be acted out by rhythmic motor behavior (88–89). That is where ritual gets into the picture. The authors "define ritual behavior as a sequence of behavior that: 1. is structured or patterned; 2. is rhythmic and repetitive (to some degree at least)...; 3. acts to synchronize affective, perceptual-cognitive, and motor processes within the central nervous system of individual participants; and 4. most particularly, synchronizes these processes among the various individual participants" (89). Based on "the literature on animal studies together with the limited studies that have been performed with humans, one can infer that there is something about repetitive rhythmic stimuli that may, under the proper conditions, bring about the unusual neural state consisting of simultaneous high discharge of both the arousal and the quiescent system" (89–90). This specific condition that leads to "both hemispheres of the brain to function simultaneously" (91), "powerfully activates the holistic operator" (90), that is one of the seven 'operators' of the mind (cf. 52). The activation of the 'holistic operator' in turn generates "the unitary experience that reconciles opposites" (91). When "ritual works (and it by no means works all the time), it powerfully relieves our existential anxiety. Furthermore, when ritual is most powerful, it relieves us of the fear of death and places us in a sense of harmony with the universe" (93). The authors repeatedly compare ritual with meditation. While ritual is normally performed by a group and "results in some greater coordination between individuals" (5), meditation can be seen as a 'private ritual' that involves communication with "a putative higher being or state of being" (6). Moreover, while ritual is a 'bottom-up' approach, meditation is a 'top-down' approach: "The bottom-up approach indicates that the initial neural stimulation is with the autonomic nervous system (either sympathetic/arousal or parasympathetic/quiescent) and proceeds to stimulation of progressively higher structures in the brain stem, midbrain, and cerebral cortex.... Thus, the rhythmic quality of ritual eventually leads to different states through activation of various brain-structures by means of either the arousal or the quiescent system" (99). The authors distinguish between 'slow' rhythmic rituals like Christian liturgy and 'rapid' rituals such as the Umbanda (99–100). The effects of "rhythmicity" in "human ceremonial ritual" (100) are further strengthened by what the authors refer to as "marked actions" like a slow bow, and they "propose that during human ceremonial ritual, the *amygdala*, which helps fix our attention, is more than normally responsive to specifically marked ritual actions" (101), resulting in what is often referred to as the 'religious awe'. Furthermore, they highlight "the effect of smell as an arousal driver" (101). According to the authors, "a liturgical sequence that employs both aspects of arousal and quiescence—some rapid songs, some slow hymns...—will allow for the participants to experience religion in the most powerful way", eventually leading them to "experience a brief break-down of the self-other dichotomy" (106). The authors are optimistic that their "theoretical framework for how ritual works" would enhance ritual efficacy by contributing to the development of rituals that are "specifically designed to affect either the quiescent or the arousal system, depending on the purpose of the ritual" (107). [MS/Florian Jeserich]

References: C.G. Jung, K.Z. Lorenz (+), C. Lévi-Strauss, R. Otto.
Examples: Christian and Jewish worship, Umbanda.
Reviews: N. Warren *CTNS* 20.2 (2000) 24–29; W.L. Proudfoot *CC* 117.31.8 (2000) 1159 f; S. Sagar *PSC* 18 (2000) 249 f; **P. Hefner *Zygon* 36.3 (2001) 477–493, K.E. Peters *Zygon* 36.3 (2001) 493–501**, and a reply by A.B. Newberg *Zygon* 36.3 (2001) 501–507.
Key-words: COG, def, eff, emo, ETH, MYT, psy.

Dartiguenave, Jean-Yves, 2001, *Rites et ritualité. Essai sur l'altération sémantique de la ritualité* (Logiques Sociales); Paris: L'Harmattan (ISBN 2-7475-0788-2) (255) (with bibliography).
[Rites and Rituality. Essay on the Semantic Modification of the Rituality]

In order to analyze the field, generally indiscriminately denoted as 'ritual', the author, a sociologist, chooses a phenomenological point of view, "i.e.,...the point of view of the internal logic which animates it. In this way, our analysis of the 'rituality' will go beyond a strict sociological approach, in order to move towards an anthropological horizon where the question about the relation between nature and culture will have a central dimension" (16–17). He uses a large number of different terms to distinguish different aspects of the field: 'rituality' (*ritualité*), 'the ritualian' (a neologism, in the form of a substantiated adjective; *le rituélique*), 'ritualism' (*ritualisme*), 'Rite' (*Rite*), 'Ritual' (*Rituel*), 'rite' (*rite*), 'ritual' (*rituel*), 'instantiation' (*instance*), 'performance' (*performance*), etc. Crucial in his argumentation is the dialectic between the process of acculturation of nature at the instantiation pole and the process of naturalization of culture at the performance pole (20–21, 248). It is here that ritualism (the conscious shaping of the general form into the particular form of the actual performance) is possible, which allows for development of rituals. "The author tries to establish the notion 'rituality' (*ritualité*) anthropologically, distinguishing it from animal ritual behavior.... He proposes to regard the 'Ritual' as a significant moment of reappropriation and reinterpretation of the 'Rite', which modifies the original finalities and significations of the latter. It is this mechanism which seems to him to be at the origin of the modifications of the contents of the 'Rite' beyond its extension in relatively identical social forms. It is also in the trajectory which goes from the 'Rite' to the 'Ritual' that he tries to point out the processes of impoverishment of the 'rituality', especially at the level of the imaginary. If he rejects the opinion according to which one would today witness a general decline of the 'Rites', he shows, on the contrary, that the impoverishment of the 'rituality' is perceptible in extreme social situations, marked by existential uncertainty and insecurity" (from the cover). [JS]

References: **J. Gagnepain (+), G. Durand (+)**, E. Goffman (+).
Key-words: def, soc, sem.

Davies, Douglas J., 1997, *Death, Ritual and Belief. The Rhetoric of Funerary Rites*; London, Washington (DC): Cassell (ISBN 0–304–33821–4, 0–304–33822–2) (viii + 216) (with index and bibliography).

The author stresses human self-consciousness and language as its key medium. He considers death a challenge to self-consciousness and language as its crucial response. 'Words of death', or funeral rites, are the adapted human response to death. They enable human beings to transform themselves and grow to meet the demands of life. The author operates under the assumption of cultural evolution and thinks that some kinds of mortuary rites are better for the growth of their participants than others. First, he discusses anthropological and sociological theories about mortuary rites with respect to human identity and social status (Chapters 1 and 2). He then deals with social aspects of grief (Chapter 3) and presents examples of reflections on death in

such different media as music, film, and architecture (Chapter 4). Then ways in which people try to control or conquer death are discussed in Chapter 5, with examples of such 'social causes' of death as suicide and euthanasia. Most civilizations have developed ideas about a life after death, and their mortuary rituals are usually closely related to them. Indian, Persian, Jewish, Islamic, ethnic, and Christian traditions are discussed in the next part of the book (Chapters 6–9). The idea of a soul or spirit is a widely held belief, with variations in many different cultures. In Chapter 10, he discusses different British traditions, as well as the ways in which nineteenth-century anthropology dealt with conceptions of the soul. Emphasizing the aspect of identity with regard to death and death rites, the author also inquires into the relation between the approach to the death of pets and the identity of their owners, as well as the identity they confer on the pets (Chapter 11). Towards the end of the book, the author writes about death as a symbol of transformation and of transcending oneself, used in many different contexts (Chapter 12). Chapter 13 deals with death within secular and technological societies. [Dorothea Lüddeckens]
Key-words: psy, idn.

De Coppet, Daniel (ed.), 1992, *Understanding Rituals* (European Association of Social Anthropologists); London, New York: Routledge (ISBN 0–415–06120–2 / 0–415–06121–0 (p)) (viii + 120) (with index).

Selected contents: Daniel de Coppet: "Introduction" (1–10); David Parkin: "Ritual as Spatial Direction and Bodily Division" (11–25); Michel Cartry: "From One Rite to Another. The Memory in Ritual and the Ethnologist's Recollection" (26–36) (*); Gerd Baumann: "Ritual Implicates 'Others'. Rereading Durkheim in a Plural Society" (97–116) (*). [MS]
Reviews: C. Hasse *TA* 27 (1993) 178; D. Sklar *AH* 20.2 (1995) 176–178; R. Parkin *JASO* 26.1 (1995) 124 f; S.-Y. Chin *RA* 24.3 (1995) 177–185.
Key-words: soc, str.

Delattre, Ronald A., 1978, 'Ritual Resourcefulness and Cultural Pluralism', *Soundings* 61:281–301.

The author claims that "[b]y pursuing the study of culture through a focus on ritual, we may make a contribution to cultural studies and also to a better understanding of the conditions essential to a healthy cultural pluralism. For ritual is a central ingredient in all culture... Ritual is present wherever humanity is present" (281). Because "[t]he state of the arts with regard to ritual studies is such that one can hardly take up the subject without specifying how one intends to use the term", the author defines ritual as "*those carefully rehearsed symbolic motions and gestures through which we regularly go, in which we articulate the felt shape and rhythm of our own humanity and of reality as we experience it, and by means of which we negotiate the terms or conditions for our presence among and our participation in the plurality of realities through which our humanity makes its passage*" (282). Based on this definition the author elaborates four aspects of ritual: "(1) ritual as 'going through motions' and gestures, (2) ritual as an articulation of human reality, (3) ritual as negotiation of relationships, and (4) ritual as passage" (282). In the first section (282–284), the author discusses S.K. Langer and C. Geertz and conceives ritual "as a paradigmatic articulation of the motions through which we go" (284). In the second section (284–287), ritual is conceived "as an *articulation* of our humanity rather than as an *expression* of it" (285). In the third section (287–288), the author argues that ritual plays a crucial role "in negotiating a wider variety of relationships essential to the working-out of our human passage through the world" (287). The fourth section is on ritual as passage (288–292). Here, the author argues: "One difference between primitive and modern rituals is that the latter initiate us into cultural and social regions that are less securely or firmly constituted and which we inhabit with less certainty and in a more tentative and insecure way" (291). By "considering some illustrations of these ritual dynamics under the conditions of modernity as they bear upon the prospects for cultural pluralism" (292), the author concludes: "Given the significance of ritual in the articulation of our humanity, the vision of a pluralistic culture can only be actualized when we appropriate adequately the potential of ritual processes" (299). [JK]

References: M. Douglas, E.H. Erikson, C. Geertz, E. Goffman, R.L. Grimes, S.K. Langer, V.W. Turner, A. van Gennep.
Key-words: def, dyn, ref.

Devisch, René, *et al.* (eds), 1995, *Le rite, source et ressources* (Publications des facultés universitaires Saint-Louis 69); Bruxelles: Facultés universitaires Saint-Louis (ISBN 2–8028–0107–4) (164) (with two bibliographies).
[Ritual. Source and Resources]

Contents: Paul Tihon: "Avant-propos" (7–9); René Devish: "Des forces aux symboles dans le rite bantou. L'interanimation entre corps, groupe et monde" (11–82); Charles Perrot: "Paroles et gestes rituels dans le Nouveau Testament" (83–103); Liliane Voyé: "Le rite en question" (105–136); Louis-Marie Chauvet: "Le rite et l'éthique. Une tension féconde" (137–155). [MS]

Reviews: G.M. Lukken *TVT* 36.4 (1996) 428 f; H.B. Meyer *ZKTh* 119.4 (1997) 487 f.

Dissanayake, Ellen, 1979, 'An Ethological View of Ritual and Art in Human Evolutionary History', *Leonardo* 12:27–31.

"Awareness that in pre-industrial societies art and ritual are intimately associated leads the author to consider a number of provocative similarities among ritualized behaviour in humans and other animals, human ritual ceremonial behaviour, and art. In these, emotionally-motivated behaviour, for example, is formalized and social bonds are strengthened and expressed. The author suggests that in human evolutionary history, ritual and art were originally interdependent. Sensuous aesthetic elements derived from functional behavioural, perceptual and physiological contexts (for example, rhythm, balance, ordering and shaping in time, improvising and metaphorical rendering) when combined with ritual ceremonial behaviour would have assisted the memorization and recitation of myth, group history and ceremonial sequences while simultaneously giving physical and psychological pleasure. From such elements (originally in the service of socially facilitative ritual behaviour) more specific and independent aesthetic features could be developed and refined, for their own sake, leading to autonomous artistic activity" (27). [JS]

Key-words: AES, ETH, emo, rht, soc, psy.

Doty, William G., 2000, *Mythography. The Study of Myths and Rituals. Second Edition*; Tuscaloosa (AL), London: The University of Alabama Press (ISBN 0–8173–1005–3 / 0–8173–1006–1 (p)) (xxi + 577) (with index and bibliography).

This is a thoroughly revised, updated, and substantially expanded version of the first edition dating from 1986. The book, with its 14 chapters, is a comprehensive review of approaches to the study of myth (mostly based on works in the English language). At the outset, the author presents a definition of the terms 'mythological corpus', 'mythologies', and 'myths' consisting of 17 features (33–34). These definitions are then theoretically 'unpacked' in the subsequent argument. Feature 16 of 'myths' is that they "may be enacted or reflected in... rituals, ceremonies, and dramas" (33). Rituals are dealt with in part 3 of the book, entitled "Embodiments, Rites, and Ceremonials" (303–404), which consists of Chapters 10–12. The text is substantially an easily accessible survey of recent literature on rituals. To begin with, the author defines 'a ritual' as follows: "A ritual, as a formal social action, is an event that utilizes patterns of sound (aural) and motion (kinesic), even color and smell, to express or communicate shared values and to inculcate or elicit them. A ritual is more sensuously immediate than most myths, except when myths are actualized in performance contexts" (306). Chapter 10, entitled "The Cosmological/Symbological Human/Social Body" (305–334), takes its inspiration from Joseph Campbell, who argued that the study of myths must also take into account its universal aspects that go beyond the historically determined (307). This leads him to a brief discussion of biogenetic and ethological approaches to the study of rituals. Moreover, it contains some reflections on the body, communication, and symbols which he calls "affectively effective communication" (332). Chapter 11 ("Yesterday's World Wide Web? Ritual as Culture's Symbolic Nexus", 335–367) is a survey of the ritual-dominant version of the myth-and-ritual school and of Victor W. Turner's ritual studies. Chapter 12 ("Sacrificial Scapegoating the Origin of Myth/Religion? Ritualizations as Necessary Gestures toward being Human", 368–404) reflects on problems of defining 'ritual' and focuses on René Girard's theory of sacrifice. Furthermore, it discusses the questions of antiritualism and postmodernity. Moreover, the author gives a summary on "How Rituals Serve Society" (398–401; 13 observations). The chapter concludes with some reflections on what the author calls 'ludic liminality': "As ludic, and as liminal, myths and rituals transpire for most of us on the margins of everyday/secular/work-consciousness. They take place in the gaps between obligatory acts, sanctions, and product-oriented technologies. As gap-fillers, they orchestrate movements from status to status and from place to place. But their betwixt-and-between position means that in them a person can have a certain distance from the compulsory. He or she can...play out alternate possibilities that otherwise would be impossible" (403). [MS]

Reviews (of the first edition): M.P. Carroll *AA* 89 (1987) 760 f; B. Brummett *CE* 36.3 (1987) 306; R.A. Segal *JAAR* 56.1 (1988) 149–152; J.L. Lucaites *JC* 38.1 (1988) 127–130; R.A. Segal *JAF* 102.403 (1989) 110.
Key-words: GEN, com, emb, sym, eth, gst, MYT, gdr, soc, def.

Douglas, Mary, 1966, *Purity and Danger. An Analysis of Concepts of Pollution and Taboo*; London: Routledge & Kegan Paul (No ISBN) (viii + 188) (with index and bibliography).

In this book, the author develops a relational approach to the concepts of taboo and purity. By way of analyzing and comparing the forms of ritual uncleanness in the comparative study of religion, the author tries "to reunite some of the separated segments" that by "human experience" have been "thus wrongly divided" (28). Hence, the author uses a systemic or structural approach as a frame for analyzing rituals and ideas of pollution and taboo. She argues that a particular set of classificatory symbols cannot be understood in isolation and "anyone approaching rituals of pollution nowadays would seek to treat a people's ideas of purity as part of a larger whole" (viii). Because "dirt is essentially disorder" and "offends against order" (2), the author tries to show that "rituals of purity and impurity create unity in experience" (2). In the first chapter (7–28), she develops the concept of ritual uncleanness by engaging the notions of sacred and profane. After criticizing James G. Frazer's evolutionary scheme, she calls for a comparative study of religious rituals. In the second chapter, "Secular Defilement" (29–40), the author argues that the European ideas of defilement and those of "primitive cultures" can be seen as expressions of the same kind of symbolic systems. Thus, the abstract definition of "dirt as matter out of place" implies "a set of ordered relations and a contravention of that order" (35), but the approach to uncleanness through order does not imply a clear-cut distinction between sacred and secular. The author addresses this problem in the third chapter (41–57) by using

"The Abominations of Leviticus" as her main example. She argues that defilement is never an isolated event and can occur only in view of a systematic ordering of such ideas as holiness as wholeness, integrity, and perfection. By claiming that "holiness is exemplified by completeness", she develops "the idea of holiness as order" (53). The fourth chapter is an analysis of European beliefs in primitive magic. Her main argument runs as follows: "As a social animal, man is a ritual animal. If ritual is suppressed in one form it crops up in others, more strongly the more intense the social interaction.... Social rituals create a reality which would be nothing without them. It is not too much to say that ritual is more to society than words are to thought. For it is very possible to know something and then find words for it. But it is impossible to have social relations without symbolic acts" (62). Moreover, the author points to the cognitive functions of ritual. It "focuses attention by framing; it enlivens the memory and links the present with the relevant past" and "changes perception because it changes the selective principles" (64). In the fifth chapter she elaborates on the problem of comparison between European and "primitive" patterns of thought. The sixth chapter, on "Powers and Dangers", again deals with the notion of disorder. Now the author focuses on the potentiality of disorder because it "also provides the materials of pattern" (94). She asserts that ritual recognizes the potency of disorder through the play on articulate and inarticulate forms and the interplay between form and formlessness. In the subsequent chapters on "External Boundaries" and "Internal Lines", the author develops the idea of society as a powerful image that has a distinct form. Using the body as a model which can stand for any bounded system with a complex structure, she defines the form and function in ritual enactment as follows: "The rituals enact the form of social relations and in giving these relations visible expression they enable people to know their own society. The rituals work upon the body politic through the symbolic medium of the physical body" (128). In the final chapter, "The System Shattered and Renewed", the author again asks "how dirt, which is normally destructive, sometimes becomes creative" (159). She comes to the conclusion that "[t]he final paradox of the search for purity is that it is an attempt to force experience into logical categories of non-contradiction. But experience is not amenable and those who make the attempt find themselves led into contradiction" (162). "Above all the subject of this chapter is impossible to discuss except in the light of men's common urge to make a unity of all their experience and to overcome distinctions and separations in acts of at-one-ment [sic]" (169). [JK]

References: **É. Durkheim** (+), M. Eliade (+), **E.E. Evans-Pritchard** (+), **J.G. Frazer** (–), E. Gellner, M. Gluckman, E. Goffman (+), J. Goody, R. Horton, W. James (+), E.R. Leach, C. Lévi-Strauss (+), L. Lévy-Bruhl (+/–), B. Malinowski (–), M. Mauss, A.R. Radcliffe-Brown (–), P. Radin, A.I. Richards, **W. Robertson Smith** (+), V.W. Turner (+), **E.B. Tylor** (–), B.R. Wilson, M. Wilson.
Examples: Rituals of purity, magic.
Reviews: T.O. Beidelmann *Anthr* 61.1–3 (1966) 907 f; M. Ginsberg *JJS* 8 (1966) 270–274; A. MacIntyre *NewSoc* 7.195 (1966) 26 f; A. Brelich *SMSR* 37.2 (1966) 263–266; Th.P. van Baaren *NTT* 21 (1966/67) 241; P.H. Gulliver *BSOAS* 30.2 (1967) 462; W. McCormack *JSSR* 6.2 (1967) 313 f; E. Ardener *Man* 2.1 (1967) 139; J.B. Tamney *SA* 28.1 (1967) 56; C. Madge *Sociol* 1.2 (1967) 209; R. Needham *TLS* (Februar) (1967) 131; M.E. Spiro *AA* 70.2 (1968) 391–393; J.-P. Roux *RHR* 174 (1968) 229; R.M. Glasse, *Homme* 9.4 (1969) 103; P.R. Kunz *RRR* 10.2 (1969) 114 f; P. Steinfels *Com* (Oktober) (1970) 49–51.
Key-words: cog, cpl, cpr, dyn, ecn, eff, emo, gdr, mng, pmc, pow, ref, rel, sem, SOC, STR, SYM.

Douglas, Mary, 1970, *Natural Symbols. Explorations in Cosmology*; London, New York: Barrie & Rockliff: The Cresset Press / Pantheon (No ISBN) (xvii + 177) (with bibliography).

"Most symbolic behaviour must work through the human body" (vii). With this statement, the author suggests the beginning of a new approach which has the following rationale: "The symbols based on the human body are used to express different social conditions. We should therefore start with a principle for classifying the latter" (vii). Then the author argues "that there is a strong tendency to replicate the social situation in symbolic form by drawing richly on bodily symbols in every possible dimension" (vii), but "that the range of situations which use the human body for expression is fairly limited. They derive essentially from the quality of social relations" (viii). Her main concern is to develop "a formula for classifying relations" which can be applied equally to all kinds of societies: "All we need to know is the way in which these relations are structured according to two independently varying criteria which I have called grid and group. Group is obvious—the experience of a bounded social unit. Grid refers to rules which relate one person to others on an ego-centred basis. Grid and group may be found together. In this case the quality of relations is ordered and clearly bounded. If group is found by itself, or grid is found without group, the quality of relations is different in each case" (viii, see also 160). Based on these concepts, the author's overall aim is to explain "why the symbolism of the body differs from one cosmology to another" (xiii). Her main thesis is "that the ideas about the human body, its potential and its weaknesses, which are found in particular social types, correspond uncannily well with ideas current in the same social types about the potential and weakness of society" (xiii–xiv). In order to develop "an approach to the study of symbolic concordances in religious expression" (xiv), the author presents her argument in eleven chapters. In Chapter 1, "Away from Ritual" (1–18), she addresses the social phenomenon of anti-ritualism and contends: "Ritual is become a bad word signifying empty conformity" (1). She perceives three phases of anti-ritualism: "First, there is the contempt of external ritual forms; second, there is the private internalising of religious experience; third, there is the move to humanist philanthropy" (7). According to the author, ritualism "is most highly developed where symbolic action is held to be most certainly efficacious" (8) and is "taken to be a concern that efficacious symbols be correctly manipulated and that the right words be pronounced in the right order" (9). In developing "a sociological approach to the problem" (11), the author states that "the most important determinant of ritualism is the experience of closed social groups" (14). In Chapter 2, "To Inner Experience" (19–36), the author develops for these purposes her concept of ritual as "pre-eminently a form of communication" (20). Here, she introduces Bernstein's discovery "how speech systems transform the experience of speakers" (20) and treats "ritual forms, like speech forms, as transmitters of culture, which are generated in social relations and which . . . exercise a constraining effect on social behaviour" (21). Following Bernstein, the author distinguishes between two basic categories of speech that are linguistically and socially distinguishable: the restricted and the elaborate code. The differences between these codes, which "depend entirely on the relation of each to the social context" (23), are correlated to patterns of family control. Based on these parameters, the author proposes a diagram with a horizontal coordinate to indicate the progression from positional to personal family control and a vertical coordinate to indicate the progression from socially restricted to elaborate speech codes (27–29). The four squares established through the horizontal and vertical coordinates are correlated to general cosmological ideas. By way of applying this model to the analysis to ritual, the author contends: "At first sight all ritual would seem to be a form of restricted code. It is a form of verbal utterance whose meanings are largely implicit; many of them are carried along standardized non-verbal channels. . . . Ritual is generally highly coded. Its units are organised to standard types in advance of use. Lexically its meanings are local and particular. Syntactically it is available to all members of the community. The syntax is rigid, it offers a small range of alternative forms" (33). "This would be fine and an end of the argument if, as was commonly held, all primitive peoples were ritualist and if the movement away from magicality were indeed able to be plotted along a graph showing more and more the effects of the division of labour on family behaviour" (34). In Chapter 3, "The Bog Irish" (37–53), the author discusses the rule of Friday abstinence among the Bog Irishman in light of her theoretical findings. She argues that "[t]he drawing of symbolic lines and boundaries is a way of bringing order into experience" (50) and that "only a ritual structure makes possible a wordless channel of communication that is not entirely incoherent" (51). In Chapter 4, "A Rule of Method" (54–64), the notion of ritual is elaborated as a restricted code. Of main concern is the question "how to use the idea of the restricted code to interpret different degrees of ritualisation" (55). Based on a diagram with grid and group as coordinates, the author aims to establish a "frame of analysis" that is "intended to express the character of social relations, the degree to which they are structured or unstructured" (59). She claims that "religious behaviour is strongly influenced by social experiences which can be studied under the head of grid and group" (62). In her attempt to limit the problem of cross-cultural comparison, the author argues that "[t]he methodological rule is merely a rough kind of safeguard against the wildest kinds of cultural selections" (64). In Chapter 5, "The Two Bodies" (65–81), the author claims: "The social body constrains the way the physical body is perceived. The physical experience of the body, always modified by the social categories through which it is known, sustains a particular view of society" (65). Moreover, she advances "the hypothesis that bodily control is an expression of social control—abandonment of bodily control in ritual responds to the requirements of a social experience which is being expressed" (70–71). In her aim "to analyse a range of symbolism under the general opposition of formal/informal" (71), the author distinguishes between the social dimension and symbolic order with regard to "the general social requirements for religious formality and informality, that is for ritualism and effervescence" (73). Her general hypothesis here is that "the inarticulateness of the social organization in itself gains symbolic expression in bodily dissociation" (74) and that "the full possibilities of abandoning conscious control are only available to the extent that the social system relaxes its control on the individual" (81). In Chapter 6, "A Test Case" (82–98), the forms of social organization among the Dinka, Nuer, and Mandari are compared to examine the thesis that "bodily control tends to be relaxed where social grid is weak" (89). More generally, the author states: "Grid and group are a function of order and constraint in social relations and these can be as easily absent in dense as in sparse populations" (97). In Chapter 7, "Sin and Society" (99–106), the author relates self and society and comes to the conclusion: "The relation of self to society varies with the constraints of grid and group: the stronger these are, the more developed the idea of formal transgression and its dangerous consequences, and the less regard is felt for the right of the inner self to be freely expressed" (102). Chapter 8, "The Problem of Evil" (107–124), argues that "if we have social units whose external boundaries are clearly marked, whose internal relations are confused, and who persist on a small scale at a low level of organization, then we should look for the active witchcraft type of cosmology" (113). In Chapter 9, "Impersonal Rules" (125–139), the author comes to the conclusion that "the secular world view is no modern development, but appears when group boundaries are weak and ego-focused grid is strong" (139). Chapter 10, "Control of Symbols" (140–155), discusses again the correlations between group and grid and returns to the opening theme of ritualism and anti-ritualism in relation to the notion of personal and impersonal powers. According to the author, anti-ritualism can only be found in forms of low social organization and a low grid. The author discusses anti-ritualism in relation to the occasion of social and personal change (144–146), the dissociation of social conditions by impersonal inflexible rules (146–150), and the emergence of revolutionary millennialism (150–155). In the final Chapter 11, "Out of the Cave" (156–167), the author states: "the argument of this book is that the elaborated code challenges its users to turn round on themselves and inspect their values, to reject some of them, and to resolve to cherish positional forms of control and communication wherever these are available" (157). By way of conceiving the current anti-ritualism as "the adoption of one set of religious symbols in place of another", which is "like a switch between restricted speech codes", the author concludes: "Two morals can be drawn from this analogy; first the duty of everyone to preserve their vision from the constraints of the restricted code when judging any social situation; second the opportunity of religious bodies to set their message in the restricted code" (166). [JK]

References: F. Barth, **B. Bernstein** (+), **É. Durkheim**, E.E. Evans-Pritchard, R. Firth, E. Goffman, C. Lévi-Strauss, G. Lienhardt, I.M. Lewis, M. Mauss, R. Otto, **W. Robertson Smith** (+), V.W. Turner, A. van Gennep.
Examples: Numerous.
Reviews: D. Martin *BJS* 21 (1970) 343 f; Anon. *CC* 87 (1970) 824 f; P. Steinfels *Com* 93.2 (1970) 49–51; S. Milburn *JASO* 1.2 (1970) 101; A. Ryan *Lis* 84.3 (1970) 314 f; K.O.L. Burridge *Man* 5.3 (1970) 53; J. Brothers *Month* 3.2.1–6 (1970) 59; **A. Edwards *NB* 51 (1970) 424–432**; J. Littlejohn *NewSoc* 395 (1970) 697; J. Raban *NS* 79 (1970) 812 f; J.G. Bishop *Theol* 73 (1970) 422 f; D.G. Macrae *TLS* 3559 (1970) 535; M.G. Silverman *AA* 73.6 (1971) 1293–1295; E.R. Leach *NYRB* 16.i (1971) 44 f; E.H. Pyle *Rel* 1.1 (1971) 72–77; S. Deshen *AJS* 77.1–6 (1971/72) 163–166; R.E.S. Tanner *HJ* 13.1 (1972) 99; **M.C. Bateson *Wor* 46.1 (1972) 98–104**; E.H. Lurkings *Eth* 85 (1973) 61; G.F. Brody *HC* 5.3 (1973) 692; T. Eagleton *Tab* 227.6929/30 (1973) 391 f; F.W. Dillistone *JTS* 25 (1974) 548–550; R. Mufti *HJ* 16.1 (1975) 90; M. Marwick *Sociol* 9.1 (1975) 132–134; A.J. Bergersen *AJS* 83.1–6 (1977/78) 1012; A. Ciattini *RIS* 21.1 (1980) 142.
Key-words: aut, COG, COM, cpr, dyn, eff, EMB, emo, idn, mng, pow, sec, SEM, SOC, SYM.

Dow, James W., 1986, 'Universal Aspects of Symbolic Healing. A Theoretical Synthesis', *American Anthropologist* 88:56–69.

The author proposes "a tentative outline of the structure of all symbolic healing, including magical healing and Western psychotherapy. The stages of symbolic healing are as follows. (1) A generalized cultural mythic world is established by universalizing the experiences of healers, initiates, or prophets, or by otherwise generalizing emotional experiences" (66). [A 'mythic world' is "a model of experiential reality" (59). "The mythic world contains the symbols that couple the social system to the self system of the patient" (63).] "(2) A healer persuades the patient that it is possible to define the patient's relationship to a particularized part of the mythic world, and makes the definition. (3) The healer attaches the patient's emotions to transactional symbols in this particularized mythic world" (66). ['Transactional symbols' are those "symbols particularized from generalized symbolic media for use in healing" (63).] "(4) The healer manipulates the transactional symbols to assist the transaction of emotion" (66). ["Emotions are the generalized media that link the self and the somatic systems" (64).] The author assumes that the structure of symbolic healing, as outlined above, "is a result of the way that human communication has been biologically organized by evolution" (66). This structure is held to be universally valid, although "[c]ultural and subcultural variations occur in (1) the rate at which paradox is resolved when establishing the healer's power to define the patient's relationship to the mythic world; (2) the symbols that make up the cultural mythic world and its structure; (3) the social role of the person who creates the personalized symbols for the therapy" (66). [MS/Florian Jeserich]

References: G. Devereux, S. Freud, C. Lévi-Strauss, N.D. Munn, T. Parsons, R. Prince, Th.J. Scheff (+), T.S. Turner, V.W. Turner.
Key-words: cog, COM, ecl, eff, EMO, exp, MYT, psy, SYM.

Drewal, Margaret Thompson, 1992, *Yoruba Ritual. Performers, Play, Agency* (African Systems of Thought); Bloomington (IN): Indiana University Press (ISBN 0–253–31817–3 / 0–253–20684–7 (p)) (xxii + 241) (with index and bibliography).

"Ritual has been said both to transform human consciousness and to alter the social statuses of participants, such as in rites of passage. This is true for the Yoruba cases examined here. In addition to these two kinds of transformation, I argue that ritual practitioners as knowledgeable human agents transform ritual itself through play and improvisation" (xiii). In her study of Yoruba rituals, the author stresses "the power of human agents to transform ritual through performance" (xiv). "Rather than privileging ritual structure as if it were some a priori 'thing', I stress the power of participants to transform ritual itself" (xiv). Throughout her study, the author (following Giddens) gives "prominence to the intentionality of actors as knowledgeable agents" (xiv). Apart from the first and the last chapter (on gender), the book focuses on "different performances to illustrate the range of operations specialists perform on rituals" (xvii). In the first chapter, "Theory and Method in the Study of Ritual Performance" (1–11), the author addresses three theoretical issues: repetition, improvisation, and change in ritual. She distinguishes "two modes of repetition that operate differently, although they are conceptually related. The broader mode of ritual repetition is the periodic restoration of an entire performance, as in annual rituals scheduled to correspond in some way to seasonal change... In this mode, the unit to be repeated is a complete whole, and long gaps of time exist between the repetitions. The other mode is the repetition that occurs within a single ritual performance, and is experienced as a steady, unbroken flow, as in regular, persistent drumming or vocalizing..." (2). Inspired by two theories of repetition that both stress transformation, the author explores "Yoruba ritual praxis as *repetition with revision*" (5), i.e. improvisation. "By improvisation I mean more specifically moment-to-moment maneuvering based on acquired in-body techniques to achieve a particular effect and/or style of performance" (7). "Improvisation is transformational, often participatory and competitive" (7). "Whenever improvisation is a performative strategy in ritual, it places ritual squarely within the domain of play. It is indeed the playing, the improvising, that engages people, drawing them into the action, constructing their relationships, thereby generating multiple and simultaneous discourses always surging between harmony/disharmony, order/disorder, integration/opposition" (7). In terms of methodology, the author proposes "a paradigmatic shift from structure to process (from an essentially spatialized view to a temporal one); from the normative to the particular and historically situated (from the timeless to the time-centered); and from the collective to the agency of named individuals. Only then can ritual as praxis be historicized" (10). "With these shifts to the particular and the individual, I was able to study ritual as transformational processes, as improvisation, in contrast to the more standard approach as a process of regularization or reproduction in which ritual is viewed more or less as reproducing the past or the cosmos in stable fashion...In such a shift, what becomes readily apparent is that in ritual there are no predictable or verifiable constants endlessly or mindlessly repeated by performers. Performance is a multilayered discourse employing multiple voices and perspectives. And as we recognize this, it should also be apparent that fieldwork itself is performance" (11). [MS/JK]

References: G. Bateson, M.E.F. Bloch (–), J.Ch. Crocker, M. de Certeau (+), M. Eliade, J. Fabian, J.W. Fernandez (+), C. Geertz, A. Gell (–), A. Giddens (+), E. Goffman, J. Goody (–), D. Handelman (–), B. Kapferer, B. Kirshenblatt-Gimblett, B. Lincoln (–), J.J. MacAloon, S.F. Moore (–), B.G. Myerhoff, S.B. Ortner (–), J.L. Peacock (–), R.A. Rappaport (–), B. Ray, M. Sahlins, **R. Schechner** (+), S.J. Tambiah (–), V.W. Turner (–).

Example: Yoruba rituals.

Reviews: **J.D.Y. Peel *Afr* 64.1 (1994) 150–166**; A.D. Buckley *CJAS* 28.3 (1994) 525 f; O.W. Lawuyi *JRA* 24.2 (1994) 189–191; L.S. Grillo *JRS* 8.2 (1994) 151; S.-Y. Chin *RA* 24.3 (1995) 177–185.

Key-words: AGN, ecn, DYN, GDR, idn, par, PMC, pow, psy, rep, rfl, tim, vir.

Drexler, Josef, 1993, *Die Illusion des Opfers. Ein wissenschaftlicher Überblick über die wichtigsten Opfertheorien ausgehend vom deleuzianischen Polyperspektivismusmodell* (Münchener ethnologische Abhandlungen 12); München: Akademischer Verlag (ISBN 3–929115–13–1) (237).

[The Illusion of Sacrifice. A Scientific Survey of the Most Important Theories of Sacrifice Proceeding from Deleuze's Modell of Polyperspectivism]

The book is based on a dissertation in social anthropology. The bulk of the book—its third chapter (17–151)—is a comprehensive review of the major and most influential theories of sacrifice (evolutionism, sociology, psychoanalysis, phenomenology of religion, ethnopsychology, cultural history, morphology of culture, theology, social anthropology, structuralism, ethology). In the fourth chapter (152–182), the author draws several conclusions from his survey. To begin with, "all theories of sacrifice fail in front of the reality of sacrifice" (152). The author altogether dismisses some theories, while he finds others to be complementary to each other and thus they can be combined in order to highlight different aspects of "a polyaspective ritual process" (154). For the author, 'sacrifice' is first of all a result of the history of scholarship (*Wissenschaftsgeschichte*), whereas it can be dismissed as a means to further scholarly endeavors: "Because sacrificial rites are linked to specific historical, economic, and socio-cultural contexts, it seems to be a desperate attempt to state a common theory of 'the sacrifice'" (160). The author regards the word 'sacrifice' as "misleading, useless, and inadequate for describing complex ritual processes such as they are encountered by a scientific observer in the ethnographic reality" (164). In order to abolish the concept of 'sacrifice', the author suggests a double strategy: first, emic concepts for 'sacrifice' such as *bulu, kuli, thysía*, and others should be elucidated in their respective contexts; secondly, these emic concepts should be linked to the category of 'ritual' (i.e. complex ritual process) (166). Because he finds that 'rituals' are performed as a means to communicate with the sacral sphere (166), the author introduces the notion of 'communication ritual' (*Kommunikationsritual*). In the final section of the book, the author sketches some features of this concept (177–182). Among other aspects, on the side of the 'ritualists' he distinguishes between actors, participants, and passers-by (*Passanten*). While some 'communication rituals' seek to establish communication, others try to abolish it. In some cases, there may be 'total communication' (*Totalkommunikation*) between the partners in the situation (e.g. men and deities); in others there is only 'partial communication' (*Partialkommunikation*) between men and deities. Whereas some 'communication rituals' are characterized by intensified forms of communications, others are merely routine ways of communicating. [MS]

Key-words: gen, hsc, COM, eth, cpl, cpr, def.

Driver, Tom Faw, 1991, *The Magic of Ritual. Our Need for Liberating Rites that Transform Our Lives and Our Communities*; San Francisco: Harper (ISBN 0–06–062096–x) (x + 270) (with index and bibliography).
2nd ed. as: Driver, Tom Faw, 1997, *Liberating Rites. Understanding the Transformative Power of Ritual*; Boulder (CO): Westview Press (ISBN 0–8133–3455–1) (xviii + 270).

The author of this book is primarily concerned with improving the quality of the rituals of the Christian church in order to make them work better for their participants. He also wants his readers to understand better how important rituals are even for the lives of modern men. To reach these goals he presents a number of perspectives on rituals, some of which are relevant for theoretical approaches. The term 'ritualization' is defined as, on the one hand, referring to "the similarity... between the behaviors of human beings and other animals", and on the other, to "the making up of behavioral routines, their coming-to-be" (15) over against 'ritual', which "connotes an already known, richly symbolic pattern of behavior, the emphasis falling less upon the making and more upon the valued pattern and its panoply of associations" (30). Ritual's roots in biology are important to him, but he warns against a one-sided "emphasis upon animal-human similarity", as well as against an "axiomatic insistence upon the categorical difference between culture and nature" (23). Even more important to the author, however, is the possibility to change the world (including existing rituals) by means of rituals and ritualizing (50–51). Part II (77–127) is about performance, which is defined as "that kind of doing in which the observation of the deed is an essential part of its doing, even if the observer be invisible or is the performer herself" (81). Also the theatrical (82) and creative (83) character of rituals are discussed here. Time and again, the author warns that rituals can be used not only constructively and for positive ends, but also destructively and for negative purposes (106, 132, 140, 191). In the third part of the book (129–191), the author discusses the "three major gifts that rituals bestow upon society... order [Rappaport, Huizinga, Leach, Langer], community [Victor Turner], and transformation [Van Gennep, Grimes, Bateson, Jennings]" (131). The "Conclusion" (193–222) focuses on the possibilities of improving

Church rituals. Appendix B (227–238) gives "Some Points in Criticism of Victor Turner". [JS]

References: R.A. Rappaport, J. Huizinga, E.R. Leach, S.K. Langer, V.W. Turner (+/–), A. van Gennep, R.L. Grimes, G. Bateson, Th.W. Jennings.
Reviews: G.M. Boone *Hom* 17.2 (1992) 31; R. Webber *CC* 109.9–16 (1992) 821; E.B. Aitken *STR* 37 (1993) 98–100; K.W. Irwin *Thom* 57.4 (1993) 700–703; L.L. Patton *JR* 73.3 (1993) 457–459; W.W. Schroeder *CRBR* 6 (1993) 506–508; **D.B. Batchelder *RLM* 28 (1994) 151–156**; L.R. Batzler *JRPR* 17.1 (1994) 48–50; M. Proctor-Smith *JRS* 8.2 (1994) 134 f.
Key-words: def, pmc, tha, eth, soc.

Driver, Tom Faw, 1994, 'Life in Performance. Reflections on Ritual, Religion, and Social Value', *Soundings* 77:63–80.

In some parts of this article, which is for the most part concerned with criticizing modern American culture, the author summarizes his position on ritual theory as follows: he sees "the world as being made up of actions" (64), thus he proposes "that the human world is constructed and made known through accumulation of numberless ritual actions" (64). He distinguishes "between primary ritual and secondary" (64). Referring to Goffman, the first "may be thought of as the ritualization of everyday life" (64), whereas by the second he means "those ceremonies that people make and perform for special occasions" (65). Ritual "is an event that takes place, an action that occurs. It is something that happens…and should be, in the first instance, valued more for itself than for anything that it might mean or come to mean" (68). "Ritual activity is a kind of schooling in learning to appreciate things for their intrinsic, and not just for their instrumental, value" (69). To clarify what for him distinguishes ritual from other performances, the author now compares ritual to a circus performance: "Circus acts, when they are good, illustrate clearly the two sides of performance…: One side is show. The other is accomplishment. Although the trapeze artist's performance is done in the circus for show, it is not only show. It is a genuine daring.… Movies and magic shows, like the arts of drama and fiction, thrive on the willing suspension of disbelief.… The circus act, by contrast, thrives on the audience's amazement at seeing the merely dreamed-of become actual.… Performance is a combination—I think I would rather say a fusion—of actuality and show. If that definition fits the circus act, it also fits ritual" (70–71). Finally, the author reflects on the relation between ritual and religion, which he sees in a rather

Durkheimian way: "Although religion and ritual are far from synonymous, there are good reasons why they always keep company. Ritual is the broader phenomenon. All religions make use of ritual, but not all ritual is religious. What is it, we may ask, that makes the association between religion and ritual so close?... The ritual, whether performed at church, temple, or home, defines, rather clearly, a kind of practice that identifies the religious community and links the devotee with the community. The unity is not only expressed but in a large part created by the ritual performance, since this provides for the group a clear and demonstrable common practice" (72–73). [JS]

References: E. Goffman (+), S.T. Coleridge, R.A. Delattre.
Key-words: def, soc, pow, idn, sec, PR1, PMC, PR2, cmp, emb.

Droogers, André, 2004, 'Enjoying and Emerging Alternative World. Ritual in Its Own Ludic Right', *Social Analysis* 48:138–154.

The author suggests that "if in analyzing ritual-like phenomena, one focuses on ritual as *the temporary emergence and playful enactment, in its own right, of a shadow reality*, the concept may stand a better chance of surviving in scholarly vocabulary" (138). Furthermore, "contrary to the usual connotation of ritual as a solemn and serious occasion, the evocation of reality might bring enjoyment and fun in its creation and performance" (138). "Rituals can serve all kinds of functions, as perceived by either participants or scholars or both, but people also repeat rituals because they offer diversion and satisfaction through the playful creation of a relevant alternative reality. The other reality has its own parameters and invites cultural experiments" (139). The author quotes his own previously (1996) published definition of play as "the capacity to deal simultaneously and subjunctively with two or more ways of classifying reality" and continues: "In experimenting with the idea of another emergent reality, ritual actors play seriously with variations, inversions, contradictions, double play, irony, incongruity, and counterrealities.... Once it has emerged, this reality begins to lead its own life, with its own characteristics, even though it remains subject to the agency of the actors" (139). Having presented and analyzed an ethnographic example, the author concludes that "enjoyment through the emergence of an alternative reality is an important dimension of ritual and presents itself as a significant reason why participants like their rituals" (148). The author presents reflections on the creation of "another reality" and its relations to normal, everyday reality and on the occasions for such creations. On such occasions, "the practice of ritual generates or creates its own emergent phenomena" (148). These on the one hand become part of a tradition, while on the other hand "inversions, deviations, and variations are all possible" (148). In the following section (149–152), the author applies "the notion of schema, taken from cognitive anthropology, and especially connectionism" (149) to an analysis of cultural repertoires. This includes reflections on issues such as ritual elements, memory, socialization and learning, simultaneity, linear/serial vs. parallel distributed schemas, routine, and globalization. The author also briefly addresses methodological issues. In his conclusion, he states: "The minimal nature of schemas allows for their creative application. Since schemas are generic, actors are challenged to apply them in their own way. Moreover, in the case of ritual, the temporary creation and enactment of an alternative reality, and the counterpoint that is posed by it, suggest that people temporarily turn the established repertoires of normal reality upside down or inside out, or exaggerate them" (153). The author argues "that ritual can be studied in its own right and is not exhaustively represented when it is reduced to societal or cultural causes or functions" (153). [MS]

References: J. Huizinga, V.W. Turner.
Example: Initiation ritual for boys among the Wagenia (Congo) in 1970.
Key-words: sec, cog, PMC, dyn, tra, agn, par.

Dulaney, Siri & Alan Page Fiske, 1994, 'Cultural Rituals and Obsessive-Compulsive Disorder. Is there a Common Psychological Mechanism?' *Ethos* 22:243–283.

This article is a study of ritual from a psychological viewpoint. The authors challenge anthropological research because of the lack of research on the content of rituals. Although they find anthropological definitions and characterizations of ritual intriguing, the authors argue that "none of this research has investigated a representative sample of world rituals and systematically compared them with nonritual activities. Without systematic comparison of rituals from around the world, we cannot determine what forms of action they actually have in common" (245). They assert that the features that typify rituals also define a psychiatric illness, namely obsessive-compulsive disorder (OCD). These shared features lead them to argue that "[i]n both cultural rituals and OCD, people simplify the world by orienting to a very small number of salient concerns and actions.... Simplification is the foundation of most religious and mythological explanation, art and memory, as well as some kinds of technology and 'magic'" (248). After stating the features of OCD, the authors give a detailed review of these features in cultural rituals, examining ethnographic materials. To answer the question of whether OCD-like features are more common in rituals than in other activities, the authors chose to determine the frequency in life-cycle transition rituals and in work; they conclude "that OCD-like features are far more prevalent in rituals than in work" (269). At the end of the article, the authors state their argument as follows: "When people acquire the combinations of elements they use and their meanings from others, and use them at times and places that are culturally prescribed, for culturally formulated purposes (and especially when they do so collectively), this performance is called a ritual. But in some people, organic damage, physiological imbalance, or sociopsychological trauma apparently causes hyperactivity of this ritual mechanism" (275). "These personal obsessions and compulsions resemble culturally constructed rituals in form and content, but lack shared meaning and collective legitimation of their constitutive efficacy.... But when it is operating normally, this ritual mechanism is what enables people to mark and constitute life transitions, to reinforce and transform social relationships, to cure illness and cope with misfortune, to express and to respond to the ineffable paradoxes in human life" (276). [JK]

References: M.E.F. Bloch, E.G. d'Aquili, M. Douglas, R. Firth, S. Freud, A. Gell, J. Goody, J. Huizinga, E. Leach, B. Malinowski, R. Needham, S.B. Ortner, A.R. Radcliffe-Brown, S.J. Tambiah, V.W. Turner, A. van Gennep.
Key-words: str, eff, myt, cpr, PSY.

Dupré, Louis, 1992, 'Ritual. The Divine Play of Time', in: Virgil Nemoianu & Robert Royal (eds), *Play, Literature, Religion. Essays in Cultural Intertextuality*, Albany (NY): State University of New York Press (ISBN 0–7914–0935–x / 0–7914–0936–8 (p)) 199–212.

In this article the author favors a phenomenological approach to the analysis of ritual and play as well as ritual and drama. According to the author, "play and ritual celebration belonged together. Always and everywhere human beings appear to have felt a need to formalize their activity, and the measured activity of play lies at the root of that self-conscious articulation of existence that we at a later stage of development are wont to refer to as 'religious' ritual" (199). After analyzing the time and myth aspects in "Ritual in Time" (200–203) and "Time in Ritual"

(203–205), the author suggests in "Time Without Ritual" (205–208) that the attitude to ritual is radically changed under the conditions of secularization in modern times: "Nature and time no longer hold the sacred meaning that men of other ages attributed to them.... The modern mentality undermines the inclination to take certain aspects of play-acting with absolute seriousness—as ritual practice requires" (205). Therefore, because of the lack of a religious substitute for the meaning-giving role of ritual, nowadays sports arena and the theater, i.e. game and drama, have replaced it. In "The Ritualization of Time in Drama (208–211), the author argues: "Drama allows us to take a temporary leave from the cares and joys of ordinary life, and language appropriately refers to such a stylized vacation as 'play'" (209). In this regard, the author traces the ritual origin of drama and its relation to time: "Like ritual, drama posits its own structured duration, separate from that indefinite passing of time in which moments merely succeed one another.... Even as the rite, the drama occurs as an act in time, yet it surpasses time by its timeless disclosures" (210). [JK]

References: H. Bergson, E. Cassirer, M. Eliade, H. Hubert, J. Huizinga, G. van der Leeuw, M. Mauss, V.W. Turner.
Key-words: emo, myt, pmc, tha, psy, sec, tim.

Eibl-Eibesfeldt, Irenäus, 1979, 'Ritual and Ritualization from a Biological Perspective', in: Mario von Cranach, *et al.* (eds), *Human Ethology. Claims and Limits of a New Discipline. Contributions to the Colloquium Sponsored by the Werner-Reimers-Stiftung*, Cambridge etc. / Paris: Cambridge University Press / Editions de la Maison des Sciences de l'Homme (ISBN 0-521-22320-2 / 0-521-29591-2 (p)) 3–55.

In the first section of this essay, the author states that it was the symbolic characteristic of rituals that has made the term 'ritual' popular among biologists. "Rituals (*Symbolhandlungen* in German) are behavior patterns which serve the function of communication and which undergo changes in the service of this function that enhance their communicative value. In other words, rituals have a signalling function which they acquire by a process called ritualization. When we speak of courtship rituals, greeting rituals, fighting rituals etc., we thus refer to a complex set of behavior patterns structured according to certain rules, whereas when we speak of the single acts involved in such a ritual we refer to expressive patterns or expressive movements. For all levels of organization the term ritualization is used when we refer to the process by which these patterns originate" (4). In the following sections, the author introduces and briefly discusses a number of key ethological concepts, such as 'adaptation', 'function', 'inborn motor patterns', 'innate releasing mechanism', 'key stimuli and releasers', 'drivers', and 'learning disposition' (4–8). The comparative method—comprising both the study of homologies (common heritage) and analogies (independent origins) in similar behavior patterns—is an important characteristic of the ethological approach (8–10). The process of ritualization draws on behavior patterns that "are usually incorporated into more complex behavorial events for which the term ritual is customary... Expressive movements and rituals thus refer to different levels of integration. In a ritual expressive movements are integrated in a more complex event which is structured in a rule-governed way" (10). "As to the origin of these patterns we can distinguish between phylogenetically evolved, culturally acquired, and individually invented signals" (10). The evolution of signals builds on "preadaptations", such as "functional acts which change their function" (e.g. patterns of nest-building serving the function of bonding), "movements expressing intention which precede an act" (e.g. opening of the mouth before biting), "displacement activities" (out-of-context activities), and "pure epiphenomena of excitation", such as trembling and sweating (11). Because ritualization "is the process by which non-communicative behavior patterns evolve into signals" (14), during that process behavioral elements may change their function, and a change of motivation may be observed (14). "In addition, movements experience a number of changes directly related to the signalling function. Signals have to be conspicuous and at the same time simple and precise so as not to be misunderstood" (14). The author provides a list comprising 11 such changes, including "[m]imic exaggeration, rhythmic repetition, fusion of elements into new patterns" (15). In the next section, the author explores "[p]hylogenetic roots of human expressive behavior" (17–21). He argues "that certain behavior patterns are innate" (21). Moreover, according to the author, "there are certain universal features" of behavoiral patterns (22). Cultural meanings derive from innate motor patterns (e.g. the movements which in many cultures accompany a 'no'-statement). Furthermore, the author claims that "we can find universal rules among which ritualistic events are structured on a higher level of integration" (26). "That functional equivalents may be substituted for one another is a characteristic of human ritual events. These can be inborn motor patterns as well as cultural ones. They are substituted according to a deep structure given as phylogenetic adaptation. It is my hypothesis that many of the diverse cultural rituals are based upon elementary strategies of social interactions which in their original form are acted out in child behavior" (28). The author illustrates this process of substitution of functional equivalents according to a deep structure by an analysis of greeting rituals and feasts, where he distinguishes three phases: the opening phase, the phase of interaction, and the phase of parting (28). "Greeting rituals and feasts provide a good example of the fact that, in spite of great cultural variation as far as the particular elaboration of the events is concerned, the basic strategies of these particular types of interaction remain cross-culturally the same. We may hypothesize that phylogenetic adaptations determine the basic structure in a fashion analogous to that by which they determine the deep grammar of language" (36). Verbal and non-verbal behavior can substitute for each other as functional equivalents, an insight that "provides a unifying theory for the study of a grammar of human social behavior" (39). Because "rituals serve the function of communication" they "thus release responses. According to these responses we can classify rituals" (39). As "some main categories of rituals" (39), the author then proceeds to provide the following examples from animal and human behavior: bonding (39–40), spacing and competing (40–44), appeasing (44–45), the conquest of fear (45), and rituals "to keep 'discipline'" (46). A brief discussion of ontogeny and "cultural pseudospecification" follows (47). The final two sections are dealing with 'therapeutic' issues pertaining to people living in big cities and the discussion of the aims and objectives of ethology. The essay culminates in the sentence: "I find it very comforting that there exists a nature of man" (55). The book also contains a comment on the paper by Rom Harré (75–80) and a reply by Eibl-Eibesfeldt (81–83). [MS]

References: E.H. Erikson, E. Goffman, K.Z. Lorenz, E.R. Leach.
Examples: Courtship rituals, everyday rituals, trance dance of the Bushmen.
Key-words: ETH, com, str, gst, cpr, def.

Elsbree, Langdon, 1982, *The Rituals of Life. Patterns in Narratives* (Series in Modern Literary Criticism); Port Washington (NY), London: Kennikat Press (ISBN 0-8046-9295-5) (viii + 145).

In his introductory chapter on "Ritual", the author explores "the concept of archetypal action for its possibilities as a synthesizing idea" (5), and in particular "the relationships between archetypal actions and ritual" (5) as a universal pattern of narratives. He argues that in this relationship "lies at least part of the explanation of the kinds of authority stories have over us, our need for them in shaping our experience, the shapes of the stories themselves, and the universalities they speak of" (5). According to him, ritual is structured behavior because it "certifies that something is being done correctly, appropriately, efficaciously" (9). Thus, he assumes that ritual also "certifies the doer, the actor, the agent: he or she, self or other, has the particular power or status, is a believable model, can be recognized as an authority" (9). Ritual is "characterized by its [sic] purposiveness, and by its agents as actors, as active participants" (9). In terms of the patterns of narratives, he assumes that "the *archetypal actions*, elementary ritual modes affecting the way we apprehend a story, suggest another approach and another set of possibilities" (14). The "essential argument throughout is that the purer the archetypal action in a work, the greater the work's hold on us as a kind of ritual" (15). According to five archetypal actions of narrative, the author divides his book into five chapters: 1. "Establishing, Consecrating a Home" (16–24), 2. "Engaging in a Contest, Fighting a Battle" (25–35), 3. "Taking a Journey" (36–50), 4. "Enduring Suffering" (51–74), and 5. "Pursuing Consummation" (75–110). In his "Conclusion" (111–134), the author discusses Archetypal Actions: "Their Interconnections and Relation to Ritual" (111–119), "Their Relationship to Criticism" (119–124), and "Their Relation to Culture" (124–132). In his "Finale", the author concludes: "There is a curious way in which each of the archetypes has its analogue in the stages of a human life and in fact is often enacted in the spirit and by character of this stage" (133). [JK]

References: E.G. d'Aquili, M. Douglas, M. Eliade, E.H. Erikson (+), J.W. Fernandez, M. Fortes, C. Geertz, A. van Gennep, M. Gluckman, E. Goffman, E.R. Leach (+), M. Mead, R. Schechner, E. Shils, V.W. Turner (+).
Key-words: eff, eth, prl.

Emigh, John, 1996, *Masked Performance. The Play of Self and Other in Ritual and Theatre*; Philadelphia: University of Pennsylvania Press (ISBN 0–8122–3058–2 / 0–8122–1336–X (p)) (xxii + 336).

In this collection of essays, the author deals with various performing traditions in Papua New Guinea, Orissa and Bali. Relying on masks and masking for their expressive power and imaginative life, the author focuses on the relationship of the mask to its wearer as "a paradigm for the relationships between the self and the other (and self and self) that lie at the heart of theatrical process [sic]" (xvii). To rethink the possibilities inherent in masked performances and their circumstances, he presents a variety of theoretical and descriptive observations on the dynamics of theatrical enactment and their ironic play with the identity of the performer and the performed. Since the mask functions as a symbol for theater, it opens up the ambiguous play between self and other. The author argues that the actor plays with the mask as if it were his or her own face and that the mask plays upon and reshapes the actor's imaginative sense of self. To focus on this aspect of masked performance, the author sets up a triad of role, mask, and text. Although the ordering of this triad differs between the various performative traditions the author presents, he claims that the essential process of finding a common ground for self and other remains the same, as do the playful and rigorous negotiation of the demands of experience, character, and text. Focusing on specific forms of masked performance, the author tries to achieve a more precise understanding of how these performances proceed within the field of paradox, ambiguity, and illusion. [JK]

References: **G. Bateson** (+), J. Clifford, M. Eliade (–), **C. Geertz**, E. Goffman, J. Grotowski, J. Huizinga (+), B. Kapferer, **R. Schechner** (+/–), E.L. Schieffelin, **V.W. Turner**, A. van Gennep.
Examples: Theater performance, masked performances.
Reviews: **N. Argenti *JMC* 2.3 (1997) 361–381**; K. Foley *ATJ* 15.2 (1998) 295 f; J. Peacock *AE* 26.3 (1999) 741.
Key-words: dyn, gst, idn, pmc, tha, pow, pr2, rel, sym, vir.

Erikson, Erik Homburger, 1977, *Toys and Reasons. Stages in the Ritualization of Experience*; New York: W.W. Norton & Company (ISBN 0–393–01123–2) (182).

This book is divided into three parts. In the first, "Play and Vision" (17–64), the author explores "a specific human capacity, grounded in man's evolution and developed in the toy world of childhood imagination, namely, to use objects endowed with special and symbolic meanings for the representation of an imagined scene in a circumscribed sphere" (42–43). By "going back to the ontogenetic beginnings of play", the author is able "to recognize... the fragility as well as the power of playfulness in the human condition, beginning with the patterns of mutual fittedness and of eager interplay between the newborn and the maternal environment" (57). After discussing "the ontogenetic patterns of playfulness", the author proceeds by addressing "phylogenetic forms of ritualization in private and in public life" in order to "help explain the life-and-death importance of human make-believe" (60). Not restricted to childhood, "the spirit of playfulness can pervade the visionary schemes which attach to human activities of utter practicality and consequence" (62). In the second part of the book, "Life Cycle and Ritualization" (65–118), the author discusses "a universal phenomenon on the borderline between playfulness and routinization, namely, that of everyday ritualized behavior as cultivated in all human societies in every stage of life" (64). 'Ritualization in everyday life' is seen as "one use of playfulness throughout life" (69). The author distinguishes between those "ritualized customs of everyday life which first formalize human playfulness" from special rituals and rites (78) or periodic ceremonies. "[N]ewly born Man, who could...fit into any number of pseudo-species and their habitats, must for that very reason be coaxed and induced to become 'speciated' during a prolonged childhood by some form of family: he must be *familiarized by ritualization* with a particular version of human existence" (79). Daily ritualization "can serve as an adaptive interplay deemed central to both the natural and the social universe" (82). It "represents a creative formalization which helps to avoid both impulsive excess and compulsive self-restriction" (82), thus accomplishing a number of important things, seven of which are listed (82–83). In one sub-chapter, "Ritualization in Everyday Life" (85–114), the author vividly sketches five stages in the ontogeny of ritualization leading from infancy to adolescence. The achievements of the former stages are integrated into the higher (or later) stages and provide basic elements for the major rituals of adult life, "which help to hold some basic institutions of society together, namely, faith in a cosmic order, a sense of law and justice, a hierarchy of ideal and evil roles, the fundamentals of technology, and ideological perspectives" (113). Therefore, there are numinous, judicious, dramatic, formal, and ideological elements in adult rituals. The third chapter, "Shared Visions" (119–175), has no direct bearing on theorizing rituals. [MS]

Reviews: C.S. Hall *CP* 22.9 (1977) 690; J.C. Hirschberg *BMC* 42.6 (1978) 531; D.E. Gilbertson & B. Coulibaly *CS* 7.1 (1978) 85; N. Tucker *NewSoc* 43.801 (1978) 328 f.
Key-words: PMC, cmp, str, idn, pow, emo, spc, PSY.

Etzioni, Amitai, 2000, 'Toward a Theory of Public Ritual', *Sociological Theory* 18:44–59.

By critically building on Durkheim, "[t]his article attempts to lay foundations for a sociological theory of holidays" (44). Moving beyond Durkheim, the author argues that (a) "*different holidays play different roles;*

indeed no two holidays serve the same societal role, and (b) *not all holidays are integrative*" (47). The author attempts to "provide a typology" of holidays that is "based on the varying societal roles fulfilled by different holidays" (47). He distinguishes between (a) "recommitment holidays", i.e. those holidays (such as Easter) that lead to an increasing commitment to "*the shared beliefs and institutions of their respective communities*" (47) and (b) "tension-management holidays" (like Mardi Gras) in which "mores that are upheld during the rest of the year are suspended" (48). The author expects "*[t]ension-management holidays that set clear time limits... to be more integrative than those that do not set such limits*" (48). Later in the paper, he discusses holiday-cycles and adds the hypothesis, that the two types of holidays "*will 'alternate', rather than holidays of one kind being followed by more of the same kind*" (53). While Durkheim had based his theory on the case-study of a very small society, a "theory of holidays applicable to complex societies" will assume that: "(a) while holidays do provide an integrative mechanism, this mechanism *may work to solidify member groups and not necessarily a whole society*...; (b) the *integrative effects of holidays on the society will depend on the relationships among such groups and the society-at-large*, which can vary from confrontational to complementary, and that (c) *these relationships can in turn be changed, and tensions 'worked through'... during holidays*" (49). Since Durkheim had assumed that holidays are public events, the author discusses the consequences of the ongoing "privatization of holidays" (52). The final sections of the paper address questions of the design (or re-engineering) of holidays and their relation to societal change. The author argues that "*religious holidays can be more radically redesigned, without losing their legitimacy, than secular ones*" (54). Moreover, he finds the hypothesis plausible "that *holidays tend to lag rather than lead societal change, and the more they lag, the more they hinder rather than enhance societal integration*" (55). [MS]

Reference: É. Durkheim (–).
Examples: Various, mostly from the USA.
Key-words: SOC, sec, dyn, par.

Fernandez, James W., 1972, 'Persuasions and Performances. Of the Beast in Every Body...And the Metaphors of Everyman', *Daedalus* 101:39–60.

This article is on the persuasion and performance of metaphors in ritual behavior. The author interprets rituals as communicative forms of religious experience and defines metaphor as "a strategic predication upon an inchoate pronoun (an I, a you, a we, a they) which makes a movement and leads to performance" (43). Moreover, he assumes that "metaphoric strategies involve the placing of self and other pronouns on continua" (44). With this strategy which "is to make it appear that the incumbent occupies a desirable or undesirable place in the continuum of whatever domain has been chosen" (45), he argues that "there is an important social use of metaphor involving the occupancy of various continua which in sum constitute a cultural quality space" (48). Therefore, the rhetoric of metaphors has the ability to "persuad[e] feelings in certain directions" (53) because the metaphor is "like synesthesia, the translation of experience from one domain into another by virtue of a common factor which can be generalized between the experiences in the two domains" (46). In distinguishing between two generalizing factors in the translation of experience, i.e. the structural and the textual, the author argues: "In the case of structural metaphor the translation between realms is based on some isomorphism of structure or similarity of relationships of parts. By textual metaphor we mean an assimilation made on the basis of similarity in feeling tone. Thus in synesthesia when we speak of music being hot we are moving from one domain of experience, that of sound, to another, that of temperature.... The metaphors in which we are interested make a movement. They take their subjects and move them along a dimension or a set of dimensions. They are not satisfied with parallel alignment, if indeed that were possible, given the inchoate nature of the pronominal subject.... Behind this discussion...lies a topographic model of society and culture.... Culture from this view is a quality of space of 'n' dimensions or continua, and society is a movement about of pronouns within this space" (47). "The point is that there is an important social use of metaphor involving the occupancy of various continua which in sum constitute a cultural quality of space. Persuasive metaphors situate us and others with whom we interact in that space" (48). Since predications have implications for the performance of ritual behavior, the author assumes that metaphors are plans for ritual behavior put into action. "If metaphors are a compensatory representation in themselves", they can become "images in the sense of plans for ritual behavior" (55). Thus, a metaphor can become "an organizing force in the performance of the rituals of entrance and exit" (55). To understand religious experiences, the author concludes, "rituals are the acting out of metaphoric predications upon inchoate pronouns which are in need of movement" (56). His main thesis in this article is "that the systematic study of those most meaningful forms in human intercommunication—metaphors—involves among many other approaches the study of the movement they make in semantic space. A sensitive ethnography must obtain the metaphors that men predicate upon themselves so as to locate the movements they desire to make in the culture they occupy" (57). [JK]

References: K. Burke (+), C. Lévi-Strauss (+).
Key-words: com, emo, gst, mng, pmc, pr1, rep, RHT, sem, spc.

Fernandez, James W., 1974, 'The Mission of Metaphor in Expressive Culture', ***Current Anthropology*** **15:119–145.**

"Every anthropologist knows that the really fine ethnographies are sensitive to local figures of speech, the chief of which is metaphor. That metaphors have been organizing principles in inquiry itself has been less apparent" (119b). According to the author, these observations necessitate a solid 'trope-ology'. "Metaphor is that elementary form which lies at the heart of social life" (132). "The elementary definition of metaphor (and metonym) from which one should work is the predication of a sign-image upon an inchoate subject" (120b). Unfortunately, the notion of 'sign-image' is nowhere clearly defined in this paper, but it seems to refer to a signal, sign, or symbols "pregnant with felt but unconceptualized meanings" (120). In what follows, the author distinguishes between seven 'missions' of metaphor. [1] Metaphor provides an identity for 'inchoate subjects' (120–122). According to the author, in "the growth of human identity, the inchoate pronouns of social life—the 'I', 'you', 'he', 'it'—gain identity by predicating some sign-image, some metaphor upon themselves" (122a). [2] The author notes "a dynamic in the lifelong search for identity, in the interplay between subject and object as the latter gives identity to the former and the former seeks to master it in turn through a new predicate" (123a). "A metaphor is a predication upon a subject of an object from a domain to which the subject belongs only by a stretch of the imagination" (123a). Hence, "the second mission of metaphor is to accomplish affective movement in inchoate pronouns" (123b). [3] "The third mission of metaphor is to move inchoate subjects into an optimum position in quality space" (124a). "The quality space of any culture can be defined by *n* dimensions or continua" (124a) that can be scaled. [4] According to the author, "metaphors are not only rhetorical devices of persuasion; they can also lead to performance" (125a). "The liturgy of any ritual is composed of a series of ceremonial scenes which may be regarded as putting into effect metaphoric predications upon the pronouns [the 'I', 'we', etc.] in the ritual.... The fourth mission of metaphor is to act as a plan for ritual behavior" (125a). "It is axiomatic to such an argument that people undertake religious experience because they desire to change the way they think about themselves and the world in which they live" (125a). "A ritual is to be analyzed...as a series of organizing images or metaphors put into operation by a series of superordinate and subordinate ceremonial scenes" (125b). [5] The "inchoateness of subjects within certain frames of reference—suburban life, early childhood, those ultimate circumstances framed by birth and death—is concretized by metaphoric predication. Such incorporation incorporates into such frames elements of other domains of experience which, if not more clearly understood, are at least more sharply felt. In a sense we may say that metaphoric predication takes an inchoate frame and incorporates into it a domain of objects and actions whose identity and action requirements we more clearly understand.... The fifth mission of metaphor, then, is to enable pronouns to fill inchoate frames by incorporating experience in the form of sign-images from a metaphoric domain aptly included in the frame. In another vocabulary, one might say that metaphor is a mediating device connecting the unconnected and bridging the gaps in causality" (126b). [6] "Metaphoric and metonymic predication in the end can only concretize a part of the inchoate whole of corporal and social experience. When the exploitation of the metaphor or metonym is fulfilled—when the condition in feeling or form of the sign-image is approximated—another metaphor appears to try to 'return us to the whole'. But of course, it only succeeds in linking the subject to a partiality or an essentially false attribution again. This repeated 'search for the whole', out of dissatisfaction, perhaps, with the 'partness' of any of our devices of representation, may be called the sixth mission of metaphor" (129a–b). [7] The author argues that "metaphoric predications upon a significant other bring about significant transformation of the inchoate subject in respect to its metonymic relationship to its parts. The seventh mission of metaphor is to rescue pronouns from a preoccupation with their parts" (131b). "On the basis of the ritual considered here and on the basis of others I have examined, I would propose that in expressive events, and in religious celebrations particularly, metaphors and metonyms are being chosen to put forth three kinds of statements: statements of adequacy, inadequacy, and transformation or transcendence of state" (131b). "Complex expressive events consist of a chain of metaphors and metonyms, often operating under the organizing effect of major metaphor. Such complexes may be analyzed (a) in matrix form, by reference to the scenes devised to put metaphoric sign-images into effect and the associations marshalled by each scene, or (b) in formula form, by reference to the transformations in subjects and objects wrought by progressions in the relations between metonymic and metaphoric predications" (133a–b). The paper includes "comments" by John Blacking, Alan Dundes, Munro S. Edmonson, K. Peter Etzkorn, George G. Haydu, Michael Kearney, Alice B. Kehoe, Franklin Loveland, Daniel N. Maltz, Michael Panoff, Richard J. Preston, Charles K. Warrinder, Roger W. Wescott, and András Zakar (133b–141a), as well as a "reply" by Fernandez (141a–143b). [MS]

References: K. Burke (+), R. Jakobson (+), C. Lévi-Strauss (+), V.W. Turner.
Examples: Christian ceremony, games and rituals among the Fang of western equatorial Africa and the inhabitants of the villages of the Asturian mountains (Spain).
Key-words: pmc, RHT, sym.

Fernandez, James W., 1977, 'The Performance of Ritual Metaphors', in: James David Sapir & Jon Christopher Crocker (eds), *The Social Use of Metaphor. Essays on the Anthropology of Rhetoric*, Philadelphia: University of Pennsylvania Press (ISBN 0-8122-7725-2) 100–131.

The author assumes that metaphorical terms are basic to ritual performances. Within a ritual performance, the use of metaphors should be taken literally. In elaborating the relationship between ritual and metaphor, the author proposes that metaphors provide organizing images that ritual action puts into effect. He argues that metaphors are not only images but also plans for ritual behavior. Thus, the actualization of metaphors in a ritual performance enables the pronouns to undergo integration and transformation in the experience of participants. Ritual becomes a form of metaphoric expression. Rejecting grammatical definitions of metaphor, the author defines metaphor semantically as a device of representation by which new meanings are learned. The strategic predication upon an inchoate pronoun leads to ritual performance. Studying the structure of associations brought into play by metaphoric predications becomes crucial for the author's study of ritual performance. In the ritual transformation of metaphor, the participant's attention shifts from one metaphoric domain to another. The experience of the performance of ritual metaphors provides different kinds of integration and individual experience. Religious metaphors are able to transform primary experiences through ritual and combine in themselves satisfactory representations of primary experiences and revitalize the social experiences. [JK]

References: K. Burke, E.E. Evans-Pritchard, C. Lévi-Strauss, V.W. Turner.
Example: Fang cult rituals of the Biwiti religious movement.
Key-words: emo, mng, pmc, rep, RHT, sem, sym.

Fernandez, James W., 1986, *Persuasions and Performances. The Play of Tropes in Culture*; Bloomington (IN): Indiana University Press (ISBN 0-253-34399-2 / 0-253-20374-0 (p)) (xv + 304) (with index and bibliography).

This book on the rhetoric of expressive culture is not a monograph but a collection of previously published articles. The title is derived from a paper originally published in 1972, which opens this collection. The book contains the following papers: "Persuasions and Performances. Of the Beast in Every Body and the Metaphors of Everyman" (3–27) (*); "The Mission of Metaphor in Expressive Culture" (28–70) (*); "Poetry in Motion. Being Moved by Amusement, Mockery, and Morality in the Asturian Mountains" (73–102); "Syllogisms of Association. Some Modern Extensions of Asturian Deepsong" (103–129); "Lexical Fields. And Some Movements About, Within, and Between Them" (130–156); "Some Reflections on Looking into Mirrors" (157–171); "Edification by Puzzlement" (172–187); "Returning to the Whole" (188–213); "The Dark at the Bottom of the Stairs. The Inchoate in Symbolic Inquiry and Some Strategies of Coping with It" (214–238); "Moving up in the World. Transcendence in Symbolic Anthropology" (239–263); "Convivial Attitudes. A Northern Spanish Kayak Festival in Its Historical Moment" (264–295). The book is divided into two parts, entitled "Persuasions" (3–70) and "Performances" (73–295), respectively. While the papers assembled in the first part of the book contain a number of theoretical statements, the articles making up the second part are "expository and not technical attempts to examine and clarify the various ideas put forth in these first two articles" (ix). In his "Introduction" (vii–xv), the author sketches some of the basic assumptions of his approach: "In my view, whatever humans are, they are certainly argumentative animals...It may be the consequence of being a very generalized animal with very little in specific adaptations to specific milieus wired into our brains. As a consequence we are required to invent ways of being—from rules and plans to world views and cosmologies—more or less appropriate to any of the diverse milieus in which we have installed ourselves. We endlessly argue over the appropriateness of those rules, plans, and world views" (vii). As social animals, the author continues, it is "our tendency... to try and maintain ourselves at the center of, or in the right position in, the social world to which we belong and whose roles we have learned to perform with satisfaction. We want to continue performing such roles... finding new roles to perform that will be even more gratifying. This maintenance of satisfying role performance by argumentative means seems to be a fundamental mission in human life.... It is the mission of our argumentative powers, I argue, to preserve our place and our gratifying performances and hence the world in which these things are lodged and to persuade others to recognize that place, that performance, and that world" (viii). The author distinguishes between "formal argument" (logical, syllogistic) and "figurative argument—or the argument of images.... This is a popular style of argument in which quite different domains are brought together in unexpected and creative ways" (viii). The book mainly deals with the latter type of argument. The author characterizes the papers of the second part as "performances not only in the sense that they examine instances of human performance in terms of the play of tropes but that they are themselves performances" (ix). He argues that these papers "take the set of ideas involved in the perspective being argued here as guides to that most challenging performance which confronts anthropology, the interpretation of field data" (ix). The author is "more interested in what tropes do than in what they are in any formal analytic sense. Here also lies the primacy of the series of essays as against the technical statement, for they all contain and seek to be grounded in 'revelatory incidents', events where tropes are actually at play and where images are actually argued by... recognizable human agents, and where the figurative actually does something to these human agents, to their relationship with others, and to their relation to their worlds as the figurative helps them define that relationship and the world" (ix). His "own particular concern here has been in how humans... construct, given their problems, identities through the argument of images and the play of tropes" (ix). "To be human is to have, to one degree or another, a problem of identity for it is to have, sooner or later, a growing sense of uncertainty—what I call here 'the inchoate'—which lies at the heart of the human condition" (ix–x). Furthermore, in his "Introduction", the author explores his notion of 'revelatory incidents' that occur during long-term participation in fieldwork (xi–xii). "The collection of essays presumes, though the point will not be argued in great detail, that humans organize their social worlds into domains of belonging and that a great deal of human life is spent in maintaining, arranging, or rearranging these domains" (xii). "It is my view that the study of the 'play of tropes' is one important way to help us to understand that dynamic" (xii). Hence, the author refers to his version of anthropology as "an-trope-ology" (xv). [JK/MS]

Reviews: D.C. Conrad *IJAS* 21.3 (1988) 515; R. Fardon *Man* 23.1 (1988) 182; T. Edwards *JRS* 3.1 (1989) 129–133; M. Ruel *JRA* 20.3 (1990) 279 f; K. Yankah *RAL* 21.1 (1990) 163; P.H. Stephenson & A. Black *RA* 19.1–4 (1991) 241; **S.J. Bowen *Sem* 91.1/2 (1992) 185–190**.
Key-words: cog, com, dyn, idn, par, pmc, rfl, RHT, sem, sym.

Fernandez, James W., 2006, 'Rhetorics', in: Jens Kreinath, Jan A.M. Snoek & Michael Stausberg (eds), *Theorizing Rituals. Vol. I: Issues, Topics, Approaches, Concepts*, (Numen Book Series 114–1), Leiden, Boston: Brill (ISBN-10: 90–04–15342–x, ISBN-13: 978–90–04–15342–4) 647–656.

The rhetorical approach to ritual rests on the assumption of persistent meaning deficit in social interaction and consequently on the view that argument is ever-present in human life in culture as men and women argue for and seek anchorage and fulfillment in particular meanings. It follows from this view that the rhetorical arts of persuasion and the gaining or changing of conviction are centrally important in the dynamics of culture. Culture we might argue is, fundamentally, the ongoing results of acts of persuasion and resultant conviction. This approach treats rituals, therefore, as complex systems of persuasion and confirmation or transformation of convictions about self and society. It studies ritual in order to understand how that persuasion is exercised and conviction is achieved through argument, whether verbal, visual or symbolic. The tropes are the long recognized elementary units of rhetorical art, metaphor, metonym, irony etc. They, from the rhetorical point of view, are the basic conceptual tools in the analysis of ritual dynamics. [James W. Fernandez]

Key-words: dyn, eff, emo, pmt, rel, RHT.

Finnegan, Ruth Hillary, 1969, 'How to Do Things with Words. Performative Utterances Among the Limba of Sierra Leone', *Man* 4:537–551.

In this article, the author applies the notion of 'performative' utterances and 'illocutionary' aspects of language as a general interpretation of speech to the Limba of Sierra Leone. Analyzing their speech acts in terms of performative utterances, the author tries to show how social relations are maintained through verbal acts of commitment or contact. With this performative approach, she wants to make a contribution "to wider discussions about the kind of analysis one can make of certain utterances referred to as 'symbolic' or 'ritual', and to controversies about the nature of language and action in non-industrial (as well as industrial) societies" (538). For this reason, the author uses two kinds of formal acts in her analysis of performative utterances. First, she discusses terms that are used for the negotiation of accepting, announcing, and pleading. Second, she analyzes such formal acts of commitment as thanking, greeting, and saying goodbye. Her main argument is that performative utterances "have not merely a descriptive or expressive force but, when publicly used in the appropriate context, are in fact a kind of action.... [T]he successful enactment of these quasi-legal utterances" are regarded "as not only performing some specific transaction or commitment on a particular occasion but as an act—not just a description—formally acknowledging a wide and often continuing social relationship" (542). After examining the Limba examples, the author questions the distinction of performative from other forms of utterance. To point towards a general illocutionary force in a variety of utterances, she recognizes the wider situations and relationships involved. She draws three conclusions: 1. "[T]his sort of approach to certain linguistic acts enables us to see them in the frame of action rather than as 'mere words', and in their functions of creating and maintaining social relationships and social situations"; 2. "[T]he present discussion is relevant for various theories put forward by social anthropologists and others about language among so-called 'primitive' peoples"; and 3. "The kind of analysis offered by Austin and followed here solves certain difficulties raised by sociologists, philosophers and others who have analysed speech in terms of a basic distinction expressed variously as that between descriptive and expressive or descriptive and symbolic" (549). In suggesting the fruitfulness of this approach for the study of religious utterances and acts, the author states that such performative analysis helps "out of the dilemma of having to allocate all speech utterances into just one or other of two categories: expressive (or symbolic or evaluative) and descriptive" (550). [JK]

References: J.L. Austin, J.H.M. Beattie, R. Firth, R. Horton, S.K. Langer, C. Lévi-Strauss, B. Malinowski, M. Mauss, S.J. Tambiah.
Example: Speech among the Limba of Sierra Leone.
Key-words: com, eff, PMT, rel, sec, soc, sym.

Finol, José Enrique, 2003, 'Le rite, morphologie et contexte', *Paragrana. Internationale Zeitschrift für Historische Anthropologie* 12 (special issue: "Rituelle Welten" = Wulf & Zirfas (eds) 2003 (*)): 88–101 (with bibliography).
[Ritual. Morphology and Context]

In this essay, the author, who introduces himself as a semiotician, confronts ritual action and ordinary, everyday action (99). The author regards the rite (*le rite*) as an action (*une action*) that can be decomposed into a number of acts (*un certain nombre des acts*) (90). According to the author, the specific character of ritual action is the result of a dialectical interplay between, on the one hand, "a certain type of action, objects, and actors", and "a specific context" on the other (90). The author finds reciprocal forces linking 'morphology' and 'context' to each other to be at work, and these forces "give the rite its particular forms of social life" (90). As for its "content", a "given number of semiotic elements" distinguish the ritual domain from that of ordinary life (91). For the author, "the rite...creates a particular micro-universe that...establishes a space, a time, actors, and meanings (*des sens*) that are completely different from those that one finds in our daily life" (91). In what follows, the author discusses ritual time and space (91–92), symbols (here following Schaff and Grimes) (92–94), ritual actors (here highlighting some differences between 'traditional' and 'contemporary' rituals) (94–95), and the ritual body (95). From this the author concludes that the rite is primarily an action directly linked to the body (95). This action can be decomposed into individual acts following a ritual syntax (96). Furthermore, ritual action is to be regarded as "a symbolic action that is able to represent and communicate to the participants certain contents (*certains contenus*) the meaning of which is to be determined by the different types of contexts, both historical and situational, pertaining to the configuration and execution of the ritual acts" (96). Finally, the author reflects on six characteristics of ritual action (96–98): (a) it is repetitive; (b) it follows a given order, (c) the sequence of which results from a specific order (a set of rules); (d) it is representative, i.e. "the acts constituting ritual action are there in place of something else" (97); (e) it is formal; and (f) it is able to "evoke" things having "a semiotic nature different from itself" (98). These reflections lead to the following binary scheme: ritual action/ordinary action // symbolic aim/pragmatic aim // prescribed/spontaneous // public/personal // symbolic/non-symbolic // sequential/non-sequential (98–99). The author concludes that by being extraordinary action "the rite wants to establish and reestablish the functioning of that which could break down daily life" (99). [MS]

References: C.M. Bell (+), R.L. Grimes (+), A. Mary (+), S. Miceli (+), V.W. Turner (+).
Examples: Life-cycle rituals from Venezuela.
Key-words: com, pr1, SEM, SYM, str, rep, spc, tim, soc.

Fischer-Lichte, Erika & Christoph Wulf (eds), 2001, *Theorien des Performativen* (Paragrana 10.1); Berlin: Akademie Verlag (ISSN 0938–0116) (334).
[Theories of Performativeness]

Selected contents: E. Fischer-Lichte & Ch. Wulf: "Vorwort" (Preface) (9); I "Sprache und Diskurs" (Language and Discourse) (11–90); II "Soziales und Geschlecht" (The Social and Gender) (91–154); Ch. Wulf & J. Zirfas: "Die performative Bildung von Gemeinschaften. Zur Hervorhebung des Sozialen in Ritualen und Ritualisierungen" (The Performative Formation of Communities. About the Emphasis on the Social in Rituals and Ritualisations) (93–116); III "Sinnlichkeit und Emotionalität" (Sensuality and Emotionality) (155–233); IV "Kunst und Medien" (Art and Media) (235–334). [JS]

Key-words: soc, gdr, emo, lan, med.

Fischer-Lichte, Erika & Christoph Wulf (eds), 2004, *Praktiken des Performativen* (Paragrana 13.1); Berlin: Akademie Verlag (ISSN 0938–0116) (309).
[Practices of Performativeness]

The chapters of this volume were written by collective Working Groups. The names of the numerous participants are mentioned in the first note to each chapter. Only the Introduction ("Vorwort") was written by the two editors of the volume alone.

Contents: [I] "Wahrnehmung und Performativität" (Perception and Performativity) (15–80); [II] "Diskursivierung des Performativen" (Discursification of the Performative) (81–127); [III] "Über das Zusammenspiel von 'Medialität' und 'Performativität'" (On the Interplay of 'Mediality' and 'Performativity') (129–185); [IV] "Differenz und Alterität im Ritual. Eine interdisziplinäre Fallstudie" (Difference and Alterity in Ritual. An Interdisciplinary Case Study) (187–249); [V] "Begehrende Körper und verkörpertes Begehren. Interdisziplinäre

Studien zu Performativität und *gender*" (Desiring Bodies and Embodied Desire. Interdisciplinary Studies on Performativity and Gender) (251–309). [JS]
Key-words: PMT, PMC, med, gdr.

Fiske, A.M. & N. Haslam, 1997, 'Is Obsessive-Compulsive Disorder a Pathology of the Human Disposition to Perform Socially Meaningful Rituals? Evidence of Similar Content', *Journal of Nervous and Mental Disease* 185:211–222.

From the authors' abstract: "This study investigated the theory that obsessive-compulsive disorder (OCD) is a pathology of the human disposition to perform culturally meaningful social rituals. We tested the hypothesis that the same actions and thoughts that are ego-dystonic in OCD are valued when they are appropriately performed in socially legitimated rituals. Two coders analyzed ethnographic descriptions of rituals, work, and another activity in each of 52 cultures. The coders recorded the presence or absence of 49 features of OCD and 19 features of other psychopathologies. The features of OCD were more likely to be present and occurred more frequently in rituals than in either control; rituals also contained more diverse kinds of OCD features. The features of other psychopathologies were less likely to be present and were less numerous in rituals than the features of OCD. Analysis of variance showed that OCD features discriminate between rituals and controls better than the features of other psychopathologies. These results suggest that there could be a psychological mechanism that operates normally in rituals, which can lead to OCD when it becomes hyperactivated" (211). [Thorsten Gieser]
References: P. Boyer, S. Freud, V.W. Turner.
Key-words: PSY, mng, cog, pmc, eff, CPR.

Fox, Steven J., 1980, 'Theoretical Implications for the Study of Interrelationships Between Ritual and Play', in: Helen B. Schwartzman (ed.), *Play and Culture. 1978 Proceedings of the Association for the Anthropological Study of Play*, West Point (NY): Leisure Press (ISBN 0-918-4385-27) 51–57.

Because the specific relationship between ritual and play is underscored in the anthropological literature, the author attempts to explore and define the parameters of this relationship, considering the ritual dimension of play and the play aspects of ritual. After discussing definitions of play and ritual, he elaborates the ritual dimensions of play: "The relationship between play and religious expression, particularly ritual behavior, is the function of a transcendental quality characteristic of both phenomena.... It should be noted, in the form of a corollary, that play functions as a counterbalance to the solemnity of many ritual acts" (53). He summarizes his argument as follows: "The ritual dimensions of play may be manifested in a variety of ways at three primary points on a continuum of integration: individual, participatory, and communal.... The extremes of the continuum are those activities in which only individuals participate, as opposed to those in which the entire community may be directly involved. An intermediate point, designated participatory, exists on the continuum to denote the selective participation of members of the community in ritual and/or play activities" (54). In considering the play aspects of ritual, the author asserts that "[b]y virtue of its integration into ritual processes, play must be, to some extent, both organized and symbolic. Under close scrutiny it may be found that the organizational bases of play, rules, are analogous to myths governing ritual. This may well be enhanced by the transcendental qualities of ritual and play; both utilize a component of 'make-believe' in their expression" (55). The author presents these interrelations in a schematic diagram with three continuums, namely activity, participatory integration, and context. For the author, "[a]ll three continua are interdependent and, therefore, modify one another within a cultural-behavioral universe. The dynamics of the relationship between ritual and play are manifest in the range of structural, expressive, and symbolic interactions that characterize these phenomena" (56). He concludes: "Often the distinction between ritual and play is not readily apparent, thereby necessitating that they be studied as interrelated behavioral phenomena" (57). [JK]

References: J.H.M. Beattie, **R. Firth** (+), J. Huizinga, E.R. Leach, **G.H. Mead** (+), **E. Norbeck** (+), V.W. Turner.
Key-words: pmc, myt, sec, sym, str.

Frankiel, Tamar, 2001, 'Prospects in Ritual Studies', *Religion* 32:75–87.

This paper is disguised as a review article (of Aune & De Marinis, *Religious and Social Ritual* [1995] and Grimes1982 (*) [revised edition 1995]). However, the author goes far beyond that task. On the basis of a discussion of the concept of liminality, the author "invites us to postulate...that rituals anticipate change; they stand on the border between this space and that, between the past and the future. Further, ritualisers make elaborate preparations for the change, using all the tools they can command. These tools may include creating the fiction that there is no change, thus defining what constitutes continuity and change. Moreover, ritual will frequently break down a situation into more and more doorways.... In order for all this to 'work', the ritual must create a ritualised body that is ready for the impending event" (80). Since the author finds that "[w]e still lack a clear method of showing *how* the ritualising body does this" (80) and in order to develop a method allowing for cross-cultural comparison, the author suggests that we should pay closer attention to cognitive linguistics (in particular, the work of Mark Johnson). In a final section, the author discusses the problem of distinguishing ritual from ritual-like behavior, warning against what he perceives to be a tendency to make theory banal (84–86). [MS]

References: C.M. Bell, Th.J. Csordas, R.L. Grimes, E.Th. Lawson, R.N. McCauley, J.Z. Smith, F. Staal, V.W. Turner.
Key-words: gen, sec, cog, DYN, cpr, emb.

Galaty, John G., 1983, 'Ceremony and Society. The Poetics of Maasai Ritual', *Man* 18:361–382.

This article is concerned with the aesthetics and semiotics of ritual as compared to other forms of art. The distinctive feature of ritual, the author proposes, "is not communication, which it shares with all domains of culture, but self-referentiality or 'aesthetics', which as a pervasive principle it shares only with the arts" (364). Similar to art, ritual "highlights itself reflexively through unusual patterns and rhythms of meaning and form: repetition, sequencing, 'figures' of action and speech, metaphor, analogy and inversion can all be used to mark an aesthetic function" (364). Because "rituals and poems are entities in which style and technique not only dominate but define a pattern of the whole", they "form selfcontained totalities with temporal and symbolic structure, in short, texts" (364). Rituals can be conceived as texts because they "creatively use aesthetic vehicles to bring into being novel and often penetrating insights with respect to their conceptual tenors, and produce signifiers that seek out but never quite attain their signifieds: in this process lies the generativity of symbols" (364). However, the author argues that the main difference between ritual and other aesthetic forms lies "not in aesthetic structure *per se* but in pragmatic enactment" (364). Therefore he contends that "[t]he pragmatics of ritual must be contrasted with the structure of ritual 'texts', as such, which—not being written—exist as the codification of the aims, rules, attitudes and events of a given rite" (364). Taken this into account the author maintains that "a ritual code cannot exhaust its meaning, since in actual performance it assumes properties of 'indexicality', by which contextual factors—the actual participants, pragmatic decisions about its enactment, the expression of emotions—lend the *event* (as opposed to the *code*) a significance of its own" (365). Therefore one needs not only to turn "to the aesthetic process of ritual, with which participants are engaged, but to the implicit power of ritual transformation by which ritual acts" (365). The main part of the paper is dedicated to the analysis of a Maasai ritual (366–377), in which the author aims to demonstrate "how the aesthetic use of semiotic functions provides the means whereby experience signifies social action" (366). According to him it is inappropriate to reduce ritual "to an expression of society since it acts on and in society by virtue of its self-referential and transformative properties" (377). Therefore he emphasizes "the iconic character of ritual in relation to society" and identifies "the functioning in ritual of synecdoches and metonyms of society, in various part/whole, cause/effect and class/member relationships" (377). If rituals are "the means whereby the social order is transformed" (379), theories of ritual signification would need to take the power of ritual transformation into account because "[t]he efficacy of ritual lies in this indeterminacy, or rather over-determinacy, since such symbols serve no one function but several by virtue of all. This aesthetic character of ritual by which it speaks with many voices is the source of its remarkable power of persuasion over individuals recruited to the intellectual and affective images it presents" (380). [JK]

References: R. Barthes (+), C. Geertz, R. Jakobson, E.R. Leach, C. Lévi-Strauss, M. Silverstein (+), P. Smith, S.J. Tambiah, V.W. Turner.
Example: Maasai sacrifice.
Key-words: AES, cpl, eff, mng, pr2, SEM, str, rfl, rht.

Gardner, D.S., 1983, 'Performativity in Ritual. The Mianmin Case', *Man* 18:346–360.

In this critical essay, the author rejects the possibility of applying the theory of speech acts to the study of ritual. By using data from certain ritual practices of male initiation of the highland Mianmin of Papua New Guinea, the author challenges the theoretical adequacy of the performative account to ritual analysis. He argues that Tambiah and Ahern have not adequately distinguished between illocutionary and perlocutionary acts, because they characterize the whole of a complex sequence of ritual acts in terms of the properties of certain parts of them. The author claims that there must be some conventions that govern the procedure and have an effect on the state of affairs. Therefore, he defines the essential characteristics of performative procedures as follows: "A procedure is performative if a correct performance, under the appropriate conditions, serves to effect a transition between two conventionally defined states; the procedure constitutes the transformation between these states. Both the procedure and the states it defines are required to be defined conventionally" (350). If one believes in ghosts or the capacity of ancestors, the author argues, then the rituals are performed not as performative acts but as a procedure in order to achieve the involvement of these ghosts or ancestors in the ritual. For this reason, rituals cannot count as performative acts in Austin's sense. In his analysis of the performativity in Mianmin initiation, the author outlines why the performative speech act theory is not only inapplicable to initiation but also generally inadequate as an account of the nature of the magical and religious rituals, which such anthropologists as Tambiah or Ahern try to explain. He concludes his analysis of the Mianmin initiation by saying that it is sufficient to counteract any suggestion that such rituals are performative "since the procedures enacted are not constitutive of the resulting state of the initiands" (355). He rejects the application of the performative speech acts for the analysis of initiation rituals: "Whether a particular procedure is performative in the required sense depends upon the place of that procedure in the lives of the people who perform it, and on their beliefs and theories about the nature of the world they inhabit. It is, moreover, only dependent upon these considerations and it is not possible for an observer to gainsay the actors in this matter. There can be no such thing as an unconscious or unrecognised performative in the accepted sense of this term. For these reasons, it seems to me unlikely that performatives, seen in their most characteristic form in the civil transactions of secular polities, play an important part in the initiation rituals usually studied by anthropologists (and, *a fortiori*, in more clearly instrumental rituals), where magical and/or religious beliefs are invariably of central importance" (355). [JK]

References: E.M. Ahern (–), J.L. Austin, F. Barth, M.E.F. Bloch, R.H. Finnegan, R.A. Rappaport, S.J. Tambiah (–), A. van Gennep.
Example: Initiation.
Key-words: com, PMT, PMC, pr2.

Gebauer, Gunter & Christoph Wulf, 1998, *Spiel—Ritual—Geste. Mimetisches Handeln in der sozialen Welt* (Rowohlts Enzyklopädie 55591); Reinbek bei Hamburg: Rowohlt Taschenbuch Verlag (ISBN 3-499-55591-3) (335) (with index and bibliography).
[Play—Ritual—Gesture. Mimetic Action in the Social World]

In this book, the authors analyze rituals, among other things, with the help of the concept of 'mimesis'. They state that through mimetic actions an individual creates his own world but simultaneously refers these mimetic actions to another (real or imagined) world that existed beforehand. In other words, mimetic actions are orientated towards models, ideals, traditions, 'reality', or recollections. According to the authors, the reason why two worlds are involved in mimetic actions is that they are performed by a material body and such performances must be interpreted. Hence, there is always the world of material actions and the world of interpretation or reference. Due to the mimetic actions' reference to another world, the authors conceive of them as inherently social actions related to other real or imagined performances. Such actions therefore involve more than one individual. In summary, they define mimetic actions as: (1) movements that refer to other movements; (2) bodily performances that are meant to represent and show something; (3) independent actions that can be understood on their own while also referring to other actions or worlds. As the authors see most social processes as based on mimetic actions, they propose that even abstract social actions (and thoughts) are grounded in the materiality of the body and its performances. Thereby a concordance between individual actions and social conceptions is achieved. Using this concept, the authors understand rituals to be created, transferred, and designed in mimetic processes. They embody and organize symbolic contents in particular places and at particular times in traditional forms and modes of action. Rituals are thus symbolic actions that are aesthetically performed and are therefore conceived of as uniting the lived and the imagined world so that both worlds appear as one world. Drawing on Goffman's concept of 'frame', the authors further state that ritual performances are meant to express/demonstrate/refer to something. This intention 'frames' ritual actions and sets them off from everyday actions. It is through the participants' common coordinated actions of the ritual performance that both their actions and intentions become similar to each other. In this way the participants socially construct and transfer meaning. [Thorsten Gieser]

References: **P. Bourdieu** (+), M. Eliade, S. Freud, E. Goffman (+), V.W. Turner, A. van Gennep.
Review: L. Nieder *Sel* 2 (1999) 33–37.
Key-words: soc, sym, AES, pmc, PR2, MIM, emo, gst.

Geertz, Clifford, 1966, 'Religion as a Cultural System', in: Michael Banton (ed.), *Anthropological Approaches to the Study of Religion*, (ASA Monographs 3), London: Travistock Publications (no ISBN [second impression, 1968: ISBN 0–422–71390–2]) 1–46.

This article concerns both cultural anthropology and the study of rituals. The author argues that religion is a cultural system based on symbolic forms, which are enacted in religious rituals. He wants to widen the traditions of social anthropology by means of a specific anthropological study of religion. In applying a semiotic approach to cultural anthropology, he defines culture as "an historically transmitted pattern of meanings embodied in symbols, a system of inherited conceptions expressed in symbolic forms by means of which men communicate, perpetuate, and develop their knowledge about and attitudes toward life" (3). Within this concept of culture, religion is "(1) a system of symbols which acts to (2) establish powerful, pervasive, and long-lasting moods and motivations in men by (3) formulating conceptions of a general order of existence and (4) clothing these conceptions with such an aura of factuality that (5) the moods and motivations seem uniquely realistic" (4). Symbol is defined as "any object, act, event, quality, or relation which serves as a vehicle for a conception—the conception is the symbol's 'meaning'" (5). The author further distinguishes between "models of 'reality'" and "models for 'reality'" (7). Cultural patterns are systems of symbols or 'models' that are representations not only of but also for the lifeworld. In placing the religious perspective as one of the cultural patterns against the background of the common sense, scientific, and aesthetic perspectives (26), religious action imbues a specific complex of symbols with persuasive authority in order to create an aura of total actuality: The sense of the 'really real' emerges in ritual because here "the world as lived and the world as imagined, fused under the agency of a single set of symbolic forms" (28). In his conclusion, the author states that the task of the anthropological study of religion is a two-fold undertaking: "first, an analysis of the system of meanings embodied in the symbols which make up the religion proper, and, second, the relating of these systems to socio-structural and psychological processes" (42). [JK]

References: **K. Burke** (+), E.E. Evans-Pritchard, É. Durkheim, R. Firth, J. Goody, C. Kluckhohn, **S.K. Langer** (+), G. Lienhardt, B. Malinowski, A.R. Radcliffe-Brown, P. Radin, E. Shils, **T. Parsons** (+).
Key-words: aes, com, emb, emo, mng, PMC, psy, rep, SEM, soc, SYM, vir.

Geertz, Clifford, 1973, *The Interpretation of Cultures. Selected Essays*; New York: Basic Books (ISBN 0-465-03425-X / 0-465-09719-7 (p)) (ix + 470) (with index).

In his Preface, the author states: "The majority of the essays are, in fact, empirical studies rather than theoretical disquisitions, for I grow uncomfortable when I get too far away from the immediancies of social life" ([vii]).
Selected contents: "Thick Description. Towards an Interpretative Theory of Culture" (3–30); "Religion as a Cultural System" (87–125) (*); "Ethos, World View, and the Analysis of Sacred Symbols" (126–141); "Ritual and Social Change. A Javanese Example" (142–169); "Deep Play. Notes on the Balinese Cockfight" (412–453). [JK/MS]

Reviews: A. Swidler *CS* 25.3 (1974) 248 f; M. Greene *HER* 44.2 (1974) 331; E. Colson *CS* 4.6 (1975) 637; W.C. Shepherd *JAAR* 43.3 (1975) 635; R. Fenn *JSSR* 13.2 (1996) 299–302.
Key-words: dyn, emo, mng, pmc, pr1, psy, sem, soc, sym.

Geertz, Clifford, 1980, *Negara. The Theatre State in Nineteenth-Century Bali*; Princeton, Oxford: Princeton University Press (ISBN 0-691-05316-2 / 0-691-00778-0 (p)) (xii + 295).

In this book the author applies the semiotic analytical method which he developed and called 'thick description' to the nineteenth-century Balinese state and its precolonial forms of social, ceremonial, and political organization. In combining historical method and anthropological analysis with political theory, the author structures his book as follows: "Introduction. Bali and Historical Method" (3–10); "Chapter 1. Political Definition. The Sources of Order" (11–25); "Chapter 2. Political Anatomy. The Internal Organization of the Ruling Class" (26–44); "Chapter 3. Political Anatomy. The Village and the State" (45–97); "Chapter 4. Political Statement. Spectacle and Ceremony" (98–120); "Conclusion. Bali and Political Theory" (121–136). In putting the ethnographic approach at the center of his analysis, the author writes: "Specifically, I will construct, both out of my own fieldwork and out of the literature, a circumstantial picture of state organization in nineteenth-century Bali and then attempt to draw from that picture a set of broad but substantive guidelines for the ordering of pre- and protohistorical material in Indonesia…generally" (7). This study is an attempt to interpret the *negara* (city-state) Bali as a theater state designed to dramatize the leading obsession in traditional Balinese culture with social inequality and social pride: "To understand the Negara is…to elaborate a poetics of power, not a mechanics.… The state drew its force, which was real enough, from its imaginative energies, its semiotic capacity to make inequality enchant" (123). The royal court functioned as a microcosm of the supernatural order and a material embodiment of political order. Therefore, the ritual life of the court became not only reflective of but also paradigmatic for social order: "The state ceremonials of classical Bali were metaphysical theatre: theatre designed to express a view of the ultimate nature of reality and, at the same time, to shape the existing conditions of life to be consonant with that reality; that is, theatre to present an ontology and, by presenting it, to make it happen—make it actual" (104). By analyzing the leading principles that organize the political anatomy of the '*negara*', the author illustrates that it is impossible to distinguish between the political and ritual aspects of the Balinese state: "Thus the royal rituals…enacted, in the form of pageant, the main themes of Balinese political thought: the center is exemplary, status is the ground of power, statecraft is a thespian [sic] art. But there is more to it than this, because the pageants were not mere aesthetic embellishments, celebrations of a domination independently existing: they were the thing itself" (120). Because in the state ceremonies the king is both a ritual object and a political actor, the author shows how the king became subject to the paradox of active passivity: "The king was also, however, a political actor, power among powers as well as sign among signs. It was the king's cult that created him, raised him from lord to icon; for, without the dramas of the theatre state, the image of composed divinity could not even take form" (131). Because in the Balinese theater state it is not possible to reduce politics to power, the author shows in his conclusions how the Balinese rituals of kingship defy the common forms of conceptualization in terms of Western political theory: "The confinement of interpretative analysis in most of contemporary anthropology to the supposedly more 'symbolic' aspect of culture is a mere prejudice, born out of the notion…, that 'symbolic' opposes to 'real' as fanciful to sober, figurative to literal.... To construe the expressions of the theatre state, to apprehend them as theory, this prejudice, along with the allied one that the dramaturgy of power is external to its workings, must be put aside. The real is as imagined as the imaginary.... The dramas of the theatre state, mimetic of themselves, were, in the end, neither illusions nor lies, neither sleight of hand nor make-believe. They were what there was" (135–136). [JK/JS]

References: G. Bateson, M.E.F. Bloch, S.J. Tambiah, V.W. Turner, M. Weber.
Examples: royal rituals.
Reviews: B. Anderson *AHR* 86.5 (1981) 1137; H.E. Wilson *CJH* 16.3 (1981) 500; H. Aveling *JAH* 15.1 (1981) 92; C. Farber *PA* 54.3 (1981) 569; S.W. Foster *AA* 84.1 (1982) 221 f; Ch.F. Keyes *AE* 9.1 (1982) 196 f; L.E.A. Howe *BSOAS* 45.1 (1982) 220; J. Walton *CS* 11.6 (1982) 625; G. Aijmer *Ethn* 47.3/4 (1982) 297; V. Valeri *JAS* 41.3 (1982) 631; S. Cederroth *ActaSoc* 26.2 (1983) 203; M. Hobart *JRAS* 1 (1983) 85; M.C. Ricklefs *JSEAS* 14.1 (1983) 184; D.N. Gellner *SAR* 3.2 (1983) 135; P.K. Manning *AJS* 89.1–6 (1983/84) 480; E. Terray *Homme* 24.1 (1984) 116; C. Warren *CanbAnth* 8.1/2 (1985) 187.
Key-words: emb, pmc, THA, pow, sem, soc, sym.

Gerhardt, Uta, 2004, 'Die zwei Gesichter des Rituals. Eine soziologische Skizze', in: Dietrich Harth & Gerrit Jasper Schenk (eds), *Ritualdynamik. Kulturübergreifende Studien zur Theorie und Geschichte rituellen Handelns*, Heidelberg: Synchron Wissenschaftsverlag der Autoren (ISBN 3-935025-43-2) (*) 49–72.
[The Two Faces of Ritual. A Sociological Outline]

This article proposes that a sociological theory of ritual should take into account the fact that ritual is not one more or less consistent phenomenon in society, but rather that two types of ritual need to be distinguished systematically. One type is representational ritual, a performance meant to impress an audience and make them feel togetherness, loyalty or commitment to a common cause. The other type is interactional ritual, a sequence of reciprocal acts which constitutes a moral order of society as it structures situational encounters. Representational ritual is treated in the literature which deals with symbolic politics and other more or less religious practices in society as such. Interactional ritual is discussed in the literature which deals with, e.g., face work in everyday settings or the give and take between a team or ensemble and its audience in the everyday theatre-like setting of social interaction. The two types of ritual represent different approaches to society and also suggest different methodologies of sociological inquiry. Whereas representational ritual signifies authoritarian society, interactional ritual is part of a democratic organization of social life. Whereas representational ritual is based on positivistic assumptions that picture the world as it presumably 'is', the idea of interactional ritual calls for a methodology of *Verstehen* (understanding) in the tradition of Max Weber. To contrast the two types of ritual, one might relate both to the image or face that is being conveyed in social life: Whereas representational ritual means that 'face' is being shown to others who supposedly are suitably impressed by the show, interactional ritual means that 'face' is being given to others who in turn are willing and able to save the face of the actor who thereby becomes indebted to others who together with him form the social world. [Uta Gerhardt]

References: H.-G. Soeffner, Th. Luckman, E. Goffman.
Key-words: exp, pmc, pow, rel, rfl, sec, SOC.

Gerholm, Tomas, 1988, 'On Ritual. A Postmodernist View', *Ethnos* 53:190–203.

"*The description of a Hindu funeral ritual in Trinidad by the West Indian writer V.S. Naipaul is used to draw attention to features of ritual in the modern world... that are not covered in classical accounts of ritual*" (191). The author briefly discusses five such features: 1. One can distinguish a "*plurality of perspectives*" in one single ritual (194). 2. The participants of the funeral "all live in a *fragmented cultural universe* combining elements from various cultural systems" (194). 3. Different experiences are shaped by the ritual, but "[n]o one has the privilege of defining for the others what the ritual, in its many details, is all about" (195). 4. There "is the hard surface of the ritual, the ruling, which is there for all to observe. It is the public face of private experience" (195). 5. There is "a transmission of tradition, almost a reinvention of it" (195). On the basis of these issues, the author criticizes the 'essentialist' views on ritual as given by Turner and Geertz. Moreover, he argues "that it may be useful to regard the Trinidad case not only as... a telling example of ritual in a postmodern world, but also as an instance of a postmodernist *perspective* on ritual" (196). The author proceeds to give a "list of desiderata" of "what one would expect from a 'theory' of or 'perspective' on or 'approach' to ritual" (197). This is what he expects: 1. "A theory of ritual should tell us what *sort* of activity it is" (197). 2. "A theory of ritual should give us an idea of the causal origins of ritual... In line with this requirement, a theory of ritual should give us an idea of how ritual is affected by non-ritual factors, how it develops and changes with changing circumstances"

(197). 3. "A theory of ritual should tell us about the effects of ritual and be specific both about how ritual works so-to-speak *in its own terms*... and how it works *in ways that may not be recognized by indigenous theory*—that is, how it produces effects in unknown and unanticipated ways" (197). 4. "A theory of ritual should preferrably be able to account for 'the native's point of view' so that we understand why we are sometimes given so much information on the 'meaning' of the ritual and sometimes so little" (198). In the final section of this essay ("Nine Theses on Ritual", 198–202), the author attempts "to sketch... an approach to ritual that answers these questions" (198). He claims that 1. ritual is "*formal, rigidly prescribed action*" (Rappaport), "a *finite province of meaning*" (Berger & Luckmann) that involves "*the focusing and intensifying of attention*" (Lewis) (198). 2. "[R]itual is instrumental action guided by men's interest in controlling and regulating the world" (Horton) and at the same time rituals "are often sophisticated exercises in semantics" (198). 3. Neither the intellectualist nor the symbolist point of view is privileged (199). 4. Moreover, the author touches on the differences between holistic and individualistic views of ritual. Regarding the "Great Divide" (199) between these points of view on 'culture' as well as ritual, the author is concerned with "the *effects* of the ritual on individual people, be they participants or observers" (200). 5. Rituals "are not usually the work of one 'author' but the result of many individual contributions... made on the basis of individual interpretations of the 'point' of the ritual and/or on the basis of the external, non-ritual use of the ritual that a certain individual may see" (Bloch) (200). 6. The author distinguishes between two ways, in which rituals may be instrumental: "One is to be instrumental in terms of a goal defined by the theory of the ritual: the *purpose* of the ritual. The other is to be instrumental in terms of a (non-ritual) goal defined by the social context of the ritual: the use of the ritual" (200). 7. Instead of asking how rituals 'work' in general, the author suggests to "put a simpler question. What is it that makes transition rites work? Essentially, what happens is that the ritual realizes a public redefinition of the initiand's status. The public focusing of attention on this redefinition is an effective measure. It works on all of those present: they see that others see" (201). 8. "It may be the experience of these well-known rituals... that is the rationale behind those rituals that also purport to be instrumental, although it is difficult to see how they could effectively be so. It is simply a case of the migration of thought patterns from one domain to another" (Horton) (201). 9. "The individual's possibility to take his distance from the official interpretation is often made too little of in analyses treating ritual as ideology in action" (201). [JK/MS]

References: J.H.M. Beattie, P.L. Berger, B. Bettelheim, M.E.F. Bloch, C. Geertz (–), R. Horton (+), B. Kapferer, E.R. Leach, G.A. Lewis (+), R.A. Rappaport (+), J. Skorupski, D. Sperber, V.W. Turner (+/–).
Example: Hindu Funeral in Trinidad.
Key-words: cmp, DEF, DYN, emo, mng, pmc, pr1, soc.

Girard, René, 1987, 'Generative Scapegoating', in: Robert G. Hamerton-Kelly (ed.), *Violent Origins. Walter Burkert, René Girard, and Jonathan Z. Smith on Ritual Killing and Cultural Formation*, Stanford: Stanford University Press (ISBN 0–8047–1370–7) (*) 73–105.

The author summarizes this article as follows: "my research always leads me to emphasize scapegoating as the generative principle of mythology, ritual, primitive religion, even culture as a whole. My paper was an attempt to show how the concrete analysis of religious material can lead back to scapegoating.... The conception of nonconscious scapegoating to which I resort is not a reductive notion. It is a dynamic principle of genesis and development that can operate as a hermeneutic tool. This principle can certainly account for those religious institutions that present visible signs of scapegoat transference in the explicit and traditional sense, but...it can also account for those religious and cultural forms that present only the most indirect signs; it can reveal that many mythical themes and many ritual actions left uninterpreted in the past are, in fact, indirect signs of scapegoating" (106). [JS]

References: J.G. Frazer, S. Freud.
Examples: Myths from the Yahuna Indians and the Ojibway Indians; the Oedipus myth.
Key-words: mng, idn, agn, eff, POW, par, exp, myt, soc.

Gladigow, Burkhard, 2004, 'Sequenzierung von Riten und die Ordnung der Rituale', in: Michael Stausberg (ed.), *Zoroastrian Rituals in Context*, (Studies in the History of Religions 102), Leiden, Boston: Brill (ISBN 90–04–13131–0; ISSN 0169–8834) 57–76.
[Sequencing of Rites and the Order of Rituals]

Typical structures of rituals have been a feature of ritual studies since Marcel Mauss. However, the further attempt to sequence rituals has yet to be undertaken. This essay presents a systematic analysis of a sequential order of ritual elements. As such, it goes beyond the well-known distinctions between different phases in rituals, for it is only by sequencing as many rites as possible (on the level of ritual elements) that specific constellations emerge, which hitherto had remained largely inconceivable. These constellations pertain to sequences of rites that are 'quoted' in other rituals, a connection between rituals by means of similar ritual sequences ('interrituality'), shortened forms of ritual sequences ('abbreviations'), and, last but not least, incorporations of rites into more extended rituals ('complexity'). A sequencing of rituals according to this scheme may indicate to what extent the composition of rituals is the result of a process of professionalization. An increasing degree of professionalization results in an increased demand, on the one hand, to control the accuracy of the ritual performance and, on the other hand, to take the reactions of participants and the audience into account. Here it is important that the participants and the audience are transformed and that they 'learn' something in the course of the temporal unfolding of a complex ritual. [Burkhard Gladigow/MS]

References: D. Baudy (+), C.M. Bell, E.G. d'Aquili (+), Ch.D. Laughlin (+), M. Mauss, J. McManus (+), S.J. Tambiah.
Example: Roman sacrifices.
Key-words: cmp, STR, CPL, tra.

Gladigow, Burkhard, 2006, 'Complexity', in: Jens Kreinath, Jan A.M. Snoek & Michael Stausberg (eds), *Theorizing Rituals. Vol. I: Issues, Topics, Approaches, Concepts*, (Numen Book Series 114–1), Leiden, Boston: Brill (ISBN-10: 90–04–15342–x, ISBN-13: 978–90–04–15342–4) 483–494.

In this article the author develops an approach to the analysis of rituals, which is based on 'complexity' as the relational structure of the elements of rituals. The author presupposes: "As a rule rituals are not determined by an 'open accumulation' of ritual elements (rites), but have a 'structure' that possesses a beginning and an end that is recognizable to actors and spectators" (483). Based on the assumption that "rituals combine typical sequences of rites into 'groups' and organize their repetitions according to schemas", the author introduces his concept of complexity: "To the extent that each of the different levels of a ritual appears with its own structure and that those levels are combined into a 'superstructure', one can speak of a complexity of rituals" (483). By way of relating the unity of rituals and their internal complexity, the author argues: "The overall structure of a ritual comprehends different patterns of an integration of the elements of diverse 'ritual levels' and thereby determines its complexity...A special problem of a 'unity' of a complex ritual (in contrast to an open stringing together of elements) lies in the different ways of integrating diverse levels in the sequence of ritual events..." (484). Then the author addresses the issues of surveyability and argues that "[c]omplexity renders rituals surveyable for actors and participants, even if the rituals seem to consist of an 'unsurveyably' large number of rites" (485). Because of their diachronic structure, rituals consist of sequences of events and therefore can "be determined by expectation, acceleration, and delay of the ritual phases. Especially in highly complex rituals, the certainty of a linear sequencing is frequently interrupted by retardations and contingencies" (486). This implies participants as well as spectators. According to the author, "the incorporation of the 'spectators' also belongs to the complexity of a ritual" (487). Moreover he argues that synchronization is a function of complexity, because it "ensures the cooperation of many actors, especially of throngs of people in diachronic succession" (488). After addressing the scope of variation and the frame of improvisation, the author discusses the process of increase in complexity. He distinguishes between two effects of increasing complexity: "A complexity of rituals can be increased under certain circumstances without there being any loss in a ritual's surveyability.... The limits of complexity can be strained, however, at the point where disparate and dysfunctional components, as well as components with different structures of complexity, are adopted" (489). Then the author introduces the notion of 'second-order' complexity and argues that in the current research "[t]oo little attention has been paid to the fact that rituals are not only internally organized and structured but that they are always related to other rituals as well or set themselves off from their rivals" (490). In this context, the author discusses the notion of interrituality. Subsequently, the issues of meaning and complexity are addressed. The essay concludes: "With an increase in internal and external complexity, a meaning of rituals 'inevitably' increases, and in large part irreversibly: a complexity of rituals is a guarantee that their meanings can be individualized and passed on" (494). [JK]

Key-words: CPL, frm, mng, STR.

Goethals, Gregor T., 1997, 'Escape From Time. Ritual Dimensions of Popular Culture', in: Stewart M. Hoover & Knut Lundby (eds), *Rethinking Media, Religion, and Culture*, Thousand Oaks (CA), London, New Delhi: SAGE Publications (ISBN (978) 0–7619–0170–1 / 0–7619–0171–X (p)) 117–132.

In this article the author re-examines the research paradigm according to which the concept of ritual can fruitfully be used to illuminate the characteristics of some events in popular culture. First, the author looks "at formal elements used to make connections between ancient ceremonies and contemporary happenings in sports and entertainment, focusing particularly on traditional rituals' exterior boundaries—space and time. A closer look at these may point up both similarities and differences. Following this, I will turn to the interior dimensions of traditional religious rites, particularly the experience of transcendence" (117–118). Referring to scholars such as Victor W. Turner, Barbara Myerhoff, Ernst Cassirer, Walter Burkert, and Jonathan Z. Smith, the author points out that rituals are patterned actions that can be distinguished from other activities because of their special framing of time and space: "Temporal boundaries, like spatial ones, are essential to ritual" (119). But these mythopoetic concepts of space and time, according to Henri Frankfort, differ in certain respects from modern ones. "Although spatial and temporal demarcations allow for some analogy between primitive rituals and contemporary cultural events, pre-modern mythologies of space and time differ radically from our own. Such differences shake up formal comparisons" (121). Next the author critically compares the interior processes of religious rituals with the corresponding processes of their secular counterparts. He starts with a benchmark first suggested by Turner: "tribal ritual framed both the serious and the playful... Today, people divide their lives into on-the-job time and leisure or play time, and the residue of liminal ritual activity, he [Turner] says, is located in our playing" (124). Leisure offers time for autotelic activities that enable the modern *homo ludens*, too, to achieve a state of self-transcendence—actually characteristic of religious experiences. But Turner's question remains: "Are all 'flows' one and do the symbols indicate different kinds of depths and flow?" (131). By dint of writings by Giamatti, Becker, and Rahner, the author finally arrives at the conclusion: "Through participation, we discover in ourselves substantially different types of flow and levels of meaning—from being a sports fan, to serious creative activity, to playing in an ultimately mysterious cosmic game whose rules are unknown" (131). [Florian Jeserich/JK]

References: E. Becker, W. Burkert, E. Cassirer, M. Csikszentmihalyi, H. Frankfort, A.B. Giamatti, W. James, B.G. Myerhoff, H. Rahner, J.Z. Smith, V.W. Turner.
Examples: Ancient Greek ceremonies, entertainment and sport events.
Key-words: cpr, exp, frm, med, mng, myt, SEC, spc, sym, tim.

Goffman, Erving, 1967, *Interaction Ritual. Essays in Face-to-Face Behavior*; Garden City (NY): Anchor Books / Doubleday (ISBN 0–385–08850–7) (270).

In this book, the author introduces a new field of research, namely the study of face-to-face interaction. He concentrates on "that class of events which occurs during co-presence and by virtue of co-presence" and studies "the glances, gestures, positionings, and verbal statements that people continuously feed into the situation, whether intended or not" (1). His aim is "to identify the countless patterns and natural sequences of behavior occurring whenever persons come into one another's immediate presence" (2). Therefore, the author advocates a "sociology of occasions", i.e.: "Social organization is the central theme, but what is organized is the co-mingling of persons and the temporary interactional enterprises that can arise therefrom" (2). He assumes that "the proper study of interaction is not the individual and his psychology, but rather the syntactical relations among the acts of different persons mutually present to one another" (2). Whereas all six chapter of this book deal with the social organization of spoken contact, only the first chapter, "On Face-Work" (5–45), specifically addresses the ritual elements of social interaction. By 'face-work' the author means "to designate the actions taken by a person to make whatever he is doing consistent with face. Face-work serves to counteract 'incidents'—that is, events whose effective symbolic implications threaten face" (12). In this context, the author uses the term 'ritual' because he deals "with acts through whose symbolic component the actor shows how worthy he is of respect or how worthy he feels others are of it" (19). Moreover, the author states: "One's face, then, is a sacred thing, and the expressive order required to sustain it is therefore a ritual one" (19). Here he introduces the notion of 'interchange' as "[t]he sequence of acts set in motion by an acknowledged threat to face, and terminating in the re-establishment of ritual equilibrium" (19), because it seems "to be a basic concrete unit of social activity and provides one natural empirical way to study interaction of all kinds" (20). As a model for interpersonal ritual behavior, the author uses such forms of interchange as challenge, offering, acceptance, and thanks (22). On this basis, he discusses the various forms and uses of face-work (24–31) and distinguishes between different ritual roles of the self (31–33). Moreover, he addresses spoken interaction (33–40) and social relationships and introduces the notions of ritual code and ritual order as tools for describing the face-to-face interaction and its consequences for social organization (42–45). [JK]

References: **G. Bateson** (+), P. Bourdieu, **G.H. Mead** (+), M. Mead, G. Simmel.
Reviews: E. Tiryakian *ASR* 33.1–6 (1968) 462; E.E. Jones *CP* 13.12 (1968) 622; B.N. Meltzer *SF* 47.1 (1968) 110; E. Hughes *AJS* 75.1–6 (1969/70) 425; M. Chastaing et al. *JPNP* 66.4 (1969) 473; F.L. Strodtbeck *AJS* 76.1–6 (1970/71) 177; M.N. Smith *SEA* 7.1 (1973) 63.
Key-words: aut, COM, dfr, emo, ETH, gst, idn, med, mng, par, pmc, PR1, psy, rel, rfl, rht, sec, SEM, soc.

Goffman, Erving, 1974, *Frame Analysis. An Essay on the Organization of Experience* (Harper Colophon Books); New York etc.: Harper & Row (SBN 06–090372–4) (xiv + 586) (with index).

This book is not on ritual theory, yet the theory developed in it is very much applicable to ritual, as the author also signals. Therefore, although only about one page (58) is devoted to "Ceremonials", it is included in this bibliography. The author first discusses the literature on which he is building (William James, Alfred Schutz and Gregory Bateson). He then declares: "My aim is to try to isolate some of the basic frameworks of understanding available in our society for making sense out of events... I start with the fact that from an individual's particular point of view, while one thing may momentarily appear to be what is really going on, in fact what is actually happening is plainly a joke, or a dream,... or a theatrical performance, and so forth" (10). In the second chapter, the concept of 'primary frameworks' is introduced, which are "seen by those who apply it as not depending on or harking back to some prior or 'original' interpretation; indeed a primary framework is one that is seen as rendering what would otherwise be a meaningless aspect of the scene into something that is meaningful" (21). There are "two broad classes of primary frameworks: natural and social. Natural frameworks identify occurrences seen as... 'purely physical'.... Social frameworks, on the other hand, provide background understanding for events that incorporate the will, aim, and controlling effort of an intelligence, a living agency, the chief one being the human being" (22). "Taken all together, the primary frameworks of a particular social group constitute a central element of its culture, especially insofar as understandings emerge concerning principal classes of schemata, the relations of these classes to one another, and the sum total of forces and agents that these interpretive designs acknowledge to be loose in the world" (27). In the third chapter the concepts 'key' and 'keying' are introduced. It takes its start in Bateson's observation "that otters not only fight with each other but also play at fighting" (40). This transformation of the primary framework 'fighting' into the derived framework 'playing' is what the author calls 'keying': "By keeping in mind these comments on animal play, one can easily turn to a central concept in frame analysis: the key. I refer here to the set of conventions by which a given activity, one already meaningful in terms of some primary framework, is transformed into something patterned on this activity but seen by the participants to be something quite else. The process of transcription can be called keying" (43–44). This, then, leads to the author's "full definition of keying", which students of rituals will recognise at once as highly relevant for rituals: "a. A systematic transformation is involved.... b. Participants in the activity are meant to know and to openly acknowledge that a systematic alteration is involved, one that will radically reconstitute what it is for them that is going on. c. Cues will be available for establishing when the transformation is to begin and when it is to end, namely, brackets in time, within which and to which the transformation is to be restricted. Similarly, spatial brackets will commonly indicate everywhere within which and nowhere outside of which the keying applies on that occasion.... e.... the systematic transformation that a particular keying introduces may alter only slightly the activity thus transformed, but it utterly changes what it is a participant would say was going on.... A keying, then, when there is one, performs a crucial role in determining what it is we think is really going on" (45). Then the author reviews "some of the basic keys employed in our society...: make-believe, contests, ceremonials, technical redoings, and regroundings" (48). In chapter four, the other possible form of transformation of frameworks is introduced: fabrication. This is defined as "the intentional effort of one or more individuals to manage activity so that a party of one or more others will be induced to have a false belief about what it is that is going on" (83). The rest of the book is mainly filled with examples and philosophical discussions of such questions as what, in the end, is real (a picture of a staged play enacting a kiss is a real picture of a real staged play enacting a real kiss, but the enacted kiss is not a real kiss, and the picture is neither a real kiss, nor a real play. Etc.). [JS]

References: W. James, A. Schutz, G. Bateson.
Reviews: G. Swanson *AAPSS* 420 (1975) 218; M.S. Davis *CS* 4.6 (1975) 599; W.A. Gamson *CS* 4.6 (1975) 603; E. Weinstein *CP* 21.5 (1976) 332; D. Jary *SR* 24.4 (1976) 917; **J. Ditton & W.W. Sharrock *Sociol* 10.2 (1976) 329–334; Anon. *T&S* 3 (1976) 119–133; I. Craib *PSS* 8.1 (1978) 79–86**; E.M. Adams *PPR* 39.4 (1979) 601 f; N.K. Denzin & **C.M. Keller *CS* 10.1 (1981) 52–60**; J. d'Amato *RA* 20.3 (1991) 149; F. Melard *RS* 23.2 (1992) 133–135; M. Dartevelle *SocTrav* 35.1 (1993) 122–125.
Key-words: com, pmc, tha, sem, mng, str, FRM, eff, spc, tim, soc.

Goody, Jack, 1977, 'Against "Ritual". Loosely Structured Thoughts on a Loosely Defined Topic', in: Sally Falk Moore & Barbara G. Myerhoff (eds), *Secular Ritual*, Assen, Amsterdam: Van Gorcum (ISBN 90-232-1457-9) (*) 25–35.

On the author's view, a "whole set of terms used in the anthropological discussion of the area generally referred to as 'religion' are virtually useless for analytic purposes and have done little but confuse the attempt to understand human behaviour" (25). In particular, this statement applies to general terms like 'magic', 'myth', and, above all, 'ritual'. The author notes two reasons for their uselessness: "In the first place, the terms are vagueness itself.... In the second place, these terms often accept, implicitly or explicitly, a dichotomous view of the world" (25). Referring to the concept of 'secular rituals', the author finds that "neither the dichotomy of religious/secular nor that of ritual or non-ritual carry much analytical weight" (28). Instead, he reminds the reader: "'Routinisation', regularisation, repetition, lie at the basis of social life itself" (28). An analytical system that cannot discriminate between different sorts of performances "is wasting our time by trivialising the study of social behavior" (29). On the one hand, the formal and repetitive character of 'ritual' leads to the assumption of eufunctional continuity (system-maintenance, group-maintenance, etc.). On the other hand, it creates "culture lag and loss of meaning" (30). Thus, while a ceremony "will repeat the physical and verbal acts associated with the earlier ceremony", "the social situation may have changed, and...the meaning will certainly have done" (30). Thus, the author suggests, "it is misleading to assert that 'rituals' provide a key to deep values more than any other type of human behaviour. Indeed, I would be tempted to argue that they conceivably provide less of a clue, . . . [for] their formality, the element of culture lag, the component of public demonstration, their role as masks of the 'true' self" (32). In the last section, since the author is "against 'ritual'", he suggests "a way out" (33). First of all, "as an opening gambit, we can attempt to translate the term ritual each time it is used" (33). Secondly, he suggests that "the structure of the ceremony, the order in which such behaviours are put together, requires particular attention" (34). This implies "the possibility of quantification" (34). Thirdly, in "the area of meaning and exegesis", there is still "a very long way to go" because everybody accepts "types of explanation and evidence for other cultures that we would not accept for our own" (34). Finally, "the function of 'ritual' can be better elucidated under changing rather than static conditions" (34). [MS]

References: R. Bocock (–), V.W. Turner (+/–), R.A. Rappaport.
Key-words: gen, mng, str, myt.

Gossen, Gary H., 1978, 'Language as Ritual Substance', in: William John Samarin (ed.), *Language in Religious Practice*, (Series in Sociolinguistics), Rowley (MA): Newbury House Publishers, Inc. (ISBN 0–88377–059–8) 40–60.

According to the author, ritual action consists of "a complex mesh of critical information rendered in several different codes at once. Some of these codes are linguistic, other nonlinguistic" (41). Therefore, he analyzes the formal language code in ritual behavior of the Chamula, a Tzotzil-speaking Mayan community in South Mexico, while recognizing the nonlinguistic and the linguistic features of their ritual language. Since the formal language of the Chamula must be present for proper interaction with the supernatural world, the author deals with this language as a ritual symbol. With Turner, he distinguishes between three different levels of ritual symbolism and organizes his essay according to these three levels. Thus, in the section on the exegetical, he deals with what the Chamulas say about their ritual language, in the second section, on operational meaning, he interprets his observations of what Chamulas do with their ritual language, and in the section of positional meaning of ritual language he asks how the ritual language fits into the whole of Chamulan life and ritual symbolism. The author is concerned with the linguistic and nonlinguistic features because he assumes that formal aspects of ritual language, including the behavioral and verbal code, provide the rituals with important substance. Thus, he regards "language as a ritual substance which shares messages with the actions and other ritual substances present in the same setting" (41). And: "In these shared ritual messages—stated in different codes—we may hope to find some crystals of essential information about the Chamula cosmos and social universe" (41). [JK]

References: J.J. Fox, **E.R. Leach** (+), **V.W. Turner** (+).
Key-words: lan, mng, sem, str, sym.

Grainger, Roger, 1974, *The Language of the Rite*; London: Darton, Longman & Todd (ISBN 0-232-51246-9) (xii + 179).

In his book, the author assumes that the rite, as a religious aspiration, is a special kind of language for speaking about god and men and the difference between them. According to him, the rite is necessary for the experience of communion that corresponds to a basic human need for a kind of self-expression and communication by including the whole person and the presence of others in the corporate awareness of a ritual. For the author, ritual is a structure that employs a certain number of fixed actions, each of which transmits a single meaning. "The rite is a structure.... Change the actions, or the order of the actions, and the rite's meaning is completely changed" (x). Since the structure of corporate rituals inhabits or introduces relationships between persons, ritual is concerned with community and the tension between individuals: "The structure of the rite allows the interaction of persons who are both interdependent and independent, and neither isolated nor confused" (xi). According to the author, freedom and spontaneity in ritual emerge from its very structure. Because of their timelessness and usefulness, he defines the function of such ordinary public rituals of the church as baptism, wedding, and funeral as follows: "Religious rites, being both dignified and traditional, present themselves as specifically appropriate for the purpose of establishing the personal by affording it public recognition. Thus religion lends public dignity to private occasions. It performs a useful service in setting up land-marks and establishing boundaries" (3). But for him religious rites are more than that: "These ordinary ceremonies of the church are able to change reality in a special way, a way that defies analysis. They are concerned, not to describe reality, but to expand it beyond description" (4). While arguing against Durkheim, the author assumes that the religious ritual can only be explained in its own terms since it is—because of its logic, structure and referents—an initiation into new possibilities. [JK/JS]

References: L. Bouyer, M. Douglas, É. Durkheim (–), M. Eliade, S. Freud, A. van Gennep, M. Gluckman, C. Lévi-Strauss, W. Robertson Smith.
Examples: Initiation, Eucharist, liturgy, theatre.
Review: Anon. *HS* 18.1 (1977) 103.
Key-words: com, dyn, lan, mng, str, sym.

Greenfield, Sidney M., 2005, 'Trance States and Accessing Implicit Memories. A Psychosocial Genomic Approach to Reconstituting Social Memory during Religious Rituals', ***Current Sociology*** **53:275–291.**

The author argues that in expanding religions of the non-Western world (1) there is a pervasiveness of trance states and other altered states of consciousness "that facilitates (2) direct communication with... the supernatural, which is (3) enlisted to provide help with practical problems" (279) and that there is "a relationship between this expanding constellation of religious attributes and the pervasive effort by peoples across the globe to recreate seemingly lost social pasts" (279). To elucidate that relationship the author summarizes findings from the neuroscience of learning and memory and reviews the distinction of different types of learning (conscious/explicit vs. non-declarative/implicit learning). He suggests that since "so much of human learning is acquired under conditions that encode emotional responses... many aspects of cultural behavior are state dependent" (283). Turning to studies of hypnosis and the basic 90- to 120-minutes rest-activity cycle (BRAC), the author holds that "[w]hile engaging in (religious) rituals that last more than one and a half to two hours (one BRAC cycle) and encouraged to go in trance, they [= people who have been displaced from the lands of their ancestors and now find themselves on the periphery] find, especially if they are actively wishing to reconstruct their social pasts, that in response to probes suggested by leaders who understand their plight, they may in fact be able to move into conscious memory aspects of long forgotten (cultural) learning" (288). [MS]

Examples: Various unspecific.
Key-words: psy, tra, pr2, emo.

Grimes, Ronald L., 1982, *Beginnings in Ritual Studies*; Lanham (MD): University Press of America (ISBN 0–8191–2210–6 / 0–8191–2211–4 (p)) (xix + 292) (with bibliography).
2nd (revised) ed.: 1995, Columbia (SC): University of South Carolina Press (ISBN-10: 1–57003–001–4, ISBN-13: 978–1–57003–001–7) (xxviii + 299).

The author announces that the essays contained in this volume "are forays into various disciplines in search of a methodology and properly defined field of ritual studies. They do not so much reflect the state of an already existing field as they constitute tentative proposals for the consolidation of one" (xii). But he approaches rituals from a particular theoretical position when he claims that students of ritual "have in common an interest in performative phenomena...in short, people and animals as they enact and embody meanings.... Ritual studies pays its fullest attention to the performative, non-verbal elements of action" (xii–xiii). The book has four parts. The first, "The Ritual Field" (1–69), "is about the hermeneutics of ritual action" (xix), about how difficult interpreting ritual is. It consists of four chapters. The first (1–17) "is an autobiographical narrative about the search for a style of studying rituals" (xix). The second, "Mapping the Field of Ritual" (19–33), provides a set of categories and questions meant to help to improve descriptions of rituals. These categories include ritual space, ritual objects, ritual time, ritual sound and language, ritual identity, and ritual action. In the final section, the author sketches a number of theoretical options in order to arrive at interpretations of rituals (32–33). In Chapter 3, "Modes of Ritual Sensibility" (35–51), the author distinguishes between six modes of ritual sensibility, which are then briefly described: ritualization, decorum, ceremony, liturgy, magic, and celebration. Chapter 4, "Defining Nascent Ritual" (53–69), comments on the following "'soft' definition for 'ritualizing', the process whereby ritual creativity is exercised: Ritualizing transpires as animated persons enact formative gestures in the face of receptivity during crucial times in founded places" (55). The second part of the book, "Ritual Process" (71–113), aims to "avoid summarizing or criticizing the discussions about ritual processes in order to illustrate some of the processes themselves" (73). These include masking, sitting, and eating. The third part, "Theories of Ritual" (115–159), has one chapter on the theories of Gotthard Booth (a psychiatrist and physician), and one on Theodor Gaster and Victor Turner. The former is significant in that Booth is not the usual author selected to represent the psychological approach; the latter, in that it not only gives summaries of the approaches of the two authors but also compares the two. Besides, both chapters are supplemented with sections that critically discuss the positions of the authors presented. These discussions show, however, that the aim of this part of the book is apparently not to present theorizing rituals for its own sake but to illustrate which contribution it may make to ritual studies generally. The last (and by far the largest) part of the book, "Ritual and Theatre" (161–266), mainly reports about the author's fieldwork on performance-oriented activities, which range from predominantly theatrical to predominantly ritual. It is clear, then, that performance theory is the predominant theoretical approach of the author. Finally, the "Afterword" (267–270) discusses the position of ritual studies to theology. [JS/MS]

References: G. Booth, Th. Gaster, V.W. Turner.
Reviews: R.A. Delattre *JAAR* 51.3 (1983) 528 f; W. Norman *SA* 44.3 (1983) 261 f; J.C. Rochelle *Zygon* 18.3 (1983) 338; **T. Frankiel *Rel* 31.1 (2001) 75–87.**
Key-words: pmc, THA, mng, sym, str, myt, DEF, emb.

Grimes, Ronald L., 1985, 'Victor Turner's Social Drama and T.S. Eliot's Ritual Drama', *Anthropologica. Journal of the Canadian Anthropology Society* N.S. 27:79–99 (with bibliography).
Republished as Chapter 8, 'Drama and Ritual Criticism', in R.L. Grimes: *Ritual Criticism. Case Studies in Its Practice, Essays on Its Theory*, Columbia 1990 (*).

"This article 'intertextualizes' a case study by Victor Turner with a play by T.S. Eliot . . . The case study [Chapter 2 in V.W. Turner 1974a (*)] . . . brings Turner's theory of social drama to bear on the confrontation between Archbishop Thomas Becket and King Henry II of England in 1170 A.D. The play [Murder in the Cathedral] is a ritual drama published by Eliot in 1935 for a commemoration of Becket's martyrdom" (79). "The reason for this comparison is to show how a theologically-based play and a theoretically-grounded analysis can imply mutual criticisms and refinements" (79–80). After an introduction follow a presentation of "Turner's Theory of Social Drama" (80–83), and analyses of "Turner's Interpretation of Becket's Social Drama" (83–85) and "T.S. Eliot's Ritual Drama" (85–91). In the last section, "Comparing a Ritual Drama and a Social Drama" (91–97), the author first plots and explains a diagram with two crossing axes at which ends "Framed (Bounded)" opposes "Unframed" and "Ritual" opposes "Drama", creating four quadrants, representing the combinations: "1 Rites" (framed ritual), "2 Plays" (framed drama), "3 Social Drama" (unframed drama), and "4 Interaction Ritual" (unframed ritual) (92). Comparing, and playing the two texts (resp. their authors, 96) off against each other then leads the author to the formulation of a number of critical statements, such as: "Eliot's drama... is not strong on narrative. Similarly, Turner's treatment of Becket contains too much narration and too little analysis for anthropologists with nomothetic goals in mind" (94), "If we allow the play to question the theory, and do not merely apply the theory to the play, we are forced to ask Turner whether it is adequate: (1) to consider either narrative or social drama as only linear; and (2) to claim that all rituals have a dramatic plot. Eliot's play helps us notice the static, circular side of Turner's interpretation. Although Eliot's play is dramatic, it makes minimum use of plot, thus calling into question Turner's treatment of all rites as narratively structured" (95–96) or "The paradigm which Turner locates historically in actors' heads can just as well be located in the Mass, in yearly Canterbury Festivals, or even in Turner's head" (96). [JS]

References: V.W. Turner, T.S. Eliot.
Examples: The two mentioned texts of V.W. Turner and T.S. Eliot.

Grimes, Ronald L., 1988a, 'Infelicitous Performances and Ritual Criticism', *Semeia* 43:103–122.

By using speech act theory as a basis for ritual criticism, the author argues that the typology of performances is applicable to various examples of 'infelicitous' ritual, since they can fail to do what participants intend them to do: "The reasons for putting speech act theory to this use are simple: (1) some of the examples used by Austin are ritualistic and (2) ritual contexts, more than any other, make use of what he calls performative utterance, that is, speech insofar as it accomplishes tasks rather than merely describing them" (104). His hypothesis is that "Austin's typology is applicable not only to things said in ritual contexts but also to things done in them, especially if the things done seem to go awry" (104). Although for the author Austin's typology is applicable to ritual as a 'performative phenomenon', it cannot explain every sort of ritual action, because rituals are more complex than speech acts. After he defines ritual as a convergence of several kinds of action, which can include various other genres, the author gives a short outline of speech act theory and its application in the performative approaches of Tambiah, Finnegan, and Ray. Arguing for the usefulness of applying the typology of "infelicitous" speech acts to ritual performance, the author gives a typology that distinguishes between nine types of infelicitous performance, i.e. misfire, abuse, ineffectuality, violation, contagion, opacity, defeat, omission, and misframe. Thus, he argues that making judgments about ritual is necessary from the participants' and from the observer's point of view. According to the author, one has also to distinguish between different kinds of failure in and of ritual. Since rituals are complex phenomena, the author argues that they seldom fail in all phases and on all levels, for different rituals might fail in different ways and at different levels. By suggesting a typology of failed performances, the author tries to show that ritual criticism has to take account of the dynamics of ritual failure by acknowledging various kinds of non-verbal gestures and different genres of ritual action. He concludes: "Analyzing ritual failure involves more than defining terms, supplying examples, or applying labels. But learning to do so is a first step toward a useful ritual criticism" (120). [JK]

References: J.L. Austin (+), R.H. Finnegan (–), C. Geertz (+), R. Girard (+), E. Goffman, B. Ray (–), J.R. Searle (+), S.J. Tambiah (+/–).
Key-words: com, dyn, PMC, pmt, rfl.

Grimes, Ronald L., 1988b, 'Ritual Criticism and Reflexivity in Fieldwork', *Journal of Ritual Studies* 2.2:217–239.

This article is about ritual criticism as an act of making judgments about rites. The aim of this paper is to reflect upon the problems of critical judgments outside the context of one's own traditions as encountered in the situation of fieldwork: "Part of the work of ritual criticism is reflecting on the ways both participants and observers decide that one way of doing a rite is more effective or appropriate than some other way" (217). Thus, the author argues that ritual traditions involve the exercise of critical judgment and there is no reason for a scholar to avoid it. Since ritual criticism is inherently value-laden, it is "a kind of cultural critique" (218). The critic's task is defined as follows: "The criticism of ritual ought to mediate between the theory and practice of it. And theorizing about ritual ought to be rooted in field study" (219). This means: "Ritual criticism is the activity of exercising judgement about a rite or some aspect of it. More precisely, it is the act of identifying and articulating the grounds—usually multiple and conflict laden—for evaluating them. Unlike ritual theories which aim to explain rites, ritual criticism may change, improve, establish, or disestablish them. Ritual criticism makes overt the 'interestedness' of enacting and interpreting rites. So it is not merely esthetic; it is also ethical and political" (220). According to the author, ritual criticism is neither ethnography nor literary criticism although it has some features in common with both; ritual criticism is involved with observation, participation, documentation as well as judgments about the adequacy, authenticity, and effectiveness of performances. In the final section (231–236), the author gives some principles which guide ritual criticism. [JK/MS]

References: T. Asad, K. Burke, T.F. Driver, Th.W. Jennings Jr. (+), R. Schechner (+).
Key-words: cmp, pmc, eff, aut, par, rep, RFL, exp.

Grimes, Ronald L., 1990, *Ritual Criticism. Case Studies in Its Practice, Essays on Its Theory* (Studies in Comparative Religion [10]); Columbia (SC): University of South Carolina Press (ISBN 0–87249–692–9) (xiii + 270) (with index and bibliography).

"The aim of this book is to demonstrate the complementarity of ritual and criticism. We shall explore case studies in which ritual and criticism require one another. Then we shall reflect on ways this mutuality alters conceptions of both ritual and criticism" (1). "The goal is... to explore styles of participant observation that can inform assessments of rites" (2). In this book, the author assumes different identities as a "scholar, critic, fieldworker, teacher, maker of rites" (3). The author argues in favor of a "circular and simultaneous" case/theory relation. The book "does not culminate in a theory, if by 'theory' one means a generalized, unified statement, subject to verification, about the causes, covariances, or other consistent relations that obtain between two items or processes observed. Rather, the cases eventuate in essays... to reflect at an order of generalization higher than that of the particular case" (4). In the first chapter, "The Ritual and Cultural Contexts of Ritual Criticism" (7–27), the author provides a number of definitions: "the term 'rite'... denotes specific enactments located in concrete times and places.... They are the actions enacted by 'ritualists' and observed and studied by 'ritologists'. The term 'rite'... refers to a set of actions widely recognized by members of a culture. Rites are differentiated... from ordinary behavior" (9). "A rite is often part of some larger whole, a ritual system or ritual tradition that includes other rites as well" (10). "'Ritual'... refers here to the general idea of which a rite is a specific instance. As such, 'ritual' does not exist, even though it is what we must try to define; ritual is an idea scholars formulate. Strictly speaking then, one would not refer to 'a' ritual or to 'rituals' but to 'ritual' and to 'a rite' or 'rites'. Ritual is what one defines in formal definitions and characterizations; rites are what people enact" (10). "The word 'ritualizing' refers to the act of deliberately cultivating rites" (10). It also refers to "the act of ... inventing rites. Ritualizing is not often socially supported. Rather, it happens in the margins" (10). "'Ritualization' ... refers to activity that is not culturally framed as ritual but which someone, often an observer, interprets as if it were potential ritual. One might think of it as infra-, quasi-, or pre-ritualistic.... Ritualization includes processes that fall below the threshold of social recognition as rites" (10). In other words, the author suggests the strategy of "dividing ritual into a 'hard', discrete sense (rites), on the one hand, and a 'soft', metaphoric sense (ritualization), on the other" (11). Subsequently, the author criticizes and rejects V.W. Turner's influential definition of 'ritual' (12–13), and he suggests identifying the 'family characteristics' of rituals (13). He provides "a list of the qualities scholars find in ritual action" as the "indicators that begin to appear when action moves in the direction of ritual" (13). He draws a chart of 15 clusters of markers that are generally held to be qualities of ritual (14). "When these qualities begin to multiply, when an activity becomes dense with them, it becomes increasingly proper to speak of it as ritualized, if not a rite as such" (14). In the next section, the author discusses the nature of criticism (15–18) and proposes the following definition: "*Ritual criticism is the interpretation of a rite or ritual system with a view to implicating its practice*" (16). "Ritual criticism is value-laden, but not merely personal" (16). "At its best it is reflexive, that is, self-critical" (17). It "goes on informally all the time, and its contexts are various—both popular and scholarly" (17). "In addition to ritualists' criticism *of* their own and other people's rites, there is criticism *by* rites" (17). Furthermore, the author discusses the practical context of ritual criticism (17–20; e.g. ritual contests, tourism, evaluative consultation) and the cultural context of ritual criticism (20–27). Here, he stresses that "the image of ritual has undergone dramatic shifts during this century" in North American religion and art (21). The author goes on to discuss Nietzsche's *Birth of Tragedy* that Ranier Friedrich had called 'the birth of ritual theory' (22). This leads him to take a brief look at postmodernism (sketching 19 points of comparison between the modern and postmodern eras). The chapter concludes: "The postmodern ethos generates a climate that encourages experimentation with the *rites* of others and thus precipitates questions about the *rights* of others: the ritual issue leads to an ethical one" (27). Chapters 2–6 are a diverse group of case studies. Chapters 7–9 take up more theoretical matters. Chapter 7, "Narrative and Ritual Criticism" (158–173), presents a critique of narrative theology and shows "(1) that it makes just as good sense to claim that the self is performatively constituted, (2) that storytelling is as akin to ritual enactment as it is to ethical behavior, (3) that time has no more privileged status than space, and (4) that narratively inspired reflection is as much a problem as it is a virtue" (160). Chapter 8, "Drama and Ritual Criticism" (174–190) (*), "puts Victor Tuner's theory of social drama in conversation with a dramatic text, T. S. Eliot's *Murder in the Cathedral*" (5) and compares Turner's and Eliot's treatment of drama (see Table 8.3. [187]). Chapter 9, "Infelicitous Performances and Ritual Criticism" (191–209) (*), reviews the application of speech act theory in ritual studies (195–198) and explores the applicability of J.L. Austin's typology of 'infelicitous performances' to examples of troublesome ritual. In doing so, the author distinguishes 9 types of infelicitous performances. These are (1) misfire (act purported but void), (2) abuse (act professed but hollow), (3) ineffectuality (act fails to precipitate anticipated empirical change), (4) violation (act effective but demeaning), (5) contagion (act leaps beyond proper boundaries), (6) opacity (act unrecognizable or unintelligible), (7) defeat (act discredits or invalidates acts of others), (8) omission (act not performed), (9) misframe (genre of act misconstrued) (204–205). The final chapter, "The Scholarly Contexts and Practices of Ritual Criticism" (210–233), first discusses practices analogous to 'ritual criticism', such as criticism in literature, theater, anthropology, liturgical theology, and religious studies (210–218). In a reflexive turn, the author then presents a criticism of (a) piece(s) of ritual criticism that he himself had written previously (218–232) and some concluding remarks (232–233). [MS/JS]

References: A. van Gennep, C. Geertz, E. Goffman, **R. Schechner, V.W. Turner.**
Examples: North American urban rituals; Christian liturgy; shamanism.
Reviews: E. Bourguignon *JSSR* 30.3 (1991) 343 f; S.G. Wieting *SA* 52.2 (1991) 214 f; B. Lex *AA* 94.1 (1992) 195; E. Badone *StudRel* 21.1 (1992) 98 f.
Key-words: pmc, THA, com, pmt, idn, eff, rep, par, rht, med, RFL, DEF.

Grimes, Ronald L., 1999, 'Jonathan Z. Smith's Theory of Ritual Space', *Religion* 29:261–273.

This essay offers a critique of J.Z. Smith 1980 (*) and 1987a (*). Among other things, the author rejects Smith's emphasis on place as a "reduction of a multidimensional phenomenon to a single, key dimension that presumably explains the whole" (267). Moreover, Smith "seems to prefer the metaphorical, social and intellectual aspect of this dimension to the literal and geographical aspects of it" (267). Furthermore, the author rejects all the reasons Smith provides for assigning an exalted position to place in his general ritual theory (268–269). He argues that "hyper-spatialising ritual theory has...the unwanted consequence of making ritual more static than it really is" (269) and states: "Ritual theory should be historically and socially grounded..." (269). Next, the author provides a summary of Smith's seven major theses and compares them with an alternative, multi-dimensional theory (269–270), followed by some reflections on different theoretical genealogies (Durkheim and Eliade vs. V.W. Turner and Van Gennep) and he exhorts the reader that "[t]he construction of theories requires attention to the metaphors that ground those theories" (270). In the final paragraph, the author states the aim of his article as follows: "I would like to counteract the tendency in ritual studies for theorists to talk past one another, or worse, never to engage one another's ideas either in public or in print" (271). [MS]

Reference: J.Z. Smith.
Key-word: SPC.

Grimes, Ronald L., 2000, 'Ritual', in: Willi Braun & Russell T. McCutcheon (eds), *Guide to the Study of Religion*, London: Cassell (ISBN 0-304-70175-0 / 0-304-70176-9 (p)) 259–270.

In the first section on "The Notion of Ritual" (252–262) the author reflects on a number of terminological issues. The second section (262–263) provides some glimpses into the history of the study of ritual. In the third section the author takes a closer (and critical) look at V.W. Turner as "An Exemplary Ritual Theorist" (263–267). In the fourth section (267–269) the author puts forward some suggestions on the future of ritual practice and the study of ritual in general. [MS]

References: R.A. Rappaport, S.J. Tambiah, **V.W. Turner**.
Key-word: GEN.

Grimes, Ronald L., 2002, 'Ritual and the Media', in: Stewart M. Hoover & Lynn Schofield Clark (eds), *Practicing Religion in the Age of the Media. Explorations in Media, Religion, and Culture*, New York: Columbia University Press (ISBN-10: 0-231-12088-5 / 0-231-12089-3 (p), ISBN-13: 978-0-231-12089-0 / 978-0-231-12088-3 (p)) 219–234.

In this essay, the author proposes a more differentiated view of the relationships between ritual and media. Today, says the author, most researchers oversimplify these relationships by either segregating ritual from media or equating the two. Reviewing the current literature on ritual and media and discussing definitions of 'ritual' for use in media research, he suggests that "performance-oriented theories offer the most provocative approaches to the interface of ritual and media. If performance is, as Richard Schechner describes it, the 'showing of a doing' or 'twice-behaved behaviour', ritual and media are species of performance having much to do with one another" (230). By asking performance-oriented questions like 'Who are the actors?', 'What constitutes on-stage and off-stage?', 'Where is the audience?', and 'What scripts dictate the performance?', the author presents a list of some of the different directions in which a study of the relationships between ritual and media could develop: 1. the media presentation of a rite; 2. a ritual event extended by media; 3. ritual actions in virtual space; 4. subjunctive/'ludic' ritualizing; 5. magical rite with media device as 'fetish'/'icon'; 6. ritualized behaviour toward electronic objects; 7. a media-delivered ritual object; 8. a media document as a certificate of ritual act; 9. ritual use of media device; 10. mediated ritual fantasy; 11. media as model for, or butt of, ritual activity. He concludes his essay by arguing that "[i]f nothing else, performance theories keep us from forgetting the obvious. They call attention to the surfaces upon which we humans inscribe meaning and on the basis of which we act" (230). [Thorsten Gieser/JS]

References: B.Ch. Alexander, V. Crapanzano, R. Schechner, J.Z. Smith.
Key-words: def, PMC, MED, vir.

Grimes, Ronald L., 2003, 'Ritual Theory and the Environment', *The Sociological Review* 51:31–45.

"Few people consider rites an effective means for saving the planet from environmental destruction" (31), but at the same time "we are witnessing the emergence of groups and individuals who consider it obvious that ritual is one, if not the, answer to the environmental conundrum" (31). Hence, the author surveys different theories of ritual in order to elucidate what ritual theory can say about the question of whether rituals are actually good for the environment. As few theories "accommodate the facts of ritual change, ritual innovation, and ritual performance" (34), he finds most theories of rituals ill equipped "to make sense of environmental ritualizing" (34). At the same time, he finds that "[t]he foundation for an ecologically relevant theory of ritual has already been partly laid" (36) in Huxley's ideas of ritualization and biogenetic structuralism. He regards the latter as "a major, provocative theory of ritual" (38), but also voices "two reservations about it" (38). The next part of the paper is a detailed discussion of Rappaport's theory (39–43). Apart from comparing Rappaport's use of the notion of performance with that of Schechner and Turner (40), he points to what he perceives as "a stunning paradox at the heart of Rappaport's sweeping vision" (41). He regards the outcome of Rappaport's theory as "an ironically sacral anthropology that has many features of a theology" (42). "The difference between Rappaport and me is that he believes he is describing 'the obvious aspects of ritual' whereas I believe he is prescribing long shots" (42). In the concluding paragraph, the author states his own credo: "For me, religious ritual is the predication of identities and differences (metaphors) so profoundly enacted that they suffuse bone and blood, thereby generating a cosmos (an oriented habitat).... This is the noetic, or even divinatory, function of ritual; ritual helps people figure out, divine, even construct a cosmos" (44). Furthermore, "neither ritual theories nor ritual systems are free of the obligation to serve the ground we walk on, the water we drink, the air we breathe. Like Rappaport, I am speaking about what rites ought or might do" (44). [MS]

References: S.J. Tambiah (−), R. Schechner, J.S. Huxley (+), Ch.D. Laughlin & E.G. d'Aquili (+/−), R.A. Rappaport (−).
Key-words: def, pmc, dyn, EFF, ECL.

Grimes, Ronald L., 2004, 'Performance Theory and the Study of Ritual', in: Peter Antes, Armin W. Geertz & Randi R. Warne (eds), *New Approaches to the Study of Religion. Volume 2: Textual, Comparative, Sociological, and Cognitive Approaches*, Berlin, New York: Walter de Gruyter 109–138.

In the first section ("The Emergence of Cultural Performance as a Category") the author briefly considers the approaches of M. Singer and C. Geertz (109–111). The second section ("The Performative Convergence") presents and discusses the contributions to performance theory by E. Goffman (112–113), V.W. Turner (113–116), and R. Schechner (116–121). The third section ("The Critical Turn") discusses the critiques of performance theories in the 1990s (121–136). The bulk of this section is devoted to a critique of C. Bell's theory. Some of the author's criticisms read as follows: "Bell's writing is replete with statements that sound like definitions even though she may intend them to be only descriptions" (123). "Although Bell is hesitant to define 'ritual' in a way that is cross-cultural or universal, she seems to have few such reservations about her own definition of 'ritualization'" (124). Moreover, he charges Bell with "conflation" (126), reification, and "circularity" (127). He criticizes Bell for an elimination of actors (127) and charges her with a misrecognition of performance (129). "She ignores the obvious fact that for Turner drama is both a source of ritual and a part of ritual, not merely an analog to it. She overlooks the fact that for me drama is less an analog to ritual than an object of study, which I compare to ritual" (130). However, he has more sympathy with Bell's approaches to performance in Bell 1997 (*) and Bell 1998 (*). He continues with a critical discussion of Bell's practice theory and her ideas about the body (131–135). While emphasizing several positive aspects of Bell's approach, he concludes: "But in the last analysis Bell does not avoid the traps she most wants to avoid: bifurcating and mediating, theorizing about ritual, positing functions and defining qualities of ritual, and constructing privileged positions for theorists themselves" (136). [MS]

References: C.M. Bell (–), C. Geertz, R. Schechner, V.W. Turner.
Key-words: PMC, pr1, emb.

Grimes, Ronald L., 2006, 'Performance', in: Jens Kreinath, Jan A.M. Snoek & Michael Stausberg (eds), *Theorizing Rituals. Vol. I: Issues, Topics, Approaches, Concepts*, (Numen Book Series 114–1), Leiden, Boston: Brill (ISBN-10: 90–04–15342–x, ISBN-13: 978–90–04–15342–4) 379–394.

Large-scale, secular cultures tend to segregate dramatic performance and ritual enactment into separate cultural domains, but there are important overlaps between them even in Westernized technocratic societies. These convergences are not mere residue left over from a primordial time when ritual and performance were supposedly one. Nor are these convergences the outcome of mere analogies—ritual perceived as if it were dramatic. The entanglement of ritual with performance

is substantial and ongoing. Theorists of ritual such as Erving Goffman, Victor Turner, and Richard Schechner have shown how society itself is performative and ritualistic. More recently, feminist and poststructural theorists such as Judith Butler have continued expanding the notion of performance, using the idea of performativity as a tool for exposing the constructedness of categories such as gender and race—both too easily construed as biological givens. In the future, theorists should take fuller account of both the constructedness and mediation of rites. [Ronald Grimes]
Key-word: PMC.

Gusfield, Joseph R. & Jerzy Michalowicz, 1984, 'Secular Symbolism. Studies in Ritual, Ceremony, and the Symbolic Order in Modern Life', *Annual Review of Sociology* 10:417–435 (with bibliography).

In this article, the work of more than 50 scholars is briefly reviewed. It aims to inform sociologists about (then) recent developments in the study of symbolism and rituals: "In the past two decades, and especially in the last few years, some sociologists and anthropologists have begun to examine a number of areas and activities in modern societies using approaches drawn from analyses of ritual, ceremony, and symbolism. In this paper, we review this kind of sociological studies in the hope of achieving a clearer understanding and some sense of direction to the use of symbolic analysis in contemporary sociology" (418). After an introduction (417–418), there follow sections on "Analyzing Symbols" (418–423), "Studies of the Institutional Order" (423–427), "Studies of Secular Ritual" (427–430), "Symbolism and Everyday Life" (430–432), "Methodological Issues" (433), a "Conclusion" (433), and the "Literature Cited" (434–435). Each of the sections is subdivided into several subsections, in which a number of authors is reviewed. The work of one of the authors (Gusfield) is mentioned in several subsections, thus positioning him implicitly within this field of research. [JS]
Key-words: SOC, SEC, SYM.

Hahn, Alois, 1977, 'Kultische und säkulare Riten und Zeremonien in soziologischer Sicht', in: Alois Hahn, *et al.* (eds), *Anthropologie des Kults. Die Bedeutung des Kults für das Überleben des Menschen*, (Veröffentlichungen der Stiftung Oratio Dominica), Freiburg, Basel, Wien: Herder (ISBN 3-451-17909-1) 51-81.
[Cultic and Secular Rites and Ceremonies from a Sociological Point of View]

In this article the author first tries to answer the question how to distinguish rituals (*Rituale*) from ceremonies (*Zeremonien*) by reviewing the definitions of several classical authors. Without at first giving definitions of either term, he does make statements about them, such as that rituals are actions, oriented at extra-empirically controlling a situation (60), that rituals are foremost a religious phenomenon (61), or that rituals are forms of action which presuppose an addressee which can be influenced (62). In the middle of the article, he summarizes as follows: "Rites (*Riten*)...are extra-empirical, repeated actions, which occur mainly there where a technical control of the circumstances for reaching emotion laden goals appear—also subjectively—impossible, so, in situations experienced as powerlessness. Furthermore...ritual actions are unlikely, when these uncontrollable circumstances are not combined with the assumption of a—no matter how weak or transient—intentionality" (65). That is then still complemented with the observation, that "rites are...directions for actions in such situations in which otherwise there is nothing one can do.... they bridge the situations which would otherwise remain without action" (67). Traditionally, rituals for dealing with situations which occur only once in the life of a person are provided by the community in which one lives, and for which they are not one time only phenomena (72), but in the last part of his paper (73-81) the author then explores how modern society, where this is no longer the case, solves that problem. Basically there is a limited number of options. Either the individual develops an *ad hoc* ritual for himself, which has the disadvantage that such individual rituals (*Individualriten*) are not recognized by one's society, or certain socially recognized professionals (such as psychiatrists) may take over (73). The current situation developed out of a shift in the understanding of nature during the Enlightenment, when rituals started to be regarded as irrational *per se* (75). Our assumption that nature is reliable, i.e. bound by laws, developed out of the theological assumption of its creation by a reliable God (77, 79). And the confirmation by the sciences that nature is reliable was at first their justification as an ideological, meaning giving system (80). When at the end of the 19th century the sciences lost this meaning giving function, they became more and more trivial (80), initiating a new era of re-mythologization and re-ritualization, even of the sciences themselves (81). [JS]

References: M. Douglas (–), N. Elias, J. Cazeneuve (+), B. Malinowski (+), É. Durkheim (+), R. Otto (+), M. Scheler (+), C. Geertz (+), F.H. Tenbruck (+), A. van Gennep, M. Foucault (+).
Example: Death rituals.
Key-words: def, sec, psy, dyn, emo, int.

Hamerton-Kelly, Robert G. (ed.), 1987, *Violent Origins. Walter Burkert, René Girard, and Jonathan Z. Smith on Ritual Killing and Cultural Formation*; Stanford: Stanford University Press (ISBN 0–8047–1370–7) (xiii + 275) (with index and bibliography).

Contents: Burton Mack: "Introduction. Religion and Ritual" (1–72) (*); René Girard: "Generative Scapegoating" (73–105) (*); Walter Burkert: "The Problem of Ritual Killing" (149–176) (*); Jonathan Z. Smith: "The Domestification of Sacrifice" (191–205) (*); Renato Rosaldo: "Anthropological Commentary" (239–244). Except for the introduction, each contribution is followed by a "Discussion" between Burton Mack, René Girard, Walter Burkert, Jonathan Z. Smith, Renato Rosaldo, John Lawrence, Robert Jewett, Terrell Butler, Frits Staal, Cesáreo Bandera, Matei Calinescu, Langdon Elsbree and Robert Hamerton-Kelly. [JS]

Reviews: E. Clemens *Eth* 98 (1988) 877; E.V. Gallagher *JAAR* 56.4 (1988) 788–790; B. Morris *Man* 23.4 (1988) 781; F. Dumas-Champion *Anthr* 84.4–6 (1989) 599.
Key-words: see the individual articles by Girard, Burkert and Smith.

Handelman, Don, 1977, 'Play and Ritual. Complementary Frames of Metacommunication', in: Antony J. Chapman & Hugh C. Foot (eds), *It's A Funny Thing, Humour*, London: Pergamon Press (ISBN 0–08–021376–6 / 0–08–021377–4) 185–192 (with bibliography).

This article is about play and ritual as systematic modes and complementary frames of meta-communication. As consistent and integral forms of social activity, the author claims, "play and ritual complement one another in the kinds of messages they communicate to the social order" (185). He defines play as a mode of organizing activity based on the reduction of available types of roles and relationships by the introduction of symbolic types and relationships. He states that on this assumption play is perceived as "a different order of reality, in form, content, and its logic of composition" (185). Because play is a meta-communicative framed activity, the frame instructs the participants to perceive what occurs within the frame as a different sort of acting and thinking. Therefore, the author defines the frame as a logical type of cognition. The passage between the logical types of play and ordinary reality is based on a paradox. If these logical types are separated by a paradox, as the author argues, there must be a level of communication that bridges the realities "separated by paradox" (186). Meta-communication is conceived as the level on which the relationship between participants is the subject of discourse. However, the author argues that the frame itself is meta-communicative, since the messages within this frame define the frame itself. Therefore, he distinguishes between two kinds of meta-communication in play. The first arises within ordinary life and bridges the different logical types, and the second kind of meta-communication arises within the play and comments on the ordinary life. Although play and ritual are complementary in their relation to the social order, there are similarities in their logic of composition. Because of its logic of composition, the author states that rituals are delineated by a distinct set of related premises on the basis of logical types of meta-communication. Its logic helps the participants to perceive what occurs within the frame based on the premises that are defined by the frame and that define it in turn. By reducing the social types to symbolic types, the ritual frame provides conceptions by means of which its reality is communicated to participants. The meta-communicative premises that bypass the paradox through the passage from one logical type to another differ in play and ritual. Whereas the premise of play is 'make-believe', that of ritual is 'let us believe'. Furthermore, the author compares ritual and play on the basis of the concept of liminality. Apart from structure as equivalent to the ordinary social order, he defines liminality as "marked by a reduction of social types and by an introduction of symbolic types" (187). As symbolic types, participants are 'masked' because they are "leveled and stripped of their social insignia" (187) as concrete selves and become anonymous beings through their collective participation in the liminal phase of a communitas. The author concludes this line of argumentation by saying that ritual and play are liminal phenomena. They transmit two kinds of meta-message, which are essential to the social order: "The first is the direct experience of a communitas-like state; and the second is what the liminal has to say about the structural, not only by contrast, but directed pointedly at the social order" (188). Summarizing the differences between play and ritual, he notes that play doubts the social order, whereas ritual integrates it. While ritual is a more stable domain of liminality, the play is a more fluid domain. There is a greater range of meta-communication in play than in ritual. Thus, the author comes to the conclusion that although play and ritual are analogous because of their frame of meta-communication, the message they transmit concerning the social order of ordinary reality is complementary: "Ritual and play are shadow images of one another in the kinds of messages they transmit to the social order. They are analogous states of cognition and perception, whose messages are complementary for the resolution of the ongoing, immoral, deviant, domain of ordinary reality. As alternative channels of meta-communication they invest social reality with the stability of hope and predictability and with the insubstantiality of the possible" (190). [JK]

References: **G. Bateson** (+), M. Douglas, A. van Gennep, M. Gluckman, E. Goffman (+), **R. Gratoff** (+), J. Huizinga (+), R.A. Rappaport, **V.W. Turner** (+).
Key-words: com, cog, sem, FRM, ref, rel.

Handelman, Don, 1979, 'Is Naven Ludic? Paradox and the Communication of Identity', in: Bruce Kapferer (ed.), *The Power of Ritual. Transition, Transformation and Transcendence in Ritual Practice*, (= *Social Analysis* 1) 177–191.

In this appreciative essay on Bateson's explanation of *naven*, the author comments on *naven* as a ludic behavior that communicates a particular kind of meta-message by the inversion of ordinary modes of communication. Although he agrees with Bateson's argument that *naven* is not a *rite de passage* but performs an inversion of social relations as a standard cultural act, he suggests that the communicative capacity of *naven* behavior to control schismogenesis can be better clarified if one analyzes the anomalous qualities of *naven* as generated by the communicative paradox of double binding. Thus, the main argument of this essay is that there are three paradoxes in the *naven* ceremony: 1. The complementarity of the *wau-laua* relationship (the relationship between mother's brother and sisters' children) is itself anomalous, 'masked', and paradoxical in Iatmul society. 2. The first anomaly is critical to the Iatmul social structure. 3. The solution of *naven* behavior to the first two paradoxes itself depends on the anomaly of play as an inversion within the mode of communication. Given that the anomalies of the *wau-laua* relationship in Iatmul society create a paradox, the author argues that there are two prototypic solutions to the dilemma of communication in the paradoxical situation of double binding. His argument runs as follows: While the meta-message of a ritual would override or supersede the paradox, the meta-message of play would invert it. As framed domains, play and ritual are able to alter perception and cognition, and their transformational properties are embodied in symbolic types that arise in situations of social inconsistency. According to the author, symbolic types are unmediated embodiments. In a double bind, the author claims, the symbolic type itself becomes the medium of communication. Thus, ritual and play are not negotiable. Although Bateson did not distinguish between ritual and play in Iatmul society, the author concludes that *naven* behavior is play rather than ritual because the basic message-unit of *naven* remains constant. Since one can analytically distinguish between ritual and play as different kinds of meta-message, the paradox in *naven* is communicated within a weak frame as play. The process of *naven* operates constantly through inversion because the participants can permanently switch *naven* behavior on or off. According to the author, then, not only is the play crucial for the working of *naven* but the *naven* behavior itself is ludic due to the constant inversion of communicative modes. [JK]

Example: *Naven* in Iatmul society.
References: **G. Bateson** (+), M. Douglas, R. Gratoff, B. Kapferer (+), R.A. Rappaport, Th.J. Scheff.
Key-words: com, frm, gdr, idn, pmc, rel, sem.

Handelman, Don, 1980, 'Re-Thinking Naven. Play and Identity', in: Helen B. Schwartzman (ed.), *Play and Culture. 1978 Proceedings of the Association for the Anthropological Study of Play*, West Point (NY): Leisure Press (ISBN 0–918–4385–27) 58–70.

To examine *naven* behavior and the play element in it, the author gives a detailed account on the *wau-laua* relationship in Bateson's analysis of the Iatmul society. He argues that "the complementariness of the wau-laua relationship is itself anomalous, 'masked', and paradoxical. The working of the relationship is also paradoxical: the wau is dominant, but also becomes a figure of submission. When this implicit submissive aspect becomes overt, wau dominance is inverted; the wau re-inverts his identity once again, by exaggerating his response, i.e. by 'playing at' the identity of 'mother' and 'wife'" (63). Through the meta-messages of 'ritual' and 'play', the cultural problem and the identity dilemma can be solved, while ritual overrides the paradox as play inverts it. The author therefore prefers to interpret *naven* behavior as play rather than as ritual, since "[t]he frame of naven behavior is weak, and the wau moves easily through it. The process of *naven* operates through inversion, which is predicated on a 'truth' which is 'false', is perhaps indeterminate, and easily transmutable.... Ritual rarely can accomplish this close and ongoing a correspondence between behavioral signals and cultural paradigms, about the nature of truth and the validity of experience. If *naven* behavior is ludic, then other of its play attributes, in part shared by ritual, make it an effective channel of meta-communication.... If *naven* behavior is play, then this raises somewhat ironic questions about the nature of Iatmul society. *Naven* behavior, as a process of play, threads through the life-spans of individuals; it weaves through a variety of cultural contexts; and it resounds within the ethos of Iatmul. As play, *naven* behavior exemplifies Douglas' (1968) idea of the joke embedded in social structure: the coherence of Iatmul social structure is dependent, in part, on the anomaly of the *wau-laua* relationship, which in turn is dependent upon the ludic for its integrity. Given the nature of play, this may be the penultimate 'jest' of the Iatmul" (68). [JK]

References: **G. Bateson** (+), M. Douglas (+), R.A. Rappaport.
Key-words: com, eff, frm, gdr, IDN, pmc, rel, soc.

Handelman, Don, 1981, 'The Ritual Clown. Attributes and Affinities', *Anthropos* 76:321–370.

In this essay, the author examines the sacred clown in four ethnographic examples of different ritual contexts in order to outline some attributes and affinities between this figure and other features in the organization of rituals. Here ritual clowns are shown to embody such crucial functions as boundary-dissolution, processuality, and reflexivity. The author rejects the view that the type 'ritual clown' is a fixture of certain rites that can be interpreted only in relation to worldviews or themes of everyday life external to the ritual context. By contrast, he interprets the ritual clown in terms of the organizational features of such rituals as a symbolic type that emerges from the ritual context and is internally composed of a set of inconsistent and contradictory attributes. Among these attributes, this figure constantly oscillates without stabilizing itself as a homogeneous composition. As a self-referential figure 'true to type', the author considers how the ritual clown, as a representation of self-transformation and a destabilizing process, evokes ambiguities of meaning by the constant oscillation between setting, crossing, and dissolving boundaries. Thus, the author asks what a ritual clown, in organizational and symbolical terms, contributes to the working and process of such rites. His view is that there are strong affinities between the organization of the symbolic type of ritual clown and the "ideas of process" in sacred or ritual contexts. Furthermore, he draws out some similarities between ritual clowns, the idea of process, and the notion of boundary. He assumes that rituals are framed activities that imply a meta-communicative message and that the boundaries of ritual frames are paradoxical, because they define and encompass the ambiguous states of liminality. [JK]

References: **G. Bateson** (+), N. Ross Crumrine (+), **M. Douglas** (+), **B. Kapferer** (+), S.K. Langer (+), E.R. Leach, A. Ortiz, **V.W. Turner** (+).
Examples: Wedding rituals, dance performance, and two seasonal calendrical rites.
Key-words: com, frm, idn, rfl, sem, str.

Handelman, Don, 1990, *Models and Mirrors. Towards an Anthropology of Public Events*; Cambridge etc.: Cambridge University Press (ISBN 0-521-35069-7 / 1-57181-165-6 (p)) (xi + 330) (with index and bibliography).
2nd. ed: 1998, New York, Oxford: Berghahn Books (ISBN 1-57181-165-6) (liv + 350).

This book concerns conceptual alternatives to ritual as a form of symbolic practice. In arguing against representational approaches in social anthropology, which tend to reduce rituals to mere epiphenomena or functions of social structure, the author introduces the notion of public events as epistemological phenomena in their own right, which equally includes 'ritual' and the 'practice of practice'. In the "Introduction" (3–81), the author discusses in three chapters the theoretical issues of public events on a theoretical level. Chapter 1, "Premises and Prepossessions" (3–21), contends that his position is "closer to a technology of events, of the identification of logics of their design, themselves embedded in cultural matrices that imbue these designs with significance and that put them to work in cultural ways" (7). He is concerned with the "logics of meta-design that potentially enable social orders to act upon or to relate to themselves in radically different ways through the substantive media of public events" (7). Moreover, he argues that "different logics of design in the constitution of public events index social orders that themselves are organized in radically different ways" (7). In terms of their sequential organization, the author argues that "[i]f public events are constructs that make order, then the logics of how they are put together is crucial to how they work, and so to that which their designs enable them to accomplish" (16). To comprehend these events, the author makes three assumptions: "First, that the relative capacities of 'doing'—of making something happen—that an event has is related to its logic of composition. Second, that the logic of composition of an event is intimately related to its organization. Third, that in order to get at the above, one must take seriously that which an event communicates about itself, as well as what an interpreter makes of this" (17). He states that public events are "constituted through their intentionality (their design, or 'structure' in an older parlance) and through their practice (their enactment or performance)" (17). They are "profoundly existential, since no event *qua* event can exist substantively as a phenomenon apart from its practice. Design and enactment are integral to one another" (17). Due to his emphasis on the synchronic perspective on public events, the author gives "epistemological primacy to design over enactment" (17). Although he merely focuses on "the logic of form through which the doing is done", he emphasizes, "all types of public events are open to fluctuation and change through their enactment. But that this is so in differing degrees, and these variations in flexibility and openness are related intimately to the logics of design of public events" (19). In Chapter 2, "Models and Mirrors" (22–62), the author distinguishes three modes of public events, namely 'modeling', 'presenting', and 're-presenting', through which one apprehends the lived-in world: "If events-that-model make change happen within themselves, that directly effects social realities, and if events-that-present are axiomatic icons of versions of such realities, then events that re-present do work of comparison and contrast in relation to social realities" (49). To apprehend the dynamic of public events, the author specifies the relationships among the different types by means of a triangular figure. Using a hypothetical "quality space" between these different types, he is able to specify his position and to argue that "the boundaries formed by the ideal interaction between the three types create a hypothetical space that encloses the qualities of all the types, and that enables their interaction so that they can cohere in different combinations and formations. Then a given public event can be said to be more like one type than the others, or to contain qualities of all the types" (60). "The event of modelling is the most clearcut; and therefore its contrasts and relationships with the other two types are distinctive and strong...However the relationship between the events of presentation and re-presentation is less stable and more ambiguous" (61). In Chapter 3, "Precariousness in Play" (63–81), the author addresses various theories of play and questions the radical disjuncture between sacred truth and frivolous falsehood, and introduces the notion of 'uncertainty' "identified with the unpredictable play of forces in flux" (63). Because play as a forceful mode of "introducing uncertainty" (67) is "infused with qualities of flux and the processual" (67) and closely related "to the very processes of change, to changeability itself" (68), the author argues that uncertainty permeates the meta-message of play in such a way that "[t]his message is...of a higher order of abstraction than that of play" (71). At the end of this chapter, the author relates public events to different kinds of social order and argues, on the basis of bureaucracy as the paradigmatic form of organizing modern societies, that "events of presentation seem associated especially with modern, bureaucratic states; events of modelling with tribal and traditional peoples; while events of re-presentation tend to an association with traditional, hierarchical societies" (77). The author develops this theoretical approach in the following chapters by means of seven case studies. Five of them appeared previously and are revised for this book. Each chapter is introduced by "Intersections" in which the author contextualizes his perception of the discussed issues in a self-reflexive manner. In the first case studies on "The Donkey Game" (86–101) and "Banana Time" (104–112), the author restudies the invention of the donkey game as occurred in a sheltered workshop in Jerusalem and the play among three middle-aged naturalized Americans in a small workplace. These forms of events are discussed in the second part (83–112) and are called "Proto-Events". They are "identifiable as special occasions, yet ones that have yet to be accorded a status of distinctive phenomena by their practitioners" (20). In the third part of this book, "Public Events" (113–269), the author discusses case studies that exemplify the three types of public events: (1) "The Palio of Siena" (116–135) as an example for events that model, (2) "Holiday Celebrations in Israeli Kindergartens (Co-author, Lea Shamgar-Handelman)" (162–189) as an example for events that present, and (3) "State Ceremonies of Israel—Remembrance Day and Independence Day (Co-author, Elihu Katz)" (191–233) as an example for events that re-present. In "Christmas Mumming in Newfoundland" (138–159), the author explores "the logic of concealment and revelation" (139) as two aspects of the playful device of inversion in the mumming practice during the 'Twelve Days' in small, rural fishing villages. In the final chapter on "Symbolic Types—Clown" (236–265 (*)), the author exemplifies his argument that "public events have logics of design that encourage particular operations" by the symbolic type of the clown as "an ambivalent figure of enticement and danger, hilarity and gravity, fun and solemnity" (236). He discusses the paradox of self-reference within the symbolic type and interprets its permeable boundaries crossing between inside and outside as later developed in terms of the Moebius strip. In the "Epilogue. Towards Media Events" (266–269), the author argues that "the study of public events... opens towards the fluid composition and rigid framing of the television screen" (266). In the modern state, information "is transmitted as images of images, copies of copies" (266–267) in such a way that "[t]he picture, the copy, must be accepted as authentic" (267). He concludes: "Like events-that-present, media events are affective rather than effective. The media event is one response to postmodern uncertainties.... Postmodern incredulity is an antisystemic response to crises in systemic organization. Yet most ironically, both the media event and the return to traditionalism seek solutions to incredulity through premises of the systemic" (269). [JK]

References: B.A. Babcock, **G. Bateson** (+), R. Bauman, W.O. Beeman (+), C.M. Bell (–), M.E.F. Bloch, P. Bourdieu, A. Cohen, M. Douglas, J.W. Fernandez, **C. Geertz** (+), A. van Gennep (+), **M. Gluckman** (+), **E. Goffman**, R.L. Grimes (–), J. Huizinga, **B. Kapferer** (+), S.K. Langer, E.R. Leach, C. Lévi-Strauss, J.J. MacAloon (–), B. Myerhoff, S.B. Ortner, R.A. Rappaport, **A.I. Richards** (+), R. Schechner, E.L. Schieffelin, **P. Smith** (+), L.E. Sullivan, S.J. Tambiah, T.S. Turner, **V.W. Turner** (+).
Examples: *Chisungu* among the Bemba (Zambia), donkey game in a Jerusalem workshop, the *Palio* of Siena, holiday celebrations in Israeli kindergartens, state ceremonies of Israel, Pakistani wedding, clowns among Pueblo Indians and Hopi.
Reviews: S. Falk *AA* 93.2 (1991) 496; J. Adler *CJS* 16.1 (1991) 91 f; F. Errington *JAR* 47.1 (1991) 121–124; D. Chaney *SR* 39.3 (1991) 675–677; P.W. Williams *ChH* 61 (1992) 283 f; M. Herzfeld *AE* 20.2 (1993) 392; M. Houseman *Man* 28.4 (1993) 836; Y.S. Carmeli *PoT* 14.1 (1993) 217 f; D. Dayan *Homme* 34.130 (1994) 158–161; **B. Kapferer *Sem* 105.3–4 (1995) 331–341**; R. Bendix *RSR* 26.1 (2000) 57; D. Pruett *DS* 2.2 (2000) 250 f.
Key-words: aut, cmp, com, cpl, def, eff, emb, FRM, med, PMC, PR1, rep, rfl, SEM, soc, STR, sym, tim.

Handelman, Don, 1993, 'Is Victor Turner Receiving his Intellectual Due?' *Journal of Ritual Studies* 7.2:117–124.

In the final section of this review article (on Alexander 1991 and Ashley 1990), the author advances his understanding of the concept of 'liminality' (121). Moreover, he identifies "two sorts of dialectical thinking embedded in Turnerian ritual", one following Gluckman ('rites of rebellion') and one open-ended, Hegelian-like (122). In the final section ("The Marketing of Victor Turner"), the author argues that "Victor Turner is not receiving his intellectual due. The indulgent application of facile renditions of liminality, anti-structure, and communitas to a vast variety of social conditions and ritual formations is burgeoning. Turner bears some responsibility for this.... Turner often repeated himself, potting and reducing his ideas to schematic diagrams that could pass more easily between disciples" (122). According to the author, "it is high time the living stop stunting the intellectual contributions of the dead Turner" (122). "A critical retrospective infused with prospective vision is overdue" (123). [MS]

Handelman, Don, 1996, 'Traps of Trans-formation. Theoretical Convergences Between Riddle and Ritual', in: Galit Hasan-Rokem & David Shulman (eds), *Untying the Knot. On Riddles and other Enigmatic Modes*, Oxford, New York: Oxford University Press (ISBN 0–19–510186–3 / 0–19–510856–6 (p)) 37–61 (with indexes and bibliography).

Since contests of riddling and riddle are sometimes part of rituals, the author traces analogies between these and his conceptualization of the logic of the ritual of trans-formation. In the first part of this article, the author outlines the structure of the ritual of trans-formation, which "is organized as a microcosm of aspects of the world that are brought into extraordinary relationships within the ritual" (38). The second part consists of a discussion of the attributes of the structure of riddles. According to the author, "the viability of the riddle depends on its relative autonomy from the everyday world of cognitive categories and the usual relationships among them" (41). Further, the structure of the riddle is both causal and processual. The puzzle of the riddle image is constituted through paradox of which the solution has to be trans-formative. In the third part, the author deals with the comparison of riddles with other enigmatic phenomena and the reason why riddles are located in rituals of trans-formation. In elaborating on convergences between riddle and ritual, the author asserts that "[f]irst, riddles may have performative, rehearsal functions, socializing their users into the logics of trans-formation that also inform certain rituals. Second, related to this, such riddles simulate the turning of paradox (and its functions of boundary maintenance) into more linear relationships of cause and effect. Third, within ritual, such riddles may act on participants as experiential, reflexive devices, either to remind them of processes at work elsewhere in a particular phase of the ritual sequence or to condense in simple form the infinitely more complex processes at work throughout the ritual sequence" (50). At the end of the article, the author presents his thoughts on the enigmatic nature of riddles. [JK]

References: R.D. Abrahams, G. Bateson, C.M. Bell, P. Smith, V.W. Turner.
Key-words: cog, com, pmc, pmt, rfl, str.

Handelman, Don, 1997, 'Rituals/Spectacles', *International Social Science Journal* 49:387–399.

In this article the author opposes two types of social action, viz. 'rituals' and 'spectacles'. "The practice of ritual is integral to cultural worlds that are organized holistically, worlds in which 'religion' constitutes the whole..." (387). The example he presents for 'ritual' is the Chisungu ritual of the Bemba of Zambia (389–390). By contrast, the spectacle is specific for the modern Western states, be they democratic or dictatorial. Of these he presents three examples: the Nuremberg rallies at the annual Nazi party day (395), the march-past of the Great October Socialist Revolution of the Soviet Union in Moscow's Red Square (396), and the Rio carnival (397). After an introduction (387–388) follow the sections "Transformation. A metalogic of ritual" (388–390), "Bureaucratic visions of order and the grounds for the modern spectacle" (390–394), "Presentation. A metalogic of spectacle" (394–398), and a short concluding one "Ritual, spectacle and resistance" (398). Rituals of change (to which the author restricts himself in this article (388)) first shatter the existing holistic world, in order to then regenerate a new, changed one (387). As opposed to this, the world in which spectacles operate is a fragmented one, which is mirrored by the spectacles (387). "I emphasize that my use of the concept of spectacle is tied closely to the relationship between bureaucracy as a system of classification and statism. In these terms, spectacle in the modern era is shaped by this relationship" (388). In other words: "Rituals of transformation, with their inner logics of change, should be distinguished radically from other 'public events', whose inner logics are closer to spectacles. Spectacles are organized like mirror-images to reflect especially composed visions of social order. The spectacle symbolizes the turn to modern social order—the rise of the state, its bureaucratic infrastructure, and the turn to totalism" (390). In the last section the author concludes that neither ritual nor spectacle are suitable to resist the bureaucratization of society. "In these emerging societies of control,... ritual will lose its relative autonomy for transformation and spectacle will at long last indeed reflect reality" (398). [JS]

Examples: The Chisungu ritual of the Bemba of Zambia; Bentham's Panopticon; the Nuremberg rallies at the annual Nazi party day; the march-past of the Great October Socialist Revolution of the Soviet Union in Moscow's Red Square; and the Rio carnival.
Key-words: def, soc, pow, sec, pmc, med, rep.

Handelman, Don, 2004, 'Re-Framing Ritual', in: Jens Kreinath, Constance Hartung & Annette Deschner (eds), *The Dynamics of Changing Rituals. The Transformation of Religious Rituals within Their Social and Cultural Context*, (Toronto Studies in Religion 29), New York etc.: Peter Lang (ISBN 0–8204–6826–6; ISSN 8756–7385) (*) 9–20.

In his article the author discusses how minor changes in rituals can theoretically be taken into account by elaborating a more dynamic concept of framing. He starts with the general assumption that "[f]raming is a central problem in understanding how rituals are organized within themselves and how they relate to the realities outside themselves" (9). The author questions the (lineal) concept of meta-communicative framing as developed by Gregory Bateson. With regard to this concept, the author identifies six problem areas: 1. "lineal framing is essentially hierarchical" (10); 2. "lineal framing is inclusive and exclusive" (11); 3. "lineal framing turns ritual into the passive recipient of change that must originate outside the ritual frame" (11); 4. "lineal framing is unidirectional" (11); 5. "the content of the lineal frame does not generate change within itself" (11); 6. "since ritual is so commonly framed in lineal terms, frames within ritual also tend to be conceptualized in this way" (12). The author challenges this concept by arguing that "[a]ny serious alternatives to lineal framing should open the frame to alteration and perhaps to change, both from its inside (its 'content', as it were) and from its outside. This criterion puts into question the lineal criteria of exclusion/inclusion and of hierarchical organization" (14). As an alternative, the author proposes the Moebius framing, which—based on a single frame—"speaks to the problem of being inside and outside the frame with virtual simultaneity, thereby opening the ritual frame to the outside world while enabling the ritual to be practiced as relatively closed" (15). Moreover, it is argued that "[t]he moebius surface or moebius ring exists through an ongoing condition of 'becoming'—in other words, it is dynamic within itself" and "if we perceive the moebius ring as a frame, then this framing is inherently dynamic, continuously relating exterior to interior, interior to exterior" (15). Taking the Moebius argument a step further, the author describes the dynamic of the Moebius frame by saying that "[t]he frame is simultaneously inside and outside, appearing and disappearing from view, always in movement, always becoming" (18). He then presents the inherent paradox of Moebius framing by saying that "the ritual—indeed, ritual practice—recursively generates its own framing which frames ritual practice. The ritual frame, then, is not an *a priori*—the frame does not exist until the frame comes into existence through the doing, the practice of framing. Yet in order to practice framing the frame must exist, which it does not. This is the paradoxicality of the existence of something that does not exist until it exists, but which must exist in order to come into existence" (18). More generally, the author concludes that "rituals characterized by moebius framing are always changing in and through practice—no matter how small the changes—even as these rituals are reproducing themselves in their gross features" (19). [JK/MS]

References: **G. Bateson** (–), C.M. Bell, É. Durkheim (–), G. Lindquist (+), S.F. Moore, B.G. Myerhoff, R.A. Rappaport, V.W. Turner.
Examples: Neo-Shamanic Rituals, a Tamil ritual drama.
Key-words: def, soc, str, com, pmc, pr2, DYN, FRM, rfl, tim.

Handelman, Don, 2006a, 'Conceptual Alternatives to "Ritual"', in: Jens Kreinath, Jan A.M. Snoek & Michael Stausberg (eds), *Theorizing Rituals. Vol. I: Issues, Topics, Approaches, Concepts*, (Numen Book Series 114–1), Leiden, Boston: Brill (ISBN-10: 90–04–15342–x, ISBN-13: 978–90–04–15342–4) 37–49.

This chapter begins with the following statement: "Conceptual alternatives to ritual should shake us out of the complacency of thinking we know what 'ritual' is, how it works, what it does" (37). According to the author, "[t]he study of 'ritual' in anthropology is dominated by two vectors: one posits universal definitions of RITUAL; the other, a plethora of ethnographic instances of 'ritual'" (37). He feels that this state of affairs "effectively blocks thinking about alternative conceptualizations" (37). These, however, require comparisons. "Universal definitions of RITUAL nullify the possibility of comparison before it begins" (37). The main problem is that the theoretical as well as the ethnographical study of ritual is based on what the author identifies as 'monothetic classification'. Because conceptual alternatives are based on comparison, they "cannot derive from a monothetic basis of classification" (38). The author argues that "one may do better to think of a field of possible forms of 'ritual'. The interior logics of these forms may help explain how these occasions do what they do" (38–39). The paper is divided in five parts. In the first part, "Basic Attributes of the Meta-Category of RITUAL" (39–41), the author contends that "if ritual is representation, then analytical attention is immediately drawn away from the event itself" (39). He observes this tendency by his critical analysis of the approaches to ritual as presented by Roy A. Rappaport (1999) (*) and Caroline Humphrey & James Laidlaw (1994) (*). He argues that one must go beyond universal definitions and pose alternative questions about rituals: "Is order made? How is order made? What sorts of order are made?" (40). In the second part, "Fields of the Possible" (42–43), the author sets up the parameter of comparison; he starts with the observation that "social orders work on themselves systemically in ongoing ways in order to adapt, correct, and change themselves and their cosmos" (42). In focusing on the relationship between the public event and social order, he considers different degrees of autonomy of public events depending on their own self-organizing capacities and argues that "the greater the autonomy of the public event from the wider world, the more likely it is that the event will be organized to effect transformations, through its own operations, that make change in that wider world" (42). From here the author extrapolates two extremes in the relationship between 'rituals' and societies and contends that "[b]etween these two extremes there opens a field of possibilities of stronger and weaker forms of public event" (43). In the third part, "Strange Conjunctions within the Field of the Possible" (43–46), the author discusses public events that mirror society. In analyzing how the 'mythopoietic cosmos' of the Yagwoia people of Papua New Guinea and the 'bureaucratic classification' of the modern nation state are reflected in the public events of these societies, the author emphasizes the similarities: "These public events are representations of dynamics that act forcefully and continually in the wider worlds within which they exist" (46). In the fourth part, "Meta-Designs. Acting on the World" (46–48), the author discusses events that model or create society. Here he compares the Chisungu ceremony of the Bemba in central Africa and the Sinhalese Suniyama exorcism and argues that the events that model have a greater degree of autonomy because they "are organized to act through their own interior dynamics on the wider world in predictive and material ways" (46). In the fifth part, "The Forming of Form" (48–49), the author concludes: "One direction towards conceptual alternatives to 'ritual' is that of a phenomenology of the forming of form.... The emphasis would be more on comparative dynamics, on the logics of forming that practice public events into existence, trying not to presuppose why this is so" (48). [JK]

Key-words: cpr, def, ter, dyn.

Handelman, Don, 2006b, 'Framing', in: Jens Kreinath, Jan A.M. Snoek & Michael Stausberg (eds), ***Theorizing Rituals. Vol. I: Issues, Topics, Approaches, Concepts,*** **(Numen Book Series 114–1), Leiden, Boston: Brill (ISBN-10: 90–04–15342–x, ISBN-13: 978–90–04–15342–4) 571–582.**

In this article, the author argues that the concept of framing is of major importance for theorizing rituals: "The idea of framing is potentially a powerful concept by means of which one can theorize ritual as different from, similar to, and interactive with not-ritual" (571). The argument is developed in two parts. In the first part, "Lineal Framing" (571–578), the author mainly discusses the approaches to framing as developed by Gregory Bateson (1956/1972) and Erving Goffman (1974) (*). According to the author, the concept of lineal framing depends upon a single premise: "that the realities of ritual are different from those of not-ritual" (571). He argues that this concept "draws immediate attention to three major issues in studying ritual: the structuring of the ritual frame, the organization of ritual within the frame, and the relationships between the interior and exterior of the frame" (572). The main problem of this concept of framing for theorizing rituals is that it sets up "a monothetic difference in value between not-ritual and ritual" and this as a consequence "turns ritual phenomena into the passive recipients of change" (573) and "[r]itual practice within the frame has little effect on the frame itself" (574). In the second part, "Fuzzier Framing" (578–582), the author discusses the idea of the Moebius surface which is used "to argue for a frame that relates to the problematic of being inside and outside the frame, as a function (to a degree) of the organization of the frame itself" (578). He defines the form of the Moebius surface and its conception as frame as follows: "The Moebius frame is twisted on itself so that the inside of the surface turns into its own outside, its outside into its inside. If the Moebius form is conceptualized as a frame, then this framing is inherently dynamic, relating exterior to interior,

interior to exterior" (578). This implies that the frame "is simultaneously inside and outside, appearing and disappearing from view, always in movement, always becoming, as of course are rituals that lend themselves to such conceptualization" (580). As a consequence, the author argues "the more conceptions of framing are made more dynamic, the more the self-organizing, autopoietic complexity of frames rises into prominence" (581). This however means that the ritual frame is prior given to the practice of framing. The author describes the paradox of dynamic framing as follows: "The ritual frame is not an a priori—the frame does not exist until the frame comes into existence through the practice of framing. Yet in order to practice framing the frame must exist, which it does not. This is the paradoxicality of the existence of something that does not exist until it exists, yet that must exist in order to come into existence" (581). [JK]

References: G. Bateson (–), E. Goffman (–).
Key-words: cpl, DYN, FRM, pr2, sem, str.

Handelman, Don & Bruce Kapferer, 1980, 'Symbolic Types, Mediation and the Transformation of Ritual Context. Sinhalese Demons and Tewa Clowns', *Semiotica* 26:44–71.

Following Turner's notion of the processual form of *rites de passage*, the authors focus on ritual as a process that transforms the ritual context and its participants. But in order to pay more attention to the dynamic properties within the processual form of rituals, they analyze especially the transformational elements of ritual and concentrate on liminal figures, which they call 'symbolic types'. The article's main thesis is that "the key dynamic in the transformational process is related to the mode and nature of mediation of symbolic types into context" (41). In contrast to the role-type as a construct of mundane reality, the authors define 'symbolic types' within ritual contexts as "internally consistent forms which are reified above context but at the same time are determinate of it, in the sense that where they appear they tend to mold context to their own internal consistency" (41). By concentrating on the different contexts and processes in transition rituals by which the symbolic types enter into their respective context, the authors argue in favor of a transformative mediation of context, namely that "the change and transformation of the type of clowns and demons is a product of the way they are mediated into context" (42). Furthermore, they claim that the major element of the symbolic types is their reflexivity because they counterpoise different but related levels of realities by containing "two or more contexts of meaning and relate them in a manner whereby one contradicts or opposes the other" (43). Through their paradoxical play with consistency and inconsistency within different contexts, "symbolic types mirror the consistency of the context in which they emerge and are concretized objects of reflection upon this consistency" (43). According to the authors, it is crucial for the transformation of the ritual as a whole, for the realization of this transformation by participants, and for the reconstitution of the symbolic type itself that "[s]ymbolic types as bearers and producers of consistency and as objects of reflection must, in rites of transition, be rendered inconsistent in themselves" (44). After discussing two examples of symbolic types—the demons in Sinhalese exorcisms and the sacred clowns in Tewa rituals—the authors summarize their main argument as follows: "Symbolic types create their context, order context, and subsume context to their consistent form. They mirror context, a function of their structuring of context, and are objects of reflection for those who are brought into unmediated contact with them.... The appearance of inconsistency within them is expressive of transformations taking place in context and is productive of further transformation" (65). The authors conclude by suggesting that "the examination of the process relating to the method and mode whereby key symbolic elements and, particularly, symbolic types are mediated into context, will provide needed insight into the ways in which rites of transformation achieve their work of transformation" (69). [JK]

References: A. van Gennep, S.K. Langer, A. Ortiz, S.J. Tambiah, **V.W. Turner** (+), N. Yalman.
Examples: Ritual clown, rituals of passage / transition rituals.
Key-words: com, cpr, DYN, frm, pmc, pr2, rel, RFL, sem, str, sym.

Harris, Solomon N., 1997, 'Ritual. Communication and Meaning', *Journal of Ritual Studies* 11.1:35–44.

In this article the author criticizes Staal's hypothesis that ritual is pure activity without meaning. The author argues that ritual is an instrument for communicating implicit symbolic meanings that go beyond explicit propositional contents of ritual as a form of social practice. Because rituals transmit information to the members of the ritualized body in encoded form, so the author contends, ritual communication is essentially confined to the members of the particular group with whom that ritual is associated. Therefore, he recognizes an asymmetry between the content of ritual communication and the propositional content of ritual. He contests the hypothesis that the extrinsic elements of rituals are identical with their symbolic meaning. Furthermore, he criticizes Staal for not differentiating between the terms 'meaningless' and 'useless', and he questions Staal's concept of meaning as intent or purpose of a deliberate action. The author concludes his argument in a Wittgensteinian vein, saying that a ritual is constituted by a system of rules in association with a particular group and its complex of values: "The rules of the ritual are, so to say, self-contained within that ritual and have no bearing on things outside that ritual.... Thus rituals are embedded in the value system of their respective groups and serve the purpose of internalizing and perpetuating that value system, or some aspect of it. Looked at in this way, the internal rules of ritual *per se*, may in the restricted sense of 'meaning' as used by Staal, be regarded as meaningless; but the ritual as an entity and as a component of the socio-cultural value system of the partic[u]lar group is meaningful" (43). [JK]

References: L. Apostel (+), C.M. Bell, M.E.F. Bloch, C. Geertz (+), E.Th. Lawson (+), **H.H. Penner** (+), R.A. Rappaport, **F. Staal** (–), S.J. Tambiah, V.W. Turner.
Example: The Vedic ritual of *Agnicayana*.
Key-words: com, mng, pr2, sem, sym.

Harrison, Simon, 1992, 'Ritual as Intellectual Property', *Man* 27:225–244.

This article discusses the existence of property rights in ritual symbolism, focusing particularly on disputes over these rights. A universe of such rights is comparable in certain respects to a prestige economy, such as the Kula system. Both manifest the same conception of property as a symbolic representation of persons. Both involve contests for the control of high-status forms of property, between political actors competing for prestige and legitimacy. Some illustrations are given of the uses of this perspective in analysing processes of change in ritual systems. [Simon Harrison/JS]

Key-words: idn, pow, aut, dyn.

Harth, Dietrich, 2005, 'Rituale, Texte, Diskurse. Eine formtheoretische Betrachtung', in: Burckhard Dücker & Hubert Roeder (eds), *Text und Ritual. Kulturwissenschaftliche Essays und Analysen von Sesostris bis Dada*, (Hermeia 8), Heidelberg: Synchron Wissenschaftsverlag der Autoren (ISBN 3–935025–76–9) 19–48.

[Rituals, Texts, Discourses. A Formtheoretical View]

In ordinary language the use of the words 'ritual', or 'text', or 'discourse' seems to refer to phenomena with a specific orderly form, a view which suggests an objective if not factual realism. But on a metalinguistic level the concept of form has to be measured against a reflective use: the same concept has an exclusive and at the same time inclusive meaning. It excludes the deformed, may it be called materia or medium (*res formandae*), and it includes in a way similar to the methods of grammatical controlling everything, may it be speech or action, in the tidy manner of discriminating between different formal categories and genres. Consequently there is neither a 'pure form' (*sensu* Frits Staal) nor a 'universal form' (*sensu* Roy Rappaport) beyond historical change. Form impresses the perception certainly as a distinctly made up whole, but in the process of (ritual) performance it displays an ever transitory feature. The essay's disagreement with some of the repeatedly discussed concepts of ritual form is played through in a variety of arguments making allusion, e.g. to the dissociation of classical text-and-ritual-dramaturgies in liturgical reform and—what is most important—to the vast convertibility (and commodification) of ritual forms and functions in late modernity. [Dietrich Harth]

References: E. Goffman, R.A. Rappaport, F. Staal.
Key-words: aes, str, PMC.

Harth, Dietrich, 2006, 'Ritual and Other Forms of Social Action', in: Jens Kreinath, Jan A.M. Snoek & Michael Stausberg (eds), *Theorizing Rituals. Vol. I: Issues, Topics, Approaches, Concepts*, (Numen Book Series 114–1), Leiden, Boston: Brill (ISBN-10: 90–04–15342–x, ISBN-13: 978–90–04–15342–4) 15–36.

Originally published in German as: 'Handlungstheoretische Aspekte der Ritualdynamik', in: Dietrich Harth & Gerrit Jasper Schenk (eds), *Ritualdynamik. Kulturübergreifende Studien zur Theorie und Geschichte rituellen Handelns*, Heidelberg: Synchron Wissenschaftsverlag der Autoren 2004 (ISBN 3–935025–43–2) (*) 95–113.

If ritual acting is seen under the premises of the social action theory a lot of concordant features can be determined. Both, ritual as well as social action, are constituted and interpreted in terms of norms and meaning. So there is no reason to deny ritual the power of meaningfully shaping social relations and situations of interacting, with the outcome, for instance, of what E. Goffman described as the tempering of risks in everyday interactions. The immediate performance of a single ritualized act may therefore be seen as an act of interpretation and at the same time of defining the particular distribution of social power and role playing. Yet, there has to be stated for all types of social action that no actor can entirely secure himself against those indeterminacies and risks which are part and parcel of all interactive encounters. The consequences are obvious and substantiate the claim of thoroughly debating the ethical values supposed to be appropriate for the given situation. Considering ritual as a type of social action poses a host of further theoretical questions. And this actually is a reminder not to forget that 'ritual as a type of social action' is a product of those scientifically justified constructivist urges by which traditions and customs are shifted on a level of reflexive concealment. [Dietrich Harth]

Key-words: def, DYN, int, mng, PMC, pow, pr1, rfl, sec, soc.

Harth, Dietrich & Gerrit Jasper Schenk (eds), 2004, *Ritualdynamik. Kulturübergreifende Studien zur Theorie und Geschichte rituellen Handelns*; Heidelberg: Synchron Wissenschaftsverlag der Autoren (ISBN 3-935025-43-2) (430) (with index).

[Ritual Dynamics. Comparative Studies in the Theory and History of Ritual Action]

Selected contents: Uta Gerhardt: "Die zwei Gesichter des Rituals. Eine soziologische Skizze" (49–72) (*); Dietrich Harth: "Handlungstheoretische Aspekte der Ritualdynamik" (95–113) (*); Christoph Wulf & Jörg Zirfas: "Performativität, Ritual und Gemeinschaft. Ein Beitrag aus erziehungswissenschaftlicher Sicht" (73–93) (*). [JK]

Key-words: gen, sec, pmc, DYN.

Hauschildt, Eberhard, 1993, 'Was ist ein Ritual? Versuch einer Definition und Typologie in konstruktivem Anschluß an die Theorie des Alltags', *Wege zum Menschen* 45:24–35. [What is a Ritual? Attempt at a Definition and Typology in Constructive Connection to the Theory of Everyday Life]

The author first recalls Iwar Werlen's three ideal types for the definition of the term 'ritual'—I: with respect to its form: a highly repetitive form of action; II: with respect to its contents: repetition of religious actions; III: with respect to its function: a mechanism for solving social problems. Since he considers even the sum of these to be insufficient, the author proposes to start from the theory of everyday life (*Theorie des Alltags*) as developed by Alfred Schütz and Thomas Luckmann. However, the definition aimed at should be more encompassing, he says, than that which Luckmann developed for religious rituals (Luckmann 1985 (*)). In the first section (26–30) of this paper, the author develops his definition of the term 'rituals'. First, rituals have in common with other behavior in everyday life that they are routinized, which reduces the attention these actions require. Secondly, routinized actions become familiar, which is their social 'sense'. Moreover, symbols point to a transcendental reality, and rituals not only use symbols, they have themselves a meaning which points towards transcendence. Furthermore, unlike symbols, they function to realize the transition into the transcendent. As opposed to everyday routinized action, the routine of ritual shifts attention from the cognitive to the performative level. The author calls this 'general defocusing' (*generelle Defocussierung*): "What steers is no longer the I but the symbolic action in its form" (29). "Rituals stand at the transition, where everyday life and transcendence come into contact. They are the expression of this transition, using a tool from everyday life: routine" (30). Thus, his definition is: "Ritual is symbolic transition-routine of everyday life by general defocusing" (30). In the second section (30–33), he distinguishes three types of ritual. That is, the relation between everyday life and transcendence may be a small, medium, or large transition. The small transitions find their expressions in daily rituals: greeting, etc. They differ from everyday routine only through their symbolic character. The medium-sized transitions are those that are new to an individual but routine for society: life cycle rituals. Large transitions are involved in those rituals that establish or confirm a society's worldview (*Alltagswelt-Ansicht*). In the third section (33–35), the author looks at a different typology of rituals and briefly discusses two more types: Christian rituals and 'new' rituals. He concludes that, whereas Christian rituals constantly interrupt the action with reflexive, cognitive parts (such as the homily [*Predigt*] in the Protestant church service), the so-called new rituals exclude these and focus exclusively on the experiential level. [JS]

References: I. Werlen, A. Schütz (+), Th. Luckman (+).
Key-words: def, rfl.

Heeschen, Volker, 1987, 'Rituelle Kommunikation in verschiedenen Kulturen', in: Wolfgang Klein (ed.), *Sprache und Ritual*, (= Zeitschrift für Literaturwissenschaft und Linguistik 17), Göttingen: Vandenhoeck & Ruprecht (ISSN 0049-8653) (*) 82–104.

[Ritual Communication in Several Cultures]

The author summarizes his arguments as follows: "In this contribution I examine the relationship of language as a means for the construction of reality and speech as a means of communication. Following evolutionary, biological theory communication is to be considered as a side effect of evolution. The problem, then, is how language evolved into being able to the expression of emotions and of social interactions. I propose that ritualized communication is the outcome of this development and that indirect or veiled speech is the principle directing the compromise between language as a means of the construction of reality and of communicative behaviour. In the course of ritualization the flexibility and creativity of speaking is restricted by the context of [the] situation, thus enabling speakers to reassuring social relationships even if situations of emotional distress and intentional interaction endanger these relationships. I contrast this notion of ritual communication with the concept of ritual as developed in social anthropology and ethnolinguistics. Research starting within the framework of human ethology has to be backed by history, demography, and social anthropology" (104). [JK]

Key-words: com, eth.

Heimbrock, Hans-Günter & H. Barbara Boudewijnse (eds), 1990, *Current Studies on Rituals. Perspectives for the Psychology of Religion* (International Series in the Psychology of Religion 2); Amsterdam, Atlanta (GA): Rodopi (ISBN 90–5183–178–1) (vii + 197).

Selected contents: H. Barbara Boudewijnse: "The Ritual Studies of Victor Turner. An Anthropological Approach and its Psychological Impact" (1–17) (*); Henri Geerts: "An Inquiry into the Meaning of Ritual Symbolism. Turner and Peirce" (19–32) (*); Hans-Günter Heimbrock: "Ritual and Transformation. A Psychoanalytic Perspective" (33–42); Heije Faber: "The Meaning of Ritual in Liturgy" (43–56); Owe Wilkström: "Ritual Studies in the History of Religions. A Challenge for the Psychology of Religion" (57–67); Jacques Janssen, Joep de Hart & Christine den Draak: "Praying as an Individualized Ritual" (71–85); Eva Ouwehand: "Women's Rituals. Reflections on Developmental Theory" (135–150); Patrick Vandermeersch: "Psychotherapeutic and Religious Rituals. The Issue of Secularization" (151–164). [JK]

Reviews: D.M. Wulff *JSSR* 31.2 (1992) 228 f; N.-P. Moritzen *ThLZ* 117.9 (1992) 698; F. Schweitzer *WZM* 44.6 (1992) 371–373.
Key-words: sem, mng, gdr, sec, psy.

Henn, Alexander, 2003, 'Zwischen Gehalt und Gestalt. Ritual und Mimesis', *Paragrana. Internationale Zeitschrift für Historische Anthropologie* 12 (special issue: "Rituelle Welten" = Wulf & Zirfas (eds) 2003 (*)):67–77 (with bibliography).
[Between Content and Form. Ritual and Mimesis]

The author proposes a notion of mimesis that goes beyond the mode of aesthetic imitation. Instead, he regards mimesis as a generative scheme of equivalences (*Erzeugungsschema von Entsprechungen*) that reduces mimesis neither to an imitation of a given content nor to the formalization of action (75). According to the author, mimesis is important in that it is situated between meaning and significance. Mimesis links sign and signified by connecting symbolical conventionality and indexical affinity (75). [MS]

References: M. Foucault, A. Gell, F. Kramer, M.T. Taussig.
Examples: Christian and Hindu rituals.
Key-words: MIM, sem, MNG, sym.

Herdt, Gilbert H. (ed.), 1982, *Rituals of Manhood. Male Initiation in Papua New Guinea*; Berkeley: University of California Press (No ISBN) (xxvi + 365) (with bibliographies per article and an index for the volume).

Contents: R.M. Keesing: "Introduction" (1–43); G.H. Herdt: "Fetish and Fantasy in Sambia Initiation" (44–98); F.J.P. Poole: "The Ritual Forging of Identity. Aspects of Person and Self in Bimin-Kuskusmin Male Initiation" (99–154); E.L. Schieffelin: "The *Bau A* Ceremonial Hunting Lodge. An Alternative to Initiation" (155–200); T.E. Hays & P.H. Hays: "Opposition and Complementarity of the Sexes in Ndembu Initiation" (201–238); P.L. Newman & D.J. Boyd: "The Making of Men. Ritual and Meaning in Awa Male Initiation" (239–285); D.B. Gewertz: "The Father Who Bore Me. The Role of *Tsambunwuro* during Chambri Initiation Ceremonies" (286–320); D.F. Tuzin: "Ritual Violence Among the Ilahita Arapesh. The Dynamics of Moral and Religious Uncertainty" (321–355). [JS]
Key-words: GDR, pow, mng, dyn.

Hockings, Paul, 1968, 'On Giving Salt to Buffaloes. Ritual as Communication', *Ethnology* 7:411–426.

This essay starts with a critique of the assumption that ritual is 'communication without information'. The author summarizes his critique as follows: "Ritual acts are necessarily repetitive but, far from erasing information, this repetition assures people that the basic values and institutions on which their society rests still retain their validity. Such a reassurance is conveyed in the symbolism of a ritual, and apparently has the effect of reducing anxiety in a community" (411). From a description of the "particular Indian ritual" of giving salt to buffaloes among the Badagas, Todas, the author emphazises that rituals transmit information in a particular way. He argues: "The kind of information which a ritual such as salt-giving presents is information not available from any other source, whether mass media or traditional oral channels. Neither government nor gossip can reassure a community on the matter of its continued existence as a community; only the periodic re-enactment of roles and the reassertion of traditional values in the indigenous ceremonies of a culture can give Badagas, Todas, and other rural communities the security of knowing that their own particular way of life is both persistent and worthwhile" (425). [JK]
Example: Giving salt to buffaloes among the Badagas, Todas.
Key-words: com, eff, idn, med, sym.

Hoëm, Ingjerd, 1998, 'Clowns, Dignity and Desire. On the Relationship Between Performance, Identity and Reflexivity', in: Felicia Hughes-Freeland & Mary M. Crain (eds), *Recasting Ritual. Performance, Media, Identity*, (European Association of Social Anthropologists), London, New York: Routledge (ISBN 0–415–18279–4 / 0–415–18280–8 (p)) (*) 21–43.

In outlining "a theoretical approach for examining relations between performances, selfhood and reflexivity", the author employs "a definition of 'performance' that focuses on playful, theatrical action" (21). The main argument is that "in the anthropological study of performance, we should seek to include the perspectives of individual actors to a greater extent than is frequently the case" (22). In contrast to Maurice Bloch, the author states: "Generally, we have seen a move away from analyses of the form and structure of the performance as an object of study in its own right, towards a greater inclusion of processes of production" (22). In line with Clifford Geertz, she points out that: "This approach opens the possibility of an explicit integration of peoples' reflexive capacities into the study of the actual interaction that produces cultural events such as those that we frequently describe as performances" (22). After presenting an empirical case on the humorous performances in Pacific societies (23–30) and projecting an alternative model of selfhood through theatre (30–38), the author concludes by saying that "a possible way to go is to include in our analyses an awareness of the fact that conceptions of agency may vary qualitatively across social spaces, and that this factor also may affect communicational patterns significantly, even within a relatively homogenous community" (40). [JK]

References: M.E.F. Bloch (–), M. Douglas, C. Geertz (+), A. Gell, E. Goffman, B. Kapferer (+), M. Sahlins, E.L. Schieffelin (+), V.W. Turner (+).
Key-words: agn, com, idn, pmc, rfl, str.

Holdrege, Barbara A. (ed.), 1990, *Ritual and Power. A Special Issue of the Journal of Ritual Studies Based on the Proceedings of the Santa Barbara Conference on Ritual and Power* (*Journal of Ritual Studies* 4.2); Pittsburgh: Department of Religious Studies, University of Pittsburgh (ISSN 0890–1112) (viii + 423).

Selected contents: Allan G. Grapard: "Preface. Ritual and Power" (1–4); Barbara A. Holdrege: "Introduction. Towards a Phenomenology of Power" (5–37); Gregor T. Goethals: "Ritual and the Representation of

Power in High and Popular Art" (149–177); Ron Grimes: "Breaking the Glass Barrier. The Power of Display" (239–261); Catherine Bell: "The Ritual Body and the Dynamics of Ritual Power" (299–313) (*). [JS]
Key-word: POW.

Hollywood, Amy, 2002, 'Performativity, Citationality, Ritualization', *History of Religions* 42:93–115.

"What I want to do here is explore the use of the term 'ritual' within the work of Butler, Austin, and Derrida in order to demonstrate the ways in which all three lean their accounts of the force of the performative on ritual. I will ask why this is so, suggest what they mean by the term, and explore the significance of their work for the understanding of ritual. I will argue that Derrida's understanding of the structures of signification offers useful suggestions for a theory of ritualization—and, by extension, of subject and materialization—grounded in the performative. The result will be both a better reading of Butler and a new account of ritual and bodily actions as performative" (96–97). According to Derrida, (bodily) actions are meaningful because of their citationality. Citationality means that signifying actions (such as rituals) do not refer to external realities but in fact generate meanings in the context of other sets of actions: Rituals cite, iterate, and (paradoxically) alter previous meaningful actions. In the final paragraph, the author concludes: "Austin argues that the right conditions are necessary for the successful performance of an illocutionary speech act; absent those conditions, the performative misfires and does not, strictly speaking, take place. Derrida, and Butler, together with ritual theorists like Asad, Bell, and Drewal, help us think about the misfiring of the performative in new ways. In changed conditions, performatives constitute new kinds of subjects and communities. Seen in this way, misfiring looks less like a danger than a possibility, one that opens room for improvisation and resistance within the very authoritarian structures (e.g., of child rearing, education, and religion) in which subjects are constituted. We do not freely choose ourselves or our communities, nor are the worlds into which we are born absolutely determinative ones in which no new meanings can be performed. Instead, subjects and communities are created and sustained by the complex interplay of sameness and difference constitutive of repetition itself" (115). [MS/Florian Jeserich]
References: T. Asad, **J.L. Austin**, C.M. Bell, P. Bourdieu, **J. Butler** (+/–), **J. Derrida**, M.Th. Drewal, M. Mauss.
Key-words: emb, hab, MNG, PMT, pow, pr1, ref, str.

Holm, Nils G., 2003, 'Ritualistics. An Overview of Research from a Religio-Psychological Perspective', in: Tore Ahlbäck & Björn Dahla (eds), *Ritualistics. Based on Papers Read at the Symposium on Religious Rituals Held at Åbo, Finland, on the July 31–August 2, 2002*, (Scripta Instituti Donneriani Aboensis 18), Åbo: Donner Institute for Research in Religious and Cultural History (ISBN 952-12-1157-1, ISSN 0582-3226) 70–81.

In this essay, the author first gives "a brief account of research into rites, before turning to my own more psychologically oriented considerations on the efficacy of rites or ritual" (71). In his "Summary" (79), the author states: "The study of rites has been influenced relatively little by psychological perspectives.... We have come to the conclusion that there is no spirituality without a connection to behaviour, which in turn always implies a body. But for the bodily rites to achieve efficacy, it is essential that they should be connected with learning processes and symbolic functions in an individual's inner existence space, to the kind of symbols that have some positive charge and meaning. Without such psychic content, the performance of a rite becomes simply an empty event which in the worst case only produces negative reactions. If, on the other hand, there is a positive memory material on the depth-psychological level of events and rites of different kinds, then the feeling of significance and relevance can reach the point where one experiences something definable as ecstasy or trance". [MS]

References: M. Argyle, T. Asad, C.M. Bell, P. Boyer, M. Douglas, É. Durkheim, M. Eliade, E.E. Evans-Pritchard, J.G. Frazer, S. Freud, C. Geertz, J. Goody, R.L. Grimes, C.G. Jung, E.Th. Lawson & R.N. McCauley, E.R. Leach, G. van der Leeuw, C. Lévi-Strauss, B. Malinowski, R. Otto, R. Pettazzoni, J.G. Platvoet, A.R. Radcliffe-Brown, D. Sperber, G. Widengren.
Key-words: gen, hsc, PSY, eff, tra.

Honko, Lauri, 1975, 'Zur Klassifikation der Riten', *Temenos* 11:61–77.
[On the Classification of Rites]

In this article, the author first discusses the classification of rituals in the third part, "Les principales attitudes rituelles", of Durkheim's *Les formes élémentaires de la vie religieuse* (1912), viz. into oblations (*sacrifice*), imitative (*mimétiques*), commemorative (*commémoratifs*) and piacular (*piaculaires*) rites. He concludes, that this attempt to classify rituals is a failure. He then discusses Van Gennep, which leads him to distinguish between *rites de passage* as a class, and as a model of rituals. In passing he mentions a number of criteria for good definitions and classifications. After some discussion of the difficulty of how to distinguish between rituals and non-rituals (*Nichtritus*), he now presents his own classification of rituals. This is based on three criteria: whether the subject of the ritual is an individual or the society; whether the ritual can be repeated, and whether it can be anticipated. The result are three classes: transition rituals (*Übergangsriten*: individual, not repeatable, expectable), calendrical rituals (*kalendarische Riten*: group, repeatable, expectable), and crisis rituals (*Krisenriten*: individual or group, not repeatable, not expectable). Within the overall class of transition rituals the subclass of initiation rituals (*Initiationszeremonien*) is of particular importance. The author divides it into three groups: initiations into age groups, secret societies, and professions. Finally, his classification is compared to the classifications proposed by a number of other scholars. [JS/Florian Jeserich]

References: E.D. Chapple & C.S. Coon (–), A. de Waal Malefijt, **É. Durkheim** (–), B.G. Glaser & A.L. Strauss, M. Gluckman, E. Norbeck, M.E. Spiro (+), M. Titiev, V.W. Turner, A. van Gennep (+).
Key-words: DEF, soc, idn, str, sec, dyn, cpr.

Honko, Lauri, 1979, 'Theories Concerning the Ritual Process', in: Lauri Honko (ed.), *Science of Religion. Studies in Methodology. Proceedings of the Study Conference of the International Association for the History of Religions, held at Turku, Finland, August 27–31, 1973*, (Religion and Reason 13), The Hague, Paris, New York: Mouton (ISBN 90–279–7782–8) 369–390.

This article has four parts: (1) an introduction, (2) a section on "The classification of rituals", (3) a section on "Process analysis and ritual", and (4) a section presenting "Three examples". The first two sections are an only slightly shorter (and probably older) English version of Honko 1975 (*). In the third section, the author compares two editions of Robert K. Merton's *Social Theory and Social Structure* from 1949 and 1968, noticing eight shifts in methodological focus, which had occurred during the intermediate ca. 20 years. He then contemplates on the effects these might have on the field of the study of ritual. In the final section, three examples of research from the field of ritual behaviour are presented, viz.: (1) "Liminal roles in the rite of passage" (a very critical presentation of Victor W. Turner's work on the Ndembu and his concepts of 'liminality' and 'communitas'), (2) "Reversal of roles in calendrical rites" (praising the work of Carsten Bergenhøj, who "suggests that the analytical model of the rite of passage can be transferred to calendrical customs" (387), a conclusion which Van Gennep himself had also drawn, of course), and (3) "The order of role-taking in crisis rites" (presenting his own role-theoretical process analysis of a Siberian shamanic healing ritual which gives rise to the following hypothesis: "the order of actualization of the different ritual roles in the shamanic seance, human as well as suprahuman roles, is constant in a particular culture and follows the rule: de-actualization of roles = actualization of roles in reverse order" (390)). The three examples thus represent the three classes of rituals which the author distinguished in the second part of this article, viz.: "rites of passage", "calendrical rites" and "crisis rites". On the pages 401–427, commentaries are found by G.J.F. Bouritius, Jacques H. Kamstra, and Anthony Jackson, as well as the discussion which took place under the chairmanship of Melford E. Spiro. [JS/Florian Jeserich]

References: C. Bergenhøj (+), E.D. Chapple & C.S. Coon, A. de Waal Malefijt, É. Durkheim (–), B.G. Glaser & A.L. Strauss, M. Gluckman (–), E. Norbeck, M. Titiev, **V.W. Turner** (+/–), A. van Gennep (+).

Key-words: DEF, soc, STR, dyn, cpr.

Houseman, Michael, 1992, 'Contrainte double et paradoxe rituel', *Cahiers critiques de thérapie familiale et de pratique de réseaux* 14:155–163.
[Double bind and ritual paradox]

This article contains the text of a presentation at the first conference on anthropology and family therapy, in Paris in 1987. In order to enable some conclusions about the usefulness of exchange between these two disciplines, the author mainly explains his audience what are some important characteristics of rituals. In order to illustrate these he uses the example of the So-ritual of the Beti from South-Cameroon, a puberty ritual for boys. After this description (155–158) follow an analysis (158–162) and some conclusions (162–163). The author points to the paradoxes created by the ritual and concludes, that these are not resolved (not even resolvable) at a cognitive level, but rather in the action of the ritual itself. It is through this action, and not through some form of communication, that the ritual is really effective: it works. In the case of initiation rituals, this work is relational: new relations are created, while old ones are resolved. Precisely because the ritual actions are not rationally understandable, but appear proper in the context of the ritual, the ritual confers a supreme knowledge, the knowledge what the reality of the ritual context is. This knowledge is a real secret, since it is ineffable and thus metaphysical, i.e. it cannot be expressed in discursive language. [JS]

Reference: G. Bateson.
Example: The So-ritual of the Beti from South-Cameroon.
Key-words: soc, psy, pow, idn, str, cog, com, pmc, PR1, REL, eff, emo.

Houseman, Michael, 1993, 'The Interactive Basis of Ritual Effectiveness in a Male Initiation Rite', in: Pascal Boyer (ed.), *Cognitive Aspects of Religious Symbolism*, Cambridge etc.: Cambridge University Press (ISBN 0-521-43288-x) 207–224.

This article is on the effect that ritual behavior has on the relationship of the participants. The author focuses on the participants' commitment to the radical changes of rights and responsibilities as they become apparent in rituals of passage. In treating the phases of the initiation ritual So of the Beti in Southern Cameroon, the author is concerned with the obvious aspects of the ritual performance of initiation more than with the ritual symbolism and its implicit signification. He wants to show "how certain organisational features of this performance, in contributing to the persuasiveness of the transformation it is supposed to effect, establish for the participants the well-foundedness of the INITIATED/UNINITIATED dichotomy" (208). In treating initiation as "a complex higher-order *form of relationship*", he distinguishes three main effects: "1. It operates a change in the pattern of relationship between the initiated and the candidates. 2. It operates another, concomitant change in the relationship between the candidates and the uninitiated. 3. It reiterates the existing pattern of relationship between initiated and uninitiated" (208). Rejecting the concept of rituals of passage as developed by A. van Gennep, the author suggests a different model, based upon a distinction between the two types of secrecy—a 'concealed secrecy' and an 'avowed secrecy'—constituting a three-person relationship in order to sketch a pattern of a dynamic relationship between relationships that is to accord with a description of the changes in relationship. In following G. Bateson, he claims that a change in the pattern of interaction is predicated upon a change in the context of interaction as an irreversible *metamorphosis* caused by the rituals of passage. In his conclusion, the author again emphasizes the participants' standpoint: "This perspective implicitly argues for an approach to ritual phenomena founded upon the recognition of dynamic relational structures intrinsic to their enactment as a whole. Such structures may be thought of as having two main characteristics: 1. They are *interactive*. In other words, they are predicated upon the complementary articulation of dissimilarities between the points of view assignable to the various categories of participants. 2. They are *complex*, that is to say, they integrate ordinarily incompatible relational patterns into novel, higher-order configurations of interdependency" (221). In this structure, the author intends to frame ritual symbolism more specifically: "I am not suggesting here that ritual symbolism is unimportant, but only that it is essentially contingent in so far as ritual effectiveness is concerned. Symbolic evocations ascribed to the *So* rite are either intrinsic to the overall relational structure its performance enacts ('emergent symbols'), in which case they are auto-referential and conceptually indefinite, or they have definite referential and conceptual content ('extrinsic symbols'), but remain subordinate to this global structural dynamic" (222). [JK]

References: G. Bateson (+), P. Bourdieu (+), R.A. Rappaport (+), P. Smith (+), S.J. Tambiah (+), V.W. Turner (–), A. van Gennep (–).
Example: The initiation ritual So of the Beti of Southern Cameroon.
Key-words: dyn, EFF, pmc, ref, REL, sem, str, sym.

Houseman, Michael, 1998, 'Painful Places. Ritual Encounters With One's Homelands', *Journal of the Royal Anthropological Institute (N.S.)* 4.3:447–467.

This article explores the role of pain in a number of ritual performances entailing the construction of characteristic connexions between people and their homelands: the English custom of Perambulation or Beating of the Bounds, die Gisaro ceremony of the Kaluli of Papua New Guinea and the initiation rites of the Australian Aranda. By focusing on the distinctive relational forms acted out in these performances, the author shows how the ritual infliction of suffering at once imbues pre-existing links with land with the immediacy of new, incontestable bodily experiences, and embeds these experiences within a wider network of ties, namely, those presupposed by the pain-inducing relationship enacted in the rituals themselves. Through such recontexualizations, the participants' attachments to the places in which they live are renewed and transformed. [Michael Houseman]

Examples: The English custom of Perambulation or Beating of the Bounds, the Gisaro ceremony of the Kaluli of Papua New Guinea, the initiation rites of the Australian Aranda.
Key-words: soc, psy, pow, idn, sym, aes, pr1, pr2, EMB, REL, eff, EMO, frm, par, tra, SPC.

Houseman, Michael, 2000, 'La percezione sociale delle azioni rituali', *Etnosistemi* 7:67–74.

Borrowing from Neisser's ideas of the 'interpersonal self', themselves deriving from Gibson's 'ecological' approach in psychology, this article argues for an account of ritual practice in terms of the perception of interactive patterning. It is submitted that in many if not most ceremonial contexts, co-ordinate performance takes precedence over individual reflection, conceptual elaboration being largely built up upon prior perceptual grounds. From the ethnographic example, a number of implications are drawn regarding the nature of ritual action and the relationship between participants' expressive behavior and their personal feelings. [Michael Houseman/MS]

Example: Ritual execution of young boys in the *labi* initiation rite of the Gbaya Kara (Central African Republic).
Key-words: str, pmc, cpl, emo, par.

Houseman, Michael, 2002, 'Dissimulation and Simulation as Forms of Religious Reflexivity', *Social Anthropology* 10:77–89.

The author wonders "whether it might not be useful to envisage the recourse to illusory devices not only in initiation rites but in rites generally as being organised around two different poles, which we might call 'dissimulation' on the one hand, and 'simulation' on the other. "In the case of 'dissimulation'...illusion is centred around the manipulation of persons. Various participants...are made to act in such a way that they are caught up in the co-ordinate patterning of each other's actions all the while being denied full access to the simulated performance they are involved in. The effectiveness of such dissimulations arises from the interdependence of the participants' respective perceptions, themselves deriving from differences in their modes of participation. On the other hand, what should rightly be called 'simulation'...is founded upon the manipulation of non-persons: animals, objects, spells and images. Its effectiveness arises from the mediating role such non-persons play in the substantiation of auto-referential trajectories in which relations of causality and representation converge" (88). Furthermore, the author suspects that what he has called 'dissimulation' "may be a regular feature of many rituals, specifically those of the *rite de passage* variety...Such episodes [as the 'discovery' of new-born babies or the 'capturing' of newly weds] invariably entail a degree of interactive staging in which for certain parties, by reason of their either being too close to the action or too far removed from it, the exact nature of the performance remains partially obscure" (88). This is also frequently encountered for what the author has called 'simulation': "[D]ivination,...sacrifice and other 'offering', 'blessing' or 'therapeutic' rituals also often entail the simulative manipulation of special objects...implying recursive circuits encompassing the officiant's ritually sanctioned aptitude for performing such acts" (88). Yet the author clarifies that he is not arguing for any sort of ritual typology because "'dissimulation' and 'simulation' may both be present in any given rite...This distinction is worth making, however, because of the different modes of reflexivity these two phenomena entail. In both cases, the participants are made partially aware of the illusory nature of the nonetheless mandatory performances they undertake.... the participants' commitment to the actuality and the necessity of these performances stems directly from their own behaviour. Conceptual indeterminacy regarding the nature of these mysterious performances is subordinated to the well-defined pragmatic conditions of their execution. In both cases, these pragmatic conditions relate to the establishment of a necessary relationship between several divergent points of view. In the case of dissimulation, implying a spatial discontinuity these points of view concern different persons interacting in different capacities simultaneously (e.g. novices, mothers). In the case of simulation, in which a temporal continuity is involved, they concern the same persons acting in different capacities at different moments (e.g. as initiators, or as novices). In the first case, reflexivity takes the form of mutual deception within the context of interactive complementarity, in the second that of a recursive circularity mediated by the manipulation of material (or discursive) artefacts" (88–89). [MS/Florian Jeserich]

References: G. Bateson (+), P. Boyer, G.H. Herdt, J.S. la Fontaine.
Examples: *Labi* male initiation of the Gbaya Kara of the Cental African Republic; *so* male initiation among the Beti of Southern Cameroon.
Key-words: idn, mng, gdr, rel, EFF, emo, RFL, aut.

Houseman, Michael, 2004, 'The Red and the Black. A Practical Experiment for Thinking about Ritual', *Social Analysis* 48:75–97.

This essay reports on the performance of an initiatory rite of the author's invention, undertaken as a practical experiment for thinking about certain recurrent features of ritual action and, specifically, of (male) initiation. In keeping with an approach which sees ritual as the enactment of special relationships, this initiation, The Red and the Black, was designed to demonstrate the importance of interactive patterning both for the structuring of ritual performance and for the participants' commitment to the relationships they ritually enact. Its meaningfulness, as well as its capacity to affect the participants' perceptions and ideas, is shown to derive less from the (minimal) explicit symbolism it employs, the beliefs it presupposes or the social functions that can be attributed to it, than from the relational entailments of the coordinate interactions it involves. Framing, simulation, secrecy, imposed suffering, symbolism, ceremonial efficacy, ritual condensation and the complex interplay of in-group and out-group perspectives, are among the issues that are illustrated and discussed. [Michael Houseman]

Key-words: str, pmc, REL, EFF, int, par.

Houseman, Michael, 2006, 'Relationality', in: Jens Kreinath, Jan A.M. Snoek & Michael Stausberg (eds), *Theorizing Rituals. Vol. I: Issues, Topics, Approaches, Concepts*, (Numen Book Series 114–1), Leiden, Boston: Brill (ISBN-10: 90–04–15342–x, ISBN-13: 978–90–04–15342–4) 413–428.

Ritual is envisaged as a distinctive way of enacting relationships; particular emphasis is thus placed upon the interactions that occur between ritual participants and the relational configurations these interactions imply. As one of what must surely be several basic organizational poles or attractors governing the perception and patterning of embodied social action, ritual is less a specific category of behavior *per se* than it is a particular process of recontextualization whose identification hinges upon personal participation and whose actualisation draws upon an interrelated set of premises pertaining to intentionality, degree of systemic closure, the link between feeling and action, the constitutive attributes of relational condensation and so forth, which are brought intro play. By means of stipulated behaviour enacting highly evocative and fundamentally ambiguous relationships, structured by interactive patterning and implying an inversion of certain pragmatic suppositions governing ordinary interaction, ritual performances afford participants with the immediate experience of highly integrative, extra-ordinary realities, sustained by self-reference and by the introduction of designated agencies and of special idioms; in doing so, these performances provide the participants with largely unassailable contexts for the

conventional reappraisal of the coordinate relationships that make up their social world. [Michael Houseman]
Key-word: REL.

Houseman, Michael & Carlo Severi, 1994, *Naven, ou le donner à voir. Essai d'interpretation de l'action rituelle* (Editions de la Maison des sciences de l'homme. Chemins de l'ethnologie); Paris: CNRS-Editions (ISBN 2-271-05171-1 / 2-7351-0543-1) (224) (with index and bibliography).
English translation and revision: *Naven or the Other Self. A Relational Approach to Ritual Action* (Studies in the History of Religions 79); Leiden: E.J. Brill 1998 (ISBN 90-04-11220-0) (xvi + 325). Abstract based on this edition.

This book is a structural re-study of the *naven* ceremony among the Iatmul of Papua New Guinea. The authors are concerned with what transforms an obviously disorganised sequence of actions and gestures into a ritual. Furthermore, they inaugurate a relational approach to ritual action. Since it is difficult for participants and observers to say what exactly a ritual is, the authors contest the commonly accepted definitions to determine the gestures and action around the Iatmul reciprocal transvestism called *naven* ('to go on view'). In order to avoid false alternatives in the study of ritual, i.e. a too general or a too specific approach, the authors want to take advantage of the possibility, "by taking a fresh look at the whole *naven* phenomenon, to propound a new approach to ritual by studying a case which did not fit in with traditional typologies. In order to arrive at further generalisations about ritual, we have sought to achieve a better understanding of one single exception" (xi). Since the authors consider the *naven* ceremony in a "two-pronged approach" (xii), namely a particular case and a means of exploring the problems raised by a theory of ritual action, they divided the book into three parts, each reflecting the dual approach in "extending the field of analysis of the preceding one" (xii). The first part, "Bateson and Naven" (1–46), concentrates on G. Bateson and situates his book *Naven* (1936) in the intellectual context of the British anthropology of its time. In so doing, they consider the concepts of message play, ritual paradox, and condensation as the theoretical aim and design of Bateson's approach to *naven* by using the *wau-laua* relationship in the Iatmul society. The second part, "Naven after Bateson" (47–162), attempts to reinterpret the *naven* as ritual in light of new ethnographic accounts by analyzing the same material. In taking the unacknowledged participation of women in the *naven* ceremony into account, the authors try to show how, e.g., the interaction between wau and laua suits a complex network of social relations and their organization as a relational structure. The third and most extensive part of this book ("Towards a Theory of Ritual Action", 163–285) addresses issues of defining ritual form (165–202), the ritual as a whole (203–222) defining ritual symbolism (223–259) and leads towards a relational approach to ritual action (261–285). It centers on general considerations of approaching ritual as a whole by defining its form and symbolism. Instead of analyzing the premises and consequences of ritualization, the authors try to concentrate on the ritual action in its own terms: "What is really necessary is to consider the organisation of ritual action itself, that is, the *form* or structure of ritualization as such. For us, the distinctive property of ritualization is to be sought in the particularly complex interactions that it brings into play. Specifically, we wish to suggest that it is the form of the *relational* field in which the protagonists are engaged which underlies the establishment of a context specific to ritual behaviour" (167). The authors give methodological priority to the ways in which action becomes ritualized, and search for the style of ritual action rather than to the ritual as a vehicle of meanings and functions. Therefore, the book's argument is directed towards a theory of ritual action as indicated in the Foreword: "A discussion leading off from the case of *naven* allows us to suggest how ritual symbolism, considered by the relational form of the rite, is based, firstly, on constant reinvention, and, secondly, on the construction of an interactive context of a particular kind. We consider lastly the symbolic 'work' of the rite, which consists in the establishment, on the basis of existing relations, of a new relationship" (xiv). In considering a series of increasingly different types of other ritual situations, the authors try "to indicate how the relational approach to the analysis of ritual action developed in this book in connection with a detailed analysis of the *naven* ceremony, may be progressively generalised to other instances of ritual behaviour" (xiv). [JK]

References: F. Barth, **G. Bateson** (+), M.E.F. Bloch (–), J.W. Fernandez, A. van Gennep (–), M. Gluckman, D. Handelman (+/–), B. Kapferer (–), E.R. Leach, C. Lévi-Strauss (+), Th. Reik, D. Sperber (+), F. Staal (–), T.S. Turner, V.W. Turner (–).
Examples: *Naven* and initiation rituals among the Iatmul of Papua New Guinea.
Reviews: P.-J. Stewart *BTTV* 155.4 (1999) 732 f; S. Harrison *JRAI* 6.1 (2000) 139; J. Robbins *Paid* 47 (2001) 254 f.
Key-words: gdr, gst, idn, pmc, pr1, REL, sem, str.

Howe, Leo, 2000, 'Risk, Ritual and Performance', ***Journal of the Royal Anthropological Institute*** **6:63–79.**

The author questions the prevalence of performance approaches in contrast to textual approaches in the study of ritual. He admits that textual approaches "insufficiently appreciate the importance of ritual's occasion", their metaphors "tend to construe ritual as an almost automatic acting out of rules based on an underlying cultural logic" and "with their emphasis on meaning, displace the doing, the performative dimension of the action" (63). "Despite a growing consensus about the merits of the notion of performance," the author thinks that "it pays inadequate attention to elements of risk that inevitably accompany performances" (63). His aim is threefold: "to make a case for the continuing significance of text; to trace some of the relations between text and performance; to comment on the neglected aspect of risk" (63). In the first section "Text and Performance" (64–67), he discusses E. Schieffelin and C. Geertz and stresses the similarities between text and performance by arguing that "they both have a definitive sequential pattern, an internal structure, and may be self-referential" (64). Then, he introduces the concept of inscription as the most significant feature of text: "Once inscription is taken into account, the relation between text and performance becomes more subtle and intricate" (64). Taking inscription as a process, he contends that "its importance lies in the fact that it is continuous. Therefore, its products are always provisional and always in the process of change as they are inscribed anew.... This introduces ideas of risk, stake, claim, strategy and competition, and it is thus pre-eminently a political process" (65). Moreover, he claims that "inscription is just as applicable to acts, skills, abilities, operations and procedures, as it is to meanings" (66). In the second section "Risk and Performance" (67–68), the author underlines the neglect of rituals as being risky: "Most rituals are staged to achieve an end, so there is always something at stake in performances. Because the outcome cannot be known in advance, success and failure (however these may be measured: instrumentally, aesthetically, evocatively, morally, etc.) are contingent" (67). In contrast to the analogies between ritual and theatre as performance, the author stresses that "risk becomes a measure of the importance and value attached to a performance. When life is at stake a ceremony to effect a cure needs to be challenging, otherwise the life is undervalued" (68). The author exemplifies his argument by analyzing a Balinese ritual and distinguishes between the extrinsic

(68–71) and intrinsic (71–75) risk. He concludes that "risk prompts a new metaphor for ritual. Ritual has been analysed as communication, drama and performance, but it is surely important to see some ritual action as test, trial, examination and contest. Although the performance metaphor is enlightening, what it presently lacks, at least in some of the ways it has been used, is the sense that, because something is at stake, it is a gamble, and that the ritual's managers must dare to conduct it. Such a gamble is only meaningful if one may lose or win something of value: the more important the value, the larger the bet, and the more significant the victory of failure" (76). [JK]

References: T. Asad, M.E.F. Bloch, C. Geertz (–), R. Schechner (–), E.L. Schieffelin (+/–), M. Strathern, S.J. Tambiah, V.W. Turner (–).
Key-words: eff, PMC, pmt, pow.

Hughes-Freeland, Felicia, 1998, 'Introduction', in: Felicia Hughes-Freeland (ed.), *Ritual, Performance, Media*, (ASA Monographs 35), London, New York: Routledge (ISBN 0–415–16337–4 / 0–415–16338–2 (p)) (*) 1–28.

The concern of this book, as the author says in the introduction, is not to define ritual as an entity of its own, but rather to consider "anthropological approaches to ritual in relation to theoretical developments in social and cultural analysis.... This book is not 'about' ritual, and its contributors do not have any interest in defining it in essential terms. Rather, the area is explored relationally to performance and/or media, and in some cases dispensed with after a cursory mention. Our object here is to find ways of thinking and writing about varieties of social practices and situations. The contributors reject the need for definitional strategies and employ ritual heuristically and contingently, as an odd-job word or a semi-descriptive term which is subordinate to the larger category of 'situated social practice...constituted and framed in relation to [its] own historical trajectories as well as to other traditions of social practice' (Gore, this volume)" (1). Further, one of the aims is "to restore the anthropological tone to debates in other, newer disciplines—cultural, performance and media studies—so as to forestall possible trivializations of theory and practice which have been maturing for over a century" (2). The author elaborates on the preliminary approaches to ritual and the connections between ritual, performance, and media. The contributions in the volume have a range of themes that deal with agency and intentionality in ritual and performance, creativity and constraint, the participatory nature of spectatorship, and the implications of different framings of relationships between reality and illusion. In the conclusion of this article, the author underlines the importance of studying ritual in connection with performance and media, since "[b]y examining ritual through the frames of performance and media, we can reconsider core questions in anthropology, to reflect on the way we arrive at our insights into the analysis and framing of social action, and to reaffirm the value of close-grained ethnography which comes from participant observation" (23). [JK]

References: E. Goffman, J. Goody, C. Humphrey & J. Laidlaw, R. Schechner, E.L. Schieffelin, S.J. Tambiah, V.W. Turner.
Key-words: agn, frm, MED, par, PMC.

Hughes-Freeland, Felicia (ed.), 1998, *Ritual, Performance, Media* (ASA Monographs 35); London, New York: Routledge (ISBN 0–415–16337–4 / 0–415–16338–2 (p)) (x + 233) (with Index).

Selected contents: Felicia Hughes-Freeland: "Introduction" (1–28) (*); Kirsten Hastrup: "Theatre as a Site of Passage. Some Reflections on the Magic of Acting" (29–45); Susanna Rostas: "From Ritualization to Performativity. The Concheros of Mexico" (85–103); Helena Wulff: "Perspectives towards Ballet Performance. Exploring, Repairing and Maintaining Frames" (104–120); Nigel Rapport: "Hard Sell. Commercial Performance and the Narration of the Self" (177–193); Edward L. Schieffelin: "Problemizing Performance" (194–207) (*); Eric Hirsch: "Bound and Unbound Entities. Reflections on the Ethnographic Perspective of Anthropology *vis-à-vis* Media and Cultural Studies" (208–229). [JK]

Review: **R. Munro *SR* 47.1 (1999) 163–172**.
Key-words: MED, PMC, tha, pr1, soc.

Hughes-Freeland, Felicia, 2006, 'Media', in: Jens Kreinath, Jan A.M. Snoek & Michael Stausberg (eds), *Theorizing Rituals. Vol. I: Issues, Topics, Approaches, Concepts*, (Numen Book Series 114–1), Leiden, Boston: Brill (ISBN-10: 90–04–15342–x, ISBN-13: 978–90–04–15342–4) 595–614.

This chapter focuses on mass-media, particularly broadcast and print technologies. It asks what contexts produced by media use ritual theory, how this theory is used, how effectively it does so, and what, if anything, have analyses of media contributed to the understanding of ritual? The

discussion is structured around four broad approaches to media which use ritual theory: the neo-functional, with a focus on social integration and the collectivity; the neo-Weberian, with a focuses on modernity; the post-Foucaultian with a focus on socially diffused power relations; and finally what I call methodological particularism, with a focus on situated ethnographic analyses and which prioritizes data over models. The chapter critiques the loose use of ritual theory in studies of the media, and suggests that this tendency might result in the restoration of the domain of the sacred and the reaffirmation of ritual as a distinctive aspect of human experience. [Felicia Hughes-Freeland]
Key-word: MED.

Hughes-Freeland, Felicia & Mary M. Crain, 1998, 'Introduction', in: Felicia Hughes-Freeland & Mary M. Crain (eds), *Recasting Ritual. Performance, Media, Identity*, (European Association of Social Anthropologists), London, New York: Routledge (ISBN 0-415-18279-4 / 0-415-18280-8 (p)) (*) 1–20.

The editors summarize the aim of this book as follows: "This volume explores ritualised action, but in doing so also addresses changes in foundational anthropological paradigms for the explanation of behaviour and society. It starts from three broad questions. First, how might anthropological analyses of ritual practice respond to the diversification of performance and audience, from live to mediated contexts? Second, what can the analysis of ritual reveal about identity politics and the relationship between power and culture in global and local practices? Third, is there a future for distinctive anthropological approaches to ritualised social action, or are we set to merge into cultural, performance and media studies?" (1). After discussing recent developments in ritual as a concept and as an analytical tool in terms of performance, media and identity (1–7), the editors point to the theme and setting of the contributions to this volume: "Our six case studies focus on ritual and identity. Several of them explore ritual and identities in relation to the media (Crain, Hughes-Freeland) while others pay more attention to identity and the performative aspects of ritual (Bovin, Hoëm, Mitchell, Rudie). The chapters present us with different ways of thinking about identity which emerge from the conjunction of ritual and/or performance" (7). By focusing on the relationship between identity production and ritual performance, the editors open up further directions of research:

"The range of events and regions discussed bring together cultural production and cultural reproduction to argue that identity must not be understood as monolithic and essential. Forms of identity which bring together the personal and the social are interactive and situational. Identity is polythetic, but it is not infinite; gender, for example, sets different kinds of limits on social actors. The contributions variously explore the scope and limits of identity production within the sphere of ritual performance, and test the hypothesis that such performance is only socially effective if it carries a sense of truth. This in turn allows a theoretical exploration of the relationship between social reality, imagination and its products, power, and fantasy as they contribute to human survival" (14). [JK]

References: C.M. Bell, C. Geertz, J.J. MacAloon, E.L. Schieffelin, V.W. Turner.
Key-words: IDN, MED, PMC, pow, pr1, rel.

Hughes-Freeland, Felicia & Mary M. Crain (eds), 1998, *Recasting Ritual. Performance, Media, Identity* (European Association of Social Anthropologists); London, New York: Routledge (ISBN 0–415–18279–4 / 0–415–18280–8 (p)) (vi + 168).

Selected contents: Felicia Hughes-Freeland & Mary M. Crain: "Introduction" (1–20) (*); Ingjerd Hoëm: "Clowns, Dignity and Desire. On the Relationship between Performance, Identity and Reflexivity" (21–43) (*); Felicia Hughes-Freeland: "From Temple to Television. The Balinese Case" (44–67). [JK]

Review: H. Mitchell *JRAI* 6.3 (2000) 527 f.
Key-words: IDN, MED, PMC, rfl, sec.

Humphrey, Caroline & James Laidlaw, 1994, *The Archetypal Actions of Ritual. A Theory of Ritual Illustrated by the Jain Rite of Worship* (Oxford Studies in Social and Cultural Anthropology); Oxford: Clarendon Press / Oxford University Press (ISBN 0–19–827788–1 / 0–19–827947–7 (p)) (ix + 293) (with index).

This book aims to propose a new theory of ritual action "by contrasting ritualized action with action which is not ritualized" (2). Instead of understanding rituals as a class of events or as an institution, the authors suggest seeing ritual as a quality or mode of action. Central to their argument is "that ritualization severs the link, present in everyday activity, between the 'intentional meaning' of the agent and the identity of the act which he or she performs" (2). They further argue "that ritual action is still 'directed', but the relation between intention and action is subtly transformed, so that it is different from action in general" (4). This transformation is made possible through the 'ritual commitment' that enables the participants to have an awareness of their ritual action, accompanied by "a conception of the action as a thing, encountered and perceived from outside" (5), in other words, as an 'archetypal' action. So, the authors state, there is no underlying meaning of the ritual that the participants share to some degree. Rather, rituals are meaningless through their 'non-intentionality' and are imposed with individual meanings by a secondary process that is nevertheless to be separated from the ritual action *per se*. The authors attempt to prove their position by analyzing the Jain daily morning *puja*, which is described in detail in Chapter 2. The concern of Chapter 3 is a critique of theories of ritual as communication, and the authors differentiate their approach from these. Next they take a look at different 'meanings of meaning', thereby referring to a comparison between ritual acts and linguistic acts. Having thus explained how locutionary and illocutionary meanings correspond to action and intention, the authors explore the units of ritual and how they can be identified as separate acts: "Both in watching and understanding the action of others, and in reflexively monitoring and understanding what we ourselves do..., we identify 'chunks' of what is done as actions... Thus the boundaries between acts are not 'given' in the physical form of what is done. To identify actions we must form an intentional understanding of them..." (92). Again comparing ritual action with everyday action, they assume that "[i]n everyday life, if you see two people doing the same thing, but with different intention in acting..., you will count these as different actions... The crucial point is that if two people do *dip puja*, the action, because ritualized, must be this alone" (95). Ritualized action is therefore also institutionalized action where "constitutive rules are accepted as determining the kinds of acts which he or she will perform" (98). These institutionalized, small, named units of ritual action together complete one another and constitute the ritual as a whole. In Chapter 5, the authors continue their elaboration by asking what exactly is prescribed in ritualized action: "we found that what people actually learn is not rules (propositions of a general kind in language) but named actions they should copy" (120). To illuminate the process of learning ritualized actions, they draw on findings from cognitive psychology and cognitive anthropology (Chapter 6). They draw a distinction between two kinds of knowledge, the practical knowledge directing activity and discursive knowledge about it. The authors come to the conclusion that something like 'collective or shared representations' exist only on the discursive level where narrative accounts of rituals can be transmitted. However, discourse about ritual need not be mastered in order to perform it. What must be learned is the performance of units of ritual action that are then bestowed with individual meaning in particular situations. The authors argue that "[p]eople do not start with models or scripts which they act out, but rather, through imitating acts which are previously named" (141). The ritualized actions thus learned appear 'natural' and 'given', i.e. people think about them in the same way as about the category of 'natural kinds' that refers to more or less superficial observable features without inherent meaning. The kinds of purposes or intentions secondarily bestowed upon ritualized acts are the topic of Chapter 7, followed in Chapter 8 by a discussion of the 'textualization of ritual' and the 'ritualization of text'. Chapter 9 is theoretically less dense; in it the authors argue that an overarching intention of rituals could be to 'mean to mean', and this posited intention is then used to interpret ethnographic data on the Jain *puja*. Finally, the authors address the role of emotions or 'emergent moods' involved in some rituals: "instead of giving discursive meanings to the act, the celebrant here becomes absorbed in the act" (227). Arguing that the spontaneous expression of mood is part of the prescribed performance, while one simultaneously becomes absorbed in the act, they conclude that "[t]he fact that the self is not only object but also subject, however, allows abstract action [i.e. movements not relevant to any particular situation] to create its own subjective 'projection'" (235). Rejecting Merleau-Ponty's notion of abstract action as having reference only to itself, the authors instead propose that even abstract actions such as ritualized actions are always situated within a particular context and thereby are bestowed with meaning, although the action *per se* is meaningless. [Thorsten Gieser]

References: C.M. Bell, Th. Gerholm, E.R. Leach, R.A. Rappaport, F. Staal.
Example: Jain *puja* in India.
Reviews: R.J. Parmentier *HR* 36.2 (1996) 166 f; F.W. Clothey *JR* 76.4 (1996) 673 f; J. Boyd & R. Williams *JRS* 10.1 (1996) 135–138; R. Gombrich *SAR* 16.1 (1996) 88–90; **C.-K. Hojbjerg *TA* 33 (1996) 147–159**; J.-R. Bowen *JRAI* 3.3 (1997) 631 f; **I. Brady *CA* 40.2 (1999) 243–248**.
Key-words: MNG, cog, pmt, PR1, cmp, agn, eff, emo, INT, tra.

Huxley, Sir Julian S. (ed.), 1966, *A Discussion on Ritualization of Behavior in Animals and Man* (Philosophical Transactions of the Royal Society, Series B 251); London: Royal Society of London (No ISBN) (280).

Selected contents: J.S. Huxley: "Introduction" (249–271); K.Z. Lorenz: "Evolution of Ritualization in the Biological and Cultural Spheres" (273–284) (*); E.R. Leach: "Ritualization in Man in Relation to Conceptual and Social Developments" (403–408). [JS]
Key-word: ETH.

Hymes, Dell, 1975, 'Breakthrough into Performance', in: Dan Ben-Amos & Kenneth S. Goldstein (eds), *Folklore. Performance and Communication*, (Approaches to Semiotics 40), The Hague, Paris: Mouton (ISBN 90–279–3143–7) 11–74.

In this essay on the performance approach to ritual, the author critically discusses N. Chomsky's use of 'performance' in transformational generative grammar in relation to the study of folklore. He defines performance as situated within a particular context and as emergent, unfolding, or arising within this context: "The concern is with performance, not as something mechanical or inferior, as in some linguistic discussion, but with performance as something creative, realized, achieved, even transcendent of the ordinary course of events" (13). Furthermore, he distinguishes between three dimensions of 'performance': "the INTERPRETABLE, THE REPORTABLE, THE REPEATABLE" (14). According to the author, these three dimensions of a performance "can be regarded as an aspect of the abilities of competent members of a culture or community. Each can also be regarded as an aspect of the circumstances facing the investigator of a culture or community" (14–15). Thus the author integrates the polarity of these aspects in the three dimensions of a performance: 1. The dimension of interpretability implies a polarity between classifying and explaining. 2. The dimension of reportability implies a polarity between reporting and describing. 3. The dimension of repeatability implies a polarity between voluntary doing and performing. Using three examples of traditional material in contemporary performances, the author distinguishes between three types of situations. The guiding questions are concerned with "the difference between knowing tradition and presenting it; between knowing what and knowing how; between knowledge, on the one hand, and motivation and identification, on the other, as components of competence in the use of language" (18). Further, he argues for a study of specific variations in performance: "There is no more an '*Ur*-performance' than there is an '*Ur*-text'. Only the systematic study of performances can disclose the true structure" (20). After presenting, analyzing, and comparing various ethnographic cases (20–68), the author concludes: "By bracketing the traditional, and stopping there, such standpoints conceal the need to breakthrough into performance in our own time. The sort of analysis attempted here suggests... a study that can transcend a conception of structure either as simply equivalent to conscious rule or as necessarily unconscious, and that can understand structure as sometimes emergent in action. From such a standpoint, the validity of structural analysis radically depends on interpretation of the praxis of those whose structure it is, and on self-awareness of the praxis of those who comprehend that structure" (71–72). [JK]

References: R.D. Abrahams, R. Bauman, F. Boas, K. Burke (+), N. Chomsky (–), E. Goffman (+), W.H. Goodenough, E. Sapir, D. Tedlock.
Example: Performance of oral narratives.
Key-words: cmp, com, PMC, rht, sem, str.

Innis, Robert E., 2004, 'The Tacit Logic of Ritual Embodiments', *Social Analysis* 48:197–212.

The first part of this paper (197–203) is a critical review of Rappaport 1999 (*). The author critically comments on the conceptual tools employed by Rappaport. In particular, he finds that Rappaport's "foregrounding of the essentially semiotic dimension of ritual by means of an appropriation of Peirce needs to be corrected and enriched by other conceptual frameworks" (203). Having pointed out some problems with Rappaport's ideas, the author proceeds "to illustrate how some elements from another philosophical project, which also oscillates between embodiment and meaning, intersect and throw light" (203) on these issues. "More specifically, I want to show how Michael Polanyi's development of the notion of 'tacit knowledge', and the correlative model of consciousness on which it is built, perspicuously foregrounds key aspects of the 'tacit logic' of ritual embodiment" (203). In the following section (203–210), the author therefore extrapolates a Polanyian theory of ritual by exploiting a number of concepts and distinctions of Polanyi's philosophy, including skill/knowledge, modes of feeling, focal vs. subsidiary awareness, articulate framework, impersonality of contemplation (as complete participation), preconceptual capacities, the construction of experienced whole, existential vs. denotative/representative meaning, verification vs. validation, interiorization, indication vs. symbolization; some of these concepts are occasionally read in the light of other theoreticians such as Dewey, Ihde, Lakoff & Johnson, and Scheffler. Similarities with and differences from the arts, especially music, are a recurrent motive in this discussion. In the final section of the paper (210–212) the author argues that publicly performed collective ('thick') rituals as studied by anthropologists "exemplify the same embodied logic" (211) as individual ('thin') modes of ritual contemplation. [MS]

References: T.F. Driver (–), N. Goodman, R.E. Ihde, G. Lakoff & M. Johnson, M. Polanyi, R.A. Rappaport (+/–), I. Scheffler.
Key-words: mng, sym, aes, emb, SEM, ref, eff, frm, par, mus.

Jackson, Anthony, 1968, 'Sound and Ritual', *Man* 3:293–299.

Referring to Needham (1967) (*), the author seeks to analyze the significance of sound in human society in general and in ritual in particular. He deals with the question "why certain sounds are picked out and deliberately used in ritual?" (294). After discussing the contrast between noise and silence as used in rituals, he seeks to explore the "correspondences between the overall structure of ritual and the particular use of structured or patterned sound" (295). He argues that sound can serve a ritual especially by marking off time. In this respect, the percussive noises, especially the drum, seems to play a significant role as the most appropriate marker of rituals: "not only can they produce an implied note of warning but they can easily break up a patterned sequence" (296). For the author, the importance of drum sounds lies in the physiological fact that the natural brain rhythms are influenced by external rhythmic stimulation so that abnormal psychological states can occur in certain cases like contact with the other world, e.g. trances or ecstasies: "The clue to the importance of the drum must lie in the capacity of rhythmic sound makers (for clapping is equally effective) for producing a feeling of contact with the other world" (297). He concludes his argument: "If ritual is seen as a striving towards contact with suprahuman powers, a transcendence of everyday reality, then it is not surprising that men will employ such means as will give them this feeling of surpassing normality" (297). [JK]

References: M. Douglas (+), É. Durkheim, M. Eliade, J.G. Frazer, E. Leach, C. Lévi-Strauss (+), **R. Needham** (+), A. van Gennep.
Key-words: aes, com, cpl, emo, frm, med, mng, psy, soc, str, tim.

James, Mervyn, 1983, 'Ritual, Drama and Social Body', *Past & Present* 98:3–29.

"This article aims to discuss a specific late medieval cult as practised in a specific context: that of the late medieval town.... The cult in question is the cult of Corpus Christi.... What I propose to discuss are the various rites which were celebrated on Corpus Christi Day, the various dramatic, theatrical manifestations which took place in connection with the occasion, and the mythology associated with both" (3). The author then argues that those who studied this phenomenon so far were rather literary scholars than historians, and that "there does seem to be lacking among most of these writers anything more than a very generalized idea of the late medieval social background against which the cult was practised and the plays performed; and very little sense of the specific social needs and pressures to which both responded. What I aim to do here... is to fill in the social dimension. Briefly, I propose to argue that the theme of Corpus Christi is society seen in terms of body; and that the concept of body provided urban societies with a mythology and ritual in terms of which the opposites of social wholeness and social differentiation could be both affirmed, and also brought into a creative tension, one with the other. The final intention of the cult was, then, to express the social bond and to contribute to social integration. From this point of view, Corpus Christi expresses the creative role of religious rite and ideology in urban societies, in which the alternative symbols and ties of lordship, lineage and faithfulness, available in countrysides, were lacking" (3–4). The author acknowledges explicitly to be indebted to the work of Mary Douglas, as well as a number of authors who wrote on the idea of the 'Body Politic'. Twice he also refers to V.W. Turner. The main part of the article is formed by a description of the indicated cult and its analysis from the announced perspective. From a ritual theoretical perspective, the article becomes most interesting towards the end, where, "[b]y way of conclusion I would like to raise some points about the abandonment of the observance of Corpus Christi, of the mythology associated with the feast, and of the cycle plays.... The critique arises from the increasingly moralistic and anti-ritualistic bent which characterizes a significant sector of urban opinion as the fifteenth century proceeds" (21). "Those who viewed the Corpus Christi plays as increasingly superfluous and potentially disruptive were also able to fasten on the tension which had always existed within the cycles between their quality as 'ritual', arising from their nature as a 'work' done for 'the honour of God and the city'; and their quality as *ludus*, that is a kind of 'play' in the literal sense: a game. As *ludus*, as game, the plays were carried into the region of popular culture: the world of mime, mumming, carnival and the rituals of reversal.... True, the sting is taken out of such presentations by the fact that they are firmly contained within the general structure of the cycle, with its dominantly orthodox tone. Nevertheless, the element of unrestrained and coarse humour, of satire and criticism which they contained, fed the sense, deeply rooted in late medieval culture, of all forms of mimetic activity as inherently improper; and as carrying implications disturbing to the established structure of deference and social order. All this is well brought out in an early fifteenth-century Wyclifite critique of the Corpus Christi drama, which both foreshadows the later Protestant criticisms and provides a dimension of depth which the latter lack. The Wyclifite preacher presents the plays as essentially rites of reversal. In them, the truths of religion are turned into stage illusions; and in the audience restraint and gravity are dissolved into emotional self-indulgence and enjoyment; men turn from reality to a game, and so become transformed from grown-ups into children. The result is a relaxation of discipline and self-control on the part of the play audiences—the more dangerous, says the Wyclifite critic, because this takes place in the context of large public assemblies. The last point probably touches the nub of the matter, and one to which the response of urban magistrates was likely to be immediate" (27–28). "The sixteenth-century privatization of the drama by the development of the stage play, the theatre and the professional actor parallels the privatization of religious and civic ritual, and arose from much the same causes. In this setting, then, the public ritual and public drama of the Corpus Christi feast no longer had any place" (29). In other words, the article documents the creation, continuation and abolition of a ritual, and theorizes on the mechanism behind its disappearance. [JS]

References: **M. Douglas** (+), V.W. Turner (+).
Example: The cult of Corpus Christi.
Key-words: idn, SOC, sec, pmc, tha, dfr, DYN.

Janowitz, Naomi, 2004, 'Do Jews Make Good Protestants? The Cross-Cultural Study of Rituals', in: Jacob K. Olupona (ed.), *Beyond Primitivism. Indigenous Religious Traditions and Modernity*, London, New York: Routledge (ISBN 0–415–27320–x / 0–415–27319–6) 23–36.

This essay discusses a number of issues raised by Tambiah (*Magic, Science, Religion, and the Scope of Rationality*, Cambridge 1990), and the author is critical of many solutions proposed by Tambiah. Moreover, the author detects a Protestant bias in many interpretations of Israelite rituals (and suggests that that predisposition in turn influences Tambiah's analysis). Since the Protestant-biased terminology seems to lead into blind alleys, the author draws on Peirce in order to come up with suggestions for an alternative terminology. She applies the terms 'icon', 'sign', and 'symbol' to the study of rituals, and sketches processes of ritual change in which earlier phases are retrospectively considered as more 'magical', and the new, substituted ones, as more 'ethical'. "These substitutions are complex mixtures of semitic signs, often with 'iconic' symbols being replaced with 'symbolical' ones" (32). *"However, a ritual must retain at some level an iconic relationship to both the source of power and the goals, or the rituals will not have any efficacy"* (33). [MS]

References: S.J. Tambiah (–), H.H. Penner (+), J.H.M. Beattie.
Examples: Scapegoat ritual from Leviticus, Hitite rituals.
Key-words: sem, eff, sym, pmt.

Jennings, Theodore W., 1982, 'On Ritual Knowledge', *Journal of Religion* 62:111–127.

In this article, the author argues that ritual is a pattern of action that cannot be subsumed under mythic or narrative forms. According to her, ritual is "a symbolic structure which is *sui generis*" (112), and ritual can be best understood as "performing noetic functions in ways peculiar to itself" (112). On the basis of these noetic functions, the author aims "to develop the basis for a theoretical/critical reflection on ritual" (112) and distinguishes between three 'moments' in this function: 1. Ritual action is a way of gaining new knowledge; the variation and alteration in ritual performance serves as an autonomous mode of noetic exploration and discovery. 2. Ritual serves to transmit knowledge; ritual repetition serves as a pedagogical mode of transmission of ritual knowledge. In providing a pattern of doing, the ritual action "does not primarily teach us to see differently but to act differently"

(117). According to the author, "[r]itual serves as a paradigm for all significant action" (118) and ritual knowledge is "the knowledge gained in bodily action, a knowledge which is a knowledge of bodily action" (119). 3. "[R]itual performance is a display of the ritual and of the participants in the ritual to an observer who is invited to see, approve, understand, or recognize the ritual action" (113). Ritual knowledge serves as the transition "between the ritual action and the attempt to gain a theoretical-critical understanding of ritual" (113). For this reason, the author distinguishes between the 'object of ritual knowledge' and the 'ritual as object of knowledge'. The 'object of ritual knowledge' is "the coordination of three kinds of action: (*a*) the ritual action, (*b*) the constituting action, (*c*) the extraritual behavior modeled by ritual action" (122). The 'ritual as the object of knowledge' is—since "the particular character of ritual knowledge invites our inquiry—that such an inquiry is or may be an extension of ritual knowledge itself" (124). Ritual action invites and directs attention and evokes a response on the part of the observer. These cognitive issues are not a violation of ritual or imported from outside, although the introduction of an outside observer might have some impact on ritual performance. Thus, it is her task "to know reflectively what is known ritually, to re-cognize ritual knowledge" (125). [JK]

References: R.L. Grimes (+), V.W. Turner (+).
Example: Liturgy.
Key-words: cmp, cog, pr1, rfl, str.

Jensen, Jeppe Sinding, 1986, 'Ritual Between Art and Control', *Temenos* 22:109–128.

The aim of this article is to present viewpoints on the meaning of ritual that can help to improve the understanding of ritual in particular and to develop a research strategy for the study of religion in general. Asserting that the history of religions is in need of theories on a broader scale, the author argues that the traditional classification of ritual under the phenomenology of religion has to be reversed. According to him, religion should become a part of the current discourse on ritual. For this purpose, he gives an overview of the various approaches that define ritual, e.g. ritual as symbolic action, language, and text, or present such theoretical approaches to the study of ritual as symbolism, structuralism, functionalism, semiotics, etc. The author stresses the importance of the concepts of reflexivity, self-referentiality, and liminality. According to him, the confusion about the meaning and function of rituals originates in the different questions and methods that provide different answers. He concludes his examination by asserting that "[s]ymbols and rituals are forms of communication and thereby a function of culture and not natural phenomena. Rituals are programs of action that mankind uses to interpret itself and the world around it" (124). [JK]

References: R.D. Abrahams, B.A. Babcock, F. Barth, P. Bourdieu, M. Douglas, M. Eliade, D.S. Gardner, C. Geertz, J. Goody, E.Th. Lawson, E.R. Leach, C. Lévi-Strauss, G.A. Lewis, B. Lincoln, H.H. Penner, R.A. Segal, M. Singer, J.Z. Smith, P. Smith, D. Sperber, F. Staal, T.S. Turner, V.W. Turner.
Key-words: gen, aes, com, def, ecl, mng, pmc, rfl, sem, str, sym.

Jeserich, Florian, 2006, 'An Invitation to "Theorizing" ***Theorizing Rituals*****. Some Suggestions for Using the Indexes', in: Jens Kreinath, Jan A.M. Snoek & Michael Stausberg (eds),** ***Theorizing Rituals. Vol. I: Issues, Topics, Approaches, Concepts*****, (Numen Book Series 114–1), Leiden, Boston: Brill (ISBN-10: 90–04–15342–x, ISBN-13: 978–90–04–15342–4) 687–713.**

This essay is intimately connected with the practice of 'theorizing'. 'Theorizing', as described by Kreinath, Snoek and Stausberg in their introduction to the volume *Theorizing Rituals*, is a form of looking at theories, approaches and concepts from both a reflexive and a reflective meta-theoretical perspective. The author argues that the use of the volume's indexes, a subject index and an index of names, helps to adopt such a position. To illustrate how the analytical indexes can be applied as tools for internally 'theorizing' *Theorizing Rituals*, he gives some examples: In the first section, entitled "Figures and Key-Figures" (688–690), the author presents some statistical data based on an analysis of the index of names. By this means, he figures out that V.W. Turner, É. Durkheim, R.A. Rappaport, S.J. Tambiah, C.M. Bell, C. Geertz, E.R. Leach, and A. van Gennep play a decisive role in guiding or molding the 'internal' discourse on ritual theory. The author then presents two exemplary features of the scholarly discourse in order to "analyze *the ways* in which the different authors are referring to each other and *the contexts* in which these mentions and citations occur.... The first one, which I call 'The Never-Ending Struggle with Durkheim' [690–697], illustrates how one can draw conclusions from looking up the entry 'Durkheim, É.' in the index of names, sorting and combining the text passages on the relevant pages. The second one, entitled 'Identity: Contexts, Concepts, and Contests' [697–710], an analysis of the entry '*identity*', illustrates how powerful a tool the subject index can be" (690). The final section ("A Prospect of Linking Internal and External Discourses", 710–713) already includes some insights from 'theorizing' the annotated bibliography at hand, thus establishing ties between the two volumes. [Florian Jeserich]

References: H.B. Boudewijnse, M. Douglas, É. Durkheim, C. Humphrey, J. Laidlaw, T.S. Turner, V.W. Turner, A. van Gennep.
Key-words: com, dyn, emo, IDN, psy, ref, rfl, sec, sem, soc, str.

Jones, Lindsay, 2000, *The Hermeneutics of Sacred Architecture. Experience, Interpretation, Comparison. Vol. I: Monumental Occasions. Reflections on the Eventfulness of Religious Architecture. Vol. II: Hermeneutical Calisthenics. A Morphology of Ritual-Architectural Priorities* (Religions of the World); Cambridge (MA): Harvard University Press (ISBN Vol. 1: 0–945454–21–x / 0–945454–22–8 (p), Vol. 2: 0–945454–23–6 / 0–945454–24–4 (p)) (xxxi + 326 / xxiv + 498) (with a foreword by Lawrence E. Sullivan and with an index and bibliography in each volume).

The author of these books is a scholar in the comparative science of religions. In his foreword, Sullivan summarizes: "These two volumes lay out in clear terms the crucial issues which must be navigated to take advantage of debates in several fields...: architecture, comparative literature, interpretation theory, history of religions, semiotics, philosophy, theology, and studies of ritual and performance. Jones cuts through these debates for his own purpose: he wants to relate architecture more closely to ritual and to the unfolding of special events. This move transforms monuments into monumental occasions and transmutes architectures into eventful encounters between special powers... and human actors in time.... He is especially keen to re-establish the viability and necessity of comparison in the human and social sciences" (xiii). "Jones argues that comparison is necessary because, unlike objectivist descriptions of architecture, which hold that sites have more or less fixed meanings, there is an endless flux between buildings and their meanings.... Since the meaning of buildings does not hold firm, should one conclude that architecture is intrinsically meaningless?... In the course of his digging, Jones uncovers grounds for an entirely different view: that of the superabundance associated with sacred architecture. Jones speaks of the superabundance of experience and the superabundance of interpretation" (xiv). "Jones... proposes some eleven sorts of relationships that exist between monuments and ritual.... These eleven nodes form an interpretative framework, or morphology, of ritual-architectural events" (xv). "The eleven-point framework develops across the several levels of orientation, commemoration, and presentation in the context of performance. It covers the way sacred architecture, in ritual events, orients participants: 1) to the universe itself by presenting a microcosmic replica; 2) to rules, precedents, standards, and convention displayed in sacred architecture; 3) to stars and heavenly bodies with which sacred architecture is aligned. Regarding the content of ritual events, sacred architecture commemorates: 4) the deities and ultimate realities housed or recalled in sacred architecture; 5) the mythical and miraculous episodes in sacred history; 6) the social order of authority and economic arrangement legitimated (or sometimes challenged) in the politics that swirl around sacred architecture; 7) the ancestors and the deceased brought to mind in the ritual commemorations held within sacred architecture. In a ritual performance sacred architecture contextualizes the presentation of: 8) theater enacted against the backdrop of sacred architecture; 9) contemplation, especially where sacred architecture becomes the focus for meditation or devotion; 10) offerings of appeasement, aiming to please sacred beings through the very process of construction; 11) pure sanctuary, a state free from imperfection" (xvi). [JS]

Key-words: com, pmc, tha, sem, mng, sym, aes, eff, pow, EMO, med, SPC, cpr.

Kapferer, Bruce, 1979, 'Introduction. Ritual Process and the Transformation of Context', in: Bruce Kapferer (ed.), *The Power of Ritual. Transition, Transformation and Transcendence in Ritual Practice*, (= *Social Analysis* 1) 3–19.

The author notes that the essays included in the volume, though they share the same interest in the dimensions of the ritual process, go beyond this notion by exploring rituals as a transitional process, because they "seek to extend an understanding of how rituals can achieve transformations in experience, identities and action for those who gather to them, both within the performative organization of the rituals themselves and in the contexts of meaning and action which extend around them" (3). These essays focus on the transformational process within ritual by examining "the nature of ritual performance, and the expressive or performative modes in which ritual symbol and action is organized in effecting ritual transformations of meaning and action" (3). The author defines transformation as "an aspect of context and of the elements (objects, actions, symbols, and identities), which compose a context" (3). Although he argues that transformation is an aspect of process, these processes do not necessarily include transformation. "The transformation of a context must involve a transformation of its constituent elements" (4). The author specifies his notion of performance: it "relates to the processes whereby a form, in this case a ritual, is translated into an action-setting involving participants and audience, or those who are bystanders, looking-in upon the action" (6). Therefore, he suggests that "the analysis of ritual as form, particularly in relation to how it effects important transformations of contexts of meaning and action, cannot be satisfactorily achieved without considering the process of its performance" (6). According to him, there are two different aspects of performance, the arrangement of space as an organisation of participants and audience into the setting of a performance, and the medium through which the symbolic object and action is carried out: 1. "The categories and roles of 'participant' and 'audience' are also subject to change in the process of performance. Such categories and roles are not stable and static properties of ritual performances" (7). 2. "Ideas, meaning and action carried through, and contained within, specific modes of expression may constitute transformations of symbolic objects and actions, and of the ideas and meaning attendant upon them, as they are carried and located in other expressive modes. The entry or merging of one performative mode of expression into another...may facilitate certain transformational processes" (8). [JK]

References: G. Bateson (+), M.E.F. Bloch, M. Douglas, E. Goffman (+), D. Handelman (+), R.A. Rappaport, E.L. Schieffelin, T.S. Turner (+), V.W. Turner (+), A. van Gennep (–).
Examples: Exorcisms, rituals of passage.
Key-words: eff, idn, mng, pmc, pmt, pr1, str.

Kapferer, Bruce (ed.), 1979, *The Power of Ritual. Transition, Transformation and Transcendence in Ritual Practice*; Adelaide (South Australia): University of Adelaide (ISSN 0155–977–X) (192) (special inaugural issue of *Social Analysis; Journal of Cultural and Social Practice*).

Selected contents: Bruce Kapferer: "Introduction. Ritual Process and the Transformation of Context" (3–19) (*); John N. Gray: "Keep the Hom Fires Burning. Sacrifices in Nepal" (81–107); Bruce Kapferer: "Entertaining Demons. Comedy, Interaction and Meaning in a Sinhalese

Healing Ritual" (108–152); Bruce Kapferer: "Emotion and Feeling in Sinhalese Healing Rites" (153–176); Don Handelman: "Is Naven Ludic? Paradox and the Communication of Identity" (177–191) (*). [JK]
Review: J.W. Fernandez *AE* 7.4 (1980) 791 f.
Key-words: mng, emo, com, idn, pmc, POW, pr1, str.

Kapferer, Bruce, 1983, *A Celebration of Demons. Exorcism and the Aesthetics of Healing in Sri Lanka*; Bloomington: Indiana University Press (ISBN 0–253–31326–0 / 0–253–20304–X (p)) (xii + 293) (foreword by Victor W. Turner) (with index and bibliography) (2nd ed. 1991).

In the Foreword, Victor W. Turner writes that this book "is a pioneering study in the emerging field of performance studies" that "aims to bring the social sciences and arts together to shape theory and methods and is cross-cultural and interdisciplinary in perspective" (ix). According to him, this approach is "combining structuralist, semiotic and processual concepts and procedures into an original and powerful mode of analysis which takes aesthetic features of ritual into full theoretical account" (ix). The author of this book explores "major Sinhalese demon ceremonies or exorcisms performed in and around the town of Galle in southern Sri Lanka" (xiii). Focusing on the description of "the ceremony of the Great Cemetery Demon", the author is concerned with "the way exorcism ritual effects key transitions and transformations in identity, experience, meaning and action" (xiii). In his approach to ritual, the author stresses "the critical importance of considering performance and especially the role of the aesthetic" (xiii). For this reason, he concentrates on music, dance, and comic drama as the key aesthetic forms in the performance of ritual exorcism. By adopting a perspective "which examines the phenomenon of the demonic and exorcism in its own terms" (xiii), the author aims at "an approach to ritual which attends to its social and political context, to the logic of ideas which are incorporated and organized within ritual performance, and to ritual performance as the *modus operandi* of these ideas and of their transformation" (2). For this reason, he "define[s] ritual as a multi-modal symbolic form, the practice of which is marked off (usually spatially and temporally) from, or within, the routine of everyday life, and which has specified, in advance of its enactment, a particular sequential ordering of acts, utterances, and events, which are essential to the recognition of the ritual by cultural members as being representative of a specific cultural type" (2). Moreover, "ritual is a social practice where ideas are produced in a determinant and dominant relation to action, and it is a practice where action is continually structured to the idea" (3). The author considers ritual performance and argues against the common structuralist or semiotic notion that performance "presupposes some concept of text" that can be analyzed "independently of its performance structure" (7). "Performance... is never mere enactment reducible to terms independent of its formation as a structure of practice" (7). He contends: "Ritual performance, as a structure of practice, is not simply the vehicle of a 'text', or a means for the expression of cultural and social meaning, or a way of communicating information which somehow lies outside it. I stress that ritual performance is itself constitutive of that which it intends, expresses, or communicates" (7). The author develops "a multifaceted approach which examines exorcism ritual both in its cultural and social milieu and in terms of the structural process of its performance" (11). He aims to elaborate "an approach to ritual which... extends our knowledge of the ritual process and the dynamics of its transformations" (11). The first part of this book consists of the following chapters: "Exorcism, Class, and Change in Urban Sri Lanka" (12–36), "Exorcists" (37–48), "Demonic Illness. Diagnosis and Social Context" (49–91), and "Exorcism and the Symbolic Identity of Women" (92–110). In these chapters, the author places exorcism practice within a broader cultural and social context as a particular Sinhalese practice that "is subject to the movement, change and dynamic, in history" (12). He focuses "on the issue of religious and ritual change as this is continually produced in a social discourse based on the contradictions and oppositions of class" (30). "The ritual authority of exorcists", he argues, "is consistent with the subversion of hierarchy as this is culturally constituted in the normal everyday world, a subversion wrought by demonic attack" (40). Based on the definition of demonic illness as a discourse, the author outlines the diagnostic practice within social context and discusses the question of "how demonic illness is generally conceptualized and some of the factors which may account for the efficacy of exorcism in the treatment of demonic illness" (49). Because in Sri Lanka "women are more often the subjects of rites of healing and cults of exorcism than are men", the author argues that women as a category "are subject to demonic attack as a function of their cultural typification, which places them in a special and significant relation to the demonic" and addresses "the symbolic identity of women, and the logic of its constitution in Sinhalese culture, as critical in accounting for the frequency of their demonic attack and exorcist treatment relative to men" (92). The remaining chapters of this book introduce various demons in Sinhalese Buddhism. In the chapter "The Demonic Illusion. Demons and the Cosmic Hierarchy" (111–128), the author argues that "[i]llusion is a major force in the process of cosmic relations and expresses the essential changeable quality of these relations and the often ambiguous and unstable character of the gods and demons" (113). Moreover, he argues that "deities can change into demons, and *vice versa*, as well as assume a variety of other forms, as can demons" (117), but they are "not only frequently ambiguous in themselves, but they also stand in an ambiguous relation to each other" (118). On the basis of this notion of demonic illusion, the author outlines the logic of the Sinhalese cosmic hierarchy: "while the demonic is immanent in the divine, the divine is also a possibility of the demonic" (124–125). This logic includes not only "a key aspect of the ambiguity of the deity, but also a key aspect of its vital power" (125). Here the ritual practice comes into play: "By acting upon and through deities, ritual can restore an order, the disorder of which can be symbolically represented through the appearance of a deity in a lower manifestation" (125). In the ethnographic chapter, "The Exorcism of the Great Cemetery Demon. Event and Structure in Major Exorcisms" (129–177), the author gives a detailed account of the organization of ritual space and the sequential order of events in this demonic exorcism. In the more theoretical chapters on "Music, Dance, and Trance" (178–206) and "The Comedy of Gods and Demons" (207–231), the author concentrates "on the aesthetic of exorcism and its role in ritual performance" (178). He argues "that transitions and transformations in meaning and experience are communicated, received, and engendered among ritual participants through the dynamic properties of the major aesthetic modes of exorcisms and by the way participant standpoint or perspective is ordered in ritual action. More generally, I approach the issue of the relation artistic form to meaning and experience" (178). He assumes that "possibilities for the ordering of experience and its meaning inhere in the structure of artistic form" (178). In the "Epilogue. A Celebration of Demons", he concludes: "The analysis of ritual without a systematic consideration of the media of performance and without an attention to the way participants are structured to the central action limits a general anthropological understanding of the nature of the ritual process" (237). [JK]

References: R. Barthes, G. Bateson (+), P.L. Berger, H. Bergson (+), M.E.F. Bloch, P. Bourdieu (+), A. Cohen, M. Douglas (+), C. Geertz, D. Handelman (+), S.K. Langer (+), E. Leach, C. Lévi-Strauss (+), Th. Luckman, C.P. MacCormack, G.H. Mead (+), S.B. Ortner, R.A. Rappaport (–), A. Schutz (+), S.J. Tambiah, V.W. Turner (+).
Reviews: A. Bharati *AA* 86.3 (1984) 728 f; R.L. Stirrat *Man* 19.4 (1984) 688 f; G. Obeyesekere *AE* 12.1 (1985) 179 f; G. Wijeyewardene *CanbAnth* 8.1/2 (1985) 223; **M. Lambek *CSSH* 27.2 (1985) 291–303**; H.L. Seneviratne *JAS* 44.3 (1985) 636 f; P. Alexander *Mank* 15.1 (1985) 72–74; S. Kokan *AFS* 45.2 (1986) 329 f; S. Bell *SAs* 9.1 (1986) 97 f.
Key-words: AES, agn, com, cpl, dnc, DYN, ecn, eff, emb, emo, GDR, idn, med, mus, PMC, POW, pr2, rel, rfl, sem, spc, STR, sym, tim.

Kapferer, Bruce, 1986, 'Performance and the Structuring of Meaning and Experience', in: Victor Witter Turner & Edward M. Bruner (eds), *The Anthropology of Experience*, Urbana (IL), Chicago: University of Illinois Press (ISBN 0–252–01236–4 / 0–252–01249–6 (p)) (*) 188–203.

In this article, the author argues that the fundamental "postulate concerning the impossibility of experiencing another's experience…is restricted to experience as comprehended and realized in the mundane world of everyday life. My argument now turns to the possibility of mutual experience in the sense of experiencing together the one experience. Such a possibility is present in many of the cultural performances we and those in other cultures recognize as art and ritual" (190–191). Crucial for such an experience of ritual is the shared participation in the same performance of the ritual. "In my usage, 'performance' constitutes a unity of text and enactment, neither being reducible to the other" (192). "The directionality of performance and the media of performance are structuring of the ritual context; together they constitute meaning of ritual, variously enable the communication of its meaning, and create the possibility for the mutual involvement of participants in the one experience, or else distance them and lead to their reflection on experience perhaps from a structured perspective outside the immediacy of the experience" (193). This is then illustrated by the example of Sinhalese exorcism in the south of Sri Lanka, which illustrates that "[M]embers of the ritual gathering are not confined within their own experience and understandings, but by their interaction they are able to stand outside themselves and interpret their experience through shared constructs and understandings" (197). The author concludes that "[i]f there is one general point underlying my argument it is the critical importance of performance in the analysis of meaning and experience. Performance as the unity of text and enactment is realized in a variety of forms, aesthetic and otherwise, which carry with them, as a potential of their structure, their own possibilities for the realization of meaning and experience. They are not necessarily reducible one to the other" (202). [JS]

References: R.D. Laing (–), M. Natanson (+), M. Dufrenne (+).
Example: Sinhalese exorcism in the south of Sri Lanka.
Key-words: STR, MNG, aes, com, PMC, cpl, EMO, med, par, rfl, tim.

Kapferer, Bruce, 1997, *The Feast of the Sorcerer. Practices of Consciousness and Power*; Chicago, London: University of Chicago Press (ISBN 0–226–42411–1 / 0–226–42413–8 (p)) (xix + 367) (with index and bibliography).

In this book, the author largely employs a phenomenological approach to ritual. At the core of his approach lies the concept of 'intentionality' drawn from Husserl. He avails himself of this concept because he contends that human beings (and their consciousness) are always directed towards other human beings and the world. There is no subject prior to an object, and *vice versa*. They are constituted simultaneously by 'being-in-the-world', such that "meaning and value (and also social and political relations) are immanent in the intentionality of human existence" (5). In other words, ritual performances—as a form of 'being-in the world'—constitute meanings by their mere enactment: "Their meaning is always in the dynamics of their situational production" (20). Since the author takes intentionality to be ambiguous, capable of either forming or destroying social relations, he focuses on the 'problematics of existence' as lived out in rituals. The book begins by situating the Sri Lankan (anti-) sorcery ritual Suniyama within its historical context (Chapter 2) in order to show how historical events and processes framed the emergence of the Suniyama. Then he locates the ritual in a Sinhalese classification system of different kinds of sorcery, sorcery practices, and people involved in sorcery. Chapter 3 presents two myths about the origin of the Suniyama that show their potentiality to be "directed toward the diverse contexts of experience and meaning in the world" (62). As the 'logos' part, myths complement practice, i.e. rituals, and therefore help to enframe and grasp, not represent, the dimensions of human reality. In Chapters 4 and 5, the author describes and interprets the Suniyama in detail, focusing on the performance character of the ritual. According to him, the nature of reality is explored (or discovered) as practices are experienced whereby the participants' bodily motions are related to the motions of their consciousness. In other words, meaning is felt through the body and inscribed on it by practice, so that it becomes "a lived knowledge and meaning" (177). It is in Chapter 5 that his phenomenological approach results in the development of the concepts of 'actuality' and 'virtuality', both being described as a space-time not radically distinct from one another. In rituals, the actuality, i.e. the reality, of everyday life is transformed by the performance of everyday activities during the ritual practices where they are controlled and more determinate in their outcome than their counterparts in actuality. Virtuality, i.e. the space-time of ritual, thus "impedes the chaos of the circumstances of life, a world that is always in flux; it attempts to set or reset the conditions from which the world develops or extends in all its changeability and expanding difference" (180). It is "a radical slowing down and entry within the constructional moments in which human beings realize themselves and their world" (180). The constitutive property of (ritual) performances are achieved by opening up "the perceptual faculties of victims [of the Suniyama], which are the keys to the intentional directions of victims and the full elaboration of consciousness" (181). Chapter 6 is an elaboration of the author's argument that ritual dynamics produce sociality. This argument is based on his assumption that agents are human beings "rooted in-the-world which is inhabited by others towards whom they are thrown and mutually oriented or acting" (185). By interpreting the Suniyama as sacrifice and gift, he examines their constititive dynamics, which involve acts of classification, differentiation and giving, acts that are at the center of social formation. The author continues the interpretation of the Suniyama by analyzing how the emotions—being "vital to their [the participants] perception and the formation of their conceptions and agency in the life world" (223)—of fear, loathing, and anger are involved in ritual practices. Finally, he concludes his elaborations with a look at the Suniyama's 'paradox of power', i.e. the ability to generate as well as destroy sociality. He thereby shows that it is the intentionality of power in sorcery which "bridges the space between persons and between persons and objects" (264). [Thorsten Gieser]

References: E.E. Evans-Pritchard, M. Gluckman, D. Handelman, B. Malinowski, M. Mauss.

Example: Suniyama ritual in Sri Lanka.
Reviews: J. Carbine *JR* 78.4 (1998) 658 f; G. Dwyer *JAR* 54.2 (1998) 252–254; M. Lambek *AA* 100.3 (1998) 834 f; D.P. Mines *AQ* 71.4 (1998) 213–215; A. Stoeckl *CambAnth* 20.1–2 (1998) 164–166; T. Borchert *SocRel* 60.1 (1999) 94 f; M. Carrithers *AE* 26.4 (1999) 1032 f; K. Garbett *Oc* 70.2 (1999) 197 f; P. Kirkup *CanbAnth* 22.2 (1999) 90 f; G. Kosack *Anthr* 94.4–6 (1999) 612; P.J. Stewart & A. Strathern *JRS* 14.1 (2000) 69; G. Tarabout *Homme* 161 (2002) 276–278.
Key-words: soc, pow, aes, pmc, pr1, dyn, myt, agn, tim, VIR.

Kapferer, Bruce, 2000, 'Sexuality and the Art of Seduction in Sinhalese Exorcism', *Ethnos* 65:5–32.

In this essay, the author presents the ritual of Sinhalese exorcism as belonging to the domain of seduction. The author's overarching concern is "to expand my understanding of these rites and of ritual more generally where erotic and seductive processes are clearly at work" (5). His focus on issues of sexuality and seduction in Sinhalese exorcisms has to be seen as "part of a larger interest in the nature of the aesthetics of ritual performance" (5). The epistemological as well as theoretical relevance of this article is due to the fact that it discusses "the harmonizing erotics of exorcism as a process that establishes a simulacrum or virtual harmonic dynamic, a reality that overcomes the reality of experience or within which the reality of experience can be reorganized or restructured" (7). For the author, this issue is important for any anthropological analysis of ritual, because "[t]he power of the erotic and the seductive is in suggestion and sometimes in the outright denial of carnal desire or interest. Depth is overridden in the delight of the poetic harmony of the surface" (7). In contrast to the modernist approaches, the author argues that "deconstructionist, poststructuralist or postmodern approaches" are gaining in strength because they "tend to insist on a greater ethnographic relativism (whereby 'ritual' as a general category is of reduced value)" (8). Related to this is "a shift away from essentializing and generalizing arguments that concentrate on the deep structures or central organizing principles of rites. The move is towards a consideration of their performance surface, of their open-endedness, dialogical ambiguities, and their diversity of interpretational possibility" (8). Therefore the author argues for "an understanding of exorcism practice as both a discourse of surfaces and depth, whereby forces of determination can be subverted and the capacity of human beings to intervene in their existential circumstances is regenerated" (8). The main part of this paper focuses on the analysis of Sinhalese rituals, called *ratayakkuma*, which "centre on women and their bodily processes" (8). The following sections addressing the ethnographic details are entitled "Myths of Sexuality and Seduction" (9–12), "The Ratayakkuma. Violent Discourses of Sexuality and Reproductive Disruption" (12–15) and "The Dance of the Seven Queens. A Ritual Discourse on the Circumstances of Female Distress" (15–18). In the section entitled "Exorcism and the Aesthetics of Seduction" (18–20), the author argues that "the erotics and seduction of exorcism aesthetics traverse emergent lines of contradiction and opposition, subverting all that which impedes the formation of encompassing harmonies and unities" (18). In "Ritual, Hierarchy, and the Logics of Contradiction" (20–26), he addresses the hierarchical dynamics and transformational logic of Sinhalese exorcism in the attempt to overcome destructive demonic forces. In describing how the aesthetic and seductive forces of ritual are able to break the paradox of contradiction, the author writes: "Seduction is a ritual tactic that avoids contradictions and oppositions. The seducer plays to create a non-threatening and non-oppositional reality in which the seducer and the seduced appear to be mutually committed" (24). In the final section "Ritual, Erotic Synthesis and the Human Determination of Determination" (26–27), the author argues that "[t]hrough ritual, human beings attempt to break the hold of forces that appear to be conditional and determinant of human existence" (26). From this follows that "[t]he demonic is itself determined and limited and exorcism practice intervenes to overcome the non-necessary determination of destructive contradictions and negations by drawing demons within an encompassing hierarchy" (26). According to him, exorcism "acts against determinations of all kinds"; it is "*par excellence* a technology of the erotic and of the seductive that manifests its potency not through contradiction or confrontation (a paradox of power) but through the arts of creative deflection, distraction, and deception. This in my view expands an understanding of the immense importance of aesthetic form not just in exorcism but perhaps in ritual practice more generally" (27). [JK]

References: C.M. Bell (–), M.E.F. Bloch (–), D. Handelman, C. Humphrey (–) & J. Laidlaw (–), R.A. Rappaport (–), S.J. Tambiah, V.W. Turner.
Example: Sinhalese exorcism ritual.
Key-words: AES, agn, DYN, eff, emb, GDR, myt, PMC, pow, pr2, str, vir.

Kapferer, Bruce, 2004, 'Ritual Dynamics and Virtual Practice. Beyond Representation and Meaning', *Social Analysis* 48:35–54.

"Ritual is one of the most used, perhaps overused, sociological categories and one of the most resistant to adequate definition" (35). Based on this assumption the author argues that "the search for the definition of ritual has been a lost cause from the outset" (36). His attempt by contrast is to propose "an approach that concentrates on ritual practice in itself and, more specifically, the formational dynamics or structuring composition of rite in which experience and meaning are constituted" (36). He emphasizes that "a focus on dynamics, rather than process, moves the understanding of ritual beyond an emphasis on symbolic meaning, reflexivity, and representation" (36). Although an "emphasis on ritual as process" as introduced by Victor W. Turner is crucial, the orientation to dynamics that the author pursues "is directed to those aspects of ritual practice that may establish not only the perceptual ground for the organization of cognition but, above all, the basis for the construction of meaning and the extension towards new horizons of meaning" (36–37). His attempt is to explain that "the virtual of ritual is a thoroughgoing reality of its own, neither a simulacrum of realities external to ritual nor an alternative reality" (37). Although it "bears a connection to ordinary, lived realities, as depth to surface", the author stresses "the virtual of rite as one in which the dynamics of cosmological, social, and personal construction—dynamics as a field of force—achieve their most intense concentration" (37). Though theories of ritual that borrowed concepts from linguistics, drama and performance theory, cybernetics or systems theory present useful insights, the author claims that "they subordinate ritual to the logic and rationale of practices that are not necessarily those of ritual, as this may be realized in a diversity of instances" (39). By way of applying some of Susanne K. Langer's concepts of dynamics and her ideas on the virtual, the author furthers the exploration of symbolic dynamics since "[t]he rites are pragmatically oriented to develop and exploit particular symbolic formations in such a way as to shape human perception and thereby transform experience" (40). The author further widens the concept of virtuality as employed by the works of Gilles Deleuze and Felix Guattari. The direction the author takes "concentrates on ritual as a virtuality, a dynamic process in and of itself with no essential representational symbolic relation to external realities—that is, a coded symbolic formation whose interpretation or meaning is ultimately reducible to the sociopolitical and psychological world outside the ritual context" (46). This approach "accentuates the internal dynamics of rite as the potency of the capacity of ritual to alter, change, or transform the existential circumstances of persons in nonritual realities" (47). According to the author "[t]he virtual is no less a reality, a fully lived reality, than ordinary realities of life. Yet it is substantially different" (47). The virtuality of rite is different from ordinary reality in two ways: It is "a kind of phantasmagoric space... a dynamic that allows for all kinds of potentialities of human experience to take shape and form" (47) and it can be regarded as critical to its *techné* as "a method for entering within life's vital processes and adjusting its dynamics" (48). He concludes that in his approach to virtuality "there is a move away from Turner's anti-structural orientation towards a dynamic of structuration. Although the representational, meaning-driven, symbolic perspective continues to be important, there is a shift to viewing ritual as a dynamic for the production of meaning rather than seeing it as necessarily predominantly meaningful in itself, a perspective that tends to overvalue ritual as representation and places a huge stress on processes such as reflexivity" (50). This concentration on dynamics "indicates some reconsideration of various performance approaches as well, while not negating their value" (50). "Rather than engaging the theatrical metaphor of performance" the author proposes that his approach "might reconceive ritual performance as a dynamic field of force in whose virtual space human psychological, cognitive, and social realities are forged anew, so that the ritual participants are both reoriented to their ordinary realities and embodied with potencies to restore or reconstruct their lived worlds" (51). [JK]

References: C.M. Bell (–), P. Bourdieu, J.W. Boyd, G. Deleuze, J. Goody, F. Guattari, D. Handelman, S.K. Langer (+), C. Lévi-Strauss, R.A. Rappaport, E.L. Schieffelin, F. Staal, V.W. Turner (+), A. van Gennep, R.G. Williams.
Key-words: AES, def, DYN, emo, pmc, rep, rfl, PR2, str, sym, tim, VIR.

Kapferer, Bruce, 2006a, 'Dynamics', in: Jens Kreinath, Jan A.M. Snoek & Michael Stausberg (eds), *Theorizing Rituals. Vol. I: Issues, Topics, Approaches, Concepts*, (Numen Book Series 114–1), Leiden, Boston: Brill (ISBN-10: 90–04–15342–x, ISBN-13: 978–90–04–15342–4) 507–522.

The essay addresses the concept of ritual as both identifying a specific class of action that can be recognized empirically and as an analytical construct whereby social action is exposed to a particular style of interpretational attitude. A broad point is that these are not easily separated, if at all. The overall direction of the essay is to argue for a concentration on dynamics instead of process. This acknowledges the importance of a processual approach, especially the work of Victor Turner in this regard developing as it does from Van Gennep. But here the move is away from any definite scheme to a concern with ritual as involving the intersection of particular kinds of dynamics. These are discussed in terms of the dynamics framing, habitus, and sacrifice. [Bruce Kapferer]

References: V.W. Turner, A. van Gennep.
Key-words: aes, DYN, rep, frm, hab.

Kapferer, Bruce, 2006b, 'Virtuality', in: Jens Kreinath, Jan A.M. Snoek & Michael Stausberg (eds), *Theorizing Rituals. Vol. I: Issues, Topics, Approaches, Concepts*, (Numen Book Series 114–1), Leiden, Boston: Brill (ISBN-10: 90–04–15342–x, ISBN-13: 978–90–04–15342–4) 671–684.

The way ritual achieves its force upon external realities and personal life trajectories has long been a concern for analysis. There are numerous valuable approaches but most posit a particular kind of interconnection between the inner realities of rite and the psychological, social and political worlds upon which ritual appears to demonstrate its effects and which are conceived of as being external to it. The argument here suggests that it is in the very disconnection between ritual realities and those which are understood as external to it that relates to the force of ritual. What is stressed is the dynamic quality of ritual as a virtuality in which it evinces machinic and technological dimensions. Through the virtual artifice of ritual the complexity of reality (grasped as chaosmic actuality) is descended into and critically reconfigured. A major example used is Sinhala anti-sorcery ritual which is concerned to readjust the space/time coordinates conditioning experience so that the anguish which is marked by sorcery can be alleviated or removed. A point that is developed is that it is in the relatively unchanging aspects of ritual that changes in experience and the orientations to non-ritual realities can be achieved. [Bruce Kapferer]

Example: Sinhala anti-sorcery ritual.
Key-words: int, DYN, VIR.

Keesing, Roger M., 1991, 'Experiments in Thinking About Ritual', *Canberra Anthropology* 14.2:60–74.

In this article, the author indulges "in some experiments in thinking about the nature of ritual as a genre of human communication" (60). He draws "mainly on the ideas of scholars outside the realm of anthropology, notably Wittgenstein, Bateson—in his incarnation as ethologist and communications theorist—Austin and Derrida. I ask what ritual is, and what its relationship is to other genres of communication. What distinguishes ritual, and how do we recognize it as such?" (60). He then opens his argument by denying the possibility that 'ritual behavior' could be distinguished from 'everyday' behavior, and illustrates this by attacking—as an example—the assumed repetitiveness of ritual, using a Wittgensteinian language game. This results in the conclusion that 'ritual' "is not distinguished by any intrinsic properties of the action performed in ritual" (62). Then, bringing in Bateson, he introduces framing: "ritual is distinguished by a communicative 'frame': that is, by a set of metacommunicative premises about the messages exchanged within the frame" (62). Such frames can be hierarchically nested. The author sees ritual as a special case of play. In other words, the frame 'this is ritual' is nested within the frame 'this is play'. This leads him to a definition of 'ritual': "Ritual is, I suggest, a genre of communication which, like play, is governed by premises of fictionality, but which, unlike play, is governed by (explicit or implicit) *scripting*. It is, moreover, canonically based on the premise that the performance is being monitored, judged and acted upon by unseen spectators, upon whose judgement hang heavy consequences. In that sense, ritual is serious, scripted play" (63). As a consequence, he understands "so-called secular rituals as being serious rather than play, precisely because they are imitations of religious rituals. That is,...the participants are themselves doing the monitoring and judging" (64). Since the author sees scripting as the essential difference between ritual and play, he argues that scripting "is itself a cultural frame, that invests acts with a particular kind of textuality" (64). He argues that the "communicative frame 'this is ritual' seems to be so basic...in our human repertoire that I am tempted to say that it is universal (as opposed to the endlessly variable acts that go on within the frame), and relatively easy recognizable across cultural boundaries. If ritual is stylized, scripted, serious play, then we can recognize it by its frame, though not by its content (just as we can recognize other genres of play)" (65). He then moves to the questions, "What do rituals 'mean'? And what do rituals 'do': that is, how does their performance transform the participants, and society?" (66). He tries to imagine how Bateson would have answered these questions. And Bateson "would have wanted to say, first of all, that ritual is not about 'things'—birth, rebirth, cosmic re-creation or what have you—but *relationships*, formal patterns that have substantive referents at different levels" (66). Rephrasing the questions, he then argues: "If ritual is a genre of communication, a frame distinguished from 'everyday life' by its premise of fictionality, and from play by its scripted seriousness, we need to ask why humans everywhere create scripts set within such a frame, and what it does to them—individually as well as collectively—when they perform, as actors or spectators, within it. The question, phrased this way, suggests that our analytical task is not simply one of deciphering encrypted structures of cultural meaning. Indeed, very few of the participants are likely to 'understand', even unconsciously, most of the meanings so encrypted" (67). "I do not believe that rituals 'work', either for individuals or for collectives, primarily because of the covert symbolic structures embedded in them. They 'work' because of the way participants think and perceive while they are in the ritual frame" (68), and this is, according to the author, based on the assumed presence of the invisible beings. This being said, the author nevertheless concludes that "[w]e do not know how or why ritual 'works'" (68). In order to try to get one step closer to an answer, he now (69) turns to two other authors: Austin and Derrida. Austin distinguishes between performative and constative utterances, but requires of both that they be serious. Derrida, on the contrary, takes " 'serious' performatives as a special and marked case of 'non-serious' ones" (69), thus in a way inverting, and thus deconstructing, Austin's position. The author now proposes, in a similar way, to deconstruct the opposition between 'everyday life' and 'ritual', by taking 'everyday life' as a special case of "a generalized category we might call 'archeo-ritual'...That is, what if we see everyday life as scripted play, framed by the communicative premise of fictionality? 'Everyday life'...then is characterized not by the absence of a frame (what we do and say is not what it appears to be) but by the implicitness and invisibility of the framing.... The actions and interactions of everyday life, in this view, are surrounded by frames of fictionality, and scripted: a special case of ritual in which participants have forgotten (or are denying) that it is a form of play and have so long memorized the script that they have forgotten (or are denying) that it exists" (70). On this view, " '[s]erious' ritual differs from play in general in being scripted, as well as 'serious'. Archeo-ritual—as Derrida might call it—is scripted play. Ritual—serious scripted play—becomes, then, the marked and special case" (71). This deconstruction "has the consequence of subverting the formal definition of ritual I proposed in the first part of the paper. I present this as a paradox, without proffering a resolution. It should be possible to define ritual in formal communicational terms, I think; but at the same time, as the deconstruction serves to remind us, the message 'This is ritual' needs to be placed within a more complex and developed theory of metacommunicative framing than the one I have sketched" (71). Finally, the author suggests that "we might learn more about rituals by studying failed rituals, or mock rituals, than successful or real ones" (71). "[C]ommunications that go wrong and expectations that are violated tell us more than smoothly orchestrated symphonies of shared meaning" (72). [JS]

References: L. Wittgenstein, G. Bateson, J.L. Austin, J. Derrida.
Key-words: def, str, sec, mng, sym, com, pmt, rel, eff, emo, FRM.

Kelly, John D. & Martha Kaplan, 1990, 'History, Structure, and Ritual', ***Annual Review of Anthropology*** **19:119–150.**

In reviewing recent contributions, the authors aim to relate concepts of history and structure to the study of ritual. They consider rituals as historical phenomena and conceive "a turn to history in the anthropology of the 1980s", "not only a turn to historical materials, but a turn from accounts set in a timeless 'ethnographic present' to accounts that find history intrinsic to their subject" (120). To indicate this paradigm shift, they "examine the fate of only three important anthropological images of ritual in the turn to history: the divine king, the cargo cult, and carnival" (121). In a first section, "Divine Kings. Ritual Making Structure?" (122–129), they argue that the rituals of divine kings were "a central image in evolutionary anthropology, and have reemerged, transformed, in the new historical anthropology" (122). The question is no longer whether divine kingship constitutes a stage to the building of nation-states or to rational thought. Rather the question of the 'new historians' is whether "rituals of kings make structure [Sahlins, Valeri, Hocart] or superstructure [Bloch]" (121). In a second section entitled "Cargo Cults. Ritual against History?" (129–136), they argue that one can observe from the divine king to the cargo cult a shift "from an image of ritual politics at the center of other societies to an image of rituals of 'others' no longer conceived as separate, but instead as connected and colonized, responding to the Western, modern, or colonial presence" (129). For that reason, "[t]he search for a general theory of cults and movements" was an important topic for "anthropological inquiry into social change, asymmetries of power, and the agency of 'others' in a real world of culture contact, capitalist encroachment, and colonialism" (129). Whereas earlier "[t]he cargo cult was an image of ritual against history, a response from the culture of the 'other' to the historical practice of the colonizers", nowadays anthropologists "seek vehicles for study of the culture and history of both colonizers and colonized" (136). In a third section, "Canival. Ritual against Structure?" (136–139), the authors address the issues of 'social drama', 'ritual process', 'communitas', and 'liminality', which by the 1970s became "influential in many related fields of ritual and historical study" (136). Finally, the authors sense a shift "[f]rom Victor Turner to Mikhail Bakthin", "from images of dialectical processes to images of deconstructive ones; from successive phases of structure and anti-structure to relations of power and resistance; from processualism to chaotics" (137). In "Conclusions. Rituals Making History" (139–141), the authors state that recently "new issues have been raised about structure, history, and ritual" (139). In connecting history, structure, and ritual, they claim that "ritual plays a crucial role in practice, as vehicle for all forms of authority" and finally suggest that "the rituals in ongoing practice are a principal site of new history being made, and that study of the plural formal potentialities of rituals could be basic to efforts to imagine possibilities for real political change" (141). [JK/Florian Jeserich]

References: M. Bakthin, M.E.F. Bloch, J. Comaroff, M.E. Combs-Schilling, M. Foucault, C. Geertz, M. Gluckman, A.M. Hocart, C. Lévi-Strauss, E. Ohnuki-Tierney, M. Sahlins, S.J. Tambiah, M.T. Taussig, V.W. Turner, V. Valeri.
Key-words: agn, dyn, eff, idn, pmc, POW, pr1, pr2, STR, tim.

Kertzer, David I., 1988, *Ritual, Politics, and Power*; New Haven (CT), London: Yale University Press (ISBN 0-300-04007-5) (xiv + 235) (with index and bibliography).

In this richly documented study—examples span the continents as well as the centuries—the author seeks to correct what he regards as the widespread tendency among social theorists to see political institutions as "simply the outcome of different interest groups competing for material resources" (174). He points out that such a modernist bias overlooks the fact that ritual is a ubiquitous part of modern political life. The modern nation-state has not escaped the need for symbolic representation but, with its expanded scale and anonymous community, made its dissemination in ritual all the more imperative. His arguments on ritual and the symbolic are grounded in the mainstream of symbolic anthropology. Two sections are devoted to "Defining Ritual" (8–9) and "Characteristics of Ritual" (9–12). Here ritual is defined as "symbolic behavior that is socially standardized and repetitive" (9). Following Victor Turner, the author notes that ritual can be a potent mechanism of legitimation because it engages people in emotionally charged social action, uniting symbols of social reality with the strong emotions that ritual performance can stir (40). Indeed, "the most effective rituals have an emotionally compelling quality to them" (99). He shows that the deepest significance of ritual is that, precisely because it is essentially nonverbal, it may promote the harmony of otherwise conflicting wills without demanding the rational response that might otherwise form the basis for further conflict. Ironically, then, ritual is to be seen less as a throwback to some primitive state than a thoroughly rational means of resolving conflict. It is at this point that the relationship between ritual and politics is particularly relevant. Since he insists that solidarity, maintained by ritual, is experiential and not cognitive, it is not an event in a society's history that simply happens but a constant process of renewal. Solidarity is not based on shared beliefs or ideas, he argues: "Ritual builds solidarity without requiring the sharing of beliefs. Solidarity is produced by people acting together, not by people thinking together" (76, also 67, 69, 96). The author approaches this theme by discussing the role of ritual first in the creation of political organizations and then in the establishment and maintenance of political legitimacy: "Far from simply reflecting existing power relations, rituals are often important in doing just the opposite, that is, in fostering beliefs about the political universe that systematically misrepresent what is going on.... What is important about the effects of ritual on cognition is as much what the rites lead us to ignore as what they lead us to see" (87). He goes on to consider how ritual is involved in the struggle for power and, in particular, how it can serve revolutionary as well as reactionary ends. For, since he claims that ritual is politically neutral, independent of the ideology of political values, it may not simply be a vehicle for creating or expressing consensus; it may also be a weapon in political struggle. Ritual is vital to challenging, as well as maintaining, the political regime. "Ritual may be vital to reaction, but it is also the lifeblood of revolution" (2). In his view, politics is a power-oriented activity, and "people can increase their power through the manipulation of ritual, just as they can lose power through ritual neglect or incompetence" (29). And, for him, the hallmark of power is the construction of reality. Since this is precisely what he sees as the function of ritual, it is clear that ritual is not just a useful resource available to the aspiring politician; it is of the very essence of political activity. [JS]

References: É. Durkheim, V.W. Turner.

Reviews: R. Hefner *AA* 90.4 (1988) 999; W. Mullins *CJPS* 21 (1988) 847 f; Caroline Anstey *IA* 64.4 (1988) 673 f; G.R. Debnam *AAPSS* 503 (1989) 154 f; M.S. Kimmel *AJS* 94.5 (1989) 1272; P.M. Hall *CS* 18.3 (1989) 377 f; M.H. Ross *JOP* 51.2 (1989) 464; R.L. Grimes *JR* 69.2 (1989) 288; G.M. Platt *JRS* 3.2 (1989) 322 f; E.S. Rawski *JSH* 23.1 (1989) 190 f; J.M. Penning *JSSR* 28.4 (1989) 548; B.L. Hanson *Per* 18.1 (1989) 39; H.M. Hintjens *PSt* 37.2 (1989) 295; D. Handelman *AE* 17.3 (1990) 559 f; E. Weber *AHR* 95.2 (1990) 454 f; G. Brana-Shute *BTLV* 146 (1990) 170 f; **G. Kourvetaris *JPMS* 18.2 (1990) 343–353**; G. Edwards *PSQ* XX.4 (1990) 863.

Key-words: def, psy, idn, soc, POW, sec, SYM, cog, com, pmc, pr1, rel, eff, EMO, rht, rep.

Klein, Wolfgang (ed.), 1987, *Sprache und Ritual* (= Zeitschrift für Literaturwissenschaft und Linguistik 17); Göttingen: Vandenhoeck & Ruprecht (ISSN 0049–8653) (149).
[Language and Ritual]

Selected contents: Iwar Werlen: "Die 'Logik' ritueller Kommunikation" [The 'Logic' of Ritual Communication] (41–81) (*); Volker Heeschen: "Rituelle Kommunikation in verschiedenen Kulturen" [Ritual Communication in Different Cultures] (82–104) (*). [JK]

Key-words: com, lan.

Köpping, Klaus-Peter (ed.), 1997, *The Games of Gods and Man. Essays in Play and Performance* (Studien zur sozialen und rituellen Morphologie 2); Hamburg: Lit (ISBN 3–8258–3467–0) (xii + 290) (with bibliographies with the articles).

Selected contents: Klaus-Peter Köpping: "The Ludic as Creative Disorder. Framing, De-framing and Boundary Crossing" (1–39); Gunter Gebauer & Christoph Wulf: "Play, Mimesis and the Body" (42–55); Don Handelman, "The Andhaka Outcome. Ludic Processes in Indian Ritual and Myth" (100–131); Klaus-Peter Köpping: "Seriousness and Ludic Creativity. Ambiguities in Greek Ritual and Myth" (151–169); Terence Turner: "The Poetic Meta-Mimesis. Ritual Clowning, Comedic Drama and Performative Representation among the Kayapayo" (173–190); Bruce Kapferer: "Ludic Powers, Determination in Game and in Play. Bali, Sri Lanka and Australia" (231–253); Bernhard Lang:

"Games Prophets Play. Street Theatre and Symbolic Acts in Biblical Israel" (257–271) [JK/MS]
Key-words: frm, mim, pmc, sym.

Köpping, Klaus-Peter, 1998, 'Inszenierung und Transgression in Ritual und Theater. Grenzprobleme der performativen Ethnologie', in: Bettina E. Schmidt & Mark Münzel (eds), *Ethnologie und Inszenierung. Ansätze zur Theaterethnologie*, (Curupina 5), Marburg: Förderverein Völkerkunde in Marburg (ISBN 3–8185–0248–x) 45–86.
[Staging and Transgression in Ritual and Theater. Boundary Problems of Performative Ethnology]

In this article, the author discusses several approaches in anthropology, critically focusing on imitation in performative and social action, the relation of different metalevels of representation, and the ambiguous notion of play. In pointing to the performative turn, the author discusses the definition, place, and boundary of the concept of performance. He deals with the possibility of deceiving the actors in the sphere of the religious, especially in ritual performances. "If this 'doing as if' is an integral element of rituals of every kind, the question is, if there is a difference to playing theater, and how we can differentiate the spheres of symbolic action, here the theatrical from the religious ritual, in the sense of a not only objective stock-taking of elements, but in regard of the state of consciousness of the actor" (48). According to the author, one has to question the clear differentiation between theater, social drama, and ritual, because theater presents itself differently. He considers play to be a middle ground between ritual and theater due to its double nature. On the one hand, the play is a staging with directors, managers, and rules; on the other hand, it includes, like any other ritual, the potential of transgression. However, the author concludes that ritual and play differ from theater in their mode of transgression. [JK]
References: G. Bateson, R. Bauman, **R. Caillois**, M. Douglas, C. Geertz, M. Gluckman, E. Goffman, J. Huizinga, E.R. Leach, **M. Leiris**, R. Schechner, G. Simmel, **V.W. Turner**, A. van Gennep, Chr. Wulf.
Key-words: frm, mim, PMC, THA, pmt, pr1, pr2, rfl, sec.

Köpping, Klaus-Peter, 2003, 'Rituelle Wirksamkeit und soziale Wirklichkeit', in: H. Schmidinger (ed.), ***Identität und Toleranz. Christliche Spiritualität im interreligiösen Spiegel*****, Insbruck, Wien: Tyrolia (ISBN 3–7022–2539–0) 170–204.**
[Ritual Efficacy and Social Reality]

This essay aims to discuss the phenomenon of 'natural religiousness' by analyzing ritual actions of Australian Aborigines and in Japanese village festivals. In doing so, the author employs a performative approach to ritual, stating that abstract ideas like 'community', 'justice', and 'beauty' can be experienced only by the performance of concrete events that can be reflected upon and transmitted. Rituals as performances are conceived of in a way akin to speech acts, i.e. they constitute social reality through its performance. Drawing on Lévi-Strauss, the author sees performances as consisting of a series of short acts that are combined in ever new ways so that rituals can adapt to ever new situations. But rituals are not only transformed through their performance; they are also capable of transforming reality. Rituals are thus a means of the constitution, foundation, and legitimation of everyday life. Following V.W. Turner, the author proposes that the liminal phase of rituals gives humans the chance to distance themselves from everyday life and thereby to reflect on it more effectively. To investigate the phenomenon of 'natural religiousness', the author then claims that it is necessary to adopt a comparative anthropological stance that derives from an analysis of the Western scientific and non-Western points of view. It is for this reason that he proceeds to describe the historical development of European discourse on the 'nature of man' together with the example of medieval festival culture. The rest of the essay deals with the two non-Western examples mentioned in the beginning. The author concludes his comparison with the assumption that, in general, ritual participants are convinced about the ritual's efficacy precisely because of, and not despite, its performance and its dramaturgical staging. [Thorsten Gieser]

References: M. Douglas, C. Lévi-Strauss, **V.W. Turner**.
Examples: medieval festival culture, Australian Aborigines rituals, Japanese village festivals.
Key-words: mng, PMC, PR1, EFF, rfl.

Köpping, Klaus-Peter & Ursula Rao (eds), 2000, *Im Rausch des Rituals. Gestaltung und Transformation der Wirklichkeit in körperlicher Performanz* (Performanzen. Interkulturelle Studien zu Ritual, Spiel und Theater 1); Münster, Hamburg, London: Lit (ISBN 3-8258-3988-5) (x + 247).
[In the Ecstasy of Ritual. Formation and Transformation of Reality in Bodily Performance]

The book is a contribution to the discussion of ritual as performative and reflexive activity. Rituals are understood as events that, through their bodily enactment as much as through the ensuing narrative discourse, become "structuring practices" of social life. Emphasis is given to the ritual as effective action, as well as to its emergent quality as risky performance. While the book's aim is to contribute to a general theoretical discussion of ritual, it also acknowledges the fact that rituals and their meanings can be understood only in the context of concrete cultural settings. Thus an introduction with a detailed review of the different positions in the debate on ritual is followed by a whole range of articles that analyze the practices of people in their concrete life situations, as well as the local negotiations in and about rituals. The articles look at ritual practices from the following points of view: 1. The reflexive quality of rituals is taken up in the analysis of local negotiations as part of the 'politics of rituals'. 2. The question of the relevance of divine intervention as reflected in indigenous discourses and its significance for the transformative potential of rituals is investigated. 3. Ritual is seen as an effective bodily performance that, through a mimetic process, brings to presence what otherwise only exists in the realm of ideas. [Ursula Rao]
Selected contents: Ursula Rao & Klaus Peter Köpping: "Die 'performative Wende'. Leben—Ritual—Theater" [The Performative Turn. Life—Ritual—Theater] (1–31) (*); Martin Gaenszle: "Sind Rituale bedeutungslos? Rituelles Sprechen im performativen Kontext" [Are Rituals Meaningless? Ritual Speech within a Performative Context] (33–44); Axel Michaels: "Ex opere operato. Zur Intentionalität promissorischer Akte in Ritualen" [Ex opere operato. On the Intentionality of Promissorical Acts in Rituals] (104–123) (*); Alexander Henn: "Exercitium—Mimesis—Interpretatio. Ritual und Bedeutung in Goa (Indien)" [Exercitium—Mimesis—Interpretatio. Ritual and Meaning in Goa (India)] (125–137); Beatrix Hauser: "Tanzen, Trinken, Transvetieren. Überlegungen zur Gestaltung und Intentionalität von Ritualen am

Beispiel der Nat-Verehrung in Myanmar (Burma)" [Dancing, Drinking, and Travesty. Considerations of the Configuration and Intentionality of Rituals exemplified by the Nat-Worship in Myanmar (Burma)] (138–155); Vincent Crapanzano: "Epilog. Fragmentarische Überlegungen zu Körper, Schmerz und Gedächtnis" [Epilogue. Fragmentary Reflections on Body, Pain, and Memory] (218–239) (*). [JK/MS]
Key-words: pmc, mng, rfl.

Köpping, Klaus-Peter & Ursula Rao, 2003a, 'Autorisierungsstrategien in ritueller Performanz. Einleitung', in: Erika Fischer-Lichte, *et al.* (eds), *Ritualität und Grenze*, Tübingen, Basel: A. Francke (ISBN 3-7720-8013-8) 211–218.
[Strategies of Authorization in Ritual Performance. Introduction]

This essay begins by stating that it has become difficult to define 'ritual' in contrast to other 'domains of action'. Moreover, the authors claim that even rituals *per se* are ambiguous due to their inherent liminality. On the one hand, rituals are capable of establishing boundaries. On the other, they are capable of transgressing and even transforming boundaries. Drawing on V.W. Turner's concept of 'liminality', the authors propose to conceive of rituals as a 'performative space' that is capable of bridging the gap of what Kapferer has called 'actuality' and 'virtuality'. As such, rituals take part in the reconstitution of social realities and are not limited in their impact to the moment of their performance. What distinguishes rituals from other performances (such as habitualized behavior) is their efficacy to establish meaning and to transform social contexts, as well as a certain reflexivity with regard to the symbolic nature of ritual communication. The authors point out, however, that even these characteristics do not always help to distinguish rituals from other performances, such as games and theater. Referring to Bateson's notion of 'framing', the authors emphasize that there are many interpretations about what the content and frame of ritual are and therefore the power to frame a ritual is always a matter of authority to be negotiated. They conclude by proposing that ambivalence is inherent in rituals and that rituals have to be ambiguous in their messages. They are like 'as if'-games in which problematic themes can be negotiated and expressed while simultaneously giving the participants the chance to step out of the frame of ritual at any time. [Thorsten Gieser]
References: G. Bateson, B. Kapferer, S.J. Tambiah, **V.W. Turner**.
Key-words: def, sec, mng, com, pmc, frm, rfl, vir.

Köpping, Klaus-Peter & Ursula Rao, 2003b, 'Zwischenräume', in: Erika Fischer-Lichte, *et al.* (eds), *Ritualität und Grenze*, Tübingen, Basel: A. Francke (ISBN 3-7720-8013-8) 235–250 (with bibliography).

The translation of the German title of this article, "Zwischenräume", could be "Gaps" or "Spaces". It refers to the subjects of (the creation as well as the transgression of) borders and liminality in rituals, as well as rituals as liminal spaces. The metaphor of the bodily skin is often used in rituals; through it, the body expresses the thoughts, feelings and emotions generated within, and through the bodily openings of the mouth and the senses it experiences the world without. Therefore the body itself can also be used as a metaphor for the society, closed in itself, yet communicating with other societies and the world 'outside'. The borders concerned in rituals, however, also include interdictions. And these too are created as well as transgressed under controlled circumstances, precisely in rituals. For borders only become real, experienced, when they are transgressed. And it is precisely in this transgression that the dangers which they try to control are turned into productive creative forces. These issues are illustrated by two examples: Japanese mask-dances, performed during the yearly harvest-festivals (Matsuri-festivals) (239–244), and exchanges of glances in the context of the confrontation with the divine in the *darshan* (244–247). In the final section (247–249) the authors restate that they wanted to elaborate upon the ritual as "border space" (*Grenzraum*), in which differences are created, but at the same time made relative or even abolished (247). "Only the transgression produces the border, thereby creating a gap, which itself, however, remains empty. Therefore the border cannot be imagined as a mark which sharply separates categories, but is—in the case of ritual—a performative gap, which enables to experience a transgression as a border experience" (248). [JS]

References: M. Foucault (+), M. Douglas (+), V.W. Turner (+).
Examples: Japanese mask-dances, performed during the yearly harvest-festivals (Matsuri-festivals), and exchanges of glances in the context of the confrontation with the divine in the *darshan*.
Key-words: str, pr2, mim, emo, frm, spc, tim.

Kreinath, Jens, 2004a, 'Theoretical Afterthoughts', in: Jens Kreinath, Constance Hartung & Annette Deschner (eds), ***The Dynamics of Changing Rituals. The Transformation of Religious Rituals within Their Social and Cultural Context,*** **(Toronto Studies in Religion 29), New York etc.: Peter Lang (ISBN 0-8204-6826-6; ISSN 8756-7385) (*) 267–282.**

The aim of these afterthoughts is to outline "an analytical matrix of the theoretical issues...on the dynamics of changing rituals" in light of this volume. Based on the observation that "rituals as events in time change constantly", the author poses the question "how one is to determine the actual degree and modality of ritual change since any modification of a single element or a particular sequence has an effect on the ritual as a whole" (267). In order to determine this degree and modality, he distinguishes between modifications and transformations as "two extreme kinds of ritual change": "Modifications are minor changes, which do not affect the identity of the ritual, whereas transformations challenge the ritual's identity.... a modification is a change in ritual, whereas a transformation is a change of ritual" (267–268). He further introduces 'identity' and 'difference' as terms that similarly "have to be conceptualized in relation to one another", because "there are no two versions of a ritual or sequences of rituals that are identical without any difference (otherwise, they would not be two versions) and there are no different versions or sequences without any identity" (268). The concepts of continuity and discontinuity are introduced to indicate the temporal dimension of ritual change. In relating these concepts to the issue of repetition, the author claims that "ritual changes...almost exclusively occur as a result of repetition because changes emerge and may become apparent only on the basis of repetition" (269). Based on this notion, he distinguishes between variation and change "as asymmetric relations between at least two versions of a ritual" and conceives variation as appearing with every repetition "without having any further significant consequences for the identity of the ritual" and change as "an irreversible process that transforms the relevant aspects of a ritual and affects its identity..." (269). He specifies the problem of ritual change by distinguishing between the changes in function, form, meaning and performance by taking the various viewpoints of the ritual participants into account: "Practitioners and observers probably perceive and interpret ritual changes differently" (271). He further discusses the concept of framing and argues that "[b]ecause ritual changes emerge from inside and from outside and the various components necessarily overlap, clear-cut distinctions of commonly used conceptions have to be placed in question" (273). After summarizing the various themes addressed in this volume, the author concludes: "Theoretical approaches concerned with issues related to the dynamics of changing rituals should be based on a highly diversified range of case studies in order to grasp the realm of possibilities within which rituals may change.... Different analytical concepts are likely to influence the modalities of how one investigates the empirical material in question. As a result, the exploration of the dynamics of changing rituals raises new questions and may also change the way one looks at rituals themselves constantly change" (282). [JK]

Key-words: DYN, frm, pmc.

Kreinath, Jens, 2004b, 'Meta-Theoretical Parameters for the Analysis and Comparison of two Recent Approaches to the Study of the Yasna', in: Michael Stausberg (ed.), *Zoroastrian Rituals in Context*, (Studies in the History of Religions 102), Leiden, Boston: Brill (ISSN 0169-8834; ISBN 90-04-13131-0) 99-136.

This paper proposes a meta-theoretical comparison of two different approaches to the study of a Zoroastrian ritual, the Yasna: the semiotic approach of William R. Darrow and the aesthetic approach of Ron G. Williams & James W. Boyd. Considering the scholarly background of these approaches, the author observes some surprising peculiarities: "Although the authors analyzed the same visual material, their approaches are mutually exclusive. Moreover, although they used similar concepts for the construction of their approaches, they addressed different contexts of the scholarly study of ritual performances" (100). Based on these observations, the author addresses a more fundamental problem, namely: "How can the differences between these theoretical approaches be explained?" (100). For this reason, the author calls for a 'higher level of abstraction', one that is able "to correlate significant historical and theoretical components and also to provide tools for an analysis of the more general issues implied" (101). Moreover, he claims that "it is necessary to compare theoretical approaches at a meta-theoretical level", which implies that an analysis on such a level "not only looks at how such approaches work and how they are constructed, but also at how they are situated in and applied to a particular field of research" (101). He therefore tries to elaborate on 'methodology', 'logic of design', and 'discourse' as such parameters that are necessary for a meta-theoretical analysis and comparison of the two approaches under scrutiny. As heuristic tools for this meta-theoretical endeavor he introduces such terms as 'theoretical approaches', 'empirical data', 'analytical concepts', and 'discursive contexts'. He further elaborates the complex and interdependent relationships between the various components involved. Using these tools, he tries to show: 1. how the approaches as presented by Darrow and by Williams & Boyd are shaped through the visual material of a staged Yasna performance as recorded on a videotape; 2. how they are constructed by use of a particular set of analytical concepts; and 3. how they participate in the different discursive contexts within the field of ritual studies. In doing so, the author analyses how theoretical approaches work within a particular field of research, how they are constructed, and how they are situated within the particular contexts of scholarly discourse. Accordingly, "a further result of the meta-theoretical comparison is its demonstration of the existence of a mutual relationship between the construction of theoretical approaches and the analysis of empirical data, as well as between the use of analytical concepts and the participation in discursive contexts. If this argument is valid, a counter-proof is necessary. That is to say, if one of the components changes, it should have an effect on the other components involved. Therefore, it is necessary to test whether, by changing one or more of the components, there is an effect on the other components involved" (135). [JK]

References: B.A. Babcock, G. Bateson, C.M. Bell (+), M.E.F. Bloch, W.R. Darrow, J.W. Fernandez, C. Geertz, E. Goffman, D. Handelman (+), M. Houseman, B. Kapferer, E.Th. Lawson, E.R. Leach, R.A. Rappaport, E.L. Schieffelin, C. Severi, D. Sperber, F. Staal, V.W. Turner, R.G. Williams & J.W. Boyd.
Example: Zoroastrian Yasna.
Key-words: pmc, AES, SEM, cog, frm, pmt, cpr, spc, rep, pr1, pr2, com.

Kreinath, Jens, 2005, 'Ritual. Theoretical Issues in the Study of Religion', *Revista de Estudos da Religião* 5:100–107 (http://www.pucsp.br/rever/rv4_2005/p_kreinath.pdf).

This essay addresses the relevance of ritual theory for the study of religion. It is argued that the emphasis on texts in the study of religion led to a misconception of rituals. According to the author, rituals, instead "have to be theorized on their own terms" (101). In taking Clifford Geertz's approach to ritual (1966 (*)) as a point of departure, the author argues that it is problematic to focus on "the meaning of religious symbols" and "the textual model as its representational frame of reference" (102). In discussing Frits Staal's approach (1979) (*), the author argues that it was his focus on "ritual as a self-referential form that rendered it problematic to analyze ritual actions as meaningful propositions comparable to language" (103). Therefore, he states, it is inappropriate "to distill the religious meaning from rituals without having analyzed the ritual actions themselves. The study of ritual is a field of its own and not simply a continuation of the study of religion" (103). The author further objects to the use of theories of semantics or syntax for theorizing ritual, because they "would fail to account for the dynamic and efficacy of ritual action" (104). He instead employs the concept of the index as proposed by Charles S. Peirce, because it "has the analytical potential to account for the complexity of the performance of ritual actions" (104). Furthermore, the author claims that the concept of the index "allows one to account for the pragmatics of ritual theory" and to conceive ritual theories as forms of a discursive practice that "shape and configure their own field of research" (105). [JK]

References: C. Geertz (–), C.S. Peirce, F. Staal (–).
Key-words: lan, mng, sec, SEM, sym.

Kreinath, Jens, 2006, 'Semiotics', in: Jens Kreinath, Jan A.M. Snoek & Michael Stausberg (eds), *Theorizing Rituals. Vol. I: Issues, Topics, Approaches, Concepts*, (Numen Book Series 114–1), Leiden, Boston: Brill (ISBN-10: 90–04–15342–x, ISBN-13: 978–90–04–15342–4) 429–470.

This article deals with the concepts of signs that are used for theorizing rituals. The author writes: "If one conceives of rituals as sign processes, as semiotics does, the questions arise (1) what concepts of signs can be used to analyze rituals, (2) what is characteristic of rituals, and (3) how do rituals differ from other forms of social action" (429). One of his main concerns is that "the various concepts of signs that are developed in modern linguistics have often been uncritically applied to the analysis of rituals" (429). Because "the very selection of linguistic concepts makes it impossible to grasp the dynamic and efficacy in the performance of ritual actions" (429–430) he argues that "a semiotic approach to ritual theory has to establish concepts of signs that are capable of addressing rituals as a form of social praxis and of dealing with the actual performance of ritual actions" (430). In order to pursue such a semiotic approach, the author reviews those approaches that he considers as paradigmatic. The argument is presented in four sections. In the first section "The Paradigm of Linguistic Signs and the Structure of Ritual Sequences" (432–436), the author discusses the approach of E. Leach as based on linguistic signs. The second section "The Meaning and Performance of Ritual Symbols" (436–446) addresses the symbolic approaches of C. Geertz and V.W. Turner. In the third section "Formalization and the Sequentiality of Ritual Action" (446–456), the approaches of M. Bloch and F. Staal are discussed in terms of how syntax and semantics are related. The fourth and final section "Performativity and Indexicality of Ritual Symbols" (456–467), takes up how the concept of indexical signs is addressed in the approaches of R.A. Rappaport and S.J. Tambiah. In his "Tentative Conclusions. Theoretical Parameters for Theorizing Semiotics of Ritual" (467–470), the author favors the concept of the index (as derived from Ch.S. Peirce and A. Gell) as alternative to the concepts of the symbolic or linguistic signs, because: "Only the concept of the index seems feasible to theorize the performance of ritual actions as a sign process by addressing those issues that are peculiar to the dynamic and efficacy in the pragmatics of ritual actions" (468). In order to specify his theoretical parameters, the author introduces the following set of features that are based on the concept of the index which he considers as suitable for theorizing the pragmatics of ritual as a sign process: sequentiality, regularity, referentiality, formality, temporality, dynamics, and efficacy. He argues that the concept of the index is able "to account for the arrangements and configurations of the various sign processes involved in the performance of ritual acts and utterances" and that it "would not only lead to a radically empirical approach to ritual but also encourage a different way of theorizing" (470). [JK]

References: M.E.F. Bloch, A. Gell, E.R. Leach, C. Geertz, Ch.S. Peirce, R.A. Rappaport, F. Staal, V.W. Turner.
Key-words: dyn, mng, pmc, SEM, str, sym.

Kreinath, Jens, Constance Hartung & Annette Deschner (eds), 2004, *The Dynamics of Changing Rituals. The Transformation of Religious Rituals within Their Social and Cultural Context* (Toronto Studies in Religion 29); New York: Peter Lang (ISBN 0–8204–6826–6; ISSN 8756–7385) (287).

Based on the assumption that "rituals are not at all static, but, on the contrary, more often subject to dynamic changes, even if their participants continue to claim that they have been the same since time immemorial" (1), the editors pose such questions as: "When do rituals change? When do they change accidentally and when are they changed intentionally? Are there particular kinds of rituals that are more stable or unstable than others? Which elements of rituals are liable to change and which are relatively stable? Who has the power or agency to change rituals intentionally? Who decides whether or not to accept a change?" (1). The editors group the articles according to four thematic constellations: 1. General Theoretical Approaches, 2. Transfer and Transformation of Ritual Contexts, 3. Recursivity and Innovation, and 4. Performance, Media, Script, and Representation. They argue that "[t]hrough the introduction of the dynamics of changing rituals, the selection of the present articles attempts to place new accents on the research in ritual studies" (2). This volume further "seeks to encourage an inquiry into the social and cultural facets and consequences of ritual performances" (3). It is argued that this new approach "can challenge the established pattern of research in ritual studies, which arose from academic reflection on the static and enduring aspects of rituals" (3). Though the articles cover a wide range of topics, the editors consider them sharing a common assumption "that while the 'framing' of a ritual—which is formed through its performance, media, script, and representation—constitutes the ritual's identity, it is not static at all but constantly undergoes change" (3). They claim that the differences between the contributions are theoretically relevant: "The comparison of different dynamics of changing rituals in different cultures—which pervades all the essays in this collection—makes clear how important it will be for ritual studies in the future to form a more complex descriptive matrix for the theoretical issues involved" (7).
Selected Contents: Don Handelman: "Re-Framing Ritual" (9–20) (*); James W. Fernandez: "Contemporary Carnival (*carnaval*) in Asturias. Visual Figuration as a 'Ritual' of Parodic Release and Democratic Revitalization" (21–39); Susanne Schröter: "Rituals of Rebellion—

Rebellion as Ritual. A Theory Reconsidered" (41–57); Dietrich Harth: "Artaud's Holy Theater. A Case for Questioning the Relations between Ritual and Stage Performance" (73–85); Klaus-Peter Köpping: "Failure of Performance or Passage to the Acting Self? Mishima's Suicide between Ritual and Theater" (97–114); Günter Thomas: "Changing Media—Changing Rituals. Media Rituals and the Transformation of Physical Presence" (115–127); Jan G. Platvoet: "Ritual as War. On the Need to De-Westernize the Concept" (243–266) (*); Jens Kreinath: "Theoretical Afterthoughts" (267–282) (*). [JK]

Review: Chr. Helland *JCR* 21 (2006) 109–111.
Key-words: cpr, soc, str, sec, mng, aes, com, pmc, tha, DYN, eff, frm, med, par, rfl, rht, tra, rep.

Kreinath, Jens, Jan Snoek & Michael Stausberg, 2006, 'Ritual Studies, Ritual Theory, Theorizing Rituals. An Introductory Essay', in: Jens Kreinath, Jan A.M. Snoek & Michael Stausberg (eds), *Theorizing Rituals. Vol. I: Issues, Topics, Approaches, Concepts*, (Numen Book Series 114–1), Leiden, Boston: Brill (ISBN-10: 90–04–15342–x, ISBN-13: 978–90–04–15342–4) xiii–xxv.

In their introductory essay, the editors propose a new approach to the field of ritual studies and ritual theory. In the first part (xiv–xvi), they outline an understanding of ritual studies as an academic discipline, "the study by scholars of rituals from not only their own culture" (xiv), before they address the way ritual theory is conceived within this field: "While theory is generally held to be a branch of ritual studies, it seems to us that in practice ritual studies largely neglect matters of theory" (xv). Hence, they attempt "to put theory more prominently on the agenda" (xv). In the second part of the essay (xvi–xxi), the editors discuss their understanding of ritual theory. They define 'ritual theories' most generally as "theories about ritual" (xvii). Questions of the definition of rituals are addressed and what is specific to rituals and what attributes rituals "share with other features of cultural organization" (xviii). Then, the editors distinguish between 'theories' and 'theoretical approaches' (xix–xxi, cf. xxi–xxii). In the third part, "From Ritual Theory to Theorizing Rituals" (xxi–xxv), they introduce the main intention of this volume, which is "to be more than a mere collection of essays presenting a panorama of available approaches to ritual theory" (xxi). 'Theorizing rituals' is conceived as a perspective rather than an abstract and coherent set of statements—a perspective

that requires "the refinement of single theories, as well as their mutual critique and competition.... It reaches beyond particular theories and takes a meta-theoretical perspective, putting the various approaches into context" (xxii). In contrast to 'ritual theory', the project of 'theorizing rituals' is described as follows: "Whereas the aim of ritual theory is to articulate a particular set of hypotheses and to draw conceptual boundaries as precisely as possible, the project of theorizing rituals is an open project" (xxii). As "an attempt to connect theory to other forms of scholarly practice" (xxiii), one of the concerns of theorizing rituals is to reach beyond the realm of theory "by entering theoretically dense fields of scholarly discourse that do not necessarily result in theoretical approaches" (xxiii). In this context, the editors introduce their understanding of 'paradigmatic concepts' which are not "linked to well-established theoretical, methodological, and academic programs" or "framed as 'theories'" (xxiv). The role of concepts is also depicted as follows: "A theoretical concept theoretically conceptualizes ritual(s), and theorizing concepts re-conceptualizes discourse" (xxv). It is further argued that the attempt to put concepts into focus "may 'reveal' something about the objects, the subjects, and the parameters of discourse" (xxv). By way of conclusion, the editors contend: "The essays assembled in this volume (and the annotated bibliography) are not intended as the final word on rituals. The assembly of these essays here allows the contours of a common field of research to emerge. Yet this field is far from being homogenous and consistent. Consistency is an important aim of theory, but theorizing must find a different way of coping with heterogeneity and with the complexity and emergent quality of scholarly discourse" (xxv). [JK]
Key-words: def, GEN, rfl, sem, ter.

Krieger, David J. & Andréa Belliger, 1998, 'Einführung', in: Andréa Belliger & David J. Krieger (eds), *Ritualtheorien. Ein einführendes Handbuch*, Opladen, Wiesbaden: Westdeutscher Verlag (ISBN 3–531–13238–5) (*) 7–33.
[Introduction]

This article is an introduction to a reader in ritual studies in German written by the editors of the volume. It has four sections. The first contains reflections on the rise of ritual studies in recent decades (7–9). The second section gives a brief survey of studies relating to seeing ritual as performance (9–17). The next section discusses approaches to ritual as communication (18–29). According to the authors, ritual is generally perceived as a distinctive level of communicative action that is characterized by specific pragmatic preconditions. These are then distinguished from the pragmatic preconditions of argumentative discourse as described by Jürgen Habermas. Contrary to Habermas, ritual is here seen as 'borderline discourse' (*Grenzdiskurs*) on which argumentation itself is ultimately based (29). The final section of the paper tentatively sketches some new perspectives. Considering the "fact" that traditional constructions of religious, cultural, and social identities are considered to be increasingly 'dysfunctional', the authors suggest that ritual studies might have an important role to play in solving problems of postmodern societies. [MS]

References: C.M. Bell (+), M. Douglas, M. Eliade (+), R.L. Grimes (+), J. Habermas (+/–), C. Humphrey & J. Laidlaw, Th. Jennings, J.G. Platvoet (+), R. Schechner (+), J.Z. Smith (+), V.W. Turner (+).
Key-words: GEN, com, pmc, pr1, sec, soc.

Krondorfer, Björn, 1992, 'Bodily Knowing, Ritual Embodiment, and Experimental Drama. From Regression to Transgression', ***Journal of Ritual Studies*** **6.2:27–38.**

This article is about the body in ritual and performance studies, with particular attention being paid to bodily knowing. The author argues that bodily knowing of ritual embodiment should be considered through the ritual qualities of regression and transgression. One of the three conceptual frameworks that are used in light of Geertz and Foucault is "the notion of an archive of cultural experience" that "allows us to examine the qualities of physical movements rather than categorizing ritual embodiment along institutional, academic, or typological lines" (30–31). The second conceptual framework, Doty's and Grimes's concept of ritual as polymorphic, "allows us to include experimental drama in the expanded field of ritual studies" (32). Through the third conceptual framework, Turner's notion of liminality, the author studies the interdependence of regression and transgression. The author argues: "Liminal spaces allow participants to explore regressive and transgressive qualities without fearing social ostracism. Participants can play with the shifting boundaries between regressive fantasies and transgressive acts" (35). [JK]

References: W.G. Doty, M. Foucault, C. Geertz, R.L. Grimes, V.W. Turner.
Key-words: emb, pmc.

La Fontaine, Jean S. (ed.), 1972, *The Interpretation of Ritual. Essays in Honour of A.I. Richards*; London: Tavistock Publications (SBN 422–73880–8) (xviii + 296).

Selected contents: Jean S. La Fontaine: "Introduction" (ix–xviii); Raymond Firth: "Verbal and Bodily Rituals of Greeting and Parting" (1–38); Esther Goody: "'Greeting', 'Begging', and the Presentation of Respect" (39–71); Jean S. La Fontaine: "Ritualization of Women's Life-Crises in Bugisu" (159–186); Monika Wilson: "The Wedding Cakes. A Study of Ritual Change" (187–201). Elizabeth Bott: "Psychoanalysis and Ceremony" (205–237); Edmund Leach: "The Structure of Symbolism" (239–275). [JK]

Reviews: K. Maddock *Oc* 43.2 (1972) 155 f; W.D. Hammond-Tooke *AS* 32.3 (1973) 199; J. Nash *SSoc* 37.2 (1973) 249; A.C. Tweedie *ASR* 18 (1974) 689; S. Webster *JPS* 83.4 (1974) 485; A. Cohen *Man* 9.1 (1974) 146; A.F. Gell *Oc* 47.3 (1977) 249 f; R. Rahmann *Anthr* 74.1/2 (1979) 265.
Key-words: dyn, gdr, sem, sym.

Laidlaw, James & Caroline Humphrey, 2006, 'Action', in: Jens Kreinath, Jan A.M. Snoek & Michael Stausberg (eds), *Theorizing Rituals. Vol. I: Issues, Topics, Approaches, Concepts*, (Numen Book Series 114–1), Leiden, Boston: Brill (ISBN-10: 90–04–15342–x, ISBN-13: 978–90–04–15342–4) 265–283.

This article reviews some recent approaches to theorizing ritual as a form of action. All dissent from the idea that ritual is best understood on the model of linguistic communication, and consider instead what if anything is distinctive about ritual in relation to philosophical and other accounts of the nature of human action. The reasons for this departure from something of an anthropological consensus are explained. Some authors whose work laid the foundations for the approaches described (Needham, Lévi-Strauss, Staal) are briefly considered. The cognitivist models of Lawson & McCauley are described, followed by our own proposal (in Humphrey & Laidlaw 1994 (*)), which not only draws on cognitive psychology but also on phenomenological and analytical philosophical theories of action, and is developed through a detailed analysis of the ethnographic example of the Jain rite of worship or *puja*. This theory proposes that ritual is distinctive, as action, due to a modification of the normal relation between intentionality and the identity of the action, which means that meaning is not inherent but must be attributed. The related work of Houseman and Severi is considered. We conclude with some questions, further research on which would clarify some points of apparent inconsistency between the works discussed. [James Laidlaw]

Key-words: AGN, cog, com, DEF, exp, INT, MNG, PR1, str, sym, ter.

Lang, Bernhard, 1988, 'Kleine Soziologie religiöser Rituale', in: Hartmut Zinser (ed.), *Religionswissenschaft. Eine Einführung*, Berlin: Reimer (ISBN 3-496-00935-7) 73–95.
[A Brief Sociology of Religious Rituals]

The article presents a brief survey of major sociological contributions to the study of rituals: group-sociology (Douglas), functionalism (Durkheim), and Marxism (Bloch). In his evaluation of functionalism, the author emphasizes play, game, and entertainment as drawbacks of classical functionalist theories. In his final section on 'ritual and history' (87–92), following Max Weber, the author discusses some long-term historical changes of rituals, esp. the 'rationalization' of rituals (from dance and prophecy to sermons and books). As a technical innovation, the invention of loudspeakers was a prerequisite of the 'intellectualization' of rituals in the nineteenth century (90). According to the author, similar developments as in the West can be traced in Buddhism, while religious ceremonies and theological erudition remained clearly separated in Hinduism (91). [MS]

References: M. Douglas (+), É. Durkheim, A.R. Radcliffe-Brown, M.E.F. Bloch, M. Weber.

Key-words: gen, SOC, cpr, cpl, med.

Laughlin, Charles D., 1990, 'Ritual and the Symbolic Function. A Summary of Biogenetic Structural Theory', *Journal of Ritual Studies* 4.1:15–39 (with bibliography).

"In this article biogenetic structural theory is summarized so that its more salient concepts may be used to explain aspects of ritual. A principle function of the human brain is the construction of a world of experience [i.e. a structure of models]. This world of experience is partially isomorphic with reality and is thoroughly symbolic in its processing" (15). "We call this entire structure of models an individual's cognized environment. This term contrasts with an individual's operational environment which is the real nature of that individual as an organism and that individual's world as an ecosystem" (16). The author distinguishes three modes of interaction between the cognized and the operational environment: the evocative mode (perception), the fulfilling mode (action), and the expressive mode (communication). Since the cognized environment is necessarily only a partial model of the operational environment, the latter is always at least partially transcendental. This is a source of uncertainty. Therefore, a society tends to build up a body of 'knowledge' about the operational environment, which goes beyond what an individual may accumulate: a cosmology. Such a cosmology takes away some of our uncertainties. A society communicates this cosmology to its members, i.e. it is incorporated into their cognized environment. Ritual is an essential technique for doing so: "By means of [cognized] symbolic and ritual techniques a cosmology comes alive in the sensory systems of individuals and leads to experiences that are interpreted in such a way as to authenticate the received view of reality" (28). Both the shared cosmology and the shared symbolic activity that rituals provide are binding the participating individuals into a community. According to the author, ritual also coordinates an individual's experiences at different levels of consciousness. He concludes: "ritual is formalized activity the intent of which is to cause transformations in the inner or outer operational environments. And, technically speaking, no transformation in the outer world can occur without producing a transformation (i.e., a restructuralization) in individuals, even if that inner transformation is no more dramatic than a change of state in the perceptual system. Paraphrasing an old adage, not only must a ritual be effective, it must be perceived to be effective by participants. But much human ritual goes beyond mere practicalities. It is intricately involved in a group's collective epistemic process. Rituals, particularly dramaturgical ones, are activities in the world that reveal the normally hidden attributes and dimensions of the operational environment. They address the limits of our zone of uncertainty as we are confronted by direct, experiential evidence of the essentially transcendental quality of our being and our world. Awareness of the existence of our zone of uncertainty is a pivotal intuition immediately apparent to anyone in any society who is prepared to reflect upon experience and limits of experience. The mysteries of death, pestilence, catastrophe, change, fertility, birth, growth, origin, failed expectations, and the like loom large in the questions addressed by cosmologies everywhere. The answers to these questions of 'ultimate concern' are commonly couched in [cognized] symbolic terms that represent the hidden forces of the cosmos that may come alive in the experience of individuals during the course of, or as a consequence of, ritual. These forces may have to be revealed to adjust their order and re-establish the natural harmony of cosmos, society, and being. Part of the re-establishment of harmony entails a shared perception of that adjustment. And the principal mechanism for assuring this shared perception is ritual" (31–32). [JS]

References: **E.G. d'Aquili** (+), **J. McManus** (+), F.J. Varela, U. Neisser, M. Webber, J. Elster, E.D. Chapple, A.F.C. Wallace, R.L. Grimes.
Key-words: com, pr2, mim, COG, sem, sym, eff, emo, rep, soc, psy.

Laughlin, Charles D., *et al.*, 1986, 'The Ritual Transformation of Experience', in: Norman K. Denzin (ed.), *Studies in Symbolic Interaction. A Research Annual* (7.A), Greenwich (CT), London: JAI Press, Inc. (ISBN 0–89232–743–x) 107–136 (with bibliography).

"In this paper, we sketch a theory based on *biogenetic structuralism* that accounts for the structure of experience" (108). "Experience seems to be phasically organized" (108). "If an experiential episode is perceived as a salient unit, then the episode may be cognized as distinct from other units of experience.... We refer to these cognized episodes of experience, and their mediating neural network as *phases*, and to the points of experiential and neural transformation between phases as *warps*" (109). Hence, the second section of this paper (108–112) discusses 'phases and warps'—a "warp is a *liminal* event" (110)—in particular, phase boundaries, emphasis on warps, and control of phases through expansion of warps. An "important point is that in any society a limited set of possible phases of consciousness is defined as normal. Members of that society are then socialized to recognize the appropriate attributes of these phases and to consider them definitive of their own and of others' mind states. This recognition operates to set boundaries on phases of consciousness typically experienced in a culture through the establishment of conditioned, internalized control of attention" (109–110). In the third part of the paper, the authors discuss "ritual and the structure of experience" (112–120). Here, they "summarize some of the principles that may account for the efficacy of ritual in warp control" (113). They identify these principles as follows: "Orientation and Enhancement of Awareness" (113), "Returning the Autonomic System" (113–115), "Types of Transformation" (115–116), "Stages of Transformation" (116–117), "Symbolic Penetration and the Theater of the Mind" (117–119), and the "Shamanic Principle" (119–120). "The induction and control of alternate phases of consciousness depends ultimately upon the transfer of information across warps between phases. We call this cross-phasing" (120). Hence, the fourth section of this paper discusses "cross-phase transference" (120–126). One technique they describe is to concentrate on a particular symbol while the warp is made: "Ritual drama may operate by means of the cross-phase transference of symbolic material. In order for drama staged in waking phase to 'come alive' in dream or trance, the focus of consciousness must remain upon at least some central aspect of the symbolism across the warp" (122). But there are "at least two methods: (1) by gradual transformation of structures prior to the appropriate warp such that the shift in cognitive organization from preceding to succeeding phases is minimized [e.g., relaxing before going to sleep in order to remain aware of dreaming], and (2) by maintaining concentration of awareness upon the symbolic material across the warp, despite the degree of disparity in organization of operating structures. These and other methods may be combined, of course, and in fact often are in ritual" (124). The fifth and final section ("Void Consciousness", 126–128) briefly discusses the "experience of ultimate awareness" that "has been reported from virtually all of the great mystical traditions" (126). [JS/MS]

References: M. Csikszentmihalyi, E.G. d'Aquili, M. Eliade, B.T. Grindal, E. Husserl, M. Merleau-Ponty, J. Piaget, V.W. Turner, A.F.C. Wallace.

Examples: Buddhist and Hindu tantrism, Sisala funeral in Ghana, !kia among the !Kung, ritual drama (North American [Sun Dance] and elsewhere), ancient Greek mystery plays, Tibetan tantric yoga, shamanism, Tibetan dream yoga, "experience of North Americans".

Key-words: cog, sym, eff, emo.

Lawson, E. Thomas, 1976, 'Ritual as Language', *Religion* 6:123–139.

In this article, the author addresses the controversy of identifying and interpreting rituals in terms of language and starts with the following methodological question: "how does one identify, interpret, and explain the meaning of a rite?" (124). By way of proposing "a specific kind of explanation of ritual" (125), the author first addresses the problem of the nature of non-verbal communication in relation to ritual. He contends: "As long as the scholar of religion concentrates on the verbal elements within the ritual, and the general symbols surrounding the ritual, it is very difficult to interpret *the rite as a whole* in terms of a theory of language" (127). He calls into question the hidden assumption that only words and symbols can reveal the semantic aspects of ritual: "To concentrate on the verbal and the symbolic elements makes a more adequate theory of ritual difficult if not impossible to develop" (128). In focusing on "the complete ritual process rather than the more specific ritual *utterances*", the author argues that "it is essential that we do not confuse data and subject matter.... As a first step in extricating ourselves from such confusion, I suggest that some important distinctions be made about the concept of ritual language" (128). He then distinguishes between four different meanings of this concept: 1. "*Language as ritual*", i.e., "ritualistic language" (129); 2. "*Ritual in language*", i.e., "the ritualistic elements within language" (129); 3. "*Language in ritual*", i.e., "the verbal elements in ritual" (129); 4. "*Ritual as language*: what this approach to ritual entails is that a theory of ritual as a whole is isomorphic with a theory of language as a whole" (130). Favoring such a theory of language as model "in terms of which to interpret ritual", the author claims that "a specific ritual is to be understood as a language unit similar to a sentence" and states: "Just as a sentence is an instance of a language system, so a ritual is an instance of a ritual system. A sentence is composed of units (or propositions) which, when the logical relations of these components are specified, makes the meaning of the whole apparent. It might very well be the case that aspects of these units are verbal utterances to be understood as performative utterances, but *how* these performatives operate in the ritual as a whole is the problem" (130). According to the author, the rationale for explaining ritual within a theory of structural linguistics is that both "ritual and language are cultural systems" (131). Since they are traditional and rule-governed, he favors a theory of ritual action conceived of as a set of semantic acts, which are formed as a syntactical unit. In elaborating a theory of ritual as a synchronic system with a surface and deep structure by employing structural linguistics, the author demands a clear distinction between competence and performance to identify and explain rituals: "Linguistic *competence* has reference to the system of rules in terms of which linguistic performance is possible. This means that a specification of linguistic competence is logically and theoretically prior to an analysis of performance" (133). Furthermore, a structural analysis of ritual makes a structural model necessary: "In the case of ritual, then, we call for the development of a theory of ritual as a synchronic system. In such a system we must distinguish between the surface and deep structure of ritual. What is done in the ritual and what semantic act is exemplified in what is done are not necessarily synonymous. Such a synchronic study may very well analyze what is unique about individual rituals for there is no reason that any particular rite is universal in form. But if it is a rite at all, it will exemplify universal principles" (134). [JK]

References: N. Chomsky (+), M. Eliade (–), J. Fontenrose, E. Gellner, **E.R. Leach** (+), J. Lyons (+), C. Lévi-Strauss, **H.H. Penner** (+), J. Piaget, B. Ray, A. van Gennep, P. Winch (–).
Examples: Prayers, rituals of supplication, rituals of passage, Christian baptism.
Key-words: cmp, COG, com, LAN, SEM, str, sym.

Lawson, E. Thomas, 1993, 'Cognitive Categories, Cultural Forms and Ritual Structures', in: Pascal Boyer (ed.), *Cognitive Aspects of Religious Symbolism*, Cambridge etc.: Cambridge University Press (ISBN 0–521–43288–x) 188–204.

This article is on the possible impact of the cognitive sciences on the theory of culture and the explanation of ritual action. The author is concerned with the problem of ritual acquisition and argues that "a theory of religious ritual action which employs the strategy of competence theorising is capable of illuminating certain aspects of the acquisition debate in the very process of laying the groundwork for an explanation in religious ritual" (189). He defines religious rituals as "instances of symbolic behaviour" (192). According to him, the competence theories are a fruitful approach because they suggest techniques for the analysis of religious ritual. He claims that "[f]rom a competence point of view, cultural systems are not simply producers of knowledge, they are also products of cognitive mechanisms and structures" (190), and "[t]he theoretical object of such analysis consists of representations in the minds of ideal ritual participants. Because they are *cognitive* representations and thus not directly accessible, the data employed in their analysis consist of peoples' *judgements* about ritual form" (192). The author asserts that such an analysis has immense advantages for cross-cultural studies of symbolic-cultural phenomena as ritual. The competence-theoretical approach developed by R. McCauley and the author "focuses upon the representation of religious *ritual action* rather than the more inclusive domain of religious *thought*, or religious *ideas*" (194). The cognitive theory of religious ritual entails "1. *A system for the representation of action.* This 'action-representation system' consists of a set of rules and categories which generate abstract structural descriptions for the representation of ritual form. 2. *A conceptual scheme.* This scheme, which contains semantic information, activates the set of universal principles and penetrates the action representation system.

3. *A set of universal principles*. These principles constrain the products of the action-representation system and feed back the results into the conceptual scheme" (196). The system for the 'representation of ritual action' involves a 'formation system' and an 'object agency filter' that generates abstract structural descriptions. A further aspect of this theory focuses on a conceptual scheme "that is represented in the minds of ritual participants in any society [which] is that set of concepts the effects of which are made manifest in cultural phenomena..." (198). Moreover, the author discusses a set of universal principles and assumes "that all religious systems involve commitments to culturally postulated superhuman agents and that all religious ritual systems involve superhuman agents at some level of description" (201). The author concludes by arguing "that with a few mechanisms (a conceptual scheme, a set of action rules and the universal principles) which represent a rich and complex set of cognitive processes we can account for both the form and content of religious ritual. This is a level of theoretical description that is complex enough to engage our attention for some time to come" (205). [JK]

References: P. Boyer (+), R.N. McCauley, D. Sperber (–).
Key-words: cog, pr1, rep, str.

Lawson, E. Thomas, 2006, 'Cognition', in: Jens Kreinath, Jan A.M. Snoek & Michael Stausberg (eds), *Theorizing Rituals. Vol. I: Issues, Topics, Approaches, Concepts*, (Numen Book Series 114–1), Leiden, Boston: Brill (ISBN-10: 90–04–15342–x, ISBN-13: 978–90–04–15342–4) 307–319.

Fundamental to a cognitive approach to religious rituals is the presumption that ritual representations employ the same cognitive resources that human beings employ in their representations of ordinary actions. For the purpose of theorizing about religious ritual form, of particular interest are those theories that lead us to a deeper understanding of how human minds represent action. Without understanding how actions are represented we will fail to understand how religious ritual actions are represented and miss some of their most interesting properties. Such theories are called competence theories. Competence theories provide important insights about how the human mind represents things and events. In fact the mind/brain seems to consist of a bundle of individually structured competencies that constrain the form that its various products assume. These cognitive capacities that competence

theories describe enable people not only to conceive of the kinds of things that there are in the world but also to act in the world in which they live. In religious ritual representations, only actions which take an object (patient) are relevant because in religious ritual systems things get done to things. There are important theoretical benefits for placing this restriction on the representations of ritual form, which have to do with discovering what is important in the ritual, which ritual act assumes prior ritual acts, who is acting as the agent of the ritual, who or what is acting as the patient, what instruments are involved, which rituals get repeated and which do not, which rituals permit substitutions and which do not, which rituals can have their effects reversed and which cannot, which rituals are more susceptible to change and which not, and so on. Essential to any action description (whether or not this action is a ritual) is the key notion of agency. It is the human ability to represent these actions which take objects (which can, of course be other agents) that provide the cognitive resources for the representation of religious ritual actions. In experimental work, Barrett and Lawson have demonstrated that the Lawson and McCauley claim, that non-cultural regularities in how actions are represented inform and constrain religious ritual participants understanding of religious ritual form, generates certain predictions which can be tested. [E. Thomas Lawson]
Key-word: COG.

Lawson, E. Thomas & Robert N. McCauley, 1990, *Rethinking Religion. Connecting Cognition and Culture*; Cambridge etc.: Cambridge University Press (ISBN 0–521–37370–0 / 0–521–43806 (p)) (ix + 194) (with index and bibliography).

In this book the authors present "an outline for a theory of ritual systems as well as a framework for a larger theory of religious systems" (171). The overarching aim of this theory is the examination of the connections between culture and cognition in general and of the relations between ritual and language in particular. The book is subdivided into seven closely connected chapters and operates at three different levels: meta-theoretical, theoretical, and substantive. On the meta-theoretical level, the authors state two theses. The first concerns the relationship between interpretation and explanation in the study of religion. In the first chapter, "Interpretation and Explanation. Problems and Promise in the Study of Religion" (12–31), and partly in the seventh, "Connecting the Cognitive and the Cultural" (170–184), the authors display their first meta-theoretical argument. In the first chapter, they discuss three different positions concerning the respective roles of interpretation and explanation (exclusivism, inclusivism, and interactionism). In contrast to exclusivistic or inclusivistic positions, they prefer a complementary approach that is able to integrate interpretation and explanation in a broader methodological framework. Finally, in the last chapter, they introduce Ernan McMullin's notion of 'structural explanation' (177–180) to characterize and explicate their own theoretical quest further. The second meta-theoretical thesis concerns what the authors call the competence approach to theorizing socio-cultural systems. They claim that symbolic-cultural systems, e.g. ritual systems, can hardly be observed directly. Hence the authors propose to study the implicit knowledge (competence) of an idealized participant instead. Thus they offer theories about the cognitive representations of religious ritual systems and of their operative principles instead of about the system itself. Accordingly, in the fourth chapter, "A Cognitive Approach to Symbolic-Cultural Systems" (60–83), the authors argue—now on a theoretical level—that the concentration on an explanatory analysis of ritual competence is promising, even though they have to leave aside the dimension of the actual performance. They insist that "it is *not* a theory of ritual acts. This theory also involves an abstraction away from the conditions of actual (ritual) practice" (77). The authors borrow the distinction between 'performance' and 'competence' from Noam Chomsky, whose linguistic theory of a generative grammar (1965) functions as their primary theoretical compass (61–68). Although Chomsky himself is deeply skeptical of attempts that try to apply his psycho-linguistic theory to socio-cultural systems (68–77), the authors use his findings for constructing their ritual theory (77–83). In doing so, they vigorously maintain in the third chapter, "Ritual as Language" (45–59) that there is a strong analogy between language and ritual: "Ritual systems are analogous to language systems and ritual systems are systems of action" (50); and insofar, as they outline in their theory of religious ritual systems, "it is the action that is the analogue of the sentence (which is the fundamental unit of linguistic analysis)" (84). This point the authors derive from the deeper insights of speech act theory and scientists such as Leach or Staal, who are discussed critically in terms of ritual and language. But contrary to Staal's (or Sperber's) approach, the authors push the analogy even further: Not only on the syntactic but also on the semantic level they ascertain parallel operations. According to the authors, symbolic systems—in this case religious rituals—are not meaningless; rather, they have a different sort of meaning. They are absolutely self-referential and therefore their meaning can only be acquired by employing a holistic approach to semantics. In the fifth and sixth chapters, "Outline of a Theory of Religious Ritual Systems" (84–136) and "Semantics and Ritual Systems" (137–169), the authors explicate and illustrate their generative theory of the representation of religious ritual actions. Every structural description of ritual action includes the following elements: ritual agents, ritual objects (which also can be ritual participants), and, of course, the agent's acts: "The *order* of elements in a structural description of a representation of a religious ritual act, then, reflects crucial logical features which pertain to actions of *any* sort.... First of all, since religious ritual acts are actions, they involve agents and their acts. In addition, we maintain...that religious rituals always involve *an object of ritual action.* Although that condition is not necessary for action generally, it is a characteristic feature of religious ritual acts" (92). Furthermore, they emphasize that "*the religion's conceptual system* determines the entities, actions, and properties which qualify as values for these symbols in the case of religious actions generally and of religious rituals in particular" (93–94). The theoretical outline results in the formulation of a speculative set of hypotheses and the ascertainment of some principles of ritual action that the authors claim are universally valid and empirically testable: 1. Rituals in which a superhuman agent acts directly ("The Principle of Superhuman Immediacy") are of cardinal importance and efficacy; in contrast to other rituals these essential ones do not require repetition. 2. The "*less active* a role the superhuman agent played in a ritual the greater the chance that ritual substitution might arise and that the ritual would become more widely available" (163). 3. "The more transcendent...and removed from everyday human affairs the superhuman agents are, the fewer and the less elaborate the corresponding religious system's rituals are likely to be" (164). On the substantive level, the authors hold the view "that the role of superhuman *agents* in religious rituals is the pivotal factor in determining a wide variety of properties which human participants attribute to those rituals and that religious ritual form is largely the product of a compromise between religions' commitments to superhuman agents and everyday views of human action" (8; see also 176). [JK/Florian Jeserich]

References: J.H.M. Beattie (–), E. Cassirer (+), **N. Chomsky** (+), M. Douglas, É. Durkheim, M. Eliade (–), R.H. Finnegan, J.G. Frazer, S. Freud, C. Geertz (–), J. Goody (–), R. Horton, S.K. Langer (+), E.R. Leach (+/–), **C. Lévi-Strauss** (+/–), B. Malinowski, G. Murray, R. Otto (–), H.H. Penner (+), R.A. Rappaport, B.C. Ray

(+/–), M.E. Spiro (–), **D. Sperber** (+/–), **F. Staal** (–), S.J. Tambiah, V.W. Turner (+/–), A. van Gennep.
Examples: Christian blessing, Vedic Rituals (Agnyadhana, Darsapurnamaseshti), Zulu rituals.
Reviews: P. Boyer *AA* 93.4 (1991) 984; J.F. Maguire *JSSR* 30.3 (1991) 344–346; A.J. Trevino *SA* 52.2 (1991) 211; J.G. Platvoet *Numen* 40.2 (1993) 189–191; **T.F. Godlove *Zygon* 28.1 (1993) 115–120; S. Glazier *RA* 23.4 (1994) 313–321**.
Key-words: AGN, CMP, COG, com, eff, def, EXP, MNG, pmt, PR1, psy, ref, REP, sec, sem, STR, SYM.

Leach, Edmund R., 1966, 'Ritualization in Man in Relation to Conceptual and Social Development', *Philosophical Transactions of the Royal Society of London* B.251:403–408.

This is a conference paper on the relation between ritual and ordinary speech as different 'communication systems'. To compare ritualization with the conceptual and social development of man, the author distinguishes between three types of human behavior, which are not generally determined in ethology: "(1) Behaviour which is directed towards specific ends and which, judged by our standards of verification, produces observable results in a strictly mechanical way...we can call this 'rational technical' behaviour. (2) Behaviour which forms part of a signalling system and which serves to 'communicate information' not because of any mechanical link between means and ends but because of the existence of a culturally defined communication code...we can call this 'communicative' behaviour. (3) Behaviour which is potent in itself in terms of the cultural convention of the actors but not potent in a rational-technical sense, as specified in (1), or alternatively behaviour which is directed towards evoking the potency of occult powers even though it is not presumed to be potent in itself...we can call this 'magical' behaviour" (403). According to the author, the term 'ritual' can embrace categories (2) and (3) because they imply characteristics of complex ritual sequences. He argues that "they have a 'structure' which is in a crude sense analogous to a prose passage in that the sequence as a whole is self-segmented into elements of decreasing scale" (404). In terms of decoding the messages embodied in ritual sequences, the author emphasizes that it is a universal feature of a ritual that its sequence "when performed 'in full' tends to be very repetitive; whatever the message may be that is supposed to be conveyed, the redundancy factor is very high" (404). The author summarizes the main points of this paper as follows: "(1) In ritual, the verbal part and the behavioural part are not separable. (2) As compared with written or writeable speech the 'language' of ritual is enormously condensed; a great variety of alternative meanings being implicit in the same category sets.... (3) We tend to think this odd because of our own speech habits, but in fact our writeable speech contains a vast amount of redundancy.... In any event in ritual sequences the ambiguity latent in the symbolic condensation tends to be eliminated again by the device of thematic repetition and variation" (408). [JK]

References: M. Fortes (–), J.G. Frazer, C. Lévi-Strauss (+), B. Malinowski, V.W. Turner.

Key-words: cpl, com, def, eth, lan, sem, str, sym.

Leach, Edmund R., 1968, 'Ritual', in: David Lawrence Sills (ed.), *International Encyclopedia of the Social Sciences* (13), New York / Chicago / London: Macmillan / Free Press / Collier-Macmillan (No ISBN) 520–526.

In this article the author gives a historical overview of the usage of the concept 'ritual'. According to him: "Ritual is clearly not a fact of nature but a concept, and definitions of concepts should be operational; the merits of any particular formula will depend upon how the concept is being used" (521). To do this, he evaluates the concepts of ritual from William Robertson Smith to Max Gluckman and from Émile Durkheim to Claude Lévi-Strauss. He considers ritual to be a form of communication: "All speech is a form of customary behaviour, but, likewise, all customary behaviour is a form of speech, a mode of communicating information.... The actions that 'say things' in this way are not as a rule intrinsically different from those that 'do things'" (523). For this reason, the author grasps ritual as a language with its own rules of grammar and syntax and inquires into the meaning of ritual symbolism. For him, one of the crucial problems is to interpret the meaning of a ritual. To interpret ritual symbols, he assumes that one has to inquire into their diverse uses both in ritual and secular contexts, and should determine, furthermore, the rules of ritual grammar and syntax. He points out: "The drama of ritual breaks up the continuum of visual experience into sets of categories with distinguishable names and thereby provides us with a conceptual apparatus for intellectual operations at an abstract and metaphysical level. Such an approach implies that we should think of ritual as a language in a quite literal sense" (524). He argues not only that ritual is a mode of social communication but also that the term 'ritual' is best used to denote the communicative aspect of social behavior. According to him, ritual as an aspect of customary behavior 'says things' rather than 'does things', but ritual also may 'do things' as well as 'say things'. After the author contrasts the diverse positions on ritual as power and on ritual as belief, he chooses the position that the ritual is prior to belief, but ritual acts are to be interpreted in the context of belief because they mean what the actors say they mean. He concludes: "It is argued that no useful distinction may be made between ritual acts and customary acts but that in discussing ritual we are concerned with aspects of behaviour that are expressive (aesthetic) rather than instrumental (technical). Ritual action, thus conceived, serves to express the status of the actor vis-à-vis his environment, both physical and social: it may also serve to alter the status of the actor. When ritual functions in this latter sense, it is a manifestation of power; thus the universal belief in the potency of ritual action is by no means an illusion" (525–526). [JK]

References: N. Chomsky, É. Durkheim, R. Firth, M. Gluckman (+), J.R. Goody, J.E. Harrison, S.L. Hooke, C. Lévi-Strauss (+), B. Malinowski, K. Marx, M. Mauss, E. Norbeck, T. Parsons (+), A.R. Radcliffe-Brown, W.R. Smith, A. van Gennep, M. Wilson.
Key-words: aes, COM, cpl, eff, eth, lan, mim, mng, pmc, pmt, pr1, sec, sem, str, sym, ter.

Leach, Edmund R., 1976, *Culture and Communication. The Logic by which Symbols are Connected. An Introduction to the Use of Structuralist Analysis in Social Anthropology* (Themes in the Social Sciences); Cambridge etc.: Cambridge University Press (ISBN 0–521–21131–X / 0–521–29052–X (p)) (105) (with index and bibliography).

This book advocates the thesis that culture communicates through the very structure of how symbols are connected. The author starts from the following assumptions: "By now my general thesis is becoming very familiar: culture communicates; the complex interconnectedness of cultural events itself conveys information to those who participate in those events" (2). His concern in this book is to discuss the question of "how anthropologists, as observers, should set about the business of deciding what customs, other than verbal customs, can be said to 'mean'" (6). He presupposes that "*all* the various non-verbal dimensions of culture... are organised in patterned sets so as to incorporate coded information in a manner analogous to the sounds and words and sentences of a natural language. I assume therefore that it is just as meaningful to talk about the grammatical rules which govern the wearing of clothes as it is to talk about the grammatical rules which govern speech utterances" (10). In the following chapters, the author introduces some of his well-known distinctions between different aspects of human behavior (natural biological / technical / expressive), his 'communication dyad' (distinguishing between index / signal; signum / natural index; symbol / sign; standardized symbol / nonce symbol; conventionally but wholly arbitrary symbol / icon), and his notion of paradigmatic transformation. Some of these distinctions are then applied to theories of magic and sorcery (29–32). In the next chapter, the author discusses boundaries of social space and time. Boundaries are crucial for determining the meaning of symbols: "When we use symbols (either verbal or non-verbal) to distinguish one class of things or actions from another we are creating artificial boundaries in a field which is 'naturally' continuous" (33). Boundaries have to be marked out, and: "It is the nature of such markers of boundaries that they are ambiguous in implication and a source of conflict and anxiety. The principle that all boundaries are *artificial* interruptions to what is naturally continuous, and that the ambiguity, which is implicit in the boundary as such, is a source of anxiety, applies to time as well as to space.... For example, at the level of concept, the change of status from 'unmarried' to 'married' is simply a switch of categories, but at the level of action the switching calls for a ritual, a crossing of social frontiers which takes place in 'no man's time'" (34). "[T]he spatial and temporal markers which actually serve as boundaries are... *abnormal, timeless, ambiguous, at the edge, sacred*" (35). "The crossing of frontiers and thresholds is always hedged about with ritual, so also is the transition from one social status to another" (35). Furthermore, the author argues "that, in all human societies, the great majority of ceremonial occasions are 'rites of transition', which mark the crossing of boundaries between one social category and another" (35). The next chapter discusses "The Material Representation of Abstract Ideas. Ritual Condensation" (37–41). Here, the author argues that "what actually *happens* is that the participants in a ritual are sharing communicative experiences through many different sensory channels simultaneously; they are acting out an ordered sequence of metaphoric events within a territorial space which has itself been ordered to provide a metaphoric context for the play acting. Verbal, musical, choreographic, and visual-aesthetic 'dimensions' are all likely to form components of the total message. When we take part in such a ritual we pick up all these messages at the same time and condense them into a single experience which we describe as 'attending a wedding'.... But the analyst must take each dimension by itself" (41). However, the author wants "to stress the added complication that, although the receiver of a ritual message is picking up information through a variety of different sensory channels simultaneously, all these different sensations add up to just one 'message'" (41). In the subsequent chapter, the author explores "Orchestral Performance as a Metaphor for Ritual Sequence" (43–45). He concludes: "In ordinary culturally defined ritual performance there is no 'composer' other than the mythological ancestors.... The performers and the listeners are the same people. We engage in ritual in order to transmit collective messages to ourselves" (45). Also in the following chapters, the author returns to rituals, and two later chapters are devoted to specific types of rituals. Chapter 17 deals with "Rites of Transition (*rites de passage*)" (77–79), and Chapter 18, the longest chapter of the entire book, with "The Logic of Sacrifice" (81–93). [JK/MS]

References: F. Barth, R. Barthes, R. Bauman, E. Cassirer, M. Douglas, E.E. Evans-Pritchard, J.W. Fernandez, R. Firth (–), C. Geertz, L. Hjelmslev, D. Hymes, R. Jakobson, **C. Lévi-Strauss** (+), B. Malinowski, M. Mauss, Ch. Morris, Ch.S. Peirce, A.R. Radcliffe-Brown, F. de Saussure, V.W. Turner, **A. van Gennep** (+).
Examples: *Rites de passage*, sacrifice.
Reviews: R.D. Leighninger *CS* 6.4 (1977) 496 f; R.E. Segal *JAAR* 46.1 (1978) 115; D. Brenneis *JAF* 92.366 (1979) 493 f.
Key-words: aes, COM, cpl, frm, lan, med, mng, mus, pmc, pmt, SEM, STR, soc, SYM, tim.

Lee, Daniel B., 2005, 'Ritual and Social Meaning and Meaninglessness of Religion', *Soziale Welt* 56:5–16.

The author argues "that the successful enactment of ritual is highly *improbable* and gains no support from subjective beliefs. I also suggest that it is *impossible* for participants in ritual to share common beliefs or intersubjectivity. Individuals may collectively perform a ritual without attaching the same belief, or any belief, to it" (5). "*Ritual is socially meaningful as a demonstration of social solidarity because it transcends the personal beliefs of individuals*... *Enacting rituals requires participants who know the right moves, possess the props, and can make the expected noises at the right moment: regardless of what they believe.* As an operation, ritual becomes socially significant when it reproduces itself in a perceptible, immanent, and redundant form. The form of ritual is closed and precludes spontaneity and freedom" (6). After a review of his examples (6–11), the author addresses several issues pertaining to the social meaning of rituals and beliefs (11–14) including the question under which circumstances religious beliefs and rituals are systematized. From all that the author derives the following theoretical conclusions: "A ritual is an imaginary performance pattern for coordinating the display of human bodies and other selected objects during scheduled real-time interactions. Society constructs the performance pattern of ritual as a solution to the problem of how participants can coordinate spontaneous displays without sharing consciousness. Ritual destroys the variety of possible human behavior by restricting spontaneity; it is the conscious attempt to socially organize a series of spontaneous selections. The complexity of ritual increases as the possibility for *meaningfully* displaying bodies is reduced by society in a selected manner that is possible but not necessary" (14). Furthermore, the author distinguishes "first order observers", i.e. participants "who have learned to expect one another to limit themselves to simulating a performance pattern established by communication" from "second order observers" who are in a position to distinguish "between a viable performance and failure" (14). (The second order observes may also be performers.) According to the author, second order observers "perceive the display of bodies and objects and consciously process their fleeting impressions with respect to an imaginary self-referential and self-constructed form of ritual" (14), i.e. the communicative meaningful connection between distinct ritual operations such as genuflections and chanting. The author distinguishes expected from unexpected display and holds that "[a] viable ritual is recognized by cultured observers as a familiar unity in difference, a perfectly continuous reproduction on the side of 'expected displays'" (15). "In the mind and heart of an individual person, religious rituals may 'mean' a great deal.... Nonetheless, religious beliefs are socially meaningless (they can make no difference in society) because a human community, having no spirit or mind, cannot possibly hold them.... Even without the existence of a collective consciousness, however, rituals remain socially meaningful because they have the symbolic power to associate, coordinate, and calibrate individuals in a visible, external, and predictable manner. This power is the result of successful communication" (15). [MS]

References: É. Durkheim (–), N. Luhmann (+).
Examples: Footwashing, baptism, expulsion and reconcialiation among the Weaverland Conference Old Order Mennonites.
Key-words: SOC, str, MNG, COM, par.

Leertouwer, L., 1973, 'Inquiry into Religious Behavior. A Theoretical Reconnaissance', in: Theodorus P. van Baaren & H.J.W. Drijvers (eds), *Religion, Culture and Methodology. Papers of the Groningen Working-group for the Study of Fun-damental Problems and Methods of Science of Religion*, (Religion and Reason 8), Den Haag, Paris: Mouton (No ISBN) 79–98.

In the first and longest section of this article, the author presents a number of fundamental objections to the way the phenomenology of religion deals with (religious) behavior (79–86). The second section discusses van Baaren's (1973) attempt to define what religious behavior really is (86–93). This leads the author to the observation "that the relationship between cultic behaviour and 'non-symbolic' behaviour is still in many respects *terra incognita*" (93). The final section briefly comments on behavioral studies in the science of religion. According to the author, in its traditional form, as regards behavior, the science of religion "has for the present more to learn than to teach" (95). "Science of religion will probably have to leave the factual pattern of behaviour largely to the social sciences... It can, however, take note of the results and make use of them in working out the normative pattern of religious behaviour, and that is what it will have to do. For now that science of religion is more and more required to explain religious behaviour to believers and unbelievers, the idealization of religious behaviour [which the science of religion has considerably contributed to, according to the author (MS)] becomes a social danger" (95–96). [MS]

References: G. van der Leeuw (–), V.W. Turner, Th.P. van Baaren (–), M.E. Spiro, H.D. Duncan.
Key-words: cpr, sec, gen, pow, rfl, exp.

Levine, Michael P., 1998, 'A Cognitive Approach to Ritual. New Method or No Method at All?' *Method and Theory in the Study of Religion* 10:30–60.

"The first part of this paper examines claims made by E. Thomas Lawson and Robert N. McCauley (1990, 1993) that are background to their argument for a new approach to studying religious ritual, and the following parts critically examine that approach" (30). The result of this critical examination reads as follows: "Their approach and ensuing theory fail on all but the empirical testability factor—a factor inconsequential without the others—though it probably fails testability too.... They also discuss methodological problems that their theory allegedly avoids and the nature of the theory's principles. In context this obfuscates the question of the fecundity and utility of their theory. No new framework is generated. Instead of fecundity there is the obvious and even the trite. A theoretically informed and empirically based research program must be judged by its results. No credible account of the significance of their analysis emerges. Their results and suggestions for further research give no reason to suppose their approach fertile" (59). [MS]

References: **E.Th. Lawson & R.N. McCauley** (–).
Key-word: cog.

Lévi-Strauss, Claude, 1990, *The Naked Man* (Mythologiques 4); Chicago: University of Chicago Press (ISBN 0–226–47496–8 (p)) (746).

French original 1971 (*L'homme nu*), Librairie Plon. First edition of the English translation: Harper & Row 1981.

In the "Finale" of the fourth and last volume of his *Mythologiques*, the author incorporates ideas about ritual that were originally put forward in the "Frazer Lecture" that he delivered in Oxford in November 1970. The section on ritual (668–684) is a reaction to his (British) critics. "How...are we to define ritual? We can say that it consists of words uttered, gestures performed and objects manipulated, independently of any gloss or commentary that might be authorized or prompted by these three forms of activity" (671). Ritual gestures and objects, however, "are given a function additional to their practical use" in that they "serve in *loco verbi*; they are a substitute for words" (671). While the "performance of gestures and the manipulation of objects are devices which allow ritual to avoid speech" (671), nonetheless "there is a great deal of speech in ritual" (672). In analyzing the question of how the ritual words say the things they are saying, the author observes two basic procedures: "parcelling out and repetition" (672). These he describes in the following terms: Ritual "indulges in these subtleties [of parcelling out], emphasizing the slightest phrases of procedures so that their performance, through its infinite attention to detail, is carried to aberrant lengths, and gives the impression of 'slow-motion' camera-work marking time to the point of stagnation, it uses another, no less striking device: at the cost of considerable verbal expenditure, it goes in for a riot of repetition: the same formula, or formulae similar in syntax or assonance, are repeated in short intervals, and are only operative, as it were, by the dozen" (673). According to the author, "the first procedure is equivalent to the second, which represents, so to speak, its extreme development" (673). The reasons for ritual to resort to these procedures leads the argument back to myth: "The fluidity of the real is such that it constantly tends to escape through the mesh and the grid that mythic thought has placed over it so as to bring out only its most contrasting features. Ritual, by fragmenting operations and repeating them unwearyingly in infinite detail, takes upon itself the laborious task of patching up holes and stopping gaps, and it thus encourages the illusion that it is possible to run counter to myth, and to move back from the discontinuous to the continuous" (674). The author advances an even more generic statement: "On the whole, the opposition between rite and myth is the same as that between living and thinking, and ritual represents a bastardization of thought, brought about by the constraints of life. It reduces, or rather vainly tries to reduce, the demands of thought to an extreme limit, which can never be reached, since it would involve the actual abolition of thought. This desperate, and inevitably unsuccessful, attempt to re-establish the continuity of lived experience...is the essence of ritual, and accounts for its distinctive characteristics" (675). These he later describes as "the characteristic mixture of stubbornness and ineffectiveness which explains the desperate, maniacal aspect of ritual" (679). Furthermore, the author briefly discusses the questions of anxiety, the emotional aspects of rituals, and the question of animal/human ritualization. On the latter question he states: "the term 'ritualization' is an inaccurate borrowing from human behaviour since, in man, ritual fulfils the opposite purpose" (682). [MS/JS]

References: V.W. Turner, E.R. Leach (–), G. Dumézil (+).
Examples: Iroquois, Fox, Pawnee, Navajo, Osage in North America.
Key-words: def, MYT, STR, eth, gst, emo.

Lewis, Gilbert A., 1980, *Day of Shining Red. An Essay on Understanding Ritual* (Cambridge Studies in Social Anthropology 27); Cambridge etc.: Cambridge University Press (ISBN 0–521–22278–8) (233) (with index, references, and an analytical table of contents).

The ethnographic starting point of the study is the question of whether it is appropriate to interpret the act of penis-bleeding that is secretly done by men among the Gnau (New Guinea) as a male 'first menstruation' (in defiance of the emic view): It is "[a] question of interpretation", as the first chapter is entitled (1–5). At several points, the author reflects on the interdependence of description and interpretation (e.g. 24–25; 216–217). This question has a number of methodological and theoretical implications that the author explicitly and systematically explores (hence the book's theoretical relevance). Chapter 2, "Problems of Ritual in General" (6–38), first argues "that no adequate case can be made for separating ritual sharply as a special kind of action distinct from others" (6). Moreover, it "cannot be demarcated by a clear boundary from other kinds of custom" (8). Both custom and ritual share the presence of imperative rules. In both cases, behavior "that might seem arbitrary was made significant by tradition or convention, at least as far as recognition of identity and the obligation to obey went" (19). "The ruling is explicit but its meaning may be implicit... The ruling is public, clear and social; its meaning may be so, or it may be indeterminate, private, various and individual" (19). Inspired by Gombrich, the author repeatedly stresses the similarities between ritual and art. For instance, "they have both been likened to language and held to express or to communicate" (9), and this is precisely the view the author consistently challenges throughout the book. As he writes in the concluding "Inventary of Themes" (216–224): "I argue that we require positive grounds before we assume that we need to look for symbolism or expression that is not apparent or explicit in the minds of the actors or in the reasons that they give for what they do" (220). He insists on distinguishing expression from communication, and rejects the interpretation of ritual as communication (32–38): "Such arguments on the communication of messages in code seem to me tenuous when there is no evidence on the part of the actors who do the rites that they understand or interpret them so. The 'meanings' provided may be a revelation of the anthropologist rather than the people" (221). Furthermore, he argues against the idea that "rites or symbols have a meaning in themselves objectively present, sometimes even a single correct meaning, waiting to be detected" (221; 117–118). Instead, he favors another similarity between ritual and art: the dimension of performance. "In ritual, as in art, he who devises or creates or performs is also spectator of what he does; and he who beholds is also active in the sense that he interprets the performance. The value of ritual lies partly in this ambiguity of the active and passive for creator, performer and beholder: the sense of an arena of constraints within which the individual is free to some extent to search out, interpret and discover implies an indeterminacy about the full significance of what is done" (38). "But the 'meaning' of a ritual performance or a play is much further off from the meaning of a purely linguistic message than it is from the 'meaning' of an event. We interpret an event at which we are present or in which we take part: we do not 'read' the event as we experience it or as we reflect on it; we do not 'decode' it to make sense of it" (34). "Ritual is not done solely to be interpreted: it is also done . . . to resolve, alter or demonstrate a situation" (35). "The analogy of ritual performance to a play suggests that we should consider response to stimuli as well as . . . the propositional meaning or communicated message" (221). According to the author, the "efficacy of substitutes or symbols [in ritual] lies in their ability to release a response, and this depends on a combination of their intrinsic attributes, the context in which they are set and the power of expectation . . . on the part of the animal or person who perceives them. This view of efficacy may lead us to question whether our search to understand ritual activities in terms of symbol, metaphor and communication is directed right" (116). Ritual "is primarily action—a way of doing, making, creating, showing, expressing, arousing—a complex form of stimulus to which people respond. Things done in ritual also have the power to arouse or to release" (118), hence ritual's appeal to emotion and feeling. Moreover, the author stresses the "alerting quality of ritual" (19–22): "A constraint is introduced into the ordinary flow of everyday life which limits freedom, requires alertness and attention: the presence of rules bounds or marks out an area as significant" (19–20). "That the rules are not self-evident in the circumstances, but artificial and requiring to be taught and learned, that they gain their validity essentially by reference to tradition, is the basis of that quality which we discern as the arbitrary or irrational in much ritual. It alerts us, the observers, as it does those to whom the ritual belongs that they are in a peculiar arena, peculiar in the intransitive sense where gestures, actions and behaviour may have significance which they would not otherwise have. Elements that are often to be observed in ritual—the aesthetic side of colour, noise and smell; the decorations, singing, the aromatic plants, the formality, stiffness or strangeness of gesture; and the tension translated by a great volume of excited chatter or by constrained silence; or the very secrecy . . . these are all elements which alert the attention and make ritual peculiar . . . We respond to these elements as observers: they are the real grounds for that unreflecting impulse which convinces us immediately, intuitively, that we deal with ritual" (20). [MS]

References: **E.H. Gombrich (+), N. Frye (+)**, J. Huizinga (+), E.R. Leach (+/–), M.E.F. Bloch (+/–), V.W. Turner (–), C. Lévi-Strauss.

Example: Penis-bleeding among the Gnau (West Sepik Province of New Guinea).
Reviews: E.G. Schwimmer *JPS* 89.4 (1980) 534 f; A. Gell *Man* 15.3 (1980) 560 f; E.L. Schieffelin *AE* 8.2 (1981) 405 f; J. Morton *AJPH* 27.2 (1981) 250 f; N. Cook *Mank* 13.1 (1981) 97 f; M.W. Young *Oc* 52.2 (1981) 160 f; C.P. MacCormack *Sociol* 15.2 (1981) 315.
Key-words: COM, pmc, pr1, mng, sym, AES, idn, frm, EFF, emo, rep, gst, rfl, gdr, def.

Lindgren, J. Ralph, 1997, 'Semiosis, Ritualization and Magic', in: J. Ralph Lindgren & Jay Knaak (eds), *Ritual and Semiotics*, (Critic of Institutions 14), New York etc.: Peter Lang (ISBN 0-8204-2805-1) 69–87.

In this article the author rejects the cognitive study of semiotics and ritual. Instead, he favors a perspective that gives primacy to practice over knowledge and to process over structure. In the general sense of the study of signs, the author takes semiotics as a study of something that one takes as standing for something else. He uses the notion of 'metaphor' as a key concept for describing the relationship between ritual and semiotics. He assumes that a metaphor is neither reducible to something else nor is its function limited to figurative speech. In other words, metaphors pervade discourse and action, as well as semiosis and ritual. Because 'semiosis' is a process whereby signs are formed and transformed, the author takes the process of semiosis as a metaphorical process. He is concerned with ritual as such a culturally produced text, which has to be interpreted by the participants through the practice of ritual performance. If practice is primary to knowledge and process is primary to structure, the author argues, ritual is similar to the metaphorical process riddled with ambiguity and instability. He takes ritual as a ritualized form of activity and regards communication as the paradigmatic sign relationship that is grounded only on convention. According to him, semiosis and ritual involve the coordination of stereotyped interactive patterns of behavior. Because the semiotic and ritual processes manifest themselves in the metaphorical pattern of syntax, semantics, and pragmatics, the argument of this article is that semiosis and ritualization can be regarded as more or less the same metaphorical processes. Semiosis is the process by which sign systems emerge, transform, and dissolve. Ritualization is the process by which privileged distinctions are established, altered, and abandoned. [JK]

References: **C.M. Bell** (+), W. Burkert (+), **J.S. Huxley** (+), E.R. Leach, C. Lévi-Strauss (–), **V.W. Turner** (+), E.M. Zuesse.
Example: Magic.
Key-words: cog, com, eth, lan, pr1, SEM, str.

Lorenz, Konrad Z., 1966, 'Evolution of Ritualization in the Biological and Cultural Spheres', in: Sir Julian S. Huxley (ed.), *A Discussion on Ritualization of Behavior in Animals and Man*, (Philosophical Transactions of the Royal Society, Series B 251), London: Royal Society of London (No ISBN) (*) 273–284.

The first section of this paper, "Ethological approach and phylogenetic ritualization" (273–278), approaches the study of 'ritual' from an evolutionistic point of view, as part of "the study of behaviour, exactly as Darwin had done" (273). This approach is in the first place comparative and selectionist, i.e. it is concerned with comparing populations of animals for finding out the features which they have (not) in common, which caused their success in the process of 'survival of the fittest'. Closer related populations tend to have more such features in common, whereas less related populations tend to have developed different such features. Already in 1898 it was rightly recognized that among such features are also ways of behavior ("coordinated motor patterns of action" (274)). Julian Huxley and Edmund Selous discovered that certain forms of behavior served the function of communication. These "communicative movements have evolved from everyday functions. The process by which they do so was termed ritualization by Julian Huxley.... the process of ritualization is one of the fastest processes of evolution known in undomesticated animals, as can be concluded from their dissimilarity in comparatively closely related species" (275). Out of the development of ordinary motor patterns into communication tools, two further functions developed: the canalization of aggression and "the formation of a bond which keeps together two or more individuals. This is achieved by most so-called greeting ceremonies... It is quite erroneous to say that such ceremonies are 'the expression of' a bond; indeed they themselves constitute it" (176). A further "characteristic of ritualized motor patterns is a change of form which the unritualized prototype underwent in the service of its new communicative function and which quite obviously was brought about by the selection pressure exerted by the survival value of communication" (276). Especially, the visual or auditory aspects are strongly exaggerated while other aspects are reduced. Through the evolution of the new, ritualized, motor pattern, it "acquires all the characteristics of an autonomous instinctive movement" (278). The second section, "Ritualization in the psycho-social evolution of human culture" (278–284), after having stressed that we "know from observation and ample experimental verification that rituals, whether phylogenetically or culturally evolved, do in fact perform the same functions of communication, of canalizing aggression, and of effecting the cohesion of pairs or groups", first pays attention to two differences between phylogenetically and culturally evolved rituals: "the mechanisms underlying the two processes and the amounts of time required by each" (279). As to the first, the "role played by genetic inheritance in the evolution and maintenance of phylogenetically evolved rituals is, of course, taken over by tradition in cultural ritualization" (280). "Habit-formation, compulsive anxiety over infractions of accepted rules, reverence and love for traditional customs—these and whatever other mechanisms there may be to ensure the permanence of culturally ritualized social norms and rites, from generation to generation, perform an analogous function in culturally ritualized social norms and rites, to genetic inheritance in the evolution of phylogenetically ritualized forms of social behaviour. Furthermore, all these mechanisms have themselves, of course, been phylogenetically evolved. Man, as Arnold Gehlen has aptly put it, is by nature a cultural creature. In other words, all his inherited norms of behaviour have been selectively moulded in phylogeny in such a way as to need being complemented by cultural tradition" (281). Human cultural rituals turn out to have exactly the same characteristics ("mimic exaggeration, redundant repetition and typical intensity") and functions ("of communication, of channelling aggression and of group cohesion (bonding)") as ritualized motor patterns in animals (281). These functions are especially prominent "in the seemingly unimportant everyday cultural rituals which we call manners" (282). Furthermore, "culturally developed social norms and rites are characters of human groups of various size much in the same manner as inherited properties evolved in phylogeny are characters of subspecies, species, genera, and higher taxonomic units.... Their divergence during historical development erects barriers between cultural units in the same sort of way as divergent evolution does between species" (282). Such cultural pseudo-speciation is "immeasurably faster than phylogenetic speciation", but nevertheless needs time (282). The article closes with the observation that this cultural differentiation easily leads to misunderstandings between people of different cultural backgrounds, with the risk of creating aggression towards outsiders, mirroring the bond it creates between insiders (283). "The dark side of pseudo-speciation is that it makes us consider the members of pseudo-species other than our own as not truly or fully human" (284). [JS]

References: **Ch. Darwin** (+), **J.S. Huxley** (+), E.H. Erikson (+).
Key-words: def, ter, soc, psy, sec, exp, COM, ETH, mim, dyn, tra, cpr.

Luckmann, Thomas, 1985, 'Riten als Bewältigung lebensweltlicher Grenzen', *Schweizer Zeitschrift für Soziologie* 3:535–550.

[Rites as Coping with Borders of the World we Live in]

In the first section of this article (535–536), the author, a sociologist, introduces his subject and gives preliminary definitions of the terms 'symbols', 'actions', 'social actions', and 'rites'. He defines 'symbols' as referring to something, not only outside itself, but rather outside the reality-domain (*Wirklichkeitsbereich*, 535) to which the symbol belongs. Then 'rites' are defined as symbolic actions, with which he wants to refer to that type of symbols which are not symbolic objects but symbolic actions (*die Handlungsform von Symbolen*, 536). That means that 'rites' are social actions, i.e. oriented towards someone else, but this someone does not belong to our daily reality-domain (*alltäglichen Wirklichkeitsbereich*, 536). In the second section (537–539) it is argued, that our experiences of reality are constantly limited by the restrictions of our senses, but that we learn to complement this by our memory of past experiences. Thus we know, when we see the front-side of a familiar object, also how its back-side looks like, although we cannot see it, because we remember to have seen it in the past. This, the author calls 'small transcendencies'. A next step is our deduction of emotions of other people from their expressions. We know, that we can ourselves cheat others in this respect, and thus probably others can mislead us as well. As opposed to 'small transcendencies', these 'middle transcendencies' cannot be verified with certainty, but that which the observed reality refers to still belongs to the same reality-domain. The third section (539–545) then discusses 'grand transcendencies', i.e. those where the signified does not belong to the same reality-domain as the signifying. From our experience, everyone knows of the reality-domain we enter when we fall asleep and dream. This reality-domain not only is different from the daily one, it also has its own, different logic. And all of us cross the border between these realities there and back again each day. In our culture, the daily reality-domain is supposed to be the more real one of the two, but this is not *a priory* necessary, and it is not so in all cultures. And there are more reality-domains. Day-dreaming is one which one enters in a state of waking, but on return to daily reality the reality of the day-dream fades away again. Some people sometimes enter even other reality-domains spontaneously, but more often people expressly learn techniques of ecstasy in order to do so intentionally and controlled. In the last cases, one usually has a clear expectation of the reality-domain one enters, based on the reports of others who have used the same technique. As opposed to sleep, these reality-domains are thus entered in a state of waking, and they keep reality priority over daily reality, once one has returned from them. Finally, death is often supposed to be a crossing-over to some other reality-domain, but that other reality-domain is only postulated on the basis precisely of human experiences of 'grand transcendencies'. The fourth section (545–549) is dedicated to symbols again. They are links between something in our daily reality (the signifying) and something in some other reality-domain (the signified). They remind us of (possibly personal immediate) experiences of that other reality-domain. But in a social context, their meaning is inter-subjectively constructed. The fifth and last section (549–550) finally turns to rites and institutions. According to the author, rites are a special form of symbols, namely symbolic *actions*. But they are also a special form of actions, namely *symbolic* actions. What makes them sociological interesting is, that they are social actions in which non-human beings are addressed and are supposed to answer. Also, in almost all societies, the daily life in the society of men is regarded subordinated under some other reality-domain, the domain of the 'great transcendencies'. Symbols thus control daily reality. Sociologically the most interesting is, that in our western society, symbols, and especially rites, are no longer part and parcel of all the institutions which guide our actions, but have obtained an institutionally specialized area: religion and science. [JS]

Key-words: def, SOC, psy, SEC, mng, SYM, com, sem, EMO.

Lüddeckens, Dorothea, 2006, 'Emotion', in: Jens Kreinath, Jan A.M. Snoek & Michael Stausberg (eds), *Theorizing Rituals. Vol. I: Issues, Topics, Approaches, Concepts*, (Numen Book Series 114–1), Leiden, Boston: Brill (ISBN-10: 90–04–15342–x, ISBN-13: 978–90–04–15342–4) 545–570.

Rituals pick up existing emotions, they change, and produce emotions. Emotions can be seen as a trigger of rituals, which might be the case with sentiments like fear or bereavement. During the ritual process, emotions change. The expression of a feeling alters the feeling itself—it can be strengthened or modified. Experiencing emotions can cause psychic processes, such as in healing rituals. Rituals can also produce emotions. This may be related to the need of rituals to be remembered, or to support the meaning and importance of the ritual event or its results. Emotions can also trigger particular actions by the participants, and they can support structures of the society. Rituals deal with emotions in the frame of their specific ritual potency. This lies first in their link to systems of symbols, which are already interrelated with emotions. It lies secondly in the sensual dimension of rituals—sensual impulses can arouse emotions through their physical impact and culture specific connotations. Thirdly, ritual structures can provoke and manipulate emotions, for example by providing space and time orientations. Fourthly, the performance dimension of rituals enables participants to express, and at the same time to experience, emotions with their bodies. [Dorothea Lüddeckens]

Key-word: EMO.

Lüger, Heinz-Helmut, 1983, 'Some Aspects of Ritual Communication', *Journal of Pragmatics* 7:695–711.

Original version: 'Formen rituellen Sprachgebrauchs', *Deutsche Sprache. Zeitschrift für Theorie, Praxis, Dokumentation* 8 (1980) 21–39 (with bibliography). English translation by Rachel Kreitz, Isabel Serle and Dave Turner.

"Ritual communication can be found in various areas of activity. It arises in a context where conventionally determined characteristics of speech stand out more prominently than individual aspects" (708). With regard to their contextual situation, "rituals, or rather, ritual characteristics represent... a specific mode of communication" (708). In this paper, the author uses the term 'ritual' "to describe a verbal action which is no longer, or is only to a limited extent, individually realized and appropriate to the specific necessities of a given situation" (697). Based on the criterion of "*reduced individualization*" (697), the paper offers a rough classification of four degrees of 'rituality' in verbal communication (cf. Table 2 on p. 709). These degrees are distinguished with regard to (a) their "ritual characteristics" and (b) "areas of communication" (709). The highest degree of 'rituality' accrues to "rituals in a restricted sense" (709). As characteristics, the author finds an exactly defined situation, the prescription of precise wording and sequencing, and explicitly formulated possibilities of sanctions. In particular, this applies to the area of "institutional performative acts" (709) (such as "religious sacraments" or procedural acts). A lower degree of 'rituality' accrues to "rituals in an extended sense" (709). Here characteristics are "standardized situational types" (709) and the "recourse to a repertoire of available formulae corresponding to situational conditions" (709) which are usually not codified. This applies first of all to so-called 'phatic acts', which one finds in the opening and concluding of conversations (greeting, etc.). The next lower degree of rituality is referred to as 'ritualizations'. These are characterized by the use of "situationally abstracted expressions" (709) and an "avoidance of particular or individual reference" (709). This refers to empty formulae as they are used, e.g., in diplomatic communiques. Another feature of 'ritualizations' is the "[r]ecourse to pre-determined schemata of expression and/or thought" (709), e.g. stereotypes that are applied in persuasive discourse. Moreover, in the case of 'ritualizations' the "standardization of the situation" (709) is not decisive (contrary to 'rituals' in a restricted and an extended sense). This applies to the usage of commonplaces, proverbs, maxims, or slogans that may, e.g., allow the participants to dispense with an individual response to a difficult situation. The lowest degree of 'rituality' is called 'routinization'. This entails a non-ritual automatization. It is non-ritual because the means-ends relationship in communication is preserved. It is to be found in standardized acts (such as asking directions). [MS]

Key-words: com, lan, pmt, rht, def.

Lukes, Steven, 1975, 'Political Ritual and Social Integration', *Sociology* 9:289–308.

Based on a summary of some anthropological disputes, the author finds that "we can extract the following definition of ritual: *rule-governed activity of a symbolic character which draws the attention of its participants to objects of thought and feeling which they hold to be of special importance*" (291). The author then sketches the Durkheimian theory and that of the "Neo-Durkheimians" (a group that the author takes to include, among others, Shils and Bellah) on political rituals. From a critical discussion he concludes "that the neo-Durkheimians have contributed virtually nothing to our understanding of the extent to which, and ways in which, modern industrial societies are integrated—first, because their conception of social integration is too simplistic, and second, because their assumption of value consensus is empirically questionable" (298). In the author's view, the neo-Durkheimian approach is to narrow both because of "the selection of the rituals they analyse, and by the analyses they offer of the rituals thus selected" (298). The author's "main positive suggestion is that political rituals should be seen as reinforcing, recreating and organizing *représentations collectives* (to use Durkheim's term), that the symbolism of political ritual *represents, inter alia,* particular models or political paradigms of society and how it functions. In this sense, such ritual plays, as Durkheim argued, a cognitive role, rendering intelligible society and social relationships, serving to organize people's knowledge of the past and present and their capacity to imagine the future. In other words, it helps to define as authoritative certain ways of seeing society: it serves to specify what in society is of special significance, it draws people's attention to certain forms of relationships and activity—and at the same time, therefore, it deflects their attention from other forms, since every way of seeing it [sic] also a way of not seeing. I suggest, in short, that we should go beyond the somewhat simplistic idea of political ritual expressing-producing-constituting value integration seen as the essence of social integration (which is the banal but widely applied aspect of Durkheim's theory) and take up instead the fertile idea that ritual has a cognitive dimension (this being, in any case, the central and original part of Durkheim's theory), though placing it (as Durkheim did not) within a class-structured, conflictual and pluralistic model of society...it suggests that such rituals can be seen as modes of exercising, or seeking to exercise, power along the cognitive dimension" (301). From these suggestions, the author derives a number of questions about political rituals and suggests viable forms of analysis (302–305). [MS]

References: É. Durkheim (+/–), M. Douglas, E.R. Leach, J. Goody, D. Sperber (+), J.H.M. Beattie, E. Shils (–), R. Bellah (–), V.W. Turner (+), R. Bocock.
Examples: British coronations, Memorial Day, public reactions to Kennedy's assassination, demonstrations, Orange Order's rituals in Northern Ireland, administrative activities in the United States, elections.
Key-words: def, soc, POW, sec, cog.

Lutkehaus, Nancy Christine & Paul B. Roscoe (eds), 1995, *Gender Rituals. Female Initiation in Melanesia*; London, New York: Routledge (ISBN 0–415–91106–0 / 0–415–91107–9 (p)) (xix + 265) (with index and bibliography).

Selected contents: Part I: "Introduction": 1. Nancy C. Lutkehaus: "Feminist Anthropology and Female Initiation in Melanesia" (3–29); Part II: "Defining Women. Gender Images in Female Initiation Rites": 2. Brigitta Hauser-Schäublin: "Puberty Rites, Women's *Naven*, and Initiation. Women's Rituals of Transition in Abelam and Iatmul Culture" (33–53); Part III: "Achieving Womanhood. The Life Cycle as Cultural Performance": 4. Kathleen Barlow: "Achieving Womanhood and the Achievements of Women in Murik Society. Cult Initiation, Gender Complementarity, and the Prestige of Women" (85–112); Part IV: "The Female Body and Life-Cycle Rites as Metaphor": 8. Nancy C. Lutkehaus: "Gender Metaphors. Female Rituals as Cultural Models in Manam" (183–204); 9. Lorraine Sexton: "Marriage as the Model for a New Initiation Ritual" (205–216); Part V: "Conclusion": 10. Paul B. Roscoe: "'Initiation' in Cross-Cultural Perspective" (219–238). [JS]
Key-word: GDR.

MacAloon, John J., 1984, 'Introduction. Cultural Performances, Culture Theory', in: John J. MacAloon (ed.), *Rite, Drama, Festival, Spectacle. Rehearsals Toward a Theory of Cultural Performance*, Philadelphia: Institute for the Study of Human Issues (ISBN 0–89727–045–2) (*) 1–15.

This article introduces a volume based on papers presented at the Seventy-sixth Burg Wartenstein Symposium on cultural performances organized by Barbara A. Babcock, Barbara G. Myerhoff, and Victor W. Turner. The aim of the conference was "to consider cultural performances in such a way as to bridge and transcend such conventional dichotomies as oral and written, public and private, doing and thinking, primitive and modern, sacred and secular, 'pop' and 'high', ludic and tragic" (1). In addition, the contributors sought "to develop typologies and historical sequences of performative genres, to judge the possibility of cross-cultural comparison, to evaluate existing analytical concepts, and to search for new conceptual tools for the investigation of performative events" (1–2). According to the editor, "[a]ll of the conferees share a commitment to the contemporary understanding of culture as 'a system of symbols and their meanings' [C. Geertz

1973 (*)]. On more particular theoretical and methodological grounds, however, there is much variation in approach. On the focal topic, we are in accord that performance is constitutive of social experience and not something merely additive or instrumental. But exactly how and how much it is constitutive remain for us subjects of feverish and fertile debate" (2). The editor further surveys concepts and contexts of cultural performance (3–10). The following statement concludes this section: "Whatever performances do, or are meant to do, they do by creating the conditions for, and by coercing the participants into, paying attention. Catharsis also may be seen as a universal property of cultural performance... in the more general sense of releasing the 'performancers' from scripted activity... back into the unmeasured or less measured realms of behavioral routine or spontaneous action" (10). Then follows a section on genre and reflexivity (10–13). The latter concept is defined as "that capacity of human beings to distance themselves from their own subjective experiences, to stand apart from and to comment on them" (11). [JK/MS]

References: B.A. Babcock, G. Bateson, K. Burke, C. Geertz (+), E. Goffman, D. Hymes, B. Kapferer, R. Schechner, M. Singer, B. Stoeltje, **V.W. Turner** (+).
Key-words: mng, PMC, sec, soc, sym, RFL.

MacAloon, John J. (ed.), 1984, *Rite, Drama, Festival, Spectacle. Rehearsals Toward a Theory of Cultural Performance*; Philadelphia: Institute for the Study of Human Issues (ISBN 0-89727-045-2) (viii + 280).

Selected contents: John J. MacAloon: "Introduction. Cultural Performances, Culture Theory" (1–15) (*); Victor Witter Turner: "Liminality and the Performative Genres" (19–41) (*); Barbara A. Babcock: "Arrange me into Disorder. Fragments and Reflections on Ritual Clowning" (102–128); Bruce Kapferer: "The Ritual Process and the Problem of Reflexivity in Sinhalese Demon Exorcisms" (179–207); John J. MacAloon: "Olympic Games and the Theory of Spectacle in Modern Societies" (241–280). [JK]

Key-words: frm, PMC, rfl, sec, sem, str.

Marglin, Frédérique Apffel, 1990, 'Refining the Body. Transformative Emotion in Ritual Dance', in: Owen M. Lynch (ed.), *Divine Passions. The Social Construction of Emotion in India*, Berkeley, Los Angeles, Oxford: University of California Press (ISBN 0–520–06647–2) 212–236.

The aim of this paper is "to reconstruct the emotional-cognitive-spiritual transformations wrought on the participants by the dance performed as part of the daily ritual in a great Hindu temple" (212). In following Tambiah's performative approach to ritual, the author argues that rituals "accomplish or perform something, a symbolic communication that, because of its manner of delivery, brings about a transformation in its participants. This transformation is the performative outcome of ritual" (213). Here the author gives a semiotic reconstruction of two dance rituals that are performed during a midday ritual and an evening ritual. In order to capture the concepts and values underlying the ritual dances, she sketches "an ideal-typical picture of the core ritual activities in the temple which center around the preparation of food offered to the deities" (214). Both ritual dances are presented in the same three-fold structure. The description of 'the cultural content of the spaciotemporal context' is followed by 'a formal analysis of the dance ritual' and the 'performative efficacy' as the 'transformation in the audience'. She argues that the ritual dance performed by women transforms the participants. The participants taste "a culturally constituted emotion that is embodied thought" (230). Moreover, "[b]odily experiences are here unified with thought; they are not relegated to a separate realm, of physiology, sensation, or nature" (230). [JK]

Reference: S.J. Tambiah.
Examples: Hindu ritual dances.
Key-words: dnc, eff, emb, EMO, pmc, pmt, sem.

Marshall, Douglas A., 2002, 'Behavior, Belonging, and Belief. A Theory of Ritual Practice', *Sociological Theory* 20:360–380.

The author wants to "propose a comprehensive, empirically credible, and theoretically fertile theory of how ritual practices transform knowledge into belief and membership into belonging" (361). His point of departure for a new model of ritual is Durkheim's theory (1912 [1995]). This model, presented in a schematic diagram, is conceptualized to combine sociological and psychological understandings of human behavior in terms of belonging and belief (361). In the first section "A Model of Ritual" (361–368), the author elaborates the several aspects of his diagram under the following headings: "Co-Presence" (361–363), "Practices" (363), "Positive and Public Rites" (363–364), "Private, Piacular and Negative Rites" (364–365), and "From Behavior to Belief and Belonging" (366–368). In the second section "Applications and Implications of the Model" (368–377), the author argues: "Ritual occurs as a socially shared response to socially shared conditions. Its mechanisms are socially instigated and mediated, its specific forms are socially determined, and even when practiced in isolation, it is as part of a socially transmitted system of belief and practice" (369). This section is again divided into subsections: 1. "The Origins of Ritual" (369–370); 2. "The Primacy of Practices" (370); 3. "A Formal Statement of the Model" (371), 4. "A Comprehensive and Extensible Theory of Ritual Practice" (371–373); 5. "Functional Substitution" (373–374); 6. "Distinctions" (374–375); 7. "New Variables—The Self and Justification" (375–377). The argument presented here, is summarized in the following way: "[T]he present model was developed with an eye toward creating a comprehensive theory of rituals, encompassing the full spectrum of ritual forms within a unified framework that is simple, useful and parsimonious" (371). "Among the most significant contributions of the explicit inclusion of psychological mechanisms in the model is the recognition of new and heretofore unnoticed mediating variables. These not only allow for fuller understanding but also suggest new research directions and predictions" (375). "Identifying the psychological mechanisms by which ritual creates belief and belonging as essentially attributional ensures that the significance of potentially competing explanations comes to the fore. Put simply, if a plausible external cause of one's state or behavior can be found, then participants will not attribute these things to the ritual focus, and the ritual's ability to create both belief and belonging will be severely compromised" (376). [JK]

Reference: É. Durkheim (+).
Key-words: exp, psy, soc.

Matthews, Gareth, 1980, 'Ritual and Religious Feelings', in: Amélie Oksenberg Rorty (ed.), *Explaining Emotions*, (Topics in Philosophy 5), Berkeley, Los Angeles, London: University of California Press (ISBN 0–520–03921–1) 339–353.

The author takes his start from a quotation of a text by Augustine: "For when men pray they do with the members of their bodies what befits suppliants... I do not know how it is... [but] that invisible inner motion which caused [these signs] is itself strengthened. And in this manner the disposition of the heart which preceded them in order that they might be made, grows stronger because they are made" (339). After an exegesis of this text, he proceeds to ask why praying is necessary at all, since God already knows the secrets of our hearts. That leads him to analyze why we need to express such feelings as gratitude or guilt in non-religious contexts. Next he shows that the fact that the other knows already what we feel makes it much easier, but by no means superfluous, to express our feelings. Bodily performances are not intended to provide information or to manipulate one's feelings. What counts, says the author, is the sincere intention and the faithful expression of one's pre-existing emotions. He concludes: "Both the puzzle Augustine begins with in the passage cited... and the puzzle he ends up with have turned out to be specious. The puzzle he ends up with is this: How can the mere motions of the body in ritual intensify religious feelings and attitudes? This puzzle is specious because it is not the mere motions of the body that have such an effect; what has, or may have, such an effect is (among other things) the sincere and understanding performance of ritual—the dramatic rehearsal of the tenets of one's faith... The puzzle Augustine begins with is then this: Why need one express, as well as simply have, feelings such as sorrow for one's sins, since God knows already what feelings one has? This puzzle is specious because it presupposes that the only (or at least the primary) reason for saying [e.g.] that I am sorry for having done something wrong is to bring about the result that someone else knows (or thinks) that I have certain feelings. But this is not so. An apology may have real point even when the person it is directed toward already knows, and I know that she or he knows, what is in my heart" (352–353). [JS/Florian Jeserich]

Reference: **Augustine** (+/–).
Example: Christian worship.
Key-words: com, pmc, pmt, pr1, eff, EMO, exp, psy, sec.

McCauley, Robert N., 2001, 'Ritual, Memory, and Emotion. Comparing Two Cognitive Hypotheses', in: Jensine Andresen (ed.), *Religion in Mind. Cognitive Perspectives on Religious Belief, Ritual, and Experience*, Cambridge etc.: Cambridge University Press (ISBN 0–521–80152–4) (*) 115–140 (with index).

This article is a discussion about the ritual frequency hypothesis and the ritual form hypothesis, both of which deal with emotional stimulation in rituals. The former thesis, developed by Harvey Whitehouse, argues that the frequency of ritual performance determines the amount of emotional stimulation that is involved in any ritual. However, the latter thesis, developed by the author and E. Thomas Lawson, underlines the importance of the knowledge of differences in ritual form that influences the emotional stimulation. The author does not challenge the issue that the crucial mnemonic variable in rituals is frequency and agrees with Whitehouse. They "share two assumptions here: (1) that participants find rituals that are loaded with sensory pageantry emotionally provocative; and (2) that this emotional provocation tends to make at least some features of these rituals more memorable than they would be otherwise. We agree, in short, about the effects of sensory pageantry and about at least one of the reasons why rituals incorporate it when they do. Our disagreements mostly concern the 'when they do' part of the previous sentence. The empirical question I want to explore is '*which* religious rituals incorporate such high levels of sensory pageantry?' or, given our common assumptions about its effects, 'which religious rituals turn up the emotional volume?'" (119). The author then discusses the 'ritual frequency hypothesis' (117–123) and the 'ritual form hypothesis' (123–133). These hypotheses differ from each other "both concerning *which* religious rituals contain elevated levels of sensory pageantry and, at least in part, concerning *why*. The ritual form hypothesis maintains that heightened sensory pageantry arises only in rituals of odd-numbered types, which characteristically spawn super-permanent effects. Ultimately, only the gods can bring about such effects, thus, in these rituals, the gods either act directly or certify the action indirectly. Consequently, each individual needs to undergo these rituals only once. Participants need to remember these special ritual episodes, but rituals of this sort also must persuade participants both of the importance of these events and of the gods' involvement. Stirring their emotions so much helps contribute to this end, too. The resulting convictions play a critical role in increasing the probabilities that participants will transmit these ideas subsequently" (133). In comparing the two hypotheses (133–138), the author reviews "two considerations that will, at least, help in assessing their comparative merits. The first concerns purely theoretical matters. The second is a brief glimpse at some relevant empirical evidence. On both counts, I shall argue that the ritual form hypothesis proves the better of the two alternatives" (133). [JK]

References: J.W. Fernandez, E.Th. Lawson, D. Sperber, F. Staal, A. van Gennep.
Key-words: cog, EMO, psy, str.

McCauley, Robert N. & E. Thomas Lawson, 2002, *Bringing Ritual to Mind. Psychological Foundations of Cultural Forms*; Cambridge etc.: Cambridge University Press (ISBN 0-521-81559-2 / 0-521-01629-0 (p)) (xiii + 236) (with index and bibliography).

In the beginning of their book, the authors review theoretical issues raised in their former work, esp. in their monograph "Rethinking Religion" (1990 (*)). In this connection, their typology of religious ritual forms is of special interest because it is crucial for an understanding of the authors' following theoretical claims. The typology, in short, describes a dichotomy between special agent rituals and special instrument or special patient rituals. But the introductory chapter (1–37) is not pure repetition. The authors present their insights in light of the newest findings in cognitive and developmental psychology. Furthermore, they use parts of the first chapter to introduce slight terminological changes and to re-negotiate definitional problems. They explain, e.g., what they mean(t) by 'religious rituals', clarifying both the 'religious' and the 'ritual' component of their *terminus technicus* (for criteria see also 144–145). Contrary to their extensive discussion of the meaning(lessness) of rituals in "Rethinking Religion", the authors now argue "that for many features of religious ritual knowledge and practice meanings simply do not seem to matter much" (36). In their new book, they would like to concentrate instead on the connections between ritual, emotion, and memory. Thus they hypothesize in the second chapter (38–89) that the performance frequency and the emotional arousal are two crucial means of enhancing memory. Where special instrument and special patient rituals rely heavily on the frequency of ritual performances to insure their memorability, special agent rituals occur only so infrequently that their recollection depends mostly upon their high level of sensory pageantry. According to the authors' cognitive alarm hypothesis, this second attractor (emotional stimulation via sensory pageantry) closely approximates the sorts of conditions that seem to make for accurate, flashbulb-like, episodic memories. Moreover, they show that these connections to enhanced memory are vital to understanding the process of culturally transmitting ritual knowledge. In the third chapter (89–124), the authors consider "two cognitive hypotheses for explaining the connections between ritual and memory dynamics. The first is the frequency hypothesis [initially launched by Harvey Whitehouse], which holds, in short, that the amount of sensory stimulation (and resulting emotional excitement) a ritual incorporates is inversely proportional to its performance frequency" (6). In addition, Whitehouse suggests that frequent repetition could also produce the so-called tedium effect: The sensory stimulation becomes habitual and, accordingly, the ritual participant's attention diminishes. The second of the two cognitive hypotheses is the "ritual form hypothesis, which holds that aspects of the representations of ritual form... explain and predict the comparative levels of sensory pageantry [which] religious rituals incorporate" (6). Moreover, the ritual form hypothesis maintains that heightened sensory pageantry arises only in special agent rituals. Because a ritual of this type characteristically spawns super-permanent effects and consequences, it must stimulate emotional excitement in order to convince the participants that something vitally important is going on and to motivate them religiously to transmit these cultural materials. In the fourth chapter (124–178) and in the first third of the fifth (183–192), the authors compare these two hypotheses' explanatory and predictive strengths by examining the empirical data provided by Whitehouse. Ultimately, the authors argue "that the ritual form hypothesis makes better sense of Whitehouse's ethnography of Kivung and splinter group rituals than his own hypothesis does" (178). This is the case because their "ritual form hypothesis possesses greater theoretical depth than the ritual frequency hypothesis, since it identifies the principal factor [viz. ritual form] determining the values of the independent [and unexplained] variable [viz. rituals' performance frequency] of the latter hypothesis" (138–139). Finally, they outline an evolutionary theory of religious ritual systems. They aim at "[i]dentifying both stable configurations and characteristic dynamic patterns" thereby trying no less than "delineating the cognitive architecture of *Homo religiosus*—not merely to understand well-known historic patterns in religious systems better but also to explain them" (8). The authors, therefore, distinguish between two general profiles of religious ritual systems: They can either be balanced or unbalanced. "The complement of rituals in a *balanced* ritual system is a bivalent configuration that includes rituals from *both* of the major two categories" (181), whereas the second "complement of rituals is unbalanced because special patient and special instrument rituals *overwhelmingly* predominate. Special agent rituals play little, if any, role" (181). Reflections on the history of culture and on the natural history of human cognition suggest that the latter complement is a relatively new form of organizing rituals and that "religious ritual systems may have exhibited a third general pattern, viz., *a second (but very old) and different sort of unbalanced system* that included only special agent rituals"

(211). This 'epidemiological' (Sperber) or evolutionary approach also suggests "that *special agent rituals must play a more fundamental role in the transmission and persistence of religion than do special patient and special instrument rituals*", because "no religious ritual system can survive without at least the periodic performance of special agent rituals capable of energizing participants and motivating them to transmit their religious systems" (212). [Florian Jeserich]

References: J.L. Barrett (+), F. Barth (+/–), P. Boyer, D. Sperber (+/–), **H. Whitehouse (+/–)**.
Examples: Rituals from various religions such as the Islamic *hajj*, Jewish *bar mitzvah*, Christian baptism, Latter Day Saints' weddings, *Kumbha Mela*, Vedic *Agnicayana*, but especially Baktaman male initiations and (in some detail) cargo cult rituals of the Pomio Kivung and their splinter groups.
Key-words: agn, cmp, COG, cpr, def, dyn, eff, EMO, exp, hab, par, pr1, pr2, rep, str.

McLeod, James R., 1990, 'Ritual in Corporate Cultural Studies. An Anthropological Approach', *Journal of Ritual Studies* 4.1:85–97.

The author argues that "it is important to be conscious of the ways in which people are using or perhaps overextending the term [ritual] as an analytical category" (86). The term has been used in many disciplines and in a multitude of contexts. While sociologists, organizational theorists, and ethologists employ the term with minimal definitional requirements and maximal use of the term, many anthropologists and students of religions are much more restrictive. The author suggests a "tripartite division" of phenomena currently classified as rituals. These are 'sacred rituals' (e.g. Incwala Ritual), 'phatic rituals' (e.g. political ritual), and 'secular rituals' (e.g. academic lectures). Furthermore, he compares the use of the term 'ritual' in classical anthropological studies of 'traditional rituals' with the use of the same term in organizational studies. In the two disciplines, the term is used in almost opposite ways. The author claims that students of 'corporate culture' have been "turning the anthropological conceptualization of ritual on its head" (89). To be "referentially defined as rituals in the traditional sense" (92), customary forms of behavior must involve all of the following characteristics: It must be conventionalized, dramatic, repetitive, communal, and have higher levels of meaning associated with the actual performance itself (92–93). The author emphasizes the difference between ceremony and ritual. "Ritual events" are distinguished from "ceremonial events" by the following traits: They are "a community or personal regeneration"; they "must demonstrate valued aspects of the social order and contribute to their perpetuation over time"; they "must link the social order to both past and future through its performance"; they "must demonstrate what is in-group symbolically and certify what is out-group symbolically"; finally, "rituals must link individuals and the group with a specific set of symbols predicated on some mythological or cosmological basis" (94). [MS]

References: J. Goody (+), E.G. d'Aquili (–), V.W. Turner (+), M. Gluckman (+).
Key-words: gen, DEF, sec.

Merkur, Daniel, 1991, 'The Discharge of Guilt. Psychoanalytic Theories of Ritual', *Journal of Ritual Studies* 5.2:15–32.

"No existing psychoanalytic theory of ritual is fully satisfactory. The theory that ritual is a culturally congenial form of compulsion neurosis is a popular misunderstanding of Freud's position and was conclusively refuted by Roheim. Three further theories start with the occurrence of a psychic trauma and its unconscious fixation. Two distinct outcomes are then possible. Either the psyche succumbs to neurosis and engages in repetition-compulsions that are symptomatic of the trauma, or the psyche copes with the trauma by engaging in play, creativity, and other healthy repetition-compulsions" (26–27). Inspired by Winnicott, the author holds that playing is the best analogy to ritual behavior. But for purposes of demarcation and definition, he thinks "it significant that ritual, in all its forms, includes an obligatory element" (23). And in combining Winnicott's position and Gay's psychoanalytical theory of learning under the guise of ritual theory, the author concludes "that both play and ritual induce ritualization of the psyche" (26). However, the author regards these theories as too general, "because neither repetition, play, nor the development of ego-structures is limited to ritual" (27). Thus the author ends by outlining his own approach. In the main, he proposes "a modification of the two theories offered by Freud ["His early theory concerned ambivalent social instincts, and his later one pertained to the primal crime" (27)]—more precisely, their reformulation in perspective of superego theory" (15). He explains that "[a] superego theory of ritual does not validate Freud's claim that ritual is a sort of group pathology, but it obliges us to regard ritual as a substitution of symbolic actions for moral undertakings. Ritual accomplishes the psychic discharge of guilt through symbolic actions.... Indeed, it is precisely because the expiation of guilt through ritual is symbolic and not genuine, that the repetition of a ritual may be necessitated" (29). [JK/Florian Jeserich]

References: E.H. Erikson, **S. Freud**, V.P. Gay, R.L. Grimes, C.G. Jung, Th. Reik, G. Roheim, J.Z. Smith, D.W. Winnicott.
Example: Zechariah's vision (Zech. 3:1,10).
Key-words: def, emo, exp, pmc, PSY, sec, sym.

Michaels, Axel, 1999, '"Le rituel pour le rituel" oder wie sinnlos sind Rituale?' in: Corina Caduff & Joanna Pfaff-Czarnecka (eds), *Rituale heute. Theorien—Kontroversen—Entwürfe*, Berlin: Dietrich Reimer (ISBN 3-496-02666-9) (*) 23–47.
[Le rituel pour le rituel—or to what Extent are Rituals Meaningless?]

The author gives a brief survey of ritual theories (23–27), and analyzes components of a Hindu initiation (27–28). In the third part (29–39), the author distinguishes five components of rituals in general: 1) Causal change (*causa transitionis*), i.e. changes pertaining to biological, physical, social or natural circumstances. "If there is neither border crossing, nor change, nor alternation, there is no ritual" (30). 2) Formal decision (*solemnis intentio*), i.e. the formal or set decision to perform the ritual (e.g. by means of an oath, a promise, or a vow). "The spontaneous, accidental, arbitrary celebration of an event in life is not yet a ritual" (30). 3) Formal criteria of action (*actiones formaliter ritorum*): to qualify as a 'ritual', the action in question must necessarily be (a) formal, stereotyped, and repeatable, (b) public, and (c) irrevocable; in many cases they may even be (d) liminal. 4) Modal criteria of action (*actiones modaliter ritorum*): *societas, religio, impressio*. These are instrumental in bringing the functional dimension of rituals about: (a) *societas* refers to those functions of rituals pertaining to society: solidarity, hierarchy, control, standardization; (b) *religio* refers to the participants awareness that the action in question is done because a transcendental value is attributed to it; (c) *impressio* refers to subjective emotions of the single participants. 5) Transformations of identity, role, status, competence (*novae classificationes; transition vitae*). Rituals produce perceptible changes in that, e.g., a new competence or social status has been gained by means of the ritual. According to the author, these five components clearly distinguish rituals from routine, sports, play, custom, theater, etc. In the final section of his paper (40–45), the author tries to reject Staal's views on the meaninglessness of ritual by appealing to neurobiology. The author finds the idea plausible that many rituals originate from actions that once upon a time were connected to such an advantage or such a pleasure gain that these were culturally transmitted as behavioral patterns, habitus, or memes. Rituals stage a primordial, elementary, archetypal state of being, and that is why they are considered as immutable. Through rituals, human beings identify themselves with the unchangeableness and timeless state, in that way resisting the uncertainty pertaining to future, life, and death. Therefore, "the meaning of ritual consists in its meaninglessness, as it does permit the staging of timelessness, unchangeableness, immortality—that is *religio*—for the mortal human being" (45). [MS]

Key-words: dyn, eth, gen, MNG, pmc, str, cmp.

Michaels, Axel, 2000, 'Ex opere operato. Zur Intentionalität promissorischer Akte in Ritualen', in: Klaus-Peter Köpping & Ursula Rao (eds), *Im Rausch des Rituals. Gestaltung und Transformation der Wirklichkeit in körperlicher Performanz*, (Performanzen. Interkulturelle Studien zu Ritual, Spiel und Theater 1), Münster, Hamburg, London: Lit (ISBN 3-8258-3988-5) (*) 104–123.

[Ex opera operato. On the Intentionality of Promissory Acts in Rituals]

According to the author, rituals (or better: ritual actions) seem to be meaningless due to their stereotypy and rigidity. The author proposes that humans aim at creating such a 'sphere of meaninglessness' in order to take part in a ritual's 'aura of unchangeability' in an ever-changing world. Furthermore, rituals—through their stability—serve the purpose of investing knowledge in a ritual in a particular context which is resistant towards changes and transferable to other contexts. The complexity of ritual actions must therefore be reduced to a few concrete and repeatable processes of actions. So, through ignoring the question of meaning, the ritual segments become meaningless. Finally, the author draws on neurophysiological findings and assumes that rituals are first and foremost a performance of meaninglessness that serves the function of 'neuronal relaxation'. He sees rituals as linked with the limbic system and thus with only limited cognitive (or conscious) access. [Thorsten Gieser]

References: J.L. Austin (+), **C. Humphrey** & **J. Laidlaw**, J.R. Searle (+), F. Staal (+/–).

Examples: Hindu, Vajrana-Buddhistic and Jainistic *puja*.

Key-words: dyn, eth, mng, pr1.

Michaels, Axel, 2006, 'Ritual and Meaning', in: Jens Kreinath, Jan A.M. Snoek & Michael Stausberg (eds), *Theorizing Rituals. Vol. I: Issues, Topics, Approaches, Concepts*, (Numen Book Series 114–1), Leiden, Boston: Brill (ISBN-10: 90–04–15342–x, ISBN-13: 978–90–04–15342–4) 247–261.

The meaninglessness of rituals only concerns the invariability of prescribed actions and the polysemy of rituals (i.e. the multiplicity of meanings). Apart from that, rituals have a great variety of meanings and functions. The tradition of commentaries demonstrates the history of the meaning that was attached to rituals. Moreover, the persistence of rituals requires that they serve some (adaptive) functions. If they were entirely without function, it would be unnecessary to transmit them (Lawson & McCauley 1990, 169). The author therefore argues that the significance of rituals lies in the fact that they often create an auratic sphere or arena of timelessness and immortality—at least in religious or semi-religious contexts. Seen from this point of view, rituals can indeed do without any specific meaning, but this in itself is not meaningless, i.e. without significance. [Axel Michaels]
Key-words: MNG, cog, ref.

Moore, Sally Falk & Barbara G. Myerhoff, 1977, 'Introduction. Secular Ritual: Forms and Meanings', in: Sally Falk Moore & Barbara G. Myerhoff (eds), *Secular Ritual*, Assen, Amsterdam: Van Gorcum (ISBN 90–232–1457–9) (*) 3–24.

The authors write that it is their "conviction that one level of meaning of many formal actions is to present or refer to the culturally postulated and the socially unquestionable. It is an attempt to reify the man-made... That which is postulated and unquestionable may but need not be religious. It may but need not have to do with mystical forces and the spirit world. Unquestionability may instead be vested in a system of authority or a political ideology or other matters. If ritual is considered a set of formal acts which deal with or refer to postulated matters about society or ideology (or matters those mounting the ritual *want* to be unquestioned) then the notion of a secular ritual is not a contradiction in terms" (22). Once this position was taken, a whole range of new questions and research topics emerged. This article attempts to give an overview of these, as well as presenting the results of the discussions that had taken place during the conference of which this volume is the result. The authors do not want to restrict attention to non-religious rituals, but rather to extend attention in order to include, besides religious, also secular rituals. Indeed, "any general answer to [theoretical questions about secular rituals] . . . is likely to apply to religious rituals as well as secular ones" (4–5). But this is not the only extension of scope they suggest. For example: "What are the implications of *new* ceremonies if past theory has been built on the ethnography of traditional rites?" they ask (4), since "[r]itual may do much more than mirror existing social arrangements and existing modes of thought. It can act to reorganize them or even help to create them" (5), because "the circumstance of having been put in the ritual form and mode, has a tradition-like effect. Even if it is performed once, for the first and only time, its stylistic rigidities, and its internal repetitions of form or content make it tradition-like" (8). Then the authors address the subject of efficacy. They distinguish doctrinal (postulated and "demonstrated" by the ritual) and operational (testable by extrinsic means) efficacy (12–13). Doctrinal efficacy is sometimes facilitated by the effect that rituals have on their participants, enabling them "to conceive the invisible referents of symbols used in rituals" (13). For religious and secular rituals, "both 'show' the unseen. Religious ritual 'shows' the existence of the other world through the display of attempts to move it. Analogously, a secular ceremony 'shows' by acting in terms of them the existence of social relationships . . . or ideas or values which are inherently invisible most of the time. It objectifies them and reifies them. It displays symbols of their existence and by implicit reference postulates and enacts their 'reality'" (14). Since "[c]ertainly one common objective of religious and secular ritual is to influence this world" (15), the authors now present "five ways of looking at the outcome of secular ritual": 1) their explicit purpose, 2) their explicit symbols and messages, 3) their implicit statements, 4) the social relationships affected, and 5) the way in which they oppose culture to chaos (16). This last point is then elaborated upon: "Social reality and social relationships are endlessly stated and restated in allegedly empty ritual behaviors, which when viewed analytically are found to convey a wealth of social agreements essential for ongoing interactions" (17). In the last section of their article, the authors turn to the definitional problem: "The issue is not one of defining words for the sake of it. That is, after all, a game all sides can play endlessly. The issue is much more serious. It is a question of which kinds of social phenomena should be distinguished, and which lumped together for the purpose of advancing the understanding of ceremony, ritual and formality in social life. That is a theoretical question, not a semantic one. It follows that since terms must be used to discuss anything, the terms used will reflect theoretical positions and analytic categories" (20). The authors conclude: "Since ritual is a good form for conveying a message as if it were unquestionable, it often is used to communicate those very things which are most in doubt.... Ritual can assert that what is culturally created and man-made is as undoubtable as physical reality. Whether a ceremony succeeds in its purpose is another question, a question about operational efficacy. But the connection between ritual and the unquestionable is often at the core of its doctrinal efficacy as much in social and political settings as in religious ones. To explore these questions, to ask about a particular ceremonial performance to what postulated and presumed truths it refers, what social relationships it involves, what doctrines it presents, what symbols it uses, raises tantalizing theoretical and methodological questions. The reward...is a glimpse into the way people in society represent their situation to themselves" (24). [JS]

References: É. Durkheim (–), S.K. Langer (+), M. Douglas (–).
Key-words: DEF, mng, sym, idn, EFF, pow, emo, rep, SEC, dyn, soc, psy.

Moore, Sally Falk & Barbara G. Myerhoff (eds), 1977, *Secular Ritual*; Assen, Amsterdam: Van Gorcum (ISBN 90–232–1457–9) (x + 293) (with bibliography).

Selected contents: Sally F. Moore & Barbara Myerhoff: "Introduction. Secular Ritual. Forms and Meanings" (3–24) (*); Jack Goody: "Against 'Ritual'. Loosely Structured Thoughts on a Loosely Defined Topic" (25–25) (*); Victor W. Turner: Variations on a Theme of Liminality" (36–52); Terence S. Turner: "Transformation, Hierarchy and Transcendence. A Reformulation of Van Gennep's Model of the Structure of Rites de Passage" (53–70) (*). [JK]

Reviews: D. Buchdahl *AA* 81.1 (1979) 180 f; C. Rivière *CIS* 67 (1979) 372; D. Hicks *Homme* 19.2 (1979) 82; G.A. Largo *JSSR* 18.1 (1979) 98–100; J.-P. Terrenoire *ASSR* 25.50–52 (1980) 320 f; A. de Ruitjer *BTTV* 136 (1980) 168; R.L. Herrick *AJS* 86.1–6 (1980/81) 396; H.J. Loth *ZRGG* 36 (1984) 81.
Key-words: def, SEC, str.

Morris, Rosalind Carmel, 2006, 'Gender', in: Jens Kreinath, Jan A.M. Snoek & Michael Stausberg (eds), *Theorizing Rituals. Vol. I: Issues, Topics, Approaches, Concepts*, (Numen Book Series 114–1), Leiden, Boston: Brill (ISBN-10: 90–04–15342–x, ISBN-13: 978–90–04–15342–4) 361–378.

This essay considers the history of theories about ritual in terms of gender. It begins with a review of the defining questions of early ritual theory, including the force of language and especially the spell, the relationship between personal transformation and social change, and the reversibility of publicity and secrecy. It then considers how these problematics have been organized in and through the analysis of particular categories of ritual, and examines the privileged place of rites of initiation in the development of a general theory about ritual. Initiation rites are generally considered to be the social mechanisms for producing and remarking gendered difference, and the paper suggests that it is therefore important to understand how and to what extent ritual theory has redoubled the demand for sexual difference as both the condition of theory and the telos of ritual. It then tracks the developments within ritual theory during the second half of the twentieth century, beginning with those theories which, influenced by linguistic pragmatics, emphasize ritual's performative dimension and its role in the constitution of sexual difference. It subsequently considers two other analytic trajectories which have departed from earlier analysis. One is concerned with the critical or resistant potentiality of ritual as a special mode of practice. The other addresses the rise of a discourse of ritual and considers its deployment within various colonial and historiographical projects, where the category of ritual works to thematize and typify disparate practices while giving to them the new value of pastness. [Rosalind Morris]

Key-word: GDR.

Munn, Nancy D., 1973, 'Symbolism in a Ritual Context. Aspects of Symbolic Action', in: John Joseph Honigmann (ed.), *Handbook of Social and Cultural Anthropology*, (Rand McNally Anthropology Series), Chicago: Rand McNally (ISBN 0-528-69996-2) 579-612.

This article is a general survey of the development of how symbols came to be conceptualized in the study of rituals and how new approaches came to be concerned with the internal structures and meanings of symbolic processes. Nevertheless, the author wants to indicate a significant shift that is relevant for ritual theory: "Looked at from the symbolic 'inside out' (rather than the functionalist 'outside in'), ritual can be seen as a symbolic intercom between the level of cultural thought and complex cultural meanings, on the one hand, and that of social action and immediate event, on the other" (579). Following this approach, she defines ritual "as a generalized medium of social interaction in which the vehicles for constructing messages are iconic symbols (acts, words, or things) that convert the load of significance or complex socio-cultural meanings embedded in and generated by the ongoing processes of social existence into a communication currency" (580). According to the author, ritual is a generalized medium of social interaction, which also links the individual to the community through the symbolic mobilisation of cultural codes. She argues: "The ritual message system consists of all the forms and rules governing these forms that pertain to the ritual process as a mode of expressive communication" (580). [JK]

References: G. Bateson, N.D. Fustel de Coulanges, É. Durkheim, C. Geertz, T. Parsons (+), A.R. Radcliffe-Brown, S.J. Tambiah, T.S. Turner (+), V.W. Turner, A. van Gennep.
Examples: marriage, rituals of passage, sacrifice.
Key-words: com, def, med, mng, pr1, sem, soc, str, SYM.

Myerhoff, Barbara G., 1990, 'The Transformation of Consciousness in Ritual Performances. Some Thoughts and Questions', in: Richard Schechner & Willa Appel (eds), *By Means of Performance. Intercultural Studies of Theatre and Ritual*, Cambridge etc.: Cambridge University Press (ISBN 0-521-32608-7 / 0-521-33915-4 (p)) (*) 245-249.

This article is on altered states of consciousness that are caused by ritual performances. The author argues that the term 'consciousness' focuses on the individual and subjective state rather than on a collective or sociological relationship. Therefore, anthropology is traditionally not regarded as the appropriate discipline for investigating the transformation of consciousness or for examining subjective experiences, such as trance, ecstasy, and possession. Although Max Gluckman considered altered states of consciousness to be esoteric knowledge outside the domain of classical social anthropology, the author prefers an 'emic' approach to ritual performance, referring to psychological studies that show that altered states of consciousness are non-linear, non-discursive, and non-linguistic. In following Susanne Langer and Clifford Geertz, she defines transformation as "a multidimensional alteration of the ordinary state of mind, overcoming barriers between thought, action, knowledge, and emotion" (246). In reference to the various approaches to ritual performance, the author argues: "Hence transformation is seldom made the explicit goal of a ritual, on whose appearance success is thought to depend.... Perhaps it is the unusual, ad hoc, volitional ritual performances—pilgrimages, conversions, healings and the like—which we should look at in considering where transformation of consciousness is an essential ingredient" (246). After discussing, R. Schechner, M. Csikszentmihalyi, R. Rappaport, and V.W. Turner, the author writes: "It should be noted here that our emphasis on 'transformation' in ritual performances inclines us towards emotionally intense and absorbing rituals, thus precludes us from attending to one of the major functions of ritual performances: that of establishing a distance from a situation or emotion" (248). She comes to the conclusion that: "It is the ludic element that is at the basis of all these questions, the play frame that embraces all performances, whether imitative, representational, transformational...The ludic is neither true nor false, nor does it suggest a specific emotional state—pleasure or pain. It simply points us to the power, the inevitability of our imaginative activities in which we have the opportunity to inscribe our fates, our desires, our stories in the air, and partly believe (to some degree) in their reality; ritual performances are testaments to our capacity to endlessly bring new possibilities into being without entirely relinquishing the old, prior understandings that have given rise to them..." (249). [JK]

References: M. Eliade, C. Geertz (+), E. Goffman (–), B. Kapferer, S.K. Langer (+), R.A. Rappaport, R. Schechner, V.W. Turner.
Examples: Rituals of passage, trance, pilgrimage.
Key-words: cog, eff, emo, frm, pmc, pow, pr1, psy, rep.

Nagendra, S.P., 1971, *The Concept of Ritual in Modern Sociological Theory*; New Delhi: Academic Journals of India (no ISBN) (xiv + 199) (with index and bibliography).

This book is an example of a Hindu religionistic approach to ritual. It is not surprising, then, to read that, according to the author, the "nearest example of the pure form of ritual is the Hindu Concept of *Nishkam* as enunciated in the Gita" (13). The first chapter is about the definition of ritual. The author gives a number of definitions, such as: "a symbolic action which is transcendentally necessary" (9) or "an enactment of the myth (anagogic symbolism)" (12) or "a specific mode of realizing the absolute, the super-cosmic in its transcendence and immanence. But since in religious traditions the absolute is always represented in a personal or psychic form (as God, Spirit, Orenda or Mana) its predominant character is that of a prescribed ceremonial. This also explains why it invariably appears as an enactment of the myth. And as the realization of the absolute would mean a transformation of nominal consubstantiality (psycho-physical) into real consubstantiality (metaphysical), the purpose of ritual is generally understood to be transubstantiation" (20–21). Logically, then, "the principle purpose of this essay is to show that modern sociological theory is unable to interpret the term 'ritual' appropriately because its positivistic bias prevents it from taking recourse to a sound theory of symbolism" (4). In the next chapters, the author presents the theories of Durkheim, Weber, Malinowski, Radcliffe-Brown, Freud and Jung. The second part of the book contains chapters on "The theory of symbolism: The semantics of ritual" (135–152), "The theory of action: Ritual as symbolic action" (153–169), and "Myth: Ritual as the enactment of myth" (170–181). "The theory of symbolism, here put forward, is largely a synthesis of the viewpoints of such scholars and thinkers as Ananda K. Coomaraswamy, Susanne K. Langer, Philip Wheelright, Carl G. Jung, and the traditional Indian semanticists, such as Anandavardhan and Mammat. The theory of action likewise is a critical reformulation of the basic assumptions of the Weberian concept of social action and the Durkheimian concept of social facts. The theory of myth, again, is an attempt at a systematic exposition of the key ideas implicit in such classical works on mythology as [those by] Joseph Campbell...Mircea Eliade...and C.G. Jung and [Karl] Kerenyi.... The work is thus mainly an attempt at interpretation and synthesis" (vii–viii). In the "Epilogue" (181–183), the author concludes: "We have tried to integrate our theory of symbolism with a general theory of action.... We have treated meaning and action as hierarchically related.... Accordingly, we have insisted on defining action in terms of meaning.... We have finally established the identity of the religious action and ritual and shown the latter to be the penultimate act, of which all other actions are reproductions. And we finally close by establishing the link between ritual and myth showing the former to be a reflection of the latter" (182–183). [JS]

Review: L. Mair *Race* 14.1 (1972) 102.
Key-words: pr1, sem, mng, sym, myt, sec, def, soc.

Needham, Rodney, 1967, 'Percussion and Transition', ***Man*** **2:606–614.**

This article starts with the concern "why is noise that is produced by striking or shaking so widely used in order to communicate with the other world?" (606). The first part of the paper addresses the first part of the question, i.e. issues of 'noise that is produced by striking or shaking'; here, the author argues that the instruments that are used in rituals are mainly percussive: "All over the world it is found that percussion, by any means whatever that will produce it, permits or accompanies communication with the other world" (607). He argues that melody, by contrast, "is far too specific and is obviously inappropriate as a criterion" (607). By way of discussing M. Dworakowska (1938) and A. Crowley (1912), he states that "[t]he reverberations produced by musical instruments thus have not only aesthetic but also bodily effects.... The sounds mark off points on a scale of intensity the effects of which range from an agonising disruption of the organism down to subliminal thrills or other bodily responses which contribute to the conscious affective appreciation of the sounds" (610–611). In addressing issues on the use of percussion in shamanic rituals, the author observes that "percussive sounds are the easiest to make, and the most obviously possible: they do not depend upon special materials, techniques, or ideas, but can readily be made with the human body alone or by its abrupt contact with any hard or resonant part of the environment" (611). The second part of the paper addresses the second part of the question, i.e. issues of 'communication with the other world' and concerns the generalizing question: "What other situations and institutionalised forms of behaviour are marked by percussion?" (611). Here the author writes that "the instruments are identified with the events, and are themselves the material symbols of them; their players may be not just normal participants but indispensable officiants at the rites and ceremonies which are distinguished by the sounds" (611). Common to these events is that they are all rites of passage, because "the class of noise-makers is associated with the formal passage from one status or condition to another" (611). The author proposes that there is "a significant connexion between percussion and transition" (611) and argues that this "is the definitive relation, and the nature of the connexion is the real problem. There is certainly no intrinsic relationship between the phenomena, yet the association is too firm for the answer to be sought in the contingent particulars of cultural tradition" (611). He further uses the concept of rituals of passage by A. van Gennep for his notion of 'transition'. According to the author, this notion offers a formally satisfactory definition of the problem. Hence he writes: "[w]hat I am dealing with is the conjunction of two primal, elementary, and fundamental features: 1) the affective impact of percussion, 2) the logical structure of category-change. According to common notions, the components pertain to two quite disparate modes of apprehension: emotion and reason" (612). "Whether or not it is agreed that there is a real problem here", the author at least claims that "there is a methodological precept which it may prove useful for the ethnographer and the theoretical social anthropologist to keep in mind, namely to pay special attention to percussion" (613). [JK]

References: R.A. Crowley, É. Durkheim, M. Dworakowska, M. Eliade, V.W. Turner, A. van Gennep.
Examples: Initiations, Shamanic rituals.
Key-words: AES, cog, com, eff, emb, EMO, frm, mus, pmc, psy, STR.

Needham, Rodney, 1985, 'Remarks on Wittgenstein and Ritual', in: Rodney Needham, *Exemplars*, Berkeley: University of California Press (ISBN 0–520–05200–5) 149–177.

In the first section of this paper (149–152), the author notes that Wittgenstein's ideas have been generally neglected by anthropologists, but that they are worth noting. The starting point is Wittgenstein's criticism "that terms such as 'descent', 'incest', 'belief', or 'anger' are vitiated because they are taken to denote monothetic classes of social facts, whereas actually they are highly polythetic and cannot therefore have the uses that are normally ascribed to them. A consequence of accepting this kind of critique is that the comparison of social facts must at first become far more difficult, if it is at all feasible in such terms; but the immense potential benefit that can follow is the attainment of a more 'perspicuous representation' of what is really at issue when we try to understand human nature and social action" (150). What Wittgenstein has to say on the concept 'ritual' is to be found in his "Remarks on Frazer's *The Golden Bough*". That is the text that the author now analyzes in order "to make what we can of his ideas in order to effect some advance in our own thoughts" (152). In the second section (153–156), he first tries to find a characteristic that would satisfy "Wittgenstein's premise…that it is possible to distinguish, by observation, ritual actions from 'animal activities' such as taking food" (153), but "in the end there seems no secure defense of the presumption that there is a particular (*eigentümlich*) aspect of social action that provides an observable index to the ritual" (154). However, Wittgenstein suggests a different approach, that of the 'family resemblances'. "In accordance with this procedure, we can say then that 'ritual' is an odd-job word; that is, it serves a variety of more or less disparate uses, yet we are tempted to describe its use as though it were a word with regular functions…It cannot be relied upon for any precise task of identification, interpretation, or comparison—as it could be if it were the monothetic concept that it is usually taken for—but this does not mean that it can have no serious use. What follows, rather, is that it has a range of uses, not a strict application corresponding to some peculiar character in the phenomena that it denotes. As a polythetic concept, 'ritual' variously combines certain characteristic features, and the task of the comparativist is to identify these features and to register the patterns into which they combine" (156). This task is more manageable when one subsumes ritual under the more general heading of symbolic action. The third section (157–160) is about the reasons behind ritual. The author reminds us that, according to Wittgenstein, "'what makes the character of ritual action is not any view or opinion [held by the participants], either right or wrong'"; as a result "the explanation of ritual cannot consist in discovering the reasons for which the participants, at any point in its development or in the course of its practice, carry it out" (157). In the fourth section (160–162), the author comments on Wittgenstein's opposition to explanation. Wittgenstein seems to be of the opinion that we only have to describe the facts as we know them, "without adding anything" (Wittgenstein) (160). Here the author does not agree: "Ethnographic reports...can hardly ever be accepted as they stand, but they call instead for a deliberate interpretation" (161). The fifth section (162–164) starts with Wittgenstein's opposition to Frazer's assumption that rituals of primitives are alien to us: "'we could very well imagine primitive practices for ourselves, and it would be an accident if they were not actually found somewhere'" (162). Wittgenstein illustrated this idea with a number of examples, which actually show that a particular motivation may be expressed in different ritual (or other) forms that we perceive as all equally comprehensive. As a corollary, this leads to the conclusion that, inversely, "we cannot infer from the form of a symbolic action what its meaning may be...and hence cannot conclude that rituals with a common form will have any common meaning or purpose" (164). The sixth section (165–170) is about origins and historical development. Wittgenstein stresses that the historical development of ritual forms is just one way of relating these forms and that "we should not assume the significance of a rite to reside in its origin alone, or that the original significance has survived only as an ineffectual relic of custom, or that the present performance of the rite provides an insufficient justification of its existence" (166). Contrary to this aspect, Wittgenstein seems to regard it as important that a ritual should have 'depth'. Analyzing these two aspects of Wittgenstein's argumentation, the author comes to the conclusion that "on the one hand... Wittgenstein has good reason to abjure an explanation by historical reconstruction; but on the other hand he has not supplied the grounds to accept that the character of a rite is to be elicited from our own experience. In particular, the character of 'depth' has not been shown to belong in a vocabulary for the comparative analysis of ritual" (169–170). The seventh section (170–174) discusses Wittgenstein's requirement that an explanation of a ritual should really explain it, not replace it by an alternative statement or label that is equally incomprehensible, as is usually done. But, as the author concludes, "the topic is still recalcitrant to a theoretical explanation" (174). In the final section (174–177), the author takes up two statements by Wittgenstein. The first is that ritual has to do "with the 'ceremonial' in contrast with the haphazard" (174). This leads the author to advocate the investigation of the property of formality wherever it is found, rather than rituals as such. The second is Wittgenstein's unwillingness to accept that rituals would always have been as meaningless as many of them seem in their current forms. The author concludes: "What calls for examination is the very assumption that the rite must have had a clear meaning once.... in the normal run of things we have no means whatever of determining any earlier meanings, let alone a single original significance for any particular rite" (176). "The question then is: Why can a rite *not* be meaningless?" (176). The author accepts that different participants may attribute different meanings to the ritual "but this contention would not settle the point at issue. What we have been looking for is a meaning that will explain the rite, and in this respect it can well be that there is no such meaning to be established.... Ritual can be self-sufficient, self-sustaining, and self-justifying. Considered in its most characteristic features, it is a kind of activity—like speech or dancing—that man as a 'ceremonial animal' happens naturally to perform" (177). [JS/MS]

Reference: **L. Wittgenstein (+)**.
Examples: Beltane, Eucharist.
Key-words: DEF, MNG, sym, exp, emo, cpr.

Ohnuki-Tierney, Emiko, 1987, *The Monkey as Mirror. Symbolic Transformations in Japanese History and Ritual*; Princeton, Oxford: Princeton University Press (ISBN 0–691–09434–9 / 0–691–09434–9 (p)) (xiv + 269) (with index and bibliography).

In the "Theoretical Setting" (3–19) that makes up part of the "Introduction", the author states: "Using Japanese culture as my example,

I examine multiple structures of meaning—that is, culture—and how they are transformed through history, on the one hand, and expressed in myth and ritual, on the other.... In examining the structures of meaning as expressed in ritual, I am particularly concerned with the construction of multiple structures of meaning as engendered by different readings of ritual performance by different social groups" (5). "To examine these relationships, I have chosen a study that consists of three interrelated parts: the monkey metaphor, the special status people, and the monkey performance. The special status people... are a heterogeneous group of people who are often referred to as outcasts in Japan. The monkey performance has been one of the traditional occupations of this social group. Both the monkey and the special status people have long been intrinsically involved in Japanese deliberations of the self and other; they have been reflexive symbols" (5–6). In the course of her investigations, the author explores "how polysemic symbols are read by ritual participants" (6). She argues "that during certain performances, the trainers from the special status group and the spectators from the dominant Japanese group read the symbols in the performance differently, so that a structure of meaning and its inversion are simultaneously present" (6). The bulk of the book investigates the (symbolic) transformations of the monkey, the special status people, and the monkey performance in the course of Japanese history. In her discussion of the monkey performance, she explores some analytical concepts: 'basic structure' (i.e., the prototype monkey performance), 'processual structure', referring to the fact that "in some types of ritual performance, the structure of meaning is transformed during the course of performance" (164), 'ritual context', "by which I mean the ritual space of the performance, encompassing social relationships in transaction and the social activities of all the participants" (164), and 'framing', "which refers to the definition of categorization of a given performance, for example as 'play', 'ritual', and the like" (164). In chapter 9, "Structures of Meaning in History, Myth, and Ritual" (209–240), the author explores some theoretical implications of her findings. "Unlike the Balinese cockfight... which does not involve heterogeneous people, the monkey performance cannot be summarized as a story the special status people tell by themselves about themselves. If a story is told, it is not always heard by the spectators the way it is told" (209). "The monkey performance of various times and places in Japanese history... defies the concept of 'multiple exegesis' of the same text. The text is not 'objectively there' to be read" (211). In the final section, the book discusses such issues as "Polysemes of Anomalous Symbols" (217–218), "Metonym and Metaphor. Transformation and Counter-Transformation" (218–221), and explores some of the historical dimensions of her long-term study. The author concludes: "The significance of the monkey as a reflexive metaphor cannot be understood without examining the changing phases of its complex structure of meaning as each phase is historically actualized" (235). According to the author, a "long-term study of a culture has another advantage. It enables us to examine the relationship between history on the one hand and a specific body of myth and a particular ritual on the other. We can also avoid an *a priori* equation of myth and ritual with history, and of historicity, or the way people conceive of history, with history itself" (235–236). [JK/MS]

References: A. Appadurai, B.A. Babcock, R. Barthes (+), G. Bateson, P.L. Berger, C. Braudel (+), M. Douglas (–), **J.W. Fernandez** (+), C. Geertz (+), E. Goffman, D. Handelman (+), K. Hastrup, J. Huizinga (+), B. Kapferer, S.K. Langer, E.R. Leach, **C. Lévi-Strauss** (+), S.F. Moore, B.G. Myerhoff, R. Needham, **M. Sahlins**, S.J. Tambiah (–), T.S. Turner, **V.W. Turner**, A. van Gennep.

Reviews: D. Handelman *AE* 15.4 (1988) 804; H. Shizumu *AFS* 47.2 (1988) 333 f; C.W. Kiefer *JAS* 47.3 (1988) 645 f; J. Robertson *JJSt* 15.2 (1989) 461 f; G.M. Wilson *AHR* 95.1 (1990) 235 f; W. Kelly *Ethnoh* 37.1 (1990) 76 f; W. Minnick *JJRS* 17.1 (1990) 92–94; W. Edwards *JDS* VII.2 (1991) 299; **D. Handelman *Sem* 119.3/4 (1998) 403–425**.

Key-words: cpl, DYN, frm, mng, pow, PMC, pmt, rfl, sem, str, SYM.

Ortner, Sherry B., 1975, 'Gods' Bodies, Gods' Food. A Symbolic Analysis of a Sherpa Ritual', in: Roy Willis (ed.), *The Interpretation of Symbolism*, (ASA Studies 3), London: Malaby Press (ISBN 0–460–14004–3) 133–169.

This article is an application of C. Geertz's symbolic approach to the Sherpa ritual and a critical evaluation of this approach. The author seeks to show how a symbolic analysis according to Geertz can be done. Moreover, she elaborates some hypotheses on the symbolic process of ritual in general. According to her, "'[a] system of symbols' remains, however, the most comprehensible way of indicating what 'a culture' is and does" (133). Using the distinction between 'model of' and 'model for', she raises three methodological questions concerning the approach of a cultural-symbolic analysis: "(1) What are the problematic realities of the culture to which the symbolic construction under analysis is addressing itself?—What is it a 'model of'? (2) What orientation (or reorientation) is it engendering towards those realities?—What is it a 'model for'? And (3) How, in its peculiar construction, does it accomplish its task in a powerful and convincing way, so that its respondents in fact accept it as an accurate rendering of 'reality', and adopt its implied orientation of attitude and/or action?" (135). The author argues that only the third question actually demands a 'symbolic analysis' as an analysis of the structure of the symbolic complex by means of various semantic devices. Therefore, she analyzes "The Problematics of the Ritual" (138–150) and "The Solutions of the Ritual" (151–164) that the Sherpa try to obtain. In her "Conclusions" (164–167), she raises some further issues about the processes of symbolic action indicated by the Sherpa ritual. Within the ritual she emphasizes the interplay between the 'symbol of' and 'symbol for' and interprets this interplay as a constant 'inter-transportation' of form and content: "Virtually every element of the ritual can be seen to function as both part of its problematic (its 'content') and part of its modes of solution (its 'form')" (166). In arguing against reductionism, she concludes: "Every aspect of a complex symbolic form is both part of its structure and part of its substance, is both being addressed by the ritual and being used by the ritual in its process of addressing other problems. We cannot, if we understand the ritual fully, emerge with a clear-cut assertion of the primacy of the social or cultural or psychological dimension of its meaning. It is the ingenuity of ritual symbolism constantly to transpose these into one another, to solve problems in each mode by means of forms derived from other modes and thus to show, ultimately, both their irreducible interdependence and the means of moving between them. Effective symbolic analysis, like effective symbolic forms, must be genuinely dialectical, sustaining this sense of the interplay between relatively autonomous yet mutually interacting and interdependent levels of structure, meaning, and experience" (167). [JK]

References: R. Benedict, K. Burke, **C. Geertz** (+), C. Lévi-Strauss, M.E. Spiro, M. Weber.
Example: Sherpa ritual of food offerings.
Key-words: eff, mng, pmc, psy, sem, soc, str, SYM, vir.

Ortner, Sherry B., 1978, *Sherpas Through Their Rituals* (Cambridge Studies in Cultural Systems 2); Cambridge etc.: Cambridge University Press (ISBN 0-521-21536-6 / 0-521-29216-6 (p)) (xii + 195) (with index and bibliography).

This book is a symbolic analysis on the ritual and social structure of the Sherpa, Himalayan highlanders who practice a variety of Mahayana Buddhism. The author offers a general interpretation of the relationship between Sherpa Buddhism and other aspects of their social life, as well as a theoretical contribution to the study of ritual and religious symbolism. Using the notion of cultural performance, she focuses on the symbolic elements of ritual in order to explore the problematic structure, relationships, and the ideas of culture within the Sherpa community. The author develops her theoretical approach to ritual symbolism in the "Introduction" (1–9). Her main assumption, which also determines the structure of the whole book, runs as follows: "Rituals do not begin with the eternal verities, but arrive at them. They begin with some cultural problems (or several at once), stated or unstated, and then work various operations upon it, arriving at 'solutions'—reorganizations and reinterpretations of the elements that produce a newly meaningful whole. The solutions (and the means of arriving at them) embody the fundamental cultural assumptions and orientations with which we are partly concerned" (2–3). In view of these assumptions, the author argues that it is important to focus on "the problems from which the ritual departs" (3). By that she means "the conflicts and contradictions of social experience and cultural meaning that are encoded in, and alluded to by, the ritual symbolism" (3). These assumptions function as organizing principles: "After a general ethnographic chapter, each subsequent chapter begins with a brief description of a cultural performance. Following the description, the rite (or in one case secular event) is then dissected, and some of its symbolic elements are used as leads or guides into exploring problematic structures, relationships, and ideas of the culture" (3). The analysis of ritual symbols leads "toward discovery of structural conflict, contradiction, and stress in the wider social and cultural world" (3). Each chapter follows this structure of the symbolic analysis: "If the first half of each chapter is a ritual-guided ethnographic account, the second half returns to the action of the ritual and asks what sorts of solutions to the problems, what sorts of experience of them are systematically constructed over the course of the event. Here we are in the realm of symbolic analysis as such, analysis of the semantic mechanisms by which the symbols and meanings are interrelated and moved toward the conclusions and resolution of the rite" (3–4). By use of multiple ritual 'lenses' as 'perspective shifter', the author wants to show that ritual "generates or regenerates a given view of the world, and engenders commitment to existing institutional structures and modes of social relationship. Ritual restores equilibrium, however unstable or antagonistic it may be" (4). Here she emphasizes the actor's point of view. According to her, the 'ritual process' is "in the first instance a matter of meaning creation for actors, whatever latent functions it may perform for the system at large" (5). Thus the author is primarily concerned with "the shaping of consciousness that takes place in ritual" (5), as well as with "the transformations of meaning/consciousness that the ritual embodies" (6). Moreover, she points out that "[t]he reshaping of consciousness or experience that takes place in ritual is by definition a reorganization of the *relationship* between the subject and what may for convenience be called reality" (9). Using Geertz's notion of the 'model of' and 'model for', she analyzes the problems and solutions, which the rituals might offer for the Sherpa community. After giving an ethnographic account of "The Surface Contours of the Sherpa World" (10–32) regarding the economy, social organization, and religion, the author uses rituals as lenses in order to emphasize the relation between religious ideology and social structure and experience: "Nyungne. Problems of Marriage, Family, and Asceticism" (33–60), "Hospitality. Problems of Exchange, Status, and Authority" (61–90), "Exorcism. Problems of Wealth, Pollution, and Reincarnation" (91–127), and "Offering Rituals. Problems of Religion, Anger, and Social Cooperation" (128–156). The final chapter ends with a brief discussion of the relationship between "Buddhism and Society" (157–169) including a consideration of the ritual mechanism (163–169). [JK]

References: K. Burke, **C. Geertz** (+), C. Lévi-Strauss, **G. Lienhardt** (+), M. Mauss, N.D. Munn, B.G. Myerhoff, M. Singer, S.J. Tambiah, T.S. Turner, **V.W. Turner** (+), A. van Gennep.
Reviews: S. Glazier *JAAR* 47.4 (1979) 703; A.E. Manzardo *JAS* 38.4 (1979) 828 f; W.H. Newell *SAs* 2.1/2 (1979) 178 f; F.K. Lehman *AE* 7.2 (1980) 384 f; C. von Fürer-Haimendorf *BSOAS* 43.1 (1980) 158 f; J.T. Hitchcock *CSSH* 22.1 (1980) 133; M.C. Goldstein *JAOS* 100.2 (1980) 216 f; G. Samuel *Man* 15.2 (1980) 400 f; **F.A. Hanson *Sem* 33.1/2 (1981) 169–178**; J. Fisher *AA* 84.3 (1982) 692 f.
Key-words: dyn, eff, emb, emo, mng, PMC, psy, sem, soc, SYM, vir.

Paige, Karen Ericksen & Jeffrey M. Paige (with the assistance of Linda Fuller and Elisabeth Magnus), 1981, *The Politics of Reproductive Ritual*; Berkeley, Los Angeles, London: University of California Press (ISBN 0–520–03071–0) (xii + 380).

In seven chapters and an introduction, based upon extensive cross-cultural research, this book presents a theory of reproductive ritual in pre-industrial societies. The authors argue that rituals are instituted by males to gain political and economic control of society through control of women's reproductive power. Chapter 1, the introduction (1–42), describes major research approaches to reproductive rituals, i.e.

psychoanalytical, transition-rite, and structural-functional, as they are associated with circumcision, menstruation rites, sex segregation, and maternal restrictions. Chapter 2, "Reproductive Ritual: A Continuation of Politics by Another Means" (43–78), outlines the argument for a political interpretation of reproductive ritual grounded in bargain-exchange theory, and the relation between available resources and the formation of fraternal interest groups. Chapter 3, "The Dilemma of Menarche: Female Puberty Rites" (79–121), describes the societal importance of menarche, attempts to manipulate it, the protection of the daughter's marriage value, premenstrual betrothals, ritual defloration, and menarchal ceremonies. Chapter 4, "Male Circumcision: The Dilemma of Fission" (122–166), suggests that male circumcision is performed as a political strategy, and describes types of fission and the family conflicts generated. Chapter 5, "The Dilemma of Legitimacy: Birth Practices" (167–208), analyzes problems of social paternity in both strong and weak fraternal interest group societies, and the relation between birth practices and community structure. Chapter 6, "Menstrual Restrictions and Sex Segregation Practices" (209–254), reviews psychoanalytic interpretations of menstrual taboos, and the political significance of menstruation as an indicator of fertility and thus of potential wealth; the ambiguities of the husband in society are illustrated by, e.g., the display of ritual disinterest in a wife's fertility. Chapter 7, "Summary and Implications for Complex Societies" (255–277), reviews the strategies for manipulating reproductive power in strong and weak societies, and discusses circumcision and birth rituals in advanced societies, the renewed interest in home births, attitudes towards menstruation; a study showing that over 50% of a sample of married women (N = 102) never had had sexual intercourse during menstruation is cited. Religious differences in attitudes towards menstruation, pregnancy, and birth practices are discussed. 3 Appendices: I) "Measures" (278–289); II) "Description of a Sample" (290–316); III) "Ethnographic Source Bibliography" (317–371). 22 Tables, 3 Figures. [JS]

Reviews: J.F. Collier *Sc* 215.4537 (1982) 1230–1232; E. Lewin *MedAnthN* 13.2 (1982) 26; M.N. Powers *SRol* 8.9 (1982) 1042–1045; J.F. Pugh *CRSA* 19.4 (1982) 612 f; K.F. Schaffer *SSQ* 63.3 (1982) 595; M. Wilson & M. Daly *HE* 10.1 (1982) 153–156; P.R. Sanday *Eth* 93 (1982/83) 436–437; E.D. Driver *CS* 12.1 (1983) 71 f; C.B. Flora *JMF* 45.4 (1983) 986 f; N. Keyfitz *SF* 61.3 (1983) 950 f; S.E. Estroff *JHPPL* 9.1 (1984) 187–189; G.C. Homans *AJS* 89.4 (1984) 941–944; **R. Collins *AJS* 89.4 (1984) 945–951**; S.K. Houseknecht *SSR* 68.3 (1984) 391–393; M.J. Casimir *Anthr* 80.4–6 (1985) 735–738.
Key-words: GDR, pow, psy, idn.

Paul, Ingwer, 1990, *Rituelle Kommunikation. Sprachliche Verfahren zur Konstitution ritueller Bedeutung und zur Organisation des Rituals* (Kommunikation und Institution 18); Tübingen: Gunter Narr (ISBN 3-87808-718-7) (308) (with bibliography).

[Ritual Communication. Linguistic Procedures for the Constitution of Ritual Meaning and for the Origanization of Ritual]

This book is mainly a discursive analysis of ritual communication that takes place within Christian worship, secular rituals, and marriage ceremonies. For his analysis, the author uses an interpretative ethnomethodology in order to consider the procedure of how ritual meaning is organized by the particular participants of a ritual communication. He assumes that 'rituality' is an anthropological universal, although the actual ritual practice is rebounded by the collective identity of the specific groups involved. In theorizing the results of his analysis of the various examples, the author tries to combine the perspective of the participants with his meta-language of description. [JK/JS]

References: G. Bateson (+), E.Th. Lawson (+), E.R. Leach (+), R.A. Rappaport (+), V.W. Turner (+), A. van Gennep, I. Werlen.
Review: G. Otto *Rhet* 12 (1993) 163 f.
Key-words: str, COM, pmt, sym, mng, rfl.

Peacock, James L., 1990, 'Ethnographic Notes on Sacred and Profane Performance', in: Richard Schechner & Willa Appel (eds), *By Means of Performance. Intercultural Studies of Theatre and Ritual*, Cambridge etc.: Cambridge University Press (ISBN 0-521-32608-7 / 0-521-33915-4 (p)) (*) 208-220.

By way of answering the question how a performance relates to life, the author writes: "A performance is not necessarily more meaningful than other events in one's life, but it is more deliberately so; a performance is, among other things, a deliberate effort to represent, to say something about something" (208). But if a performance is understood as "an action which attempts to communicate meaning, then it is never purely 'form'" (208); a rigid distinction between form and content is seen as problematic. The author argues that the term 'sacred performance' is an oxymoron. "The sacred cannot... be 'performed'. Any reduction of meaning to form deprives that form of meaning; to perform the 'sacred' necessarily is to profane it. Yet the sacred becomes real only as embodied in form" (208). While focusing on the difference in the relationship between form and experience that is associated with sacred and profane performances, his purpose is to raise questions about the patterning of human experience. After discussing the case of the Primitive Baptists in the Blue Ridge Mountains of North Carolina and Virginia and comparing it to the Javanese *ludruk* theatre, the author concludes: "To symbolize is human, and to symbolize entails separating (and therefore struggling to reunite) form, meaning, and context. While all humans endeavor to arrange some kind of integration among these elements, the endeavor is perhaps most challenging for those who as history evolves toward differentiation and complexity, are distinguished as 'performers', and, therefore, must relate their 'performances' to the rest of their experience; for them, the universal task of integrating form, meaning, and context becomes the personal task of rendering form meaningful while performing then subsuming this intensely concentrated unity of form and meaning within a wider unity which is life. The question posed in this paper is whether sacralization of performance makes a difference in this endeavor. Comparison of two varieties of performance experience drawn from fieldwork suggests that sacralization does make a difference" (220). [JK]

Examples: Primitive Baptists' Communion, the Indonesian *ludruk* theatre.
Key-words: com, emo, mng, pmc, sec, str.

Penner, Hans H., 1969, 'Myth and Ritual. A Wasteland or Forest of Symbols', *History and Theory* 8:46–57.

In this article the author presents a historical outline of the different methods of understanding myth and ritual in anthropology and in the history of religions. He concludes: "On the one hand, an anthropological-functional method which attempts to explain myth and ritual by reference to social or psychological realities either does not explain religion or explains society or psychology by reference to myth and ritual. On the other hand, historians of religions attempting to work out a non-reductionistic method have described myths as referring to the sacred, which in itself is not an object of inquiry. We have been describing myths as symbols of symbols, and find ourselves lost in a forest of symbols without reference. In both approaches it is clear that the problem of the cognitive content of myths has been suspended or rejected. Furthermore, it can be shown that if the historian of religions attempts to use his method in order to explain myth and ritual as a function of the sacred, he faces the same functional fallacy in anthropology. Finally, it is the referent, or object, of myth and ritual as symbolic expressions that remains the central problem in both disciplines" (57). [JK]

References: M. Eliade, J. Fontenrose, J.G. Frazer, Th. Gaster, J.E. Harrison, C. Kluckhohn, E. Leach (–), C. Lévi-Strauss (+), V.W. Turner, J. Wach.
Key-words: cog, exp, MYT, psy, soc, str, sym.

Penner, Hans H., 1985, 'Language, Ritual, and Meaning', *Numen* 32:1–16.

In this essay the author questions Staal's hypothesis of the meaninglessness of rituals (1979 (*)). According to Staal, rituals are meaningless "because rituals do not refer to anything, they have no reference" (2). Using Frege's distinction between meaning and reference, the author argues that a theory of meaning must include reference but cannot be based upon reference: "What Staal overlooks in his general overview and criticism of contemporary theories of ritual is that all of them assume that rituals must refer to something in order to have meaning" (3). According to the author, the analysis of 'meaning' is a semantic or semiological issue. Using the linguistic approaches of Saussure and Beneviste, he concludes: "If ritual is viewed as the foundation of syntax, the origin of syntax, and if ritual is thought of as meaningless (for itself), then how do we explain the appearance of the sign? Conversely, if ritual is defined as a sign system in the context of semiotics, then meaning is inherent in the system. In such a system 'there is neither signified without signifier nor signifier without signified'. If ritual is meaningless, then it is not a semiotic system. If rituals are not semiotic systems, then they do not contain or involve syntactic or semantic components. Staal...does not argue that rituals are not semiological systems. On the contrary, he argues that rituals do have a syntax, but they are meaningless. Given the...evidence from linguists, Staal's position is simply wrong" (10–11). [JK]

References: G. Frege (+), C. Lévi-Strauss (+), F. de Saussure (+), **F. Staal** (–).
Key-words: lan, MNG, ref, sem, str.

Penner, Hans H., 1989, 'Rationality, Ritual, and Science', in: Jacob Neusner, Ernest S. Frerichs & Paul Virgil McCracken Fletsher (eds), *Religion, Science, and Magic. In Concert and in Conflict*, Oxford, New York: Oxford University Press (ISBN 0–19–505603–5 / 0–19–507911–6 (p)) 11–24.

After an introduction on the classical debate over the distinction between "magic, science, and religion" (11–13), the author poses his thesis: "ever since Frazer, explanations and arguments about religion, ritual, and science have assumed a specific idea about rationality" (13). The first section then presents "The Symbolic Approach to Ritual" (14–17), the approach taken by such scholars as Leach, Beattie, C. Geertz, Goody, Douglas, and V.W. Turner. It is based on the distinction between "rational behavior" (science) and "ritual behavior". "In brief, ritual actions are not to be taken as behavior that is rational—that is, a means-end action. Rituals express desires and needs as ends in themselves" (15). Such explanations are normally formulated in functionalist terms. "As far as I know, the critique, based upon Hempel's analysis of functional explanations, has not been demolished. I shall therefore conclude... that such explanations of ritual are either invalid, tautological, or trivial" (17). The second section presents "The Rationalist Approach to Ritual" (17–19). Here we find such scholars as Horton, Carnap, Hempel, Nagel, and Braithwaite. The problem with this model is "the notion of 'correspondence rules', which relate invariant observational statements to unobservable entities in theoretical statements. These rules, however, were never worked out in a satisfactory way.... What is ironic about all this is that from the very beginning the hypothetico-deductive model with its notion of correspondence rules was used to mark off scientific knowledge from traditional religious thought" (19). Since these two approaches are the major ones used to explain ritual, "it is clear that we do not have a coherent theory or set of hypotheses for explaining ritual" (19). The third section therefore investigates "The Concept of Rationality in Studies of Ritual" (20–22), since that seems to be the source of the problems. The author quotes Godelier's definition of rationality, which is characteristic of most scholars' understanding of the concept: "A person is considered rational when (a) he pursues ends that are mutually coherent, and (b) he employs means that are appropriate to the ends pursued" (20). He then discusses Hempel's comments on the subject. Hempel first points out that the rationality of a decision is independent of both the (in)correctness and the (in)completeness of the information on which it is based, and then asks: "But while the information basis of a rational action thus need not be true, should there not at least be good reasons for believing it true?" Some writers "do in fact require this as a necessary condition for rational action", but Hempel will not impose this requirement (21). The author now argues that the traditional position—taken by the symbolist, as well as some rationalist authors discussed—requires "good reasons" or "adequate evidential support" for believing in the adequacy of the means for reaching the pursued ends, and that these authors deny that there could be such reasons or such support for believing in the adequacy of rituals, though the participants do. This seems unfair. Some other rationalist authors, however, accept that "ritual actions qualify as rational even though such actions are based upon incomplete or false empirical assumptions" (22). But, as Hempel puts it, "[i]f this is generally the case, then the assumption of rationality could not possibly be violated; any apparent violation would be taken to show only that our conjectures about the agent's beliefs, or those about his objectives, or both would be mistaken" (22). This is also undesirable. In the final section, "Conclusion" (22–24), the author now asks: "Who decides what ends are coherent, and who judges whether the means are appropriate?" (23). In the argumentation so far, it was the scholars. However, "[u]pon reflection the answer is clear; it is the believer/actor who decides" (23). But that allows the author to give two examples in which the decision about rational or irrational results in utterly counter-intuitive answers. That dilemma is resolved by adopting Moor's definition of rationality: "1. S's belief is an irrational belief if and only if S has the belief and realizes . . . that there are little or no grounds for the truth of the belief but overwhelming grounds for the falsity of the belief. 2. S's belief is a rational belief if and only if S's belief is not irrational. 3. S's action is an irrational action if and only if S's action is based at least in part on S's irrational beliefs. 4. S's action is a rational action if and only if S's action is not irrational" (23). This definition "does allow us to assert . . . that traditional religious thought and action are as rational as modern scientific thought and action" (23). "It may well be that the beliefs are mistaken, but we must then insist . . . that such mistaken beliefs do not entail irrationality, or sheer non-rational expressiveness. Moreover, once we begin our analysis from this view we shall note that beliefs and actions are to be explained from within a massive network of rational beliefs and actions. Ritual beliefs and actions will have to be explained holistically as elements within a rational system" (24). [JS]

References: E.R. Leach, J.H.M. Beattie, C. Geertz, J. Goody, M. Douglas, V.W. Turner, R. Horton, R. Carnap, E. Nagel, R.B. Braithwaite, C.G. Hempel, J.H. Moor.
Key-words: sym, EXP, pr1.

Pentikäinen, Juha, 1979, 'The Symbolism of Liminality', in: Haralds Biezais (ed.), *Religious Symbols and their Functions. Based on Papers read at the Symposion on Religious Symbols and their Functions held at Åbo on the 28th–30th of August 1978*, (Scripta Instituti Donneriani Aboensis 10), Stockholm: Almquist & Wiksell International (ISBN 91-22-00199-9) 154–166.

This article consists of seven sections, which make independent statements, related to liminality. The first section is about Arnold van Gennep. The author reviews some of the current criticisms of Van Gennep's work *Les rites de passage* (1909) and in turn criticizes the critics by stating that Van Gennep "has in general been regarded as a prefunctionalist" (155), but the author "would prefer to consider him as a *prestructuralist*" (155), which is then underpinned with some arguments. The second section summarizes what Victor W. Turner wrote about liminality. The third section describes the structure of a Karelian wedding ceremony, dividing the process for both the girl and the boy into 6 stages, which the author distributes as three times two over the three phases separation, transition, and incorporation. He therefore isolates "smaller units of analysis" (157) which he terms 'ritual movements'. In the fourth section, the author claims that "[r]itual behaviour is always the communication of the symbols which transmit religious or other messages to the participants aware of their meanings" (158) and then quotes Firth, V.W. Turner and Geertz concerning symbolism. The fifth section presents the concepts emic and etic. The author underlines that in "the *emic* study of the ritual we put a great emphasis on ideas, interpretations, attitudes, feelings, and meanings" (160) and with that he pleads not only for studying the ritual behavior but also the "cognitive and conative knowledge" (160) underlying it. These cognitive elements he tries to grasp with his concepts of 'world view' and 'ritual repertoire'. The sixth section discusses the phenomenon that those who die a bad death, or children who die before they have been ritually incorporated in the community, are in many cultures supposed not to enter the realm of the dead, and thus to remain in a kind of permanent liminality. The seventh and final section extends the concept of liminality to those who live on the margin of society: "many authors, painters, and musicians seem to live a kind of continuous marginality. They also seem to enjoy their way of life and put a great emphasis on their marginal exceptional experiences which seem to be a necessary catalysator for their creativity" (163). He illustrates this with the example of Marina Takalo. [JS/Florian Jeserich]

References: R.D. Abrahams, R. Firth, C. Geertz, M. Gluckman, L. Honko, A. van Gennep, **V.W. Turner**.
Examples: A Karelian wedding ceremony, Marina Takalo.
Key-words: str, mng, sym, cog.

Pertierra, Raul, 1987, 'Ritual and the Constitution of Social Structure', *Mankind* 17:199–211.

By way of introduction, the author states: "How social structures are constituted and reproduced by the action orientations of social actors, remains one of the basic questions in the social sciences" (199). He contends that "ritual action is central to the constitution of social structure. Its importance lies in the ability of ritual to transform a context through the performative use of language and through other symbolic practices" (199). Therefore he argues "a theory of ritual action is essential for understanding the relationship between the internal demands and the external consequences of social action" (199). He distinguishes between rituals and ceremonials, because, for him, rituals have a transformative character, whereas ceremonials are commemorative: "Both ritual and ceremonial may involve religious and secular aspects, but the former involves a transformation or transmutation of its elements into a new mode, while the latter reflects or translates existing social relations" (200). Because rituals "are situationally and institutionally bound", they "derive their meaning and their efficacy in the context of their performance, rather than in the intentions of the performers or in the instrumental consequences of their actions" (200). After giving an account on how ritual is related to social structure, rational action, discourse and meaning, he argues that "rituals structure social relations, including relations of domination, authorize practices and organize dispositions towards and attitudes in the world" (205). Therefore, "[r]ituals embed discursive and symbolic actions in social structures and convert them into authoritative practices" (210). The author concludes by saying that "no theory of action will be adequate unless it gives a full account of the role and contribution of ritual to the constitution of social structure" (210–211). [JK]

References: M.E.F. Bloch, R. Bocock, P. Bourdieu, É. Durkheim, C. Geertz, J. Habermas, B. Kapferer, R.A. Rappaport, V.W. Turner.
Key-words: eff, hab, pmc, pmt, pow, pr1, sec, SOC.

Platvoet, Jan G., 1995, 'Ritual in Plural and Pluralist Societies. Instruments for Analysis', in: Jan Platvoet & Karel van der Toorn (eds), *Pluralism and Identity. Studies in Ritual Behaviour*, (Studies in the History of Religions 65), Leiden, New York, Köln: E.J. Brill (ISBN 90–04–10373–2) (*) 25–51.

The aim of this article is to develop a "ritual theory which may be applied also to cultural and religious plurality" (25) and a " 'substantive' operational definition of ritual for the comparative study of religions" (26) that includes "religious as well as secular ritual behaviour" (25). The author gives a provisional definition of ritual and elaborates on thirteen dimensions, made up of traits and functions, that are typical and "serve as the diacritical features by which we may identify a ritual, even if they do not always, strictly speaking, actually constitute it" (27). After explaining these dimensions—namely the interaction, the collective, the customary, traditionalising innovation, the expressive, the communicative, the symbolic, the multi-media, the performance, the performative, the aesthetic, the strategic and the integrative dimensions—the author discusses the definition of ritual in plural and pluralist societies, concerning esp. the anthropological analysis of ritual. At the end of the article, the author defines ritual, which involves both communicative and strategic functions, as: "that ordered sequence of stylized social behaviour that may be distinguished from ordinary interaction by its alerting qualities which enable it to focus the attention of its audiences—its congregation as well as a wider public—onto itself and cause them to perceive it as a special event, performed at a special place and/or time, for a special occasion and/or with a special message. It effects this by the use of the appropriate, culturally specific, consonant complexes of polysemous core symbols, of which it enacts several redundant transformations by multi-media performance, thereby achieving not only the smooth transmission of a multitude of messages—some overt, most of them covert—and stimuli, but also serving the strategic purposes—most often latent, sometimes manifest—of those who perform it *ad intra*, within unified congregations or *ad extra* as well as *ad intra* in situations of plurality" (41–42). Appendix One:

"Definitions of Ritual, Chronologically Ordered" (42–45); Appendix Two: "A Brief History of Anthropological Theory on Ritual as Expressing Social Structure" (45–47). [JK]

References: E.M. Ahern, Th.P. van Baaren, G. Baumann, C.M. Bell, M.E.F. Bloch, P. Bourdieu, M. Douglas, É. Durkheim, J.W. Fernandez, C. Geertz, A. van Gennep, J. Goody, R.L. Grimes, B. Kapferer, D.I. Kertzer, E.Th. Lawson, E.R. Leach, G.A. Lewis, J.J. MacAloon, S.F. Moore, B.G. Myerhoff, D. Parkin, R. Schechner, J.Z. Smith, F. Staal, L.E. Sullivan, S.J. Tambiah, V.W. Turner.

Key-words: aes, com, DEF, eth, hsc, idn, med, pmc, pmt, pow, sec, SOC, str, sym.

Platvoet, Jan G., 2004, 'Ritual as War. On the Need to De-Westernize the Concept', in: Jens Kreinath, Constance Hartung & Annette Deschner (eds), *The Dynamics of Changing Rituals. The Transformation of Religious Rituals within Their Social and Cultural Context*, (Toronto Studies in Religion 29), New York: Peter Lang (ISBN 0-8204-6826-6 / ISSN 8756-738) 243–266.

This article problematizes the eurocentrism in the Western concept of 'ritual' and makes the case for reconsidering its adequacy and validity. The author assumes that "[r]itual is habitually seen as repetitive religious behavior solidifying the society or congregation in which it is celebrated" (243). Although "valid for most, but not for all, rituals", he argues that "they may be a way of exploding a society and of waging war upon one's enemies" and "[i]t has taken Western scholars of religions a long time to discover these secular, non-repetitive, explosive rituals" (243). Based on this assumption he aims to 'de-Westernize' the commonly used concept of 'ritual' so that it can "serve as an adequate tool for research into the generality of the ritual behavior of humankind, both religious and secular" (243). He structures his contribution as follows: "I first discuss the root cause of why we need to de-westernize ritual and the other core concepts of *Religionswissenschaft* [245–249]. I introduce my argument with an example from the study of the indigenous religions of Africa. Secondly, I suggest that we need to develop an ethological science of religions with ritual as its pivotal notion [249–252]. Thirdly, I survey three shifts in ritual theory. The first is that from an 'exclusive' definition—ritual being tied exclusively to religion—to an inclusive one: the category of 'ritual' comprising 'ritualizing' communicative behavior of both religious and secular kinds [252–255]. The second shift is that from Émile Durkheim's theory of ritual as solidifying society to that of

Catherine Bell of ritual as 'redemptive hegemony,' that is, as maintaining its 'order' by being full of well-hidden violence [255–257]. And the third is from noting that ritual may solidify society not only by hiding its violent face, but also by being openly violent, aggressive and destructive of society [257–258]. I demonstrate the latter from a series of politico-religious rituals in India between 1984 and 1992, which all aimed at liberating the god Rama from his Muslim jail [258–261]" (243–244). In his conclusion the author suggests that "'[r]ituals of war' are not limited only to plural societies with histories of 'communal violence'" (261) but that "rituals of war, confrontation and exclusion are endemic in all religions" (262). In his view, "[d]iscerning that rituals may be openly violent, and integrating that awareness into the analytical notion of 'ritual,' represents... a significant step in the de-westernization of this *etic* category in *Religionswissenschaft* as an academic discipline for the comparative study of religions and their rituals, as well as in 'ritual studies'" (262). [JK]

References: C.M. Bell (+), P. Bourdieu, É. Durkheim (–), C. Geertz, E. Goffman, S.F. Moore, B.G. Myerhoff, A.R. Radcliffe-Brown, V.W. Turner.
Example: Destruction of the Babri mosque in Ayodhya.
Key-words: def, eth, hsc, POW, rfl, sec, soc, TER.

Platvoet, Jan G., 2006, 'Ritual, Religious and Secular', in: Jens Kreinath, Jan A.M. Snoek & Michael Stausberg (eds), *Theorizing Rituals. Vol. I: Issues, Topics, Approaches, Concepts*, (Numen Book Series 114–1), Leiden, Boston: Brill (ISBN-10: 90–04–15342–x, ISBN-13: 978–90–04–15342–4) 161–205.

'Ritual' has by now established a virtual monopoly, terminological, conceptual and theoretical, for itself in the semantic field of terms denoting not only actions by means of which believers presume that they communicate with meta-empirical realms and beings, but also in clusters designating secular modes of expressive behavior, social as well as solitary. The purposes, and parts, of this essay are three. The aim of the first and largest part is to present preliminary data on when, how and why the *etic*, or scholarly, concept of 'ritual' began to serve as an imaginative theoretical construct for specific heuristic, analytical and theoretical purposes in the academic study of, first, the social interaction, postulated by believers, between themselves and meta-empirical worlds, and soon also for secular communication between humans, humans and animals, and between animals, and even for solitary, expressive,

but non-communicative behavior of humans and animals. The ulterior purpose is to develop a historical approach to the methodological problem of whether or not one should adopt an 'exclusive' or 'inclusive' definition of ritual, i.e. restrict it to religiously inspired behavior, or include secular stylized interaction also into it. Its outcome is that that issue, however important it is in itself, is not so much determined by reflection on methodology or the practicalities of research as by the wider semantic and symbolic processes in the societies of which scholars of religions happen to be part. I suggest that the terminology of the study of religions and ritual studies has been much more determined by processes of semantic change in Northwest European languages in the 19th and 20th centuries, and by other contingencies of our cultural histories, than by reflexive methodologies. Even so, the goal of the second part is to argue for an inclusive approach to the methodology of the study of ritual on pragmatic grounds, and thus move towards a pragmatics of ritual studies. The third part briefly address the politics of defining 'ritual', be it only in the conclusion, for neither the semantic developments described in the first part, nor the advocacy of an inclusive approach in the second, are innocent of the use of (symbolic) power in human societies. [Jan G. Platvoet]
Key-words: com, cpl, cmp, def, eth, hsc, SEC, soc, sym, TER.

Platvoet, Jan G. & Karel van der Toorn (eds), 1995, *Pluralism and Identity. Studies in Ritual Behaviour* (Studies in the History of Religions 67); Leiden, New York, Köln: E.J. Brill (ISBN 90-04-10373-2) (vi + 376) (with indexes).

Selected contents: Jan Platvoet & Karel van der Toorn: "Ritual Responses to Plurality and Pluralism" (3–21); Jan Platvoet: "Ritual in Plural and Pluralist Societies. Instruments for Analysis" (25–51) (*); Jan Snoek: "Similarity and Demarcation" (53–67) (*); Jan Platvoet & Karel van der Toorn: "Pluralism and Identity. An Epilogue" (349–360). [JK]

Reviews: M. Ruel *JRA* 26.4 (1996) 437–440; G. Rouwhorst *NTT* 50 (1996) 329 f; H. Stoks *TVT* 36.3 (1996) 325 f; L. Minnema *BTLV* 58.3 (1997) 353; A. Kanafani-Zahar *ASSR* 44/106 (1999) 90–92.
Key-words: def, cpr, exp, idn, sec, soc.

Prattis, Ian, 2001, 'Understanding Symbolic Process—Metaphor, Vibration, Form', ***Journal of Ritual Studies*** **15.1:38–54.**

According to the author, who introduces himself as "a meditation teacher" (38), symbols "are communication vehicles that operate as pointers to the unknown, and as mediators between different levels of consciousness and reality" (39). "There is a cycle of understanding here which proceeds from symbols in the human unconscious to mythology then to ritual enactment. The argument is that the deep mind in the unconscious projects symbols into mythology which then become the basis of liturgical reinforcement. The liturgical acting out of the myths thus enables the devotee to experience, with awareness, the power of the symbols being liturgically enacted" (39). In a subsequent section, this process is described as "[t]he movement... from metaphor to vibration and finally to form" (41). "The progression from metaphor in the mind to vibration in the body is essential..." (42). The "midpoint" of this process "usually involved entry into an altered state of consciousness (A.S.C.), so that the individual experiences an oceanic sense of interconnectedness... Without the experience of this state... behavioral restructuring and personal transformation is highly unlikely" (42). It turns into "embodied consciousness" (43). "In all meditation traditions it is constantly emphasized that the vehicle for transformation is oneself.... This is a metonymic process in which the microcosm (body) contains all the information about the macrocosm (cosmos).... Fully knowing the body means knowing the wonders of the universe" (44). In a subsequent section the author discusses "a number of loose threads hanging in the present essay" (46). These include "the deep hunger for ritual in our society" (46), processes of intercultural "symbolic appropriation" (48), "symbolic transformation" (49), and, finally, the "going beyond symbol" (50). In all these discussions the notion of 'archetype' features prominently. [MS]

References: J. Campbell, C. Geertz, **C.G. Jung** (+), Ch.D. Laughlin (+), C. Lévi-Strauss (–), V.W. Turner (+), R. Wagner.
Examples: Eagle Dance, the Eucharist.
Key-words: eff, myt, psy, sym.

Price, S. Michael, 1988, 'Ritual, Meaning, and Subjectivity. Studying Ritual as Human Religious Expression', ***Epoche*** **16:11–32.**

The paper is basically a critique of Frits Staal's essay, "The Meaninglessness of Ritual" (1979 (*)). The critique is based on different readings of Vedic materials, informed by an Eliadean type of the history of religions, and tries to get rid of "the musty halls of positivist objectivism" (32). According to the author, ritual is "full of significance, since it is a tenacious and vital part of human activity. What meaning ritual has may be intuitive, symbolic, subjective, and ineffable.... Our business as students of religion is to understand how ritual is meaningful; how it assists us in expressing ourselves and our relation to our world and to the Transcendent; and how its ubiquity reflects the fundamental human need to symbolize and express our relation to what we understand as the Transcendent.... It is...a question of subjective experience. As we describe it, soberly, and as objectively as we can, we are describing the real experience of a real person or group of people. As we describe, we are expressing our own subjective experience of 'the other'" (31). Apart from criticizing Staal, the author briefly discusses Jonathan Z. Smith's book, *To Take Place* (1987 (*)), whom he finds to exalt place rather too much (25). [MS]

References: F. Staal (–), J.Z. Smith (–), M. Eliade (+), C. Geertz (+).
Key-words: MNG, cpl, rfl.

Rao, Ursula, 2006, 'Ritual in Society', in: Jens Kreinath, Jan A.M. Snoek & Michael Stausberg (eds), *Theorizing Rituals. Vol. I: Issues, Topics, Approaches, Concepts*, (Numen Book Series 114–1), Leiden, Boston: Brill (ISBN-10: 90–04–15342–x, ISBN-13: 978–90–04–15342–4) 143–160.

The article "ritual in society" addresses the way ritual is embedded in a larger social context. More specifically, it discusses the relevance of rituals for the making and unmaking of power relations, by way of reviewing the contribution of various influential studies. Three interconnections between ritual and social order are addressed: firstly, the way authority within the ritual is established with reference to and with effect for other social contexts; secondly, the relevance ritual experiences have for the recreation of the social, and thirdly, the way meaning given to rituals or sequences within rituals relates to, reshapes and renegotiates elements of a cultural repertoire. The debate about rituals' affects on the social order is set within the framework of recent theories on the performativity of rituals. Against the assumption that rituals represent, naturalize and internalize a stable social order—typically found in the first half of the twentieth century—the article draws attention to the power of concrete ritual performances to reenact, change and manipulate the social in non-determinate, open and potentially risky ways. Although the article argues that ritual frames are flexible and that there are shifts in the way concrete ritual performances relate to social context, it does not deny that redundancy, regularity and stereotypy are important and typical elements of ritual. To understand the particular character of ritual performances we need to understand the complex relation between stability and flexibility in ritual. Negotiations of and in rituals do not only address questions of power and authority, they also focus on the elasticity of the ritual frame (which again has implications for the way ritual is related to power). [Ursula Rao]

Key-words: com, cpl, dyn, emo, frm, pmc, pmt, pow, pr1, rfl, SOC, str, sym.

Rao, Ursula & Klaus-Peter Köpping, 2000, 'Die "performative Wende". Leben—Ritual—Theater', in: Klaus-Peter Köpping & Ursula Rao (eds), *Im Rausch des Rituals. Gestaltung und Transformation der Wirklichkeit in körperlicher Performanz*, (Performanzen. Interkulturelle Studien zu Ritual, Spiel und Theater 1), Münster, Hamburg, London: Lit (ISBN 3-8258-3988-5) (*) 1–31 (with bibliography).

[The 'Performative Turn'. Life—Ritual—Theater]

In their introductory essay, the authors consider the performative turn in the study of rituals. They start with the observation that in recent times the use of the concept of ritual becomes loosened. According to them, rituals are nowadays conceived as any kind of formalized behavior which is authoritative in character and tradition-like in form. At the same time rituals are also conceived as based on a particular notion of transformative power. This broadens the approach to ritual while including those aspects of performance that are related to theater and the arts in general. According to the authors, rituals are currently discussed within the framework of performance theories including such topics as "ritual in theater", "theater as ritual" or "the theatricality of ritual" (1). In order to contextualize this turn in ritual studies, the authors give a short sketch of the history of the concepts of performance, event, and praxis. In discussing the concept of event as performance, they address the changeability and negotiateability of structures: "The performance is the event in which structure and practice come together, while reality emerges through a structured adaptation of the world" (3). Based on the assumption that structure exists only in the moment of its realization, the authors favor a dynamic concept of performative events so that a clear-cut definition of ritual becomes impossible. As a result, the authors argue that the functions and meanings of social actions do not appear as "transcendent categories" but as "discursive positioned practice orientations" (3). In their emphasis on the notion of a "contextual situated practice" (3), the authors aim to shift the focus towards a view that accounts for the particular actors, their positions and different understandings of the events that in reverse constitute the social reality as an emerging interplay of divergent perceptions. In their attempt to foster the performance study of rituals as embedded in local contexts, the authors see themselves confronted with a paradox: "On the one hand, the attempt is made to foster a cultural comparative perspective by way of viewing the different culturally positioned establishments of ritual. On the other hand, the contextual analysis calls into question the possibility of a general, contextually displaced concept of ritual" (3). As the authors argue, this paradox cannot be satisfactorily resolved. They perceive their contribution as homage to Roger Caillois and consider ritual as a combination of obsession (or ecstasy) and mimicry. This is reflected in the title of this volume: *Im Rausch des Rituals* (In the Ecstasy of Ritual). The main part of the introduction consists of five parts. In the first part, "*Wider die Auflösung des Ritualbegriffs*" (Against the Dissolution of the Concept of Ritual) (4–7), the authors discuss the approaches of Mary Douglas, Jack Goody, and Gilbert Lewis and take the concept of framing as a basic condition of performative action to emphasize the transformative power of ritual. (6). In the second part, "*Rituale als transformative Performanzen*" (Rituals as Transformative Performances) (7–11), the authors take up Victor Turner's concept of 'ritual process' and Clifford Geertz's concept of 'dramatic performance' and propose the equivocality of meaning as specific for rituals. In the third part, "*Zwischen Sein und Schein. Zur Problematik des Theatralen*" (Between Reality and Illusion. The Problem of the Theatrical) (11–18), the authors compare the various components of ritual and theater and their various transitions in form and content. Here, they address the issues of meaning and efficacy in ritual and theatrical performances. The fourth part, "*Rituelle Praxis und die Frage ihrer Bedeutung*" (Ritual Practice and the Question of its Meaning) (18–21), tackles the notion of the meaninglessness of rituals as developed by Caroline Humphrey & James Laidlaw. In the final part, entitled "*Die Übermächtigung und Ermächtigung des Körpers im Ritual*" (The Overpowerment and Empowerment of the Body in Ritual) (21–27), the authors deal with the notions of ritual embodiment and ritual mimesis as they are related to pain and memory. In this context, they see the specificity of rituals in the modality of how they are performed: "Through the formalism of its highly reflective action—which is based on an elaborate traditional codification of body movements—the ritual performance sets up a transformation, which does not...hide the truth or simulate the reality by way of representation. It rather reveals 'another' reality" (24). By way of conclusion, the authors state: "In a holistic view on the different intellectual and practice-oriented approaches to ritual and the positioning of the performances within the current discourse, it is possible to interpret ritual as *practice* in its cultural contexts" (27). [JK]

References: R. Bauman, M.E.F. Bloch, **R. Caillois** (+), M. Douglas, É. Durkheim, C. Geertz, Th. Gerholm, A. Giddens, E. Goffman, J. Goody (+/–), **C. Humphrey & J. Laidlaw**, B. Kapferer, L. Kendall, **S.K. Langer**, G.A. Lewis (+), F.A. Marglin, S.F. Moore & B. Myerhoff, **P. Radin** (+), E.L. Schieffelin, S.J. Tambiah, V.W. Turner, T.S. Turner.

Key-words: AUT, dyn, eff, emb, frm, mim, mng, PMC, tha, pr1, pr2, rfl, sec, soc.

Rappaport, Roy A., 1968, *Pigs for the Ancestors. Ritual in the Ecology of a New Guinea People*; New Haven, London: Yale University Press (ISBN 0–300–00850–3 / 0–300–01378–7 (p)) (xx + 311) (foreword by Andrew P. Vayda) (with index and bibliography).

The first chapter of this book, "Ritual, Ecology, and Systems" (1–7), forms an introduction that lays out what the book will present: the main concern of this study "is not with the part ritual plays in relationships occurring within a congregation. It is concerned, rather, with how ritual affects relationships between a congregation and entities external to it" (1). Among the Tsembaga, a group of Maring-speaking people living in the Bismarck Mountains of New Guinea, which the author studied, "ritual not only expresses symbolically the relationships of a congregation to components of its environment but also enters into these relationships in empirically measurable ways" (3). "Ritual will be regarded here as a mechanism, or set of mechanisms, that regulates some of the relationships of the Tsembaga with components of their environment" (4). "The rituals upon which this study focuses are interpreted as part of the distinctive means by which a population, the Tsembaga, relates to the other components of its ecosystem and to other local human populations that occupy areas outside the boundaries of Tsembaga territory" (6). The next chapter (8–31) provides an introduction to the Tsembaga, followed by chapters discussing their relations with the immediate environment (32–98), other local populations (99–152), and their ritual cycle (153–223). Based on the preceding material, Chapter 6, "Ritual and the Regulation of Ecological Systems" (224–242), formulates an ecological theory of ritual. First, the author distinguishes two (sub)systems, "the ecosystem and the regional system, with the local population participating in both" (226–227). While the former refers to "a demarcated portion of the biosphere that includes living organisms and nonliving substances interacting" (225), the latter refers to the exchange between neighboring groups. "It has been argued in this study that Maring ritual is of great importance in articulating the local and regional subsystems. The timing of the ritual cycle is largely dependent upon changes in the states of components of the local ecosystem.... Maring ritual... operates not only as a homeostat—maintaining a number of variables that comprise the total system within ranges of viability—but also as a transducer—'translating' changes in the state of one subsystem into information and energy that can produce changes in the second subsystem" (229). After having thus summarized the results of the previous chapters, the author finally formulates a number of questions of a more general kind: "In the light of the analysis presented in this study it may be asked whether rituals have peculiar virtues that make them particularly well suited to function as homeostats and transducers. I can offer only brief and highly speculative suggestions here" (233). But it is precisely these suggestions that comprise his theory. First, he notices that the execution of a ritual is a binary signal: the ritual is executed, or it is not. As such, it is a very simple signal, summarizing a much more complex state of affairs (234–235). It is an unambiguous signal, easy to recognize (235). The author then poses the question of what advantage sanctity confers upon such a signal, and argues that, because of the attitude of the people concerned towards sanctity, sanctification "may enhance the reliability of symbolically communicated information" (236). Furthermore, sanctity "is a functional alternative to political power" (237) and thus may function also in environments, such as the Maring population, where political authority is virtually absent. Here "compliance with the conventions is ensured, or at least encouraged, by their sanctity" (237). Finally, the author distinguishes "two models of the environment... significant in ecological studies... the 'operational' and the 'cognized'. The operational model is that which the anthropologist constructs through observation and measurement of empirical entities, events, and material relationships.... The cognized model is the model of the environment conceived by the people who act in it. The two models are overlapping, but not identical" (237–238).

To this point, he had presented the operational model alone, but now the author takes up the cognized model: "the important question concerning the cognized model, since it serves as a guide to action, is not the extent to which it conforms to 'reality' (i.e. is identical with or isomorphic with the operational model), but the extent to which it elicits behavior that is appropriate to the material situation of the actors, and it is against this functional and adaptive criterion that we may assess it" (239). "The cognized model of the environment, then, is understood by the functional anthropologist to be part of a population's means of adjusting to its environment" (239). This model, as "native epistemology may be of considerable importance in evolutionary processes" (241). The author concludes with the statement that the "study of man the culture-bearer cannot be separated from the study of man as a species among species" (242). [JS/MS]

Reviews: R.F. Salisbury *AAPSS* 380 (1968) 202 f; M. Strathern *Man* 3.4 (1968) 687 f; J.B. Watson *AA* 71.3 (1969) 527–529; A. Strathern *BSOAS* 32.1 (1969) 204 f; H.C. Wilson *JAS* 28.3 (1969) 658 f; A. Ploeg *JPS* 78.2 (1969) 271 f; S. Robbins *Ethnoh* 18.2 (1971) 167 f; C. Henfrey *NewSoc* 17.451 (1971) 876 f; **M. McArthur *Oc* 45.2 (1974) 89–123; G. Petersen *DA* 5.3 (1980) 255–259**; A. Strathern *AE* 12.2 (1985) 374 f; P.D. Dwyer *Oc* 56.2 (1985) 151–154; T.E. Hays *AA* 89 (1987) 754 f.
Key-words: com, cog, sem, eth, pow, ecn, ECL, soc.

Rappaport, Roy A., 1971, 'Ritual, Sanctity and Cybernetics', *American Anthropologist* 73:59–76.

In this essay the author investigates the role that ritual and sanctity play in cybernetics. His thesis is that the role of the sacred in human communication and in the regulation of social and ecological systems is approached through ritual. On the basis of his earlier ethnographic studies on Tsembaga ritual and belief (1968 (*)), the author focuses mainly on the formal characteristics of ritual that make them suitable to communicate and regulate complex social and ecological systems. His argument is that the ritual cycle that operates as a homeostatic of the local ecological subsystems is closely connected to the cycles of the social and ecological system. Focusing on the function of ritual as homeostasis and communication devices, the author defines ritual as a mode of communication distinguished from other modes by its distinctive code of conventionalized display. According to the author, ritual content and ritual occurrence are involved in communication. They are both important in regulatory operation. Due to their formal characteristics, the author argues that rituals are suitable for communication and regulatory functions. Moreover, he relates the concept of sanctity to a problem of symbolic communication. Because a signal is not intrinsic to its referent, he argues that there is a connection between sanctity and the characteristics of human communication. Because the relationship of the signal to its referent can differ, the author assumes that sanctity is "*the quality of unquestionable truthfulness imputed by the faithful to unverifiable propositions*" (69). Because sanctity is thus not a property of objects but of the discourse about objects, he considers sanctity to be non-discursive. In his conclusion, the author states that because regulation depends on communication, questions about the relationship between sanctity and communication are questions about the relationship between sanctity and regulation. He concludes that the concept of the sacred makes symbolic communication possible, and therefore also social and ecological orders which are dependent on that. [JK]

References: **G. Bateson** (+), E.H. Erikson (+), S. Freud, E. Goffman, E.R. Leach.
Examples: ritual dance, festival, ancestor rituals.
Key-words: COM, def, ECL, ref, rep, sem, soc, str, sym.

Rappaport, Roy A., 1974, 'The Obvious Aspects of Ritual', *Cambridge Anthropology* 2:3–69.

In this article, the author advances a ritual theory in which he defines those elements of ritual he regards as obvious: "This paper is not about the symbols of which most human rituals are in large part made... It is concerned with the obvious rather than the hidden aspects of ritual" (3). "One of the points" that the author shall try to make is "that there is at the heart of ritual a relationship that has a logically necessary outcome. This is to say that a certain meaning or function is intrinsic to the very structure of ritual, and that ritual imposes, or is an attempt... to impose logical necessity upon the vagrant affairs of the world" (4). To consider "what may be functionally particular to ritual would first require consideration of ritual's form" (4). The author argues that "it becomes apparent through consideration of ritual's form that ritual is not simply an alternative way to express certain things, but that certain things can be expressed only in ritual" (5). Because of this, the author takes "ritual to be *the* basic social act" (5). In contrasting "the depth of ritual with ritual's surface", the author claims that "the surfaces of ritual are *not* symbolic, or at least not entirely so", which seems "to be one of its most interesting and important characteristics, for through ritual some of the embarrassments and difficulties of symbolic communication are overcome" (5). In order to develop this argument, the author points out what he considers the obvious features of ritual but at the same time he emphasizes that "[n]o single feature of ritual is peculiar to ritual. It is in the conjunction of its features that it is unique..." (6). First and foremost, he takes formality as "an obvious aspect of all rituals: both observers and actors identify acts as ritual in part by their formality" (6). This in reverse means: "While ritual is characterised by its formality all that is formal, stereotyped, repetative [sic] or decorous is not ritual" (8). Secondly, he addresses performance and argues that "performance as well as formality is necessary to ritual. Performance is the second *sine qua non* of ritual, for if there is no performance there is no ritual" (8). This however does not imply the reverse, because "not all formal performance is ritual" (8). In taking drama as an example, the author argues that "dramas have audiences, ritual have congregations. An audience watches a drama, a congregation participates in a ritual" (8). These distinctions lead the author to consider two different forms of communication involved in ritual: "There seem to be two broad classes of messages transmitted in ritual" (11). He refers to these transmissions as indexical and symbolical messages: "Whereas the indexical is concerned with the immediate the canonical is concerned with the enduring" (12). Although the author adopts C.S. Peirce's classification of signs in symbols, icons, and indices (12), he only distinguishes between two classes of information that are transmitted in ritual: "All rituals...carry indexical information, information concerning the current states of the participants, often if not always transmitted indexically rather than symbolically. The second class, the canonical, is concerned with enduring aspects of nature, society or cosmos, and is encoded in apparently invariant aspects of liturgical orders. The invariance of a liturgy may be an icon of the seeming changelessness of the canonical information that it incorporates or even an index of its actual changelessness, but canonical information itself rests ultimately upon symbols" (16). The author continues by addressing the representation of analogical processes by digital signals: "Reduction of the continuous and complex to the binary through ritual occurrence is also important in the transition of individuals from one state or condition to another" (20). This implies that "[t]he occurrence of ritual not only articulates what it itself distinguishes...It also aids in the transduction of information between unlike systems" (23). The author then employs J.L. Austin's theory of speech acts to address the performativeness of ritual: "Ritual...not only ensures the correctness of the performative enactment; it also makes the performatives it carries explicit..." (28). For the author the meta-performative aspect of ritual is crucial: "Perhaps the most important reason for considering the performativeness of ritual is... that certain rituals are not themselves obviously performative but may make performatives possible" (29). Here, the author develops his concept of 'liturgical order', which "refers both to the more or less invariant sequences of formal acts and utterances that comprise single rituals and to the sequence of rituals that make up ritual cycles and series" (30). To perform a liturgical order "which is by definition a relatively *invariant* sequence of acts and utterances *encoded by someone other* than the performer himself, is to *conform* to it, authority or directive is *intrinsic* to liturgical order" (30–31). This again implies that "*by performing a liturgical order the performer accepts, and indicates to himself and to others that he accepts, whatever is encoded in the canons of the liturgical order in which he is participating*" (31). Acceptance is of crucial importance here, it is "a *public act*, visible to both the witnesses and the performer himself" and it "not only is not belief, it does not even imply belief" (34). A further function of liturgical performances is "to establish conventional understandings, rules and norms in accordance with which everyday behaviour is supposed to proceed, not to control that behaviour directly" (35). He further summarizes that "ritual is unique in at once establishing conventions, that is to say enunciating and accepting them, and in insulating them from usage" (38). This implies: "*We judge the state of affairs by the degree to which it conforms to the stipulations of the performative ritual*" (39–40). Then, the author again addresses the fact that rituals consist of the conjunctions of acts and utterances, which "suggests that not all messages are communicated equally well by all media" (40). By way of relating this conjunction to the indexical and canonical messages, the author states: "Whereas acts and substances represent substantially that which is of the here and now, the words of liturgy can connect the here and now to the past, or even to the beginning of time, and to the future, or even to the time's end" (42). This means that the different ritual media of communication complement each other: "The canonical and the indexical come together in the *substance* of the *formal* posture or gesture" (42). Because of that the author claims that "ritual may contain within itself a paradigm of creation" (42). By relating this paradigm of creation to the establishment of conventions the author argues: "In the ritual union of form and substance there is a reunion of convention with the nature from which words have alienated, but never freed it" (45). After some further suggestions on how liturgical orders have regular structures analogue to the rules of grammar, the author relates the invariance of liturgical orders to the notion of the sacred. He contends: "The invariance of ritual, which antedates the development of language, is the foundation of convention, for through it conventions are not only emunciated [sic], accepted, invested with morality, and naturalised, but also sanctified. Indeed, the sacred itself emerges out of liturgical invariance" (55). Then, the author relates the sacred to the numinous: "The canons of liturgy, in which are encoded both propositions concerning that which is ultimately sacred and sentences concerning temporal social orders may, then, receive in the rituals in which they are enunciated the support of numinous emotions" (59). Both are conceived as complementary to one another: "It is of interest that sacred propositions and numinous experiences are the inverse of each other. Ultimate sacred propositions are discursive but not material, numinous experiences are material...but not discursive" (60). Ritual, in this respect, "is an intrinsic part of an ultimate corrective loop in which the sacred and the numinous...are united in whole living systems" (62). The author concludes by saying that "[i]t is in its structure that ritual is distinctive and it is from its structure that its unique functions arise. Its world-founding properties derive from the simple relationship at its center: that of the performer to his own performance of an invariant, non-instrumental emotionally significant order that he himself did not encode. This relationship is, as it were, the 'atom of ritual', and virtually everything that I have argued is implied, if not entailed, by it" (63–64). [JK]

References: **J.F. Austin**, **G. Bateson** (+), **M.E.F. Bloch** (+), É. Durkheim, M. Eliade, E.H. Erikson, R.H. Finnegan, R. Firth, E. Goffman, J. Goody, **E.R. Leach** (+/–), J. Lyons, **Ch.S. Peirce** (+), J.R. Searle, **S.J. Tambiah** (+), P. Tillich, **V.W. Turner** (+/–), **A. van Gennep**, A.F.C. Wallace.
Key-words: cog, COM, def, dyn, ecl, eff, emb, emo, mng, PAR, pmc, PMT, psy, RFL, SEM, soc, STR, sym, TIM.

Rappaport, Roy A., 1978, 'Adaptation and the Structure of Ritual', in: Nicholas Blurton Jones & Vernon Reynolds (eds), *Human Behaviour and Adaptation*, London: Tylor & Francis (ISBN 0–850–6613–74) 77–102.

The author argues that ritual has variant as well as invariant components that can be called 'canonical' and 'self-referential'. The invariance of the liturgical order is bound to "eternal aspects of the social and cosmological order", whereas the variance of ritual indicates "the current states of the performers, expressing, by association, the relationship of the performers to the invariant order encoded in the canon" (81). The author argues that the performance of a liturgical order indicates the conformity to this order. Further, the performer accepts the codes of the canons as he takes part in the performance. The author distinguishes acceptance from belief: belief is subjective, whereas acceptance is a public act. "Acceptance entails obligation, and whether or not a man abides by what he has accepted, he has obligated himself to do so" (85). Consequently, "in its very form ritual does not merely symbolize but *embodies* social contract, and as such is the fundamental social act—that upon which society is founded" (86). Through utterances, rituals "bring states of affairs into being" (86). Inherent in rituals, creation leads to the invariance of ritual from which sanctity comes. The very characteristic of sanctity, namely its unquestionableness, is reflected in the conventional aspects of society, like authority, correctness, propriety, etc. Like the sacred, the numinous is an aspect of the Holy. "The union in ritual of the numinous, a product of emotion, with the sacred, a product of language, suggests possible grounds for the notion of the divine" (95). The author concludes his analysis with the statement: "The sacred and the numinous, the discursive and the non-discursive, the rational and the affective, structure and communitas make up wholes.... Human adaptation resides ultimately in wholes through the mobilization of which the ambitions of separate men may be subordinated to common interest...It is through such wholes that the conflicts between individual men and their societies are mediated. Wholeness, holiness and adaptiveness are one and the same" (101). [JK]

Key-words: COM, ecl, emb, par, PMC, pmt, rfl, soc, str, sym.

Rappaport, Roy A., 1979, *Ecology, Meaning and Religion*; Berkeley: North Atlantic Books (ISBN 0-938190-28-8 / 0-938190-27-x (p)) (xi + 259) (with a bibliography per chapter and an index).

This volume consists of seven essays, written between 1962 and 1977. Only one of them ("On Cognized Models", 97–144) was not published before. Most are on culture in general, but two deal explicitly with ritual. The first of these, "Ritual Regulation of Environmental Relations among a New Guinea People" (27–42), was first published in 1967; it is a short version of his 1968 book, *Pigs for the Ancestors*. The second, "The Obvious Aspects of Ritual" (173–221), is an expanded version of an article that was published in 1974 (*). [JS]

References: J.L. Austin (+), J.R. Searle (+), J. Skorupski (+), Ch.S. Peirce (+).

Reviews: D. Tuzin *AA* 83.2 (1981) 403; J.F. Hopgood *AE* 9.3 (1982) 588 f; J. Fabian, and reply by R.A. Rappaport *CA* 23.2 (1982) 205; **R. Hefner *CSSH* 25.3 (1983) 547–556**; R.E. Segal *JAAR* 54.2 (1986) 387.
Key-words: COM, PMC, PMT, sem, str, ecl, eth, eff, emo, par, dyn, def, soc.

Rappaport, Roy A., 1980, 'Concluding Comments on Ritual and Reflexivity', *Semiotica* 30:181–193.

According to the author, most of the papers in this volume of Semiotica "are primarily concerned with the significance of the reflexive actions of myth and ritual in the construction of personal and/or social identity" (181). To begin with, he comments on the essay by Myerhoff and Metzger and their attempt to "enlarge our understanding by likening the reflexivity of another genre, journal writing, to these more traditional forms, particularly to rites of passage" (181). Moreover, he contrasts journal writing to cases of the ritual use of mirrors dealt with by Fernandez in his essay. "It may be, in sum, that in writing a journal one writes oneself, but to write oneself is not necessarily to right oneself. To rite oneself is not necessarily to right oneself either, but it may be suggested that the certainties of ritual provide in most instances a safer and more reliable mode of self-construction than does the journal" (185). A further point of comparison concerns the matter of participation: "One does not participate in a journal, one merely writes it, and writing constructs nothing larger than the self" (186). However, "in performing a ritual one participates in it. To participate is by definition to become part of something larger that the self. When one performs a ritual, one not only constructs oneself but also participates in the construction of a larger public order" (187). In the subsequent section, the author comments on "the place of ritual's reflexivity in the construction of public orders *per se*" (187). According to the author, "the form that is ritual is intrinsically reflexive in nature. The term 'reflexive' points, minimally, to the effects of an action upon an actor. Now note: if the order of acts performed and utterances voiced by the actor is not encoded by him, his performance perforce confirms to that order. That is to say that he is subordinating himself to the order that the ritual encodes simply by performing it.... The reflexive act of subordination also establishes that to which there is subordination. To exist, a liturgical order must be performed. Liturgical orders, the orders encoded in ritual, are *substantiated*—provided substance, or realized—made into *res* only in instances of their performance. The relationship of performer to performance is extraordinarily intimate, or even inextricable. By participating in a ritual, the performer becomes part of an order which is utterly dependent for its very existence upon instances, such as [t]his, of its performance" (187). Moreover, according to the author, "the effects of such performances proceed in two directions at once, and in the selfsame acts. On the one hand, the performer is incorporated into an order; on the other, that very order is established. If reflexivity supposes that subject and direct object, so to speak, are one and the same, the double action of ritual should perhaps count as 'hyper-reflexive'" (187). In what follows, the author explores "the relationship of reflexivity to performativeness" (188). This implies questions of morality. "We see here an elaboration of the dual direction of the effects of ritual's reflexivity. In establishing orders on the one hand and in incorporating participants into them on the other, ritual generates the morality of the relationship in which they stand" (189). Moreover: "Sanctity is also established by ritual's reflexivity" (189). In the final section of the paper, the author suggests "that the notion of the divine has at least four features": a) It "is not material in any ordinary sense"; b) "it not only exists, but possesses 'being'"; c) "it is efficacious"; and d) "it is something like alive" (190). The author argues "that the first three of these qualities are supplied by fundamental linguistic processes as they are expressed in ritual's utterances, the last by the emotions generated in ritual" (190). [JK/MS]

References: J.L. Austin, B.A. Babcock (+), M.E.F. Bloch (+), C. Geertz, J.W. Fernandez (+), D. Handelman (+), B. Kapferer (+), B.G. Myerhoff (+), V.W. Turner.
Examples: Rituals of passage, liturgies.
Key-words: eff, idn, PAR, pmc, pmt, pow, RFL, SEM, soc, str.

Rappaport, Roy A., 1992, 'Ritual, Time, and Eternity', *Zygon* 27:5–30.

This article is on the modalities in which time and eternity are organized and constructed by ritual and the entailments of its liturgical order. The author wants to suggest ways "in which conceptions of eternity are also implicit in ritual" and to "propose ways in which liturgical orders construct temporal orders composed of alternations of time and eternity" (7). Because the liturgical orders of rituals and sequences of rituals divide the continuous duration into distinct periods, the author suggests that "ritual distinguishes two temporal conditions: (1) that prevailing in mundane periods and (2) that prevailing during the intervals between them" (5). Thus liturgical orders are "more or less fixed sequences of acts and utterances, following each other 'in order'" (8). On the basis of this notion, the author distinguishes between three dimensions in which liturgical order is realized: the sequential, the synchronic, and the hierarchic dimensions of liturgical order. In terms of the construction of time, he doubts both that there is a "universal temporal sense guiding all humans" and that "the sense of time is fully constructed *ex nihilo* by each culture for itself" (10). Thus, his argument is based on a chiasm and runs as follows: "Nature is a source of temporal raw material, and societies may, of course, found time upon the periodicities of nature; but this does not propose that human time is simply natural" (10). And: "Although cultures may make use of a range of natural cyclicities in their construction of time, time needs always to be constructed. The materials out of which it is constructed, moreover, are not limited to natural recurrences" (10). However, he argues that "[M]ost natural processes are continuous rather than discontinuous" (11), but "[i]n dividing the continuous duration into distinct periods, liturgy provides the wherewithal of succession and further provides for those successions to be joined into larger wholes" (12). Thus the construction of time is given by the distinction of the two temporal conditions of "ordinary periodic time and extraordinary intervallic time" (12). On the basis of the comparison of liturgical order and digital operations of a computer, the author distinguishes between such temporal sequences as recurrence and alteration: "Whatever the recurrence structure of mundane time may be, *overall* temporal structure, when constituted by a liturgical order, is an alteration between mundane time and 'time out of time'" (14). Moreover, he argues that the liturgical order of rituals not only reflects the periodicity of mundane time, but also reverses and imposes recurrence upon the mundane processes of an arbitrary periodicity. But those sequences imposed by liturgical orders "differ not only in shape, length, and the bases for the occurrence of their constituent rituals, but also in the frequency of the rituals composing them, in the regularity of their occurrence, and in the length of individual rites" (18). Although ritual performance involves organic, social, and cosmic time, the ritual time of the 'communitas' is based on tempo and coordination that is organized within the social time: "*The interactions of the social unit assume temporal frequencies and degrees of coordination characteristic of the internal dynamics of single organisms*" (23). Furthermore, the author argues that eternity is a "recurrence without end" because eternity is constructed through the invariance of the ritual's form: "In ritual, one returns ever again to that which never changes, to that which is punctiliously repeated in every performance" (25). Liturgical time is a time out of ordinary time and a product of invariant recurrence in ritual because of the changeless repetition of its liturgical order. [JK/JS]

References: B.A. Babcock, M. Eliade, E. Leach (+), V.W. Turner (+), A. van Gennep (+).

Key-words: com, STR, sym, rep, sem, soc, mng, par, cpl, TIM.

Rappaport, Roy A., 1999, *Ritual and Religion in the Making of Humanity* (Cambridge Studies in Social and Cultural Anthropology 110); Cambridge etc.: Cambridge University Press (ISBN 0–521–22873–5 / 0–521–29690–0 (p)) (xix + 535) (with index and bibliography).

This posthumously published book is the theoretical legacy of this anthropologist. It contains a good number of ideas that he had published in previous writings (and that are annotated under the respective titles in this bibliography). In the book's 14 chapters, the author unfolds a comprehensive theory of religion. Because, according to him, "the Holy and its elements are generated in and integrated by ritual, they will be approached through ritual" (24). Therefore, ritual plays a crucial role in this theory of religion. The titles of the chapters are as follows: 1) "Introduction" (1–22); 2) "The Ritual Form" (23–68); 3) "Self-referential Messages" (69–106); 4) "Enactments of Meaning" (107–138); 5) "Word and Act, Form and Substance" (139–164); 6) "Time and Liturgical Order" (169–215); 7) "Intervals, Eternity and Communitas" (216–235); 8) "Simultaneity and Hierarchy" (236–276); 9) "The Idea of the Sacred" (277–312); 10) "Sanctification" (313–343); 11) "Truth and Order" (344–370); 12) "The Numinous, the Holy, and the Divine" (371–405); 13) "Religion in Adaptation" (406–437); and 14) "The Breaking of the Holy and its Salvation" (438–461). Virtually every chapter is relevant to theorizing rituals, and in most if not all chapters rituals are explicitly discussed. The book needs a closer scrutiny than can be given in this abstract, which will mostly concentrate on Chapter 2. Here, to begin with, the author takes "the term 'ritual' to denote *the performance of more or less invariant sequences of formal acts and utterances not entirely encoded by the performers*" (24). He explicitly adds: "this definition encompasses much more than religious behavior" (24). Moreover, it "encompasses not only human rituals" (25). On the other hand, "as inclusive as this definition may be, not all behavior plausibly called 'religious' fits comfortably within its terms... as all ritual is not religious, not all religious acts are ritual" (25). According to the author, ritual is a specific structure, or form, that, in a unique fashion, relates five features. As such, these features are not peculiar to ritual, but, in a specific formal relationship, they constitute ritual. These features are: 1) "encoding by other than performers" (32–33); 2) formality in the sense of decorum (33–36); 3) invariance (more of less) (36–37); 4) performance (37–46); and 5) formality (vs. physical efficacy) (46–50). The author emphasizes that his formal definition of ritual is consequential for its substance as well: "Inasmuch as the substance of ritual is infinitely various, this must mean that these meanings and effects follow from ritual's universal form" (30). Moreover: "*The ritual form... adds something to the substance of ritual, something that the symbolically encoded substance by itself cannot express*" (31). Ritual is seen as a specific form of communication: "The form which is ritual is surely without communicational equivalents" (137). Several chapters of the book explore aspects of ritual communication that he also refers to as 'auto-communication', for "the transmitters of ritual's message are always among their most important receivers" (51). Ritual form relates to ritual content as frame (Goffman), context marker (Bateson), or metamessage, and if the ritual form, as the author assumes, is universal, "*then it is plausible to assume that the metamessages intrinsic to that form are also universal*" (31). Ritual "*is without equivalents or even... without alternatives*" (31), it is "*the social act basic to humanity*" (31). This is so because, as the author argues in the different chapters of the book, "*the performance of more or less invariant sequences of formal acts and utterances not entirely encoded by the performers logically entails the establishment of convention, the sealing of social contract, the construction of integrated conventional order we shall call* Logoi..., *the investment of whatever it encoded with morality, the construction of time and eternity; the representation of a paradigm of creation, the generation of the concept of the sacred and the sanctification of conventional order, the generation of theories of the occult, the evocation of numinous experience, the awareness of the divine, the grasp of the holy, and the construction of orders of meaning transcending the semantic.* These and other secondary entailments derivative from them inhere, as it were, in the form which we have defined as ritual and... reveal themselves as we unpack that definition" (27). [MS]

References: G. Bateson, M.E.F. Bloch, E. Goffman, E.R. Leach (–), C. Lévi-Strauss, S.J. Tambiah, R. Firth, J.W. Fernandez, Ch.S. Peirce, V.W. Turner, and many others.
Examples: Maring ritual, Catholic Mass, carnival.
Reviews: E. Turner *JAR* 55.4 (1999) 588 f; R. Bellah *JSSR* 38.4 (1999) 569 f; **A. Strathern & P. Stewart *SocAn* 43.3 (1999) 116–121**; A. Yengoyan *AA* 102.2 (2000) 404; D. Dalton *AQ* 74.1 (2001) 48 f; F.S. Adeney *JRS* 16.1 (2002) 126 f.; E. Paquette *Reli* 25 (2002) 349–352; R. Parmentier *HR* 43/2 (2003) 162–164.
Key-words: COM, PMC, PMT, SYM, STR, eth, emo, eff, PAR, TIM, ECL, SEC, DEF, gst, mng.

Ray, Benjamin Caleb, 1973, '"Performative Utterances" in African Rituals', *History of Religions* 13:16–35.

In this paper the author uses the wider relevance of the performative approach to analyze ritual language. Together with the specific query concerning the importance of performative utterance in creating and maintaining social relations through rituals, the author attends to the performative aspects of ritual language among the Dinka of the southern Sudan and the Dogon of central Mali. According to him, these rituals seem to be well suited for this kind of analysis "both because of their 'active' linguistic character and because of the extensive linguistic information about them in anthropological accounts" (17). Thus he assumes that the notion of performative utterance will illuminate the meaning of rituals "by noticing what is being *done* through the use of *words*" (17). On the basis of the relationship between words and deeds, the author argues that this 'performative' approach is helpful to see that language is crucial for the mechanism of these rites, in which one does something through saying something, and how the belief in such an instrumentality of words can intelligibly be understood. He criticizes Beattie for confusing the relation between ritual words and ritual deeds and thus for misunderstanding Austin's distinction between illocutionary and perlocutionary acts. Instead of looking for the ritual behavior in external psychological or sociological consequences, the author prefers the 'performative' approach because it directs the researcher's attention to the internal verbal structure of the ritual as the place of its meaning and purpose. He concludes: "One of the advantages of the 'performative' approach is that it avoids immediately importing the observer's theoretical framework into the analysis of ritual language and directs our attention to a firm bridgehead of shared linguistic realities. Only on this basis, I would contend, can we make serious progress in understanding the language of alien ritual systems" (35). [JK]

References: **J.L. Austin** (+), J.H.M. Beattie (–), M. Douglas, **R.H. Finnegan** (+), G. Leenhardt (+), B. Malinowski (+), S.J. Tambiah (–).
Example: Sacrifice.
Key-words: eff, mng, PMC, soc, str.

Reeves, Edward B. & Robert A. Bylund, 1989, 'Social Density and Public Ritual in Non-Industrial Communities. A Cross-Cultural Analysis', *The Sociological Quarterly* 30:225–244.

"An implication of Durkheimian theory—that different types of rites and the elaborateness of public rituals are determined by social density—is emperically tested, using data available for 183 non-industrial communities derived from Murdock's Standard Cross-Cultural Sample" (225). "The results of the analysis support the Durkheimian thesis that social density is an important determinant of ritual activity. Social density was found to be negatively related to the occurrence of crisis rites and positively related to the occurrence of calendrical rites and ritual elaboration" (238). "The present analysis indicates that social density is a more significant determinant of ritual activity than is either political hierarchy or the division of labor, two factors often considered to have leading importance.... One theoretical position that is definitely not supported by the findings is the social evolutionist idea that ritual activity must decline with increasing complexity in the division of labor" (238). "The findings of this study have useful implications when extended to modern complex societies. Where social relations are diffuse, tenuous, and irregular we might expect to find a higher incidence of ritual emphasizing crisis and threat.... On the other hand, the use of secular ritual in collectivist societies which have an apparatus for high surveillance would be comparable with the connection between high social density and the occurrence of regularly-scheduled rites which focus on the maintenance of societal structure. Similarly, it should be possible to explore the positive relation between social density and ritual elaboration in bureaucratic settings. Collectivist societies like the Soviet Union have highly elaborated secular rituals, such as the personality cult of Lenin, more so than occurs in decentralized societies such as England, France, or the United States" (238–239). The article is followed by an appendix (239–241), notes (241–242) and a bibliography (242–244). [JS]

Reference: É. Durkheim (+).
Key-word: SOC.

Reeves, Edward B. & Robert A. Bylund, 1992, 'Anonymity and the Rise of Universal Occasions for Religious Ritual. An Extension of Durkheimian Theory', *Journal for the Scientific Study of Religion* 31:113–130 (with bibliography).

The authors observe that Durkheim already noted that religious beliefs of people with a low population density are more specific and concrete than those of people with a high population density, where "religious beliefs take on a universal character" (113). The authors seem to imply that since high density populations develop out of low density ones, it follows that religious ideas with a universal character developed out of more concrete ones. "We shall call the process that brings about this transformation 'universalization'" (114). The purpose of the study presented in this paper is to determine whether this process of universalization claimed by Durkheim for religious ideas, also occurs in religious action (i.e. rituals). The hypothesis therefore is that "[l]ow density and limited differentiation should result in rituals which are held on irregular, ad hoc occasions where typically there is a specific (localized) sense of crisis. Conversely, the greater the density and differentiation in society, the greater the likelihood that rituals will be held in regular occasions following some standardized temporal scheme which transcends the particular circumstances of a local group" (114). The authors then introduce Schutz's distinction between intimates (people one knows well), consociates, and contemporaries (people one does not know personally at all) in order to differentiate between low population density societies (where most people are intimates) and high density ones (where most people are contemporaries only, but some are consociates and even intimates). "Urban, industrial societies have another characteristic that confuses the issue we wish to explore. The sacred in the United States and in similar societies is differentiated into secular as well as religious dimensions. Thus, we have mostly secular rituals, such as presidential nomination conventions and law court proceedings, as well as fully religious rituals" (116). To circumvent these complications, the authors decided to confine their "empirical analysis to non-industrial societies where rituals are almost always of a religious nature" (116). They then give some examples that confirm that "low-density societies... have exclusively ad hoc rites, while high-density societies... practice calendrical rites. In comparison... medium-density societies... practice both ad hoc and calendrical rites" (117). They explain this thus: "Ad hoc crisis rites are a kind of informal interaction which is most characteristic of an intimate social environment, while calendrical rites correspond to formal interaction that is associated with a multi-party, anonymous social setting" (118). And continue: "We wish then to propose here that change from ad hoc crisis rites to calendrical rites is analogous to the change, noted by Durkheim, from concrete conceptions of sacred beings to the 'international gods'. To see society as a mixture of intimates, consociates, and contemporaries existing in varying proportions contributes a new dimension of understanding to Durkheim's theory of religious universalization" (118). They then test their theory on a sample of 148 non-industrial societies, derived from the Standard Cross-Cultural Sample, designed by Murdock and White. As independent variables they choose population density, the degree of technical specialization, the extent of political hierarchy, and the reliance upon money exchange (122), while the universalization of ritual occasions (operationalized as the extent to which calendrical rituals were more frequent than crisis rituals) was the dependent variable (121). "An analysis of the decomposition of effects in the path model showed that many of the causal relations we hypothesized were supported... In some cases the non-significance of these relations was an artifact, we suspect, of the small sample size and the fairly strong correlation among the independent variables... Population density was found to have the largest effect and the only significant direct effect (beta = 0.20) on the occurrence of universalized ritual occasions" (123). "The present research indicates that universal ritual occasions synchronize interactions between persons who are socially differentiated and anonymous. This type of ritual creates a basis for recognizing anonymous others as co-members of large, diffuse social groups. It does not occur on occasions of individual or local group crisis, and hence does not necessarily signify a homogeneous emotional and cognitive experience. Greater latitude is given to individuals as far as their motivations for participation are concerned" (124–125). This conclusion contradicts what urban sociologists have generally thought, namely "that the function of religion in cities is to provide a basis for community, that is, for the playing out of face-to-face relationships, and to contribute to heightened experiences of intimacy, in order to offset the feeling of alienation which urban life is said to promote. To this argument we are tempted to suggest a counter. The intimacy which modern religious ritual is supposed to achieve might be more apparent than real, a *semblance* of intimacy which is fostered by the synchronization and formal interaction that universal ritual occasions provide" (127). [JS]

References: **É. Durkheim (+)**, A. Schutz (+).
Key-words: def, SOC, psy, sec, emo, par.

Riner, Reed D., 1978, 'Information Management. A System Model of Ritual and Play', in: Michael A. Salter (ed.), *Play. Anthropological Perspectives*, (Proceedings of the Association for the Anthropological Study of Play 1977), West Point (NY): Leisure Press (ISBN 0–918438–16–0) 42–52.

This article is an analysis of ritual and play based on General System Theory. According to this theory, "ritual and play behaviors are polar expressions of a single behavioral process whose objective is to keep informational inputs within an optimum range" (42). The author gives three ethological studies, namely the presenting ritual of the hamadryas baboon, the threat ritual of the gorilla, and the rain dance of the chimpanzee, in order to show that "ritual and play behaviors have a common origin" (47). After analyzing the common behaviors and operations with the system theory, the author develops a model, according to which the difference of ritual and play behavior from other need satisfaction behaviors lies in a method of information management. "This system approach to play and ritual behaviors emphasizes adequate information as an autonomous basic need for all adapting systems. It argues for pre-cultural, indeed pre-hominoid, origins of play and ritual, and for the trans-human and trans-cultural expression of the same process" (51). A further implication of this model asserts that the mixture of play and ritual is to be found in all performances, which enrich some informational inputs and reduce simultaneously others. [JK]

Key-words: com, cog, pmc, str, eth.

Roberts, Janine, 1988, 'Setting the Frame. Definition, Functions, and Typology of Rituals', in: Evan Imber-Black, Janine Roberts & Richard A. Whiting (eds), *Rituals in Family and Family Therapy*, New York, London: Norton (ISBN 0–393–70064–x) 3–46.

The context for this article is given in the title of the volume: family therapy. Therefore, the author starts from the observations: "Ritual has been used as such a general term both popularly and across academic disciplines that the problem of definition has to be addressed. For use clinically in family therapy, ritual needs to be defined narrowly enough to distinguish it from other types of interventions, yet broadly enough to encompass the range of ritual interventions that families and clinicians can create. I will look first at how the term has already been used in the field of family therapy, then return to ritual's roots in anthropology, and emerge with the definition of ritual that is used in this book" (3). A review of the literature on "Ritual as Used in Systems Family Therapy" (3–6) follows which summarizes the work of Mara Selvini Palazzoli and others from the "Milan group", as well as Onno van der Hart (from the Netherlands). She then turns to "Ritual as Used in Anthropology" (6–8), mentioning Victor Turner, Moore & Myerhoff, Rappaport, and Van Gennep. This leads to her "Working Definition of Ritual": "Rituals are coevolved symbolic acts that include not only the ceremonial aspects of the actual presentation of the ritual, but the process of preparing for it as well. It may or may not include words, but does have both open and closed parts which are 'held' together by a guiding metaphor. Repetition can be a part of rituals through either the content, the form, or the occasion. There should be enough space in therapeutic rituals for the incorporation of multiple meanings by various family members and clinicians, as well as a variety of levels of participation" (8). As opposed to her initial statement, this does not conclude the paper, but only the first of the three major sections: "The Problem of Definition" (3–11). After a case example (8–11), she continues with the second main section, which deals with the "Functions of Rituals" (11–25). Here she states that "[r]ituals provide 'frameworks for expectancy' (Douglas, 1966 [*]) where, through the use of repetition, familiarity, and transformation of what is already known, new behaviors, actions, and meanings can occur" (11). In the subsection, "Structure, Action and Meaning: Ritual as Intercom" (13–16), we read: "At the same time that the transition is made and marked, there is space in the celebration for new traditions to be established" (14). And she concludes this subsection: "Combining both the cultural perspective and social perspective of anthropology: Ritual works as both a maintainer and creator of social structure for individuals, families and social communities, as well as a maintainer and creator of world view [sic]. It can mediate between the two arenas of structure and meaning so that each defines, reflects, and elucidates the other" (15–16). In the next subsection, "Other Functions of Rituals" (16–20), she mentions: "Ritual can incorporate both sides of contradictions so that they can be managed simultaneously" (16); "Ritual may provide a way for people to find support and containment for strong emotions (Scheff, 1979 [*])" (16); "Social coordination among individuals, families, and communities and among past, present and future can be facilitated by ritual" (18); and "ritual supports transitions (Van der Hart, 1983; Van Gennep, 1960)" (19). In the subsection, "How Rituals Work for Individuals" (20–21), she reviews "the neurobiological impact of participation in rituals" (20). The subsection, "Functions of Ritual and Family Therapy" (21–22), first states: "The functions of rituals have important implications for the use of ritual in family therapy precisely because they offer many possibilities for holding duality" (e.g. "the change/no change dilemma [in therapy]") (21). These are then discussed. After another case example (22–24), this section closes with the subsection, "Differences Between

How Therapeutic Rituals and Cultural Rituals Work" (24–25), which title, by the way, introduces an interesting suggestion for the classification of rituals. She is of the opinion that the differences between these two kinds of rituals are significant. The third and last main section is "Rituals, Families, and the Therapy Process" (25–43). It contains the subsections "Assessment of Family Ritual Behavior" (25–26), "Typology of Family Rituals" (26–33), "Family Celebrations, Family Traditions, Life Cycle Rituals and Day-to-Day Life" (33–36), "Symptomatic Behavior as Ritual" (36–37), "Therapy as Ritual" (where Van Gennep's tripartite structure is seen in therapy; 37–42), "Ritual Typology and the Therapy Process" (42–43), and "Creating Therapeutic Rituals" (which mainly refers the reader to the Chapters 2 and 3 of the volume; 43). The whole of this last main section is tailored to therapeutic ritual specifically. [JS]

References: **M.S. Palazzoli**, O. van der Hart, V.W. Turner, S.F. Moore, B.G. Myerhoff, R.A. Rappaport, A. van Gennep, M. Douglas, A.R. Radcliffe-Brown, E.G. d'Aquili, Ch.D. Laughlin, J. McManus.
Example: Family therapy.
Key-words: DEF, frm, PSY, mng, str.

Roth, Andrew L., 1995, '"Men Wearing Masks". Issues of Description in the Analysis of Ritual', ***Sociological Theory*** **13:301–327.**

The argument of this article is based on the assumptions that "[t]he lack of consensus about the analysis of ritual stems from the absence of an explicitly formulated, shared set of procedures for investigating it" (302). The author observes that "the variation of empirical foci is paralleled by an equal diversity of methodological approaches", and each approach "constitutes an attempt to face—more or less explicitly—the twin issues of (1) *identifying* some phenomenon as ritual and, having done so, (2) determining how to *describe* it" (302). The author considers three methodological approaches by way of formulating a set of three questions: 1. "*Is ritual described from a 'solidaristic' or an 'agonistic' perspective?*" (302); 2. "*Is ritual action described from a 'compositional' or a 'functional' perspective?*" (302); 3. "*Is ritual identified as an 'aspect' of action or a 'type' of it?*" (303). According to the author, these questions constitute a framework for analyzing ritual, which is descriptive as well as prescriptive, because it "describes how social scientists have studied ritual" and prescribes how "ritual should be investigated in terms of its significance as and for social action" (303). Based on this framework, the author aims "to show that advances in our understanding of how ritual functions will depend on our developing the analytic tools necessary to describe ritual as a distinctive type of social action, with properties that differentiate it from other types of action" (303). Hence the author contends: "What the analyst observes can only be understood in terms of elements extrinsic to the ritual actions themselves. This approach raises the question of how analysts demonstrate the *relevance* of observations and inferences about the organization and significance of ritual through their description of it" (304). In the first section, entitled "'Solidaristic' versus 'Agonistic' Perspectives on Ritual" (304–309), the author discusses E. Shils & M. Young and S. Lukes who illustrate the basic features of these perspectives as well as M. Gluckman and J. Alexander as alternatives who either argue "that ritual has *both* solidaristic and agonistic functions, depending on the level of analysis" or posit "that the function of ritual is contingent, so that... the outcome may be solidaristic or agonistic" (306). The second section, entitled "'Compositional' versus 'Functional' Approaches to Ritual" (309–315), discusses A. van Gennep and É. Durkheim who emphasize respectively the composition and the function of ritual. Here, the author argues that "[a] compositional emphasis highlights the structure and dynamics of ritual as a process, while a functional emphasis underscores the social consequences of, and references for, that process" (309–310). V.W. Turner is taken as an approach that combines the compositional and functional accounts of Van Gennep and Durkheim. In the third section on "Ritual as an 'Aspect' or a Type of Social Action" (315–320), the author argues that "the distinction between ritual as either an aspect or a type of social action provides an initial pointer to deeper issues involved in the description and analysis not only of ritual, but of social action more generally. To treat ritual as an aspect of social action typically involves identifying it in terms of single—but pervasive—attributes, such as 'interaction', 'symbols', or 'power'" (315). As alternatives to E. Goffman who functions as an example for analyzing ritual as an aspect of action, the author discusses T. Parsons and C. Bell who conceive ritual as a type of social action. In the forth section "Observation and Inference. The Problem of Adequate Description" (320–325), the author addresses the description of ritual as social activity and contrasts the descriptive approach of C. Geertz with the observational approach of H. Sacks. According to him, "[l]ike ritual, description is socially organized and involves choices: Describing is, itself, a course of conduct" (321). In favoring the latter approach the author suggests that "[i]nstead of analyzing symbols and their meanings in terms of abstract, symbolic *systems*, the analyst would observe how (or, indeed, whether) the participants themselves orient to symbols at any given instance in the ritual" (323). The author argues in favor of the compositional analysis of ritual as a type of social action and with reference to Van Gennep that "the study of ritual can progress as a descriptive enterprise with scientific credibility, where the warrant for the descriptions would originate not from the theoretical constructs of the analysts, but from the indigenous practices of the participants" (324). The author concludes that ritual "will necessarily be constituted as observable actions and sequences of actions, and it is in the details of these actions and sequences that analysts should search for evidence of ritual's enduring, if variable, sociological relevance" (325). [JK]

References: J.C. Alexander, C.M. Bell (+), É. Durkheim, C. Geertz, M. Gluckman, E. Goffman (–), S. Lukes, T. Parsons, E. Shils, V.W. Turner, A. van Gennep (+), M. Young.
Key-words: cpr, DEF, pr1, SOC, STR, sym.

Rothenbuhler, Eric W., 1998, *Ritual Communication. From Everyday Conversation to Mediated Ceremony*; Thousand Oaks (CA): Sage Publications (ISBN 0–7619–1586–9 / 0–7619–1587–7 (p)) (xv + 159) (with indexes and bibliography).

This book has two parts, "What Is Ritual?" and "Ritual in Communication Research", each containing 6 short chapters, while Chapter 13, "The Necessity of Ritual to Humane Living" (129–131), "discusses a belief that motivated this work, a belief…that ritual is necessary to humane living together" (x). Since the book claims also to be "a bibliographic essay" (ix), it closes with a bibliography of no less that 417 items. In the "Preface", the author gives first an "Overview" of the book (ix–xi) and then makes his "Theoretical Agenda" explicit (xi–xiii): "This book is intended as a contribution to the tradition of debunking utilitarianism, to identifying the independent, arational roles played by symbols, meanings, and ideas. For the present purposes, I locate the origin of that tradition with Émile Durkheim…" (xi). "I hope to rehabilitate ritual among those who treat it with suspicion. I want to point out its ubiquity and usefulness. I want to demonstrate its beauty and power. I want to point out that among the devices for order, it is one of the most gentle and most available to rational reform when it is needed" (xiii). The "Preface" starts thus: "This is a book on ritual, on the literature of ritual studies, on the use of the term *ritual* in the literature of communication studies, on ritual as a communicative phenomenon, and on communication as a ritual phenomenon. It is concerned with rituals as things, ritual ways of doing things, and ritual as a concept. It is a bibliographic essay, and an exercise in theory" (ix). In the first chapter, "Descriptions and Definitional Strategy" (3–6), it is made clear that both "rituals as events and the ritual aspects of ongoing social activities" (4) will be the subject of the book. The second chapter, "Definitions" (7–27), first discusses 15 "Common Terms of Definition" (7–25) in order to conclude in the second section, "A Communicative Principle and a Final Definition" (25–27), with the author's definition: "Ritual is the voluntary performance of appropriately patterned behaviour to symbolically effect or participate in the serious life" (27). Chapter 3 discusses "Five Inadequate Concepts" (28–35) and Chapter 4 "Four Only Partly Adequate Concepts" (36–45), while Chapter 5 addresses "Some Special Problems in the Study of Ritual", namely "Social Change" (46–50) and "Inventing Rituals" (50–52). The first part is concluded by Chapter 6, discussing "Communication Theory and Ritual Problems" (53–69) of which the author states, that it "is more explicitly devoted to original theoretical work than any other chapter in the book. In that chapter, I explicate a propositional argument leading to the conclusion that ritual is one of the strongest forms of communicative effectiveness we can identify, and show its effectiveness works through its communicative devices" (x). The second part opens with Chapter 7, "Five Contributions of the Ritual Concept to Communication Studies" (73–77), followed by Chapter 8 "Mediated Communication in Ritual Form" (78–88), Chapter 9 "Ritual Functions of Mediated Culture" (89–95), Chapter 10 "Political, Rhetorical, and Civic Rituals" (96–104), and Chapter 11 "Ritual Communication Forms in Everyday Secular Life" (105–116), to conclude with Chapter 12 "Ritual Conceptions of Culture and Communication" (117–128). The author summarizes: "The first half [of the book] begins by exploring definitions of ritual, works through the ritual studies literature, and concludes with a discussion of ritual as communication. The second half begins with the usefulness for communication studies of the idea of ritual, works through the communication studies literature, and concludes with a discussion of communication as ritual" (x). [JS]

References: **É. Durkheim** (+), **J.C. Alexander** (+), R.L. Grimes (+), and many others.

Reviews: J. Smith *EJC* 15.1 (2000) 98 f; S. Jain *SocBul* 49.1 (2000) 148.

Key-words: GEN, DEF, soc, psy, sec, mng, sym, aes, COM, eth, pmc, pr1, dyn, eff, MED.

Sax, William, 2006, 'Agency', in: Jens Kreinath, Jan A.M. Snoek & Michael Stausberg (eds), *Theorizing Rituals. Vol. I: Issues, Topics, Approaches, Concepts*, (Numen Book Series 114–1), Leiden, Boston: Brill (ISBN-10: 90–04–15342–x, ISBN-13: 978–90–04–15342–4) 473–481.

In social theory generally, 'agency' is usually thought of as a property of individual persons. Moreover, it is often confused with topics like 'free will' and 'resistance'. In this article, the author maintains that these tendencies derive from an uncritical individualism, and that when one accepts a straightforward definition of agency as 'the capacity to effect change in the external world', one sees that ritual agents are often complex rather than individual, that ritual agency is often distributed among multiple actors and institutions, and that indigenous or 'emic' models attributing ritual agency to non-human beings are consistent with such a definition. The author argues that individual human agency is not the only kind of agency, that rituals themselves might have a distinctive kind of agency, and that ritual theorists should also give some thought to distributed, complex, non-human, and supernatural forms of agency. He illustrates his argument with examples from the history of ritual theory, and from his own fieldwork amongst the 'divine kings' of the central Himalayas: local gods whose agency is built up, as it were, from subordinate forms of agency distributed amongst individuals, families, clans, and other kinds of associations in the region. The author argues that public ritual is precisely the point at which complex agency is articulated and confirmed. [William Sax]

Key-words: aes, AGN, pow, soc, spc.

Scarduelli, Pietro, 2000, 'Introduzione', in: Pietro Scarduelli (ed.), *Antropologia del rito. Interpretazioni e spiegazioni*, (Nuova Didattica), Torino: Bollati Boringhieri (ISBN 88–339–5651–2) 9–66 (with bibliography).

This introductory essay to an edited volume on ritual studies can be divided into two parts. In the first part (9–57) the author delineates the development of ritual theory from the 19th century to the 1980s, while the second part (57–61) provides a discussion of the different essays contained in the volume, followed by a bibliography (62–66). In his genealogy of ritual theories the author traces three lines of continuity from the 19th through the 20th centuries: an intellectualist approach, an emotional approach, and one focusing on social dynamics (17). On the other hand, the author also identifies some approaches that have no precursors among 19th century theoreticians, in particular ethology and structuralism. Moreover, the author points to the meta-theoretical option to devise explanations of ritual on a different level from the conscious efforts of the social actors themselves (40) and he stresses the impact of linguistics on several ritual theories (43). "All the theoretical models taken into consideration here (psychological, sociological, communication, structuralist, performative, intellectualist, and textual approaches) can be traced back to two fundamental meta-theoretical options: the interpretative option... [and] the explanatory option..." (49). The author then proceeds by contrasting these options and by discussing their respective implications and consequences (49–52). That leads over to a discussion of the unconscious in cultural representations and the differences between indigenous interpretations and the models of the observers (52–57). Several theoreticians are discussed quite extensively; these are listed below under "References". [MS]

References: É. Durkheim, R. Firth, J.G. Frazer, C. Geertz, M. Gluckman, R. Horton, E.R. Leach, B. Malinowski, R.R. Marett, D. Middleton & E.H. Winter, A.R. Radcliffe-Brown, R.A. Rappaport, J. Skorupski, P. Smith, B. Spencer, S.J. Tambiah, V.W. Turner, E.B. Tylor, V. Valeri.
Key-words: GEN, hsc.

Schäfer, Alfred & Michael Wimmer (eds), 1998, *Rituale und Ritualisierungen* (Grenzüberschreitungen 1); Opladen: Leske & Budrich (ISBN 3-8100-2171-7) (227).
[Rituals and Ritualizations]

Contents: Michael Wimmer & Alfred Schäfer: "Einleitung. Zur Aktualität des Ritualbegriffs" (9–47) (*); Bernhard Streck: "Ritual und Fremdverstehen" (49–60); Ivo Strecker: "Auf dem Weg zu einer rhetorischen Ritualtheorie" (61–93) (*); Hermann Pfütze: "'Ohne Rand und Band'. Zur nachlassenden Bestätigungskraft von Ritualen" (95–108); Konrad Thomas: "Ritual und Vergessen. Zu René Girards Theorem der méconnaissance" (109–115) (*); Edith Seiffert: "Ritual total. Über Ritualisierung in der Psychoanalyse" (117–127); Hans Bosse: "Der Forscher wird eingesperrt. Kreative Wandlungsprozesse eines Zwangsrituals" (129–163); Alfred Schäfer: "Rituelle Subjektivierungen" (165–181); Hermann Timm: "Alle Jahre wieder. Die rituelle Lebensrundung im Christentum" (183–191); Thomas Macho: "Robinsons Tag. Notizen zur Faszinationsgeschichte nationaler Feiertage" (193–208); Wolfgang Braungart: "Zur Ritualität der ästhetischen Moderne. Eine kleine

Polemik und einige Beobachtungen zur Kunst der Mittellage bei Eduard Möricke" (209–227). [MS]

Schaller, Joseph J., 1988, 'Performative Language Theory. An Exercise in the Analysis of Ritual', *Worship* 62:415–432.

With a focus on the nature of ritual language and its particular use in liturgical rites similar and dissimilar to other forms of ordinary social communication, the author outlines a perspective on ritual language as a performative mode of communication. As a principal advantage of the performative language theory, he emphasizes in his study of liturgical rites the relationship of meaning and text in the context of ritual. In reference to the speech act theory, he understands liturgy as a ritual performance in which the text is essentially related to the ritual act. Furthermore, he argues that in the light of this theory one has to assume that in performative uses of language the existential situation of participants can be changed, and that a different state is established through the performative way of communicating. In considering language as performative, the author argues that it is important to view the liturgical texts in their ritual context and uncover their pragmatic meaning. On this basis, text and ritual performance are mutually and circularly dependent: "The ritual itself defines a 'world of meaning', a subclass of performance considered 'appropriate' within the situation established by the very performance of the ritual. In this way, the ritual not only forms the context for the text, but the text also reciprocally 'informs' the ritual, allowing the participants to come to a more profound understanding of the meaning of the actions they are performing" (420). Thus he concludes that through performativity one can reflect on the manner in which text and context in ritual performances exist interdependently. [JK]

References: C. Geertz, R.A. Rappaport, B. Ray, **W.T. Wheelock** (+).
Examples: Liturgy, rite of anointing, prayer.
Key-words: com, lan, mng, PMT, pr1.

Schechner, Richard, 1966, 'Approaches to Theory/Criticism', *Tulane Drama Review* 10.4:20–53.

In the first part of this article (21–28), the author reviews "the Cambridge Anthropologists" and what he summarizes as their thesis: there had once existed "a Primal Ritual from which they felt both Attic tragedy and the surviving rituals derived" (21–22). After analyzing why it "held such power", ("It can be compressed, codified, and generalized: it is teachable. It is self-repairing... It seems to explain everything...") (26) he discards it ("In short, the thesis is brilliant, speculative criticism. But it is no more than that.... perhaps it is time to abandon the Cambridge thesis altogether..." (26)). He does not want to replace it by another origin theory, but instead focuses on ritual in relation to theater, play, games and sports. "Together these five comprise the public performance activities of men" (27) which are all primeval activities, so that there is no reason to look at one as the origin of another. In the second part of the article (28–39), these five activities are then analyzed and compared, on the basis of certain characteristics: special ordering of time, special value for objects, non-productive, rules, special place, appeal to other, audience, self-assertive, self transcendent, completed, performed by group, symbolic reality, and scripted (summarized in a table on page 35). As a result, the five activities are subdivided into three groups: play (in which the rules are established by the player) and ritual (in which the rules are given by an authority) are two extremes between which games, sports and theater form the third, intermediate group of 'middle terms'. "In the middle terms the rules [the space, the conventions, the play (script), the director (of a theater play)] exist as [concentric] frames: some rules say what *must* be done and others what *must not* be done. Between these frames there is freedom" (37). But "the frames are not static—even within a single production" (38). The third and last part of the article (39–53) is about "models of play construction", and thus not related to ritual, but purely to theater. [JS]

References: F. Fergusson, J.E. Harrison, G. Murray, F.M. Cornford, J.G. Frazer, P.W. Pickard-Cambridge.
Key-words: def, myt, PMC, tha, frm, SPC, TIM.

Schechner, Richard, 1970, 'Actuals. A Look Into Performance Theory', in: Alan Cheuse & Richard Koffler (eds), *The Rarer Action. Essays in Honor of Francis Fergusson*, New Brunswick (NJ): Rutgers University Press (ISBN 8135–0670–0) 97–135.
Reprinted in: *Essays on Performance Theory, 1970–1976*; New York: Drama Book Specialists 1977 (*), 3–35 and in: *Performance Theory. Revised and Expanded Edition*; New York, London: Routledge 1988 (*), 35–67.

This article opens with a description of a ritual combat among the Tiwi from North Australia (97–98), then discusses Plato's and Aristotle's concept of art as mimetic, i.e. as coming after the event it depicts (99–100), moves on to signal a renewed interest in 'primitive' men and cultures in order to present four characteristic "yearnings which have triggered not only an interest in primitive peoples but artistic movements that concretize that interest" (101), namely: "(1) *Wholeness....* (2) *Process. Organic Growth....* (3) *Concreteness....* (4) *Religious/Transcendental Experience*" (101–102). The author then introduces the terms 'actuals' (102) and 'actualizing' (103) without precisely defining them, but we can think of 'actuals' as particularly realistic performances, such as rituals, and 'actualizing' (which he compares with Eliade's concept of 'reactualizing') clearly is the activity of 'doing' an 'actual'. "Understanding actualization means understanding both the creative condition and the artwork, the actual. Among primitive peoples the creative condition is identical with trances, dances, ecstasies; in short, shamanism" (103). This leads to descriptions of shamanism (103–105), from which he moves to a model of experience. Experience "is not segregated on hierarchical planes. It is not that everything is the same, but that all things are part of one wholeness and that among things unlimited exchanges and transformations are possible" (106). It is "here and now but other-worldly" (106). Then follow two more examples of rituals: the "puberty initiation of eastern Australia called a *bora*" and "a cycle called the *hevehe* [with] the Elema of New Guinea" (107). In the context of the *hevehe*, he notes: "The spirit moves only when a man is in the mask. Conversely a man dances well only when he is moved by the spirit. Two autonomous, symbiotic existences interpenetrate each other" (109). "The *hevehe* cycle mixes the ceremonial and the personal without diluting or blending either. A mask dances because it is alive. A man dances because he is animated by the mask" (112). "...the apparently opposite actuals of Australia and New Guinea are founded on the same belief in multiple, valid, equivalent, and reciprocating realities. The actuals are here and now, efficacious, and irrevocable" (113). Against the background of these examples, the author now proposes that "an actual has five basic elements, and each is found both in our own actuals and those of primitive peoples: (1) *organic growth*, something happens *here and now*; (2) *consequential, irremediable*, and *irrevocable* acts, exchanges, or situations; (3) *contest*, something is *at stake* for the performers and often for the spectators; (4) *initiation*, a *change in status* for participants; (5) space is used *concretely* and *organically*" (114–115). The remainder of the essay is devoted to the discussion of each of these five elements. They are illustrated by examples from experimental theater performances (1. The Living Theatre's *Paradise now*; 2. Ralph Ortiz's *The Sky Is Falling*; 3. *Dionysus in 69*; 4. *The Constant Prince*; 5. The Performance Group's

Makbeth [1969]). The last element is also illustrated with the "Fiji initiation called *nanda*" (125–128). At the last pages (130–132), the author returns to his model of experience, which "shows each element as different dimensions of the same plane" (130) and now adds a second version to it, which is adapted to the theater. It shows that in the experimental theater context, performers, text/action, director, time, space, and audience all interact with each other. He ends: "Mimetic theater has given us great masterpieces. Mimetic acting is a major tradition. There are other kinds of performances, however. Of these, 'actuals' relate practices among primitive 'whole-seeking' peoples and parts of our own population, particularly the young" (132). [JS]

References: Plato, Aristotle, **M. Eliade** (+), J. Rothenberg, A. Lommel, E. Cassirer, **F.E. Williams** (+).
Examples: The Tiwi (North Australia), Shamanism, the *bora* (eastern Australia), the *hevehe* (Elema, New Guinea), the *nanda* (Fiji), experimental theatre.
Key-words: aes, PMC, tha, mim, emo, spc, tim, dnc.

Schechner, Richard, 1973, 'Drama, Script, Theatre, and Performance', *The Drama Review* 17:5–36.
Revised version in: *Essays on Performance Theory, 1970–1976*; New York: Drama Book Specialists 1977 (*), 36–62. The abstract is based on this version.

In the first part (36–48) of this article, the author first looks back to Paleolithic times in order to see how ritual and theater developed from then on, to the Greeks, the Renaissance, and finally modernity. His conclusion is that only in the Renaissance was the relation between action and text reversed. Formerly, the action was the central issue, and the script was used as a tool to help transmit how the action had to be done. But from the Renaissance onwards, the text gets prime importance, and the action is interpretation of the script. After contemplating on definition issues (38), he defines four terms: drama, script, theater, and performance. The drama is the central issue (idea, plot) transmitted from the author to the performers in the form of a more specific script. The performers then convert the script into an even more concrete theater production, which is realized in a number of actual performances (together with an audience). "Drama is the domain of the author, composer, scenarist; script is the domain of the teacher, guru, shaman, master; theatre is the domain of the performers; performance is the domain of the audience. Clearly, in many situations, the author is also the guru and the performer; in some situations the performer is also the audience" (39). Then follows an excursus on theatrical productions (40–43) and some examples, including ethnographic ones: Bali (43–44), New Guinea (45), and Sri Lanka (46–48). These serve to illustrate that there exist cases where one of the four concepts is absent, thus making clear what the differences between them are. In the second part (49–61), the author elaborates on the relation between performance, ritual, and play, arguing again from the Paleolithic, ethological evolutionary perspective. "Some animals, such as bees and ants, are rich in ritualized behavior but absolutely bereft of play. No species that I know of plays without also having a wide repertory of ritual behavior. But it is only in the primates that play and ritual coincide, mix, combine; it is only in man and closely related species that the aesthetic sense is consciously developed. The only theory of aesthetics that I can tolerate is one in which aesthetics is considered a specific coordination of play and ritual" (52–53). He then elaborates on the relation between play and hunting behavior, both being performances. "Hunting is inherently, not metaphorically, theatrical/dramatic" (56). He concludes by reformulating "from a structural basis what I previously adduced from prehistory" (57). Throughout the paper, statements are sometimes made concerning framing or keying, although without reference to either Bateson or Goffman or these technical terms (39, 48, 53, 56–57, 58). But on these last pages it is especially the fuzziness of the borders between the categories concerned that is stressed: "A cat with a captured mouse is 'playing' with its prey; it is also completing the hunting process. Chimps will convert play behavior into serious behavior and back again, so that a play chase suddenly erupts into a fight, the fight is resolved by gestures of dominance and submission, this 'contract' is 'ratified' by mutual grooming and soon enough there is another playful chase. In humans, the situation is the most complicated.... when the seriousness is taken away from the play, the playing grows sloppy and dull, not fun" (58). Indeed, "playful activity constantly generates rules.... In other words..., all play is 'scripted'" (58). He concludes: "It is my belief that performance and theatre are universal, but that drama is not. I think that drama may develop independently of performance and theatre, as a special instance of performance and theatre. (All performance events have 'scripts'.)" (60). [JS]

References: K.Z. Lorenz, N. Tinbergen, J.S. Huxley, J. Huizinga.
Examples: Bali, New Guinea, Sri Lanka.
Key-words: PMC, tha, pr1, pr2, mim, cmp, aes, ETH, pow, def, dyn, frm.

Schechner, Richard, 1974, 'From Ritual to Theatre and Back. The Structure/Process of the Efficacy-Entertainment Dyad', *Educational Theatre Journal* 26:455–480.
Revised version in: *Essays on Performance Theory, 1970–1976*; New York: Drama Book Specialists 1977 (*), 63–98 and in: *Performance Theory. Revised and Expanded Edition*; New York, London: Routledge 1988 (*), 106–152.

In the first section of this article (455–460), the author describes the *kaiko* celebration of the Tsembaga of Highlands New Guinea, based on Rappaport 1968 (*), and comments on it: "The performance is a transformation of combat techniques into entertainment.... But the Tsembaga dance is a dance, and clearly so to every one present at it" (456). "The *kaiko* entertainments are a ritual display, not simply a doing but *a showing of a doing*. Furthermore, this showing is both actual (= the trading and giving of goods resulting in a new imbalance) and symbolic (= the reaffirmation of alliances made concrete in the debtor-creditor relationship). The entertainment itself is a vehicle for debtors and creditors to exchange places; it is also the occasion for a market; and it is fun" (456–457). There follow comments on theater and a short description of the *Engwura* cycle of the Arunta of Australia, based on Spencer & Gillen's report. In the second section (461–471), the author starts with a description of a ritual that he himself observed in 1972 at Kurumugl in the Eastern Highlands of New Guinea, indicating its difference from the *kaiko* of the Tsembaga as follows: "...the ritual [*kaiko*] functions without the Tsembaga being explicitly aware of its function;...there are neither performance theorists nor critics among the Tsembaga. At Kurumugl the people know what the ritual does and why it was established—to inhibit warfare among feuding groups. The ritual at Kurumugl is already traveling along the continuum toward theatre in the modern sense. Knowing what the ritual does is a very important step in the development of theatre from ritual" (461). And that development is what he wants to trace. Analyzing the Kurumugl example, he concludes: "In the New Guinea Highlands, at first under the pressure of the colonial police, later under its own momentum, warfare is transformed into dancing. As [certain, mentioned] activities grow in importance, entertainment as such takes over from efficacy as the reason for the performance. It is not only that creditors and debtors need to exchange roles, but also that people want to show off; it is not only to get results that the dances are staged, but also because people like dancing for its own sake. Efficacy and entertainment are opposed to each other, but they form a binary system, a continuum" (467). "The basic opposition is between efficacy and entertainment, not between ritual and theatre.... No performance is pure efficacy or pure entertainment. The matter is complicated because one can look at specific performances from several vantages: changing perspective changes classification" (468). The third section (471–480) starts with a summary of the previous two: "(1) in some social settings ritual performances are part of ecosystems and mediate political relations, group hierarchy, and economics; (2) in other settings ritual performances begin to take on qualities of show business; (3) there is a dialectical-dyadic continuum linking efficacy to entertainment—both are present in all performances, but in each performance one or the other is dominant; (4) in different societies, at different times, either efficacy or entertainment dominates, the two being in a braided relationship to each other" (471). Then follows a reference to a twelfth-century interpretation of the Mass as a theatrical performance (471), but "[b]ecause of its all-inclusive hold on its congregation the Mass was not theatre in the classical or modern sense. Theatre comes into existence when a separation occurs between audience and performers.... The audience is free to attend or stay away—and if it stays away it is the theatre that suffers, not the would-be audience. In ritual, staying away means rejecting the congregation—or being rejected by it...To put it another way: ritual is an event upon which its participants depend; theatre is an event which depends on its participants" (473). Then follows the example of the dance of the Mudmen, performed as a tourist entertainment three times a week in Asaro, a village about seventy miles east of Kurumugl. "The people of Asaro don't know what their dance is any more. Surely it's not to frighten enemies—it attracts tourists. It has no relationship to the spirits of the dead who appear only before dawn, and the tourists come a little after midday.... In short, the dance will approach those Western standards of entertainment represented by the tastes of the audience, and the benefits will rise accordingly. Presently, the Asaroans perform a traditional ritual emptied of its efficacy but not yet regarded as a theatrical entertainment" (474). This is followed by brief mention of some more examples of rituals that are performed for tourists (the Grassmen of Kenetisarobe), both in a version for tourists and one for insiders (the Ketchak in Bali), or partly open to tourists and partly for insiders only (the Abuang in Bali) (474–475). "Surely the tourist trade has influenced so-called 'genuine' performances in Bali and elsewhere.... But even traditional performances vary greatly from generation to generation—an oral tradition is flexible, able to absorb many personal variations within set parameters" (475). The author now moves to examples of rituals performed on stage in America: whirling dervishes from Turkey and "Shingon Buddhist monks...with 'ceremonies, music, and epics of ancient Japan'" (479). His conclusion is that "[a]ny ritual can be lifted from its original setting and performed as theatre—just as any everyday event can be. This is possible because context, not fundamental structure, distinguishes ritual, entertainment, and ordinary life from each other. The differences among them arise from the agreement (conscious or unexpressed) between performers and spectators" (479). The opposite has been tried: a "move from theatre to ritual marks Grotowski's work and that of the Living Theatre. But the rituals created were unstable because they were not attached to actual social structures outside theatre" (480). The last section (480–481) shortly describes the (then) most recent production of The Performance Group: Brecht's *Mother Courage*. [JS]

References: R.A. Rappaport, B. Spencer & F.J. Gillen, K.Z. Lorenz, I. Eibl-Eibesfeldt.
Examples: The *kaiko* celebration of the Tsembaga and a ritual in **Kurumugl**, both in the Highlands New Guinea; the *Engwura* cycle of the Arunta of Australia; the Mass; the dance of the Mudmen in Asaro, New Guinea; the Grassmen of Kenetisarobe, New Guinea; the Ketchak and the Abuang in Bali.
Key-words: aes, PMC, THA, frm, EFF, par, rfl, ecl, DYN, dnc.

Schechner, Richard, 1977, *Essays on Performance Theory, 1970–1976*; New York: Drama Book Specialists (ISBN 0–910482–81–0 / 0–910482–88–8 (p)) (x + 212) (with bibliography).
Revised edition: Routledge, New York 1988 (*).

From the Introduction: "Performance is a very inclusive notion of action; theatre is only one node on a continuum that reaches from ritualization in animal behavior (including humans) through performances in everyday life—greetings, displays of emotion, family scenes and so on—to rites, ceremonies and performances: large-scale theatrical events" (1). The "deep structures [of theatre] include preparations for performance both on the part of the performers (training, rehearsal, preparations immediately before going on) and spectators (deciding to attend, dressing, going, settling in, waiting) and what happens after a performance. These cooling off procedures are less studied but very important. They include spreading the news of the performance, evaluating it (getting it 'into' the system of ordinary life), putting the space to rest, returning the performers to ordinary life" (1–2). "Because the theatre is subjunctive, liminal, dangerous, duplicitous it must be hedged in with conventions: means of making the place and the event safe. In safe precincts at safe times actions can be carried to extremes, even for fun" (2).

Contents: "Actuals. A Look into Performance Theory" (1970) (3–35) (*); "Drama, Script, Theatre and Performance" (Revised version of the 1973 edition) (36–62) (*); "From Ritual to Theatre and Back. The Structure / Process of the Efficacy-Entertainment Dyad" (revised version of the 1974 edition) (63–98) (*); [with Cynthia Mintz]: "Kinesics and Performance" (1973) (99–107); "Towards a Poetics of Performance" (revised version of a lecture presented in 1975) (108–139); "Selective Inattention" (1976) (140–156); "Ethology and Theatre" (first published here) (157–201). [JS]

Key-words: PMC, tha, str, frm, par, rfl.

Schechner, Richard, 1981, 'Performers and Spectators Transported and Transformed', *The Kenyon Review* 3:83–113.

The author first sketches the breadth of the concept 'performance' and then states: "performance activities are fundamentally processual: there will always be a certain proportion of them in the process of transformation, categorically undefinable. But all performances... share at least one underlying quality. Performance behavior isn't free and easy. Performance behavior is known and/or practiced behavior... either rehearsed, previously known, learned by osmosis since early childhood, revealed during the performance by masters, guides, gurus, or elders, or generated by rules that govern the outcomes as in improvisatory theater or sports" (84). He then discusses the principally dynamic character of performances within longer traditions: "the performance process is a continuous rejecting and replacing" (85–86). Then a first example is given: Quesalid, the Kwakiutl who wanted to expose the shamans and ended up being himself a successful one. "Quesalid... was transformed into what he had set out to expose" (87). The second example is that of an actor who played the role of Narad-muni at the Ramlila of Ramnagar, India, for many years. Over the years, he identified himself, and was identified by others, more and more with the sage he played. "This man is not Narad-muni, but also he is not not Narad-muni" (88). These are examples of slow transformation processes caused by the performances in which these people take part. The author relates this process to what Csikszentmihalyi calls "flow" (89–90). However, "[a]cting, in most cases, is the art of temporary transformation: not only the journey out but also the return. Quesalid and Narad both, over the long run, gave in to their roles...And some roles effect a swift and permanent transformation, as in initiation rites and other 'rites of passage'" (90). That brings him to the second section of his paper (91–97), which starts with a definition of the two prototypes: "I call performances where performers are changed 'transformations' and those where performers are returned to their starting places 'transportations'" (91). But long series of transportations may cause a transformation, as was shown by the first two examples. As an example of a transformation performance, he now relates an initiation ritual in Papua-New Guinea. This gives him the opportunity to reflect on the relation between the candidate(s) who are transformed and the other performers who are transported: "People are accustomed to calling transportation performances 'theater' and transformation performances 'ritual'. But this neat separation doesn't hold up. Mostly the two kinds of performances coexist in the same event.... Those who no longer change...effect the changes wrought in the transformation" (94). And then the author switches to the analysis of the roles of the audiences and their interaction with those who are transported or transformed: "Spectators at transformation performances usually have a stake in seeing that the performance succeeds.... Thus in transformation performances the attention of the transported and the spectators converges on the transformed. This convergence of attention, and direct stake in the performance, is why so many transformation performances use audience participation" (95–96). This section concludes with the enumeration of "the four variables operating in every performance: 1) whether the performance is efficacious,...or whether it is fictive...; 2) the status of the roles within a performance; 3) the status of the persons playing the roles...And, finally, 4) the quality of the performance measured by the mastery performers have over whatever skills are demanded" (97). The last section (97–113) gives four more examples to illustrate the theory previously outlined and to elaborate upon it. The examples are: Athenian theatre in the fifth century BC, Sanskrit drama and "much contemporary Indian theater", Japanese Noh, and modern American theater. In the first of these examples, it is the performers (actors and authors) who are transformed (into losers and a winner) while being watched by the spectators and judges. In the second example, there is only transportation: performers and spectators cooperate in perfect harmony. Here a "successful performance is one where both the levels of skill (preparers) and understanding (partakers) are high and equal" (103). This is also the case in Noh, but here, "unless the spectators know what's going on through specific instruction in Noh the *hana* [= flower, that what the performance should produce, JS] is missing.... This is different from the Indian situation where mutuality but not special knowledge is required.... the Noh spectator must become a *connoisseur* or he will fail the performance" (109). As opposed to this, what EuroAmerican theater "asks of its audience is not special knowledge but responsivity. The historic sources of this theatre are not so much religious ritual or initiatory ordeals but popular entertainments" (109–110). Here the "performer is transported while individual spectators experience their own reactions at the level of private responses.... There is no collective work set out for the audience to do or participate in" (110). "In each of the others the audience has a definite collective role to play.... The only thing close to this kind of celebratory play/work in our culture is what fans do at football, baseball, boxing, or other sports events" (111). [JS]

Reference: M. Csikszentmihalyi.
Examples: Quesalid, the Kwakiutl shaman; Narad-muni at the Ramlila of Ramnagar, India; an initiation ritual in Papua-New Guinea; Athenian theatre in the fifth century BC; Sanskrit drama and "much contemporary Indian theater"; Japanese Noh; and modern American theatre.
Key-words: PMC, THA, pr1, pr2, mim, cmp, aes, agn, eff, emo, PAR, DYN, def, soc.

Schechner, Richard, 1982, 'Collective Reflexivity. Restoration of Behavior', in: Jay Ruby (ed.), *A Crack in the Mirror. Reflexive Perspectives in Anthropology*, Philadelphia: University of Pennsylvania Press (ISBN 0–8122–7815–1) 39–81.

This essay explores the notion of 'restored behavior', which is introduced in the following terms: "Restored behavior is living behavior treated as a film editor treats strips of film. These strips can be rearranged, reconstructed; they are independent of the causal systems (psychological, social, technological) that brought them into existence: they achieve a life of their own" (39). "Restored behavior is used in all kinds of performances from shamanism, exorcism, and trance to ritual theatre and aesthetic theatre, from initiation rites to liminal social dramas, from psychoanalysis to newer therapies...In fact, the use of restored behavior is the main characteristic of performance. The practitioners of all these arts, rites, and healings assume that some sort of behavior—organized sequences of events, scripted actions, known texts, scored movies, strips—exists separately from the performers" (40). "Restored behavior is symbolic and reflexive...Performance means: never for the first time" (40). The author distinguishes between three "performative systems" (41–47), and this "model has implications for a unified theory of ritual" (46). a) The first system consists of an I that becomes "someone else, or myself in another state of being" (41). This "repetition of individual or social facts in the future indicative" corresponds to "ritual in the ethological sense" (46). b) The form found in many traditional performances consists of the "repetition of a given or traditional performance" and corresponds to "ritual in the social and religious sense", but "also those aesthetic performances that share in a necessity of unchangeability" (46). c) The third system is "performance based in a previous performance", e.g. "theater in which the mise-en-scene [sic] is developed during rehearsals", "rituals that enact or commemorate myth or folklore", "ethnographic films", and "neoclassical or ancient traditional forms 'recovered' for modern audiences" (43). "What is recalled are earlier performances: history not being what happened but what is encoded and transmitted. Performance is...behavior itself and carries with it a kernel of originality, making it the subject for further interpretation, the source of further history. That is why ritual is so much more powerful than myth. Ritual lives—is performed—or it isn't, while myths die and lie around libraries" (43). Here, the "performance itself is the text" (46), and the corresponding rehearsals are "doubly reflexive" (46). "Rituals disguise themselves as restorations of actual events when, in fact, they are restorations of earlier rituals" (46). This form of performance is "ritual in the symbolic sense" (46). Particular performances can combine or be between different modes. "As performances they are played in the indicative mood, but as performances of something they are in the subjunctive mood. The difference between animal ritual and human ritual is that animals are always performing what they are, while humans almost always perform what they are not" (47). In the subsequent sections, the author extensively discusses and compares the film on the *agnicayana* made by Staal and Gardner (47–53), the reinvention of Indian dance called Bharatanatyam (47–55), and the 'restored village' theme parks in North America (56–65). "The theory explaining all this will come from theater specialists or from social scientists learned in theater...Preparing to do theater includes either memorizing a score of gestures, sounds, and movements and/or achieving a mood where apparently 'external' gestures, sounds and movements 'take over' the performer as in trance. This basic theatrical process is universal. Everywhere, behavior that is other is transformed into the performer's own; alienated or objectified parts of the performer's self—either his private self or his social self—are reintegrated and shown publicly in a total display. The process has two parts and a conclusion" (65). Here an analogy is drawn with the three stages of 'the ritual process', leading the author to assume: "Theater is an 'artificial species' of ritual" (66). Thereafter, the author discusses workshop-rehearsals, distinguishing between two basic methods (66–74). "The rehearsal process is a basic machine for the restoration of behavior. It is no accident that this process is the same in theater as it is in ritual" (74). In the following section, the author sketches "a theory that includes the ontogenesis of individuals, the social action of ritual, and the symbolic, even fictive, action of art. Clearly these overlap: their underlying process is identical. A performance 'takes place' in the 'not me... not not me' between performers; between performers and script; between performers, script, and environment; between performers, script, environment, and audience" (76). In the final section, the author once again discusses the film by Staal and Gardner and problems of reflexivity in fieldwork (77–81). [MS]

References: F. Staal (–), C. Geertz (+), E. Goffman (+/–), B. Myerhoff, R.A. Rappaport (+), **V.W. Turner** (+), D.W. Winnicott (+).
Examples: "The Fire Altar" (film by Staal and Gardner), Bharatanatyam, theme parks with restored villages, a ritual from the Sepik River area of Papua New Guineas, modern theatre.
Key-words: PMC, RFL, eth, myt, aut, gst, emo, pr2, aut, par, frm.

Schechner, Richard, 1987, 'The Future of Ritual', *Journal of Ritual Studies* 1.1:5–33.

The aim of this article is to study violence in rituals—in human as well as animal rituals—and to show the relatedness of theater and ritual. The author argues that ritual and theater resemble each other and that violence plays a prominent role in both. This violence is at the same time sexual. "The violence of 'real life' is anything but redemptive. In order to tolerate it at all humans are constantly 'making something out' of quotidian violence" (10). One of the main functions of ritual is, according to the author, to deal with crises. The repetitive, rhythmic, exaggerated, concentrated, simplified, and spectacle qualities of rituals enable the stimulation of the brain with opium-like endorphins, such that the relief of individual and collective anxieties is achieved. Further, the author points out, following Girard, that ritual sublimates violence. Accordingly, "[r]itual process permeates the social, religious and aesthetic life of all cultures. The same may be said of theater. Theater and ritual comprise a braided twin-system. Certain cultures, historical periods and individual genres emphasize the one or the other.... What distinguishes the one from the other in any given performance is context, including what the audience expects, who the sponsoring agents are and what the occasion for the performance is" (16). The author concludes his article by interpreting the human liminality: "Human liminality exists betwixt and between the ethological, the neurological, and the social. In this way people elaborate their conceptual-artistic possibilities. These artful elaborations have been decisive in human history since paleolithic times. They appear always to have been fundamentally erotic and violent" (30). [JK]

References: S. Freud, A. van Gennep, R. Girard, V.W. Turner.
Key-words: ETH, pmc, THA, pow, psy, soc.

Schechner, Richard, 1988a, *Performance Theory. Revised and Expanded Edition*; London, New York: Routledge (ISBN 0-415-90092-1 / 0-415-90093-x) (xv + 304) (with index and bibliography).

First published as *Essays on Performance Theory, 1970–1976*; New York: Drama Book Specialists. (1977) (*) (x + 212).
New Edition 2003, edited and including a new essay "Rasaesthetics" (333–367).

In the "Author's note", it is stated: "The differences between this edition of *Performance Theory* and the one published in 1977 are considerable. One old essay and one new one are added to the collection: 'Approaches' (1966) and 'Magnitudes of Performance' (1987). One essay, 'Kinesis and Performance' has been dropped. I've balanced necessary revisions with my wish to preserve the trajectory of my thinking about performance over the more than twenty years these essays span (1966–1987)" (ix). In the "Introduction. The Fan and the Web" ([xii]–xv), the author states: "This isn't a potluck book. The essays are organized around a system that can be configured as both a fan and a web" (xiii). The fan-model described a continuum of performance ("an inclusive term") reaching from the ritualization of animals, through art-making process, play, performance in everyday life, sports, entertainments, eruption and revolution of crisis, and shamanism to rites and ceremonies and

performances of great magnitude. "The web is the same system seen more dynamically. Instead of being spread out along a continuum, each node interacts with the others" (xiii). The author mentions 9 'nodes': 1) prehistoric shamanism and rites, 2) historic shamanism and rites, 3) origins of theater in Eurasia, Africa, the Pacific, and Asia, 4) origins of European theater, 5) contemporary environmental theater, 6) dialogic and body-oriented psychotherapies, 7) ethological studies of theater, 8) performance in everyday life, and 9) play and crisis behavior. "Connections among items 1 through 4 can be investigated historically and may be linked to performances around the world from Paleolithic times onward. Connections among items 6 through 9 reveal 'deep structures' of performance" (xiii). Both models (fan and web) are also represented in graphical form. Furthermore, the author states: "My method is similar to that of the Aborigines who credit dreams with a reality as powerful and important as events experienced while awake. Or is it the other way round? I know that analyses could be made separating out planes of reality; but sometimes—especially in the theater—it is necessary to live as if 'as if' = 'is'" (xiii).
Contents: 1. "Approaches" (1–34); 2. "Actuals" (35–67) (*); 3. "Drama, Script, Theatre, and Performance" (68–105) (*); 4. "From Ritual to Theatre and Back. The Efficacy-Entertainment Braid" (106–152) (*); 5. "Towards a Poetics of Performance" (153–186); 6. "Selective Inattention" (187–206); 7. "Ethology and Theatre" (207–250); 8. "Magnitudes of Performance" (251–288) (*). [MS]

Reviews: T. Whittock *BJA* 29.4 (1989) 378 f; E. Dissayanake *Man* 24.4 (1989) 693; M.J. Sidnell *MD* 34.4 (1991) 569 f.
Key-words: eth, PMC, tha, EFF.

Schechner, Richard, 1988b, 'Playing', *Play and Culture* 1:3–19.

This article deals with "the various processes of playing" in order to "shift the emphasis in play studies away from concentration on the genres of play" (3). After addressing the problem in defining play, the author argues that this problem "is not intractable if 'play acts' are measured against six templates: structure, process, experience, function, ideology and frame" (4). According to him: "Play acts, players, spectators, and observers can be independently analyzed in terms of each of these templates" (5). The author has not the ambition to develop a unified theory of play but instead he analyzes "three key aspects: multiple realities, dark play, and generating performances" (5). The first aspect is discussed in "Maya-Lila. Playing's Multiple Realities" (6–12), here, he contrasts the differences between the Western and Indian concepts of play and reality. "Maya-lila is fundamentally a performative-creative act of continuous playing where ultimate positivist distinctions between true and false, real and unreal, cannot be made" (7). In the second section (12–14), the author describes instances of what he calls 'dark play': "Dark play may be conscious playing, but it can also be playing in the dark when some or even all of the players don't know they are playing. Dark play occurs when contradictory realities coexist, each seemingly capable to challenge the other out..." (5). Dark play "(a) is physically risky, (b) involves intentional confusion or concealment of the frame 'this is play', (c) may continue actions from early childhood, (d) only occasionally demands make-believe, (e) plays out alternative selves" (14). The third aspect, "Generating Performances" (15–16), does not concern "finished performances of theatre, dance, sports, rituals and popular entertainments" but "focus on some aspects of the processes for generating performances" (15). The theme that connects dark play, Western ideas of play, and the maya-lila theory is 'provisionality', that is, "the unsteadiness, slipperiness, porosity, unreliability, and ontological riskiness of the realities projected or created by playing" (15). In his "Conclusions" (16–18), the author argues "Playing is a creative destabilizing action that frequently does not declare its existence, even less its intentions" (16). According to him "it's much too limiting, too tight, too certain to build play theories around notions of play genres, identifiable 'things'.... presently we need to stop looking so hard at play, or play genres, and investigate *playing*, the ongoing underlying process of off-balancing, loosening, bending, twisting, reconfiguring, and transforming—the permeating, eruptive/disruptive energy and mood below, behind, and to the sides of focused attention" (18). [JK]

References: G. Bateson, M. Czikszentmihalyi, D. Handelman (–), J. Huizinga, **V.W. Turner** (+).
Key-words: cpr, frm, PMC.

Schechner, Richard, 1988c, 'Victor Turner's Last Adventure', in: Victor W. Turner (ed.), *The Anthropology of Performance*, (Performance Studies Series 4), New York: PAJ Publications (A Division of Performing Arts Journal) (ISBN 1–55554–000–7 / 1–55554–001–5 (p)) (*) 7–20.

The author argues that ritual "has been so variously defined—as concept, praxis, process, ideology, yearning, religious experience, function—that it means very little because it can mean too much.

Reviewing some of the literature about ritual... shows that ritual can be looked at [in] five different ways: 1) as part of the development of organisms... 2) as structure... 3) as performance process... 4) as experience... 5) as a set of operations in human social and religious life" (10). He concentrates "on what was preoccupying Turner at the moment of his sudden death" (8). In particular, he comments on the final essay of the collection ("Body, Brain, and Culture") in which Turner had "laid out his evolutionary approach to ritual" (10) and taken up ideas from ethology, sociobiology, and biostructuralism. He discusses Turner's idea of genetic 'coadaptation' and raises some doubts on his approach: "I am uncomfortable with his attempt to relocate and thereby resolve the 'problems' of ritual action in the workings of evolution, or, more specifically, the human brain" (16). "Turner's coadaptive compromise seems over-generously Christian" (17). "I am saying what I think Turner might have been coming to. He realized that an organ of contemplation—even in the human brain—is not capable of absolute self-examination. The brain will go crazy (or mystically fuzzy) dealing with too many layers of metatextural reflexivity. But the brain might either create an exterior organ of thought or actively seek to come into contact with non-human others with whom it could communicate. Many experiments point in these directions. And it's not only with apes and dolphins that we want to talk. It would seem that if humans are to survive the next step is communication with some genuinely thoughtful other" (19). [MS]

Reference: V.W. Turner.
Key-words: eth, rfl.

Schechner, Richard, 1991, 'Magnitudes of Performance', in: Richard Schechner & Willa Appel (eds), *By Means of Performance. Intercultural Studies of Theatre and Ritual*, Cambridge etc.: Cambridge University Press (ISBN 0–521–32608–7 / 0–521–33915–4 (p)) 19–49.

Slightly revised version of that, first published in R. Schechner: *Performance Theory. Revised and Expanded Edition*, London, New York 1988a (*), 251–288. The original version of 1988 was reprinted in: *Performance Theory, Revised and Expanded Edition. With a New Preface by the Author*, London, New York: Routledge 2003, 290–332. Page numbers refer to the editions of (1988 / 1991 / 2003). Abstract based on the 1991 version.

This article opens with the assertion that "at the descriptive level there is no detail of performance that occurs everywhere under all circumstances. Nor is it easy to specify limitations on what is, or could be treated as, performance" (251 / 19 / 290). Then a table is presented that plots events against time and space, serving to demonstrate how wide the field of performances is. The author then takes the position that, "caveats taken, there are two meanings of 'ritual' that can be applied to the study of performance, the ethological and the neurological" (–/ 24 /–). The first section of the article ("A figure for all genres", 251–257 / 19–25 / 290–296) closes with the statement: "My aim is to indicate what the magnitudes of performances are and where each magnitude of performance takes place" (257 / 25 / 296). The second section ("Insiders-Outsiders", 257–261 / 25–28 / 296–301) discusses the insider-outsider opposition: the differences between performers and audiences. "These differences are not just exercises in the 'emic/etic' pitfalls of fieldwork. The great big gap between what a performance is to people inside from what it is to people outside conditions all the thinking about performance" (260 / 27 / 300). The author then distinguishes between "professional performers" and "Goffman performers". But "there are actually two kinds of Goffman performers: the ones who conceal, as conmen do; and the ones who don't know they are performing. Of this second type there are two subdivisions: ordinary people playing their 'life roles'... and those whose particular actions have been framed as a performance [by others]" (260–261 / 28 / 300). In the third section ("Birdwhistell and Ekman", 261–265 / 28–32 / 301–306), the author compares the work of Ray Birdwhistell and Paul Ekman. Birdwhistell studied facial gestures ('kinemes'), and found that these are culture-specific. Ekman showed that the expression by actors of six basic emotions elicited emotion-specific activity in the autonomic nervous system (ANS). He did two experiments. In the first, the actors "were told precisely which muscles to contract... constructing facial prototypes of emotion muscle by muscle, in the other, subjects were asked to experience each of the six emotions by reliving a past emotional experience for 30 seconds" (263 / 30 / 303). "What is truly surprising about Ekman's experiment is not that emotional recall works, but that... mechanical acting worked better than getting the actor to feel" (264 / 31 / 305). This suggests that "deep acting" (body language) "exists at the ANS level" and therefore that "acting may engage the old-mammalian and reptilian brains" (265 / 31 / 305). These experiments lead to four important conclusions: 1) There exists a "universal language" of "basic emotions". 2) "This 'language of emotions' is nonverbal and consists of facial displays, vocal cries, body postures (freezes) and movements (stamping, rushing, crouching). 3) There is a corresponding universal system in nerve and brain process—and this system probably underlies what anthropologists have called ritual. 4. "The culture-specific kinemes that Birdwhistell finds are built on top of the 'universal language of emotions'" (265 / 31–32 / 306–306). This leads the author to the conclusion, that "performances 'take place' all along the continuum from brain events to public events of great spatial and temporal magnitude" (265 / 32 / 306). The next section ("The Natyasastra", 266–274 / 32–36 / 306–315) presents the Natyasastra and later Indian texts that describe nine basic emotions and how performers should express them. These texts "insist on what Ekman's experiments show:...feelings can lead to stage action while the practice of specific stage exercises can arouse feelings in the actor. In a definable way the performer can be moved by her/his own performance.... [Acting] is not only the means by which the audience gets the performance but also the way in which the actors get it—the 'it' being not only gestures but feelings as well" (270 / 35 / 312–314). The next section ("Lying and the performer's three halves", 274–275 / 37–38 / 315–317) analyzes the phenomenon of lying. This leads to the conclusion that there are in a performer not only two 'persons' involved: the acting one and the feeling one, but even a third: the "outside observing and to some degree controlling" one. In the next section ("Brain lateralization and performance", 275–278 / 38–41 / 318–321), this leads to the conclusion that it is precisely the presence of this consciously controlling 'I' that distinguishes "between performances that are so only contextually and those that the performer is consciously of manufacturing" (275–276 / 38 / 318). The final section ("Performativity, theatricality, and narrativity", 278–283 / 41–45 / 321–327) gives the "seven 'performance magnitudes' or levels": 1) Brain event, 2) Microbit, 3) Bit, 4) Sign, 5) Scene, 6) Drama, and 7) Macrodrama (282 / 44 / 325–326). Higher levels are always built out of the components from one of the lower levels. Rituals are to be located at level 6, and Victor Turner's "social dramas" at level 7. "Performance magnitude means not only size and duration but also extension across cultural boundaries and penetration to the deepest strata of historical, personal, and neurological experience" (283 / 45 / 327). [JS]

References: R. Birdwhistell, P. Ekman, E. Goffman.
Key-words: com, PMC, tha, pr1, pr2, emb, cmp, aes, ETH, frm, EMO, par, gst, rfl, spc, tim, dyn, def, soc, psy.

Schechner, Richard, 1993, *The Future of Ritual. Writings on Culture and Performance*; London, New York: Routledge (ISBN 0–415–04689–0 / 0–415–04690–4 (p)) (x + 283) (with index).

Contents: 1. "Introduction. Jayaganesh and the Avant-Garde" (1–23); 2. "Playing" (24–44) (*); 3. "The Street is the Stage" (45–93); 4. "Waehma, Space, Time, Identity, and Theatre at New Pascua Arizona" (94–130); 5. "Striding Through the Cosmos. Movement, Belief, Politics, and Place in the Ramlila of Ramnagar" (131–183); 6. "Wayang Kulit in the Colonial Margin" (184–227); 7. "The Future of Ritual" (228–265) (*). [JS/JK]

Reviews: O. Najera-Ramirez *AA* 96.2 (1994) 466; R. Martin *AH* 20.1 (1995) 80 f; P. Greenhill *JRS* 9.1 (1995) 136–138; S.-Y. Chin *RA* 24.3 (1995) 177–185.
Key-words: PMC, idn, spc, tim.

Schechner, Richard, 1994, 'Ritual and Performance', in: Tim Ingold (ed.), *Companion Encyclopedia of Anthropology*, London, New York: Routledge (ISBN 0–415–02137–5 / 0–415–16421–4 (p)) 613–647.

According to the author, ritual and performance are interrelated since rituals are performed and theatrical performances are ritualized. The difference between them is in context and emphasis rather than in function: "Rituals emphasize efficacy… Theatre emphasizes entertainment" (613). For the author, the historical and thematic relationship between ritual and theater consists essentially in the interplay between efficacy and entertainment. He assumes that efficacy and entertainment form two poles of a continuum, whether a specific performance is theater or ritual depends primarily on context and function: "A performance is called theatre or ritual because of where it is performed, by whom, and under what circumstances" (622). Ritual and theater are conceived as the two poles of a continuum, there is no performance that can be described either as pure efficacy or as pure entertainment: "The matter is complex because one can look at specific performances from several vantage points, and to change perspectives is also to change one's characterization of the event" (623). In keeping with European theater, the author develops a dynamic model of the relationship between ritual and theater, which he regards as being applicable to all cultures: "[d]uring each historical period in every culture either entertainment or efficacy is dominant; but the situation is never static: one rises while the other declines. The changes in the relationship between entertainment and efficacy are part of the overall pattern of social change. Performance is more than a mirror of social change, however; it participates in the complex process that *creates* change" (624). Similar to efficacy and entertainment, the author describes the relationship between performers and spectators within a performance as dynamical: "The relationship between performers, spectators, and performance, like that between entertainment and efficacy, is dynamic, moulded by specific social, cultural, and historical developments" (626). He applies Victor Turner's concept of 'social drama' with its fourfold structure of breach, crisis, redressive action, and reintegration, to aesthetic drama. On this basis he develops an infinite loop model of a permanent intervening relation between social drama and aesthetic drama. He reaches the conclusion that ritual, aesthetic, and social performances are closely related to each other: "Ritual is part of the warp and woof of every kind of performance, sacred and secular, aesthetic and social" (643). [JK]

References: K. Burke, E. Goffman, M. Gluckman, R.A. Rappaport, M. Singer, V.W. Turner.
Examples: Social drama, rituals of passage.
Key-words: aes, cpr, DYN, eff, eth, PMC, tha, pmt, soc.

Schechner, Richard, 2002, *Performance Studies. An Introduction*; London, New York: Routledge (ISBN 0–415–14620–8 / 0–415–14621–6 (p)) (x + 289) (with index and bibliography). Reprinted 2003.

This book is intended as an introduction to the open field of performance studies meant to be used in the classroom. The author introduces himself as "a Jewish Hindu Buddhist atheist living in New York" (1), etc. While the main text includes almost no quotations, this richly illustrated book contains many boxes providing background information about persons, events, things, and excerpts from books and articles in order to present other voices, ideas, and interruptions. The book is divided into eight chapters: "What is Performance Studies" (1–21); "What is Performance" (22–44); "Ritual" (45–78); "Play" (79–109); "Performativity" (110–142); "Performing" (143–187); "Performance Processes" (188–225); and "Global and Intercultural Performance" (226–283). All chapters are provided with suggested reading, "things to think about", and "things to do". In the chapter on ritual, the author introduces 'rituals' as "memories in action" (45), and briefly introduces the complex relationship between ritual and play (45). He then illustrates the varieties of ritual (45–46), and the (spurious) distinction between 'sacred' and 'secular' rituals (47–49). According to the author, rituals can be understood from at least four perspectives, namely structures, functions, processes, and experiences (49). Furthermore, he wants to explain (sic) rituals from an evolutionary perspective and, hence, discusses animal and human ritual (51–57), the latter going beyond the former as they mark a society's calendar and transport a person from one life phase to another (57). This leads to a presentation of Victor W. Turner's theory (57–71) by adding a number of different examples, including his observation of a two-day pig kill celebration in Papua New Guinea in 1972 (69–71). The author briefly introduces his 'efficacy-entertainment dyad' (71). According to him, "[t]he shift from ritual to aesthetic performance occurs when a participating community fragments into occasional paying customers. The move from aesthetic performance to ritual happens when an audience of individuals is transformed into a community" (72). In a further chapter, the author discusses changing rituals and the invention of new ones (72–74). Apart from being invented, "older rituals have long provided grist for the artistic mill or have been used as a kind of popular entertainment" (74), and, "at first influenced by colonialism and later by globalization, artists have drawn on the rituals of many cultures for use in their own new works" (77). [MS]

Key-words: gen, PMC, PMT, pr1, pr2, str, aes, eff, emo, aut, par, spc, tim, sec.

Schechner, Richard & Willa Appel (eds), 1990, *By Means of Performance. Intercultural Studies of Theatre and Ritual*; Cambridge etc.: Cambridge University Press (ISBN 0–521–32608–7 / 0–521–33915–4 (p)) (xv + 298).

Selected contents: Richard Schechner: "Introduction" (1–7) (*); Victor W. Turner: "Are There Universals of Performance in Myth, Ritual, and Drama?" (8–18) (*); Richard Schechner: "Magnitudes of Performance" (19–49) (*); Colin Turnbull: "Liminality. A Synthesis of Subjective and Objective Experience" (50–81); Paul Bouissac: "The Profanation of the Sacred in Circus Clown Performances" (194–207); James L. Peacock: "Ethnographic Notes on Sacred and Profane Performance" (208–220) (*); Yi-Fu Tuan: "Space and Context" (236–244); Barbara G. Myerhoff:

"The Transformation of Consciousness in Ritual Performances. Some Thoughts and Questions" (245–249) (*); Herbert Blau: "Universals of Performance; or Amortizing Play" (250–272). [JK]

Reviews: E. Bruner *AA* 93.4 (1991) 966; J.J. Pawlik *Anthr* 86.4–6 (1991) 644; J.R. Brandon *BTLV* 147.2/3 (1991) 344–346; B.C. Alexander *HR* 31.3 (1992) 323 f; E.L. Schieffelin *AE* 21.3 (1994) 668 f.
Key-words: PMC, tha.

Schechner, Richard & Willa Appel, 1990, 'Introduction', in: Richard Schechner & Willa Appel (eds), *By Means of Performance. Intercultural Studies of Theatre and Ritual*, Cambridge etc.: Cambridge University Press (ISBN 0–521–32608–7 / 0–521–33915–4 (p)) (*) 1–7.

This volume, which is dedicated to Victor W. Turner, is "a further step in the process of exploring some of the interweavings of ritual and theatre" (1). The aim of this volume "was to approach the genres of theatre, dance, music, sports, and ritual as a single, coherent group, *as performance*" (3). One of the core questions is "whether or not the same methodological tools and approaches could be used" (3) to understand different forms or genres of performance. The attempt was to "lay the groundwork for proposing general principles or, as Turner called them, 'universals of performance'" (3). The issue involved is divided "into six specific areas of interest" (3): "*Transformation of being and/or consciousness.* Either permanently, as in initiation rites, or temporarily as in aesthetic theatre and trance dancing a performer—and sometimes spectators too—are changed by means of performance. How does this change come about? How is it made part of a performance?" (4). "*Intensity of performance....* Understanding intensity of performance is finding out how performances build, how they draw spectators in (or intentionally keep them out), how space, scripts, sounds, movements—the whole *mise-en-scène*—are managed" (4). "*Audience-performer interactions.* How does an audience provide the context for a performance? When a performance moves to a new place encountering new audiences (on tour, for example), even if everything is kept the same, the performance changes. The same happens when an audience is imported, as when tourists or anthropologists see 'the real thing'. Aside from these questions of context, there is a wide range of audience behavior from full participation as in many rituals and festivals to the sharp separation of stage from audience in the proscenium theatre.... The reception of a performance varies according to how much individual spectators know about what's going on" (4). "*The whole performance sequence.* Generally Western scholars have paid more attention to the 'show'" (4). "But every performance event is part of a systematic sequence of occurrences. Performance includes six or seven phases: training, rehearsal (and/or workshop), warm-up, the performance, cool-down, and aftermath. Not all performances in all cultures include all these phases—but finding out what is emphasized and what is omitted is very instructive" (5). "*Transmission of performance knowledge.* Performance consists of mostly oral traditions. Even where there is written drama, the arts of performing...are passed down through direct oral transmission. Precisely how these traditions are passed on in various cultures and different genres is of central importance" (5). "*How are performances evaluated?* This is a very sticky problem because criteria vary from culture to culture, genre to genre. Are there any 'universal', or at least general, principles to be used to determine whether performances are 'good' or 'bad'? Do we go by the standards applied inside a given culture and if so, do we use what performers have to say or what critics, scholars, and audiences say (recognizing that these opinions are often at odds)? Also, to whom are evaluations directed—to the performers, to would-be spectators, to scholars?" (6). [JK]

Key-words: aes, dyn, emb, PMC, str, tim, tra.

Scheff, Thomas J., 1977, 'The Distancing of Emotion in Ritual', *Current Anthropology* 18:483–505 (with bibliography).

This article starts by reminding us, that there are generally two attitudes towards ritual: the positive one, confirming its social or psychological function, and the negative one, regarding rituals as useless remnants of the past. The author notes that especially the scholars taking the last view "emphasize cognitive and verbal aspects, however, to the virtual exclusion of emotions.... None of these authors indexes any of the main emotions I shall discuss: grief, fear, shame, and anger" (484). He then announces that he will "argue that ritual performs a vital function: the appropriate distancing of emotion. I shall propose a theory of ritual and its associated myth as dramatic forms for coping with universal emotional distresses" (484). After summarizing Freud's theory of catharsis concerning the mechanism of the healing process in cases of suppressed emotions (484–485), he announces that he will "offer a new theory of catharsis that retains Freud's major concepts but introduces two new elements. The first is a precise definition of catharsis, and the second is the concept of distancing" (485). He then defines "catharsis as the discharge of one or more of four distressful emotions: grief, fear, embarrassment, or anger. These emotions are physical states of tension in the body produced by stress.... In the absence of interference, these tension states will be spontaneously discharged by convulsive, involuntary bodily processes...This definition of catharsis is unusual in making a sharp distinction between emotion as distress and emotion as discharge.... Distress and discharge are, however, two different and in fact opposite processes" (485). The next section discusses "the concept of distancing as it is used in discussions of drama" (485). Here, three points in a continuum are named: underdistanced dramas (where the audience is completely drawn into the emotions presented), overdistanced drama (the opposite of underdistanced ones: those which do not involve the emotions of the audience at all), and those which have esthetic distance (where the audience experiences emotions but is not overwhelmed by them) (485–486). The author now applies this concept to the context of emotional distress and suggests that at "esthetic distance, one is both participant in, and observer of, one's own distress, so that one can go in and out freely.... One seems to be both deeply immersed in a powerful feeling from the past and at the same time observing oneself feeling" (486). The next section shows that "emotional distress is unavoidably and repeatedly generated in the process of living, for both children and adults. Since there are usually powerful external and internal controls on the discharge of this distress, most persons accumulate repressed emotion. In traditional societies, it seems likely that ritual, with its associated myth, provided a context that was both a psychologically enabling and a socially acceptable occasion for repeated catharsis" (488). This leads the author to define 'ritual', for the purpose of this paper, "as the distanced reenactment of situations of emotional distress that are virtually universal in a given culture.... there are three central elements in this definition: recurring shared emotional distress, a distancing device, and discharge" (488). Those in our culture who value rituals positively seem to stress the cases in which rituals generate esthetic distance, whereas those who value them negatively seem to stress the cases of overdistancing (and sometimes: underdistancing). The next section discusses two examples: funeral rituals and curing rituals. In the final section, the author moves from description to suggesting a possible way to improve the effectiveness of ritual in our modern western culture: "Perhaps the key to the effectiveness of ritual is that there are two different types of distancing devices—those that increase distance, and those that decrease it. For occasions in which the members of a community are overdistanced from emotion, which is the predominating case in modern societies, a ritual which decreases distance by evoking past scenes of collective distress is required" (490). As was announced on the first page of this article, it "was sent for comment to 50 scholars. The responses are printed below [490–500] and are followed by a reply by the author [500–504]". Among those who replied are Don Handelman (493), Bruce Kapferer (495–496), and Jan van Baal (498–499). [JS]

Reference: **S. Freud.**
Examples: Funeral rituals, curing rituals.
Key-words: aes, pr1, eff, EMO, med, myt, def, PSY.

Scheffler, Israel, 1981, 'Ritual and Reference', *Synthese* 46:421–437.

The "topic in this paper is the interpretation of ritual" (421). However, instead of presenting a "comprehensive theory of ritual", the author limits his argument to an "exploratory discussion of its symbolic functioning alone" (421). In particular, he addresses "the symbolic character of ritual, assuming indeed that it is multiply symbolic, that is, symbolic at once in diverse modes" (421). Following Ernst Cassirer, the author speculates that "the strength of ritual…may lie just in this fact that it is anchored by multiple referential bonds to objects" (421). He further considers "five modes of ritual symbolization or reference" (421): a) 'denotation', b) 'exemplification', c) 'expression'—all three taken from Nelson Goodman's study of the arts—plus d) 'mention-selection' and e) 're-enactment'. a) Ritual gestures, including verbal gestures, "may denote or represent historical occurrences, or occurrences thought to be historical" (422), and also ritual objects may "function symbolically and…stand for or denote in a wide variety of ways" (422). b) "Not every ritual gesture denotes, but normally every such gesture has firm specifications or prescriptions that it must satisfy" (422). Moreover, "every successful performance is an example of the rite in question, i.e. it literally exemplifies it" (422). This implies "not only that it satisfies the relevant specifications for the rite in question but that it constitutes a *sample* of it, thus referring to it" (422). The question of the specifications for rites leads to a discussion of the notation of rituals (422–423), which in turn leads the author to address "two differences between art and ritual" (424). These concern the finite number of rites in a given cultural-religious system (424) and the specific constraints imposed on the performer of rituals (424–427). c) A rite may also "metaphorically exemplify. In this way it enters the domain of expression" (427). "Expression is not a matter of what the symbol denotes or characterizes but of what denotes or characterizes it" (428). "And whatever a given rite may in fact portray, it may simultaneously exemplify, literally or metaphorically, quite different things" (428). d) A discussion of the problem of 'mimetic identification' (429–431) leads him to the concept of 'mention-selection': "The mimetic gesture portraying the act of a god, is in such capacity *denotative*. In addition, however, it mention-selects representations of the same act, itself included. But then, by confusion of such mention-selection with denotation, the gesture in question is itself taken to be the act of a god, and not merely the portrayal of such act" (432). e) On the basis of 'commemorative rituals' that "center on particular events in sacred story" (433), the author develops the notion of re-enactment in order to describe "the relation of a ritual performance to its past replicas" (434). The author argues that this kind of reference or 'allusion' to past replicas is a further symbolic mode of reference, which is "neither denotation, nor exemplification, nor expression, nor mention-selection" (434), because a ritual performance as the author suggests "alludes to its own past kin, just as it may point back to a commemorated event" (435). [JK/MS]

References: J.L. Austin, E. Cassirer, **N. Goodman** (+), H. Frankfort, T. Jacobson, **S.K. Langer.**
Key-words: AES, exp, gst, mim, pmc, REF, SEM, SYM.

Scheffler, Israel, 1993, 'Ritual Change', *Revue Internationale de Philosophie* 46:151–160.

In this contribution, the author discusses the question of how different modes of ritual change can be specified, particularly: "When does a change in a rite become a change of the rite?" (151). His main assumption is that rites are "multiple rather than singular symbolic entities" (151). By this he means that they are "identified by practice not with single performances but rather with groups of performances satisfying certain specifications" (151). Due to such specifications, rites "lay down conditions that must be satisfied, defining a right and a wrong way of doing things if the rite is to be realized" (151). Therefore, the author rejects the view that a rite can be simply identified by its rigidity because identity is "a matter of definitive specification" whereas rigidity "concerns rather the attitude taken toward the rite as defined" (152). Thus the identity of a ritual is assured when "a fluid practice crystallizes sufficiently to articulate defining specifications" (153). But the origination of ritual categories and their dissolution is "neither change in a rite, nor is it change of a rite, for there was here no rite to begin with" (153). Besides mere variation of ritual specifications or alteration of frequency, "there may be a change in the mode of performance of a rite which does not violate the ritual specifications in force" (154). Another 'change in a rite' can be "the growth or promulgation of a new set of specifications to replace the old" (154), but this change cannot be considered a 'change of the rite'. Although "the ruling of a relevant authority at a given time" (155) is a definitive specification of a rite, the author considers this case to be a further 'change in a rite'. By contrast, a 'change of the rite' might instead "be understood as replacement of one rite, definitively specified by performance, by another rite, so specified, for effecting a given function" (155). Aside from the change of a rite's role or function, the author considers also the change of reference of the semantic changes of a rite to be "the alteration not of its constitutive performances but of their references, whether denotative or exemplificational or expressive" (157). Depending on various factors of reference in a given cultural system, the semantic change might be regarded as 'change in a rite' or as 'change of the rite'. According to the author, the reference to, or the exemplification of, certain governing specifications that a rite satisfies or not is the only relevant criterion for distinguishing between these different modes of ritual change and ritual identity as well, for "ritual performances not only comply with but also exemplify ritual specifications" (159). [JK]

References: E. Cassirer (–), N. Goodman (+).

Key-words: aes, DYN, emo, exp, gst, pmc, ref, sem, str, sym.

Scheffler, Israel, 1997, *Symbolic Worlds. Art, Science, Language, Ritual*; Cambridge etc.: Cambridge University Press (ISBN 0–521–56425–5) (214) (with index).

Most sections of this book have already appeared as articles in journals or volumes of proceedings. In his (new) chapter, "Introduction and Background" (3–10), the author defines his main concern as follows: "Symbolism is a primary characteristic of mind, displayed in every variety of thought and department of culture. This book explores aspects of symbolic function in language, science, and art as well as ritual, play, and the forming of worldviews" (3). As the author readily points out, his "account of human nature as ever active and symbol forming has drawn heavily upon the work of the great pragmatic philosophers" (4), such as Peirce, James, Mead, and Dewey. Moreover, he acknowledges his intellectual debt to Cassirer and, most of all, Goodman. The author rejects "the restrictions of philosophy to logic, science, or languages as objects of study. My interest is after all to further the theory of symbolism. Such theory needs to obey strict methodological canons even as it studies all sorts of symbolic phenomena falling outside the purview of logical discourse. A theory must yield understanding, explanation, or insight" (5–6). Apart from Goodman's notions of 'denotation' and 'exemplification', a "further and novel semantic thread that runs through a number of treatments to follow is the notion of mention-selection... This notion applies to the use of a symbol to refer not only to its instances, but also to its companion symbols" (7). In the second chapter (11–21), he introduces this notion as relating "a term not to what it denotes but rather to parallel representations of a suitable kind", i.e., "to those representations that it appropriately captions" (11). The book has six sections: "Symbol and Reference" (3–21), "Symbol and Ambiguity" (23–63), "Symbol and Metaphor" (65–94), "Symbol, Play, and Art" (95–126), "Symbol and Ritual" (127–160), "Symbol and Reality" (161–209), the last section being a debate with Goodman. The section on ritual contains a revised version of his papers "Ritual and Reference" (*) and "Ritual Change" (*). The new version of the former paper adds some introductory remarks and discusses the contribution of Cassirer and Langer to understanding ritual (129–132). In the "Introduction" to the volume, the author remarks: "Abstracting from the social and historical context of ritual in order to concentrate on its semantic functions, this section emphasizes the cognitive roles of ritual" (9). [MS]

References: E. Cassirer, **N. Goodman** (+/–), S.K. Langer.
Key-words: SYM, SEM, pmc, lan, mim, rep, gst, REF, cog.

Schieffelin, Edward, 1985, 'Performance and the Cultural Construction of Reality', *American Ethnologist* 12:707–724.

The purpose of this article is to show the limitations of meaning-centered analyses of ritual and to emphasize the importance of nondiscursive rhetorical and performative aspects. The author does not merely assess the crucial role that nondiscursive elements play in the efficacy of ritual, but—like other authors, such as Bloch and especially Kapferer before him—to show how these ritual elements work. To challenge the tendency to conceive rituals as cultural texts, coded communication, or a structure of meanings, the author analyzes the Kaluli curing séances as emergent social constructions. In these séances, "*the force of the transformation comes across on the nondiscursive dramaturgical and rhetorical levels of performance. The spirit medium and audience together co-create a new reality that recontextualizes particular problematical social circumstances and enables action to be taken in regard to them*" (707). Thus, "the meaning of ritual performance is only partly resident in the symbols and symbolic structures of which it is constructed . . . the meanings of the symbols and of the rite itself are created during the performance, evoked in the participants' imagination in the negotiation between the principal performers and the participants . . . rituals do not exist in a vacuum of structural scripts and frames" (722). And it is precisely this creative process of completing the vividly displayed, highly emotional, but only fragmentary symbolic material that renders rituals effective. [JK/Florian Jeserich]

References: M.E.F. Bloch (+/–), C. Geertz (–), B. Kapferer (+), C. Lévi-Strauss, S.B. Ortner.
Example: Kaluli curing séances.
Key-words: agn, DYN, EFF, emo, MNG, par, PMC, pmt, RHT, str, SYM.

Schieffelin, Edward, 1996, 'On Failure and Performance. Throwing the Medium Out of the Seance', in: Carol Laderman & Marina Roseman (eds), *The Performance of Healing*, London, New York: Routledge (ISBN 0–415–91200–8) 59–89 (with bibliography).

According to the author, the anthropological study of ritual has turned from studying the ritual enactment in terms of "structure of representation to seeing them as processes of practice and performance" (59). This emphasis appeals to those interested in "the nature and power of ritual experience because it is concerned . . . with actions more than with text, with illocutionary rather than with propositional force—with the social construction, rather than just representation, of reality. The performative perspective is also fundamentally concerned with something anthropologists have always found elusive and hard to deal with: the creation of presence. Performances . . . create and make present realities vivid enough to beguile, amuse or terrify" (59). According to the author, the crucial question is: "What is involved in the performative creation of presence, verisimilitude, and social effectiveness, and how is this involved in the social construction of reality?" (60). Before he develops his argument on the basis of a particular ethnographic example, the author distinguishes "two principal modes of usage for the term 'performance'" (60): a) "a display of expressive competence by one or more performers addressed to an audience" (60), and b) "the fundamental practices and performativity of everyday life" (61). However, the author argues that there are 'continuities' between both notions. "First, at the level of experience in everyday life, it is possible to move from one mode to the other" (61). Second, the theatrical performances are based on principles derived from everyday performances (61–62). "The main business of this essay...is to develop and explore a mode of performative analysis through elucidation of a particular ethnographic example" (62). This, the author claims, may reveal "the inner construction of a particular 'ritual' or 'theatrical' experience involved" and "the particular ways (at least performatively) a people constructs its own particular social reality" (62). In his ethnographic analysis, the author introduces "a series of determinative issues" (64): 'emergence', "what happens by virtue of performance" (64); 'agenda', "what the people who observe or participate in a performance expect to accomplish through it" (65); 'form', "any domain of consistency of performance" (65); 'means', "any conventional and/or aesthetic device which may be strategically used to produce particular effects" (65); 'strategy', "the way in which means are used within a performance to accomplish performance intentions" (66); 'embodiment', and 'historicity' or 'contingency', which "is usually the most neglected aspect of performance, yet...one of the most essential. Ritual performances are never timeless. They are ephemeral—they only happen once" (66). From a discussion of a particular (failed) performance, the author concludes: "the enactment of all ceremonial (or theatrical) performances is inherently risky. This is because they are necessarily subject to the variable competencies of the major performers, the competing agendas and ongoing evaluations of all the participants, as well as unforeseen contingency and blind luck" (80). "Successful mastery of the risks of performing is "a necessary condition for the creation of performative authority" (80). While the "authority of performance is not necessarily ephemeral" (80), "[p]erformative authority is a fundamental condition of emergence. The emergent is what performance as performance brings about in social reality—and thus in historical experience" (81). According to the author, "it might be argued that performativity is of crucial importance in highly contingent, dialogic, and improvisational kinds of performance" (82), such as the one he analyzed. "Nevertheless, the articulation of ritual structure within social reality, insofar as it is actually enacted, is unavoidably a performative process" (82). In the final part of the essay, the author reconsiders the way the concept of 'performance' "may be useful in anthropology" (82), taking ethnocentric implications into consideration. According to him, "[t]he issue is: 'What are the performative dimensions of the social construction of reality: how are local enactments articulated in the world?' The issue is... about the relative movement of moral and cosmological relationships, power and experience" (83). He concludes with a methodological-epistemological statement: "If, as I believe, ethnographic understanding is more of the nature of annotated translation than sociological reduction, then it is through this kind of tracking or alteration between our perspectives and that of the Other, rather than the reduction of the Other's to ours, that we reach our fullest comprehension of our mutual humanity. Within the limits of the objectives of this paper, however, my point has been to show how a performative analysis can contribute to understanding the emergence of consequential realities in the historical world" (84). [JK/MS]

References: G. Bateson, R. Bauman (+), M.E.F. Bloch (+), P. Bourdieu (+), M.Th. Drewal (+), E. Goffman (+), D. Hymes (+), B. Kapferer (+), B. Kirshblatt-Gimblett, S.B. Ortner, R.A. Rappaport, M. Sahlins, R. Schechner, S.J. Tambiah, V.W. Turner (+).
Example: A spirit seance observed in 1976 among the Kaluli people of Papua New Guinea.
Key-words: aes, agn cmp, com, DYN, eff, emo, PMC, tha, PMT, pr2, pow, rep, soc, str, tim.

Schieffelin, Edward, 1998, 'Problematizing Performance', in: Felicia Hughes-Freeland (ed.), *Ritual, Performance, Media*, (ASA Monographs 35), London, New York: Routledge (ISBN 0–415–16337–4 / 0–415–16338–2 (p)) (*) 194–207.

This article is a critical discussion of the study of cultural performances, indicating a shift "away from studying them as systems of representations... to looking at them as processes of practice and performance" (194). The author starts with the observation that there is "a growing dissatisfaction with purely symbolic approaches to understand materials like rituals" (194), because performance "deals with actions more than text: with habits of the body more than structures of symbols, with illocutionary rather than propositional force, with the social construction of reality rather than its representation" (194). Regarding the theatrical relation between performer and spectator, the author calls into question the Western notion of theater. For this reason, he stresses the notion of performance as used in two ways in the social science. First, performance is a compound of "particular 'symbolic' or 'aesthetic' activities, such as ritual or theatrical and folk artistic activities, which are enacted as intentional expressive productions in established local genres" (194). "'Performance' in this usage refers to the particular kind of performative event treated as an aesthetic whole in a larger social context" (195). Secondly, in the line of Erving Goffman performance refers to "performativity itself: the expressive processes of strategic impression management and structured improvisation through which human beings normally articulate their purposes, situations and relationships in everyday social life. Here the notion of performance converges with implications of theories of practice" (195). According to the author, both usages characterize performance with "conscious intent" (196). In discussing the concept of 'ritualization' as developed by Caroline Humphrey & James Laidlaw (1994) (*), who "explicitly exclude 'performance' from their discussion" (196), the author stresses the contingency that is inherent in any performance and any performative activity in the social construction of reality. He argues that "any performance (indeed any performative activity) is inherently a contingent process" (197). "Everything (in ritual no less than theatre), from the observance of the correct procedures to the resonance of the symbolism, the heightening of emotion, the sense of transformation, all depend on whether the performers and other participants can 'bring it off'. It is always possible the performance may fail. Thus 'performance' is always inherently *interactive*, and fundamentally *risky*" (198). In contrasting text and performance, the author argues that "the character of performance as accomplishment together with its interactive quality and element of risk" helps to differentiate it from the notion of text, arguing that "performance can never be text, and its unique strategic properties are destroyed when it is considered as, or reduced to, text. To be sure, performances share some qualities with texts. They have beginnings, middles, and ends, they have internal structure, may refer to themselves, etc. But it is precisely the performativity of performance for which there is no analogue in text" (198). Regarding the relation between performance and practice, the author sees closeness between them because of their moment of improvisation and states: "performance embodies *the expressive dimension of the strategic articulation of practice*. The italicized expression here could stand as our definition of performativity itself. It is manifest in the expressive aspect of the 'way' something is done on a particular occasion.... Thus performativity is located at the creative, *improvisatory* edge of practice in the moment it is carried out" (199). Then the author questions in the section "The Theatrical Relation between Performer and Spectator in the Social Sciences" (200–204) the suitability of the traditional Western concept of the performance-audience relationship for cross-cultural comparison. He argues that popular assumptions about the "nature of the relationship between theatre audience and performers in conventional western theatre form probably the most problematic part of the extension of theatre metaphors and performative ways of thinking into social science theory" (202). "Yet understanding the precise nature of this relationship in a performance event is fundamental to understanding the structure and character of the event itself.... It is for this reason that it is important to make the relationship between the participants and others in performative events a central subject in ethnographic investigation" (204). The author argues that "these relationships need careful investigation—both in formal performances and in everyday life—because it is within these relationships that the fundamental epistemological and ontological relations of any society are likely to be implicated and worked out: because this is the creative edge where reality is socially constructed" (204). In relation to performance and performativity, the author concludes that "any ethnography of performance is inherently addressing the issue of the social construction of reality, and that, in fact, performativity is not only endemic to human being-in-the-world but fundamental to the process of constructing a human reality.... The central issue of performativity, whether in ritual performance, theatrical entertainment or the social articulation of ordinary human situations, is the imaginative creation of a human world" (205). [JK]

References: R. Bauman (+), P. Bourdieu (+), E. Goffman (+), C. Humphrey & J. Laidlaw (–), L. Kendall (+), R. Schechner (+/–).
Key-words: aes, DYN, eff, emo, hab, PAR, PMC, THA, pmt, pr1, soc, sym, tim.

Schieffelin, Edward, 2006, 'Participation', in: Jens Kreinath, Jan A.M. Snoek & Michael Stausberg (eds), *Theorizing Rituals. Vol. I: Issues, Topics, Approaches, Concepts*, (Numen Book Series 114–1), Leiden, Boston: Brill (ISBN-10: 90–04–15342–x, ISBN-13: 978–90–04–15342–4) 615–625.

This paper is more a meditation on the nature of participation than a review of the historical literature on the subject. Most discussions of participation have focused on ceremonial contexts (Durkheim and Levy-Bruhl are the classics). Taking a partly phenomenological approach, this paper tries to show how participation is an integral part of everyday (as well as ritual) activity and is integral to both individual and group experience. Participation is taken to entail an 'epistemological posture' towards the world radically opposed to the epistemology of articulate cognitive experience that sees the world as 'alter'—as 'standing-over-against-consciousness'—commonly privileged in western thought. As a mode of being-in-the-world participation is thus not grounded in a sense of being thrust into the world so much as in a sense of being identified with, and submitted to it as part-to-a-greater-whole. While the perception of alterity is our means of grasping the world, participation is the means by which we experience its being and reality. [Edward Schieffelin]

Key-words: soc, emo, PAR, tim.

Schilbrack, Kevin (ed.), 2004, *Thinking through Rituals. Philosophical Perspectives*; London, New York: Routledge (ISBN 0–415–29058–9 / 0–415–29059–7) (IX, 278).

As the editor points out in his "Introduction", his goal in this book "is to argue that there are rich and extensive philosophical resources available with which one might build bridges between ritual and thought, between practice and belief, and between body and mind" (1).
Contents: Kevin Schilbrack: "Introduction. On the Use of Philosophy in the Study of Rituals" (1–30); Nick Crossley: "Ritual, Body Technique, and (Inter)Subjectivity" (31–51); Amy Hollywood: "Practice, Belief, and Feminist Philosophy of Religion" (52–70); Ladelle McWhorter: "Rites of Passing. Foucault, Power, and Same-Sex Commitment Ceremonies" (71–96); Brian Clack: "Scapegoat Rituals in Wittgensteinian Perspective" (97–112); Michael L. Raposa: "Ritual Inquiry. The Pragmatic Logic of Religious Practice" (113–127); Kevin Schilbrack: "Ritual Metaphysics" (128–147); Robert McCauley: "Philosophical Naturalism and the Cognitive Approach to Ritual" (148–171); Frits Staal: "Theories and Facts on Ritual Simultaneities" (172–187); T.C. Kline III: "Moral Cultivation through Ritual Participation. Xunzi's Philosophy of Ritual" (188–206); Jonardon Ganeri: "The Ritual Roots of Moral Reason. Lessons from Mimamsa" (207–223); Steven Kepnes: "Ritual Gives Rise to Thought. Liturgical Reasoning in Modern Jewish Philosophy" (224–237); Charles Taliaferro: "Ritual and Christian Philosophy" (238–250); Peter van Ness: "Religious Rituals, Spiritually Disciplined Practices, and Health" (251–272). [MS]

Key-words: pow, pr1, cog, emo.

Schjødt, Jens Peter, 1986, 'Initiation and the Classification of Rituals', *Temenos* 22:93–108.

The author starts with the statement that "[t]his article presents a formal and structural definition of the phenomenon of initiation in order to distinguish it from other categories. It begins with the use of the term by certain leading scholars. My proposal will, therefore, be purely theoretical and (I hope) valuable as a tool for a more precise terminology and a more useful classification of rituals.... This article is primarily concerned not with function but with structure and symbolism from a semantic point of view, and with classifications" (93). The author then discusses Van Gennep, Eliade, Victor W. Turner, Honko, and Terence S. Turner. This leads him to the conclusion, that *rites de passage* have a sequence, not of three, but of five stages (98). He agrees with Van Baal, that all rituals have this structure, and thus proposes to drop the term *rites de passage* altogether. He distinguishes three categories of rituals on the basis of the "quality of [the] non-liminal level" in the initial and final phases (100–101), viz. calendrical rituals (initial phase: zero, final phase: zero), crisis rituals (negative-zero), and initiation rituals (zero-positive). Towards the end of the paper he gives a list of six constitutive elements which together characterize initiation rituals: "1. The object of the transition is one or more individuals, but not the whole society. 2. There is a qualitative difference between the level of the initial and the final phases, the latter being higher than the former. 3. The transformation of the objects that takes place is in principle irreversible. 4. The 'thing' gained through the transitional phase of initiation is always something that can be associated with knowledge or capabilities of a religious or magical kind, i.e. numinous knowledge which is necessary in order to fulfill the demands of the new existence. 5. The horizontal structure of the chain of events is organized in a tripartite sequence, including symbolic elements (often symbols of dying) that separate from the initial phase, symbolic elements of transition, and symbolic elements (often symbols of rebirth) that integrate the person to the final phase. 6. The relation between the two non-liminal phases and the liminal is symbolized by a number of analogous pairs of binary oppositions" (103–104). However, as he points out, "It is decisive to note in this characterization that one element is missing completely, namely an element that could show us that it is in fact a ritual we are facing. This is, of course, intended, because it is easy to find myths and other narratives which have this very structure. This implies that what we face here is not restricted to some categories of rituals but in fact represents an ideological structure that can be found in myths and other kinds of religious expression" (104). [JS/MS]

References: M. Eliade (+/–), **L. Honko (+)**, T.S. Turner, V.W. Turner (+/–), J. van Baal, **A. van Gennep**.
Key-words: DEF, myt, STR, mng, sym.

Schmidt, Francis, 1994, 'Des inepties tolérables. La raison des rites de John Spencer (1685) à W. Robertson Smith (1889)', *Archives de science sociale des religions* 85:121–136.
[On Permissable Follies. The Reason of Rites from John Spencer (1685) to W. Robertson Smith (1889)]

The paper aims at contributing to an 'archaeology' of a widespread repugnance at ritual in the intellectual history of Europe in general and in the study of religions (*Religionswissenschaft*) in particular. As a turning point towards a recognition of the importance of rituals ("rites") the author draws attention to the book *De Legibus Hebraeorum Ritualibus* (1685) by the Anglican theologian and scholar of Hebrew, John Spencer. The article outlines *De Legibus*. In this book, Spencer undertook to demonstrate that far from being the result of divine arbitrariness, rituals were based on reason. Spencer distinguishes between those rituals that have a celestial origin (and are to be retained by the Anglican Church) and most others that were invented by human beings (and need not be retained, contrary to the claims of Judaism and the Roman Church). By inverting the traditional argument of plagiarism, Spencer claims that many Mosaic laws were actually borrowed from Egypt and had been maintained for pedagogical reasons. In a final section, Schmidt traces the fortuna of Spencer's book from Johann Meyer (1693) down to W. Robertson Smith (1889). [MS]

Key-word: hsc.

Seeman, Don, 2004, 'Otherwise Than Meaning. On the Generosity of Ritual', *Social Analysis* 48:55–71.

"As a hermeneutic enterprise, cultural anthropology tends to assume that ordered and coherent meaning is *the* primary desideratum of social life. Ritual practice plays a primarily supportive role whenever meaning has been threatened or called into question by pain or by circumstance. In this view, ritual generates meaning" (55). The author challenges this hermeneutic tradition that, according to him, theorizes ritual as theodicy, i.e., as "the attempt to make sense of suffering" (58) or, in more general terms, "as justification of culture" (59). Since he regards Geertz and Weber as the main protagonists of this tradition the paper starts with a review of their views (56–59). He juxtaposes this meaning-oriented hermeneutic tradition with an experience-oriented phenomenological approach (60) and engages Levinas' "phenomenology of pain" (59) that emphasizes "the uselessness of suffering, which resists theodicy (read 'culture') in precisely the same way that pain resists human consciousness" (59). Suffering cannot be "domesticated" by culture/ritual "as a machine for the generation of meaning" (60). In the final section of the paper (62–70) the author then juxtaposes "Levinas (and thus also Weber and Geertz) with a twentieth century ritual virtuoso named Kalonymos Shapira, whose holocaust writings exemplify the relationship between ritual and uselesness in an extreme social setting" (63), that of the Warsaw Ghetto. "Shapira's work bears comparison with Levinas's, and lends support to the idea that our preoccupation with meaning may stem from a particular religious genealogy of social theory. Ritual can be analyzed as a ground of intersubjectivity or transcendence rather than meaning, which makes it more akin to medicine, in Levinas's terms, than to theodicy" (55 [from the author's abstract]). "Levinas also argues—and this is where I think we can learn the most from him—that there are moments in which ritual practice constitutes a break, a reaching for the interhuman. This is what I mean by the generosity of ritual" (70). [MS]

References: T. Asad, P. Bourdieu, C. Geertz (–), **E. Levinas** (+) M. Weber (–).
Key-word: MNG, EMO.

Segal, Robert Alan, 2000, 'Making the Myth-Ritualist Theory Scientific', *Religion* 30:259–271.

Working from his base in ancient Greek religion, Walter Burkert has come to propose a theory of religion generally. That theory rests on the work of ethologists and, more recently, of sociobiologists. While concentrating on ritual, which for him is the heart of religion, Burkert links ritual to myth to offer his own version of the myth-ritualist theory. Rejecting the old-fashioned view, epitomized by J.G. Frazer, that myth and ritual function to spur the crops to grow, he maintains that the two function at once to unify society and to alleviate anxiety. Their function is sociological and psychological rather than magical. Put another way, their function is symbolic rather than practical. For Burkert, as for

Frazer, myth-ritualism arose in the stage of agriculture, but for Burkert it is tied to the prior stage of hunting. How original is Burkert's theory of myth-ritualism and of religion? Why does he turn to ethology in particular? If he is seeking to provide a scientific theory of religion, what does he mean by 'scientific'? [Robert A. Segal]

References: W. Burkert, J.G. Frazer.
Key-words: eth, exp, myt.

Segal, Robert Alan, 2005, 'Myth and Ritual', in: John R. Hinnells (ed.), *The Routledge Companion to the Study of Religion*, London, New York: Routledge (ISBN 0–415–33310–5, 0–415–33311–3 (p)) 355–378.

This chapter is divided into three sections. Section one discusses myth (355–366). Section two, entitled "myth and ritual", reviews myth-ritualist theory (366–369). Section three, dealing with ritual (369–375), reviews main ritual theories (see under References, below) and concludes: "In the nineteenth century ritual was assumed to be the 'primitive' counterpart to modern technology, which rendered it superfluous and, worse, impossible. In the twentieth century ritual has been seen as almost anything but the outdated counterpart to technology. Ritual, it has been maintained, is about the human world and not just about the physical world. Consequently, its function is not physical but social, psychological, or existential. Even for cognitive psychologists, the focus is now on how humans think ritually, not on what ritual is intended to do" (375). [MS]

References: V.W. Turner, W. Burkert, E.R. Leach, R.A. Rappaport, P. Boyer.
Key-words: gen, hsc, myt, ter.

Segal, Robert Alan, 2006, 'Myth and Ritual', in: Jens Kreinath, Jan A.M. Snoek & Michael Stausberg (eds), *Theorizing Rituals. Vol. I: Issues, Topics, Approaches, Concepts*, (Numen Book Series 114–1), Leiden, Boston: Brill (ISBN-10: 90–04–15342–x, ISBN-13: 978–90–04–15342–4) 101–121.

According to the myth and ritual, or myth-ritualist, theory, myth is tied to ritual. Myth is not just a statement but an action. The most uncompromising form of the theory maintains that all myths have accompanying rituals and all rituals have accompanying myths. In tamer versions, some myths may be without accompanying rituals or some rituals without accompanying myths. Whatever the tie between myth

and ritual, the myth-ritualist theory is distinct from other theories of myth and from other theories of ritual in focusing on the tie. This essay traces the history of the theory, starting with its creation by William Robertson Smith and then its development by J.G. Frazer and in turn Jane Harrison and S.H. Hooke. The application of the theory to the ancient world as a whole and subsequently to the whole world is then presented. The application of the theory outside of religion is considered next. Contemporary revisions of the theory by Claude Lévi-Strauss, René Girard, and Walter Burkert follow. Finally, some suggestions for further development of the theory are offered. [Robert A. Segal]
Key-words: gen, hsc, MYT, ter.

Severi, Carlo, 1993a, *La memoria rituale. Follia e immagine del Bianco in una tradizione sciamanica amerindiana* (Idee 7); Florence: La Nuova Italia (ISBN 88-221-1250-4) (273).
[The Ritual Memory. Folly and Images of the White in an Amerindian Shamanic Tradition]

This is a book on the birth, the ritual usage and the persistence of an image of the White in a Mesoamerican (Cuna) shamanic tradition. While the author advocates an anthropological approach that insists on the analysis of specific objects instead of making far-reaching general assumptions (4–5), the book raises some theoretical questions: "What maintains and what cancels the memory of a society? How is that sort of shared knowledge, which we call tradition, preserved in time? This problem... is at the center of the research of which this book takes stock" (8–9). To resolve that problem, the author introduces the notion of ritual memory (*la memoria rituale*). According to the author, "the ritual practice (*la pratica rituale*) of an Amerindian shaman... consists precisely in establishing a relationship between those two aspects which myth, as an abstract object, excludes. The two poles of this relationship are... the representation of individual experience (in general created by pain, uncertainty, and disorientation) and... a particular form... of historical memory" (19). This particular form of historical memory is linked to the ritual context. "Thus, the ritual memory interprets the private experience by referring it to the memory of the group, and in this way preservers traces of that which the myth does not record" (19). According to the author, the shamanic tradition aims at the elaboration of a specific form of memory that only ritual action (*l'azione rituale*), and the chants transcribing it, are able to preserve. For two reasons, the author calls this the 'ritual memory': "Not only because it is entrusted...to the form imposed by its utterance (*enunciazione*), but also because by preserving...the remembrance (*il ricordo*) of a painful past it cyclically renews the illusion of a future victory" (42). [MS]

Example: Cuna shamanism.
Reviews: J. Galinier *JSAm* 80 (1994) 335–338; G. Townsley *Homme* 36.138 (1996) 186.
Key-words: pmc, pmt, pr1, pr2, sym, cmp, eff, EMO, myt, tra.

Severi, Carlo, 1993b, 'Talking About Souls. On the Pragmatic Construction of Meaning in Cuna Ritual Language', in: Pascal Boyer (ed.), *Cognitive Aspects of Religious Symbolism*, Cambridge etc.: Cambridge University Press (ISBN 0–521–43288–x) 165–181.
Almost identical English version of Chapter 6: "*Parlar d'anime*" [Talking about Souls] of his *La memoria rituale*, 1993, 221–247.

Whereas S.J. Tambiah vouches for the priority of semantics over pragmatics in the study of ritual, the author of this article argues that the reverse often holds true. Based on his Cuna case, he tries to show that "rules about the ceremonial use of language (reflecting a specific categorisation of ritual speakers and of their addressees) play an essential role in the generation of ritual symbolism, and suggest a new approach, focused on the pragmatic construction of meaning" (166) within ritual contexts. To illustrate his approach, the author studies "the case of the Cuna society, where a complex religious category [*purpa*], usually translated as 'soul' or 'spiritual presence', may seem almost meaningless in ordinary talk, and yet plays a crucial role in the shamanistic representation of the human experience" (165). In the course of the essay, the author seeks to show that the use of a special ritual language (*purpa-namakke*) transforms the meaning of *purpa*: A vague, simple, yet meaningless category becomes a meaningful and highly complex one if contextualized in the dynamic process of a ritual performance. And since the author follows R. Carnap's minimal definition of pragmatics "the study of aspects of language that *require* reference to the users of it" (180), he also takes into account the various relations expressed in the ritual performance: The web of relationships between the ritual chanter, the ill person, the auxiliary spirits, and the shamanistic chant plays an essential role in the generation of ritual symbolism and meaning. "Thus, the pragmatic dimension of the ritual recitation, that is, the study of *purpa-namakke* as a sequence of actions which define the ritual speaker and his addressee, is not only a useful tool for understanding what *purpa* can mean; the rules concerning *purpa-namakke* in fact establish and designate the conditions for generating its meaning" (179). In a sense, "the study of the generation of the meaning of *purpa* coincides with the study of the construction of this context" (177). [JK/Florian Jeserich]

Reference: M.E.F. Bloch, S.J. Tambiah (+/–).
Example: Cuna shamanism.
Key-words: com, cpl, dyn, eff, emo, LAN, MNG, pmc, pr1, rel, SEM, str, sym.

Severi, Carlo, 2002, 'Memory, Reflexivity and Belief. Reflections on the Ritual Use of Language', *Social Anthropology* 10:23–40.

This is an attempt to extend the approach to ritual theory as advanced by the author and Michael Houseman in 1994 (*). While that theory was "based entirely on the analysis of sequences of actions", this essay aims at "the study of ritual situations of a different kind, where action seems to play a less important role, and is replaced, through the recitation of chants, by a special use of language" (25). By analyzing a Cuna song or shamanistic performance, the author arrives at two conclusions pertaining to ritual in general: a) Concerning "the 'special context' which frames ritual linguistic communication: ritual enunciation always involves the metamorphosis... of its enunciator. We can answer the first question we have posed (How can we describe, in formal terms, the special context that makes ritual communication different from ordinary life?) as follows: the ritual context... is different from ordinary communication because it brings the pragmatics [sic] aspect of communication to the foreground, through a reflexive definition of the enunciator. It makes the enunciator a complex figure, made up by the condensation of contradictory identities" (37). b) By comparing ritual and theater, the author arrives at his second point: "Ritual action builds a particular kind of fiction, a special context for communication, where any positive answer will imply doubt and uncertainty, and vice versa. Everybody is supposed to believe it, and yet no one can really be sure" (38). The author concludes "that linguistic communication becomes ritualised when a particular way to elaborate a complex image of the enunciator is made to unleash that particular tension between belief and doubt that defines a ritual-reflexive stance. The context of the ritual use of language is not defined solely by the use of any specific linguistic form, but rather by the reflexive elaboration of the image of the speaker, and by its perlocutionnary [sic] effect: that particular tension between faith and doubt that characterises any belief" (39). [MS]

References: J.A. Austin, M. Houseman & C. Severi, C. Humphrey & J. Laidlaw, E.R. Leach (+), C. Lévi-Strauss, P. Smith (+), S.J. Tambiah.
Example: Shamanism in general and Cuna shamanism in particular.
Key-words: PMC, tha, pmt, par, eff, LAN, COM, RFL, cpl, REL.

Severi, Carlo, 2006, 'Language', in: Jens Kreinath, Jan A.M. Snoek & Michael Stausberg (eds), *Theorizing Rituals. Vol. I: Issues, Topics, Approaches, Concepts*, (Numen Book Series 114–1), Leiden, Boston: Brill (ISBN-10: 90–04–15342–x, ISBN-13: 978–90–04–15342–4) 583–593.

The author states: "Since Bronislaw Malinowski... the analysis of ritual action and the study of language have been closely related in the field of anthropology. Language has been seen as a paradigmatic model in three respects: "as a way to study the construction of meaning in the ritual context, as an image of the internal order that structures ritual actions, and eventually as a pragmatic context for understanding the effectiveness of ritual" (583). Accordingly, the essay is structured in three parts. In the first part, "Ritual, Language, and the Construction of Meaning" (583–588), the author distinguishes between two approaches to the study of meaning in language: the intellectualist and the semiological. According to him, they both "deny or minimize certain properties of ritual which in the eyes of the participants are essential" (584). In both approaches "the concern is always with the premises or consequences of ritual", but not with "the organization of ritual action itself" (584). In addressing the process of the construction of meaning the author discusses Claude Lévi-Strauss' approach to the problem of ritual form. After contrasting this approach with the approaches of Victor W. Turner and Roy Rappaport, the author concludes "the analogy between ritual and linguistic phenomena is not satisfying, at least insofar as its application is restricted to semantics" (588). In the second part, "Language as an Image of Order" (588–590), the author addresses syntax as an account to study the relationship between language and ritual. Here he starts with the analogy between ritual and music as conceived by Frits Staal and then shortly discusses the cognitive approach of E. Thomas Lawson and Robert N. McCauley. In the third part, "Language and Ritual Interaction" (590–593), the author writes, "the linguistic model, which has been based successively on semantic and syntactic structures, leads now to another approach, one based on the construction of a special pragmatic context of communication" (591). He proposes a new perspective that moves "from the study of actions *in loco verbi* to the study of *verba in loco actus*". The author concludes by saying: "From this new perspective—once the analogy of linguistic structures, syntactic or semantic, has shown its limits—the 'internal form' of ritual action becomes a matter of context, identification, and pragmatics" (593). [JK/MS]

References: C. Lévi-Strauss, F. Staal.
Key-words: eff, LAN, mng, mus, pr1, sem, str.

Sharf, Robert H., 2005, 'Ritual', in: Donald S. Lopez Jr. (ed.), *Critical Terms for the Study of Buddhism*, Chicago, London: University of Chicago Press (ISBN 0–226–49314–8, 0–226–49315–6 (p)) 245–270.

The chapter opens with some reflections on the way the term 'ritual' is commonly used, followed by "a *précis* of a large and sophisticated body of theory about ritual that has developed over the last century" (249). Reviewing the critique of the category ritual, the author argues that "[r]itual begins to look less like a text and more like music—difficult to describe in words yet easily recognizable" (251). "Ritual... is more like music than like language insofar as it is impossible to extract content from form. Moreover, as with music, anyone conversant in a tradition of ritual practice is able to discern the difference between an accomplished performance and a mediocre one" (251). As "a ritual event is rendered a singularity that cannot be translated into another medium" (252), several scholars have attempted non-representational approaches to ritual. According to the author, a problem with these non-representational approaches is that notions advanced by these theoreticians "are parasitic upon, and thus ultimately reaffirm, the very dichotomies they try to resolve. Moreover, while performative and nonrepresentational approaches aim to overcome the parochialisms and limitations of Western enlightenment thought, they remain allied with the modernist project insofar as they transform ontological issues into questions of epistemology" (252). Contrary to many theorists, the author holds, "native ritualists... will claim that their performances are in fact instrumental—that ritual changes not just the view of the world but the world itself" (252). "The so-called performative approaches to ritual offered to date... turn out to be predicated on the very dichotomies they have tried to avoid..." (252). The author goes on to explore the notion of play (253–257) and argues: "Ritual might then be viewed as a special form of adult play. It entails the manipulation of metalinguistic framing rules that govern signs and meanings such that a given object or action does not denote what it would normally denote. In doing so, religious rituals may blur the map-territory relation" (256). "Ritual recreates the situation of early childhood play in all its enthralling seriousness and intensity...dichotomies are intentionally confounded, creating a transitory world...Insofar as this is accomplished through manipulation of the metalinguistic cues implicit in all social exchange, and insofar as the emergence of the social self is coincidental to the acquisition of precisely such metalinguistic cues, ritual exposes the transitional nature—the betwixt-and-betweenness—of social reality. The world created in ritual is, according to this analysis, no more 'empty' than the world of everyday life" (257). This line of analysis is then applied to two sets of Buddhist rituals. [MS]

References: C.M. Bell, M.E.F. Bloch, R.L. Grimes, R.A. Rappaport, R. Schechner, S.J. Tambiah, V.W. Turner.
Examples: Buddhist darshan, Chan/Zen.
Key-words: PMC, frm, eff, mng, mus.

Shaughnessy, James D. (ed.), 1973, *The Roots of Ritual*; Grand Rapids (MI): Eerdmans (ISBN 0-8028-1509-X) (251) (with index and bibliography).

Selected contents: J.Ch. Crocker: 'Ritual and the Development of Social Structure. Liminality and Inversion' (47–86) (*); Margaret Mead: 'Ritual and Social Crisis' (87–101); P.J. Quinn: 'Ritual and the Definition of Space' (103–119); J.Z. Smith: 'The Influence of Symbols upon Social Change. A Place on Which to Stand' (121–143); A. Kavanagh: 'The Role of Ritual in Personal Development' (145–160); E. Fischer: 'Ritual as Communication' (161–184); R.N. Bellah: 'Liturgy and Experience' (217–234). [JS]

Reviews: J. Wilson *JSSR* 13.3 (1974) 379 f; N. Mitchell *ThSt* 35.1 (1974) 212; P.W. Hoon *USQR* 29.3/4 (1974) 281–285; D.F. Payne *EQ* 47 (1975) 63; Robin Gill *SJTh* 28.3 (1975) 294–295.
Key-words: soc, psy, com, emo, spc.

Sinding-Larsen, Staale, 1984, *Iconography and Ritual. A Study of Analytical Perspectives*; Oslo: Universitetsforlaget (ISBN 82-00-07306-8 / 82-00-07184-7 (p)) (210).

In this book the author focuses on ritual-connected iconography and inscriptions within the Roman Catholic church. Employing a systemic approach, he analyzes the relationships between liturgy, iconography, and participants. His basic assumption is that "[p]articipation in the liturgy...was defined as an essential instrument to achieve one's salvation. It is a logical conclusion, then, that the pictorial decoration of a church or a chapel...should be directly connected with the liturgy. The liturgy was and is defined as a 'depository of faith', the expression of all dogmas and important doctrines and also to a large extent of the spiritual attitudes of any special period towards them" (9). After having outlined his approach (Part I), the author begins introducing the reader to the functional context of Christian iconography (Part II) by clarifying the terms 'theology', 'Church', 'tradition', and 'liturgy'. In the main part of his book (Part III), the author analyzes the liturgy-iconography-participant-system into its different constituent parts (1. General Characteristics of the Iconography; 2. Description of the Subject; 3. The Subject and Its References; 4. Interrelation between Iconographical Subjects; 5. Text References; 6. The Liturgical Space; 7. Space Relations; 8. Ritual and the Perception of Pictoral Arrangement; 9. Ritual Focus; 10. Conception of Sacred Images; 11. Iconography as a Medium for Messages; 12. The User's Role; 13. Planning, Production, Resources; 14. Organizational Iconography; 15. The Ritual Dimension). In the last part of the book (Part IV) he summarizes his approach. The author proposes a 'reconstructive context analysis', which he understands to be an "analysis of an historical situation from its own viewpoints in its own terms" (46). To analyze the different viewpoints of the participants in liturgy, the context of everyday life of these people has to be accounted for: "Liturgy can be roughly described as a regulated system of texts to be read or sung and of a limited number of actions. Images, however, will usually evoke wider fields of experience and association than the written word and simple actions will normally do. Consequently, iconography will tend to be more actively attributed with non-liturgical and non-theological notions. Affective values of everyday experience and personal devotion will be easily brought in" (15). The power to evoke certain experiences and associations is further explored by the author with the help of psychological findings on perceptual processes: "It may be assumed that ritual to some extent exerts a regulating effect on the perceptual interaction between the messages processed by the ritual, the iconographical structures intended to respond to them, and the conceptualization on those participating in the ritual" (130). Examining a particular example he concludes: "The public and ritual site of the Pesaro painting and the official symbols included in it... alert the onlooker to linking up intuitively... what he sees in the picture with other symbols that have alerted him on comparable occassions, e.g. when he has been witnessing or taking part in State processions and other rituals which, as they all were, were focused on Mass" (169). In conclusion, rituals regulate the perception of participants by focusing their attention on certain aspects of the iconography in such a way that the ritual system "alerts particular sensitivity to ritual messages and proneness to conform to their demands" (130). [Thorsten Gieser]

References: E.R. Leach (–), J. Skorupski (+/–), V.W. Turner.
Example: Liturgy and iconography of the Roman Catholic church.
Reviews: R. Cormack *JTS* 37 (1986) 697; A.J. Blasi *RRR* 28.2 (1986) 202 f; G. Strohmaier-Wiederanders *ThLZ* 111 (1986) 136.
Key-words: mng, sym, aes, cog, pmc, rep, com.

Smart, Ninian, 1972, *The Concept of Worship* (New Studies in the Philosophy of Religion); London, Basingstoke: Macmillan (ISBN 333–10273–8) (x + 77).

"The aim of this monograph is to explore the concept of worship. In some degree the method is linguistic, but it is aimed also to place the activity of worship in the milieu of religious practices and beliefs" (ix). "To worship is to perform a piece of ritual" (5), and "ritual typically has to do with overt, and chiefly bodily, action" (5). "The usage of physical movements in ritual supplies a range of gestures, and these in a way constitute a language" (7). Worship is also "a relational activity: one cannot worship oneself" (26–27). Moreover, "the ritual of worship expresses the superiority of the Focus [of worshipping] to the worshipper(s)" (27), and "the ritual also performatively sustains or is part of the power of the Focus" (27). Worship "expresses the numinous experience and the Focus of worship is awe-inspiring" (44). The "Focus of worship is unseen, i.e. transcends any particular manifestations of it that there may be" (44). And "the superiority of the Focus gives it greater power than the worshipper" (44). "All this implies the personalised character of the Focus", and "it becomes evident that the foci of worship, God or the gods, need to be understood in the context provided by worship. That is, there is an internal relationship between the concepts of god and of worship" (51). Therefore, the first part of the book (1–52) is devoted to "Worshipping", and the second part (53–75) to "God's Existence". [MS/JS]

Reviews: J.T. Stahl *CSR* 3.3 (1973) 298; F.C. Coplestone *HS* 14.2 (1973) 219; S. Brown *Mind* 84 (1975) 472.
Key-words: pmt, pr1, gst, emo.

Smith, Jonathan Zittel, 1980, 'The Bare Facts of Ritual', *History of Religions* 20:112–127.
First delivered as a Woodward Court Lecture at the University of Chicago in 1977.
Reprinted in: Jonazath Z. Smith: *Imagining Religion. From Babylon to Jonestown*, Chicago, London: University of Chicago Press, 1982 (ISBN 0–226–76358–7/0–226–76360–9), 53–65.
German translation: "Ritual und Realität", in: Andréa Belliger & David J. Krieger (eds): *Ritualtheorien. Ein einführendes Handbuch*, Opladen, Wiesbaden: Westdeutscher Verlag 1998 (ISBN 3–531–13238–5) (*) 213–226.

Smith asks for the relation between ideal and reality with respect to rituals. What happens if something coincidental, a kind of 'accident', occurs within a cult? Smith takes a report of Plutarch: How does the Priestess of Athena Polias react when donkey drivers ask for the first time within the temple area for something to drink? "No, for I fear it will get into the ritual" (113). With this answer, she refuses because of the powerful capacity of rituals for routinization. Whether a coincidence is ritually integrated into a cult or not, is not due to what happens but is the result of a decision. A ritual is thus "a difficult strategy of choice" (117). This notion "requires us to perceive ritual as a human labor, struggling with matters of incongruity" (117). There is a selection from reality: in the ritual, an idealized, perfect reality is practiced. Hence, the author suggests "that, among other things, *ritual represents the creation of a controlled environment* where the variables...of ordinary life have been displaced *precisely* because they are felt to be so overwhelmingly present and powerful. *Ritual is a means of performing the way things ought to be in conscious tension to the way things are in such a way that this ritualized perfection is recollected in the ordinary, uncontrolled, course of things*" (125). According to the author, "[t]here is a 'gnostic' dimension to ritual. It provides the means for demonstrating that we know what ought to have been done.... Ritual provides an occasion for reflection and rationalization on the fact that what ought to have been done was not done, what ought to have taken place did not occur. From such a perspective, ritual is not best understood as congruent with something else—a magical imitation of desired ends, a translation of emotions, a symbolic acting out of ideas, a dramatization of a text, or the like. Ritual gains force where incongruency is perceived" (125) [the 1982 reprint continues: "...and thought about" (63)]. Smith turns the theory "likes produces likes" upside down: rituals represent no congruence, but incongruence. [Dorothea Lüddeckens/MS]

References: A. van Gennep, S. Freud.
Examples: Stories about ritual from antiquity and modern literature; boar-hunting rituals especially from paleo-Siberian peoples.
Key-words: myt, rep, soc, mng, sym, emo, ecl, spc, tim.

Smith, Jonathan Zittel, 1987a, *To Take Place. Toward Theory in Ritual* (Chicago Studies in the History of Judaism); Chicago, London: University of Chicago Press (ISBN 0–226–76359–5 / 0–226–76361–7 (p)) (xvii + 183) (with index).

In his "Preface" the author states: "In the work before you, the primary question will be a matter of theory: the issue of ritual and its relation to space" (xii). However, it is only in the fifth and last chapter of this book (96–117) that it becomes clear what the function of the other chapters was. It is here that the author comes to discuss the concepts 'myth' and 'ritual', and their mutual relation. From the Reformation to the end of the nineteenth century, they have been used predominantly by Protestants, and regarded as opposed and mutually exclusive, since myths were analyzed in order to demonstrate that 'the others' in the end held similar ideas as 'we', whereas 'rituals' were used to show how much 'they' differed from 'us'. Only from the end of the nineteenth century onwards did scholars try to reconcile the two, ascribing a communicative function to rituals and assuming the myths to be the scripts enacted in rituals. This the author regards as an unhappy move, leading us away from understanding rituals. On his view, "[r]ritual is, first and foremost, a mode of paying attention. It is a process for marking interest" (103). Hence its relation to place: "The temple serves as a focusing lens, establishing the possibility of significance by directing attention, by requiring the perception of difference. Within the temple, the ordinary...becomes significant, becomes 'sacred', simply by being there. A ritual object or action becomes sacred by having attention focused on it in a highly marked way. From such a point of view, there is nothing that is inherently sacred or profane. These are not substantive categories, but rather situational ones. Sacrality is, above all, a category of emplacement" (104). "Ritual is, above all, an assertion of difference. Ritual is a means of performing the way things ought to be in conscious tension to the way things are. Ritual relies for its power on the fact that it is concerned with quite ordinary activities placed within an extraordinary setting" (109). According to the author, "ritual is not best understood as congruent with something else ... Ritual gains force when incongruency is perceived and thought about" (109–110). "Ritual is a relationship of difference between 'nows'—the now of everyday life and the now of ritual place; the simultaneity, but not the coexistence, of 'here' and 'there'.... One is invited to think of the potentialities of the one 'now' in terms of the other; but the one cannot become the other. Ritual, concerned primarily with difference, ... is systemic hierarchy par excellence" (110). Ritual, therefore, is very different from myth: "If ritual is concerned with the elaboration of relative difference that is never overcome, myth begins with absolute duality (for our purposes best expressed as the duality of 'then' and 'now'); its mode is not that of simultaneity, but rather of transformation. In myth, ... the one becomes the other" (112). There are cases, however, where myth and ritual occur in combination. Of these, there are two kinds: those where a myth (i.e. a process in time) is transformed into ritual (i.e. place)—such as in the case of the gods of the Australian Aranda, who created the world in its present form (Chapter 1; 1–23)—and those where a ritual (i.e. a place) is turned into a myth (i.e. presented as a process in time)—such as the case of the rituals performed at the sacred places in Jerusalem in the fourth century, which were sublimated into the calendar of the Christian Year (Chapter 4; 74–95). Pure ritual, however—such as the Temple ritual described in Ezekiel 40–48 (Chapter 3; 47–73)—is related to place alone, not to time, where place should be understood "not simply in the sense of environmental generation, but also in the sense of social location, of genealogy, kinship, authority, superordination, and subordination" (Chapter 2; 24–46, here 46). [JS/MS]

References: M. Eliade (–), I. Kant (+), É. Durkheim (+), S. Freud (+), C. Lévi-Strauss (+).
Examples: Aranda, the temple ritual of Ezekiel 40–48, the Christian rituals in Jerusalem in the 4th century.
Reviews: C.S. Littleton *AA* 90.3 (1988) 769; D. Kertzer *AQ* 62.1 (1989) 45; J. Rogerson *Theol* 745 (1989) 67; **K.-W. Bolle *HR* 30.2 (1990) 204–212**; J. Baldovin *JRS* 6.2 (1992) 137 f.
Key-words: pmc, pow, SPC, MYT, def, tim.

Smith, Jonathan Zittel, 1987b, 'The Domestication of Sacrifice', in: Robert G. Hamerton-Kelly (ed.), *Violent Origins. Walter Burkert, René Girard, and Jonathan Z. Smith on Ritual Killing and Cultural Formation*, Stanford: Stanford University Press (ISBN 0–8047–1370–7) (*) 191–205.

In the first part of this paper, the author discusses ritual in general; only in the second part does he focus on animal sacrifice in particular. Reviewing definitions of 'ritual' by Freud and Lévi-Strauss, he comes to the conclusion that "both insist that ritual activities are an exaggeration of everyday activities, but an exaggeration that reduces rather than enlarges, that clarifies by miniaturizing in order to achieve sharp focus" (194). Quoting himself, he then takes the position, that in culture in general, and thus also in religion, what counts is not originality, but rather repetition. In culture, "there is no text, it is all commentary;... there is no primordium, it is all history;... all is application.... we are dealing with historical processes of reinterpretation, with tradition" (196). With respect to the phenomenon of animal sacrifice, he is of the opinion that this is a rather recent phenomenon, which developed only in agrarian cultures: it did not develop from hunting, but on the contrary, it is the ritualized form of the everyday act of selective killing of domesticated animals, which characterizes the breeding of cattle. [JS]

References: S. Freud (+), C. Lévi-Strauss (+), A.E. Jensen (+).
Key-words: str, dyn.

Smith, Jonathan Zittel, 1998, 'Constructing a Small Place', in: Benjamin Z. Kedar & Raphael Jehudah Zwi Werblowsky (eds), *Sacred Space. Shrine, City, Land. Proceedings from the International Conference in Memory of Joshua Prawer held in Jerusalem, June 8–13, 1992*, New York: New York University Press (ISBN 0–8147–4680–2) 18–31.

"The activity of transposition is one of the basic building blocks of ritual and a central object of ritual thought. The capacity to alter common denotations in order to enlarge potential connotations within the boundaries of ritual is one of the features that marks off its space as 'sacred'. Transposition is a paradigmatic process set within the largely syntagmatic series of actions which characterize ritual. The respects in which 'this' might, under some circumstances, also be a 'that' gives rise to thought which plays across the gaps of like and unlike... Seen in this light, ritual is a prime mode of exploring the systematics of difference in relation to processes of transformation and identification" (18). In this essay, the author discusses a specific technique of transposition, namely 'miniaturization' (e.g. the construction of small-scale replicas of religious buildings, or the replacement of sacrifice by ink-making or of a book by amulets). After a historical study of some of such processes of miniaturization, the author concludes with a rather general statement: "As major theorists of ritual from Freud to Lévi-Strauss have rightly maintained, ritual, with its characteristic strategies for achieving focus and its typical concern for 'microadjustment', is often itself a miniaturization and, simultaneously, an exaggeration of everyday actions. Miniaturization, when applied to ritual—as in the case of the Magical Papyri—then becomes a sort of *ritual of ritual*, existing, among other loci, in a space best described as discursive or intellectual" (29). [MS]

Reference: C. Lévi-Strauss (+).
Examples: The Church of the Holy Sepulchre and its replicas in the West; the decline of animal sacrifice in late antiquity and the Greek Magical Papyri.
Key-words: str, sym, aut, SPC, rfl.

Smith, Pierre, 1982, 'Aspects of the Organization of Rites', in: Michel Izard & Pierre Smith (eds), *Between Belief and Transgression. Structuralist Essays in Religion, History and Myth*, Chicago, London: University of Chicago Press (ISBN 0–226–38861–1) 103–128.

Originally published as: 'Aspects de l'organisation des rites' in: Michel Izard & Pierre Smith (eds), *La fonction symbolique. Essais d'anthropologie*, (Bibliothèque des sciences humaines), Paris: Gallimard 1979 (ISBN 2–07–028621–5), 139–170.

The author argues that ritual phenomena "cannot be reduced to a simply [sic] display of social mechanisms, a faithful reflection of myths, or even a confused forest of diversely associated symbols" (103). His aim is "to clarify their incredible complexity and their captivating strangeness...by trying to find the principles of their own specific elaboration" (103). To this end, he examines two aspects, a) the "focalizing elements" of rites and b) their "integration into systems" (104). a) "Focalizing elements of the rite...are those acts around which the different sequences revolve and are organized" (104), i.e. these operations that cannot be reduced to mere symbolic action but make things 'really happen' when the rite is performed. Thus, "the kernel of rituals lies...in their encounter with...a certain kind of 'snare for thought' [*piège à pensée*]" (106). However, such 'snares for thought' (like bullroarers) only become 'sacred objects' when they "are made part of a preconceived ritual schema" (108). b) Concerning the formal organization of rites, the author states: "Every rite is linked to circumstances which determine how it is performed, and these circumstances themselves form series. The various rites associated with circumstances of the same series tend to form a system, that is, to respond to, oppose, complete, or repeat each other in a way that is certainly more evident... than is the case with those connected to circumstances belonging to different series. On the other hand, it seems that no society limits its ritual activities to a single series of circumstances, and it follows that several ritual systems generally coexist within the same culture. As a first hypothesis, we can schematically distinguish and define four universal series of circumstances apt to determine the characteristics of ritual systems. For every rite is tied either to periodical or occasional circumstances; and these circumstances can, in either case, primarily effect either the life of the collectivity or that of individuals" (108). Those rites "that are connected with a series of periodical circumstances form a system along an axis of the syntagmatic type; each rite in the series will necessarily be preceded and followed by another in a clearly determined order which will be repeated with each recurrence of the cycle" (108). "Occasional rites, on the other hand, react to time's surprises, to circumstances which are foreseeable only from a statistical point of view. They form a system along the axis of the paradigmatic type, offering a number of types of ritual responses to various situations" (109). As "different societies develop these systems to unequal degrees, and each one elaborates them in its own way" (109), these systems form "a significant dimension of any culture" (109) and invite comparison. Moreover, in every culture "complex and diverse links" (110) between the co-existing ritual systems are established. "In a general way, a single type of ritual act, such as sacrifice, initiation, prayer, or the display of ritual masks, can be integrated, either centrally or accessorily, to various systems, differently interconnected among themselves, and in this way receive different colorings or orientations" (110). [MS]

References: C. Lévi-Strauss (+/–), M. Gluckman (–), A. Dundes (–), H. Kuper (–).
Examples: All from Africa: the Bedik in Senegal, Rwanda, the Ncwala among the Swazi.
Key-words: STR, cpl, idn, tim, myt, cpr, ecn.

Snoek, Joannes Augustinus Maria, 1987, *Initiations. A Methodological Approach to the Application of Classification and Definition Theory in the Study of Rituals*; Pijnacker: Dutch Efficiency Bureau (ISBN 90–6231–150–4) (xv + 237).

This thesis is an attempt to establish a methodology for constructing definitions. This is exemplified with regard to the term 'initiations' (sic). After a discussion of the pioneering studies of initiations (Schurtz, Webster, 12–24), the author provides a survey of classification and definition theory (25–56). This leads to a discussion of previous classifications of rituals (57–89). These are dismissed as "mainly formulations of intuitive ideas" (89). The subsequent chapter reviews the work of some scholarly authorities on 'initiations' (90–147) and investigates the way in which this term is actually used by these scholars: which features they consider to be typical for initiations (intension of the term) and which phenomena they refer to as such (extension of the term). This leads to a stipulative definition of 'initiations' (148–175), operating with the 'characters' or features of 'initiations' provided by the review of existing scholarship. The resulting definition by identification reads as follows: "Initiations are all those, and only those, *rites de passage*, limited in time, and involving at least one subject participant, which are nonrecurrent transitions in time for their individual objects (the candidates)" (169, 173). As rituals of passage, initiations are considered to be a subclass of rituals. (Rituals are defined as "ritual processes, oriented towards an object, having some function(s) for that object", 148). According to the author, rituals of passage have a tripartite structure, and the "object" of an 'initiation' must be "an individual person: the candidate" (173). By the notion 'transitions in time', the author refers to a change in one or more of the candidate's status(es) (173). Moreover, initiations "are first-time rituals which cannot be repeated" (174). Apart from these monothetic characteristics that are derived from the definition-by-identification, the term has some eight polythetic characteristics that are independent of the definition-by-identification but part of a definition-by-description. E.g.: "Through an initiation, one usually becomes a member of a group" (174). The term 'initiations' usually denotes rituals "accompanying the coming of age, becoming a member of a 'secret' society, or a shaman.... Other Lifecycle and Inaugural Rituals, such as birth, marriage, parenthood, funeral, and enthronement rituals, may be so as well" (174). In order to arrive at these definitions, the author also formulates a refined classification of 'rituals' (88). [MS/JS]

References: H. Schurtz, H. Webster, A. van Gennep, W.B. Kristensen, M. Eliade, A.E. Jensen.
Key-words: hsc, ter, DEF, STR, gdr, cpr, tim.

Snoek, Joannes Augustinus Maria, 1995, 'Similarity and Demarcation', in: Jan G. Platvoet & Karel van der Toorn (eds), *Pluralism and Identity. Studies in Ritual Behaviour*, (Studies in the History of Religions (*Numen* Book Series) 67), Leiden, New York, Köln: E.J. Brill (ISBN 90–04–10373–2) (*) 53–67.

This article poses the general theory that "the more the groups from which one wishes to distinguish oneself (the out-groups) are similar to one's own group (the in-group), the more rigidly will the distinguishing characteristics be formulated, and the more attention will be paid to these characteristics" (54). First it is shown that this theory is supported by group dynamics theory, and that when the groups concerned are religious groups, the differences between their religions may well be used as demarcating characteristics. What makes this theory relevant for ritual theory is that different groups may also distinguish themselves through differences between their respective ritual practices. The first example presented in the paper to illustrate the theory (different Grand Lodges within Freemasonry) supports the thesis. The second example (different Pentecostal groups) shows that "when (especially perceived) similarity approaches identity, demarcation sharply drops to zero" (66). In that case, the groups may come to merge, thus loosing their separate identity. [JS]

Examples: Freemasonry, Pentacostal groups.
Key-words: com, IDN, pow, rep, soc.

Snoek, Joannes Augustinus Maria, 2003, 'Performance, Performativity, and Practice. Against Terminological Confusion in Ritual Studies', *Paragrana. Internationale Zeitschrift für Historische Anthropologie* 12 (special issue: "Rituelle Welten" = Wulf & Zirfas (eds) 2003 (*)):78–87 (with bibliography).

This article discusses some terminological issues in theorizing rituals. The terms discussed "are: 'performance', 'performativity', and 'practice', the last one both in the sense of 'action' or 'praxis', and in the sense of 'embodiment', as indications of four different types of ritual theories. This paper is not about the contents of these theories, but about the desirability to distinguish them, and the difficulty to do so as a result of confusing terminology" (78). Short summaries are then given of the theories, indicated by the terms 'Performance' (79–80), 'Performativity' (80), 'Practice (Action)' (81), and 'Practice (Embodiment)' (81–82) "in order to point out their main features and differences" (79). Each of these theories generates its own kind of questions, and at the end of each of these sections, examples of such questions are given. The section 'Relation and Distinction' (82–83) then argues why it makes sense to keep these terms and the theories they refer to distinct, among others because "in order to be able to investigate their relations, one first has to distinguish them" (82). The last section, 'Confusion' (83–85) discusses the difficulties which arise from translating these terms into German, where words exist which sound similar but mean something different, while the words which are proper translations of the English ones sometimes seem unrelated to the English words. It also shows, however, that native English speakers also sometimes confuse the terms, using for example 'performance' when 'performative ritual' is intended. [JS]

References: S.J. Tambiah (+), R. Schechner (+), M.E.F. Bloch (+), C.M. Bell (+/–), Chr. Wulf (+).
Key-words: def, PMC, PMT, PR1, PR2, mim, emb, cmp.

Snoek, Joannes Augustinus Maria, 2006, 'Defining "Ritual"', in: Jens Kreinath, Jan A.M. Snoek & Michael Stausberg (eds), *Theorizing Rituals. Vol. I: Issues, Topics, Approaches, Concepts*, (Numen Book Series 114–1), Leiden, Boston: Brill (ISBN-10: 90–04–15342–x, ISBN-13: 978–90–04–15342–4) 3–14.

This article is not about what 'rituals' are, but about the procedure to construct a definition of such terms as 'rituals' in such a way that the term can be used scholarly in a particular context. It is shown that all actually existing definitions contain at least some characteristics which are not of a classical (Aristotelian) nature, but rather polythetic and/or fuzzy. Therefore, they always have fuzzy boundaries. It is also shown that those characteristics of 'rituals' which actually happen to be classical ones are by no means sufficient to define the term in a way which comes close to its traditional use. Therefore, inclusion of at least some polythetic and/or fuzzy ones is unavoidably. Furthermore, six closely related but different concepts, useful for describing ritual activities, are

discussed. Methodologically it would be ideal to use unambiguously a different term for each one of them, and thus also to use the word 'rituals' for only one concept, as opposed to the current practice. The article closes with a demonstration of the method proposed to construct the type of definition intended, resulting in one possible definition. [JS]
References: L.A. Zadeh (+), R. Needham, M.E. Spiro (+), C.M. Bell, R.L. Grimes.
Key-word: DEF.

Soeffner, Hans-Georg, 1988, 'Rituale des Antiritualismus. Materialien für Außeralltägliches', in: Hans Ulrich Gumbrecht & Klaus Ludwig Pfeiffer (eds), *Materialität der Kommunikation*, (Suhrkamp-Taschenbuch Wissenschaft 750), Frankfurt a. M.: Suhrkamp (ISBN 3-518-28350-2) 519–546.
[Rituals of Antiritualism. Materials for the Extraordinary]

Contrary to small-scale societies, in societies characterized by 'second-hand' forms of interaction and organizations, rituals can no longer be controlled and directly maintained by all participants; rather, the organization of rituals has to be able to maintain itself. Thus it is no longer society that forms and transmits rituals, but the performance of interaction-rituals establishes the possibility of creating temporary interaction-communities. In complex societies, knowledge becomes more and more 'depersonalized' and 'mediated'. Therefore, it easily gets detached from its chain of transmission, and many ritualized gestures and other forms of ritualized expression now transport 'structural meanings and effects' that have almost nothing to do with the situations in which they are going to be used. In the empty space (*Leerstelle*) that is created by their being detached from their original context, they can be charged with new symbolic content. This, however, does not effect the former horizon of meaning that has fallen into oblivion. According to the author, there are institutionalized forms of behavior whose *raison d'être* remains unconscious, regarding both its reason of its origin and the reason for its transmission. However, in many cases the quest for the content of single rituals distracts from the insight that formal structures of 'orientation' that are of paramount importance for social organization are established and consolidated through rituals. Ritual behavior is formalized, predictable, and thus can be considered an older relative of rational calculation. In this essay, the author seeks to show that far from living in an age of committed anti-ritualism, we are living in an age of an obscure ritualism (*in einem undurchschauten*

Ritualismus). He makes this point by analyzing what he considers to be two extreme forms of this attitude: forms of ritualized anti-ritualism, and the transformations of a dated version of a rite by way of a naive, inflationary ritualism. [MS]

References: M. Douglas (–), A. Gehlen, H. Plessner, E. Goffman.
Examples: Mass-demonstrations; travels of pope John-Paul II.
Key-words: pr2, str, gst, SOC.

Soeffner, Hans-Georg (with editorial assistance from Ulrike Krämer), 1992, *Die Ordnung der Rituale. Die Auslegung des Alltags 2* (Suhrkamp-Taschenbuch Wissenschaft 993); Frankfurt a. M.: Suhrkamp (ISBN 3–518–28593–9) (216) (2nd Edition: 1995).
Eng. transl. by Mara Luckmann: *The Order of Rituals. The Interpretation of Everyday Life*, New Brunswick (NJ): Transaction Publishers 1997 (xvii + 176) (ISBN 1–560–00184–4).

In his introduction to this collection of 'sociological novels', the author, a sociologist, introduces the basic problem he tries to tackle in these essays: the question of the autonomous social subject, and the problem of how societies that are (presumably) based on individualism are held together. According to the author, social order has to be constantly produced, and his investigation is mainly concerned with the forms of social expression or staging. Those traditional forms need to be constantly transformed into action. In turn, those forms constantly connect each action to traditional patterns that transmit their own meaning and contain the knowledge and intentions of previous generations. There is no clear distinction between 'form' and 'content' of action; rather, action has its own genres (similar to literature). The forms of everyday routine create their own sort of reality. At the same time, those forms and rituals serve as patterns for articulating a specific view of reality and as trigger-patterns (*Auslösungsmuster*) for a rather static sequence of actions. Every society has different collections of such mechanisms of ignition (*Zündungsmechanismen*) that make it possible to come to terms with future events (7–13). One of the 'sociological novels' in this collection of essays, investigating a specific genre of action, is a reprint of Soeffner 1988 (*). [MS]

Reviews: R.S. Perinbanayagan *AJS* 104.1 (1998) 270; J. Blau *HR* 51.4 (1998) 563–566; G. Vowinckel *KZfSS* 51.1 (1999) 155; M. Luckmann & D. Hartmann *SF* 77.4 (1999) 1691 f.
Key-words: str, mim, emb, str, rfl, soc.

Sørensen, Jesper, 2001, 'Magi og rituell effikacitet. En kognitiv tilgang', ***Religionsvidenskabeligt Tidsskrift*** **38:59–71.**
[Magic and Ritual Efficacy. A Cognitive Approach]

The author first sketches what he regards as the two main approaches in the previous study of ritual: the intellectualist and the symbolist approaches (59–62). In the following two sections, he discusses the differences between ritual and non-ritual action (62–67). According to the author, contrary to non-ritual action, ritual action possesses none (or very few) domain-specific expectations connecting the state of affairs prior to the respective (ritual) action and the very (ritual) action itself. Moreover, there are no (or few) intuitive representations connecting the respective (ritual) action with its desired/expected result (65). According to the author, these characteristics of ritual action have two effects: the making of perceptual and associative connections between the action and its desired/expected results as well as the creation of symbolic interpretations connecting the diagnostic and prognostic aspects of the action (66). In the final section, these observations are applied to a new interpretation of magic (67–70). [MS]

References: J.H.M. Beattie, P. Boyer, M. Douglas, É. Durkheim, E.E. Evans-Pritchard, J.G. Frazer, C. Humphrey & J. Laidlaw (+), J. Skorupski, V.W. Turner, E.B. Tylor.
Example: Azande.
Key-words: PR1, EFF, cog.

Sørensen, Jesper, 2003, 'The Question of Ritual. A Cognitive Approach', in: Tore Ahlbäck & Björn Dahla (eds), ***Ritualistics. Based on Papers Read at the Symposium on Religious Rituals Held at Åbo, Finland, on the July 31–August 2, 2002*****, (Scripta Instituti Donneriani Aboensis 18), Åbo: Donner Institute for Research in Religious and Cultural History (ISBN 952-12-1157-1, ISSN 0582-3226) 207–220.**

The author ends his "article with a short list of propositions summarising the preceding argument: 1) Ritual should not be seen as a kind of language... Language is dependent on a system of conventional symbolic reference meant to communicate, whereas ritual is a type of action meant to *do* something. 2) Ritual and ritualisation as a mode of behaviour is found among animals and humans alike and therefore forms a very basic, possibly innate behavioural modality in humans. This explains why it is spontaneously produced and found in all human groups. 3) By violation of domain-specific expectations, rituals provoke the search for other possible clues for the purpose or meaning of the ritual action. 4) Two strategies are involved: (a) basic perceptual features are utilised to construct iconic and indexical relations; (b) symbolic interpretations are formed, constrained but not determined by these basic structures. In the case of religious rituals, symbolical interpretations tend to be drawn from a culture's stock of religious representations and facilitate new religious interpretations to emerge. 5) Finally, rituals not only enable the construction of symbolic interpretation, but also facilitate the dissolution and deconstruction of already established interpretations. Rituals can in this respect be understood as generators of symbolic meaning... because they are actions that violate intuitive expectations and deconstruct established symbolic reference and thereby give rise to alternative hermeneutic strategies used to construct representations of meaning and function" (218–219). [MS]

References: F. Barth, I. Eibl-Eibesfeldt, C. Humphrey & J. Laidlaw, D. Sperber, V.W. Turner.
Key-words: COG, eth.

Sørensen, Jesper, 2005, 'Ritual as Action and Symbolic Expression', in: Eyolf Østrem, *et al.* (eds), *Genre and Ritual. The Cultural Heritage of Medieval Rituals*, Copenhagen: Museum Tusculanum Press (ISBN: 87-635-0241-0) 49–63.

Instead of attempting "to provide a definition of ritual based on necessary and sufficient conditions" the author suggests exploring "a *prototype* theory of ritual and ritualization" (49). First, however, the author reviews "some of the traditional approaches to ritual in anthropology and the study of religion" (49), i.e. what he refers to as the intellectualist and the symbolist approaches respectively (49–51). He holds "that a good starting point" for an investigation on some characteristics of ritual and ritualization "is the simple observation that ritual is a type of action. First, as other types of action, rituals involve bodily movements governed by motor programmes" (sic) (51). Secondly, as other actions, "rituals are meant to affect the world..." (52). "Finally prototypical actions also involve an agent with intentions..." (52). In order to find out where ritual action differs from ordinary action, the author looks at human ethology (52–56) and cognition (56–62). With regard to ethology, he concludes "that ethology tells us that ritualization consists in the transformation of functional behavior into demonstration or communication; that a substantial part of this communication is universal and based on innate and unconscious expressions and responses; that ritualization entails a weakening of emotions and a decoupling from immediate functions that enable the development of symbolic communication; and that rituals consist in a mix between universal and biological fixed expressions and cultural symbols" (56). The discussion of cognition is very similar to the one in Sørensen 2001 (*). "If we apply the discussion of rituals from ethology and cognitive science to the model of action, we find two major transformations. First, there is a tendency to invest in the biologically evolved communicative aspects of actions and directly perceptible features of the actions, such as spatial contiguity and similarity. Second, we find a new interpretational strategy using symbolic interpretations, whether culturally specified or idiosyncratic. As domain-specific relations are bypassed, the relative importance of direct perceptual clues is emphasised" (61). "Ritualization in the broad sense of the term involving basic physical communication can be understood in this light, as a search for perceptual features of information in lack of a direct functional element in the actions performed. Ritual thereby functions as a bridgehead to symbolic communication" (61). While rituals on the one hand stimulate the construction of symbolic interpretations, these very interpretations are always "underdetermined by the actions performed..." (62). "Rituals are therefore sources of both continuous construction of new meaning through symbolic interpretation and sources of constant deconstruction of already established meaning" (62). The concluding section (63) offers three observations on the relation between ritual action and the aesthetic genres. [MS]

References: W. Burkert, T. Deacon (+), É. Durkheim (–), I. Eibl-Eibesfeldt, P. Ekman, C. Humphrey & J. Laidlaw (+), E.R. Leach, K.Z. Lorenz (+), R. Schechner, F. Staal (+).
Example: Magic.
Key-words: def, mng, cog, ETH, int, pr1.

Sørensen, Jørgen Podemann, 1993, 'Ritualistics. A New Discipline in the History of Religions', in: Tore Ahlbäck (ed.), *The Problem of Ritual. Based on Papers Read at the Symposium on Religious Rites Held at Åbo, Finland on the 13th–16th of August 1991*, (Scripta Instituti Donneriani Aboensis 15), Åbo: The Donner Institute for Research in Religious and Cultural History (ISBN 951-650-196-6) (*) 9–25.

"The novel aim of this paper is to define a discipline, i.e. an analytical level, analogous with the analysis defined by such linguistic disciplines as phonetics, morphology, syntax and semantics" (9). At the same time, this 'new discipline' is to be considered as a subdiscipline of the history of religions. "Religion is probably as complex as language, and it is therefore appropriate that the comparative study of religion should not content itself with interesting themes, but also aim at distinguishing levels of analysis, thus dividing itself into subdisciplines" (10–11). The discussion of some examples from the history of religions leads the author to conclude that "considerable clarification is obtained by isolating the ritual level" (16–17) in these cases, whereas discussing them on a wider, "all-embracing level, vaguely defined as 'religion'" (16) has led to much confusion. However, to clearly distinguish the 'level of ritual' from other levels, a definition of 'ritual' is required. "In order to be useful a definition must, I believe, imply some sort of relation between the characteristics it joins together" (18), i.e., it must be more than "a collection of adjectives and other characteristics that may often be applied to ritual" (18). "In the case of ritual, this could be obtained if the formal characteristics were related to the purpose of ritual" (18). According to the author, it is "safe to say that all rituals aim somehow at governing the course of events; they are intended to work on whatever object they have, to change it or to maintain it" (18). Thus rituals are a form of 'expressive actions' (Leach), that is, communication, but: "Ritual is communication only in the sense that it represents something; it refers, signifies and makes sense... It is designed to work" and "it acts by means of exactly those features that make it akin to communication: by representing" (19). Therefore, 'ritual' is defined as "representative acts designed to change or maintain their object, thus distinguishing ritual from all other kinds of communication and from all other kinds of action" (19–20). The emphasis is thus placed on "ritual efficacy" and "ritual dynamics" (20). In defining 'ritual' the author has "at the same time defined the field of ritualistics—not as a methodological monopoly, but as a distinct level of analysis. Ritualistics is the study of ritual dynamics, i.e., of the way representations are put to work in rituals" (21). Ritualistics is also concerned with the question of meaning in rituals. "In ordinary communication, meaning is the end product; in ritual, meaning is a means towards whatever end or purpose it has.—We may also observe that the ritual is made up of meaning or meanings; it is through their meaning that the statements are considered efficacious. Meaning is to ritual very much what sound is to language" (23). [MS]

References: E.M. Zuesse (–), **E.R. Leach (+)**, V.W. Turner, F. Staal (+/–).

Examples: Rituals among the Lepachas of Sikkim, the idea of god among the Maasai, the centennial discussion on monotheist tendencies in ancient Egyptian religion, the debate on ancient Egyptian kingship.
Key-words: com, EFF, ref, str, cpl, def, dyn.

Sørensen, Jørgen Podemann, 2003, 'The Rhetoric of Ritual', in: Tore Ahlbäck & Björn Dahla (eds), *Ritualistics. Based on Papers Read at the Symposium on Religious Rituals Held at Åbo, Finland, on the July 31–August 2, 2002*, (Scripta Instituti Donneriani Aboensis 18), Åbo: Donner Institute for Research in Religious and Cultural History (ISBN 952-12-1157-1, ISSN 0582-3226) 149–161.

"[T]his is what I think ritual is: an activity formally situated at that point zero where every move and every word become efficacious because they deal with things in their 'state of not yet being'. The role of religious representations in ritual is to dramatize the countdown to that turning point and sometimes also to express and secure the order of images the priest wishes to see when he re-emerges from the primeval darkness of the sanctuary. There are multiple ways in which rites thus rhetorically situate themselves at the turning point, from which things may be produced, renewed, or controlled. This paper could not account for more than a few... varieties... What I may perhaps hope to have demonstrated is that the framework of the rhetoric of ritual may serve not only to unify important theoretical issues and analytical devices in ritual studies, but also to clarify and reformulate a consistent approach to the comparative study of ritual" (159). [MS]

References: C.M. Bell, J.G. Frazer, M. Mauss, J.P. Sørensen, V.W. Turner.
Examples: Spells, prayer, sacrifices, purifications; Egypt, Maori, Islam, Confucianism, Daoism.
Key-words: EFF, RHT, CPR, myt.

Sørensen, Jørgen Podemann, 2006, 'Efficacy', in: Jens Kreinath, Jan A.M. Snoek & Michael Stausberg (eds), *Theorizing Rituals. Vol. I: Issues, Topics, Approaches, Concepts*, (Numen Book Series 114-1), Leiden, Boston: Brill (ISBN-10: 90-04-15342-x, ISBN-13: 978-90-04-15342-4) 523–531.

In 1902, Hubert and Mauss defined rituals as "actes traditionnels d'une efficacité *sui generis*." The kind of efficacy they (rightly) took as constituent of ritual as such, was obviously the postulated efficacy implicit in any ritual act or speech, but through functionalism, the concept became

mixed up with ideas of the 'positive latent function' of ritual. While Radcliffe-Brown considered local ideas that a ritual would actually entail some result as largely outside the scope of social anthropology, Malinowski took a more ambiguous view, and modern anthropologists have often inherited his dream of a unified study of ritual form and function. Through Bourdieu, who spoke of the 'social magic' of ritual, Catherine Bell came to use the word efficacy exclusively in the sense of a positive contribution to social structure, misrecognized by ritualists and ritual public alike. This paper argues that ritual efficacy should be studied at the level of rhetoric. Some rituals obviously are illocutionary acts in the sense of J.L. Austin, and what constitutes ritual in general is a distinct dramatic rhetoric that constructs itself as an illocutionary and *eo ipso* an efficacious act. Efficacy is the formative principle of ritual, and the religious symbols and ideas in a ritual are there not to explain or motivate ritual action, but as rhetorical means to render it efficacious. Without this rhetoric of postulated efficacy, the 'social magic' or 'misrecognized efficacy' of Bourdieu and Bell would hardly be possible. [Jørgen Podemann Sørensen]
Key-words: EFF, pmt, pr1, RHT.

Sperber, Dan, 1975, *Rethinking Symbolism* (Cambridge Studies in Social Anthropology); Cambridge etc. / Paris: Cambridge University Press / Hermann (ISBN 0-521-20834-3 / 0-521-09967-6 (p)) (153) (with bibliography).
Translation by Alice L. Morton of: *Le symbolisme en general* (Collection Savoir); Paris: Hermann 1974 (ISBN 2-7056-5771-1) (163).

This book is on symbolism, rather than on ritual. However, the author explicitly reminds us that "I have...accepted that symbolism was ritual as well as verbal" (110). His theorizing of symbolism therefore implicitly is also a theorizing of ritual, be it from a specific perspective. That perspective is a cognitive approach to the mechanism of how our brain 'symbolises'. The author suggests that the brain uses two mechanisms, the conceptual and the symbolic, to deal with inputs. At first, the "conceptual mechanism constructs and evaluates conceptual representations by means of (1) its input—exogenous (perceptions) or endogenous (memorised information); (2) the system of semantic categories; (3) the active memory; (4) encyclopaedic entries corresponding to the semantic categories used in representations...Those conceptual representations that have failed to be regularly constructed and evaluated constitute the input to the symbolic mechanism.... The symbolic mechanism deals in two stages with the defective conceptual representations that are submitted to it. Firstly, it modifies their focal structure: it shifts the attention from the statements describing the new information to the unfulfilled conditions that have made the representation defective. [Elsewhere (Chapter 4), the author refers to this mechanism as the "putting in quotes" of the information concerned.] Secondly, it explores the passive memory in search of information capable of re-establishing the unfulfilled conditions. At the end of this process of evocation, information thus found is submitted to the conceptual mechanism which uses it together with the previously unfulfilled condition to reconstruct a new conceptual representation. The latter is the interpretation of the initial symbolic representation. The output of the symbolic mechanism thus serves as the input to the conceptual mechanism. In other words, the symbolic mechanism is a feedback device coupled to the conceptual mechanism" (141–142). The book has five chapters. The first, "Symbolism and Language" (1–16), has an introductory character. The second, "Hidden Meanings" (17–50), and third, "Absent Meaning" (51–84), deal with resp. V.W. Turner & Freud and Lévi-Strauss. In the fourth, "Symbolism and Knowledge" (85–113), the way the brain deals with information is analyzed, while in the last chapter, "The Symbolic Mechanism" (115–149), the theory of the author, or rather his metatheory, "a framework within which a theory of symbolism may be constructed" (148), is formulated. [JS/MS]

References: V.W. Turner (+/–), S. Freud (–), C. Lévi-Strauss (–).
Examples: The Dorze (Ethiopia), sacrifice.
Reviews: A. Marras *ERGS* 33 (1976) 335; K.H. Basso *LS* 5 (1976) 240; D. Chaney *Sociol* 10.2 (1976) 395; T.O. Beidelmann *Anthr* 72.3/4 (1977) 622–624; R. Breen *CambAnth* 3.3 (1977) 81; G.I. Wurtzel *ERGS* 34 (1977) 231; A. Gell *Oc* 47.3 (1977) 249 f; J. Ennew *SR* 25.1 (1977) 173; R.A. Segal *JAAR* 46.4 (1978) 610.
Key-words: mng, SYM, cog, sem, cpl, rep.

Staal, Frits, 1979, 'The Meaninglessness of Ritual', *Numen* 26:2–22.

In this article the author is concerned with the theoretical implications of a Vedic ritual. He rejects the view that rituals have any meaning and argues that it is an "erroneous assumption about ritual... that it consists in symbolic activities which refer to something else" (3). According to him, it is characteristic of a ritual performance that "it is self-contained and self-absorbed" (3). Thus the performers are totally absorbed by the proper execution of the complex rules of ritual activity: "Their primary concern, if not obsession, is with rules. There are no symbolic meanings going through their minds when they are engaged in performing ritual" (3). Thus the author defines 'ritual' as a pure activity because it is governed by rules similar to the syntax of language: "Ritual, then, is primarily activity. It is an activity governed by explicit rules. The important thing is what you do, not what you think, believe or say" (4). Assuming that "the only cultural values rituals transmit are rituals" (8), the author restates his thesis with slight changes of meaning: "Ritual is pure activity, without meaning or goal.... Things are either for their own sake, or for the sake of something else.... To say that ritual is for its own sake is to say that it is meaningless, without function, aim or goal, or also that it constitutes its own aim or goal.... In ritual activity, the rules count, but not the result. In ordinary activity it is the other way around.... What is essential in the ceremony is the precise and faultless execution, in accordance with rules, of numerous rites and recitations" (9). "In ritual activity, the activity itself is all that counts" (10). However, the author even goes further by assuming that: "The meaninglessness of ritual explains the variety of meanings attached to it. It could not be otherwise.... However, though a ritual activity may resemble a meaningful non-ritual activity, this does not imply that it must itself be meaningful" (12). In the second part of this article, the author introduces the ritual syntax: "If ritual consists in the precise execution of rules, it must be possible to know what its rules are" (15). On the assumption that "a ritual consists of smaller units", which the author calls "rites" (17), he distinguishes between 'embedding' and 'modification' as main features of ritual structure. Moreover, because of the similarity between ritual rules and the rules of syntax, the author argues for the ritual origin of syntax: "syntax comes from ritual" (19). But language differs from ritual because in language "meanings and sounds are related to each other through a vast and complicated domain of structured rules: syntax" (19). According to the author, rituals "fail to express meaning, but reflect syntactic structure in its pure form, hence pure activity" (21). [JK]

References: W. Burkert, R. Caillois, H. Hubert, J. Huizinga, J.S. Huxley, C. Lévi-Strauss, M. Mauss (+), A. van Gennep.
Example: Vedic ritual.
Key-words: cpl, MNG, ref, sem, sym, str.

Staal, Frits, 1989, *Rules Without Meaning. Ritual, Mantras, and the Human Sciences* (Toronto Studies in Religion 4); New York etc.: Peter Lang (ISBN 0–8204–0553–1) (xix + 490) (with index of names and bibliography).

Indian edition: *Ritual and Mantras. Rules Without Meaning*, Delhi: Motilal Banarsidass 1996 (xix + 490) (ISBN 81–208–1411–8).

As the author states in the "Preface" to this book, his aim is "to go beyond mere description and offer explanations" (xiii). The core of the book is a discussion of "Ritual" (= Part II; 61–190) and "Mantras" (= Part III; 191–346), both topics having been "strangely neglected in the theoretical sciences" (xiv). This abstract will focus mainly on Part II ("Ritual"). The central parts of the book are framed by two parts that discuss matters of 'theory', 'science', 'explanation', 'hypotheses', and related issues. Starting from the assumption that the concepts 'meaning' and 'rules' play an important role in "the analysis of ritual and mantras", Part I ("Methods, Meanings and Rules"; 1–60) gives a brief survey of discussions in philosophy and linguistics about those concepts. The author stresses the Indian origin of linguistics and discusses Panini (6th or 5th century B.C.E.) alongside Chomsky and Wittgenstein. He argues: "To refer to the meaning of rules is not prohibited but can be misleading and confusing, and it is clearer and more helpful to our understanding to say that such rules... are without meaning" (60). Part II ("Ritual") starts with some reflections on the priority of theories as compared to definitions (61–62). The author describes his procedure as follows: "We will start with Vedic ritual which comprises data of which no one has denied that they come under ritual. There are, moreover, Indian terms which demarcate this domain and distinguish it from other things... We shall discuss characteristics and properties of Vedic ritual and then sketch a proposal for a theory. Subsequently we shall try to find out whether the proposed hypothesis is applicable to other undoubted rituals, and to things of which some people have claimed that they are rituals, although others have been doubtful. This latter undertaking will be an extensive enterprise, and we shall be concerned only with a first beginning. New data will be needed to test our hypothesis" (64). The author then proceeds to sketch Vedic ritual(s) and to discuss some basic (Vedic) rites, and the structure of (Vedic) ritual with its "indefinite complexity" (91). This is achieved by 'recursive rules' and the techniques of 'inserting' and 'embedding' (91–99). This leads him to a discussion of "Ritual and Grammar"

(101–114). Here he first provides more abstract models of describing the 'syntactic' structures that he had observed in Vedic rituals. The author finds that "the occurrence in the syntax of both ritual and language of specific and unobvious rules . . . is sufficiently striking to demand an explanation" (110). He argues that ritual must be the cause since "for Early Man, ritual was at least as important as language is for us. Ritual, after all, is much older than language. Unlike language, it can originate on all fours. It is common among animals" (111). In language, however, "syntax is older than semantics" (112), a view that he claims is supported by "many facts" and "Vedic ritual itself" (112). "The view that syntax has a ritual origin and is older than semantics would explain why there is syntax in ritual, why there is an independent level of syntax in linguistics, why language is so unlogical and . . . why language pictures the world in such a roundabout fashion" (114). These hypotheses lead him to the question of 'meaning' in and "Interpretations of Ritual" (115–140). He emphatically rejects the "widespread assumption about ritual . . . that it consists in symbolic activities which refer to something else. It is characteristic of ritual performance, however, that it is self-contained and self-absorbed" (115). According to the author, ritual "is primarily activity. It is an activity governed by explicit rules. The important thing is what you do, not what you think, believe or say" (116). The author continues to review some "Indian interpretations" of, or speculations on, ritual, especially from the Brahmans (117–122), contrasting them with "Western interpretations" (122–131), esp. from the sociology of religion. According to the author, these interpretations are misleading because the authors were Christians "and assumed accordingly that it [i.e. ritual] symbolized religious truths and values" (124). Moreover, "these different unsuccessful attempts at characterizing ritual teach a lesson already known to philosophers: symbolization requires minds and beliefs. Therefore, to grant that ritual is prior to belief, but to persist in trying to interpret it in terms of symbols is a hopeless task. If ritual is prior to belief, as it happens to be in the scheme of evolution, it must be interpreted in different terms" (131). The remaining part of the chapter on "The Meaninglessness of Ritual" (131–140) reprints his famous essay from 1979 (*). The next chapter ("Anthropology Without Asia"; 141–155) is a critical discussion of two major anthropological contributions to the study of rituals (by Firth and Turner). In general terms, the author argues that in order to achieve a fresh perspective on ritual, we "should detach it in particular from those domains where our culture and history have been predisposed to place it: in the realms of religion and society" (141). This "methodological prerequisite" (141) is supported by "the concept of ritualization that has been adopted in the description of animal behavior" (142). In the subsequent chapter ("Syntax, Semantics and Performatives"; 157–163), the author argues that Tambiah (1979), "by advocating a rule-oriented approach, somewhat misleadingly called performative, went significantly beyond the semantic approach that is characteristic of almost all anthropological work on ritual" (163). In so doing, Tambiah "paved the way for a syntactic approach that may ultimately lead to a scientific study of ritual" (163). The 'syntactic approach' leads the author to discover "numerous similarities between music and ritual" (165), which he explores in the final chapter ("Music and Ritual"; 165–190) of Part II (on 'ritual'). This comparison is part of his project to "dissociate rituals from religious services" which is intended to "a general reclassification of the ritual phenomena" (183). "The preponderant and enduring characteristics of music and ritual are that they consist in formal structures of sounds and acts that can be studied most effectively and fruitfully by adopting a syntactic approach. These sounds and acts are like the letter symbols of mathematics in that they are abstract and can therefore be interpreted in any way we like" (186). "In the scheme of evolution, music is obviously much older than myth. If there is a link between the two, it can only be that myth has adopted structures inherent in music. Since ritual displays similar structures, this explains the parallelisms between myth and ritual that have often been mentioned but that do not signify anything" (187). In Part III (on 'mantras'), he deepens some of his main ideas on ritual. Again, he criticizes the ideas of performativity (now also with respect to Wheelock) and performance ("Performatives, Pragmatics, and Performance"; 237–251). "Performance Theory, at the time of writing an American favorite, exhibits all the faults of the empiricist caricature of scientific method" (247). "When we study mantras or ritual, we are primarily interested in competence—in what the ritualists know and not only in what they do" (249). He concludes this section by stating: "A sociologist or political scientist may explain why in the seventies and eighties, many American social scientists have been fascinated by the study of performance. It may not be accidental that these scholars belong to the society that reelected a President noted for performance, not for competence" (251). Furthermore, the author argues "that chance plays an important role in ritual" (346; see also "Mantras by Chance", 295–311). In the first chapter of Part IV ("The Human Sciences"), the author argues that the Indian contributions to the sciences of ritual and grammar "have not only been outstanding, but unique" (365). "There is nothing in contemporary research that resembles or even approaches the scientific achievements of the Srauta Sutras unless it is derived from these sutras, such as Hubert and Mauss (1897–1898)" (366). In the subsequent chapter ("Oral Traditions"; 369–385), the author argues that the "sciences of ritual and grammar were born in the context of these oral traditions and it is likely that hey were also created without the help of writing" (379). The next chapter discusses "Religions" (387–419). According to the author, the "inapplicability of Western notions of religion to the traditions of Asia has not only led to piecemeal errors of labeling, identification and classification, to conceptual confusion and to some name-calling. It is also responsible for something more extraordinary: the creation of so-called religions" (393). After a critique of "The Myth of Two Civilizations" (421–432), the author draws some "Conclusions" (433–454). Now a "provisional definition" of ritual is provided: "Ritual may be defined, in approximate terms, as a system of acts and sounds, related to each other in accordance with rules without reference to meaning" (433). "Ritual rules are sometimes the same, and sometime different from the rules of language discovered in linguistics. Two features characterize them: (1) they are recursive and can generate infinitely many structures; and (2) they correlate sounds an acts in such a manner as to approximate a one-one-correspondence" (433–434). "The definition needs to be tested in non-Asian civilizations and among non-human animals" (434). "My present guess is that human ritual differs from animal ritual in the greater degree of its involvement with mantras" (436). The author goes on to reconstruct an evolutionary "development from ritual via mantras to language" (437). This hypothesis confirms the idea "that ritual and mantras are not languages . . . because they originated prior to language in the scheme of evolution" (437). The final section discusses the question of universals. "The meaninglessness of ritual and the myth of the two cultures are two tips of the iceberg of human nature. What remains under water is not only the roots of religion, but an even more ancient archaic obsession with language and its symbol-generating and mythopoetic functions. This reflects the nature of man as the unique creature that is endowed with language and loves to talk" (453). [MS]

References: A.J. Ayer, W. Burkert, R. Carnap, N. Chomsky (+), W. Dilthey (–), É. Durkheim (–), I. Eibl-Eibesfeldt, R. Firth (–), M. Foucault, H.-G. Gadamer (–), C. Geertz (–), J. Goody, J.C. Heesterman, H. Hubert & M. Mauss (+), M. Heidegger,

R.A. Hinde, R. Jakobson (+), G. Joos, C. Lévi-Strauss, K.Z. Lorenz, B. Malinowski (+), G. Obeyesekere, Panini (+), H.H. Penner (–), J.Z. Smith (+) S.J. Tambiah (+/–), V.W. Turner (–), M. Weber (–), L. Wittgenstein.
Examples: Vedic ritual, Taoist ritual.
Reviews: **S.N. Balagangadhara *CD* 4.1 (1991) 98–106**; B.K. Smith *JRS* 5.2 (1991) 141–143; **A. Grapard, B.L. Mack & I. Strenski *Rel* 21 (1991) 207–234** (with a reply by Staal: Staal 1991); P.J. Griffiths *HR* 31 (1992) 412–414; G. Yocum *RSR* 19.1 (1993) 90; M. Calkowski *AE* 21.4 (1994) 921 f.
Key-words: DEF, EXP, mng, sem, str, ETH, mus, myt, pmt, pmc, SEC.

Staiano, Kathryn Vance, 1979, 'A Semiotic Approach to Ritual Drama', *Semiotica* 28:225–246.

Despite various difficulties in the analysis of religious symbols, the author argues in favor of a semiotic approach to analyzing certain signs as they appear in such 'cultural texts' as myths and rituals. Signs as religious symbols are conceived to direct ritual action depending on the cultural texts from which they are taken. Thus the author defines religious symbols as polysemous, affective, and prescriptive signs. The potency of symbols is derived from their multireferential or multivocal nature and their ability to encode a special model of reality. In analyzing the specific signs as they appear in myths as 'cultural texts', the author tries to gain access to a community's image or model of the world through the decipherment of their religious symbols. Through the placement of such signs within these cultural texts, according to the author, the signification implies that these texts organize and direct ritual actions. Because signs cannot be considered apart from the context in which they occur, the author examines the structure of mythical narratives. These cultural texts provide the chief context for the occurrence of religious symbols within rituals, the relationships between certain signs of the cultural text, and the ritual actions that are prescribed by their myth as their underlying structure. [JK]

References: J.W. Fernandez, C. Geertz, E.R. Leach, C. Lévi-Strauss, N.D. Munn, V.W. Turner.
Key-words: myt, pmc, sem, str, sym.

Stark, Rodney, 2001, 'Gods, Rituals, and the Moral Order', *Journal for the Scientific Study of Religion* 40:619–636.

Based on a comparative survey of world cultures, the author argues (against Durkheim's claims) that "*participation in religious rituals per se has little independent impact on morality and none when done on behalf of gods conceived as unconscious essences, or as conscious gods of small scope and lacking moral concerns*" (619). [MS]

Reference: É. Durkheim (–).
Key-word: SOC.

Stausberg, Michael, 2002, 'Rituel et religion', in: Pierre Gisel & Jean-Marc Tétaz (eds), *Théories de la religion*, (Religions en perspective 12), Genève: Labor et Fides (ISBN 2–8309–1051–6) 106–128.
[Ritual and Religion]

This chapter surveys different ways of theorizing the relationship between religion and ritual in the developments of theories of religion and theories of ritual. Moreover, it raises some epistemological and terminological issues. [MS]

References: C.M. Bell, M. Douglas, É. Durkheim, R.L. Grimes, J.S. Huxley, J.P. Sørensen, G. van der Leeuw, W. Robertson Smith, V.W. Turner.
Key-words: gen, hsc, def, TER.

Stausberg, Michael, 2003, 'Ritual Orders and Ritologiques. A Terminological Quest for some Neglected Fields of Study', in: Tore Ahlbäck & Björn Dahla (eds), *Ritualistics. Based on Papers Read at the Symposium on Religious Rituals Held at Åbo, Finland, on the July 31–August 2, 2002*, (Scripta Instituti Donneriani Aboensis 18), Åbo: Donner Institute for Research in Religious and Cultural History (ISBN 952–12–1157–1, ISSN 0582–3226) 221–242.

This paper proposes to devote greater theoretical attention to the field of study hitherto designated as 'ritual density', 'ritual systems', 'ritual tradition', 'ceremonial', 'ceremonial patterns', 'ceremonial wholes', 'liturgical orders', 'organization of rites', 'series of rituals', and critically discusses previous theoretical attempts to conceptualize it. The author suggests calling the study of such "orders of rituals" "ritologiques". The paper concludes by sketching series of possibly useful concepts: "Transrituality / interrituality // archirituals / pararituals / hyper-rituals" (238). [MS]

References: C.M. Bell, E.Th. Lawson & R.N. McCauley, N. Luhmann, C. Lévi-Strauss, A. van Gennep, R.A. Rappaport.
Key-words: gen, def, str, cog, cpl, tra, mus.

Stausberg, Michael, 2006, 'Reflexivity', in: Jens Kreinath, Jan A.M. Snoek & Michael Stausberg (eds), *Theorizing Rituals. Vol. I: Issues, Topics, Approaches, Concepts*, (Numen Book Series 114–1), Leiden, Boston: Brill (ISBN-10: 90–04–15342–x, ISBN-13: 978–90–04–15342–4) 627–646.

This chapter starts from the observation that many ritual theories could be held to implicitly deny the occurrence of reflexivity in rituals (627). On the other hand, 'reflexivity' has turned into a key-term in the humanities (628). However, this chapter doubts whether one shared notion of 'reflexivity' underlies the varieties of ways in which the term is currently used. "In contradistinction to the bulk of the existing literature, this paper will not try to, implicitly or explicitly, impose one reading of the term. The ambition of the present chapter is much more modest: it is to create awareness of some of the various ways by which 'reflexivity' has been, and can be, employed in ritual theories and theorizing rituals" (629). The chapter then proceeds by seeking to distinguish between the notions of 'reflection' and 'reflexivity' (629–631). The remaining sections of the chapter engage these notions with respect to both rituals and ritual theories. With regard to rituals, the chapter sketches different modes of reflection as promoted by rituals as well as various reflexive media (such as mirrors and mask), reflexive ceremonial and behavioral patterns, the reflexive dimension of performance as well as some other instances that may trigger experiences of reflexivity (such as boredom and observation) (632–637). The following section critically engages Luhmann's distinction of three types of self-reference (basic self-reference, reflexivity, and reflection) for the study of rituals (637–640). The next section (640–642) seeks openings for a reflexive approach to ritual theory, pointing to the theoretical impasse created by some assumptions of ritual theory (such as the idea that ritual is the non-ordinary *par excellence*). The final section of the chapter (642–645) discusses the relations between reflexive modernization (Beck, Giddens), ritual theory, and contemporary forms of ritualization. [MS]

References: U. Beck, C.M. Bell (+), A. Giddens, D. Handelman, M. Houseman, B. Kapferer, B. Latour & S. Woolgar, N. Luhmann (+/–), M. Merleau-Ponty, R. Schechner, V.W. Turner.
Key-words: idn, pmc, frm, par, RFL.

Stausberg, Michael (ed.), 2006, '"Ritual". A Lexicographic Survey of Some Related Terms from an Emic Perspective', in: Jens Kreinath, Jan A.M. Snoek & Michael Stausberg (eds), *Theorizing Rituals. Vol. I: Issues, Topics, Approaches, Concepts*, (Numen Book Series 114–1), Leiden, Boston: Brill (ISBN-10: 90–04–15342–x, ISBN-13: 978–90–04–15342–4) 51–98.

The chapter starts by recalling the Western roots and semantic developments of the term 'ritual'. As a majority of ritual theorists seem to assume the universality of 'rituals' as a cultural phenomenon, this chapter then addresses the question whether one also finds terminological equivalents to 'ritual' in other languages that would support the idea of rituals constituting conceptually distinct spheres. The bulk of the chapter is constituted by 18 brief essays that explore the possible occurrence of emic equivalents to the term 'rituals' in a number of languages (see examples, below). These essays (original pieces of research written by specialists on the relevant languages) are followed by some comparative, systematic, and semantic reflections on the essays assembled in this chapter. [MS]

References: C.M. Bell, G.A. Lewis, F. Staal.
Examples: Akkadian, Anishnabe, Arabic, Chinese, Egyptian, Greek, Hebrew, Hittite, Hopi, Japanese, Mongolian, Old Norse, Persian, Sami, Sanskrit, Tamil, Tibetan, and Turkish terms for 'ritual'.
Key-word: TER.

Stolz, Fritz, 1997, 'Von der Begattung zur Heiligen Hochzeit, vom Beuteteilen zum Abendmahl—kulturelle Gestaltungen natürlicher Prozesse', in: Fritz Stolz (ed.), *Homo naturaliter religiosus. Gehört Religion notwendig zum Mensch-Sein?*, (Studia Religiosa Helvetica / Jahrbuch 3), Bern etc.: Peter Lang (ISBN 3–906759–23–7) 39–64.
[From Copulation to Sacred Marriage, from the Division of Prey to the Lord's Supper—Cultural Shapings of Natural Processes]

This essay explores the religious, and ritual, continuation, or transformation, of two key biological mechanisms: food intake and sexuality. Both have a biological effect. At the same time, they are the starting point for secondary motivations and effects, human communication, and social order. While all this can also be observed among primates, the author argues that this process has gained in dynamics in the course of human evolution. Language allowed for new forms of communication, but even in human, and especially religious, communication, eating and sexuality serve as major "points of crystallization" (48). The investigation of the religious, and ritual, significance of eating and sexuality in Ancient Oriental-Jewish-Christian symbol systems leads the author to conclude that the different aspects of food intake and sexuality—the primary effects, secondary motivations, communication, and the creation of social order—are highly variable (e.g. the primary effects can dominate, or they can recede entirely into the background) (61). Ultimately, however, the historian cannot answer the question of whether culture can be completely cut off from nature (61). [MS]

Key-words: com, ETH, cpl, med, soc, tra.

Strathern, Andrew & Pamela J. Stewart, 1998, 'Embodiment and Communication. Two Frames for the Analysis of Ritual', *Social Anthropology* 6:237–251.

The purpose of this paper is to "compare the analysis of ritual from two different perspectives, embodiment and communication" (237). With regard to the former, the authors "are concerned with the putative effect of rituals on the participants themselves and the environments to which they are linked", with regard to the latter, they "consider the communicative purposes of the actors in rituals *vis à vis* their social context as well as the powers to which the rituals may be directed" (237). Assuming that these two issues are related with one another, the authors argue that they are "not dealing with alternative modes of overall analysis but with modes that may be seen as complementary in their impact" (237). According to the authors, embodiment refers to "the anchoring of certain social values and dispositions in and through the body, with primary reference to the human body" and ritual to "the repetitive, ordered performance of certain embodied actions similarly attached to social values and purposes" (237). In contrast to C. Bell, they argue that embodiment means not bodily experience but "the entry of the social into the human body" (238). In the main part of their paper, the authors analyze the female spirit cult in Hagen by addressing its performance details (241–243), its mythological background (243–245), and the *hambua hatya*, a human sacrifice ritual in Duna (246–247). In the paragraphs entitled "Towards the Symbolic. Elementary and Complex Codifications of Embodiment" (248), the authors argue that the ritual context of embodiment is useful for studying embodiment and communication: "Ritual practices are inevitably a special kind of embodied practices, ones that are tied to a sliding scale of significations, from index to symbol in Peircean terms. It is the movement from index to symbol that we equate with a movement from elementary to complex. As index the body remains itself; as symbol it becomes the vehicle for trope expansion" (248). In their "Conclusion. Trans-Cultural Logics of Embodiment and Communication" (248–250), the authors summarize the argument by saying that "[t]he Hagen and Duna rituals display obvious differences at the level of their details. In a wider sense, however, they show similarities in their logics. They are concerned with cosmic renewal, shown in the avoidance of infertility and sickness" (248). After discussing the similarities and differences in terms of the periodicities of the ritual cycles for renewal and the directionality and emphasis in these renewals in the bodies of the performers, the authors argue that these logics depend "on the idea of communication, since there must be a process of communication between the human body and the cosmic forces" (249). [JK]

References: F. Barth, C.M. Bell (–), Th.J. Csordas, B. Malinowski, R.A. Rappaport (+).
Examples: Female spirit cult in Hagen, human sacrifice ritual in Duna, both in Papua New Guinea.
Key-words: COM, EMB, gdr, mng, SEM, sym.

Strecker, Ivo, 1988, *The Social Practice of Symbolization. An Anthropological Analysis* (London School of Economics. Monographs on Social Anthropology 60); London, Atlantic Highlands (NJ): Athlone Press (ISBN 0–485–19557–7) (ix + 246) (with index and bibliography).

Based on fieldwork among the Hamar of southern Ethiopia, this work addresses symbolism and pragmatics of communication. The author primarily focuses on methodological problems of the interpretation of symbolism in ritual as relevant for anthropological research. In the first part of this volume, entitled "Ritual and Symbolism" (10–26), he indicates the shift from the symbolic product to the principles of symbolic production (10–11) and addresses the crucial role that symbols and rituals play in the analysis of social systems (11–15). He argues that the study of ritual and symbolism is bound up with problems of anthropological description: "Actions which we call 'ritual' tend to provide a pitfall for the ethnographer, because in the practice of fieldwork ritual is often relatively easy to observe" (13). Because of its visibility, "ritual is prone to lead him towards a bias in perception", but "this bias, which initially stems only from practical reasons, soon becomes a bias with theoretical implications" (14). Although the author assumes that ritual can be used "as an analytical indicator which allows an insight into the inner differentiation or anatomy of a social system", he argues that "there are serious analytical limitations. Ritual belongs, after all, to what has come to be called since Marx the superstructure (*Überbau*) of society. Ritual is ideology in action" (14). "Any anthropological description", he continues, "which does not take this into account and uncritically bases its generalizations on observations from the realm of ritual is bound to present not the true but the ideological form of society" (14–15). After discussing the analytical use of ritual in the works of M. Gluckman and V.W. Turner (15–18) and the theory of ritual symbolism presented by Turner (18–22), he formulates a general critique of this approach (22–26). According to the author, Turner is wrong because he "treated multivocality only as the effect and not as the cause of symbolization" (24). As point of departure, the author argues: "Yet if we want to explain symbolism in ritual we must also include in our analysis the cause of symbolism, the authors of symbolic statements who think symbolically and know and anticipate the multivocality of the statements which they create. We must think of people as actors who do not only think of their own interests but also of the interests of others, and who therefore choose at specific moments to communicate not by means of univocal signs but rather by means of multivocal symbols. We have to try to understand the processes which go into symbolic codification. Once we have understood the practice of symbolic coding or, as I have called it in this study, the practice of symbolization, then we will also be able to cope with symbolic statements more competently and use our findings for an analysis of the social system" (25). In the second part, entitled "The Cognitive Basis of Symbolization" (27–57), the author develops symbolism as a cognitive mechanism following D. Sperber (27–35). After addressing issues of focalization and displacement (35–43), he discusses H.P. Grice and his concepts of evocation and implicature (43–50). Then he returns to Sperber and takes irony as a test case for symbolization (50–57). The third and main part of this volume is entitled "Symbolization as a Social Practice" (58–170) and starts with the discussion of P. Brown's & S. Levinson's theory of politeness (60–69). The author then discusses at length the concept of symbolization within the strategies of politeness (69–154) followed by a modification and extension of Brown's and Levinson's model (154–170). The forth part "Symbolization and Social Domination" (171–202) deals with speaking and social domination in Hamar (173–184) and strategies of politeness (184–202). The fifth part of the volume, entitled "Symbolization and Ritual" (203–225) returns to the problem of symbolism in ritual and explains the Hamar rite of passage by the theory of symbolization (205–212). In addressing the limits of explaining symbolism (212–225), the author writes: "The ethnographer is a stranger, a foreigner in an alien culture where, at first, he has no inkling of the order of things. Only through a long and complex process of learning does he come to know the order and in turn reaches the ability to recognize and understand the displacement of things" (214). He argues that "[o]nly as the ethnographer joins in the life of the people, takes part in their practical activities, shares sorrow and joy and health and sickness with them, and as gradually a history of joint experience develops, can he hope that people will begin to communicate with him as they communicate with each other; that is, indirectly by way of implicature" (224). Based on these findings the author concludes: "When this level of discourse has been reached, adequate communication about ritual symbolism becomes possible because now the ethnographer and the people can converse without being afraid of ever breaking what I might perhaps call the 'law of symbolism': that no one may reduce a symbolic statement to any single meaning" (225). [JK]

References: J.L. Austin, P. Bourdieu, **P. Brown & S. Levinson**, É. Durkheim, M. Gluckman, H.P. Grice, A.R. Radcliffe-Brown, E. Sapir, J.R. Searle, **D. Sperber**, V.W. Turner (–).
Review: J. Abbink *Anthr* 85.1–3 (1990) 274.
Key-words: COG, com, pmc, pmt, pr1, RFL, RHT, sem, soc, SYM.

Strecker, Ivo, 1998, 'Auf dem Weg zu einer rhetorischen Ritualtheorie', in: Alfred Schäfer & Michael Wimmer (eds), *Rituale und Ritualisierungen*, (Grenzüberschreitungen 1), Opladen: Leske & Budrich (ISBN 3810021717) (*) 61–93.
[Towards a Rhetoric Theory of Ritual]

Basically, this paper reviews some of the author's previously published works (from 1969, 1971 and 1988 (*)). It mainly consists of quotations from these earlier publications. Moreover, the contributions of some other scholars (Sperber, Grice, Brown, Bourdieu) are reviewed. The review of these contributions dealing with the characteristics of rituals and problems of meaning and symbolization leads the author to notice an irony in the fact that none of the scholars realized the importance of rhetoric in analyzing linguistic pragmatics. Behind many of the problems that were discussed by himself and other scholars, the author now identifies rhetoric in a broader sense of the term, i.e. including different forms of action in communication. [MS]

References: I. Strecker (+), P. Bourdieu, E. Goffman, H.P. Grice, D. Sperber.
Key-words: mng, sym, RHT, com.

Strenski, Ivan, 2003, *Theology and the First Theory of Sacrifice* (Numen Book Series. Studies in the History of Religions 98); Leiden, Boston: Brill (ISBN 90-04-13559-6 / ISSN 0169-8834) (ix + 248) (with index).

This is an attempt at "historizing the theory of sacrifice" seeking "to discover the various 'politics' of theorizing sacrifice—understood broadly as the enabling conditions either facilitating the theorizing of sacrifice or disabling a potential theory of sacrifice" (16). "With theory and talk about theory so abundant these days, a pause to take stock of them as historical realities might help us understand better what we do and what needs to be done in further theorizing" (14). The book focuses mainly on the theory devised by Hubert and Mauss, the "first" full-blown and highly influential theory (rather than mere theoretical or theological account) of sacrifice. The book tries "to give an account of how the 'first theory' of sacrifice came into being within the context of an intellectual, institutional and religious rivalry" (228). Besides arguments and principles, conspirations and deceit are elements of this history. Apart from Hubert and Mauss, the author presents a number of rival theoretical attempts. [MS]

Reference: H. Hubert & M. Mauss.
Example: Sacrifice.
Key-word: hsc.

Sullivan, Lawrence E., 1986, 'Sound and Senses. Toward a Hermeneutics of Performance', *History of Religions* 26:1–33.

This essay "reconnoiters some theories of performance from several points of view... The following pages interpret some interpreters of performance" (1). Hence, it is an attempt in hermeneutics, an interpretation of the interpreters. The essay consists of three sections. In the first (2–14), the author observes "some of the issues that float in the air where various branches of the academy discuss performance" (2). Here the author observes that despite "their differences, it might be argued that all of these theories make several common claims about the nature of performance.... Most important, I would argue all of these theories of performance attempt to grasp the quiddity of symbolic action; they seek to understand what sets performance of the human condition apart from brute behavior" (5). Based on his reading of these theories, the author contends "that the 'quality of knowledge' that underlies performance and sets it apart from behavior is seen to have at least these three characteristics: it is self-constituting, it is signified in genre (i.e., it is manifest in specific articulations of symbolic form), and it brings synesthesia into play" (6). In what follows, the author surveys the way different groups of theorists evaluate synesthesia and self-constitution (7–14). In the second part of his paper (14–27), the author discusses "some strikingly original interpretations of human performance among native South American cultures. These views are not presented as quaint cultural examples from which to extract the hard core of precultural [sic] truth. Rather, here are people's systematic thoughts about their own meaning, about the nature and value of their acts, and about the process of understanding" (15). The third and final section of the paper (28–33) presents some observations on "similarities between hermeneutics of performance in academic culture and the South American. In both instances, the act of interpretation is an act, a performance. Hermeneutics is not a species of knowledge that transcends culture. It cannot be. It is the work of understanding that makes culture. As such, hermeneutics in academic culture bears some affinity with jazz, drama, sports, moral action, and healing. Hermeneutics serves as a resource for culture because it is based not on preference but on a valued order of knowledge that, even if implicit, is, nonetheless, comprehensive. The reflexivity of performance brings this order to the surface in order to critique or judge it" (28). "How one arrives at and interprets the specific knowledge that grounds a culture's performance is a hermeneutical question. It is a hermeneutics driven not by a conflict of readings so much as by a conflict in the meaning of our own acts. Like performance, then, hermeneutics is also self-constituting" (29). "The South American views challenge another assumption about human performance and understanding. Even if performances are self-constituting... cultural performances need not be self-instituted... That is, human performance is an interpretation, a symbolic act of understanding the original event by reenacting it" (30). The paper concludes with the following thesis: "Cultures are interpretations of themselves, including reflections on their process of understanding. All cultures interpret their interpreters. For the moment in academic culture, hermeneutics and entertainment seem to have misplaced their compatibility. However, the act of genuinely understanding the plural cultures that characterize our modern world promises to be a good show" (33). [MS/JK]

References: J.L. Austin, B.A. Babcock, G. Bateson, P. Bourdieu, K. Burke, M. Csikszentmihalyi, M. Eliade, C. Geertz, E. Goffman, D. Hymes, R. Jakobson, E.R. Leach, J.J. MacAloon, R. Schechner, J.R. Searle, M. Singer, S.J. Tambiah, T.S. Turner, V.W. Turner.
Examples: Several performances among South American people; drama, dance, Jazz, sports.
Key-words: com, med, aes, mng, PMC, pr2, rfl, soc, sym.

Tambiah, Stanley Jeyaraja, 1968, 'The Magical Power of Words', *Man* (N.S.) 3:175–208.

The author emphasizes the relevance of linguistics for anthropological approaches to ritual. Because "ritual words are at least as important as other kinds of ritual act" (176), it is necessary to study especially the role of verbal behavior in ritual. Following Edmund Leach, the author defines ritual as "a complex of words and actions (including the manipulation of objects)" (184). Thus the author highlights the interconnection network between actions and words, thereby calling into question the simple identity of word and deed as postulated by linguistic philosophy. That is to say, the metaphoric and metonymic use of language in the magical act—which the author equates with ritual—is only a technique to imitate or simulate practical actions. Exactly this expressive property of the magical words is the secret of their efficacy and power, whereas the primary function of the ordinary language is communication. [JK/Florian Jeserich]

References: J.G. Frazer (–), R. Jakobson, E.R. Leach, C. Lévi-Strauss, **B. Malinowski** (+/–), M. Mauss, V.W. Turner.
Examples: Sinhalese healing ritual, Trobriand magic rituals.
Key-words: com, PMT, pow, eff, pr1, ter.

Tambiah, Stanley Jeyaraja, 1973, 'Form and Meaning of Magical Acts. A Point of View', in: Robin Horton & Ruth Finnegan (eds), *Modes of Thought. Essays on Thinking in Western and Non-Western Societies*, London: Faber & Faber (ISBN 0–571–09544–5) 199–229.

Although both magic and science use the analogical mode of thought, their validity should be measured and verified by different standards. "Magical acts...constitute 'performative' acts by which a property is imperatively transferred to a recipient object or person on an analogical basis. Magical acts are ritual acts, and ritual acts are in turn performative acts whose positive and creative meaning is missed and whose persuasive validity is misjudged if they are subjected to that kind of empirical verification associated with scientific activity" (199). The author exemplifies his assertions with ethnographic data on the Azande, who used analogy in their rites concerning material substances. After summarizing the meaning and types of analogy, he advances the thesis that "in ritual operations by word and object manipulation, the analogical action conforms to the 'persuasive' rather than the 'scientific' model" (212). The combination of word and deed in most 'magical rites' is guided by ritual acts, which are performative acts by means of analogical reasoning. At the end of the article, the author notes: "By simply naming rituals of non-Western societies as 'magic', and the substances they use as 'medicines' and 'drugs', we cannot thereby attribute to the phenomena so named, by virtue of that naming, characteristics that may be peculiar to one's own contemporary civilization" (228). [JK]

References: E.E. Evans-Pritchard, B. Malinowski, V.W. Turner, F. de Saussure, R. Horton, M. Weber.
Key-words: cmp, exp, pmt, pr1, eff.

Tambiah, Stanley Jeyaraja, 1981, 'A Performative Approach to Ritual', *Proceedings of the British Academy* 65:113–169.

The author treats the dual aspect of rituals as performance. On the one hand, ritual "reproduces in its repeated enactments certain seemingly invariant and stereotyped sequences", and on the other hand, "no one performance of a rite, however rigidly prescribed, is exactly the same as another performance" (115). Although one cannot separate ritual from non-ritual absolutely, he tries to find relative contrasting features in order to distinguish between certain kinds of social activity. Accordingly, Tambiah ventures a working definition of ritual: "Ritual is a culturally constructed system of symbolic communication. It is constituted of patterned and ordered sequences of words and acts, often expressed in multiple media, whose content and arrangement are characterized in varying degree by formality (conventionality), stereotypy (rigidity), condensation (fusion), and redundancy (repetition). Ritual action in its constitutive features is performative in these three senses: in the Austinian sense of performative wherein saying something is also doing something as a conventional act; in the quite different sense of a staged performance that uses multiple media by which the participants experience the event intensively; and in the third sense of indexical values—I derive this concept from Peirce—being attached to and inferred by actors during the performance" (119). [JK]

References: J.L. Austin, Ch.S. Peirce.
Key-words: DEF, com, cpl, PMT, PMC, pr1, SEM, sym, vir.

Tambiah, Stanley Jeyaraja, 1985, *Culture, Thought, and Social Action. An Anthropological Perspective*; Cambridge (MA), London: Harvard University Press (ISBN 0–674–17969–2) (411).

Selected contents: "The Magical Power of Words" (17–59) (*); "Form and Meaning of Magical Acts" (60–86) (*); "A Thai Cult of Healing" (87–122); "A Performative Approach to Ritual" (123–166) (*); "Animals Are Good to Think and Good to Prohibit" (169–211); "From Varna to Caste through Mixed Unions" (212–251); "On Flying Witches and Flying Canoes. The Coding of Male and Female Values" (287–315); "A Reformulation of Geertz's Conception of the Theater State" (316–338); "An Anthropologist's Creed" (339–358). [JK/MS]

Key-words: com, cpl, cmp, exp, PMT, pmc, tha, pow, eff, pr1, sem, sym.

Terrin, Aldo Natale, 1999, *Il rito. Antropologia e fenomenologia della ritualità* (Le scienze umane); Brescia: Morcelliana (ISBN 88–372–1751–x) (444) (with index and bibliography).
[Ritual. Anthropology and Phenomenology of Ritualness]

This massive volume is divided into two main parts. Part one is entitled "Anthropology of rite" (19–187), and part two "Phenomenology of ritualness [*ritualità*]" (189–402). Part one has three chapters. Chapter 1 reviews main approaches to the definition, classification, and interpretation of rites (19–65). The author sketches the socio-functionalist, psychoanalytic and cathartic, structuralist and cognitivist, ethological and ecological, micro-sociological and (last but not least) expressive-ludic-symbolic interpretations (50–64). The latter interpretation builds on the "phenomenological" (28) definition proposed by the author: "...phenomenologically speaking, a rite is a sacred and repetitive action that is composed of a *drómenon* (action) and a *legómenon* (word, myth). In it and in the conjunction of word and action a 'holistic' way of acting manifests itself...This ritual action seeks to realize the *legómenon* (the myth) by means of the structure of a symbolic-mythical play where an indisputable premise asserts itself according to which *x signifies y in the context ct*, i.e., where something stands for something else" (29). Chapter 2 takes a closer look at main socio-functionalist theories of ritual in anthropology (67–102). The author argues that most of the anthropologists always pursue an alibi, "a somewhere else where to seek the significance of rite" (102). In chapter three the author discusses ethological and ecological approaches to ritualization and rite (103–142). The fourth chapter of part one is entitled "The rite: by necessity and by play" (143–187). This chapter is the theoretical cornerstone of the book. In it, the author argues that the rite is "co-natural with the human being" (143) and he advances a model of "incarnation" for understanding rites (143). The author emphasizes that necessity and play are the two main ingredients of rites (155). According to the author, rite and life are interdependent. The rite has no purpose beyond itself (173). As play it transposes reality and by going beyond the 'as if' it creates its own reality (179). "The realization of the rite coincides with the passage from the 'as if' to the 'that is it' here and now" (179). "The religious rite . . . serves to create a provisional but real transposition of the world . . ." (187). The second, phenomenological, part of the book comprises chapters on "space and rite" (191–216), "time and rite" (217–256), "rite and music" (257–300), and "rite and theatre" (301–352). The final chapter discusses rites and performance in post-modern contexts between dispersion and "quest for a holistic meaning" (353–402). [MS]

References: G. Bateson, C.M. Bell, M.E.F. Bloch, W. Burkert, E.G. d'Aquili, É. Durkheim, M. Eliade, E.E. Evans-Pritchard, M. Fortes, J.G. Frazer, S. Freud, C. Geertz, R. Girard, M. Gluckman, R.L. Grimes, J.E. Harrison, J. Huizinga, J.S. Huxley, S.K. Langer, E.Th. Lawson, C. Lévi-Strauss, K.Z. Lorenz, B. Malinowski, J. McManus, B.G. Myerhoff, A.R. Radcliffe-Brown, R.A. Rappaport, R. Schechner, J.Z. Smith, F. Staal, S.J. Tambiah, V.W. Turner.
Examples: Various.
Key-words: GEN, hsc, DEF, myt, sec, eth, pmc, THA, SPC, TIM, mus.

Thomas, Günter, 1998, *Medien—Ritual—Religion. Zur religiösen Funktion des Fernsehens* (Suhrkamp Taschenbuch Wissenschaft 1370); Frankfurt a. M.: Suhrkamp (ISBN 3-518-28970-5) (723) (with index and bibliography).
[Media—Ritual—Religion. On the Religious Function of Television]

In this book the author explores religious, and especially ritual, dimensions of television. His main argument runs as follows: The institution of television, in its unity of production, presentation, and reception, is to be understood as a ritual-liturgical order consisting of various differentiated single rituals. This order could be defined as religious with regard to functions and characteristics. After having introduced theological conceptions of this topic at the beginning of the book, the author elaborates his argument in the main section. He begins with a critical evaluation of contributions to ritual and religious dimensions of television so far. Then he continues by discussing various complex and multifaceted definitions of 'culture', 'religion', and 'ritual' with respect to their relevance to television issues. It is here that the author argues that religion (and television) is best seen as a strong ritualized symbolic system that produces encompassing cosmologies for society. Following Geertz, he focuses on the ability of religious symbols to span and connect different spheres of reality in order to form 'common sense'. In ritual, as in watching television, one leaves the reality of everyday life behind to enter a ritually-established space of experience where the lived and the imagined world are amalgamated into a single system of symbolic forms. Thereby, a temporarily limited 'imagined community' is created among viewers on the one hand as well as between viewers and producers on the other. In contrast to rituals, where physical presence is necessary, television needs only what the author calls 'medial presence', i.e. the inclusion of viewers in cinematic space through their bodily reactions to the program. In this way, a process of 'secondary secularization' is initiated that is characterized by more reflexivity, more intense feelings of 'contingency', a more voluntary nature of participation, and a growing indirect control of bodily affects instead of the direct control of ritual bodies. These elaborations are completed by the system theoretic approach to rituals of Roy Rappaport. By analyzing mechanisms and processes of communication in ritual, the author shows further similarities between ritual and television. In Part IV, the author gives two examples of religious and ritual dimensions of television, first the liturgical order of television programs and, second, the cosmology produced through television programs, which are discussed with the help of the elaborations from the previous chapters. Finally, the author concludes his book with a summary of his findings, perspectives for further research, and the implications of his findings for the theological frame outlined in the introduction. [Thorsten Gieser]

References: **C. Geertz**, **R.A. Rappaport**, V.W. Turner.
Review: M.L. Pirner *ZPT* 51.3 (1999) 331 f.
Key-words: myt, soc, str, sec, sym, com, eth, emb, cpl, emo, MED, spc, tim, rfl.

Thomas, Günter, 2000, 'Secondary Ritualization in a Postliterate Culture. Reconsidering and Expanding Walter Ong's Contribution on "Secondary Orality"', *Soundings. An Interdisciplinary Journal* 83.2:385–409.

In this article, the author builds up on the work of Walter Ong and Jan Assmann. After the "Introduction" (385) follows a first section "The Transition from Orality to Literacy" (386–388) in which Ong's ideas to this subject are presented. "In oral cultures, the inevitable problem of retaining and retrieving knowledge is mastered by the use of mnemonic aids like patterning, rhythm, and formula.... Continuity in the flow of thought and persistent focus of attention has to be ensured by uninterruptedness, redundancy, repetition, and slow progress of thought" (386). "The spoken word unites people in physical co-presence as listeners and creates a unity with the speaker" (387). "The advent of the alphabet changed the picture as did the invention of print" (387). "The tool of writing... [separates] the writer and the recipient... It liberates from the controlling power of presence in real interaction" (387). But "Ong's insights into the character of primary orality can be and have to be supplemented with observations concerning the place of ritual within the overall economy of oral communication in preliterate cultures" (388). Therefore, in the second section, "The Connection of Orality, Ritual, and Cultural Memory" (388–389), Assmann's concept of 'cultural memory' is summarized. "The shift from oral culture to chirographic culture is at the same time a shift from ritual coherence to textual coherence as a way of holding the world together" (389). "Assmann emphasizes the important role of ritual in oral societies and traces the transformations in the formation of cultural identity brought about by writing" (389). In the next section, "'Secondary Orality' in a Media Age" (390–395), the author first summarizes Ong's conceptualization of 'secondary orality' (390–391). "However, a close and precise reconstruction of Ong's account of secondary orality faces a complex of problems" (391). In order to avoid these, the author chooses to concentrate on one particular type of secondary orality, namely that found in radio and television, which he calls "audiovisual orality" (392). According to the author, audiovisual orality "is in its own way formulaic and replete with repetition. Enabling visual and oral presence without physical presence, it simulates immediacy and creates community by providing a shared experience, a shared field of perception. Based on self-consciousness and reflexivity, it deliberately plays with the border between fiction and life. It revitalizes a dramatic polarization of virtues and vices and offers endless combat between heroes and villains both in its mythic narratives as well as in its real life stories. Within its ongoing, never-ending performance of these narratives, audiovisual orality brings back flat characters yet places them in very linear plots. By describing the world from a perspective beyond one's own world, television creates a consensual field, articulates a social self, and monitors society's self-image. It allows one to play with the safety of 'not being there' and the thrill and immediacy of 'being there'" (395). In analogy to Ong's concept of 'secondary orality', the author now develops in the next section "The Concept and Place of 'Secondary Ritualization'" (395–398). "'Secondary ritualization' substitutes the physical copresence of participants with an audiovisual means of presence and assumes a much higher degree of reflexivity in ritual communication—even though it is rarely identified as 'ritual'. Physical presence is replaced by technological means of mediated presence" (396). The author then reflects on the similarities and differences between audiovisual orality and traditional rituals, summing up eight points (397–398). The next section poses the question about the relation between "'Secondary Orality' and Cultural Memory" (398–399). The academic world, and other sections of our society, may still be based on literacy. "There is little doubt, however, that for most people in our society who live most of their lives in a common sense world, television is the leading distributor and conveyor of interpretation and meaning.... The knowledge that builds up individual and cultural self-identity needs not only to exist and to be stored, but to circulate and to be performed in discourses. It needs to be accessible to 'everyone'. The communication processes that circulate it need to be rooted in the practice of everyday life. From this perspective, processes of 'secondary ritualization' in television have to an extent taken over the function of constructing cultural memory" (399). The article closes with some "Concluding Remarks and Questions" (399–400). "The concept of 'secondary ritualization' owes very much to Walter Ong's work in rhetoric. It can, however, introduce an important distinction into the field of ritual studies. On the one hand, it can help to confine the inflationary use of the concept 'ritual', and on the other hand, it opens up new venues for the analysis of contemporary media culture" (400). [JS]

References: W. Ong (+), J. Assmann (+), R.L. Grimes (+).
Key-words: def, soc, pow, idn, str, sec, com, cpl, dyn, MED, par, RFL, tra, spc, tim.

Thomas, Günter, 2006, 'Communication', in: Jens Kreinath, Jan A.M. Snoek & Michael Stausberg (eds), *Theorizing Rituals. Vol. I: Issues, Topics, Approaches, Concepts*, (Numen Book Series 114–1), Leiden, Boston: Brill (ISBN-10: 90–04–15342–x, ISBN-13: 978–90–04–15342–4) 321–343.

This chapter explores the concept of communication in regard to ritual. In a first step the author tries to map the field and proposes an ordering pattern for structuring the broad variety of theoretical approaches which in some way or the other conceptualize ritual as a communication process. The second step consists of a conceptual exposition and elaboration of two essential concepts: communication and perception. Based on this exposition, in a third step, a 'thick theoretical description' of the ritual way of communication is provided: Ritual is a complex, highly plastic, and amazingly evolutionary 'successful' form of communication that addresses essential and inescapable problems and paradoxes of communication processes in social life. As a consequence, rituals are still present today in all societal subsystems, ranging from religion to law, education, sport, the arts, science, and economics. Seen in the light of communication theory, the form of ritual is one elementary mechanism to connect multiple psychic systems and social systems and serves to deal with the inherent risks of communication. And yet, since ritual manages the risks of communication within the medium of communication, it always is in danger of creating the problems it attempts to solve: the 'ritual way of communicating' can fail. [Günter Thomas]

References: R.L. Grimes, R.A. Rappaport, J.A.M. Snoek, R. Needham, D. Handelman, J.Z. Smith, E.R. Leach, B. Gladigow, C. Humphrey & J. Laidlaw.
Examples: Christian Mass, Lord's Supper.
Key-words: COM, cpl, dyn, emb, frm, med, par, rfl, str.

Toren, Christina, 1993, 'Sign Into Symbol, Symbol as Sign. Cognitive Aspects of a Social Process', in: Pascal Boyer (ed.), *Cognitive Aspects of Religious Symbolism*, Cambridge etc.: Cambridge University Press (ISBN 0–521–43288–X) 147–164.

The author calls into question the common anthropological assumption of a domain called 'the symbolic' as demarcated by ritual. She states that this assumption depends on a conventional *a priori* distinction between sign and symbol. According to the author, the notion of ritual action as symbolic should be understood as the product of a progressive cognitive construction. Considering the example of Fijian kava-drinking, the author points out that only older children and adults fully understand and construct the symbolic meaning of rituals. For them the above/below axis, e.g., not only describes the space inside buildings but symbolically represents the hierarchical relations within family and society. For younger children, in contrast, above/below is nothing more than a 'sign'; it refers to nothing but itself. For this reason the author argues for a developmental process of cognitive differentiation between sign and symbol. Sign and symbol make up, so to speak, the two poles of a progressive continuum of meaning. Her core argument ends as follows: "If, as I argue, ritual comes to stand for something other than itself as the outcome of a developmental process, this implies that our received anthropological notion of the symbolic inevitably distorts our analysis of 'the meaning' of ritual. For such meaning as is ascribed to any given ritualised behaviour by ourselves and others lies not only in the ritual process itself, but in the very developmental process through which persons make meaning out of ritual. *This is a process which in its nature is always unfinished, for meaning is always capable of further elaboration*" (159–160). Besides a critical consideration of recent approaches, the author concludes with some suggestions for understanding ritual: "As the product of human cognitive processes, 'meaning' cannot be located anywhere outside the minds of human subjects, for it is only momentarily instantiated in the product of their interactions. This is not to imply, absurdly, that meaning is so labile as to preclude communication and the continuity of communication, but rather that it is always in the process of 'becoming'" (163). And this dynamic sheds light on the notion of ritual as rule-governed behavior as well, because "it is only when we understand the process through which 'the symbolic' is cognitively constructed that we can also understand the coercive power of ritual" (147, cf. 161). [JK/Florian Jeserich]

References: M.E.F. Bloch (–), P. Bourdieu (–), G.A. Lewis (–), J. Piaget, M. Sahlins (–), D. Sperber (–), L.S. Vygotsky, H.R. Wagner.
Example: Fijian kava ritual.
Key-words: COG, com, mng, POW, sem, str, sym, dyn, soc.

Travers, Andrew, 1982, 'Ritual Power in Interaction', ***Symbolic Interaction*** **5:277–286 (with bibliography).**

After a short introduction to the article (277–278) follows a summary of Goffman's theory of the concept "ritualness" (278) and an introduction to the two examples: "Punks, Nurses, and Pollution" (279). The substance of the article are the descriptions of these two case studies: "Ritual Power through Pollution: Punks" (279–282) and "Ritual Power through Socialization: Nurses" (282–284). The article ends with some conclusions in the section "Ritual Power" (284–285). The author wants "to develop Erving Goffman's idea that persons are ritual beings by concentrating on how persons may acquire 'ritualness' through their interactional conduct.... The description of punks and nurses will show how Goffman's notion of ritualness can be further refined into a new concept for interaction, 'ritual power'. This I define as a variable quantity of Goffman's 'ritualness', derived from interaction conduct, and often done so deliberately" (277). The author wants to "theorise from" the data (278), which material "is used for inventing rather than 'testing' theory" (279). "Now punks go after ritual power by desacralizing themselves where nurses travel in an opposite direction in order to escape the contaminants with which their work brings them into contact. Nurses, therefore, can be said to sacralize themselves in just as deliberate and far-reaching [a] way as punks do the reverse" (282). The author summarizes as follows: "Ritual power may now be defined as the amount of 'ritualness' a person has within interaction, and as such it is something more than the ritualness that Goffman has said must be respected between persons. So ritual power can be won from interactional conduct alone and is not just a property to be lost or, at best, after being lost, restored to a former level. (It should be noted here of course, that, since ritual power belongs primarily to interactions, it is not the same as status, which is given to a person rather than generated by himself out of his conduct alone.)" (284). [JS]

References: **E. Goffman, M. Douglas**.
Key-words: soc, POW, idn, sec, pr1, pr2, emb, agn.

Turner, Terence S., 1977, 'Transformation, Hierarchy and Transcendence. A Reformulation of Van Gennep's Model of the Structure of *Rites de Passage*', in: Sally Falk Moore & Barbara G. Myerhoff (eds), *Secular Ritual*, Assen, Amsterdam: Van Gorcum (ISBN 90–232–1457–9) (*) 53–70.

The author summarizes his theory (or model, as he calls it) as follows: "Rather than a simple triadic sequence,... the elementary structure of *rites de passage* identified by Van Gennep is really composed of a pair of cross-cutting binary contrasts. These can be conceived as intersecting vertical and horizontal axes. The horizontal axis consists of the contrast between two categories (e.g., 'boy' and 'man') between which the passage takes place. The vertical axis comprises the relationship between this pair of categories and the higher-level transformational principles that regulate the passage between them. The point is that the structure of *rites de passage* models both of these axes simultaneously, in a way that defines each as a function of the other. The rites of separation and aggregation, in other words, mark the vertical (inter-level) separation between the level at which the initial and final social states or status-identities of the transition are defined and the higher level comprised by the principle of transformation between them, as well as the horizontal (intra-level) separation from the first of the two statuses and aggregation with the second. The liminal phase of the ritual, as this implies, is the direct expression of the higher level of transcendent, transformational principles which form the ground and mechanism of the social transition in question.... The contents of the liminal stage are...defined by the model as situationally and culturally dependent variables. The common features of the expression of the variable content of liminal rites are accounted for on the basis of the relative transcendental (hierarchical) relationship of the principles expressed by such rites in any given instance to the lower-level relations or states comprising the terminal points" (68–69). [JS]

References: A. van Gennep (+), V.W. Turner (+), M. Gluckman (–).
Key-words: pmc, pr2, STR, rel, EFF.

Turner, Terence S., 2006, 'Structure, Process, Form', in: Jens Kreinath, Jan A.M. Snoek & Michael Stausberg (eds), *Theorizing Rituals. Vol. I: Issues, Topics, Approaches, Concepts*, (Numen Book Series 114–1), Leiden, Boston: Brill (ISBN-10: 90–04–15342–x, ISBN-13: 978–90–04–15342–4) 207–246.

This chapter presents a review and critique of Anthropological theories of ritual, beginning with Durkheim and the *Année Sociologique*, and selectively covering later French, British, German and American ideas about the structural and formal aspects of ritual and the dynamics of ritual process. The emphasis is on constructing a synthetic theory using the valuable contributions of each of these approaches together with more recent theoretical ideas drawn from linguistic pragmatics (e.g., objectification), ethology and social interaction analysis (framing, efficacy), the theory of tropes, phenomenological approaches to subjective-objective interaction, and hermeneutic concepts of interpretation (e.g., intentionality and meaning). A major point of the analysis is that there is no incompatibility between structural, formal and interpretative analyses, if they are consistently reformulated as aspects of activity or praxis in its objective, subjective and social respects. On the contrary, a praxiological approach may show the way to integrate semiotic notions of signification, hermeneutic and phenomenological notions of meaning and subjectivity, and social interactionist concepts of framing and efficacy. [Terence Turner]

Key-words: STR, frm, eff, eth, rht, mng, sem, pr1.

Turner, Victor Witter, 1967, *The Forest of Symbols. Aspects of Ndembu Ritual*; Ithaca (NY): Cornell University Press (No ISBN) (xii + 405).

This volume brings together a number of articles published previously, as well as one new chapter, "Mukanda: The Rite of Circumcision" (151–279), on ritual theory and on the rituals of the Ndembu. The first part contains those more concerned with theory; the second part, the more descriptive ones. However, "the theoretical part contains much descriptive material, and the descriptions are interwoven with theoretical passages" (1). Already in the "Introduction" (1–16), the author presents some of his now classical positions. He distinguishes, for the Ndembu, between life-crisis rituals and rituals of affliction (6). Life-crisis rituals are defined as rituals that mark "an important point in the physical or social development of an individual, such as birth, puberty, or death" (7). Rituals of affliction are not explicitly defined, but in the section describing them (9–11) we read: "whenever an individual has been divined to have been 'caught' by...a spirit, he or she becomes the subject of an elaborate ritual, which many people from far and near attend, devised at once to propitiate and to get rid of the spirit that is thought to be causing the trouble" (9). "Then, if one has undergone successful treatment, one is entitled to become a minor 'doctor' when the same ritual is performed for other people, perhaps progressing in time to the role of principal doctor. Thus, the way to religious fame is through affliction" (10). According to the author, the Ndembu know three kinds of affliction, each with its own ritual treatment, corresponding to hunting cults, fertility cults, and curative cults (10–11), which are then described. The first chapter, "Symbols in Ndembu Ritual" (19–47), presents much theoretical material on symbolism. It contains one of the most quoted statements by the author: "By 'ritual' I mean prescribed formal behavior for occasions not given over to technological routine, having reference to beliefs in mystical beings or powers. The symbol is the smallest unit of ritual which still retains the specific properties of ritual behavior; it is the ultimate unit of specific structure in a ritual context" (19). And also: "Each kind of ritual is a patterned process in time, the units of which are symbolic objects and serialized items of symbolic behavior" (45). The second chapter, "Ritual Symbolism, Morality, and Social Structure among the Ndembu" (48–58), is again on symbolism. It contains such statements as: "It must not be forgotten that ritual symbols are not merely signs representing known things; they are felt to possess ritual efficacy, to be charged with power from unknown sources, and to be capable of acting on persons and groups coming in contact with them in such a way as to change them for the better or in a desired direction. Symbols, in short, have an orectic as well as a cognitive function. They elicit emotion and express and mobilize desire" (54). Chapter 3 (59–92) is about color classification. Chapter 4 is one of the most famous papers by the author on ritual theory: "Betwixt and Between. The Liminal Period in Rites de Passage" (93–111). Here he introduces the concepts "betwixt and between" (97), "liminality" (95–100), and "comity" (100–101) (which will later in his work evolve into 'communitas'). The remaining chapters are less theoretically dense. [JS/MS]

Example: The Ndembu.
Reviews: J.L. Peacock *AA* 70.5 (1968) 984 f; L. Bloom *JMAS* 6.1–4 (1968) 290 f; W. Hirschberg *Kairos* 10 (1968) 308; G. Calame-Griaule *SSI* 7.6 (1968) 51; K.O.L. Burridge *Oc* 39.4 (1969) 331 f; P.H. Gulliver *BSOAS* 33.2 (1970) 437; R.E.S. Tanner *HJ* 11.1 (1970) 88; B. Ben-Amos *WF* 29.2 (1970) 134.
Key-words: cmp, mng, SYM, STR, eff, emo, def.

Turner, Victor Witter, 1969, *The Ritual Process. Structure and Anti-Structure* (The Lewis Henry Morgan Lectures at the University of Rochester 1966); Chicago: Routledge & Kegan Paul (ISBN 0-7100-6765-8) (viii + 213) (with index and bibliography).

In this book the author attempts to place his research on the Ndembu of northwestern Zambia in the context of ritual theory. In the two opening chapters, the author gives a detailed ethnographic survey of two Ndembu rituals. In doing so, he wants to "stress how certain regularities that emerged from the analysis of numerical data, such as village genealogies and censuses and records of succession to office and inheritance of property, became fully intelligible only in the light of values embodied and expressed in symbols at ritual performances" (8). In the first chapter, "Planes of Classification in a Ritual of Life and Death" (1–43), he explores "the semantics of ritual symbols in *Isoma*, a ritual of the Ndembu", and constructs "from the observational and exegetical data a model of the semantic structure of this symbolism" (10). His method and procedure, "to begin with particulars and move to generalization" (10), is the reverse of the structural approach of scholars who "explain specific rituals as exemplifying or expressing the 'structural models' they find in the myths" (14). By contrast, the author favors an indigenous exegesis of symbols. For this reason, he attempts "to penetrate the inner structure of ideas" contained in the *Isoma* ritual: "It is therefore *necessary* to begin at the other end, with the basic building-blocks, the 'molecules', of ritual. These I shall call 'symbols'..." (14). Based on an analysis of the processual form or pattern of the *Isoma* ritual, the author points out various triadic and dyadic structural features of classification involved in this ritual. He concludes: "In other types of ritual contexts other classifications apply.... What is really needed, for the Ndembu and, indeed, for any other culture, is a typology of culturally recognized and stereotyped situations, in which the symbols utilized are classified according to the goal structure of the specific situation. There is no single hierarchy of classifications that may be regarded as pervading all types of situations" (41). The second chapter is on the "Paradoxes of Twinship in Ndembu Ritual" (44–93). The author summarizes: "An event, such as twinning, that falls outside the orthodox classifications of society is, paradoxically, made the ritual occasion for an exhibition of values that relate to the community as a whole, as a homogeneous, unstructured unity that transcends its differentiations and contradictions" (92). He continues by addressing the dramatic structure of his book: "This theme, of the dualism between 'structure' and 'communitas', and their ultimate resolution in 'societas', seen as process rather then timeless entity, dominates the next three chapters of this book" (92). In the following chapter, "Liminality and Communitas" (94–130), the author further elaborates an issue that "is in the first place represented by the nature and characteristics of what Arnold van Gennep (1960) has called the 'liminal phase' of *rites de passage*" (94). The author defines the two concepts introduced in this chapter as follows: 1) "The attributes of liminality or of liminal *personae* ('threshold people') are necessary ambiguous, since this condition and these persons elude or slip through the network of classifications that normally locate states and positions in cultural space. Liminal entities are neither here nor there; they are betwixt and between the positions assigned and arrayed by law, custom, convention, and ceremonial" (95). 2) "I prefer the Latin term 'communitas' to 'community', to distinguish this modality of social relationship from an 'area of common living'. The distinction between structure and communitas is not simply the familiar one between 'secular' and 'sacred', or that, for example, between politics and religion" (96). "It is rather a matter of giving recognition to an essential and generic human bond, without which there could be *no* society. Liminality implies that the high could not be high unless the low existed, and he who is high must experience what it is like to be low" (97). Moreover, the author argues that "communitas has an existential quality; it involves the whole man in his relation to other whole men. Structure, on the other hand, has cognitive quality;...it is essentially a set of classifications, a model for thinking about culture and nature and ordering one's public life" (127). He sets up the relation between both as follows: "Communitas breaks in through the interstices of structure, in liminality; at the edge of structure, in marginality; and from beneath structure, in inferiority" (128). Thus, "the distinction between structure and communitas exists and obtains symbolic expression in the cultural attributes of liminality, marginality, and inferiority" (130). In the fourth chapter, "Communitas. Model and Process" (131–165), the author stresses the modalities of communitas. Thus he distinguishes between different modes of communitas: 1) the existential or spontaneous, 2) the normative, and 3) the ideological (132) and applies this distinction in his comparison of various cases in cross-cultural perspective. In the concluding chapter, "Humility and Hierarchy. The Liminality of Status Elevation and Reversal" (166–203), the author focuses on liminality as both "phase and status" (167). In terms of structure and process, he distinguishes between "two main types of liminality", namely, the "*rituals of status elevation*" and the "*rituals of status reversal*" (167). At the end of this chapter, the author summarizes his argument as follows: "Society (*societas*) seems to be a process rather than a thing—a dialectical process with successive phases of structure and communitas.... Persons starved of one in their functional day-to-day activities seek it in ritual liminality. The structurally inferior aspire to symbolic structural superiority in ritual; the structurally superior aspire to symbolic communitas and undergo penance to achieve it" (203). [JK]

References: M. Douglas (+), É. Durkheim (–), M. Eliade (+), E.E. Evans-Pritchard (+), M. Fortes (+/–), **A. van Gennep** (+), M. Gluckman (+/–), E. Goffman (+), R. Needham, A.I. Richards (+), **C. Lévi-Strauss** (–), M. Wilson (+).

Examples: Healing rituals, *rites de passage*, initiation, joking relations.
Reviews: B. Anderson *ActaSoc* 13.4 (1970) 281; T.O. Beidelmann *Anthr* 65.1/2 (1970) 322; N. Abercrombie *Month* 3.1.1–6 (1970) 306; P.H. Gulliver *BSOAS* 34.1 (1971) 195; P.M. Gardner *JAF* 84.334 (1971) 450; F.B. Welbourn *JRA* 4.1 (1971) 69; I.M. Lewis *Man* 6.2 (1971) 306; **Th. Schwartz *AA* 74.4 (1972) 904–908**; J.-C. Muller *CJAS* 12.3 (1978) 485; A. Soucy *CanbAnth* 1.1 (2000) 152 f.
Key-words: cmp, cog, dyn, emb, ecl, emo, mng, PMC, rel, STR, SYM, tim.

Turner, Victor Witter, 1974a, *Dramas, Fields, and Metaphors. Symbolic Action in Human Society* (Symbol, Myth, and Ritual 6); Ithaca (NY): Cornell University Press (ISBN 0–8014–0816–4 / 0–8014–9151–7 (p)) (309) (with bibliographies to the chapters, and index).

This volume brings together seven essays, which, with the exception of the second, were presented as lectures and/or published between 1967 and 1974: 1) "Social Dramas and Ritual Metaphors", 2) "Religious Paradigms and Political Action. Thomas Becket at the Council of Northampton", 3) "Hidalgo. History as Social Drama", 4) "The Word of the Dogon" (first published as a review in *Social Science Information* 7.6 [1968], 55–61), 5) "Pilgrimages as Social Processes" (first published as "The Center Out There. Pilgrims' Goal" in *History of Religions* 12.3 [1973], 191–230), 6) "Passages, Margins, and Poverty. Religious Symbols of Communitas" (first published in *Worship* 46 [1972], 390–412 + 432–494), and 7) "Metaphors of Anti-structure in Religious Culture" (first published in Allan W. Eister (ed.): *Changing Perspectives in the Scientific Study of Religion*, New York 1974). In his "Preface", the author writes: "'Dramas', 'passages', 'action', 'processes'—these are the key words in the titles of the essays in this book. Alongside them are such terms as 'metaphors' and 'paradigms'. The book attempts in fact to probe and describe the ways in which social actions of various kinds acquire form through the metaphors and paradigms in their actors' heads (put there by explicit teaching and implicit generalization from social experience), and, in certain intensive circumstances, generate unprecedented forms that bequeath history new metaphors and paradigms" (13). We find here also his well-known concept of liminoidity defined: "In the evolution of man's symbolic 'cultural' action, we must seek those processes which correspond to open-endedness in biological evolution. I think we have found them in those liminal, or 'liminoid' (postindustrial-revolution), forms of symbolic action, those genres of free-time activity, in which all previous standards and models are subjected to criticism, and fresh new ways of describing and interpreting sociocultural experience are formulated. The first of these forms are expressed in philosophy and science, the second in art and religion" (15). "Because [the modern arts and sciences] are outside the arenas of direct industrial production, because they constitute the 'liminoid' analogues of liminal processes and phenomena in tribal and early agrarian societies, their very outsiderhood disengages them from direct functional action on the minds and behavior of a society's members" (16). Finally, the author introduces the terms of the title of the volume: "In the present context, 'fields' are the abstract cultural domains where paradigms are formulated, established, and come into conflict. Such paradigms consist of sets of 'rules' from which many kinds of sequences of social action may be generated but which further specify what sequences must be excluded. Paradigm conflict arises over exclusion rules. 'Arenas' are the concrete settings in which paradigms become transformed into metaphors and symbols with reference to which political power is mobilized and in which there is a trial of strength between influential paradigm-bearers. 'Social dramas' represent the phased process of their contestation. These abstract formulations underlie the essays that make up the book" (17). [JS]

Reference: A. van Gennep.
Examples: Thomas Becket, Hidalgo, Dogon, pilgrimage.
Reviews: G.E. Swanson *CS* 4.3 (1975) 308; R.W. Friedrichs *JSSR* 14.1 (1975) 67–70; **J.W. Fernandez *JSSR* 14.2 (1975) 191–197**; R.B. Taylor *CSR* 6.2/3 (1976) 250; N.S. Hopkins *IJCS* 17 (1976) 317; R.S. Ellwood *JAAR* 44.1 (1976) 193; B. Kapferer *SoRA* 9 (1976) 170.
Key-words: sym, str, eth, pow, med, spc, cpr, soc, emo.

Turner, Victor Witter, 1974b, 'Symbols and Social Experience in Religious Ritual', *Studia Missionalia* 23:1–21.

The author begins by repeating his thesis "that religious ritual is composed of symbols, verbal and non-verbal, which might be described as its 'units or molecules'" (1). In what follows, he reviews the "vast but confused literature" around the terms 'symbol', 'sign', and 'signal', "to which several scientific and humanistic disciplines have contributed" (1). In particular, he refers to "a few useful definitions and distinctions from the new discipline of 'semiotics'" (2). By way of example, he explores terms such as 'symbol', 'sign vehicle' and 'sign', '*signifiant*' and '*signifié*', 'token' and 'type' (2–3). The author denies that a simple 'sign' model is adequate for the analysis of rituals, for "there is not just a single denotatum, but several denotata; not one designatum, but several designata" (7). Instead, he opts for the concept of a 'multivocal symbol'. Symbols are multivocal in that they are susceptible of many meanings and significations. A 'multivocal symbol' is characterized by three aspects: "The multivocal symbol is composed of: 1. a symbol vehicle which is iconic in that at least one of its sensory perceptible characteristics can be readily associated with at least one of its denotations (e.g. white sap = milk = matriliny...); 2. a set of denotations, or primary meanings—not usually a single denotation; 3. a set of designations or connotations implied in addition to the primary meaning(s) of the symbol" (8). Besides this multivocality of a ritual symbol, the author stresses its polarization of meaning. These, however, are "not the only 'structural' properties of ritual symbols. Such properties have to be derived from the various dimensions of meaning we can detect in the symbols" (10). Based on his work on African religion, he distinguishes between "three major dimensions of significance—(a) the exegetic, (b), the operational and (c) the positional" (11). These are defined in the following terms: a) "The exegetical dimension consists of the whole corpus of explanations of a particular symbol's or a chain of symbol's meaning offered by indigenous informants" (11). b) "In the operational dimension a symbol's meaning is equated (*à la* Wittgenstein) with its use—here we observe not only what ritual participants say about it but also what they do with it" (12). c) "In the positional dimension we see the meaning of a symbol as derived from its relationship to other symbols in a specific cluster or gestalt of symbols whose elements acquire much of their meaning from their position in its structure, from their relationship to other symbols" (12–13). Concerning the exegetic dimension, he argues that "the meaning of a symbol is built up by analogy and association on three semantic foundations, which we may call its (a) nominal, (b) subtantial and (c) artifactual semantic bases. (a) The nominal basis is represented by the name assigned to the symbol in ritual contexts, in non-ritual contexts, or in both sets of contexts. (b) The substantial basis, in the case of objects used as symbols, consists in their culturally selected natural and material properties. (c) The artificial basis is represented by the symbolic object after it has been worked upon, fashioned or treated by purposive human activity; in short, when it becomes a cultural artifact" (13–14). The utility of these distinctions is then illustrated with Ndembu rituals. In a concluding section, the author argues that whereas actors use symbols in believing that there is some irreducible mystery to them, the observers take the multivocal symbols as univocal signs while believing that all things in the cosmos are ultimately knowable (19). "A non-verbal symbol as against a lingual sign has many disadvantages, including cumbersomeness, but it does have the advantage of being able to stand, however enigmatically, for what can be known by intuition rather than mediately through concepts" (20). [JK/MS]

References: M. Douglas, S.K. Langer, C. Lévi-Strauss (–), **U. Weinreich** (+).
Examples: Ndembu rituals.
Key-words: emo, mng, pmt, SEM, sym.

Turner, Victor Witter, 1974c, 'Liminal to Liminoid in Play, Flow, and Ritual. An Essay in Comparative Symbology', *Rice University Studies* 60:53–92.
Reprinted in: V.W. Turner: *From Ritual to Theatre. The Human Seriousness of Play*, 1982 (*) 20–60.

This essay seeks to introduce a new discipline called 'comparative symbology': the comparative study or interpretation of symbols (53). After stating the meaning of this discipline and its difference from 'semiotics', 'semiology', and 'symbolic anthropology', the author discusses Arnold van Gennep's *rites de passage* in order to elaborate his concept of liminality. He is especially interested in the blurring and merging of distinctions, social relations, rights and obligations, and the social order that enable cultural creativity. Furthermore, he examines the concepts of work, play, and leisure in different societies while paying special attention to their relation to the Industrial Revolution. In this aspect, 'work' in societies, which are studied by anthropologists, refers to ritual and sometimes myth and includes an element of 'play'. "The point is, though, that these 'play' or 'ludic' aspects of tribal and agrarian ritual and myth are, as Durkheim says, '*de la vie sérieuse*', that is, they are intrinsically connected with the 'work' of the collectivity in performing symbolic actions and manipulating symbolic objects" (64). Moreover, the author argues that one has to examine 'play' in order to differentiate between liminal and 'liminoid', since liminal is related to obligation whereas liminoid is related to choice. Liminality is mostly to be found in tribal and agrarian societies, which possess the quality of 'communitas'. 'Communitas', which can be distinguished as spontaneous, ideological, and normative, on the author's view, can be compared to the notion of 'flow' developed by Csikszentmihalyi and McAloon. "In societies before the Industrial Revolution, ritual could always have a 'flow' quality for total communities (tribes, moieties, clans, lineages, families, etc.); in post-Industrial societies, when ritual gave way to individualism and rationalism, the flow experience was pushed mainly into the leisure genres of art, sport, games, pastimes, etc." (89–90). [JK/JS]

References: R.D. Abrahams, R. Barthes, R. Bauman, M. Buber, M. Csikszentmihalyi, É. Durkheim, A. van Gennep (+), J.J. MacAloon, J. Piaget, M. Singer, M. Weber.
Key-words: mng, PMC, sec, soc, sem, str, SYM.

Turner, Victor Witter, 1975, 'Ritual as Communication and Potency. A Ndembu Case Study', in: Caroline E. Hill (ed.), *Symbols and Society. Essays on Belief Systems in Action*, (Southern Anthropological Society Proceedings 9), Athens (GA): University of Georgia Press (ISBN 0–820–3037–12) 58–81.

According to the author, Leach's typology of behavior related to ritual (1966), namely 'rational technical' behavior, 'communicative' behavior, and 'magical' behavior, "helps us to understand the cognitive, but not the affective and conative aspects of such ritual" (59). Based on the example of the Ndembu hunting ritual, Mukaala, the author aims to show the complex system of ritual that includes a symbolic structure, a semantic structure, a telic structure, and a role structure. After elaborating on the phases and episodes precisely and interpreting the meanings in Mukaala, he discusses the ritual symbols. "Such symbols raise a problem of meaning and a problem of efficacy. The first takes us into the cosmology and ideology of the specific culture whose members operate the sets of symbols we are considering; the second raises problems for the psychologist, and may have universal human implications" (78). Further, the ultimate aim of Ndembu rituals "is to enable the members of Ndembu society to think feelingly and feel coherently about their mutual relationships in hut, village, chiefdom, and bush. Symbolic activities and objects are thus more than components of signaling systems, they are switchpoints of social action" (80). [JK]

References: **E.R. Leach** (+), G. Lienhardt.
Example: Ndembu hunting ritual (Mukaala).
Key-words: com, cog, eff, emo, eth, mng, psy, soc, sym, str.

Turner, Victor Witter, 1977, 'Frame, Flow, and Reflection. Ritual and Drama as Public Liminality', in: Michel Benamou & Charles Caramello (eds), *Performance in Postmodern Culture*, (Theories of Contemporary Culture 1), Madison (WI): Coda Press Inc. (ISBN 0–930956–00–1) 33–55.

This essay focuses on the notion of public reflexivity in the form of a performance. The author considers public reflexivity and is concerned with liminality. According to him, liminality is "full of potency and potentiality" and may also be "full of experiment and play" and public reflexivity "takes the form of a performance" and is also concerned with what he has called 'liminality' (33). He focuses especially on the public reflexivity of rituals, in which the society critiques and questions itself. These public rites, which have to do with public liminality, are performed in a framed space and time. As an example of these public rituals, the author elaborates on carnival. "Carnivals differ from rituals in... that they seem to be more flexibly responsive to social and even societal change, change in the major political and economic structures" (39). Then he turns to another reflexive genre that is related to liminality, namely stage drama. The author asserts that drama is to be considered in terms of flow, though it is "liminoid" rather than liminal. After stating the difference between the concepts 'liminoid' and 'liminal', he concludes that "liminal genres put much stress on social frames, plural reflexivity, and mass flow, shared flow while liminoid genres emphasize idiosyncratic framing, individual reflexivity, subjective flow, and see the social as problem not datum" (52). [JK]

References: P.L. Berger, **M. Csikszentmihalyi** (+), N.Z. Davis, **A. van Gennep** (+), E. Goffman (+), Th. Luckman, R. Schechner.
Key-words: frm, mng, pmc, pow, psy, RFL, sem, spc, soc, sym, tim.

Turner, Victor Witter, 1979, 'Dramatic Ritual / Ritual Drama. Performance and Reflexive Anthropology', ***Kenyon Review*** **1.3:80–93.**

Reprinted in: V.W. Turner: *From Ritual to Theatre. The Human Seriousness of Play*, 1982 (*) 89–101.

The paper starts with the following statements: "I've long thought that teaching and learning anthropology should be more fun than they often are. Perhaps we should not merely read and comment on ethnographies, but actually perform them" (80 [89 (pagenumbers in square brackets refer to the reprint)]). According to the author, one possibility of getting beyond the restrictions imposed by the conventional anthropological genres, such as the monographs, "may be to turn the more interesting portions of ethnographies into playscripts, then to act them out in class, and finally to turn back to ethnographies armed with the understanding that comes from 'getting inside the skin' of members of other cultures, rather than merely 'taking the role of the other' in one's own culture. A whole new set of problems is generated by this apparently simple process. For each of its three stages (ethnography into playscript, script into performance, performance into meta-ethnography) reveals many of the frailties of anthropology" (81 [90]). The author "was given an opportunity to test these speculations in practice" (81 [90]) when he, together with Alland and Goffman, was taking part in a workshop organized by Schechner, and the rest of the paper is a reflection on what happened during this workshop that aimed to "'explore the interface between ritual and the theatre...between social and aesthetic drama', and other limina between the social sciences and performing arts" (81 [90–91]). Although the term drama has been criticized, the author is still convinced that social drama is to be found at every level of social organization. "[D]ramas induce and contain reflexive processes and generate cultural frames in which reflexivity can find a legitimate place" (83 [93]). "The movement from ethnography to performance is a process of pragmatic reflexivity" (92 [100]) dissolving the Cartesian dualism of subject and object. He concludes that "[i]f anthropologists are ever to take ethnodramatics seriously,... [w]e will have to become performers ourselves, and bring to human, existential fulfillment what have hitherto been only mentalistic protocols" (93 [101]). [JK/MS]

References: E. Goffman, R. Schechner.
Key-words: pmc, THA, pr1, aut, emo, rfl.

Turner, Victor Witter, 1982, *From Ritual to Theatre. The Human Seriousness of Play* (Performance Studies Series 1); New York: PAJ Publications (A Division of Performing Arts Journal) (ISBN 0-933826-16-8 / 0-933826-17-6 (p)) (127) (with a short bibliography per essay and an index for the volume).

The Introduction of this volume is largely autobiographical. It opens with the statement that: "The essays in this book chart my personal voyage of discovery from traditional anthropological studies of ritual performance to a lively interest in modern theatre, particularly experimental theatre" (7). At the point where the author describes his fieldwork in Africa, he includes a summary of his concept of "social drama" (10) and then argues that "theatre owes its specific genesis to the third phase of social drama" (12). It follows a section on Wilhelm Dilthey (12–15), after which he describes Richards Schechner's experimental theatre (15–16). After an interlude on the etymology of the word 'experience' (16–18), he draws the themes presented together in the statement: "'Experimental' theatre is nothing less than 'performed',

in other words, 'restored' experience, that moment in the experiential process...in which meaning emerges through 'reliving' the original experience (often a social drama subjectively perceived), and is given an appropriate aesthetic form. This form then becomes a piece of communicable wisdom, assisting others...to understand better not only themselves but also the times and cultural conditions which compose their general 'experience' of reality" (18). "The ethnographies, literatures, ritual, and theatrical traditions of the world now lie open to us as the basis for a new transcultural communicative synthesis through performance.... We *can* learn from experience—from the enactment and performance of the culturally transmitted experiences of others—peoples of the Heath as well as of the Book" (18–19).
Contents: "Introduction" (7–19); "Liminal to Liminoid, in Play, Flow, Ritual. An Essay in Comparative Symbology" (20–60) (*); "Social Dramas and Stories About Them" (61–88); "Dramatic Ritual / Ritual Drama. Performative and Reflexive Anthropology" (89–101) (*); "Acting in Everyday Life and Everyday Life in Acting" (102–123). [JS/MS]

Reviews: A.T. Kachel *JSSR* 22.4 (1983) 386 f; J.L. Peacock *AA* 87.3 (1985) 685 f.
Key-words: pmc, THA, pr2, sym, rfl, aut.

Turner, Victor Witter (ed.), 1982, *Celebration. Studies in Festivity and Ritual*; Washington (DC): Smithsonian Institution Press (ISBN 0–87474–920–4) (318).

Selected contents: Victor W. Turner: "Introduction" (11–30); Victor W. Turner & Edith Turner: "Religious Celebrations" (201–219) (*); John J. MacAloon: "Sociation and Sociability in Political Celebrations" (255–271); Ronald L. Grimes: "The Lifeblood of Public Ritual. Fiestas and Public Exploration Projects" (272–283). [JK]

Reviews: J. Bamberger *Sc* 218.4578 (1982) 1212; J. Stewart *AE* 11.1 (1984) 195 f; E.A. Early *WF* 43.4 (1984) 265; P. Alexander *Mank* 15.1 (1985) 72.
Key-words: pmc, sec.

Turner, Victor Witter, 1984, 'Liminality and the Performative Genres', in: John J. MacAloon (ed.), *Rite, Drama, Festival, Spectacle. Rehearsals Toward a Theory of Cultural Performance*, Philadelphia: Institute for the Study of Human Issues (ISBN 0–89727–045–2) (*) 19–41.

The aim of this article is to "discuss what have been varyingly described as performative genres, cultural performances, modes of exhibition or presentation—such as ritual, carnival, theater, and film—as commentaries and critiques on, or as celebrations of, different dimensions of human relatedness" (19). Using grammatical terminology, the author refers to these performative genres as 'subjunctive moods'. This cultural subjunctivity is related to liminality. The author is especially interested in liminality with public character, so he argues that "[p]ublic liminality is governed by public subjunctivity. For a while almost anything goes..." (21). According to him, prescientific cultures have established metapatterns and frames through their rituals in order to view themselves from new perspectives and to create a new language. The term 'reflexivity' also suits to these processes, which the author calls 'social drama': "It is in social dramas that plural reflexivity begins" (23). Although his usage of the term 'drama' is criticized by other scholars for assigning it "to regular courses of events that become publicly visible through some breach of a norm ordinarily held to be binding" (23), he holds that his "contention is that social dramas are the raw stuff out of which theater comes to be created as societies develop in scale and complexity and out of which it is continually regenerated. For I would assert that the social drama form is, indeed, universal, though it may be culturally elaborated in different ways in different societies" (24). The distinctive quality of performative genres lies, according to the author, in the process, where subjectively the actor is in flux and cognitive discriminations are made. "Whether the script is by an individual playwright or is 'tradition' itself, it usually comments on social relationships, cultural values, and moral issues. The actors do not take part in the formulation of the author's messages; rather, they activate those messages by the flow quality of their performance—a flow that engages the audience as well, impressing on its members the 'message' of the total production" (27). To illustrate this argument, the author gives a detailed report on the Japanese Noh drama and the novel, on which most of the plots of this drama are based. [JK]

References: G. Bateson, E. Goffman, A. van Gennep.
Key-words: pmc, tha, frm, rfl.

Turner, Victor Witter, 1985a, 'The Anthropology of Performance', in: Victor Witter Turner (ed. by Edith L.B. Turner), *On the Edge of the Bush. Anthropology as Experience*, (The Anthropology of Form and Meaning), Tucson (AZ): The University of Arizona Press (ISBN 0-8165-0949-2) 177–204.

In her prologue to this volume, Edith Turner, the author's widow, writes of this article: "The essay 'The Anthropology of Performance', written for his seminar in 1980, now published for the first time, lays out the new development, in which he integrates his concept of the social drama with the processual reflexive character of postmodern drama. He leads on to the richness and subtleties of contemporary social performances, where communitas, though 'intrinsically dynamic, is never quite realized' (p. 190). It is through Dilthey's dynamic view of '*Weltanschauung*' and of 'lived experience' that Vic shows us the next step, which takes us to the anthropology of experience" (14). Starting with a discussion of postmodernism, the author reviews a wealth of authors, such as Jean Gebser, George Spindler, Sally Moore, Richard Schechner, Erving Goffman, Ronald Grimes, Charles Hockett, Edmund Leach, Noam Chomsky, Dell Hymes, Theodore Schwartz, D.M. MacKay, Robert Hinde, and finally and most extensively, Wilhelm Dilthey. He summarizes his concept of social drama, which he defines here as "units of aharmonic or disharmonic social process, arising in conflict situations. Typically, they have four main phases of public action. These are: 1) breach... 2) crisis... 3) redressive action... 4) reintegration... or irreparable schism" (180). He discusses the differences and similarities between his use of the term 'ritual' and the definitions advanced by Schechner, Goffman, and Grimes (180). He compares his concept of social drama with theater, and states that "[f]or me the dramaturgical phase begins when crises arise in the daily flow of social action. Thus, if daily living is a kind of theater, social drama is a kind of meta-theater" (181). It is in the third phase of social drama, redressive action, that ritual, besides law (itself highly ritualized) has its place. The author now elaborates on the differences between the modern and the postmodern approach to the social sciences, resulting in the statement where performance comes in: "Time is coming to be seen as an essential dimension of being as well as multiperspectival, no longer merely as a linear continuum conceived in spatial terms. With the postmodern dislodgement of spatialized thinking and ideal models of cognitive social structures from their position of exegetical preeminence, there is occurring a major move towards the study of processes, not as exemplifying compliance with or deviation from normative models both etic and emic, but as performances. Performances are never amorphous or openended, they have diachronic structure, a beginning, a sequence of overlapping but isolable phases, and an end. But their structure is not that of an abstract system; it is generated out of the dialectical oppositions of process and of levels of process" (185). He then distinguishes between "'social' performances (including social dramas) and 'cultural' performances (including aesthetic or stage dramas)" (187). A discussion of theories of nonverbal communication follows, "because the genres we shall study in this essay, ritual, carnival, theater, spectacle, film, and so forth, contain a high proportion of nonverbal symbols" (187). A passionate passage now leads over to a discussion of Dilthey: "Communitas is the implicit law of wholeness arising out of the relations between totalities.... The process of striving toward and resistance against the fulfillment of the natural law of communitas necessitates that the unit of history and of anthropology...and also the unit of their analysis is drama, not culture or archive. And performances, particularly dramatic performances, are the manifestations *par excellence* of human social process. In saying these things I reveal myself an adherent of the epistemological tradition which stresses what Wilhelm Dilthey calls 'lived experience'" (190). The analysis of Dilthey's work fills the remaining 14 pages. Concepts that are significant for ritual theory are mentioned in the process, such as reflexivity (196, 199, 201), meaning (196, 201, 203), medium (200), force (201), mimesis (201), cognition (202). Finally, the author summarizes: "Now I see the social drama, in its full formal development, its full phase structure, as a process of converting particular values and ends, distributed over a range of actors, into a system (which may be temporary or provisional) of shared or consensual meaning. The redressive phase, in which feedback is provided by the scanning mechanisms of law and religious ritual, is a time in which an interpretation is put upon the events leading up to and constituting the phase of crisis" (203). [JS]

References: J. Gebser, G. Spindler, S.F. Moore, R. Schechner, E. Goffman, R.L. Grimes, Ch. Hockett, E.R. Leach, N. Chomsky, D. Hymes, Th. Schwartz, D.M. MacKay, R.A. Hinde, W. Dilthey.
Key-words: PMC, tha, mim, cog, mng, eth, med, rfl, tim, dyn, def, soc.

Turner, Victor Witter, 1985b, 'Epilogue. Are there Universals of Performance in Myth, Ritual, and Drama?' in: Victor Witter Turner (ed. by Edith L.B. Turner), *On the Edge of the Bush. Anthropology as Experience*, (The Anthropology of Form and Meaning), Tucson (AZ): The University of Arizona Press (ISBN 0–8165–0949–2) 291–301.

Reprinted as: 'Are There Universals of Performance in Myth, Ritual, and Drama?' in: Richard Schechner & Willa Appel (eds), *By Means of Performance. Intercultural Studies of Theatre and Ritual*, Cambridge, New York: Cambridge University Press 1990 (ISBN 0–521–32608–7 / 0–521–33915–4 (p)) 8–18.

In his essay the author discusses the developmental relationship between ritual and theater and stresses the relationship of both to social drama as different forms of social mirrors with a certain degree of self-reflexivity. He assumes that "both ritual and theatre crucially involve liminal events and processes and have an important aspect of social metacommentary" (291). After restating his main thesis on the tripartite structure of the ritual process as mirroring a social drama, the author touches on the experimental theater of Grotowski and Schechner and gives a short sketch of a neurobiological interpretation of performance, or what he calls the anthropology of experience. In defending his model of social drama, which he has drawn from literature, against the critique of his teachers, Firth and Gluckman, the author discusses Geertz's textual and dramatic approaches, which Geertz used to distinguish between 'real life' and 'on stage' as different modes of acting. But some of the misunderstandings and contradictions emerging from this double approach, as the author argues, can be resolved by viewing these modes as "components of a dynamic system of interdependence between social drama and cultural performance" (300). After presenting a model of a bisected figure of a loop to indicate the interrelationship of social drama and stage drama, the author finally notes that "the interrelation of social drama and stage drama is not an endless, cyclical, repetitive pattern; it is a spiral one. The spiralling process is responsive to inventions and the changes in the modes of production in a given society" (301). [JK]

Examples: Theatre, rituals of passage.
References: K. Burke, E.G. d'Aquili, É. Durkheim, R. Firth, C. Geertz (–), M. Gluckman, E. Goffman, J. Grotowski, B.G. Myerhoff, **R. Schechner** (+), A. van Gennep.
Key-words: dyn eth, pmc, tha, rfl, str, sym.

Turner, Victor Witter, 1988, *The Anthropology of Performance* (Performance Studies Series 4); New York: PAJ Publications (A Division of Performing Arts Journal) (ISBN 1–55554–000–7 / 1–55554–001–5 (p)) (185) (2nd edition; 1st edition 1987) (with index).

This volume brings together seven essays that have been published previously, but no acknowledgments are provided.
Contents: "Images and Reflections. Ritual, Drama, Carnival, Film, and Spectacle in Cultural Performance" (21–32); "Social Dramas in Brazilian Umbanda. The Dialectics of Meaning" (33–71); "The Anthropology of Performance" (72–98) (*); "Rokujo's Jealousy. Liminality and the Performative Genres" (99–122); "Carnaval in Rio. Dionysian Drama in an Industrializing Society" (123–138); (with Edith L.B. Turner:) "Performing Ethnography" (139–155); "Body, Brain, and Culture" (156–178). The papers are preceded by an introduction by Richard Schechner, entitled "Victor Turner's Last Adventure" (7–20) (*). [MS]
Key-words: PMC, eth.

Turner, Victor Witter & Edward M. Bruner (eds), 1986, *The Anthropology of Experience*; Urbana (IL), Chicago: University of Illinois Press (ISBN 0–252–01236–4 / 0–252–01249–6 (p)) (391).

Selected contents: Edward M. Bruner: "Experience and Its Expressions" (3–30); Victor W. Turner: "Dewey, Dilthey, and Drama. An Essay in the Anthropology of Experience" (33–44); Roger D. Abrahams: "Ordinary and Extraordinary Experience" (45–72); James W. Fernandez: "The Argument of Images and the Experience of Returning to the Whole" (159–187); Bruce Kapferer: "Performance and the Structuring of Meaning and Experience" (188–203) (*); Richard Schechner: "Magnitudes of Performance" (344–369) (*); Clifford Geertz: "Making Experiences, Authoring Selves" (373–380). [JK]
Reviews: R.A. Paul *AE* 14.3 (1987) 464–465; M. Jackson *ANZJS* 23.3 (1987) 456; J.L. Peacock *JAF* 100.397 (1987) 342; W.E.A. van Beek *BTLV* 145 (1989) 571; P. Knecht *JJRS* 16.1 (1989) 86–88; S. Glazier *RA* 19.1–4 (1991) 41.
Key-words: aut, emo, idn, mng.

Turner, Victor Witter & Edith Turner, 1982, 'Religious Celebrations', in: Victor Witter Turner (ed.), *Celebration. Studies in Festivity and Ritual*, Washington (DC): Smithsonian Institution Press (ISBN 0-87474-920-4 / 0-87474-919-0 (p)) (*) 201–219 (with bibliography).

The volume in which this article was published had "its origin in an exhibition of celebratory objects culled from museum collections, [but] it should be noted that virtually all of the objects in the exhibit were once components in one or other of the phases of the ritual process... They owe their character not only to the idiosyncrasy of the cultural tradition forming their original context but also to their function within the tripartite, transformative process" (203). The authors open this article by reviewing the etymological roots of the term 'religion' and its use in classical antiquity, after which follows their own "extended definition" (201). Then they state that "[a]nthropologists usually call religious practices 'ritual'. To celebrate is to perform ritual publicly and formally... Rituals celebrate or commemorate transhuman powers" (201). It follows a summary of Arnold van Gennep's "epoch-making book, *Les Rites de Passage*, the importance of which scholars have hardly begun to grasp" (202), and a summary of V.W. Turners ideas about liminality. A distinction is made between rituals with a "public and open or secret and sequestered" (203) liminal phase. "Public liminality is often the major phase in seasonal or calendrical rituals... As contrasted with initiation rituals and rituals of the life cycle, these seasonal festivals do not emphasize the symbolism of birth, maturation, death, and rebirth—that is, of linear developments—but rather... develop a 'metalanguage', nonverbal as well as verbal, which enables participants and spectators to realize how far they have fallen short of or transgressed their own ideal standards... By this means, societies renew themselves at the source of festal joy, having purified themselves through collective self-criticism and jocund reflexivity" (203). Then follows a discussion of "the three features of liminality...: communication of the sacra, ludic recombination, and communitas" (203–206). A substantial part of the article discusses four examples of religious celebration (206–217). "A common thread can be seen to run through the[se] four examples...: Jivaro headhunting celebration, the Plains Indians' Ghost Dance, Protestant meetings, and Catholic Holy Week solemn celebrations. All recognize a transhuman controlling power that may be either personal or impersonal. In societies or contexts in which such power is regarded as impersonal, anthropologists customarily describe it as *magic*, and those who manipulate the power are magicians. Wherever power is personalized, as Deity, gods, spirits, demons, genii, ancestral shades, ghosts, or the like, anthropologists speak of *religion*. By this definition, the celebrations we have considered contain both magical and religious procedures. The four rituals are concerned with danger, either subjective or objective.... Deity, danger, protection, salvation seem then to be ingredients of a wide range of religious celebrations" (217–218). [JS]

Reference: A. van Gennep.
Examples: Jivaro headhunting celebration, the Plains Indians' Ghost Dance, Protestant meetings, Catholic Holy Week solemn celebrations.
Key-words: def, str, sec, com, rfl.

Tybjerg, Tove, 2001, 'Myter, ritualer og videnskaber. Wilhelm Mannhardt og Jane Ellen Harrison', *Religionsvidenskabeligt Tidsskrift* 38:5–18.
[Myths, Rituals, and Sciences. Wilhelm Mannhardt and Jane Ellen Harrison]

The article presents Mannhardt's and Harrison's contributions to the myth-ritual-debate and assigns them important places in the development towards a greater emphasis on ritual in the study of religion. The author emphasizes their background in folklore and archaeology respectively and draws attention to their research methodologies (Mannhardt's questionnaire), teaching style, and use of images (Harrison). [MS]

References: W. Mannhardt, J.E. Harrison.
Key-words: hsc, myt.

Uhl, Florian & Artur R. Boelderl (eds), 1999, *Rituale. Zugänge zu einem Phänomen* (Schriften der Österreichischen Gesellschaft für Religionsphilosophie 1); Düsseldorf, Bonn: Parerga (ISBN 3-930450-44-5) (263).
[Rituals. Approaches to a Phenomenon]

Selected Contents: Thomas Luckmann: "Phänomenologische Überlegungen zu Ritual und Symbol" (11–28); Hans Kraml: "Ritual. Spracherklärungen zu den Grundlagen gesellschaftlicher Wirklichkeit" (29–41); Clemens Sedak: "Rituale. Weisen der Welterzeugung" (43–62); Herbert Muck: "Zur Handlungsfähigkeit der Feiernden im Umgang mit Ritualisierungen" (129–144); Johann Figl: "Religiöse Rituale—ein unbewältigtes Thema der Philosophie" (187–205); Florian Uhl:

"Rituale—Aspekte eines interdisziplinären Diskurses in der Religionsphilosophie" (207–260). [JK]
Key-words: lan, sym.

Van Baaren, Theodorus P., 1983, 'A Short Meditation Upon the Theme of Ritual', *Nederlands Theologisch Tijdschrift* 37 (special issue: *Analysis and Interpretation of Rites. Essays to D.J. Hoens*, edited by J.G. Platvoet):189–190.

In this short article the author gives in condensed form the ideas he held on what the term 'ritual' refers to, as well as about what characteristics are found in most or all rituals. He distinguishes between secular ceremonial and religious ritual, but suggests that they may also be referred to as social or religious ritual. "We must remember though that the line of demarcation between these two cannot always be clearly defined" (189). He regards ritual behavior as symbolic and ritual as "always a form of communication", but warns against taking communication to be the same as community (189). On the other hand, since communication implies "the bridging of a gulf", every ritual necessarily shares liminality in V.W. Turner's sense (189). After contemplating how historians of religions should deal with the religious character of rituals, he mentions "the three 'laws' of ritual that I once formulated for the first time during a discussion at the study conference in Turku: 1. As the distance between the two persons, groups or corporate bodies concerned increases, the ritual extends and grows more complicated. 2. Every ritual is inclined to expand and to annex continually increasing fields of human behaviour. 3. Every ritual runs the danger to succumb to its own top-heaviness, because its practical consequences may become impossible to comply with" (190). [JS/MS]
Key-words: DEF, sec, dyn.

Verkuyl, Henk J., 1997, 'On Syntactic and Semantic Considerations in the Study of Ritual', in: Dick van der Meij (ed.), *India and Beyond. Aspects of Literature, Meaning, Ritual and Thought. Essays in Honor of Frits Staal*, (Studies from the International Institute for Asian Studies), London, New York: Kegan Paul International (ISBN 0–7103–0602–4) 620–635.

In his contribution on the semiotic study on formal language, the author tries "to take away some of the naturalness of the assumption that a strict distinction can be made between form and meaning, and thus between syntax and semantics" (620). Regarding Staal's hypothesis on the meaninglessness of rituals, he introduces his argument as follows: "I have no idea how much of what I am going to say really bears on the main hypotheses of Staal's work on ritual. After all he underscores the point that he considers ritual as an activity rather than as a language. But here, I think, one should be careful: only if language is defined as a system of forms and their meanings, may one claim that rituals are *not* languages on the ground that they are just systems of meaningless forms. In that sense, it becomes natural to focus on rituals as systems of activity. Yet, the very fact that Staal attributes a syntax to ritual implies that it is possible to attach meanings to its expressions even if the meaning of the forms is reduced to their own form itself. One may study syntax without semantics, but that does not mean that there can be no meanings. The basic question becomes whether there are sufficiently developed theories of meaning to provide meanings to apparently meaningless forms, or whether the forms are assigned a sort of 'zero-meaning' as in Chomsky's work" (620–621). [JK]

References: N. Chomsky (+), F. Staal (–).
Key-words: MNG, pr1, sem, str.

Von Ins, Jürg, 2001, *Der Rhythmus des Rituals. Grundlagen einer ethnologischen Ritualsemiotik, entwickelt am Beispiel des Ndëpp der Lebu (Senegal)*; Berlin: Reimer (ISBN 3–496–02708–8) (399).

[The Rhythm of Ritual. Foundations of an Ethnological Semiotics of Ritual Developed on the Example of the Ndëpp of Lebu (Senegal)]

This volume is an attempt to cover "a fundamental lack of social scientific theories of ritual" (19). In order to document ethnographically singular ritual performances, the author develops a specific method for studying rituals. Based on a multimedia documentation of rituals, he proposes a process oriented and semiotic-ethnographic method: the semiotic protocol (*das semiotische Protokoll*). He claims that the novelty of this method is "that it enables one to document ritual processes without previously differentiating categorically between environmental and bodily specific, action oriented and cognitive sub-processes. The ritual semiotic documentation method enables one to present synchronic and diachronic sub-processes in the way in which they interact under various perspectives of participants. This method avoids the un-reflected linearization of events and disavows a step away from the level of textual representation" (19). According to the author, this new method sets up the design of this volume which opens up a methodological position that enables one to go back and forth between the theory and praxis of documentation. In this vein, the volume is divided in three sections. The first section "The Lebu. History and Ethnography" (17–50) gives an overview of the history and society of the Lebu. The author presents in the second section "Ndëpp and the Religion of Lebu" (51–210) the ethnographic studies and theoretical positions about the Ndëpp rituals, theories and approaches to the study of rituals as well as his new method. He then applies in the third and last section "Ethnographic and Ethnologic Explication" (211–383) his method to the Ndëpp rituals and presents his interpretation based on his new ritual semiotic method. Of primary ritual theoretical relevance is Chapter 6, entitled "Theories of Ritual" (151–172). Here the author discusses in social scientific terms some aspects of ritual, e.g. ritual action as correlation of thought (152–154), ritual as restriction (154–155), ritual as stabilizing institution (155–157), ritual as a mode of communication (158), ritual as interaction with transcendent and immanent partners (158–159), ritual and language (159–161), ritual as expressive action (161–162), ritual as process (162–164), ritually synchronized experience (164) and ritually regulated ecological systems (164–165). He then continues to introduce such ritological key concepts as ritualization (168–170) and ritual self-regulation (171–172). Chapter 7, which is also of primary relevance, is entitled "Methodology. Semiotics as Ritological Method" (173–200). Here, the author discusses aspects of sign processes (174), ritualization between dyadic and triadic concepts of sign (175), the semiotic function circle model (*Funktionskreismodell*) (176), and semiotic definitions of communication (176–179). Furthermore, the author addresses the semiotics of forms of reference in ritual processes as semantics, pragmatics and syntax (179–180). In his elaboration on multivocality of the ritual sign process, the author gives details about the issues of rhythm (181–184) and frame (184–191) as well as about the epistemology of ritual processes (191–195) and rituals as sign processes (195–200). After the author has discussed his ethnographic method (201–202) and the protocol procedures of his new method (203–210), he gives an interpretation of the Ndëpp ritual (213–256). In Chapter 11 the author discusses the methodological outcome of his study in terms of a semiotics of ritual (257–260). He summarizes his method as follows: "In contrast to all existing ritual theories based on ritual types, the method, developed here, conveys an access to the understanding of ritual process as interplay between the relative invariant ritual structure and the changing situations, which are brought by the participants of every ritual performance. As an instrument of documentation and ritual analysis, the semiotic function circle model has proven itself, as it allows to conceive people, structures and 'imaginative' instances on the same level and as intersections of one network of relations" (257). [JK]

References: C.M. Bell, E.G. d'Aquili, U. Eco, R.H. Finnegan, C. Geertz, M. Gluckman, E. Goffman, J. Goody, R.L. Grimes, R.R. Jackson, E.R. Leach, M. Mauss, R. Needham, Ch.S. Peirce, R.A. Rappaport, S.J. Tambiah, V.W. Turner, I. Werlen, R.E. Wiedenmann.
Example: Ndëpp healing ritual of the Lebu.
Key-words: com, frm, lan, med, pmc, rep, str, SEM, tim.

Wallace, Anthony F.C., 1966, *Religion. An Anthropological View*; New York: Random House (No ISBN) (xv + 300) (with index and bibliography).

Since the author sees religion as primarily ritual, this book is actually mainly about ritual. It has five chapters. The first, "Introduction: Some General Theories of Religion" (3–51), "briefly outlines some of the traditional anthropological theories of religion" (vii). The second, "The Anatomy of Religion: The Fundamental Pattern, the Four Major Types, and the Thirteen Regional Traditions" (52–101), "undertakes to analyze the categories under which religion is described and to make a rough and ready classification of religious institutions and culture areas" (vii). The third, "The Goals of Religion: Ritual, Myth, and the Transformations of State" (102–166), "states the major goals of religious ritual and the ritual devices for achieving these goals" (vii). The fourth, "The Functions of Religion: Relations among Cause, Intention, and Effect" (167–215), "reviews some of the currently available information on the functions of religion" (vii). And in the fifth and last chapter, "The Processes of Religion: Origins, the Ritual Process, History, and Evolution" (216–270), "considerations of processes of long-term historical and evolutionary change in religion are presented, in conjunction with a statement of a theory of the ritual process" (vii). This summary, then, will from here on concentrate on the first part of the last chapter (216–242) in which the author presents his theory. The section "The Origins of Ritual" (216–233) argues that rituals are already observable in both mammals and birds, as well as in Neanderthal and Cro-Magnon men. "Originally... ritual served to prepare the lower [than human] animals for efficient execution of the intricate individual and social behaviors involved in combat, food-getting, and reproduction. Ritual continued to serve these same functions in early man" (232–233). The section "The Ritual Process" (233–242) then builds up the author's theory from this basis. This theory is condensed in the formulation of a definition of 'ritual': "stereotyped communication, solitary or interpersonal, which reduces anxiety, prepares the organism to act, and (in social rituals) coordinates the preparation for action among several organisms, and which does all this more quickly and reliably than can be accomplished (given the characteristics of the organisms and the circumstance) by non-stereotyped, informational communication" (236). After this statement, the author further comments on aspects of the content of human rituals, viz. their information and their meaning (236–239). Finally, he describes "the ritual learning process" (239–242) which, in his opinion, "seems to involve a special five-stage process" (239), viz. pre-learning, separation, suggestion, execution, and maintenance (240–241). On the last page of the book, six conclusions are formulated: "1. Ritual is instrumentally primary and belief system is secondary. 2. Ritual aims at accomplishing five types of transformation of state: technological, therapeutic, ideological, salvational, and revitalizational. 3. The function of ritual is to prepare a human being for the efficient performance of a task by communicating an image of a highly organized world system, already described in the belief system, and by suggesting a role during a ritual learning process which follows the law of dissociation. 4. In a viable religion, appropriately fitted rituals and belief systems accomplish those transformations of state that are functionally necessary to the development and maintenance of the kind of society that exists or that the ritual practitioners want. 5. Scientific belief and secular ritual, in a long-continuing evolutionary process, are restricting the application of religious belief and ritual, both theistic and nontheistic, to the ideological, salvational, and revitalizational spheres, and are increasingly replacing religious ritual and belief even in these areas. 6. Viable faiths of the future will be nontheistic and will not 'deify' either person or state" (270). [JS]

Reviews: W.H. Anderson *RRR* 9 (1967) 62; R.L. Means *SA* 28 (1967) 104–107; A. Hultkrantz *HR* 9 (1970) 344–347.

Key-words: def, soc, psy, sec, mng, sym, cog, COM, ETH, emb, dyn, eff.

Werlen, Iwar, 1984, *Ritual und Sprache. Zum Verhältnis von Sprechen und Handeln in Ritualen*; Tübingen: Gunter Narr Verlag (ISBN 3–87808–188–x) (411) (with index and bibliography).
[Ritual and Language. On the Relation between Speech and Action in Rituals]

In this book, the author wants to examine the action-character of speech, on the basis of one particular kind of actions: rituals (15). The first chapter (21–89) is about the definition of 'Ritual'. Here he discusses a number of classical definitions (a.o. those by Gluckman, Malinowski, Leach, Victor Turner, Durkheim, Cazeneuve, Parsons, Goffman, Lorenz, Fortes, Goody, and Moore & Myerhoff) before formulating one himself: "[Ritual is] an expressive institutionalized action or sequence of actions" (81), whereby he asserts explicitly that he takes performativity as an aspect of institutionalization. Then, the three terms of the definition (action, expressivity, and institutionalization) are once more reviewed. The second chapter (90–147) deals with the action-theory of language. It reviews a.o. such authors as Pike, Austin, Searle and Saussure, but Tambiah is remarkably absent. Then follow three chapters with examples: Chapter 3 (148–229) about the Roman Catholic mass, Chapter 4 (230–323) about Goffman's concept of ritual and the startings and endings of conversations as rituals, and Chapter 5 (324–372) about the expression of politeness in speech, illustrating the ritual aspect of speech. The last chapter (373–380) formulates some conclusions, a.o. that the relation between action and speech is not always the same, and that there are different such relations, not only from one type of action to another (e.g. the mass vs. a conversation), but also within one and the same type of action, *in casu* ritual: "divine words and human words, prayer by a priest or a believer, sermons, reading and recitation are not only different forms of action, but also of speech" (380). [JS]

References: M. Gluckman, B. Malinowski, E.R. Leach, V.W. Turner, É. Durkheim, J. Cazeneuve, T. Parsons, E. Goffman, K.Z. Lorenz, M. Fortes, J. Goody, S.F. Moore & B.G. Myerhoff, K.L. Pike, J.L. Austin, J.R. Searle, F. de Saussure.
Examples: the Roman Catholic mass, the startings and endings of conversations, the expression of politeness in speech.
Key-words: def, LAN, PMT, PR1, pr2, mim, emb, cmp, sem, rht.

Werlen, Iwar, 1987, 'Die "Logik" ritueller Kommunikation', in: Wolfgang Klein (ed.), *Sprache und Ritual*, (= Zeitschrift für Literaturwissenschaft und Linguistik 17), Göttingen: Vandenhoeck & Ruprecht (ISSN 0049–8653) (*) 41–81.
[The "Logic" of Ritual Communication]

According to the author, the ritual can be defined by three criteria: institutionalization, symbolic nature, and action. In this article, he analyzes Lutheran services and doctor-patient interactions, focusing on the relationship between institutionalization and symbolic nature. "This paper deals... with the organization of only partially pre-structured rituals and with the disclosure of the meaning of a ritual in interaction" (81). [JK]

Examples: Lutheran services and doctor-patient interactions.
Key-words: com, mng, pr1.

Wheelock, Wade T., 1982, 'The Problem of Ritual Language. From Information to Situation', *Journal of the American Academy of Religion* 50:49–71.

The author raises the problem of how ritual language can be described adequately. For him the crucial point consists in the embodiment of utterances in the context of ritual action because ritual is neither a speechless act nor an enacted thought. Since ritual language not only communicates ideas but also is used to achieve the intent of ritual action, the author understands ritual as an inseparable combination of articulate speech and purposeful action. He defines ritual language as "that set of utterances which is intimately and essentially connected with the action context of ritual" (50). Because he presupposes that adopting general categories used for the description of language can solve the problem of describing ritual language, he applies the theory of speech acts to the analysis of utterances in the context of ritual action. Nevertheless, the author wants to maintain a clear-cut distinction between the speech acts of ordinary language and the 'extraordinary' characteristics of ritual speech acts. For him the language of ritual is often a fixed and prescribed text, similar to a liturgy. But also the context of ritual action is mostly standardized because ritual is recognizable as a stereotyped kind of linguistic behavior within a predetermined and paradigmatic situation. Because in ritual language the text of ritual precedes the actual enactment of a ritual situation and therefore creates its own context, text and context become manifest simultaneously:

"In general, then, ritual utterances serve both to engender a particular state of affairs, and at the same time express recognition of its reality" (58). But one of the most characteristic differences between these types of speech acts is that ritual utterances convey almost no information. Therefore, the author wants to mark "a broad distinction between all those speech acts whose fundamental intention is the communication of information between a speaker and a hearer, and those speech acts whose intention is to create and allow the participation in a known and repeatable situation. This thesis implies that the language of any ritual must be primarily understood and described as 'situating' rather than as 'informing' speech" (59). [JK/JS]

References: M. Douglas, M. Eliade (–), R.H. Finnegan, F. Heiler (–), G. van der Leeuw (–), G. Lienhardt, M. Mead, S.J. Tambiah (+), V.W. Turner.
Examples: Vedic high cults, sacrifices and wish-offerings, Jewish and Christian liturgies, Navaho curing ceremonies.
Key-words: com, LAN, pmt, sem.

Whitehouse, Harvey, 2002, 'Religious Reflexivity and Transmissive Frequency', ***Social Anthropology*** **10:91–103.**

"I have argued that in highly routinised regimes, rituals are in a very real sense 'empty procedures', in relation to which a reflexive stance is not automatic. In such traditions, explicit religious knowledge typically takes the form of official dogma and exegesis, the reproduction of which does not necessarily entail processes of reflexivity. Less commonly, as in the case of the Jain *puja*, such official exegesis is lacking and repetitive rituals can, in the real world, appear to be empty procedures and nothing more. It follows that both Christians and Jains are capable of being profoundly unreflexive participants in their religions. As such, there may be little occasion for doubt.... Paradoxically, it is the official purveyors of routinised religions (the gurus and the priests), dealing as heavily as they do in explicit forms of religious knowledge, who are most prone to reflexivity in general, and doubts or crises of faith more particular. The more practice-based forms of lay participation may generate considerable fewer opportunities for reflexivity and scepticism. / Rare, climatic rituals [e.g. Melanesian initiations] produce a very different story. Such practices are never empty procedures because participants are forced into processes of reflexivity, throught [sic] which all valued religious knowledge is generated. Even if such knowledge is verbally stateable, it is often only fully intelligible to those who have generated exegetical interpretations of their own, through personal experiences of participation in rituals. In view of this, native exegesis, where it exists, only ever scratches the surface of what people know about their rituals.... Such forms of religious transmission, premised as they are on processes of reflexivity, are liable to generate doubts. Indeed, in religious traditions operating in this way, such as the initiatory ordeals of certain Melanesian fertility cults, the deliberate construction of veils of deceit, and the transmission of partial truths, are integral to the discovery of seemingly deeper insights, occult powers and mysteries" (101–102). In the course of his investigation, the author distinguishes between "five levels of knowledge in relation to frequently-repeated rituals" (98) and "four main types of religious knowledge" sustained by rare, climatic rituals (101). [MS]

References: F. Barth, **C. Humphrey & J. Laidlaw** (–).
Examples: Christian services, Jain *puja*, Melanese initiations.
Key-words: COG, RFL, emo, par, tim.

Whitehouse, Harvey, 2006, 'Transmission', in: Jens Kreinath, Jan A.M. Snoek & Michael Stausberg (eds), *Theorizing Rituals. Vol. I: Issues, Topics, Approaches, Concepts*, (Numen Book Series 114–1), Leiden, Boston: Brill (ISBN-10: 90–04–15342–x, ISBN-13: 978–90–04–15342–4) 657–669.

The study of how rituals are transmitted across space and time has received a major boost in recent years from the cognitive science of religion—an emerging field that focuses on the role of universal cognitive architecture in generation and reproduction of religious practices and concepts. Two main kinds of project are discussed in this chapter: those concerned with the effects of tacit intuitive cognitive mechanisms on the nature and form of ritual actions and those that attend to the variable activation of context-sensitive cognitive operations, such as explicit memory systems and analogical thinking, that influence the construction of ritual exegesis. Some of the complex connections between these aspects of ritual transmission are also briefly considered. [Harvey Whitehouse]

Key-word: TRA.

Wiedenmann, Rainer E., 1989, 'Tropen rituellen Sozialverhaltens. Zu einem sozio-semiotischen Modell', *Sociologia Internationalis* 27:195–220.
[Tropes of Ritual Social Behavior. Towards a Socio-Semiotic Modell]

In rejecting the thesis of so-called pan-semiotism, the author argues that system theory and operative hermeneutic semiotics are helpful to interpret the relation between the sociological observable aspects of ritual action and the level of its cultural and scientific interpretation. For this reason, he uses the concept of a semiotics of tripartite signs and its differentiation into possible sign relations as a key variable for the analysis of socio-semiotic and cultural-semiotic processes. The author seeks to demonstrate how semiotics can be helpful for the structural and functional analysis of ritual action. After outlining the tripartite semiotic and operational hermeneutic as complementary analytical concepts, the author suggests that ritual behavior is directed by selection and combination as its different modes of intentionality. On the basis of a tropological axis as a first analytic parameter, the author argues that the field of ritual performance has to be studied according to the different modes as extended between the poles of paradigma and syntagma. Thus metaphor and metonymy are conceived as different tropes of the ritual process. On the basis of archaeology and teleology as another axis, ritual action has to be understood within the possible realm of symbolic innovation and substantialistic reification of the expressive forms of ritual performance. In his conclusion, the author outlines a four-dimensional typology of ritual behavior, which is based on both the axis of metaphor and metonymy and the axis of archaeology and teleology. Nevertheless, he concludes that it requires further parameters to grasp the realm of ritual dynamics. [JK]

References: E.G. d'Aquili (+), R. Bocock, **M. Douglas** (+), **É. Durkheim**, J.W. Fernandez (+), R. Firth, A. van Gennep, M. Gluckman, E. Goffman (–), R.L. Grimes, G.C. Homans, W. Jetter, Ch.D. Laughlin (+), E.R. Leach, C. Lévi-Strauss (+/–), G.H. Mead (–), R. Merton (–), R.A. Rappaport, M. Sahlins, **V.W. Turner** (+), I. Werlen.
Key-words: dyn, pmc, pr1, rht, SEM, soc, str.

Wiedenmann, Rainer E., 1991, *Ritual und Sinntransformation. Ein Beitrag zur Semiotik soziokultureller Interpenetrationsprozesse* (Soziologische Schriften 57); Berlin: Duncker & Humblot (ISBN 3–428–07327–4) (329).
[Ritual and the Transformation of Meaning. A Contribution to the Semiotics of Socio-Cultural Interpenetration Processes]

The author uses a semiotic approach for his interpretation of the interrelation between ritual and the transformation of meaning in modern societies. His main focus is the socio-cultural transformation that emerges through ritual behavior. To articulate a typology of ritual transformation, he defines ritual as an expressive, stylized, repetitive, and redundant behavior that functions as language. Because of the transitional character of ritual behavior and the ambiguous situation of transition, ritual is a process of expressive transition. The author has a twofold thesis: 1) a critique of the sociological approaches to ritual transition and 2) a semiotic conceptualization of the socio-cultural processes of ritual transition within a semiotic typology. He gives a critical overview of some sociological approaches to ritual and argues that the sociological theory of ritual action has to take account of a semiotic differentiation of the expressive transition within a ritual situation. According to him, ritual change is not merely an epiphenomenon of social change. He criticizes recent theories of deritualization and ritualization and tries to reestablish Mary Douglas's comparative-synchronistic approach with its 'grid'-'group' schema. To compare rituals, the author uses a semiotic concept of ritual symbolism. Although the author emphasizes the correlation between cultural reality and social structure on the basis of a bodily symbolism, he criticizes Douglas for marginalizing the cultural-semantic dimension in favor of the systematic demands of social structure. In his classification of various relations between ritual and rationality, the author is concerned with the cultural dimension of rituals. For this reason, he combines monistic and pluralistic parameters with static and dynamic approaches. To compare and conceptualize the 'rational' semantic of ritual behavior, he uses the semiotic concept of sign as a frame of reference that can function as a structural and functional variable. To grasp the dynamic of the cultural semantic of ritual behavior, he drafts a cultural-semiotic typology of the ritual transformation of meaning. Therefore, he defines ritual as a medium of communication in its semantic, syntactic, and pragmatic dimensions. In sketching a tropological typology of ritual semiosis, the author treats the teleology and archaeology of lineal processes and the metaphoric and metonymic of ritual, and discusses the concept of sign and semiotic method, because he wants to treat ritual behavior and ritual change as a controlled process of varying intersystemic processes of transformation. [JK/JS]

References: R. Bellah, P.L. Berger, **M. Douglas (+/–)**, É. Durkheim, E. Goffman, J. Goody, E.R. Leach (+), Th. Luckman, T. Parsons (–), M. Sahlins, V.W. Turner (+), A. van Gennep (+), M. Weber.
Key-words: com, cpr, DYN, eff, eth, mng, pr2, rht, SEM, soc, str, sym.

Williams, Ron G. & James W. Boyd, 1993, *Ritual Art and Knowledge. Aesthetic Theory and Zoroastrian Ritual* (Studies in Comparative Religion); Columbia (SC): University of South Carolina Press (ISBN 0–87249–857–3) (xv + 200) (with bibliographical references and index).

This book by a philosopher and a historian of religion is a theoretical contribution to the aesthetic aspects of Zoroastrian rituals, where ritual is viewed through the lens of aesthetics. It is based mostly on fieldwork with a Zoroastrian high priest. In viewing the Zoroastrian rituals as artworks, the authors apply categories from the philosophy of art to the various dramatic, visual, gestural, musical, and literary dimensions of ritual. They define ritual as a mode of expression not reducible to other forms of religious communication. Thus they analyze the ritual performance as *sui generis* composition of physical, imaginative, and symbolic aspects. In the first part on "Ritual Spaces" (13–57), the authors distinguish between the physical, virtual, and meaning spaces by emphasizing the virtual features of ritual images. They give a detailed survey of the ritual as an artwork by interpreting the ritual as 1) a set of physical objects and events, 2) a presentational illusion or hyperreality, and 3) a representational model according to its different aspects. In their analysis of the special powers of ritual within the complex interaction of its elements, they focus on those features that lie outside the realm of concept, proposition, or reference. Therefore, rituals provide integrative environments as a result of the virtual power of the ritual images that are internally connected with their physical and linguistic features. In the part on "Ritual Knowledge" (59–155), the authors distinguish between two stances that the practitioner may take towards ritual practice. They argue that religious ritual has a noetic function and is a *sui generis* mode for the discovery and expression of knowledge. In using recent theories of metaphor, they question the argument that the ritual's noetic function is only given by change or variation. In analyzing the role of repetition in more or less unchanging rituals, they argue that ritual repetition has a noetic function because the repetition can function as a tool for a practitioner's acquisition of ritual knowledge. In comparing the universality of repetition in ritual with that of a dramatic performance, they draw the parallels between rituals and artworks and suggest that "*repetition is an essential feature of ritual activity; invariance belongs to the very nature of ritual as it does to certain forms of artwork*" (72). Thus they understand ritual as a masterpiece and emphasize the ritual commitment to invariance and right repetition. They claim that this commitment to invariance, and not the invariance of its performance, is a necessary condition for the acquisition of ritual knowledge. However, they point out that invariance is the key to the ritual's noetic function. This noetic function is based on the interplay of the various art forms and aesthetic categories within the ritual performance. Furthermore, the authors distinguish between luring, focusing, conveying, and opposing potentiating dimensions of ritual metaphors. They argue that "a ritual masterpiece can act as horizon, both patterning (focusing and conveying) and providing the means for the transcendence of pattern (luring, opposing, potentiating)" (101). In the final section of their methodological remarks, the authors distinguish between the ritual act and the theory of the act in order to consider the shift from act to theory and to mark the limits of theory as well. In favoring an interpretation that avoids reductionism by attending to the ritual gestures, they point out: "We have theorized in order to see more clearly and appreciate more profoundly, but none of this effort replaces the ritual act and what it makes manifest: the difference between event and word, between life and reflection" (155). [JK]

References: R.H. Davis, G. Deleuze & F. Guattari, T.F. Driver, W.G. Doty (+), **N. Goodman** (+), R.L. Grimes (+), **Th.W. Jennings** (–), **S.K. Langer** (+), R.A. Rappaport (+/–), B.K. Smith (+), J.Z. Smith, F. Staal (–), S.J. Tambiah (+), V.W. Turner (+/–), A. van Gennep (+), W.T. Wheelock.
Examples: Zoroastrian high liturgy Yasna, Afrinagan.
Reviews: A.-M. Gaston *JAS* 53.4 (1994) 1310 f; M. Hutter *Numen* 41 (1994) 326 f; G.-P. Strayer *JRS* 9.1 (1995) 142; P. Chelkowski *IJMES* 28.2 (1996) 258 f.
Key-words: AES, cmp, cog, eff, gst, mng, ref, sem, spc, tim, VIR.

Williams, Ron G. & James W. Boyd, 2006, 'Aesthetics', in: Jens Kreinath, Jan A.M. Snoek & Michael Stausberg (eds), *Theorizing Rituals. Vol. I: Issues, Topics, Approaches, Concepts*, (Numen Book Series 114–1), Leiden, Boston: Brill (ISBN-10: 90–04–15342–x, ISBN-13: 978–90–04–15342–4) 285–305.

Relying on the fact that many rites employ artful means, this essay illustrates the relevance and importance of using philosophical aesthetic theories in the study of ritual. This approach seeks to provide a better understanding of the powers of artful rituals, while also helping to address important issues in the field of ritual studies. Beginning with methodological reflections, the essay summarizes a variety of aesthetic theories and enumerates some of the powers of art. To illustrate the application of aesthetic theories to particular rituals, the following themes are discussed: ritual liminality and the virtual in art; artful integration and ritual contextualization; ritual knowledge and the notion of artistic masterpiece; and the aesthetic theory of formalism and its relation to ritual purity. This leads to a discussion of the historical and metaphysical contexts of various aesthetic theories and their compatibility or incompatibility with the metaphysical assumptions underlying two specific ritual traditions, Zoroastrianism and Shinto. Finally, an approach to the study of ritual based on the philosophy of Gilles Deleuze is offered as an alternative to the previously discussed aesthetic theories. The essay concludes with some speculative thoughts concerning the broader question: what is it about ritual practices and the arts that explains why they so often intersect? [Ron Williams & James Boyd]
References: G. Deleuze & F. Guattari, S.K. Langer.
Key-word: AES.

Wilson, Edward O., 1978, *On Human Nature*; Cambridge (MA): Harvard University Press (ISBN 0–674–63441–1) (xii + 260).

This book has a chapter (Chapter 8: "Religion", 169–193) which discusses religion and ritual, specifically exploring how religious practices confer biological advantages. Sociobiology attempts to account for the origin of religion "by the principle of natural selection acting on the genetically evolving material structure of the brain" (192). [JS]
Key-word: eth.

Wimmer, Michael & Alfred Schäfer, 1998, 'Einleitung. Zur Aktualität des Ritualbegriffs', in: Alfred Schäfer & Michael Wimmer (eds), *Rituale und Ritualisierungen*, (Grenzüberschreitungen 1), Opladen: Leske & Budrich (ISBN 3-8100-2171-7) (*) 9-47.
[Introduction. On the Timeliness of the Concept of Ritual]

Apart from offering brief summaries of the essays collected in this volume (39–45), in their introductory essay the editors address some theoretical issues. In the first section, the authors argue that the notion of 'ritual' has gained a new relevance exactly at the time when the classical idea of subjectivity was questioned (13). Moreover, they claim that the notion of ritual may help to deconstruct notions of subjectivity that regard alterity as a danger rather than as the very condition of subjectivity (17). In the next section, the authors discuss some theories of modernity and modernization and their respective (implicit or explicit) ideas about ritual (17–23). This leads to a discussion of ritual and communication. Here the authors argue that ritual links nature to culture and constructs culture in such a way that it is perceived as if it were nature. Viewed from this angle, modernization has not really installed an autonomous subject but rather a loss of the self; de-ritualization means de-symbolization and "Weltverlust" (*loss of world*) (28). Ritual staging, the authors argue, mostly occurs in situations that require confident self-affirmations of the subject in question. Rituals achieve that aim by not transcending the relations between the self on the one hand and the transcendent and social conditions on the other (30). These thoughts place into question both traditional aims of pedagogy and recent attempts to apply rituals in pedagogical contexts (30–32). This leads to a discussion of the relationship between rituals and rules. In this context, the authors define 'ritualization' as the making of rules in such a way that the freedom of interpretation and enactment on the part of concerned parties is seriously restricted when following these rules. According to the authors, 'ritual' occurs when the question of the meaning of 'ritualization' is raised (33). Concerning the question of meaning, the authors stress latency, i.e. a system of symbolic references that transcends the intentions of the concerned parties (34). In the following section, the authors elucidate some implications of their main thesis, according to which rituals refer to situations in which individuals are posited in an arrangement that sets them in relation to

a transcendent (such as the social, the inexpressible, the holy) that in turn cannot be reduced to mere subjectivity (37–38). [MS]
Key-words: com, pr1, rel, idn, agn, par, rfl, def.

Winkelman, Michael, 1986, 'Trance States. A Theoretical Model and Cross-Cultural Analysis', *Ethos* 14:174–203 (with bibliography).

"This paper presents a psychophysiological model of trance states and relates these changes to the basic structure and physiology of the brain [175–178]. It is argued that a wide variety of trance induction techniques lead to a state of parasympathetic dominance in which the frontal cortex is dominated by slow wave patterns originating in the limbic system and related projections into the frontal parts of the brain. Psychophysiological research on the effects of a variety of trance induction procedures is reviewed to illustrate that these procedures have the consequence of inducing this set of changes in psychophysiology [178–183]. Clinical and neurophysiological research on the nature of human temporal lobe function and dysfunction is reviewed to illustrate that the physiological patterns of conditions frequently labeled as pathological are similar to the psychophysiology of trance states [183–186]. Analyses of cross-cultural data on trance state induction procedures and characteristics are presented [186–192]. The model of a single type of trance state associated with magico-religious practitioners is tested and shown to be significantly better than a model representing trance states as discrete types, supporting the theoretical position that there is a common set of psychophysiological changes underlying a variety of trance induction techniques. The differences that do exist among practitioners with respect to trances illustrate a polarity between the deliberately induced trance states and those apparently resulting from psychophysiological predispositions toward entering trance states. The relationship of trance-type labeling (for example, soul journey/flight, possession) to variables indicative of temporal lobe discharges [192–195] and variables assessing social conditions [196–198] indicates that possession trances are significantly associated with both symptoms of temporal lobe discharge and with the presence of political integration beyond the local community" (174–175). [JS]
Key-words: psy, sec, exp, cog, eth, emb, emo, med.

Wulf, Christoph, 2006, 'Praxis', in: Jens Kreinath, Jan A.M. Snoek & Michael Stausberg (eds), *Theorizing Rituals. Vol. I: Issues, Topics, Approaches, Concepts*, (Numen Book Series 114–1), Leiden, Boston: Brill (ISBN-10: 90–04–15342–x, ISBN-13: 978–90–04–15342–4) 395–411.

In ritual studies praxis is a central concept that embraces many different dimensions. The concept is used to bridge the opposition between thought and action. It is a construction aimed at overcoming the aforementioned dichotomy. In this paper, praxis refers to ritual praxis stressing its performative aspects. Since praxis focuses on the *mise en scène* and the staging of the ritual action, this perspective leads to a consideration of the body and of the aesthetic aspects of the ritual performance. Ritual praxis implies the knowledge of how to perform a ritual. This knowledge is not theoretical but practical. This raises the question concerning what the characteristics of practical knowledge are and how it is acquired. Here the concepts of habitus and mimesis are of central importance. They refer to issues of desire and power and the negotiation of difference in ritual praxis. Ritual praxis is a construct that is relevant to the entire spectrum of ritual acts. Besides signifying intentional ritual acts performed by subjects and groups, the term 'ritual praxis' also refers to that more or less conscious practical knowledge that forms the basis of ritual acts. Ritual praxis understood in this sense encompasses the classical great rituals of religion, politics, and culture, as well as everyday rituals. It encompasses the areas of liturgy, ceremony, celebration, convention, and ritualization, and it is applicable to rituals of transition, institutional rituals, seasonal rituals, rituals of intensification, rituals of opposition, and interactive rituals. [Christoph Wulf]

Key-words: PR1, PR2, MIM, EMB, CMP, pmc, aes, hab, pow.

Wulf, Christoph, *et al.* (eds), 2001, *Das Soziale als Ritual. Zur performativen Bildung von Gemeinschaften*; Opladen: Leske & Budrich (ISBN 3–8100–3132–1) (387) (with index and bibliography).

[The Social as Ritual. On the Performative Formation of Communities]

This book is a qualitative, ethnographic study of the urban life of school children (aged 10–13) in central Berlin around the turn of the millennium. However, in his introduction (7–17), Christoph Wulf, the main editor, states that the materials presented in these studies aim at developing a multidimensional and performative notion of ritual. Moreover, Wulf enumerates some 30 characteristics that, in his eyes, rituals 'are' or 'do'; e.g. rituals are cultural performances and as such are bodily, performative, expressive, symbolic, rule-governed, etc., etc.; they do take place in social spaces, create and change social orders and hierarchies, etc., etc. (7–8). Furthermore, he argues that "rituals and ritualizations" are of paramount importance for creating social relationships. This also includes education and socialization. "Forms and possibilities of social action are gained and developed in ritual situations" (10). He then raises the question of the relationships between different ritual practices and 'styles'. To investigate this question, the book studies "selected processes of performative creations of communities" (10) in families, peer groups, schools, child cultures, and media. Here the book focuses mainly on 'micro-rituals', such as meals in a family setting or entertainments during breaks in a school setting. The authors explore and apply a number of different methods to investigate such processes. The book contains chapters on the city as a performative space (Birgit Althans; 19–36), the family as a ritual living space (Kathrin Audehm & Jörg Zirfas; 37–118), ritual transitions in everyday life at school (Michael Göhlich & Monika Wagner-Willi; 119–204), recess games as instances of performative child culture (Anja Tervoore; 205–248), and ritual media events in peer groups (Constanze Bausch & Stephan Sting; 249–323). Of special theoretical interest is Christoph Wulf's essay on ritual action as mimetic knowledge (325–338). Here he distinguishes between four stages within mimetic processes, leading from its preconditions (such as gestures that the children have learned during infancy) up to the reconstruction of mimetic events in ethnographic research. In a final chapter (339–347), Christoph Wulf and Jörg Zirfas sketch some perspectives that they feel should be explored in further studies of the performative dimension of rituals: complexity, scenic performances, the ludic, corporeality, mimesis, power, regularity (*Regelhaftigkeit*), iconology, macro-rituals, and the sacred (*das Heilige*). [MS]

References: P. Bourdieu (+), J. Butler, E. Goffman (+), N. Goodman (+), V.W. Turner.

Key-words: PMC, PMT, SOC, gen, PR2, MIM, emb, hab, CPL, pow, gst, sec.

Wulf, Christoph & Jörg Zirfas (eds), 2003, *Rituelle Welten* (special issue of *Paragrana. Internationale Zeitschrift für Historische Anthropologie* 12); Berlin: Akademie Verlag (ISSN 0938–0116) (683).
[Ritual Worlds]

Selected contents: Christoph Wulf & Jörg Zirfas: "Anthropologie und Ritual. Eine Einleitung" (11–28); Ulrike Brunotte: "Ritual und Erlebnis. Theorien der Initiation und ihre Aktualität in der Moderne" (29–53) (*); Alexander Henn: "Zwischen Gehalt und Gestalt. Ritual und Mimesis" (67–77) (*); Joannes Snoek: "Performance, Performativity, and Practice. Against Terminological Confusion in Ritual Studies" (78–87) (*); José Enrique Finol: "Le rite, morphologie et contexte" (88–101) (*); Ivo Strecker: "Die Magie des Rituals" (114–132); Mary Douglas: "Nostalgie für Levy-Bruhl: Denken in Kreisen" (158–183) (*); William Sax: "Heilungsrituale: Ein kritischer performativer Ansatz" (385–404); Maren Hoffmeister: "'Ich konnte nicht anders, es war stärker'. Das Ritual als Zwang" (423–442); Günter Thomas: "Der gefesselte Blick. Körper, Raum und Präsenz im Medienritual" (599–620). [JS]

Key-words: soc, pow, psy, idn, sec, gdr, PMC, pmt, pr1, pr2, mim, sem, dyn, eff, emo, MED.

Wulf, Christoph & Jörg Zirfas, 2004, 'Performativität, Ritual und Gemeinschaft. Ein Beitrag aus erziehungswissenschaftlicher Sicht', in: Gerrit Jasper Schenk & Dietrich Harth (eds), *Ritualdynamik. Kulturübergreifende Studien zur Theorie und Geschichte rituellen Handelns*, Heidelberg: Synchron Wissenschaftsverlag der Autoren (ISBN 3–935025–43–2) (*) 73–93.
[Performativity, Ritual, and Community. A Contribution from an Educationalist Perspective]

In the first section of their paper the authors state that their study focuses on the formation of communities. The authors criticize prior research for their emphasis on the symbolic dimension of rituals; instead they wish to emphasize their performative dimension, i.e., the "performative processes of interaction and formation of meaning" (73). According to the authors, understanding rituals as performances puts the focus on their forms of action and staging, they are to be understood as "social institutions with a performative surplus that comes to light in the dramaturgy and organization of ritual interactions and their effects, in their scenic-mimetic expressivity, the performance and staging dimensions of social action and the practical knowledge of social action" (74). Communities are not to be understood in terms of their storing of traditions and symbolic knowledge, but rather as "spaces of interaction and dramatic fields of action that are constituted by rituals as symbolic stagings in conjunctive spaces of experience" (74). The authors hold that rituals "frame specific practices in ordinary life in such a manner that they can be experienced as something extraordinary" (75); that is especially relevant with regard to experiences of difference (breaches, transitions, crises). According to the authors rituals are characterized by four formal features: framing, repetitiveness, homogeneity, and publicity (75–76). Furthermore, they briefly discuss the concepts of liminality, operationality, symbolism, and their creation of a specific form of reality (76). While rituals of transition emphasize various forms of transition, there is another category of rituals that reinforce the cohesion of extant groups (*Sozialitäten*), here referred to as "connective rituals" (77). The second section of their paper (77–82) juxtaposes the performative and the hermeneutic approaches in educational science. In order to throw light on the constitution of societies in everyday life rituals, the authors analyze shared meals (83–86). The final section of the paper outlines eight aspects of further research with respect to rituals (86–91): (1) the constitution of reality; (2) scenic staging; (3) the ludic dimension; (4) the sacred; (5) corporeality; (6) mimesis; (7) rules; (8) power. [MS]

References: J.L. Austin, R. Barthes, C.M. Bell, P. Bourdieu, J. Butler, J. Cazeneuve, E. Fischer-Lichte, C. Geertz, E. Goffman, N. Luhmann, R. Schechner, D. Sperber, I. Strecker, V.W. Turner.
Example: Verbal interaction over lunch in a Berlin family.
Key-words: gen, soc, sec, soc, mng, pmc, pmt, pr2, dyn, emo, frm, rfl, mim.

Wuthnow, Robert, 1987, *Meaning and Moral Order. Explorations in Cultural Analysis*; Berkeley, Los Angeles, London: University of California Press (ISBN 0–520–05950–6) (xiii + 435) (with indexes and bibliography).

In this book, the author concentrates on four theoretical approaches, four levels of cultural analysis: the subjective, the structural, the dramaturgic, and the institutional. After the first, introductory, chapter (1–17) follows one chapter (18–65, 66–96, 97–144 resp.) on each of the first three approaches, and then five chapters (145–185, 186–214, 215–264, 265–298, 299–330 resp.) dealing with the last one. Ritual is presented explicitly in Chapter 4 about the dramaturgic approach. In its first section ("The Nature of Ritual", 98–109) the author does not start with a definition of 'ritual', but nevertheless makes a number of statements about the ways in which in his view previous authors have misunderstood or misrepresented 'ritual', statements from which his own conception of 'ritual' becomes apparent. In the end he then defines 'ritual' as: "a symbolic-expressive aspect of behavior that communicates something about social relations, often in a relatively dramatic or formal manner" (109). This is an unusually broad definition, and thus he clarifies: "This definition incorporates the idea that ritual must not be seen as a discrete category of behavior but as an analytic dimension that may be present to some degree in all behavior. It emphasizes the communicative properties of behavior and the fact that ritual often communicates more effectively because it conforms to certain stylized or embellished patterns of behavior. Also worth underscoring is the idea that ritual is essentially social: although it may express emotions or intentions, it clearly assists in articulating and regulating the nature of social relations. Thus, ritual can legitimately be approached at the dramaturgic level...rather than treating it simply in terms of its subjective origins or meanings" (109). Both in this section and in the next ("The Social Context of Ritual", 109–123) it becomes clear that the author has a thoroughly secular conception of 'ritual' ("rituals such as etiquette, protocol, or ceremonial display in formal organizations" (110)). The third section ("An Empirical Case: 'Holocaust' as Moral Ritual", 123–140) consequently gives a secular example: the simultaneously watching by 120 million Americans (nearly two-thirds of the adult population of the USA) of the television serial "Holocaust" on four successive evenings in mid April 1978, analyzed from the dramaturgic perspective as a ritual. The last section of this chapter ("The Problem of Meaning (Again)", 140–144) starts with reminding us that "Ritual is a symbolic act, a gesture performed for expressive rather than purely instrumental purposes" (140). The book contains a number of further pertinent statements about 'ritual', but it would be a mistake to assume that this chapter which is explicitly about 'ritual' exhausts the meaning of this monograph for theorizing 'rituals'. The four theoretical approaches discussed and exemplified by various materials are on several occasions also referred to as levels of cultural analysis, levels which to some extent may all be useful for the analysis of any cultural phenomenon. Thus, especially the institutional level—presented in this book most exhaustively—stressing for example the role of the acquisition of resources as a decisive factor for the success or failure of a cultural phenomenon to perpetuate itself, shows many aspects which clearly apply to many 'rituals'. [JS/MS]

References: B. Malinowski (–), E. Goffman (+), É. Durkheim (–), J.W. Mayer & B. Rowan (+), M. Douglas (+), H. Miner (+).
Examples: Various, including watching the television serial "Holocaust".
Key-words: def, soc, psy, str, sec, MNG, sym, COM, PMC, REL, sem, dyn, emo, INT, RFL, ECN, gst.

Young-Laughlin, Judi & Charles D. Laughlin, 1988, 'How Masks Work, or Masks Work How?' *Journal of Ritual Studies* 2.1:59–86.

"Masking is ubiquitous to the culture areas of the world and is a symbolic activity inextricably associated cross-culturally with cosmological drama and shamanic ritual. Our question is, 'Masks work how?' In Part 1, we place masks within their physical, cultural and cosmological context so as to view the activity of masking as part of a wider symbolic process. Masks are seen to be transformations of face. In Part 2, the work of masking is realized as a transformation of experience, and is related to a general cycle of meaning in culture whereby cosmological beliefs give rise to direct experience, and experience verifies and vivifies cosmology. And in Part 3 the 'how' of masking is explained using a biogenetic structural perspective which traces the possible transformations of brain that may occur within the wearer and audience and that may mediate a variety of mask-related experiences." [Abstract from the article.]

Key-words: med, emo, mng, aes, eth.

Zuesse, Evan M., 1975, 'Meditation on Ritual', *Journal of the American Academy of Religion* 43:517–530.

This article wants to give a general introduction into the phenomenon 'ritual'. At the end, the author summarizes that "...the purpose of this essay is a modest one: it is enough if we have shown that there is in the mere act of religious ceremonial a wealth of significance insufficiently appreciated up to now. Whatever may be the errors or inadequacies of this preliminary statement, it is important to understand that there is in the ritual gesture as such (even without going into the specific cultural and religious content of the rite) a remarkably rich and focused insight into the nature of the spiritual universe and of human life. This distinctive way of 'seizing' existence can be endlessly explored and meditated on in speculative and mythic exegesis in different religions, or on the contrary can be ignored or denied on the intellectual level, but it continues to work its magic in a covert way that can only be fully understood in the very experience itself" (530). [JS]

References: E. Husserl, S.K. Langer (+), M. Eliade (+), E. Cassirer, O.F. Bollnow (+), L. Lévy-Bruhl, M. Merleau-Ponty, S. Freud (–).

Key-words: gen, myt, str, MNG, aes, PMC, PR1, cmp, rel, emo, par, rfl, gst, spc, tim.

PART B

SECONDARY LITERATURE
(84 items)

Ackerman, Robert, 1975, 'Frazer on Myth and Ritual', ***Journal of the History of Ideas*** **36:115–134.**

Ackerman, Robert, 1987, ***J.G. Frazer. His Life and Work*****; Cambridge, New York: Cambridge University Press (ISBN 0–521–34093–4) (x + 348 + [10] p. of plates) (with index).**

Ackerman, Robert, 1991, ***The Myth and Ritual School. J.G. Frazer and the Cambridge Ritualists*** **(Theorists of Myth 2); New York: Garland Publisher (ISBN 0–8240–6249–3) (xii + 253) (reprinted New York: Routledge 2002).**

Alexander, Bobby Chris, 1991, ***Victor Turner Revisited. Ritual as Social Change*** **(American Academy of Religion: Academy Series 74); Atlanta (GA): Scholars Press (ISBN 1–55540–600–9 / 1–55540–601–7 (p)) (ix + 191) (with index and bibliography).**
Review: D. Handelman *JRS* 7.2 (1993) 117–124; Rejoinder: *JRS* 8.2 (1994) 161–163.

Ashley, Kathleen M. (ed.), 1990, ***Victor Turner and the Construction of Cultural Criticism. Between Literature and Anthropology*****; Bloomington (IN): Indiana University Press (ISBN 0–253–31003–2 / 0–253–20594–8 (p)) (xxii + 185) (with index and bibliography).**

Selected Contents: Part II: "Turner's Theory and Practice". Ronald L. Grimes: "Victor Turner's Definition, Theory, and Sense of Ritual" (141–146) (*); Frederick Turner: "'Hyperion to a Satyr'. Criticism and Anti-structure in the Work of Victor Turner" (147–162); Edith Turner: "The Literary Roots of Victor Turner's Anthropology" (163–169). [MS]
Review: D. Handelman *JRS* 7.2 (1993) 117–124.

Barbosa de Almeida, M.W., 1992, 'On Turner on Lévi-Strauss', ***Current Anthropology*** **33:60–63.**

Belier, Wouter W., 1994, 'Arnold van Gennep and the Rise of French Sociology of Religion', ***Numen*** **41:141–162 (with bibliography).**

Belmont, Nicole, 1974, ***Arnold van Gennep. Créateur de l'ethnographie française*** **(Petite Bibliothèque Payot; Collection Science de l'Homme 232); Paris: Payot (ISBN 2–228–32320–9) (187).**
= idem: *Arnold van Gennep. The Creator of French Ethnography*, Chicago, London: University of Chicago Press 1979 (vi + 167) (ISBN 0–226–04216–2).

Boudewijnse, H. Barbara, 1990, 'The Ritual Studies of Victor Turner. An Anthropological Approach and its Psychological Impact', in: Hans-Günter Heimbrock & H. Barbara Boudewijnse (eds), ***Current Studies on Rituals. Perspectives for the Psychology of Religion*****, (International Series in the Psychology of Religion 2), Amsterdam, Atlanta (GA): Rodopi (ISBN 90–5183–178–1) (*) 1–18.**

Boudewijnse, H. Barbara (ed.), 1994, ***De erfenis van Victor Turner*** **(Special issue of** ***Antropologische Verkenningen*** **13.4) (69).**
[The legacy of Victor Turner]

Brunotte, Ulrike, 2001, 'Das Ritual als Medium "göttlicher Gemeinschaft". Die Entdeckung des Sozialen bei Robertson Smith und Jane Ellen Harrison', in: Erika Fischer-Lichte, ***et al.*** **(eds),** ***Wahrnehmung und Medialität*****, (Theatralität 3), Tübingen, Basel: Francke (ISBN 3–7720–2943–4) 85–102.**

Brunotte, Ulrike, 2003, 'Ritual und Erlebnis. Theorien der Initiation und ihre Aktualität in der Moderne', ***Paragrana. Internationale Zeitschrift für Historische Anthropologie*** **12 (special issue: "Rituelle Welten" = Wulf & Zirfas (eds) 2003 (*)):29–53.**

Discusses Harrison, Schurtz, Blüher, V.W. Turner, Bettelheim and Eliade. [JS]

Buswell III, James O., 1979, 'Javanese Ritual and Geertz's Interpretation. A Rebuttal', in: John Hill Morgan (ed.), *Understanding Religion and Culture. Anthropological and Theological Perspectives*, Washington (DC): University Press of America (ISBN 0–8191–0848–0) 181–194.

Bynum, Caroline Walker, 1984, 'Women's Stories, Women's Symbols. A Critique of Victor Turner's Theory of Liminality', in: Robert L. Moore & Frank E. Reynolds (eds), *Anthropology and the Study of Religion*, (Studies in Religion and Society), Chicago: Center for the Scientific Study of Religion (ISBN 0–913348–20–1 / 0–913348–21–x (p)) 105–125.
Reprinted in: Ronald L. Grimes (ed.): *Readings in Ritual Studies*, Upper Saddle River (NJ): Prentice-Hall 1996 (ISBN 0–02–347253–7) 71–86.

Calame, C., 2003, 'Le rite d'initiation tribale comme catégorie anthropologique (Van Gennep et Platon)', *Revue de l'Histoire des Religions* 220:5–62.

Calder III, William Musgrave (ed.), 1991, *The Cambridge Ritualists Reconsidered. Proceedings of the First Oldfather Conference, held on the campus of the University of Illinois at Urbana-Champaign, April 27–30, 1989* (Illinois Classical Studies. Supplement 2 / Illinois Studies in the History of Classical Scholarship 1); Atlanta (GA): Scholars Press (ISBN 1–55540–605–x) (xii + 295).

Campany, Robert F., 1992, 'Xunzi and Durkheim as Theorists of Ritual Practice', in: Frank E. Reynolds & David Tracy (eds), *Discourse and Practice*, Albany (NY): State University of New York Presss (ISBN 0–7914–1023–4 / 0–7914–1024–2 (p)) 197–231.
Reprinted in: Ronald L. Grimes (ed.): *Readings in Ritual Studies*, Upper Saddle River (NJ): Prentice-Hall 1996 (ISBN 0–02–347253–7) 86–103.

Capps, Donald, 1979, 'Erikson's Theory of Religious Ritual. The Case of the Excommunication of Ann Hibbens', *Journal for the Scientific Study of Religion* 18:337–349.

Carey, James W., 1975, 'Communication and Culture. Review Essay of Clifford Geertz' "The Interpretation of Cultures"', *Communication Research* 2:173–191.

Carpentier, Martha C., 1994, 'Jane Ellen Harrison and the Ritual Theory', *Journal of Ritual Studies* 8:11–26.

Collins, Mary, 1976, 'Ritual Symbols and the Ritual Process. The Work of Victor Turner', *Worship* 50:336–346.

Cunningham, Adrian & Ivan Strenski (eds), 1991, 'Ritual as Such. Frits Staal's Rules Without Meaning', *Religion* 21:207–234.

This is a review-symposium on Staal 1989 (*). Contents: Allan G. Grapard: "Rule-Governed Activity vs. Rule-Creating Activity" (207–212); Burton L. Mack: "Staal's Gauntlet and the Queen" (213–218); Ivan Strenski: "What's Rite? Evolution, Exchange and the Big Picture" (219–225); Frits Staal: "Within Ritual, About Ritual and Beyond" (227–234). [JK]

Dawe, Alan, 1973, 'The Underworld-View of Erving Goffman. Review Article', *British Journal of Sociology* 24:246–253.

Deflem, Mathieu, 1991, 'Ritual, Anti-Structure, and Religion. A Discussion of Victor Turner's Processual Symbolic Analysis', *Journal for the Scientific Study of Religion* 30:1–25.

Douglas, Mary, 2003, 'Nostalgie für Lévy-Bruhl. Denken in Kreisen', *Paragrana. Internationale Zeitschrift für Historische Anthropologie* 12 (special issue: "Rituelle Welten" = Wulf & Zirfas (eds) 2003 (*)):158–183.

Fardon, Richard, 1999, *Mary Douglas. An Intellectual Biography*; London, New York: Routledge (ISBN 0–415–04092–2 / 0–415–04093–0 (p)) (315) (with index and bibliography).

Förster, Till, 2003, 'Victor Turners Ritualtheorie. Eine ethnologische Lektüre', *Theologische Literaturzeitung* 128:703–716.

Förster, Till, 2004, 'From Rationality to Creativity. Ritual Activity and Religious Experience in the Work of Edward Evans-Pritchard (1902–1973) and Victor Turner (1920–1983)', in: Frieder Ludwig & Afe Adogame (eds), *European Traditions in the Study of Religion in Africa*, Wiesbaden: Harrassowitz (ISBN: 3–447–05002–0) 245–253.

Frankiel, Tamar, 2001, 'Prospects in Ritual Studies', *Religion* 32:75–87.

This paper is disguised as a review article of Aune & De Marinis, *Religious and Social Ritual* [1995] and Grimes 1982 (*) [revised edition 1995]. For an abstract see Part A. [MS]

Gay, Volney Patrick, 1979, *Freud on Ritual. Reconstruction and Critique* (Dissertation Series. American Academy of Religion); Missoula (MT): Scholars Press (ISBN 0–891–30282–4) (ix + 212) (originally presented as the author's thesis, University of Chicago, 1976).

Gay, Volney Patrick, 1983, 'Ritual and Self-Esteem in Victor Turner and Heinz Kohut', *Zygon* 18:271–282.

Geerts, Henri, 1990, 'An Inquiry into the Meaning of Ritual Symbolism. Turner and Peirce', in: Hans-Günter Heimbrock & H. Barbara Boudewijnse (eds), *Current Studies on Rituals. Perspectives for the Psychology of Religion*, (International Series in the Psychology of Religion 2), Amsterdam, Atlanta (GA): Rodopi (ISBN 90–5183–178–1) (*) 19–32.

Gellner, David N., 1999, 'Religion, Politik und Ritual. Betrachtungen zu Geertz und Bloch', in: Corina Caduff & Joanna Pfaff-Czarnecka (eds), *Rituale heute. Theorien—Kontroversen—Entwürfe*, Berlin: Dietrich Reimer (ISBN 3–496–02666–9) (*) 49–72.

Ghosh, A., 1987, 'Tambiah on Ritual', *Contributions to Indian Sociology* 21:217–223.

Gibson, James E., 1991, 'Celebration and Transgression. Nietzsche on Ritual', ***Journal of Ritual Studies*** **5:1–32.**

Giobellina-Brumana, F. & E.-E. Gonzalez, 1981, 'Mito : Rito :: Levi-Strauss : Mary Douglas', ***Revista Española de Antropologia Americana*** **11:245–257.**

Grimes, Ronald L., 1976, 'Ritual Studies. A Comparative Review of Theodor Gaster and Victor Turner', ***Religious Studies Review*** **2:13–25.**

Grimes, Ronald L., 1985, 'Victor Turner's Social Drama and T.S. Eliot's Ritual Drama', ***Anthropologica, Journal of the Canadian Anthropology Society*** **N.S. 27:79–99 (with bibliography).**

For an abstract see Part A.

Grimes, Ronald L., 1990, 'Victor Turner's Definition, Theory, and Sense of Ritual', in: Kathleen M. Ashley (ed.), ***Victor Turner and the Construction of Cultural Criticism. Between Literature and Anthropology*****, Bloomington (IN): Indiana University Press (ISBN 0–253–31003–2 / 0–253–20594–8) (*) 141–146.**

Grimes, Ronald L., 1999, 'Jonathan Z. Smith's Theory of Ritual Space', ***Religion*** **29:261–273.**

For an abstract see Part A.

Handelman, Don, 1976, 'Some Contributions of Max Gluckman to Anthropological Thought', in: Myron J. Aronoff (ed.), ***Freedom and Constraint. A Memorial Tribute to Max Gluckman*****, Assen: Van Gorcum (ISBN 90–232–1392–0) 7–14.**

Handelman, Don, 1993, 'Is Victor Turner Receiving his Intellectual Due?' ***Journal of Ritual Studies*** **7:117–124.**

This is a review article on Alexander 1991 and Ashley 1990. For an abstract see Part A. [MS]

Héran, François, 1994, 'Rite et méconnaissance. Notes sur la théorie religieuse de l'action chez Pareto et Weber', *Archives de sciences sociales des religions* 85:137–152.

Hockey, J., 2002, 'The Importance of Being Intuitive. Arnold van Gennep's The Rites of Passage', *Morality* 7:210–217.

Isenberg, Sheldon & Dennis E. Owen, 1977, 'Bodies, Natural and Contrived. The Work of Mary Douglas', *Religious Studies Review* 3:1–16.

Kalocsai, Csilla, 2000, 'The Incursive Nomadism of Victor W. Turner. Reinterpretations of Ritual, Drama and Performance', *http://classes.yale.edu/anth500a/projects/project_sites/00_Kalocsai/* version of 5/5/2000: 15 pages (accessed 9/2/2003) (with an annotated bibliography on V.W. Turner of 4 items, and a bibliography of secondary literature about him of 14 items).

Kapferer, Bruce, 1987, 'The Anthropology of Max Gluckman', in: Bruce Kapferer (ed.), *Power, Process and Transformation. Essays in Memory of Max Gluckman*, (Social Analysis. Special Issues Series 22), Adelaide: Department of Anthropology, University of Adelaide (No ISBN) 3–21.

Levine, Michael P., 1998, 'A Cognitive Approach to Ritual. New Method or No Method at All?' *Method and Theory in the Study of Religion* 10:30–60.

About E. Thomas Lawson and Robert N. McCauley (1990, 1993). For an abstract see Part A. [MS]

Mack, Burton L., 1987, 'Introduction. Religion and Ritual', in: Robert G. Hamerton-Kelly (ed.), *Violent Origins. Walter Burkert, René Girard, and Jonathan Z. Smith on Ritual Killing and Cultural Formation*, Stanford: Stanford University Press (ISBN 0–8047–1370–7) (*) 1–70.

Summarizes the theories of René Girard, Walter Burkert, and Jonathan Z. Smith. [JS]

Malley, Brian & Justin L. Barrett, 2003, 'Can Ritual Form be Predicted from Religious Belief? A Test of the Lawson-McCauley Hypotheses', *Journal of Ritual Studies* 17.2:1–14.

Manning, Phil, 1989, 'Ritual Talk', *Sociology* 23:365–385.

"In this paper, I look at Erving Goffman's account of the way the self is displayed in everyday talk." (365). [MS]

Matthews, Gareth, 1981, 'Comments on Israel Scheffler', *Synthese* 46:439–444.

A commentary on Scheffler 1981 (*). [MS]

Messer, Ellen & Michael Lambek (eds), 2001, *Ecology and the Sacred. Engaging the Anthropology of Roy A. Rappaport*; Ann Arbor (MI): University of Michigan Press (ISBN 0–472–11170–1) (viii + 364).

Selected Contents: Ellen Messer: "Thinking and Engaging the Whole. The Anthropology of Roy A. Rappaport" (1–45); Robert I. Levy: "The Life and Death of Ritual. Reflections on Some Ethnographic and Historical Phenomena in the Light of Roy Rappaport's Analysis of Ritual" (145–169); Peter K. Gluck: "New Ways in Death and Dying. Transformation of Body and Text in Late Modern American Judaism. A Kaddish for Roy 'Skip' Rappaport" (170–192); James L. Peacock: "Belief Beheld. Inside and Outside, Insider and Outsider in the Anthropology of Religion" (207–226); Thomas J. Csordas: "Notes for a Cybernetics of the Holy" (227–243); Michael Lambek: "Rappaport on Religion. A Social Anthropological Reading" (244–273); Gillian Gillison: "Reflections on Pigs for the Ancestors" (291–299); Polly Wiessner and Akii Tumu: "Averting the Bush Fire Day: Ain's Cult Revisited" (300–323). [JK]

Michaels, Axel (ed.), 1997, *Klassiker der Religionswissenschaft. Von Friedrich Schleiermacher bis Mircea Eliade*; München: Beck (ISBN 3–406–42813–4) (427) (with indexes and bibliographies).
[Classics of the Sciences of Religions. From Friedrich Schleiermacher to Mircea Eliade]

Included are articles about life, work and influence of a.o. Robertson Smith, Frazer, Freud, Durkheim, Mauss, Van Gennep, V.W. Turner, and Eliade. [JS]

Miller, Diane L., 1982, 'Ritual in the Work of Durkheim and Goffman. The Link between the Micro and the Macro', *Humanity and Society* 6:122–134.

Nagendra, S.P., 1970, 'Max Weber's Theory of Ritual', *Indian Journal of Sociology* 1:173–184.

Neubert, Frank, 2004, 'Übergänge. Tod und Sünde bei Robert Hertz im Kontext durkheimianischer Religionssoziologie', *Zeitschrift für Religionswissenschaft* 12:61–77.

From the journal's abstract: "Hertz presents a theory of transitions which differs in some central points from the results of van Gennep and Turner. It is the aim of this essay to show these differences, and to present them in the light of Durkheimian sociology of religion and its interpretation by the Collège de sociologie." [MS]

Olson, Carl, 1994, 'Eroticism, Violence, and Sacrifice. A Post-modern Theory of Religion and Ritual', *Method and Theory in the Study of Religion* 6:231–250.

Reviews the theory of George Bataille and applies it to the Sun Dance of the Sioux. [MS]

Owen, Dennis E., 1998, 'Ritual Studies as Ritual Practice. Catherine Bell's Challenge to Students of Ritual', *Religious Studies Review* 24:23–30.

This review covers Bell 1992 (*) and Bell 1997 (*) plus two further publications by M.E. Combs-Schilling and S. Starr Sered respectively. [MS]

Piette, Albert, 1997, 'Pour une anthropologie comparée des rituels. Rencontre avec des "batesoniens"', *Terrain* 29:139–150.

In order to find out if 'ritual' is "un concept opératoire, dirscriminant" (141) the author starts from the assumption that the notion of 'ritual' refers to a specific contextual frame. Therefore, he presents some authors and their thoughts on 'frame/framing' and related problems: Gregory Bateson (141–143), Victor W. Turner (143–144), Richard Schechner (144–146), Barbara Babcock and Susan Stewart (146), John MacAloon (146–147), and Erving Goffman (147–149). [MS]

Platvoet, Jan G., 1983, 'The Study of Rites in the Netherlands', ***Nederlands Theologisch Tijdschrift*** **37 (special issue:** ***Analysis and Interpretation of Rites. Essays to D.J. Hoens*****, edited by J.G. Platvoet):177–188.**

Discusses the theories of D.J. Hoens, J. van Baal and W.E.A. van Beek, and to a lesser extent those of C.J. Bleeker, P.D. Chantepie de la Saussaye, H.Th. Obbink, W.B. Kristensen, C.P. Tiele, G. van der Leeuw, K.A.H. Hidding, Th.P. van Baaren, L. Leertouwer, A.J. Vink, and J.P.B. de Josselin de Jong. It also introduces the other contributions in this volume by Th.P. van Baaren, W.E.A. van Beek, J.G. Platvoet, W. van Wetering, J.H. Kamstra, J. van Baal, D.C. Mulder and J.D.J. Waardenburg. [JS]

Price, S. Michael, 1988, 'Ritual, Meaning, and Subjectivity. Studying Ritual as Human Religious Expression', ***Epoche*** **16:11–32.**

On Frits Staal. For an abstract see Part A.

Renard, Jean B., 1986, 'Les rites de passage. Une constante anthropologique', ***Etudes théologiques et religieuses*** **61:227–238.**

Robbins, Joel, 2001, 'Ritual Communication and Linguistic Ideology. A Reading and Partial Reformulation of Rappaport's Theory of Ritual', ***Current Anthropology*** **42:591–614.**

Schechner, Richard, 1988, 'Victor Turner's Last Adventure', in: Victor W. Turner, ***The Anthropology of Performance*****, (Performance Studies Series 4), New York: PAJ Publications (A Division of Performing Arts Journal) (ISBN 1–55554–000–7 / 1–55554–001–5 (p)) (*) 7–20.**

For an abstract see Part A.

Segal, Robert Alan, 1983, 'Victor Turner's Theory of Ritual', *Zygon* 18:327–335.
Reprinted in: Robert A. Segal: *Religion and the Social Sciences. Essays on the Confrontation*, (Brown Studies in Religion 3), Atlanta (GA): Scholars Press 1989 (ISBN 1–555–40295–x) 137–146.

Segal, Robert Alan, 2000, 'Making the Myth-Ritualist Theory Scientific', *Religion* 30:259–271.

For an abstract see Part A.

Stagl, Justin, 1983, 'Übergangsriten und Statuspassagen. Überlegungen zu Arnold van Genneps "Les rites de passage"', in: Karl Acham (ed.), *Gesellschaftliche Prozesse*, Graz: Akademische Verlags- und Druckanstalt (ISBN 2–201–01224–6) 83–96.

Strenski, Ivan, 1996, 'The Rise of Ritual and the Hegemony of Myth. Sylvain Lévi, the Durkheimians and Max Müller', in: Lauri L. Patton & Wendy Doniger (eds), *Myth and Method* (Studies in Religion and Culture), Charlottesville (VA), London: University Press of Virginia (ISBN 0–813–91656–9 / 0–813–91657–7 (p)) 52–81.

Strenski, Ivan, 1997, 'The Social and Intellectual Origins of Hubert and Mauss's Theory of Ritual Sacrifice', in: Dick van der Meij (ed.), *India and Beyond. Aspects of Literature, Meaning, Ritual and Thought. Essays in Honour of Frits Staal*, (Studies from the International Institute for Asian Studies), London, New York: Kegan Paul International (ISBN 0–7103–0602–4) 511–537.

Strenski, Ivan, 2002, *Contesting Sacrifice. Religion, Nationalism, and Social Thought in France*; Chicago, London: University of Chicago Press (ISBN 0–226–77736–7) (ix + 228) (with index).

Strenski, Ivan, 2003, *Theology and the First Theory of Sacrifice* (Numen Book Series. Studies in the History of Religions 98); Leiden, Boston: Brill (ISBN 90–04–13559–6 / ISSN 0169–8834) (ix + 248) (with index).

Apart from Hubert and Mauss, the author presents a number of rival theoretical attempts. For an abstract see Part A. [MS]

Tambiah, Stanley Jeyaraja, 2002, *Edmund Leach. An Anthropological Life*; Cambridge etc.: Cambridge University Press (ISBN 0–521–80824–3) (538).

Thomas, Konrad, 1998, 'Ritual und Vergessen. Zu René Girards Theorem der *méconnaissance*', in: Alfred Schäfer & Michael Wimmer (eds), *Rituale und Ritualisierungen*, (Grenzüberschreitungen 1), Opladen: Leske & Budrich (ISBN 3–8100–2171–7) (*) 109–115.

Tufis, Paula, 2001, 'Conditia ritului de trecere in contemporaneitate', *Revista Romana de Sociologie* 12:517–523.
[The Conditions of Passage Rites in the Contemporary World; in Rumanian]

Discusses Arnold van Gennep, Gaston Wagner, Max Gluckman, Julian Pitt-Rivers, and Arnold Niederer.

Tybjerg, Tove, 1993, 'Wilhelm Mannhardt. A Pioneer in the Study of Rituals', in: Tore Ahlbäck (ed.), *The Problem of Ritual. Based on Papers Read at the Symposium on Religious Rites Held at Åbo, Finland, on the 13th–16th of August 1991*, (Scripta Instituti Donneriani Aboensis 15), Åbo: The Donner Institute for Research in Religious and Cultural History (ISBN 951–650–196–6) (*) 27–37.

Tybjerg, Tove, 2001, 'Myter, ritualer og videnskaber: Wilhelm Mannhardt og Jane Ellen Harrison', *Religionsvidenskabeligt Tidsskrift* 38:5–18.

For an abstract see Part A.

Verkuyl, Henk J., 1997, 'On Syntactic and Semantic Considerations in the Study of Ritual', in: Dick van der Meij (ed.), *India and Beyond. Aspects of Literature, Meaning, Ritual and Thought. Essays in Honor of Frits Staal*, (Studies from the International Institute for Asian Studies), London, New York: Kegan Paul International (ISBN 0–7103–0602–4) 620–635.

On Frits Staal and Noam Chomsky. For an abstract see Part A.

Warfield, Rawls A., 2001, 'Durkheim's Treatment of Practice. Concrete Practice vs. Representations as the Foundation of Reason', *Journal of Classical Sociology* 1:33–68.

Wiebe, Donald, 2004, 'Can Science Fabricate Meaning? On Ritual, Religion, and the Academic Study of Religion', in: Timothy Light & Brian C. Wilson (eds), *Religion as a Human Capacity. A Festschrift in Honor of E. Thomas Lawson*, (Numen Book Series. Studies in the History of Religions 99), Leiden, Boston: Brill (ISBN 90–04–12676–7) 89–103.

A critical discussion of Rappaport 1999 (*). [MS]

Wulf, Christoph, Michael Göhlich & Jörg Zirfas (eds), 2001, *Grundlagen des Performativen. Eine Einführung in die Zusammenhänge von Sprache, Macht und Handeln*; Weinheim, München: Juventa-Verlag (ISBN 3–7799–1075–6) (318) (with index and abstracts).

This volume features the theories of Austin (Michael Göhlich: "Performative Äußerungen. John L. Austins Begriff als Instrument erziehlungswissenschaftlicher Forschung"; 25–46), Habermas (Michael Göhlich and Jörg Zirfas: "Kommunikatives Handeln in der Lebenswelt. Die Theorie der performativen Einstellung von Jürgen Habermas; 47–73), Derrida (Jörg Zirfas: "Dem Anderen gerecht werden. Das Performative und die Dekonstruktion bei Jacques Derrida"; 75–100), Bourdieu (Kathrin Audehm: "Die Macht der Sprache. Performative Magie bei Pierre Bourdieu"; 101–128); Foucault (Birgit Althans: "Transformationen des Individuums. Michael Foucault als Performer seines Diskurses und die Pädagogik der Selbstsorge"; 129–155), Butler (Anja Tervooren: "Körper, Inszenierung und Geschlecht. Judith Butlers Konzept der Performativität"; 157–180), Mead (Benjamin Jörrisen: "Aufführungen der Sozialität. Aspekte des Performativen in der Sozialphilosophie Georg Herbert Meads"; 181–201), Goffman (Constanze Bausch: "Die Inszenierung des Sozialen. Erving Goffman und das Performative"; 203–225), Turner (Monika Wagner-Willi: "Liminalität und soziales Drama. Die Ritualtheorie von Victor Turner"; 227–251), and Wulf & Gebauer (Christoph Wulf: "Mimesis und Performatives Handeln. Gunter Gebauers und Christoph Wulfs Konzeption mimetischen Handelns in der sozialen Welt"; 253–272). The volume also contains short biographies of the theoreticians (273–278). [MS]

Zumwalt, Rosemary, 1982, 'Arnold van Gennep. The Hermit of Bourg-la-Reine', ***American Anthropologist*** **84:299–313 (with bibliography).**

PART C

LEXICON ARTICLES
(96 items)

Alexander, Bobby Chris, 1987, 'Ceremony', in: Mircea Eliade (ed.), *The Encyclopedia of Religion* (3), New York, London: MacMillan Publishing Company (ISBN 0–02–909720–7 (vol. 3) / 0–02–909480–1 (set.)) 179–183.

Allen, Davina A., E.M. Jackson & Cassandra Lorius, 1993, 'Ritual', in: Kenneth McLeish (ed.), *Bloomsbury Guide to Human Thought*, London: Bloomsbury Publishing Limited (ISBN 0–7475–0991–3) 644–646.

Anon., 1992a, 'Rites of Passage', in: Rosemary Goring (ed.), *Chambers Dictionary of Beliefs and Religions*, Edinburgh, New York: Chambers (ISBN 0–550–15000–5) 442.

Anon., 1992b, 'Rituals', in: Rosemary Goring (ed.), *Chambers Dictionary of Beliefs and Religions*, Edinburgh, New York: Chambers (ISBN 0–550–15000–5) 442–443.

Anon., 1992c, 'Worship', in: Rosemary Goring (ed.), *Chambers Dictionary of Beliefs and Religions*, Edinburgh, New York: Chambers (ISBN 0–550–15000–5) 567.

Anon., 1995, 'Resistance through Ritual', in: David Jary, *et al.* (eds), *Collins Dictionary of Sociology*, Glasgow: HarperCollins (ISBN 0–00–470804–0) 555–556 (2nd edition).

Anon., 1998, 'Ritual', in: Gordon Marshall (ed.), *A Dictionary of Sociology*, Oxford, New York: Oxford University Press (ISBN 0–19–280081–7) 569–570 (2nd edition).

Anon., 1999a, 'Liturgie', in: John Bowker (ed.), *Das Oxford-Lexikon der Weltreligionen*, (übersetzt und bearb.), Düsseldorf: Patmos (ISBN 3-491-72406-6) 603-604.

Anon., 1999b, 'Riten', in: John Bowker (ed.), *Das Oxford-Lexikon der Weltreligionen*, (übersetzt und bearb.), Düsseldorf: Patmos (ISBN 3-491-72406-6) 842.

Anon., 1999c, 'Ritual', in: John Bowker (ed.), *Das Oxford-Lexikon der Weltreligionen*, (übersetzt und bearb.), Düsseldorf: Patmos (ISBN 3-491-72406-6) 843-844.

Anon., 1999d, 'Übergangsriten', in: John Bowker (ed.), *Das Oxford-Lexikon der Weltreligionen*, (übersetzt und bearb.), Düsseldorf: Patmos (ISBN 3-491-72406-6) 1031-1032.

Anwar, Ghazala, 1999, 'Worship', in: Serenity Young (ed.), *Encyclopedia of Women and World Religion* (2), New York: Macmillan Reference USA (ISBN 0-02-864608-8) 1070-1072.

Auffarth, Christoph, 2000, 'Ritual', in: Christoph Auffarth, Jutta Bernard & Hubert Mohr (eds), *Metzler Lexikon Religion* (3), Stuttgart, Weimar: Metzler (ISBN 3-476-01553-x) 219-220.

Barnard, Alan & Jonathan Spencer, 1996, 'Rite of Passage', in: Alan Barnard & Jonathan Spencer (eds), *Encyclopedia of Social and Cultural Anthropology*, London, New York: Routledge (ISBN 0-415-09996-X) 489-490.

Baudy, Dorothea, 2001a, 'Kult/Kultus, I. Religionswissenschaftlich', in: Hans Dieter Betz, *et al.* (eds), *Die Religion in Geschichte und Gegenwart. Handwörterbuch für Theologie und Religionswissenschaft* (4), Tübingen: Mohr Siebeck (ISBN 3-16-146944-5) 1799-1802 (4th edition).

Baudy, Dorothea, 2001b, 'Kult/Kultus, II. Forschungsgeschichtlich', in: Hans Dieter Betz, *et al.* (eds), *Die Religion in Geschichte und Gegenwart. Handwörterbuch für Theologie und Religionswissenschaft* (4), Tübingen: Mohr Siebeck (ISBN: 3–16–146944–5) 1802–1806 (4th edition).

Baumann, Richard, 1989, 'Performance', in: Erik Barnouw (ed.), *International Encyclopedia of Communications* (3), Oxford, New York: Oxford University Press (ISBN 0–19–505804–6) 262–266.

Bayes, Paul, 1986, 'Drama and Worship', in: J.G. Davies (ed.), *A New Dictionary of Liturgy & Worship*, London: SCM Press Ltd (ISBN 0–334–02207–X) 214–216 (with bibliography).

Bell, Catherine M., 2005, 'Ritual [Further Considerations]', in: Lindsay Jones (ed.), *The Encyclopedia of Religion. Second Edition* (11), Detroit etc.: Thomson Gale (ISBN 0–02–865980–5) 7848–7856 (with bibliography).

For an abstract see Part A.

Bendlin, Andreas, 2001, 'Ritual, I. Begriff', in: Hubert Cancik & Helmuth Schneider (eds), *Der Neue Pauly. Enzyklopädie der Antike* (10), Stuttgart, Weimar: Metzler (ISBN 3–476–01480–0 (vol. 10) / 3–476–01470–3 (set)) 1024.

Brandon, Samuel G.F., 1973, 'Religious Ritual', in: Philip Paul Wiener (ed.), *Dictionary of the History of Ideas. Studies of Selected Pivotal Ideas* (4), New York: Charles Scribner's Sons (ISBN 0–684–13293–1) 99.

Burke, Kenneth, 1968, 'Interaction, III. Dramatism', in: David Lawrence Sills (ed.), *International Encyclopedia of the Social Sciences* (7), New York / Chicago / London: Macmillan / The Free Press / Collier-Macmillan (No ISBN) 445–452 (with bibliography).

Calmard, Jean, 1995, 'Rituel (théâtre)', in: Michel Corvin (ed.), *Dictionnaire encyclopédique du théâtre* (2), Paris: Bordas (ISBN 2-04-027134-1) 772–774 (with bibliography).

Colombo, A. & S. Offelli, 1982, 'Rito', in: Carlo Giacon (ed.), *Enciclopedia filosofica* (7), Roma: Lucarini (No ISBN) 155–156.

Colpe, Carsten, 1992, 'Ritus, 1. Religionsgeschichtlich', in: Erwin Fahlbusch, *et al.* (eds), *Evangelisches Kirchenlexikon. Internationale theologische Enzyklopädie* (3), Göttingen: Vandenhoeck & Ruprecht (ISBN 3-525-50137-4 (vol.3)) 1661–1662 (3rd edition) (with bibliography).

Davies, J.G., 1986, 'Cult, Cultus', in: J.G. Davies (ed.), *A New Dictionary of Liturgy & Worship*, London: SCM Press Ltd (ISBN 0-334-02207-x) 202–203.

Di Nola, Alfonso M., 1973a, 'Culto', in: Alfonso M. di Nola, Maurilio Adriani & Enrico Chiavacci (eds), *Enciclopedia delle religioni* (2), Firenze: Vallecchi editore (No ISBN) 532–539.

Di Nola, Alfonso M., 1973b, 'Liturgia', in: Alfonso M. di Nola, Maurilio Adriani & Enrico Chiavacci (eds), *Enciclopedia delle religioni* (3), Firenze: Valecchi editore (No ISBN) 1534–1537.

Di Nola, Alfonso M., 1973c, 'Ripetizione rituale', in: Alfonso M. di Nola, Maurilio Adriani & Enrico Chiavacci (eds), *Enciclopedia delle religioni* (5), Firenze: Valecchi editore (No ISBN) 383–420.

Di Nola, Alfonso M., 1973d, 'Rito', in: Alfonso M. di Nola, Maurilio Adriani & Enrico Chiavacci (eds), *Enciclopedia delle religioni* (5), Firenze: Valecchi editore (No ISBN) 428–440.

Elsas, Christoph, 1989, 'Initiationsriten, 1. Religionsgeschichtlich', in: Erwin Fahlbusch, *et al.* (eds), *Evangelisches Kirchenlexikon. Internationale theologische Enzyklopädie* (2), Göttingen: Vandenhoeck & Ruprecht (ISBN 3-525-50132-3 (vol. 2)) 664–666 (with bibliography).

Evans, Elizabeth S., 1996, 'Ritual', in: David Levinson & Melvin Ember (eds), *Encyclopedia of Cultural Anthropology* (3), New York: Henry Holt and Company (ISBN 0–8050–2877–3) 1120–1123.

Fisher, Paul, 1986, 'Culture and Worship', in: J.G. Davies (ed.), *A New Dictionary of Liturgy & Worship*, London: SCM Press Ltd (ISBN 0–334–02207–x) 203–205.

Gerlitz, Peter, 1987, 'Initiation/Initiationsriten', in: Gerhard Müller & Gerhard Krause (eds), *Theologische Realenzyklopädie* (16), Berlin, New York: Walter de Gruyter & Co. (ISBN 3–11–011159–4) 156–162 (with bibliography).

Gladigow, Burkhard, 1998, 'Ritual, komplexes', in: Hubert Cancik, Burkhard Gladigow & Karl-Heinz Kohl (eds), *Handbuch religionswissenschaftlicher Grundbegriffe* (4), Stuttgart, Berlin, Köln: W. Kohlhammer (ISBN 3–17–009556–0) 458–460.

Glazier, Stephen D., 1995, 'Religion. Beliefs, Symbols and Rituals', in: Frank N. Magill (ed.), *International Encyclopedia of Sociology* (2), London, Chicago: Salem Press Inc. (ISBN 1–884964–45–1) 1094–1097.

Green, A.E., 1995a, 'Rite of Passage', in: Martin Banham (ed.), *The Cambridge Guide to Theatre*, Cambridge etc.: Cambridge University Press (ISBN 0–521–43437–8) 922.

Green, A.E., 1995b, 'Ritual', in: Martin Banham (ed.), *The Cambridge Guide to Theatre*, Cambridge etc.: Cambridge University Press (ISBN 0–521–434378) 922–925 (with bibliography).

Grimes, Ronald L., 1987, 'Ritual Studies', in: Mircea Eliade (ed.), *The Encyclopedia of Religion* (12), New York: Macmillan (ISBN 0–02–897135–3) 422–425.

Grimes, Ronald L., 2002, 'Ritual', in: Joseph L. Price & Donald W. Musser (eds), *A New Handbook of Christian Theology*, New York: Abingdon Press (ISBN 0–687–27802–3) 413–415 (revised edition; 1st ed. 1992).

Grünschloß, Andreas, 1987, 'Initiation', in: Karl Müller & Theo Sundermeier (eds), *Lexikon missionstheologischer Grundbegriffe*, Berlin: Dietrich Reimer (ISBN 3–496–0911–x) 168–176 (with bibliography).

Gutmann, Hans-Martin, 2001, 'Ritual', in: Norbert Mette & Folkert Rickers (eds), *Lexikon der Religionspädagogik* (2), Neukirchen-Vluyn: Neukirchener (ISBN 3–7887–1745–9) 1853–1857 (with bibliography).

Hegland, Mary Elaine, 1999, 'Ritual', in: Serenity Young (ed.), *Encyclopedia of Women and World Religion* (2), New York: Macmillan Reference USA (ISBN 0–02–864608–8) 844–846.

Hozier, Anthony, 2002, 'Ritual', in: Colin Chambers (ed.), *The Continuum Companion to Twentieth Century Theatre*, London, New York: Continuum (ISBN 0–8264–4959–x) 649–650 (with bibliography).

Jackson, E.M., 1993, 'Cult', in: Kenneth McLeish (ed.), *Bloomsbury Guide to Human Thought*, London: Bloomsbury Publishing Limited (ISBN 0–7475–0991–3) 177–178.

Jennings Jr., Theodore W., 1987, 'Liturgy', in: Mircea Eliade (ed.), *The Encyclopedia of Religion* (8), New York, London: MacMillan Publishing Company (ISBN 0–02–909480–1) 580–583.

Joyce, R.A., 2001, 'Ritual and Symbolism, Archaeology of', in: Neil J. Smelser & Paul B. Baltes (eds), *International Encyclopedia of the Social & Behavioral Sciences* (20), Amsterdam etc.: Elsevier Science Ltd. (ISBN 0–08–043076–7 (set)) 13371–13375 (with bibliography).

Kelleher, Margaret Mary, 1987a, 'Ritual', in: Joseph A. Komonchak, Mary Collins & Dermont A. Lane (eds), *The New Dictionary of Theology*, Dublin: Gill and Macmillan (ISBN 0–7171–1552–6) 906–907 (with bibliography).

Kelleher, Margaret Mary, 1987b, 'Worship', in: Joseph A. Komonchak, Mary Collins & Dermont A. Lane (eds), *The New Dictionary of Theology*, Dublin: Gill and Macmillan (ISBN 0–7171–1552–6) 1105–1106 (with bibliography).

Köpping, Klaus-Peter, 2003, 'Ritual and Theatre', in: Dennis Kennedy (ed.), *The Oxford Encyclopedia of Theatre and Performance* (2), Oxford: Oxford University Press (ISBN 0–19–860174–3 (set); 0–19–860671–0 (Vol. 2)) 1139–1141.

Kramer, Fritz W., 2000, 'Ritual', in: Bernhard Streck (ed.), *Wörterbuch der Ethnologie*, Wuppertal: Edition Trickster im Peter Hammer Verlag (ISBN 3–87294–857–1) 210–213 (2nd edition).

Lang, Bernhard, 1993, 'Kult', in: Hubert Cancik, Burkhard Gladigow & Karl-Heinz Kohl (eds), *Handbuch religionswissenschaftlicher Grundbegriffe* (3), Stuttgart, Berlin, Köln: W. Kohlhammer (ISBN 3–17–010531–0 (set) / 3–17–009555–2 (vol.3)) 474–488.

Lang, Bernhard, 1998, 'Ritual/Ritus', in: Hubert Cancik, Burkhard Gladigow & Karl-Heinz Kohl (eds), *Handbuch religionswissenschaftlicher Grundbegriffe* (4), Stuttgart; Berlin; Köln: W. Kohlhammer (ISBN 3–17–009556–0) 442–458.

Leach, Edmund R., 1968, 'Ritual', in: David Lawrence Sills (ed.), *International Encyclopedia of the Social Sciences* (13), New York / Chicago / London: Macmillan / Free Press / Collier-Macmillan (No ISBN) 520–526.

For an abstract see Part A.

Madden, Lawrence J., 1990, 'Liturgy', in: Peter E. Fink (ed.), *The New Dictionary of Sacramental Worship*, (A Michael Glazier Book), Collegeville: The Liturgical Press (ISBN 0–8146–5788–5) 740–742 (with bibliography).

Meslin, Michel, 1997, 'Les rites', in: Frédéric Lenoir (ed.), *Encyclopédie des religions* (2: Thèmes), Paris: Bayard Éditions (ISBN 2–227–31093–6 (vol. 2)) 1947–1956.

Meyer-Blanck, Michael, 2002, 'II.1.1 Zeichen—Riten—Symbolhandlungen', in: Gottfried Bitter, *et al.* (eds), *Neues Handbuch religionspädagogischer Grundbegriffe*, München: Kösel (ISBN 3-466-36598-8 / ISBN 3-466-36597-X (p)) 61–64.

Mischung, Roland & Klaus-Peter Köpping, 1999, 'Ritus, Ritual', in: Wolfgang Müller (ed.), *Wörterbuch der Völkerkunde*, Berlin: Dietrich Reimer (ISBN 3-496-02650-2) 316–317.

Mitchell, Jon P., 1996, 'Ritual', in: Alan Barnard & Jonathan Spencer (eds), *Encyclopedia of Social and Cultural Anthropology*, London, New York: Routledge (ISBN 0-415-09996-x) 490–493.

Muller, J.-C., 1991, 'Rite de passage', in: Pierre Bonte & Michel Izard (eds), *Dictionnaire de l'ethnologie et de l'anthropologie*, Paris: Presses universitaires de France (ISBN 2-13-043383-9) 633–634.

Münzel, Mark, 2000, 'Fest', in: Bernhard Streck (ed.), *Wörterbuch der Ethnologie*, (2. und erweiterte Auflage), Wuppertal: Edition Trickster im Peter Hammer Verlag (ISBN 3-87294-857-1) 67–73 (2nd edition).

Myerhoff, Barbara G., Linda A. Camino & Edith Turner, 1987, 'Rites of Passage: An Overview', in: Mircea Eliade (ed.), *Encyclopedia of Religion* (12), New York: MacMillan Publishers Company (ISBN 0-02-909830-0 (vol. 12) / 0-02-909480-1 (set)) 380–386.

Newton, Denise, 1986, 'Sociology and Worship', in: J.G. Davies (ed.), *A New Dictionary of Liturgy & Worship*, London: SCM Press Ltd (ISBN 0-334-02207-x) 493–497 (with bibliography).

O'Grady, Kathleen, 1999, 'Ritual Studies', in: Serenity Young (ed.), *Encyclopedia of Women and World Religion* (2), New York: Macmillan Reference USA (ISBN 0-02-864608-8) 846–848.

Parkin, D., 2001, 'Ritual', in: Neil J. Smelser & Paul B. Baltes (eds), *International Encyclopedia of the Social & Behavioral Sciences* (20), Amsterdam etc.: Elsevier Science Ltd. (ISBN 0-08-043076-7 (set)) 13368-13371 (with bibliography).

Rappaport, Roy A., 1989, 'Ritual', in: Erik Barnouw, *et al.* (eds), *International Encyclopedia of Communication* (3), Oxford, New York: Oxford University Press (ISBN 0-19-505804-6 (vol. 3) / 0-19-504994-2 (set)) 467-473 (with bibliography).

Renger, Johannes, 1999, 'Kult, Kultus', in: Hubert Cancik & Helmuth Schneider (eds), *Der neue Pauly. Enzyklopädie der Antike* (6), Stuttgart, Weimar: J.B. Metzler (ISBN 3-476-01476-2 (vol. 6) / 3-476-01470-3 (set)) 891-892.

Rzepkowski, Horst, 1992a, 'Rites de Passage', in: Horst Rzepkowski (ed.), *Lexikon der Mission. Geschichte, Theologie, Ethnologie*, Graz, Wien, Köln: Styria (ISBN 3-222-12052-8) 368 (with bibliography).

Rzepkowski, Horst, 1992b, 'Ritus', in: Horst Rzepkowski (ed.), *Lexikon der Mission. Geschichte, Theologie, Ethnologie*, Graz, Wien, Köln: Styria (ISBN 3-222-12052-8) 368-369 (with bibliography).

Saint-Jean, Raymond, 1988, 'Rites', in: Marcel Viller, André Rayez & A. Derville (eds), *Dictionnaire de spiritualité ascétique et mystique. Doctrine et histoire* (13), Paris: Beauchesne (No ISBN) 686-692.

Schechner, Richard, 1987, 'Drama. Performance and Ritual', in: Mircea Eliade (ed.), *The Encyclopedia of Religion* (4), New York, London: MacMillan Publishing Company (ISBN 0-02-909730-4 (vol.4) / 0-02-909480-1 (set)) 436-446.

Schievenhövel, Wulf, 1999, 'Ritualisierung', in: Wolfgang Müller (ed.), *Wörterbuch der Völkerkunde* (3), Berlin: Dietrich Reimer (ISBN 3-496-02650-2) 316-317 (3rd edition).

Schmidt, Bettina, 1999, 'Kult', in: Wolfgang Müller (ed.), *Wörterbuch der Völkerkunde* (3), Berlin: Dietrich Reimer (ISBN 3–496–02650–2) 218–219 (3rd edition).

Schmidt-Biggemann, W., 1976, 'Kult', in: Joachim Ritter & Karlfried Gründer (eds), *Historisches Wörterbuch der Philosophie* (4), Basel, Stuttgart: Schwabe & Co. (ISBN 3–7965–0115–x (set)) 1300–1309.

Schuh, Franzjosef, 1992, 'Ritual', in: Manfred Brauneck & Gérard Schneilin (eds), *Theaterlexikon. Begriffe und Epochen, Bühnen und Ensembles*, (Rowohlts enzyklopädie), Reinbek: Rowohlt (ISBN 3–499–55465–8) 795–797 (3rd edition) (with bibliography).

Searle, Mark, 1992, 'Ritual', in: Cheslyn Jones, *et al.* (eds), *The Study of Liturgy*, Oxford, New York: Oxford University Press (ISBN 0–19–520922–2 (p)) 51–58 (revised edition) (with bibliography).

Sigrist, Christian, 1992, 'Ritus', in: Joachim Ritter & Karlfried Gründer (eds), *Historisches Wörterbuch der Philosophie* (8), Basel: Schwabe und Co. (ISBN 3–7965–0115–x (set)) 1052–1058.

Smith, Pierre, 1991, 'Rite', in: Pierre Bonte & Michel Izard (eds), *Dictionnaire de l'ethnologie et de l'anthropologie*, Paris: Presses universitaires de France (ISBN 2–13–043383–9) 630–633.

Snjezana, Zoric, 1999, 'Ritual', in: Peter Prechtl & Franz-Peter Burkard (eds), *Metzler Philosophie Lexikon. Begriffe und Definitionen*, Stuttgart, Weimar: J.B. Metzler (ISBN 3–476–01679–x) 517–518 (2nd edition).

Staal, Frits, 2001, 'Ritual', in: John F.A. Sawyer & J.M.Y. Simpson (eds), *Concise Encyclopedia of Language and Religion*, Amsterdam etc.: Elsevier (ISBN 0–08–043167–4) 310–313.

Stephenson, Barry, 2005, 'Rites of Passage [Further Considerations]', in: Lindsay Jones (ed.), *The Encyclopedia of Religion*. (11), Detroit etc.: Thomson Gale (ISBN 0–02–865980–5) 7801–7804 (2nd edition).

Sundermaier, Theo, 1998, 'Ritus I', in: Gerhard Müller, Horst Balz & Gerhard Krause (eds), *Theologische Realenzyklopädie* (29), Berlin, New York: Walter de Gruyter (ISBN 3–11–016127–3 (vol. 29)) 259–265.

Thomas, Terence, 1995a, 'Rites of Passage', in: John R. Hinnells (ed.), *A New Dictionary of Religions*, Oxford, Cambridge: Blackwell Reference (ISBN 0–631–18139–3) 426–427 (2nd edition).

Thomas, Terence, 1995b, 'Ritual', in: John R. Hinnells (ed.), *A New Dictionary of Religions*, Oxford, Cambridge: Blackwell Reference (ISBN 0–631–18139–3) 427–428 (2nd edition).

Turner, Victor Witter, 1987, 'Rites of Passage. A Few Definitions', in: Mircea Eliade (ed.), *The Encyclopedia of Religion* (12), New York: MacMillan Publishing Company (ISBN 0–02–909830–0 (vol. 12) / 0–02–909480–1 (set)) 386–387.

Ukpokodu, Peter, 1995, 'Rites of Passage and Aging', in: Frank N. Magill (ed.), *International Encyclopedia of Sociology* (2), London, Chicago: Salem Press Inc. (ISBN 1–884964–45–1) 1129–1133.

Wettstein, Howard, 1998, 'Ritual', in: Edward Craig (ed.), *Routledge Encyclopedia of Philosophy* (8), London, New York: Routledge (ISBN 0415–18713–3 (vol. 8) / 0415–07310–3 (set)) 338–341.

White, R. Kerry, 1995, 'Ritual', in: R. Kerry White (ed.), *An Annotated Dictionary of Technical, Historical and Stylistic Terms Relating to Theatre and Drama. A Handbook of Dramaturgy*, Lewiston, Queenston, Lampeter: The Edwin Mellen Press (ISBN 0–7734–8873–1 / 0–7734–8989–4 (p)) 173 (with bibliography).

Wickler, Wolfgang, 1992, 'Ritualisierung', in: Joachim Ritter & Karlfried Gründer (eds), *Historisches Wörterbuch der Philosophie* (8), Basel: Schwabe und Co. (ISBN 3–7965–0115–x (set)) 1050–1051.

Winthrop, Robert H., 1991a, 'Rite of Passage', in: *Dictionary of Concepts in Cultural Anthropology*, (Reference Sources for the Social Sciences and Humanities 11), New York etc.: Greenwood Press (ISBN 0–313–24280–1) 242–245.

Winthrop, Robert H., 1991b, 'Ritual', in: *Dictionary of Concepts in Cultural Anthropology*, (Reference Sources for the Social Sciences and Humanities 11), New York etc.: Greenwood Press (ISBN 0–313–24280–1) 245–250.

Worgul, George S., 1990, 'Ritual', in: Peter E. Fink (ed.), *The New Dictionary of Sacramental Worship*, (A Michael Glazier Book), Collegeville: The Liturgical Press (ISBN 0–8146–5788–5) 1101–1106 (with bibliography).

Wulf, Christoph, 1997, 'Ritual', in: Christoph Wulf (ed.), *Vom Menschen. Handbuch Historische Anthropologie*, Weinheim, Basel: Beltz (ISBN 3–407–83136–6) 1029–1037.

Wybrew, Hugh, 1992, 'Ceremonial', in: Cheslyn Jones, *et al.* (eds), *The Study of Liturgy*, Oxford, New York: Oxford University Press (ISBN 0–19–520922–2 (p)) 485–493.

Zimmerman, Joyce Ann, 2002, 'Liturgie, I. Phänomenologisch', in: Hans Dieter Betz, *et al.* (eds), *Die Religion in Geschichte und Gegenwart. Handwörterbuch für Theologie und Religionswissenschaft* (5), Tübingen: Mohr Siebeck (ISBN 3–16–146945–3) 430–432 (4th edition).

Zuesse, Evan M., 1987, 'Ritual', in: Mircea Eliade (ed.), *The Encyclopedia of Religion* (12), New York: Macmillan (ISBN 0–02–897135–3) 405–422.

PART D

READERS
(8 items)

Belliger, Andréa & David J. Krieger (eds), 1998, *Ritualtheorien. Ein einführendes Handbuch*; Opladen, Wiesbaden: Westdeutscher Verlag (ISBN 3-531-13238-5) (485) (with index and bibliography).
[Theories of Ritual. An Introductory Compendium]

Most papers contained in this reader can also be found in Grimes 1996 (= *Readings in Ritual Studies*) with the exception of the introductory essay, the section from Humphrey and Laidlaw (1994 = *The Archetypal Actions of Ritual*), the essay by Jan Platvoet (1995 = "Ritual in Plural and Pluralist Societies"), and the paper by Grimes which has been written specially for this reader. The reader has two sections: I. "Allgemeine Ritualtheorien" (General Theories of Ritual); II. "Ritual in Gesellschaft und Kultur" (Ritual in Society and Culture).
Contents of part I: David J. Krieger & Andréa Belliger: "Einführung" (7–33) (*); Catherine Bell (from 1992 (*)): "Ritualkonstruktion" (37–47); Albert Bergesen (1984): "Die rituelle Ordnung" (49–76); Mary Douglas (from 1966 (*)): "Ritual, Reinheit und Gefährdung" (77–97); Clifford Geertz (1971/1973, from 1973 (*)): "'Deep Play'—Ritual als kulturelle Performance" (99–118); Ronald Grimes (from 1982 (*)): "Typen ritueller Erfahrung" (119–134); Caroline Humphrey & James Laidlaw (from 1994 (*)): "Die rituelle Einstellung" (135–155); Theodore W. Jennings, Jr. (1982): "Rituelles Wissen" (157–172) (*); Jan Platvoet (1995): "Das Ritual in pluralistischen Gesellschaften" (173–190) (*); Roy A. Rappaport (from 1974 (*) / 1979 (*)): "Ritual und performative Sprache" (191–211); Jonathan Z. Smith (1980): "Ritual und Realität" (213–226) (*); Stanley J. Tambiah (1981): "Eine performative Theorie des Rituals" (227–250) (*); Victor W. Turner (from 1969 (*)): "Liminalität und Communitas" (251–262).
The second part contains mostly contributions to ritual studies. Hence, its contents are not listed here, with one exception: Christian Bromberger (1995): "Fußball als Weltsicht und als Ritual", which, contrary

to all the other papers in this section, is not included in Grimes 1996. [MS/JK]

Carter, Jeffrey (ed.), 2003, *Understanding Religious Sacrifice. A Reader* (Controversies in the Study of Religion); London: Continuum (ISBN 0–8264–4879–8 / 0–8264–4880–1 (p)) (xi + 467) (with index and bibliography).

As the editor states in his "Postscript" (449–453), "[t]he aim of this anthology has been to present the range of theoretical positions scholars have put forward in their attempts to understand sacrifice and sacrificial phenomena. Organized chronologically, it has spelled out the development of one controversy that has helped define the study of religion since its earliest days. In the end, much remains of the work of critiquing the old in service of re-constructing the new" (452–453). Apart from a general introduction by the editor (1–11), this reader contains excerpts from the work of 25 theoreticians: Edward Burnett Tylor (1874), Herbert Spencer (1882), William Robertson Smith (1894), James G. Frazer (1911/1915), Henri Hubert & Marcel Mauss (1899 [1964]), Edward A. Westermarck (1912), Émile Durkheim (1912 [1965]), Sigmund Freud (1913 [1950]), Gerardus van der Leeuw (1933 [1986]), Georges Bataille (1949 [1991]), Adolf E. Jensen (1951 [1969]), Edward E. Evans-Pritchard (1954), Walter Burkert (1972 [1983] (*)), René Girard (1972 [1977]), Jan van Baal (1976), Victor W. Turner (1977), Luc de Heusch (1985), Valerio Valeri (1985), Jonathan Z. Smith (1987 (= 1987a (*)), Robert J. Daly (1990), Bruce Lincoln (1991), Nancy Jay (1992), William Beers (1992), Maurice Bloch (1992 (from 1992 (*)), John D. Levenson (1993). The editor has provided a short introduction to every excerpt where he outlines the theory and gives some general information on the respective scholar. [MS]

Grimes, Ronald L. (ed.), 1996, *Readings in Ritual Studies*; Upper Saddle River: Prentice Hall (ISBN 0–02–347253–7) (xvi + 577).

In his introduction (xiii–xvi), the editor sketches the dramatic change in ritual's reputation since the mid-1960s and the recent interdisciplinary discussion that this book "aims to illustrate and foster" (xv). "Its selections represent the most current scholarly thinking on the topic of ritual. Though it includes brief selections from those who fundamentally shaped the field in the first half of the twentieth century…it focuses

on more recent writers from a variety of disciplines, including religious studies, anthropology, theology, history, psychology, law, media studies, ethology, performance studies, literature, and the arts" (xv). Not all articles deal with theory. However, the editor states: "Generally, I have favored sections that combine theoretical breadth with the concrete particulars that can be provided by ethnographic, textual, or historical research" (xv). The articles are followed by an appendix, "Classification of the Selections" (567–577). This classification is divided into four groups: I. "Ritual Components" (11 sections); II. "Ritual Types" (16 sections); III: "Rites by Location" (4 sections with many sub-sections); and IV: "Disciplines Used to Study Ritual" (18 sections). The 43 articles contained in this reader are arranged in alphabetical order.
Contents: Barbara A. Babcock (1984): "Arrange me into Disorder: Fragments and Reflections on Ritual Clowning" (1–21); Catherine Bell (from 1992 (*)): "Constructing Ritual" (21–33); Diane Bell (1981): "Women's Business Is Hard Work: Central Australian Aboriginal Women's Love Rituals" (33–48); Albert Bergesen (1984): "Political Witch-Hunt Rituals" (48–61); Walter Burkert (from 1972 (*) / 1983): "The Function and Transformation of Ritual Killing" (62–71); Caroline Walker Bynum (1984): "Women's Stories, Women's Symbols: A Critique of Victor Turner's Theory of Liminality" (71–86) (*); Robert F. Campany (1992): "Xunzi and Durkheim as Theorists of Ritual Practice" (86–103) (*); M. Elaine Combs-Schilling (1991): "Etching Patriarchal Rule: Ritual Dye, Erotic Potency, and the Maroccan Monarchy" (104–118); Vincent Crapanzano (1980), "Rite of Return: Circumcision in Marocco" (118–131); Eugene d'Aquili, Charles D. Laughlin Jr. [& John McManus] (from 1979 (*)): "The Neurobiology of Myth and Ritual" (132–146); Robbie E. Davis-Floyd (1994): "Rituals in the Hospital: Giving Birth the American Way" (146–158); Mary Douglas (from 1966 (*)): "Dirt: Purity and Danger"; Tom F. Driver (from 1991 (*)): "Transformation: The Magic of Ritual" (170–187); Emile Durkheim (1915): "Ritual, Magic, and the Sacred" (188–193); Mircea Eliade (1959): "Ritual and Myth" (194–201); Erik H. Erikson (1968): "The Development of Ritualization" (201–211); Sigmund Freud (1959): "Obsessive Actions and Religious Practices" (212–217); Clifford Geertz (from 1973 (*)): "Deep Play: Notes on the Balinese Cockfight" (217–229); Sam D. Gill (1987): "Disenchantment: A Religious Abduction" (230–239); René Girard (1977): "Violence and the Sacred: Sacrifice" (239–256); Gregory T. Goethals (1981): "Ritual: Ceremony and Super-Sunday" (257–268); Erving Goffman (from 1967 (*)): "Interaction Ritual: Deference and

Demeanor" (268–279); Ronald L. Grimes (from 1990 (*)): "Ritual Criticism and Infelicitous Performances" (279–293); Don Handelman & Lea Shamgar-Handelman (1990): "Holiday Celebrations in Israeli Kindergartens" (293–307); Richard F. Hardin (1983): "'Ritual' in Recent Literary Criticism: The Elusive Sense of Community" (308–324); Theodore W. Jennings Jr. (1982): "On Ritual Knowledge" (324–334) (*); David I. Kertzer (from 1988 (*)): "Ritual, Politics, and Power" (335–352); John Laird (1988): "Women and Ritual in Family Therapy" (353–367); Claude Lévi-Strauss (1963 / 1967): "The Effectiveness of Symbols" (368–378); John J. McAloon (from 1984 (*)), "Olympic Games and the Theory of Spectacle in Modern Societies" (378–392); Barbara G. Myerhoff (1984): "Death in Due Time: Construction of Self and Culture in Ritual Drama" (393–412); Manuel H. Peña (1980): "Ritual Structure in a Chicano Dance" (412–427); Roy A. Rappaport (1974 (*) / from 1979 (*)): "The Obvious Aspects of Ritual" (427–440); Richard Schechner (1985): "Restoration of Behavior" (441–458); Bardwell Smith (1992): "Buddhism and Abortion in Contemporary Japan: Mizuko Kuyo and the Confrontation with Death" (458–473); Jonathan Z. Smith (1980 (*) / from 1982): "The Bare Facts of Ritual" (473–483); Frits Staal (1979): "The Meaninglessness of Ritual" (483–494) (*); Stanley J. Tambiah (1981/1979): "A Performative Approach to Ritual" (495–511) (*); Victor W. Turner (from 1969 (*)): "Liminality and Communitas" (511–519); Victor W. Turner (from 1967 (*)): "Symbols in Ndembu Ritual" (520–529); Arnold van Gennep (1960): "Territorial Passage and the Classification of Rites" (529–536); Melanie Wallendorf & Eric J. Arnould (1991): "Consumption Rituals of Thanksgiving Day" (536–551); Peter A. Winn (1991): "Legal Ritual" (552–565). [MS]

Harvey, Graham (ed.), 2005, *Ritual and Religious Belief. A Reader* (Critical Categories in the Study of Religion); London: Equinox (ISBN-10: 1–904768–16–4 / 1–904768–17–2 (p); ISBN-13: 978–1–904768–16–6 / 978–1–904768–17–3 (p)) (ix + 292).

Contents: Graham Harvey: "Introduction" (1–16); Part 1: Exemplifying the Problem: Martin Luther: "The Sacraments of Holy Baptism and of the Altar"; Reform Rabbis in the USA: "The Pittsburgh Conference 'Declaration of Principles'" (18–21/22–24); Part 2: Surveying the discussion: Jonathan Z. Smith: "To Take Place" (26–50) (from 1987a (*)); Part 3: Relating Ritual to Actions and Ideas: Maurice Bloch: "Myth" (52–60); Stanley J. Tambiah: "Malinowski's Demarcations and his Exposition of the Magical Art" (61–77); Kieran Flanagan: "Holy and Unholy Rites: Lies and Mistakes in Liturgy" (78–86); Ian Reader: "Cleaning Floors and Sweeping the Mind" (87–104); Margaret J. King: "Instruction and Delight: Theme Parks and Education" (105–123); Edward L. Schieffelin: "Problematizing Performance" (124–138) (1998 (*)); Peter Stallybrass and Allon White: "Introduction" [from Stallybrass & White (eds): *The Politics and Poetics of Trangression*, Cornell University Press 1986] (139–162); Gerrie ter Haar: "Ritual as Communication: A Study of African Christian Communities in the Bijlmer District of Amsterdam" (163–188); David I. Kertzer: "The Rites of Power" (189–201) (from 1988 (*)); Susan S. Sered: "Ritual Expertise in the Modern World" (202–217); Carlo Severi: "Memory, Reflexivity and Belief: Reflections on the Ritual Use of Language" (218–240) (2002 (*)); Part 4: Conclusion: Reflecting our Categories: Malcolm Ruel: "Christians as Believers" (242–264); Catherine Bell: "Ritual Reification" (265–285) (from 1992 (*)). [MS/Knut Melvær]

Schechner, Richard & Mady Schuman (eds), 1976, *Ritual, Play, and Performance. Readings in the Social Sciences/Theatre*; New York: Seabury Press (ISBN 0-8164-9285-9) (xviii + 230).

This book is an edition of formerly edited essays and articles: Richard Schechner: "Introduction: The Fan and the Web" (xv–xviii) (from 1977 (*) / 1988a (*)); I. Ethology: Alland Alexander Jr: "The Roots of Art" (5–17); Konrad Lorenz: "Habit, Ritual, and Magic" (18–34); George Schaller: "The Chest-Beating Sequence of the Mountain Gorilla" (35–39); Jane van Lawick-Goodall: "The Rain Dance" (40–45); II. Play: Johan Huizinga: "Nature and Significance of Play as a Cultural Phenomenon" (46–66); Gregory Bateson: "A Theory of Play and Fantasy" (67–73); Claude Lévi-Strauss: "The Science of the Concrete" (74–74); III. Ritual and Performance in Everyday Life: Ray L. Birdwhistell: "It Depends on the Point of View" (80–88); Erving Goffman: "Performances" (89–96); Victor W. Turner: "Social Dramas and Ritual Metaphors" (97–120); IV. Shamanism, Trance, Meditation: A.F. Anisimov: "The Shaman's Tent of the Evenks" (125–138); E.T. Kirby: "The Shamanistic Origins of Popular Entertainments" (139–149); Jane Belo: "Trance Experience in Bali" (150–161); V. Rites, Ceremonies, Performances: Richard A. Gould: "Desert Rituals and the Sacred Life" (166–185); Jerzy Grotowski: "The Theatre's New Testament"

(186–195); Richard Schechner: "From Ritual to Theatre and Back" (196–222) (1974 (*)). [JK]

Reviews: R. Wulbert *SSR* 63.1 (1978) 242–246; C. Turnbull & N. Garner *AQ* 52.4 (1979) 222.

Segal, Robert Alan (ed.), 1996, *Ritual and Myth. Robertson Smith, Frazer, Hooke, and Harrison* (Theories of Myth 5); New York, London: Garland (ISBN 0–8153–2259–3) (xi + 410).

The author writes in his introduction to this reprint edition of some major contributions to the myth and ritual theory: "Because the myth-ritualist theory maintains that myths and rituals operate in tandem, it has repeatedly been castigated by those who argue that the two phenomena operate independently of each other and come together only episodically. This volume therefore includes selections from not only the leading myth-ritualists but also critics and revisionists" (xiii). Selected Contents: William Bascom: "The Myth-Ritual Theory" (1–12); Samuel G.F. Brandon: "The Myth and Ritual Position Critically Considered" (12–43); James G. Frazer: "The Myth of Adonis" (97–106); James G. Frazer: "The Ritual of Adonis" (107–143); Richard F. Hardin: "'Ritual' in Recent Criticism: The Elusive Sense of Community" (170–186); Jane Harrison: "Introduction" [from: *Themis*] (187–201); S.H. Hooke: "The Myth and Ritual Pattern of the Ancient East" (203–217); Stanley Edgar Hyman: "The Ritual View of Myth and the Mythic" (218–228); Phyllis M. Kaberry: "Myth and Ritual: Some Recent Theories" (230–242); Clyde Kluckhohn: "Myths and Rituals. A General Theory" (243–277); Hans H. Penner: "Myth and Ritual. A Wasteland or a Forest of Symbols" (334–345) (*); Lord Raglan: "Myth and Ritual" (346–353); William Robertson Smith: "Introduction. The Subject and the Method of Inquiry" [from: *Lectures on the Religion of the Semites*] (355–382). [JK]

Review: H. Munson *MTSR* 11.2 (1999) 160–163.

Segal, Robert Alan (ed.), 1998, *The Myth and Ritual Theory. An Anthology*; Malden (Mass), Oxford: Blackwell Publishers (ISBN 0–631–20679–5 / 0–631–20680–9) (ix + 473) (with index and further reading).

In his introduction (1–13), the editor states: "The myth and ritual, or myth-ritualist, theory maintains that myths and rituals operate together.

The theory claims not that myths and ritual happen to go hand in hand but that they must. In its most uncompromising form, the theory contends that myths and rituals cannot exist without each other. In a milder form, the theory asserts that myths and rituals originally exist together but may subsequently go their separate ways. In its mildest form, the theory maintains that myths and rituals can arise separately but subsequently coalesce" (1). The introduction then sketches the development of the theory from its original formulation, through its different applications, to its revisions.

Selected Contents: I. Original Formulation of the Theory: William Robertson Smith (1889): "Lectures on the Religion of the Semites" (17–34); II. Development of the Theory: James Frazer (1922): "The Golden Bough" (35–57); Jane Harrisson (1912): "Themis" (58–82); S.H. Hooke (1933): "The Myth and Ritual Pattern of the Ancient East" (83–92); III. Application of the Theory to the Ancient World; IV. Application of the Theory World Wide; V. Application of the Theory to Literature; VI. Revisions of the Theory: Theodor H. Gaster (1961): "Thespis" (307–312); Clyde Kluckhohn (1942): "Myths and Rituals. A General Theory" (313–340); Walter Burkert (from 1972 (*) /1983): "Homo Necans" (341–346); Claude Lévi-Strauss (1963): "Structure and Dialectics" (347–355); VII. Evaluations of the Theory: William Ridgeway (1915): "The Dramas and Dramatic Dances of Non-European Races" (359–378); James Frazer (1921): "Introduction to Apollodorus, *The Library*" (379–380); H.J. Rose (1959): "The Evidence of Divine Kings in Greece" (381–387); S.G.F. Brandon (1958): "The Myth and Ritual Position Critically Examined" (388–411); William Bascom (1957): "The Myth-Ritual Theory" (412–427); Joseph Fontenrose (1966): "The Ritual Theory of Myth" (428–459); H.S. Versnel (1993): "Prospects" (460–467). The editor supplies brief introductions to each chapter and provides further bibliographical references. [MS]

Reviews: W.M. Calder *RSR* 24.4 (1998) 387; G. Aijmer *JAI* 5.2 (1999) 314; C.R. Phillips *Rel* 29 (1999) 299–301.

Wirth, Udo (ed.), 2002, *Performanz. Zwischen Sprachphilosophie und Kulturwissenschaften* (Suhrkamp Taschenbuch Wissenschaft 1575); Frankfurt a. M.: Suhrkamp (ISBN 3-518-29175-0) (436).

[Performance. Between Philosophy of Language and the Science of Culture]

Selected contents: Udo Wirth: "Der Performanzbegriff im Spannungsfeld von Illokution, Iteration und Indexikalität" (9–60); Erving Goffman: "Modulen und Modulation" (185–192); Victor W. Turner (1979): "Dramatisches Ritual, rituelles Theater. Performative und reflexive Ethnologie" (193–209) (*); Stanley J. Tambiah (1981): "Eine performative Theorie des Rituals" (210–242) (*); Wolfgang Iser: "Mimesis und Performanz" (243–261); Umberto Eco: "Semiotik der Theateraufführung" (262–276); Erika Fischer-Lichte: "Grenzgänge und Tauschhandel. Auf dem Wege zu einer performativen Kultur" (277–300); Judith Butler: "Performative Akte und Geschlechterkonstruktion. Phänomenologie und feministische Theorie" (301–320). [JK]

PART E

BIBLIOGRAPHIES
(5 items)

Arlen, Shelley, 1990, *The Cambridge Ritualists. An Annotated Bibliography of the Works by and about Jane Ellen Harrison, Gilbert Murray, Francis M. Cornford, and Arthur Bernard Cook*; Metuchen (NJ), London: Scarecrow Press (ISBN 0–8108–2373–x) (x + 414) (with indexes).

The first section of this bibliography provides a brief introduction to the Cambridge Ritualists [1–5], followed by sections listing general surveys and bibliographic works on myth and myth criticism (5–6 [= entries 1–14]) and general works about the Cambridge Ritualists (7–17 [= entries 15–86]). The next chapters deal with the main protagonists of the school (Jane Ellen Harrison, Gilbert Murray, Francis M. Cornford, Arthur Bernard Cook). Each section provides a portrait and a brief introduction to the respective scholar. This bibliography lists books and pamphlets, translations, articles, and reviews by the respective scholar as well as critical, biographical, and miscellaneous works about him/her, followed by obituaries and biographical entries in encyclopedias. In total, it numbers 2019 entries, most of them annotated with brief summaries. The work is provided with several indexes. [MS]

Grimes, Ronald L., 1984, 'Sources for the Study of Ritual', *Religious Studies Review* 10:134–145.

This article is a kind of pre-release of some material of the author's 1985 bibliography ("the full bibliography is forthcoming" (134)), discussing the ideas behind it. The author states that he "collected almost 1,600 English-language items dating from 1960 to the present" (134). He then presents the way in which he classified these items, viz. in 1. Ritual Components (with 10 sub-categories), 2. Ritual Types (with 16 sub-categories), 3. Ritual Descriptions ("rites interpreted with primary reference to specific traditions, systems, periods, or geographical areas", no sub-categories), and 4. General Works in Various Field-Clusters (with 10 sub-categories). "Both the classification and sheer number of items present problems. For the purpose of this essay I can deal only with the classification problems by identifying a few illustrative ones. As for the list, I have chosen to reduce it programmatically. I do not try so much to reflect as to shape the field by singling out some works and skipping over others. My aim is to indicate topics and directions for fruitful research rather than identify representative examples of scholarship" (134). Then follow sections on the four main classes presented before (134–141) and a list of "References" (141–145) with 199 selected items in plain alphabetical order. [JS]

Grimes, Ronald L., 1985, *Research in Ritual Studies. A Programmatic Essay and Bibliography* (ATLA Bibliographic Series 14); Metuchen (NJ), London: The American Theological Library Association & The Scarecrow Press (ISBN 0-8108-1762-4) (ix + 165) (with an "author index").

All in all, this bibliography lists 1633 items. These are arranged in four sections: 1. "Ritual Components" (37–67) with 10 sub-sections (action; space; time; objects; symbol, metaphor; group; self; divine beings; language; quality, quantity, theme); 2. "Ritual Types" (68–116) with 16 sub-sections (rites of passage; marriage rites; funerary rites; festivals; pilgrimage; purification; civil ceremony; rituals of exchange; sacrifice; worship; magic; healing rites; interaction rites; meditation rites; rites of inversion; ritual drama); 3. "Ritual Descriptions (rites interpreted with primary reference to specific traditions, systems, periods, or geographical areas)" (117–125); 4. "General Works in Various Field Clusters" (126–150) with 10 sub-sections (religious studies, theology, ethics, history of religions, liturgics; anthropology, ethnography, ethology, folklore; sociology, social psychology, political science; literature, literary criticism; philosophy; history, classics; communications, kinesics, linguistics; psychology, medicine, biology, physics, genetics; education; theatre, arts, music). The "Programmatic Essay" (1–18; with extensive references: 18–33) tries "to shape the field by singling out some works and skipping over others. My aim is to indicate topics and directions for fruitful research rather than identify representative examples of scholarship" (3). [MS]

Review: P. Bernabeo *JRS* 1.1 (1987) 150–152.

Grimes, Ronald L., 1987, 'Key Words in Searching for Data on Ritual', *Journal of Ritual Studies* 1.2:139–145.

"Using computerized data bases to locate materials on rituals is not as easy as one might think" (139). Therefore, the essay presents a list of 187 keywords that "may help both solve and illustrate the problem of doing elementary bibliographical searches" (139). This list consists of keywords from the following domains: the most obvious general terms ('rites'; 'rituals'; 'ceremonies'; etc.), "ritual types" (e.g. 'funerals'; 'weddings'); "ritual actions" ('blessing'; 'gift-giving'; etc.), some 'specific rites' (but only those are listed that "have become more generalized, less tradition-specific in their usage" [139], e.g. 'baptism'; 'Sabbath'; 'puja', while 'Akitu' and 'Hajj' are not given), and a number of "ritual objects". The author further reminds us that "many rites are catalogued under the name of deities to which they pertain" (139), such as 'Dionysus, rites of'. "Further, religious and political personages should not be overlooked: priests, healers, rabbis, queens, chiefs, etc., for they are sometimes treated in terms of their ritual functions" (139–140). The list widely neglects terms from the realm of theory. Thus, while the author regards words such as 'blood', 'bones', and 'hair' as "key words in searching for data on ritual", terms such as 'communication', 'flow', 'liminality', 'performance', 'performativity', 'transformation' are not listed. [MS]

McVann, Mark, 1995, 'General Introductory Bibliography for Ritual Studies', in: Mark McVann & Bruce J. Malina (eds), *Transformations, Passages, and Processes. Ritual Approaches to Biblical Texts*, (Semeia 67), Atlanta (GA): Scholars Press (No ISBN) 227–232.

The author provided this "briefly annotated bibliography" for "biblical scholars interested in further reading in the area of ritual studies" (227). That means that it does not aim to restrict itself to literature in the domain of ritual theory. However, of the 18 monographs by 14 authors then presented, 13 are also included in our current bibliography. The five other ones are: (1) Robert L. Cohn: *The Shape of Sacred Space. Four Biblical Studies* (AAR Studies in Religion 23), Chico (CA): Scholars Press 1981; (2) Howard Eilberg-Schwartz: *The Savage in Judaism. An Anthropology of Israelite Religion and Ancient Judaism*, Bloomington: Indiana University Press 1990; (3) René Girard: *La violence et le sacré* 1972 = *Violence and the Sacred*, trans. Patrick Gregory, John Hopkins University Press, Baltimore

1977; (4) Bruce Lincoln: *Discourse and the Construction of Society. Comparative Studies of Myth, Ritual, and Classification*, New York, Oxford: Oxford University Press 1989; and (5) Arnold van Gennep: *Les rites de passage. Étude systématique des rites*, Paris: Librairie Critique Emile Nourry 1909 = *The Rites of Passage*, London 1960. [JS/MS]

APPENDICES

APPENDIX A

CHRONOLOGICAL LISTING OF ITEMS IN THE BIBLIOGRAPHY (all 620 items)

In this list, the indication between brackets after each item refers to the part of the bibliography in which the item can be found:

Part A: Primary Literature
Part B: Secondary Literature
Pert C: Lexicon Articles
Part D: Readers, or
Part E: Bibliographies

In the case of the items included in Part A, it is also indicated if it concerns a monograph (**A**), an edited volume (*A*), or an article (A).

Some articles from Part A have also been copied (though without the abstract) in Part B or C: 11 are included in both Part A and Part B (R.L. Grimes 1985, S.M. Price 1988, R. Schechner 1988(c), D. Handelman 1993, H.J. Verkuyl 1997, M.P. Levine 1998, R.L. Grimes 1999, R.A. Segal 2000, T. Frankiel 2001, T. Tybjerg 2001, I. Strenski 2003), while 2 are included in both Part A and Part C (E.R. Leach 1968 and C.M. Bell 2005). These are listed here as (A & B) or (A & C) respectively.

1966
J.H.M. Beattie 1966 (A)
M. Douglas 1966 (**A**)
C. Geertz 1966 (A)
J.S. Huxley (ed.) 1966 (*A*)
E.R. Leach 1966 (A)
K.Z. Lorenz 1966 (A)
R. Schechner 1966 (A)
A.F.C. Wallace 1966 (**A**)

1967
E. Goffman 1967 (**A**)
R. Needham 1967 (A)
V.W. Turner 1967 (**A**)

1968
K. Burke 1968 (C)
P. Hockings 1968 (A)
A. Jackson 1968 (A)

E.R. Leach 1968 (A & C)
R.A. Rappaport 1968 (**A**)
S.J. Tambiah 1968 (A)

1969
R.H. Finnegan 1969 (A)
H.H. Penner 1969 (A)
V.W. Turner 1969 (**A**)

1970
J.H.M. Beattie 1970 (A)
R. Bocock 1970 (A)
N.R. Crumrine 1970 (A)
M. Douglas 1970 (**A**)
S.P. Nagendra 1970 (B)
R. Schechner 1970 (A)

1971
J. Cazeneuve 1971 (**A**)
M. Csikszentmihalyi & S. Bennett 1971 (A)
S.P. Nagendra 1971 (**A**)
R.A. Rappaport 1971 (A)

1972
W. Burkert 1972 (**A**)
J.W. Fernandez 1972 (A)
J.S. la Fontaine (ed.) 1972 (*A*)
N. Smart 1972 (**A**)

1973
S.G.F. Brandon 1973 (C)
J.C. Crocker 1973 (A)
A. Dawe 1973 (B)
A.M. di Nola 1973a (C)
A.M. di Nola 1973b (C)
A.M. di Nola 1973c (C)
A.M. di Nola 1973d (C)
C. Geertz 1973 (**A**)
L. Leertouwer 1973 (A)
N.D. Munn 1973 (A)
B.C. Ray 1973 (A)
R. Schechner 1973 (A)
J.D. Shaughnessy (ed.) 1973 (A)
S.J. Tambiah 1973 (A)

1974
M.C. Bateson 1974 (A)
N. Belmont 1974 (B)
M.E.F. Bloch 1974 (A)
R. Bocock 1974 (**A**)
J.W. Fernandez 1974 (A)
E. Goffman 1974 (**A**)
R. Grainger 1974 (**A**)
R.A. Rappaport 1974 (A)
V.W. Turner 1974a (**A**)
V.W. Turner 1974b (A)
V.W. Turner 1974c (A)
R. Schechner 1974 (A)

1975
R. Ackerman 1975 (B)
R. Bauman 1975 (A)
P. Bourdieu 1975 (A)
S.G.F. Brandon 1975 (**A**)
J.W. Carey 1975 (B)
E.G. d'Aquili & C.D. Laughlin 1975 (A)
L. Honko 1975 (A)
D. Hymes 1975 (A)
S. Lukes 1975 (A)
S.B. Ortner 1975 (A)
D. Sperber 1975 (**A**)
V.W. Turner 1975 (A)
E.M. Zuesse 1975 (A)

1976
M. Collins 1976 (B)
R.L. Grimes 1976 (B)

D. Handelman 1976 (B)
E.T. Lawson 1976 (A)
E.R. Leach 1976 (**A**)
R. Schechner & M. Schuman 1976 (D)
W. Schmidt-Biggemann 1976 (C)

1977
E.H. Erikson 1977 (**A**)
J.W. Fernandez 1977 (A)
J. Goody 1977 (A)
A. Hahn 1977 (A)
D. Handelman 1977 (A)
S. Isenberg & D.E. Owen 1977 (B)
S.F. Moore & B.G. Myerhoff 1977 (A)
S.F. Moore & B.G. Myerhoff (eds) 1977 (*A*)
R. Schechner 1977 (**A**)
T.J. Scheff 1977 (A)
T.S. Turner 1977 (A)
V.W. Turner 1977 (A)

1978
B.A. Babcock 1978 (A)
R.A. Delattre 1978 (A)
G.H. Gossen 1978 (A)
S.B. Ortner 1978 (**A**)
R.A. Rappaport 1978 (A)
R.D. Riner 1978 (A)
E.O. Wilson 1978 (**A**)

1979
E.M. Ahern 1979 (A)
J.O. Buswell III 1979 (B)
D. Capps 1979 (B)
A. Cohen 1979 (A)
E.G. d'Aquili, C.D. Laughlin Jr. & J. McManus (eds) 1979 (A)
E. Dissanayake 1979 (A)
I. Eibl-Eibesfeldt 1979 (A)
V.P. Gay 1979 (B)
D. Handelman 1979 (A)
L. Honko 1979 (A)
B. Kapferer 1979 (A)
B. Kapferer (ed.) 1979 (*A*)
J. Pentikäinen 1979 (A)
R.A. Rappaport 1979 (**A**)
F. Staal 1979 (A)
K.V. Staiano 1979 (A)
V.W. Turner 1979 (A)

1980
F.B. Bird 1980 (A)
K. Blanchard 1980 (A)
S.J. Fox 1980 (A)
C. Geertz 1980 (**A**)
D. Handelman 1980 (A)
D. Handelman & B. Kapferer 1980 (A)
G.A. Lewis 1980 (**A**)
G. Matthews 1980 (A)
R.A. Rappaport 1980 (A)
J.Z. Smith 1980 (A)

1981
F. Giobellina-Brumana & E.-E. Gonzalez 1981 (B)
D. Handelman 1981 (A)
G. Matthews 1981 (B)
K.E. Paige & J.M. Paige 1981 (**A**)
R. Schechner 1981 (A)
I. Scheffler 1981 (A)
S.J. Tambiah 1981 (A)

1982
P. Bourdieu 1982 (A)
A. Colombo & S. Offelli 1982 (C)
L. Elsbree 1982 (**A**)
R.L. Grimes 1982 (**A**)
G.H. Herdt (ed.) 1982 (*A*)
T.W. Jennings 1982 (A)
D.L. Miller 1982 (B)
R. Schechner 1982 (A)
P. Smith 1982 (A)
A. Travers 1982 (A)
V.W. Turner 1982 (**A**)
V.W. Turner (ed.) 1982 (A)
V.W. Turner & E. Turner 1982 (A)
W.T. Wheelock 1982 (A)
R. Zumwalt 1982 (B)

1983
N.R. Crumrine 1983 (A)
T.J. Csordas 1983 (A)
E.G. d'Aquili 1983 (A)
J.G. Galaty 1983 (A)
D.S. Gardner 1983 (A)
V.P. Gay 1983 (B)
M. James 1983 (A)
B. Kapferer 1983 (**A**)
H.-H. Lüger 1983 (A)
J.G. Platvoet 1983 (B)
R.A. Segal 1983 (B)
J. Stagl 1983 (B)
T.P. van Baaren 1983 (A)

1984
E.M. Bruner (ed.) 1984 (*A*)
C.W. Bynum 1984 (B)
R.L. Grimes 1984 (E)
J.R. Gusfield & J. Michalowicz 1984 (A)
J.J. MacAloon 1984 (A)
J.J. MacAloon (ed.) 1984 (*A*)
S. Sinding-Larsen 1984 (**A**)
V.W. Turner 1984 (A)
I. Werlen 1984 (**A**)

1985
A.J. Blasi 1985 (A)
E.G. d'Aquili 1985 (A)
R.L. Grimes 1985 (E)
R.L. Grimes 1985 (A & B)
T. Luckmann 1985 (A)
R. Needham 1985 (A)
H.H. Penner 1985 (A)
E. Schieffelin 1985 (A)
S.J. Tambiah 1985 (**A**)
V.W. Turner 1985a (A)
V.W. Turner 1985b (A)

1986
P. Bayes 1986 (C)
M.E.F. Bloch 1986 (**A**)
J.G. Davies 1986 (C)
J.W. Dow 1986 (A)
J.W. Fernandez 1986 (**A**)
P. Fisher 1986 (C)
J.S. Jensen 1986 (A)
B. Kapferer 1986 (A)
C.D. Laughlin, *et al.* 1986 (A)
D. Newton 1986 (C)
J.B. Renard 1986 (B)
J.P. Schjødt 1986 (A)
L.E. Sullivan 1986 (A)
V.W. Turner & E.M. Bruner (eds) 1986 (*A*)
M. Winkelman 1986 (A)

1987
R. Ackerman 1987 (B)
B.C. Alexander 1987 (C)

M.E.F. Bloch 1987 (A)
W. Burkert 1987 (A)
D. Cannadine & S. Price (eds) 1987 (*A*)
P. Gerlitz 1987 (C)
A. Ghosh 1987 (B)
R. Girard 1987 (A)
R.L. Grimes 1987 (C)
R.L. Grimes 1987 (E)
A. Grünschloß 1987 (C)
R.G. Hamerton-Kelly (ed.) 1987 (*A*)
V. Heeschen 1987 (A)
T.W. Jennings Jr. 1987 (C)
B. Kapferer 1987 (B)
M.M. Kelleher 1987a (C)
M.M. Kelleher 1987b (C)
W. Klein (ed.) 1987 (*A*)
B.L. Mack 1987 (B)
B.G. Myerhoff, L.A. Camino & E. Turner 1987 (C)
E. Ohnuki-Tierney 1987 (**A**)
R. Pertierra 1987 (A)
R. Schechner 1987 (A)
R. Schechner 1987 (C)
J.Z. Smith 1987a (**A**)
J.Z. Smith 1987b (A)
J.A.M. Snoek 1987 (**A**)
V.W. Turner 1987 (C)
I. Werlen 1987 (A)
R. Wuthnow 1987 (**A**)
E.M. Zuesse 1987 (C)

1988

T. Asad 1988 (A)
S.H. Blackburn 1988 (**A**)
D. Cheal 1988 (A)
T. Gerholm 1988 (A)
R.L. Grimes 1988a (A)
R.L. Grimes 1988b (A)
D.I. Kertzer 1988 (**A**)
B. Lang 1988 (A)
S.M. Price 1988 (A & B)
J. Roberts 1988 (A)
R. Saint-Jean 1988 (C)
J.J. Schaller 1988 (A)
R. Schechner 1988a (**A**)
R. Schechner 1988b (A)
R. Schechner 1988c (A & B)
H.-G. Soeffner 1988 (A)
I. Strecker 1988 (**A**)
V.W. Turner 1988 (**A**)
J. Young-Laughlin & C.D. Laughlin 1988 (A)

1989

R. Baumann 1989 (C)
M.E.F. Bloch 1989 (**A**)
C. Elsas 1989 (C)
P. Manning 1989 (B)
H.H. Penner 1989 (A)
R.A. Rappaport 1989 (C)
E.B. Reeves & R.A. Bylund 1989 (A)
F. Staal 1989 (**A**)
R.E. Wiedenmann 1989 (A)

1990

S. Arlen 1990 (E)
K.M. Ashley 1990 (B)
R. Bauman & C.L. Briggs 1990 (A)
C.M. Bell 1990 (A)
A.-M. Blondeau & K. Schipper (eds) 1990 / [1990] / 1995 (*A*)
H.B. Boudewijnse 1990 (B)
H. Geerts 1990 (B)
R.L. Grimes 1990 (**A**)
R.L. Grimes 1990 (B)

D. Handelman 1990 (**A**)
H.-G. Heimbrock & H.B. Boudewijnse (eds) 1990 (*A*)
B.A. Holdrege (ed.) 1990 (*A*)
J.D. Kelly & M. Kaplan 1990 (A)
C.D. Laughlin 1990 (A)
E.T. Lawson & R.N. McCauley 1990 (**A**)
C. Lévi-Strauss 1990 (**A**)
L.J. Madden 1990 (C)
F.A. Marglin 1990 (A)
J.R. McLeod 1990 (A)
B.G. Myerhoff 1990 (A)
I. Paul 1990 (**A**)
J.L. Peacock 1990 (A)
R. Schechner & W. Appel (eds) 1990 (*A*)
R. Schechner & W. Appel 1990 (A)
G.S. Worgul 1990 (C)

1991
R. Ackerman 1991 (B)
B.C. Alexander 1991 (B)
W.M. Calder III 1991 (B)
A. Cunningham & I. Strenski 1991 (B)
M. Deflem 1991 (B)
T.F. Driver 1991 (**A**)
J.E. Gibson 1991 (B)
R.M. Keesing 1991 (A)
D. Merkur 1991 (A)
J.-C. Muller 1991 (C)
R. Schechner 1991 (A)
P. Smith 1991 (C)
R.E. Wiedenmann 1991 (**A**)
R.H. Winthrop 1991a (C)
R.H. Winthrop 1991b (C)

1992
Anon. 1992a (C)
Anon. 1992b (C)
Anon. 1992c (C)
P.J. Anttonen 1992 (A)
G. Baumann 1992 (A)
C.M. Bell 1992 (**A**)
M.E.F. Bloch 1992 (**A**)
R.F. Campany 1992 (B)
M. Cartry 1992 (A)
C. Colpe 1992 (C)
M.W.B. de Almeida 1992 (B)
D. de Coppet (ed.) 1992 (*A*)
M.T. Drewal 1992 (**A**)
L. Dupré 1992 (A)
S. Harrison 1992 (A)
M. Houseman 1992 (A)
B. Krondorfer 1992 (A)
R.A. Rappaport 1992 (A)
E.B. Reeves & R.A. Bylund 1992 (A)
H. Rzepkowski 1992a (C)
H. Rzepkowski 1992b (C)
F. Schuh 1992 (C)
M. Searle 1992 (C)
C. Sigrist 1992 (C)
H.-G. Soeffner 1992 (**A**)
W. Wickler 1992 (C)
H. Wybrew 1992 (C)

1993
T. Ahlbäck (ed.) 1993 (*A*)
D.A. Allen, E.M. Jackson & C. Lorius 1993 (C)
W.O. Beeman 1993 (A)
C.M. Bell 1993 (A)
J. Comaroff & J. Comaroff 1993 (A)
J. Drexler 1993 (**A**)
D. Handelman 1993 (A & B)
E. Hauschildt 1993 (A)

M. Houseman 1993 (A)
E.M. Jackson 1993 (C)
B. Lang 1993 (C)
E.T. Lawson 1993 (A)
R. Schechner 1993 (**A**)
I. Scheffler 1993 (A)
C. Severi 1993a (**A**)
C. Severi 1993b (A)
J.P. Sørensen 1993 (A)
C. Toren 1993 (A)
T. Tybjerg 1993 (B)
R.G. Williams & J.W. Boyd 1993 (**A**)

1994

W.W. Belier 1994 (B)
H.B. Boudewijnse 1994 (B)
P. Boyer 1994 (**A**)
M.C. Carpentier 1994 (B)
T.F. Driver 1994 (A)
S. Dulaney & A.P. Fiske 1994 (A)
F. Héran 1994 (B)
M. Houseman & C. Severi 1994 (**A**)
C. Humphrey & J. Laidlaw 1994 (**A**)
C. Olson 1994 (B)
R. Schechner 1994 (A)
F. Schmidt 1994 (A)

1995

Anon. 1995 (C)
F.B. Bird 1995 (A)
H.B. Boudewijnse 1995 (A)
J. Calmard 1995 (C)
R. Devisch, *et al.* (eds) 1995 (*A*)
S.D. Glazier 1995 (C)
A.E. Green 1995a (C)
A.E. Green 1995b (C)
N.C. Lutkehaus & P.B. Roscoe (eds) 1995 (*A*)
M. McVann 1995 (E)
J.G. Platvoet 1995 (A)
J.G. Platvoet & K.v.d. Toorn (eds) 1995 (*A*)
A.L. Roth 1995 (A)
J.A.M. Snoek 1995 (A)
T. Thomas 1995a (C)
T. Thomas 1995b (C)
P. Ukpokodu 1995 (C)
R.K. White 1995 (C)

1996

A. Barnard & J. Spencer 1996 (C)
W. Braungart 1996 (**A**)
W. Burkert 1996 (**A**)
J. Emigh 1996 (**A**)
E.S. Evans 1996 (C)
R.L. Grimes 1996 (D)
D. Handelman 1996 (A)
J.P. Mitchell 1996 (C)
E. Schieffelin 1996 (A)
R.A. Segal 1996 (D)
I. Strenski 1996 (B)

1997

B.C. Alexander 1997 (A)
C.M. Bell 1997 (**A**)
D.J. Davies 1997 (**A**)
A.M. Fiske & N. Haslam 1997 (A)
G.T. Goethals 1997 (A)
D. Handelman 1997 (A)
S.N. Harris 1997 (A)
B. Kapferer 1997 (**A**)
K.-P. Köpping (ed.) 1997 (*A*)
J.R. Lindgren 1997 (A)
M. Meslin 1997 (C)

A. Michaels 1997 (B)
A. Piette 1997 (B)
I. Scheffler 1997 (**A**)
F. Stolz 1997 (A)
I. Strenski 1997 (B)
H.J. Verkuyl 1997 (A & B)
C. Wulf 1997 (C)

1998
Anon. 1998 (C)
A. Baranowski 1998 (A)
D. Baudy 1998 (**A**)
C.M. Bell 1998 (A)
A. Belliger & D.J. Krieger 1998 (D)
H.B. Boudewijnse 1998 (A)
J.N. Bremmer 1998 (A)
F.W. Clothey 1998 (A)
E. Collins 1998 (A)
G. Gebauer & C. Wulf 1998 (**A**)
B. Gladigow 1998 (C)
I. Hoëm 1998 (A)
M. Houseman 1998 (A)
F. Hughes-Freeland 1998 (A)
F. Hughes-Freeland (ed.) 1998 (*A*)
F. Hughes-Freeland & M.M. Crain 1998 (A)
F. Hughes-Freeland & M.M. Crain (eds) 1998 (*A*)
K.-P. Köpping 1998 (A)
D.J. Krieger & A. Belliger 1998 (A)
B. Lang 1998 (C)
M.P. Levine 1998 (A & B)
D.E. Owen 1998 (B)
E.W. Rothenbuhler 1998 (**A**)
A. Schäfer & M. Wimmer (eds) 1998 (*A*)
E. Schieffelin 1998 (A)
R.A. Segal 1998 (D)
J.Z. Smith 1998 (A)
A. Strathern & P.J. Stewart 1998 (A)
I. Strecker 1998 (A)
T. Sundermaier 1998 (C)
G. Thomas 1998 (**A**)
K. Thomas 1998 (B)
H. Wettstein 1998 (C)
M. Wimmer & A. Schäfer 1998 (A)

1999
Anon. 1999a (C)
Anon. 1999b (C)
Anon. 1999c (C)
Anon. 1999d (C)
G. Anwar 1999 (C)
C. Auffarth 1999 (A)
B. Barthelmes & H. de la Motte-Haber (eds) 1999 (*A*)
C. Caduff & J. Pfaff-Czarnecka (eds) 1999 (*A*)
E.G. d'Aquili & A.B. Newberg 1999 (**A**)
R. Fardon 1999 (B)
D.N. Gellner 1999 (B)
R.L. Grimes 1999 (A & B)
M.E. Hegland 1999 (C)
A. Michaels 1999 (A)
R. Mischung & K.-P. Köpping 1999 (C)
K. O'Grady 1999 (C)
R.A. Rappaport 1999 (**A**)
J. Renger 1999 (C)
W. Schievenhövel 1999 (C)
B. Schmidt 1999 (C)
Z. Snjezana 1999 (C)
A.N. Terrin 1999 (**A**)

F. Uhl & A.R. Boelderl (eds) 1999 (*A*)

2000

C. Auffarth 2000 (C)
V. Crapanzano 2000 (A)
W.G. Doty 2000 (**A**)
A. Etzioni 2000 (A)
R.L. Grimes 2000 (A)
M. Houseman 2000 (A)
L. Howe 2000 (A)
L. Jones 2000 (**A**)
C. Kalocsai 2000 (B)
B. Kapferer 2000 (A)
K.-P. Köpping & U. Rao (eds) 2000 (*A*)
F.W. Kramer 2000 (C)
A. Michaels 2000 (A)
M. Münzel 2000 (C)
U. Rao & K.-P. Köpping 2000 (A)
P. Scarduelli 2000 (A)
R.A. Segal 2000 (A & B)
G. Thomas 2000 (A)

2001

L.M. Ahearn 2001 (A)
J. Andresen (ed.) 2001 (*A*)
J.L. Barrett & E.T. Lawson 2001 (A)
D. Baudy 2001a (C)
D. Baudy 2001b (C)
A. Bendlin 2001 (C)
U. Brunotte 2001 (B)
P. Buc 2001 (**A**)
M.S.-Y. Chwe 2001 (**A**)
L. Csaszi 2001 (A)
J.-Y. Dartiguenave 2001 (**A**)
E. Fischer-Lichte & C. Wulf (eds) 2001 (*A*)
T. Frankiel 2001 (A & B)
H.-M. Gutmann 2001 (C)
R.A. Joyce 2001 (C)
R.N. McCauley 2001 (A)
E. Messer & M. Lambek 2001 (B)
D. Parkin 2001 (C)
I. Prattis 2001 (A)
J. Robbins 2001 (B)
J. Sørensen 2001 (A)
F. Staal 2001 (C)
R. Stark 2001 (A)
P. Tufis 2001 (B)
T. Tybjerg 2001 (A & B)
J. von Ins 2001 (**A**)
R.A. Warfield 2001 (B)
C. Wulf, *et al.* (eds) 2001 (*A*)
C. Wulf, M. Göhlich & J. Zirfas 2001 (B)

2002

M. Argyle 2002 (A)
J.L. Barrett 2002 (A)
W. Burkert 2002 (A)
R.L. Grimes 2002 (A)
R.L. Grimes 2002 (C)
J. Hockey 2002 (B)
A. Hollywood 2002 (A)
M. Houseman 2002 (A)
A. Hozier 2002 (C)
D.A. Marshall 2002 (A)
R.N. McCauley & E.T. Lawson 2002 (**A**)
M. Meyer-Blanck 2002 (C)
R. Schechner 2002 (**A**)
C. Severi 2002 (A)
M. Stausberg 2002 (A)
I. Strenski 2002 (B)
S.J. Tambiah 2002 (B)
H. Whitehouse 2002 (A)

U. Wirth 2002 (D)
J.A. Zimmerman 2002 (C)

2003
R.N. Bellah 2003 (A)
G. Brown 2003 (A)
U. Brunotte 2003 (B)
C. Calame 2003 (B)
J. Carter 2003 (D)
U. Dahm 2003 (**A**)
M. Douglas 2003 (B)
J.E. Finol 2003 (A)
T. Förster 2003 (B)
R.L. Grimes 2003 (A)
A. Henn 2003 (A)
N.G. Holm 2003 (A)
K.-P. Köpping 2003 (A)
K.-P. Köpping 2003 (C)
K.-P. Köpping & U. Rao 2003a (A)
K.-P. Köpping & U. Rao 2003b (A)
B. Malley & J.L. Barrett 2003 (B)
J.A.M. Snoek 2003 (A)
J. Sørensen 2003 (A)
J.P. Sørensen 2003 (A)
M. Stausberg 2003 (A)
I. Strenski 2003 (A & B)
C. Wulf & J. Zirfas (eds) 2003 (*A*)

2004
J.C. Alexander 2004 (A)
T.S. Chambers 2004 (A)
J. Cole 2004 (A)
A. Droogers 2004 (A)
E. Fischer-Lichte & C. Wulf (eds) 2004 (*A*)
T. Förster 2004 (B)
U. Gerhardt 2004 (A)
B. Gladigow 2004 (A)
R.L. Grimes 2004 (A)
D. Handelman 2004 (A)
D. Harth & G.J. Schenk (eds) 2004 (*A*)
M. Houseman 2004 (A)
R.E. Innis 2004 (A)
N. Janowitz 2004 (A)
B. Kapferer 2004 (A)
J. Kreinath 2004a (A)
J. Kreinath 2004b (A)
J. Kreinath, C. Hartung & A. Deschner (eds) 2004 (*A*)
F. Neubert 2004 (B)
J.G. Platvoet 2004 (A)
K. Schilbrack (ed.) 2004 (*A*)
D. Seeman 2004 (A)
D. Wiebe 2004 (B)
C. Wulf & J. Zirfas 2004 (A)

2005
C. Alcorta & R. Sosis 2005 (A)
C.M. Bell 2005 (A & C)
S.M. Greenfield 2005 (A)
D. Harth 2005 (A)
G. Harvey 2005 (D)
J. Kreinath 2005 (A)
D.B. Lee 2005 (A)
R.A. Segal 2005 (A)
R.H. Sharf 2005 (A)
J. Sørensen 2005 (A)
B. Stephenson 2005 (C)

Chapters from *Theorizing Rituals* Vol. I (2006)
D. Baudy 2006 (A)
C.M. Bell 2006 (A)
M.E.F. Bloch 2006 (A)
H.B. Boudewijnse 2006 (A)

J.W. Fernandez 2006 (A)
B. Gladigow 2006 (A)
R.L. Grimes 2006 (A)
D. Handelman 2006a (A)
D. Handelman 2006b (A)
D. Harth 2006 (A)
M. Houseman 2006 (A)
F. Hughes-Freeland 2006 (A)
F. Jeserich 2006 (A)
B. Kapferer 2006a (A)
B. Kapferer 2006b (A)
J. Kreinath 2006 (A)
J. Kreinath, J. Snoek & M. Stausberg 2006 (A)
J. Laidlaw & C. Humphrey 2006 (A)
E.T. Lawson 2006 (A)
D. Lüddeckens 2006 (A)
A. Michaels 2006 (A)
R.C. Morris 2006 (A)
J.G. Platvoet 2006 (A)
U. Rao 2006 (A)
W. Sax 2006 (A)
E. Schieffelin 2006 (A)
R.A. Segal 2006 (A)
C. Severi 2006 (A)
J.A.M. Snoek 2006 (A)
J.P. Sørensen 2006 (A)
M. Stausberg 2006 (A)
M. Stausberg 2006 (ed.) (A)
G. Thomas 2006 (A)
T.S. Turner 2006 (A)
H. Whitehouse 2006 (A)
R.G. Williams & J.W. Boyd 2006 (A)
C. Wulf 2006 (A)

APPENDIX B

ITEMS IN THE BIBLIOGRAPHY OF PRIMARY LITERATURE (= PART A) RELATED TO KEY-WORDS

Subjects indicated by key-words are listed here in the following order:

A. General Subjects;
B. Subjects Discussed in Volume I, in the order of the chapters in that volume;
C. Relevant Subjects, Not Directly Covered in Volume I, in alphabetical order.

For an alphabetically ordered list of the key-words see the Introduction (xv–xvii).

A. General Subjects

General and Introductory (gen)

B.C. Alexander 1997; Barthelmes & De la Motte-Haber (eds) 1999; Bell 1997; 2005; Bellah 2003; Buc 2001; Collins 1998; Doty 2000; Drexler 1993; Frankiel 2001; Goody 1977; Grimes 2000; Harth & Schenk (eds) 2004; Holm 2003; Jensen 1986; Kreinath *et al.* 2006; Krieger & Belliger 1998; Lang 1988; Leertouwer 1973; McLeod 1990; Michaels 1999; Rothenbuhler 1998; Scarduelli 2000; Schechner 2002; Segal 2005; 2006; Stausberg 2002; 2003; Terrin 1999; Wulf *et al.* (eds) 2001; Wulf & Zirfas 2004; Zuesse 1975.

History of Scholarship (hsc)

Bell 1992; 1997; Drexler 1993; Holm 2003; Platvoet 1995; 2004; 2006; Scarduelli 2000; Schmidt 1994; Segal 2005; 2006; Snoek 1987; Stausberg 2002; Strenski 2003; Terrin 1999; Tybjerg 2001.

History of the Term 'Ritual' (ter)
Asad 1988; Boudewijnse 1995; 1998; Bremmer 1998; Collins 1998; Handelman 2006a; Kreinath *et al.* 2006; Laidlaw & Humphrey 2006; Leach 1968; Lorenz 1966; Platvoet 2004; 2006; Segal 2005; 2006; Snoek 1987; Stausberg 2002; 2006b; Tambiah 1968.

B. Subjects Discussed in Volume I

In the order of the chapters in that volume.

1.1 Definition and Classification (def)

Ahearn 2001; Anttonen 1992; Asad 1988; Beattie 1966; Bell 1992; 1993; Bird 1980; 1995; Blasi 1985; Boudewijnse 1998; Boyer 1994; Brown 2003; Buc 2001; Burkert 1987; Cheal 1988; Collins 1998; Crocker 1973; D'Aquili 1985; D'Aquili & Newberg 1999; Dartiguenave 2001; Delattre 1978; Doty 2000; Drexler 1993; Driver 1991; 1994; Eibl-Eibesfeldt 1979; Gerholm 1988; Grimes 1982; 1990; 2002; 2003; Hahn 1977; Handelman 1990; 1997; 2004; 2006a; Harth 2006; Hauschildt 1993; Honko 1975; 1979; Jensen 1986; Kapferer 2004; Keesing 1991; Kertzer 1988; Köpping & Rao 2003a; Kreinath *et al.* 2006; Laidlaw & Humphrey 2006; Lawson & McCauley 1990; Leach 1966; Lévi-Strauss 1990; Lewis 1980; Lorenz 1966; Luckmann 1985; Lüger 1983; Lukes 1975; McCauley & Lawson 2002; McLeod 1990; Merkur 1991; Moore & Myerhoff 1977; Moore & Myerhoff (eds) 1977; Munn 1973; Nagendra 1971; Needham 1985; Platvoet 1995; 2004; 2006; Platvoet & Van der Toorn (eds) 1995; Rappaport 1971; 1974; 1979; 1999; Reeves & Bylund 1992; Roberts 1988; Roth 1995; Rothenbuhler 1998; Schechner 1966; 1973; 1981; 1991; Scheff 1977; Schjødt 1986; J.Z. Smith 1987a; Snoek 1987; 2003; 2006; J. Sørensen 2005; J.P. Sørensen 1993; Staal 1989; Stausberg 2002; 2003; Tambiah 1981; Terrin 1999; Thomas 2000; V.W. Turner 1967; 1985a; V.W. Turner & E. Turner 1982; Van Baaren 1983; Wallace 1966; Werlen 1984; Wimmer & Schäfer 1998; Wuthnow 1987.

2.1 Myth and Ritual (myt)

Ahlbäck (ed.) 1993; Baudy 1998; Beattie 1966; 1970; Brandon 1975; Burkert 1972; 1996; 2002; Cazeneuve 1971; D'Aquili 1983; D'Aquili *et al.* (eds) 1979; D'Aquili & Newberg 1999; Doty 2000; Dow 1986; Dulaney & Fiske 1994; Dupré 1992; Fox 1980; Girard 1987; Goethals 1997; Goody 1977; Grimes 1982; Kapferer 1997; 2000; Lévi-Strauss

1990; Nagendra 1971; Penner 1969; Prattis 2001; Schechner 1966; 1982; Scheff 1977; Schjødt 1986; Segal 2000; 2005; 2006; Severi 1993a; J.Z. Smith 1980; 1987a; P. Smith 1982; J.P. Sørensen 2003; Staal 1989; Staiano 1979; Terrin 1999; Thomas 1998; Tybjerg 2001; Zuesse 1975.

2.2 Ritual and Psyche (Psychology) (psy)

Ahlbäck (ed.) 1993; Argyle 2002; Barthelmes & De la Motte-Haber (eds) 1999; Boudewijnse 2006; Burkert 1972; Cohen 1979; Crapanzano 2000; Csikszentmihalyi & Bennett 1971; Csordas 1983; D'Aquili & Laughlin 1975; D'Aquili *et al.* (eds) 1979; D'Aquili & Newberg 1999; Davies 1997; Dissanayake 1979; Dow 1986; Drewal 1992; Dulaney & Fiske 1994; Dupré 1992; Erikson 1977; Fiske & Haslam 1997; Geertz 1966; 1973; Goffman 1967; Greenfield 2005; Hahn 1977; Heimbrock & Boudewijnse (eds) 1990; Holm 2003; Houseman 1992; 1998; Jackson 1968; Jeserich 2006; Kertzer 1988; Laughlin 1990; Lawson & McCauley 1990; Lorenz 1966; Luckmann 1985; Marshall 2002; Matthews 1980; McCauley 2001; Merkur 1991; Moore & Myerhoff 1977; Myerhoff 1990; Needham 1967; Ortner 1975; 1978; Paige & Paige 1981; Penner 1969; Prattis 2001; Rappaport 1974; Reeves & Bylund 1992; Roberts 1988; Rothenbuhler 1998; Schechner 1987; 1991; Scheff 1977; Shaughnessy (ed.) 1973; V.W. Turner 1975; 1977; Wallace 1966; Winkelman 1986; Wulf & Zirfas (eds) 2003; Wuthnow 1987.

2.3 Ritual in Society (Sociology) (soc)

J.C. Alexander 2004; Argyle 2002; Bauman 1975; Bell 1993; Bellah 2003; Bloch 1986; 1987; 1989; 1992; Bocock 1970; 1974; Boudewijnse 2006; Bourdieu 1975; Bruner (ed.) 1984; Burkert 1972; 1987; 1996; Cannadine & Price (eds) 1987; Cheal 1988; Chwe 2001; Cohen 1979; Cole 2004; Crocker 1973; Csaszi 2001; Csikszentmihalyi & Bennett 1971; D'Aquili 1985; D'Aquili *et al.* (eds) 1979; Dartiguenave 2001; De Coppet (ed.) 1992; Dissanayake 1979; Doty 2000; Douglas 1966; 1970; Driver 1991; 1994; Etzioni 2000; Finnegan 1969; Finol 2003; Fischer-Lichte & Wulf (eds) 2001; Gebauer & Wulf 1998; Geertz 1966; 1973; 1980; Gerhardt 2004; Gerholm 1988; Girard 1987; Goffman 1967; 1974; Gusfield & Michalowicz 1984; Handelman 1980; 1990; 1997; 2004; Harth 2006; Honko 1975; 1979; Houseman 1992; 1998; Hughes-Freeland (ed.) 1998; Jackson 1968; James 1983; Jeserich 2006; Kapferer 1997; Kertzer 1988; Kreinath *et al.* (eds) 2004; Krieger & Belliger 1998; Lang 1988; Laughlin 1990; Leach 1976; Lee 2005; Lorenz

1966; Luckmann 1985; Lukes 1975; MacAloon 1984; Marshall 2002; Moore & Myerhoff 1977; Munn 1973; Nagendra 1971; Ortner 1975; 1978; Penner 1969; Pertierra 1987; Platvoet 1995; 2004; 2006; Platvoet & Van der Toorn (eds) 1995; Rao 2006; Rao & Köpping 2000; Rappaport 1968; 1971; 1974; 1978; 1979; 1980; 1992; Ray 1973; Reeves & Bylund 1989; 1992; Roth 1995; Rothenbuhler 1998; Sax 2006; Schechner 1981; 1987; 1991; 1994; Schieffelin 1996; 1998; 2006; Shaughnessy (ed.) 1973; J.Z. Smith 1980; Snoek 1995; H.-G. Soeffner 1988; 1992; Stark 2001; Stolz 1997; Strecker 1988; Sullivan 1986; Thomas 1998; 2000; Toren 1993; Travers 1982; V.W. Turner 1974a; 1974c; 1975; 1977; 1985a; Wallace 1966; Wiedenmann 1989; 1991; Wulf *et al.* (eds) 2001; Wulf & Zirfas (eds) 2003; 2004; Wuthnow 1987.

2.4 Ritual: Religious and Secular (sec)

J.C. Alexander 2004; Asad 1988; Bateson 1974; Bird 1980; Blasi 1985; Bocock 1970; 1974; Boudewijnse 1998; Boyer 1994; Braungart 1996; Bruner (ed.) 1984; Cheal 1988; Douglas 1970; Driver 1994; Droogers 2004; Dupré 1992; Etzioni 2000; Finnegan 1969; Fox 1980; Frankiel 2001; Gerhardt 2004; Goethals 1997; Goffman 1967; Gusfield & Michalowicz 1984; Hahn 1977; Handelman 1997; Harth 2006; Harth & Schenk (eds) 2004; Heimbrock & Boudewijnse (eds) 1990; Honko 1975; Hughes-Freeland & Crain (eds) 1998; James 1983; Jeserich 2006; Keesing 1991; Kertzer 1988; Köpping 1998; Köpping & Rao 2003a; Kreinath 2005; Kreinath *et al.* (eds) 2004; Krieger & Belliger 1998; Lawson & McCauley 1990; Leach 1968; Leertouwer 1973; Lorenz 1966; Luckmann 1985; Lukes 1975; MacAloon 1984; MacAloon (ed.) 1984; Matthews 1980; McLeod 1990; Merkur 1991; Moore & Myerhoff 1977; Moore & Myerhoff (eds) 1977; Nagendra 1971; Peacock 1990; Pertierra 1987; Platvoet 1995; 2004; 2006; Platvoet & Van der Toorn (eds) 1995; Rao & Köpping 2000; Rappaport 1999; Reeves & Bylund 1992; Rothenbuhler 1998; Schechner 2002; Staal 1989; Terrin 1999; Thomas 1998; 2000; Travers 1982; V.W. Turner 1974c; V.W. Turner (ed.) 1982; V.W. Turner & E. Turner 1982; Van Baaren 1983; Wallace 1966; Winkelman 1986; Wulf *et al.* (eds) 2001; Wulf & Zirfas (eds) 2003; 2004; Wuthnow 1987.

2.5 Structure, Process, Form (including Syntax, Sequence, Repetition) (str)

Anttonen 1992; Babcock 1978; Baranowski 1998; Bateson 1974; Baudy 1998; Bauman 1975; Bell 1990; Bird 1980; Blanchard 1980; Bloch

1987; 1992; 2006; Blondeau & Schipper (eds) 1990 / [1990] / 1995; Boyer 1994; Braungart 1996; Burkert 1972; 2002; Caduff & Pfaff-Czarnecka (eds) 1999; Cartry 1992; Chwe 2001; Crocker 1973; Dahm 2003; D'Aquili 1985; De Coppet (ed.) 1992; Douglas 1966; Dulaney & Fiske 1994; Eibl-Eibesfeldt 1979; Erikson 1977; Finol 2003; Fox 1980; Galaty 1983; Gladigow 2004; 2006; Goffman 1974; Goody 1977; Gossen 1978; Grainger 1974; Grimes 1982; Handelman 1981; 1990; 1996; 2004; 2006b; Handelman & Kapferer 1980; Harth 2005; Hoëm 1998; Hollywood 2002; Honko 1975; 1979; Houseman 1992; 1993; 2000; 2004; Houseman & Severi 1994; Hymes 1975; Jackson 1968; Jennings 1982; Jensen 1986; Jeserich 2006; Kapferer 1979; 1983; 1986; 2000; 2004; Kapferer (ed.) 1979; Keesing 1991; Kelly & Kaplan 1990; Köpping & Rao 2003b; Kreinath 2006; Kreinath *et al.* (eds) 2004; Laidlaw & Humphrey 2006; Lawson 1976; 1993; Lawson & McCauley 1990; Leach 1966; 1968; 1976; Lee 2005; Lévi-Strauss 1990; Lindgren 1997; MacAloon (ed.) 1984; McCauley 2001; McCauley & Lawson 2002; Michaels 1999; Moore & Myerhoff (eds) 1977; Munn 1973; Needham 1967; Ohnuki-Tierney 1987; Ortner 1975; Paul 1990; Peacock 1990; Penner 1969; 1985; Pentikäinen 1979; Platvoet 1995; Rao 2006; Rappaport 1971; 1974; 1978; 1979; 1980; 1992; 1999; Ray 1973; Riner 1978; Roberts 1988; Roth 1995; Schechner 1977; 2002; Schechner & Appel 1990; Scheffler 1993; Schieffelin 1985; 1996; Schjødt 1986; Severi 1993b; 2006; J.Z. Smith 1987b; 1998; P. Smith 1982; Snoek 1987; H.-G. Soeffner 1988; 1992; J.P. Sørensen 1993; Staal 1979; 1989; Staiano 1979; Stausberg 2003; Thomas 1998; 2000; 2006; Toren 1993; T.S. Turner 1977; 2006; V.W. Turner 1967; 1969; 1974a; 1974c; 1975; 1985b; V.W. Turner & E. Turner 1982; Verkuyl 1997; Von Ins 2001; Wiedenmann 1989; 1991; Wuthnow 1987; Zuesse 1975.

2.6 Ritual and Meaning (including Meaninglessness / Semantics) (mng)

Ahearn 2001; Anttonen 1992; Asad 1988; Auffarth 1999; Baranowski 1998; Bateson 1974; Bell 1992; Bird 1995; Bloch 1986; 1987; 1992; 2006; Bocock 1974; Boudewijnse 1995; 1998; Boyer 1994; Brown 2003; Caduff & Pfaff-Czarnecka (eds) 1999; Cheal 1988; Chwe 2001; Clothey 1998; Cole 2004; Dahm 2003; Douglas 1966; 1970; Fernandez 1972; 1977; Fiske & Haslam 1997; Galaty 1983; Geertz 1966; 1973; Gerholm 1988; Girard 1987; Gladigow 2006; Goethals 1997; Goffman 1967; 1974; Goody 1977; Gossen 1978; Grainger 1974; Grimes 1982; Harris 1997; Harth 2006; Heimbrock & Boudewijnse (eds) 1990; Henn

2003; Herdt (ed.) 1982; Hollywood 2002; Houseman 2002; Humphrey & Laidlaw 1994; Innis 2004; Jackson 1968; Jensen 1986; Jones 2000; Kapferer 1979; 1986; Kapferer (ed.) 1979; Keesing 1991; Köpping 2003; Köpping & Rao (eds) 2000; 2003a; Kreinath 2005; 2006; Kreinath *et al.* (eds) 2004; Laidlaw & Humphrey 2006; Lawson & McCauley 1990; Leach 1968; 1976; Lee 2005; Lewis 1980; Luckmann 1985; MacAloon 1984; Michaels 1999; 2000; 2006; Moore & Myerhoff 1977; Munn 1973; Nagendra 1971; Needham 1985; Ohnuki-Tierney 1987; Ortner 1975; 1978; Paul 1990; Peacock 1990; Penner 1985; Pentikäinen 1979; Price 1988; Rao & Köpping 2000; Rappaport 1974; 1992; 1999; Ray 1973; Roberts 1988; Rothenbuhler 1998; Schaller 1988; Schieffelin 1985; Schjødt 1986; Seeman 2004; Severi 1993b; 2006; Sharf 2005; Sinding-Larsen 1984; J.Z. Smith 1980; J. Sørensen 2005; Sperber 1975; Staal 1979; 1989; Strathern & Stewart 1998; Strecker 1998; Sullivan 1986; Toren 1993; T.S. Turner 2006; V.W. Turner 1967; 1969; 1974b; 1974c; 1975; 1977; 1985a; V.W. Turner & Bruner (eds) 1986; Verkuyl 1997; Wallace 1966; Werlen 1987; Wiedenmann 1991; Williams & Boyd 1993; Wulf & Zirfas 2004; Wuthnow 1987; Young-Laughlin & Laughlin 1988; Zuesse 1975.

3.1 Action

See pr1 under 3.8 Praxis.

3.2 Aesthetics (aes)

Barthelmes & De la Motte-Haber (eds) 1999; Brandon 1975; Braungart 1996; Dahm 2003; Dissanayake 1979; Galaty 1983; Gebauer & Wulf 1998; Geertz 1966; Harth 2005; Houseman 1998; Innis 2004; Jackson 1968; Jensen 1986; Jones 2000; Kapferer 1983; 1986; 1997; 2000; 2004; 2006a; Kreinath 2004b; Kreinath *et al.* (eds) 2004; Leach 1968; 1976; Lewis 1980; Needham 1967; Platvoet 1995; Rothenbuhler 1998; Sax 2006; Schechner 1970; 1973; 1974; 1981; 1991; 1994; 2002; Schechner & Appel 1990; Scheff 1977; Scheffler 1981; 1993; Schieffelin 1996; 1998; Sinding-Larsen 1984; Sullivan 1986; Williams & Boyd 1993; 2006; Wulf 2006; Young-Laughlin & Laughlin 1988; Zuesse 1975.

3.3 Cognition (cog)

Alcorta & Sosis 2005; Andresen (ed.) 2001; Baranowski 1998; Barrett 2002; Barrett & Lawson 2001; Bloch 1989; 2006; Boudewijnse 2006; Boyer 1994; D'Aquili 1983; D'Aquili *et al.* (eds) 1979; D'Aquili & Newberg 1999; Douglas 1966; 1970; Dow 1986; Droogers 2004; Fernandez

1986; Fiske & Haslam 1997; Frankiel 2001; Handelman 1977; 1996; Houseman 1992; Humphrey & Laidlaw 1994; Jennings 1982; Kertzer 1988; Kreinath 2004b; Laidlaw & Humphrey 2006; Laughlin 1990; Laughlin *et al.* 1986; Lawson 1976; 1993; 2006; Lawson & McCauley 1990; Levine 1998; Lindgren 1997; Lukes 1975; McCauley 2001; McCauley & Lawson 2002; Michaels 2006; Myerhoff 1990; Needham 1967; Penner 1969; Pentikäinen 1979; Rappaport 1968; 1974; Riner 1978; Scheffler 1997; Schilbrack (ed.) 2004; Sinding-Larsen 1984; J. Sørensen 2001; 2003; 2005; Sperber 1975; Stausberg 2003; Strecker 1988; Toren 1993; V.W. Turner 1969; 1975; 1985a; Wallace 1966; Whitehouse 2002; Williams & Boyd 1993; Winkelman 1986.

3.4 Communication (com)

Ahern 1979; Alcorta & Sosis 2005; J.C. Alexander 2004; Argyle 2002; Auffarth 1999; Babcock 1978; Bateson 1974; Baudy 1998; Bauman 1975; Bauman & Briggs 1990; Beattie 1966; 1970; Bird 1995; Blasi 1985; Bloch 1974; 1986; 1989; Boudewijnse 2006; Bourdieu 1975; Braungart 1996; Bruner (ed.) 1984; Burkert 1972; 1987; 1996; Chwe 2001; Crocker 1973; Csaszi 2001; Dahm 2003; Doty 2000; Douglas 1970; Dow 1986; Drexler 1993; Eibl-Eibesfeldt 1979; Fernandez 1972; 1986; Finnegan 1969; Finol 2003; Gardner 1983; Geertz 1966; Goffman 1967; 1974; Grainger 1974; Grimes 1988a; 1990; Handelman 1977; 1979; 1980; 1981; 1990; 1996; 2004; Handelman & Kapferer 1980; Harris 1997; Heeschen 1987; Hockings 1968; Hoëm 1998; Houseman 1992; Hymes 1975; Jackson 1968; Jensen 1986; Jeserich 2006; Jones 2000; Kapferer 1983; 1986; Kapferer (ed.) 1979; Keesing 1991; Kertzer 1988; Klein (ed.) 1987; Köpping & Rao 2003a; Kreinath 2004b; Kreinath *et al.* (eds) 2004; Krieger & Belliger 1998; Laidlaw & Humphrey 2006; Laughlin 1990; Lawson 1976; Lawson & McCauley 1990; Leach 1966; 1968; 1976; Lee 2005; Lewis 1980; Lindgren 1997; Lorenz 1966; Luckmann 1985; Lüger 1983; Matthews 1980; Munn 1973; Needham 1967; Paul 1990; Peacock 1990; Platvoet 1995; 2006; Rao 2006; Rappaport 1968; 1971; 1974; 1978; 1979; 1992; 1999; Riner 1978; Rothenbuhler 1998; Schaller 1988; Schechner 1991; Schieffelin 1996; Severi 1993b; 2002; Shaughnessy (ed.) 1973; Sinding-Larsen 1984; Snoek 1995; J.P. Sørensen 1993; Stolz 1997; Strathern & Stewart 1998; Strecker 1988; 1998; Sullivan 1986; Tambiah 1968; 1981; 1985; Thomas 1998; 2000; 2006; Toren 1993; V.W. Turner 1975; V.W. Turner & E. Turner 1982; Von Ins 2001; Wallace 1966; Werlen 1987; Wheelock 1982; Wiedenmann 1991; Wimmer & Schäfer 1998; Wuthnow 1987.

3.5 Ethology (eth)

Bateson 1974; Baudy 1998; 2006; Bell 1992; Bird 1995; Boyer 1994; Braungart 1996; Burkert 1972; 1987; 1996; 2002; Dahm 2003; D'Aquili 1983; 1985; D'Aquili & Laughlin 1975; D'Aquili *et al.* (eds) 1979; D'Aquili & Newberg 1999; Dissanayake 1979; Doty 2000; Drexler 1993; Driver 1991; Eibl-Eibesfeldt 1979; Elsbree 1982; Goffman 1967; Heeschen 1987; Huxley (ed.) 1966; Leach 1966; 1968; Lévi-Strauss 1990; Lindgren 1997; Lorenz 1966; Michaels 1999; 2000; Platvoet 1995; 2004; 2006; Rappaport 1968; 1979; 1999; Riner 1978; Rothenbuhler 1998; Schechner 1973; 1982; 1987; 1988a; 1988c; 1991; 1994; Segal 2000; J. Sørensen 2003; 2005; Staal 1989; Stolz 1997; Terrin 1999; Thomas 1998; T.S. Turner 2006; V.W. Turner 1974a; 1975; 1985a; 1985b; 1988; Wallace 1966; Wiedenmann 1991; Wilson 1978; Winkelman 1986; Young-Laughlin & Laughlin 1988.

3.6 Gender (gdr)

Ahearn 2001; Bloch 1986; Blondeau & Schipper (eds) 1990 / [1990] / 1995; Doty 2000; Douglas 1966; Drewal 1992; Fischer-Lichte & Wulf (eds) 2001; 2004; Handelman 1979; 1980; Heimbrock & Boudewijnse (eds) 1990; Herdt (ed.) 1982; Houseman 2002; Houseman & Severi 1994; Kapferer 1983; 2000; La Fontaine (ed.) 1972; Lewis 1980; Lutkehaus & Roscoe (eds) 1995; Morris 2006; Paige & Paige 1981; Snoek 1987; Strathern & Stewart 1998; Wulf & Zirfas (eds) 2003.

3.7 Performance (and Performativity) (pmc, tha, pmt)

Performance / Theatre / Play (pmc): J.C. Alexander 2004; Barthelmes & De la Motte-Haber (eds) 1999; Bauman 1975; Bauman & Briggs 1990; Beattie 1966; 1970; Beeman 1993; Bell 1992; 1993; 1998; Bird 1980; 1995; Blackburn 1988; Blanchard 1980; Bloch 1974; Bocock 1974; Braungart 1996; Brown 2003; Bruner (ed.) 1984; Chambers 2004; Collins 1998; Crumrine 1983; Csikszentmihalyi & Bennett 1971; Douglas 1966; Drewal 1992; Driver 1991; 1994; Droogers 2004; Dupré 1992; Emigh 1996; Erikson 1977; Fernandez 1972; 1974; 1977; 1986; Fischer-Lichte & Wulf (eds) 2004; Fiske & Haslam 1997; Fox 1980; Gardner 1983; Gebauer & Wulf 1998; Geertz 1966; 1973; 1980; Gerhardt 2004; Gerholm 1988; Goffman 1967; 1974; Grimes 1982; 1988a; 1988b; 1990; 2002; 2003; 2004; 2006; Handelman 1979; 1980; 1990; 1996; 1997; 2004; Handelman & Kapferer 1980; Harth 2005; 2006; Harth & Schenk (eds) 2004; Hoëm 1998; Houseman 1992; 1993; 2000; 2004; Houseman & Severi 1994; Howe 2000; Hughes-Freeland 1998;

Hughes-Freeland (ed.) 1998; Hughes-Freeland & Crain 1998; Hughes-Freeland & Crain (eds) 1998; Hymes 1975; James 1983; Jensen 1986; Jones 2000; Kapferer 1979; 1983; 1986; 1997; 2000; 2004; Kapferer (ed.) 1979; Kelly & Kaplan 1990; Kertzer 1988; Köpping (ed.) 1997; 1998; 2003; Köpping & Rao (eds) 2000; 2003a; Kreinath 2004a; 2004b; 2006; Kreinath *et al.* (eds) 2004; Krieger & Belliger 1998; Krondorfer 1992; Leach 1968; 1976; Lewis 1980; MacAloon 1984; MacAloon (ed.) 1984; Marglin 1990; Matthews 1980; Merkur 1991; Michaels 1999; Myerhoff 1990; Needham 1967; Ohnuki-Tierney 1987; Ortner 1975; 1978; Peacock 1990; Pertierra 1987; Platvoet 1995; Rao 2006; Rao & Köpping 2000; Rappaport 1974; 1978; 1979; 1980; 1999; Ray 1973; Riner 1978; Rothenbuhler 1998; Schechner 1966; 1970; 1973; 1974; 1977; 1981; 1982; 1987; 1988a; 1988b; 1991; 1993; 1994; 2002; Schechner & Appel 1990; Schechner & Appel (eds) 1990; Scheffler 1981; 1993; 1997; Schieffelin 1985; 1996; 1998; Severi 1993a; 1993b; 2002; Sharf 2005; Sinding-Larsen 1984; J.Z. Smith 1987a; Snoek 2003; Staal 1989; Staiano 1979; Stausberg 2006a; Strecker 1988; Sullivan 1986; Tambiah 1981; 1985; Terrin 1999; T.S. Turner 1977; V.W. Turner 1969; 1974c; 1977; 1979; 1982; 1984; 1985a; 1985b; 1988; V.W. Turner (ed.) 1982; Von Ins 2001; Wiedenmann 1989; Wulf 2006; Wulf *et al.* (eds) 2001; Wulf & Zirfas (eds) 2003; 2004; Wuthnow 1987; Zuesse 1975.

Theatre and the theatrical (tha): Beeman 1993; Bird 1980; 1995; Driver 1991; Dupré 1992; Emigh 1996; Geertz 1980; Goffman 1974; Grimes 1982; 1990; Hughes-Freeland (ed.) 1998; James 1983; Jones 2000; Köpping 1998; Kreinath *et al.* (eds) 2004; Rao & Köpping 2000; Schechner 1966; 1970; 1973; 1974; 1977; 1981; 1987; 1988a; 1991; 1994; Schechner & Appel (eds) 1990; Schieffelin 1996; 1998; Severi 2002; Tambiah 1985; Terrin 1999; V.W. Turner 1979; 1982; 1984; 1985a; 1985b.

Performativity (pmt): Ahern 1979; Bauman & Briggs 1990; Beattie 1966; 1970; Bird 1995; Blackburn 1988; Bloch 1974; 1986; Bourdieu 1975; 1982; Collins 1998; Fernandez 2006; Finnegan 1969; Fischer-Lichte & Wulf (eds) 2004; Gardner 1983; Grimes 1988a; 1990; Handelman 1996; Hollywood 2002; Howe 2000; Humphrey & Laidlaw 1994; Janowitz 2004; Kapferer 1979; Keesing 1991; Köpping 1998; Kreinath 2004b; Lawson & McCauley 1990; Leach 1968; 1976; Lüger 1983; Marglin 1990; Matthews 1980; Ohnuki-Tierney 1987; Paul 1990; Pertierra 1987; Platvoet 1995; Rao 2006; Rappaport 1974; 1978; 1979; 1980; 1999; Schaller 1988; Schechner 1994; 2002; Schieffelin 1985; 1996; 1998; Severi 1993a; 2002; Smart 1972; Snoek 2003; J.P.

Sørensen 2006; Staal 1989; Strecker 1988; Tambiah 1968; 1973; 1981; 1985; V.W. Turner 1974b; Werlen 1984; Wheelock 1982; Wulf *et al.* (eds) 2001; Wulf & Zirfas (eds) 2003; 2004.

3.8 Praxis (Action, Mimesis, Embodiment, Competence) (pr1, pr2, mim, emb, cmp)

Praxis in the sense of Action (pr1): Ahearn 2001; J.C. Alexander 2004; Asad 1988; Bauman 1975; Bell 1990; 1992; 1998; Bird 1995; Bocock 1970; 1974; Boudewijnse 1995; Braungart 1996; Brown 2003; Cheal 1988; Crocker 1973; Dahm 2003; Driver 1994; Elsbree 1982; Fernandez 1972; Finol 2003; Geertz 1973; Gerholm 1988; Goffman 1967; Grimes 2004; Handelman 1990; Harth 2006; Hollywood 2002; Houseman 1992; 1998; Houseman & Severi 1994; Hughes-Freeland (ed.) 1998; Hughes-Freeland & Crain 1998; Humphrey & Laidlaw 1994; Jennings 1982; Kapferer 1979; 1997; Kapferer (ed.) 1979; Kelly & Kaplan 1990; Kertzer 1988; Köpping 1998; 2003; Kreinath 2004b; Krieger & Belliger 1998; Laidlaw & Humphrey 2006; Lawson 1993; Lawson & McCauley 1990; Leach 1968; Lewis 1980; Lindgren 1997; Matthews 1980; McCauley & Lawson 2002; Michaels 2000; Munn 1973; Myerhoff 1990; Nagendra 1971; Penner 1989; Pertierra 1987; Rao 2006; Rao & Köpping 2000; Roth 1995; Rothenbuhler 1998; Schaller 1988; Schechner 1973; 1981; 1991; 2002; Scheff 1977; Schieffelin 1998; Schilbrack (ed.) 2004; Severi 1993a; 1993b; 2006; Smart 1972; Snoek 2003; J. Sørensen 2001; 2005; J.P. Sørensen 2006; Strecker 1988; Tambiah 1968; 1973; 1981; 1985; Travers 1982; T.S. Turner 2006; V.W. Turner 1979; Verkuyl 1997; Werlen 1984; 1987; Wiedenmann 1989; Wimmer & Schäfer 1998; Wulf 2006; Wulf & Zirfas (eds) 2003; Zuesse 1975.

Praxis in the sense of Mimesis, Embodiment, Competence (pr2): Asad 1988; Blackburn 1988; Bourdieu 1982; Collins 1998; Driver 1994; Emigh 1996; Galaty 1983; Gardner 1983; Gebauer & Wulf 1998; Greenfield 2005; Handelman 2004; 2006b; Handelman & Kapferer 1980; Harris 1997; Houseman 1998; Kapferer 1983; 2000; 2004; Kelly & Kaplan 1990; Köpping 1998; Köpping & Rao 2003b; Kreinath 2004b; Laughlin 1990; McCauley & Lawson 2002; Rao & Köpping 2000; Schechner 1973; 1981; 1982; 1991; 2002; Schieffelin 1996; Severi 1993a; Snoek 2003; H.-G. Soeffner 1988; Sullivan 1986; Travers 1982; T.S. Turner 1977; V.W. Turner 1982; Werlen 1984; Wiedenmann 1991; Wulf 2006; Wulf *et al.* (eds) 2001; Wulf & Zirfas (eds) 2003; 2004.

Mimesis (mim): Bell 1992; Braungart 1996; Burkert 1972; Gebauer & Wulf 1998; Henn 2003; Köpping (ed.) 1997; 1998; Köpping & Rao 2003b; Laughlin 1990; Leach 1968; Lorenz 1966; Rao & Köpping 2000; Schechner 1970; 1973; 1981; Scheffler 1981; 1997; Snoek 2003; H.-G. Soeffner 1992; V.W. Turner 1985a; Werlen 1984; Wulf 2006; Wulf *et al.* (eds) 2001; Wulf & Zirfas (eds) 2003; 2004.
Embodiment (emb): Bell 1990; 1992; 1993; 2006; Bourdieu 1982; Clothey 1998; Crapanzano 2000; Doty 2000; Douglas 1970; Driver 1994; Frankiel 2001; Geertz 1966; 1980; Grimes 1982; 2004; Handelman 1990; Hollywood 2002; Houseman 1998; Innis 2004; Kapferer 1983; 2000; Krondorfer 1992; Marglin 1990; Needham 1967; Ortner 1978; Rao & Köpping 2000; Rappaport 1974; 1978; Schechner 1991; Schechner & Appel 1990; Snoek 2003; H.-G. Soeffner 1992; Strathern & Stewart 1998; Thomas 1998; 2006; Travers 1982; V.W. Turner 1969; Wallace 1966; Werlen 1984; Winkelman 1986; Wulf 2006; Wulf *et al.* (eds) 2001.
Competence (cmp): Asad 1988; Barrett & Lawson 2001; Baumann 1992; Bell 1993; Blackburn 1988; Cartry 1992; Clothey 1998; Driver 1994; Erikson 1977; Gerholm 1988; Gladigow 2004; Grimes 1988b; Handelman 1990; Humphrey & Laidlaw 1994; Hymes 1975; Jennings 1982; Lawson 1976; Lawson & McCauley 1990; McCauley & Lawson 2002; Michaels 1999; Platvoet 2006; Schechner 1973; 1981; 1991; Schieffelin 1996; Severi 1993a; Snoek 2003; Tambiah 1973; 1985; V.W. Turner 1967; 1969; Werlen 1984; Williams & Boyd 1993; Wulf 2006; Zuesse 1975.

3.9 Relationality (rel)

Babcock 1978; Crocker 1973; Crumrine 1983; Douglas 1966; Emigh 1996; Fernandez 2006; Finnegan 1969; Gerhardt 2004; Goffman 1967; Handelman 1977; 1979; 1980; Handelman & Kapferer 1980; Houseman 1992; 1993; 1998; 2002; 2004; 2006; Houseman & Severi 1994; Hughes-Freeland & Crain 1998; Kapferer 1983; Keesing 1991; Kertzer 1988; Severi 1993b; 2002; T.S. Turner 1977; V.W. Turner 1969; Wimmer & Schäfer 1998; Wuthnow 1987; Zuesse 1975.

3.10 Semiotics (sem)

Babcock 1978; Bateson 1974; Bloch 1974; 1986; 1987; 1989; 1992; Braungart 1996; Crapanzano 2000; Dahm 2003; Dartiguenave 2001; Douglas 1966; 1970; Fernandez 1972; 1977; 1986; Finol 2003; Galaty 1983; Geertz 1966; 1973; 1980; Goffman 1967; 1974; Gossen 1978;

Handelman 1977; 1979; 1981; 1990; 2006b; Handelman & Kapferer 1980; Harris 1997; Heimbrock & Boudewijnse (eds) 1990; Henn 2003; Houseman 1993; Houseman & Severi 1994; Hymes 1975; Innis 2004; Janowitz 2004; Jensen 1986; Jeserich 2006; Jones 2000; Kapferer 1983; Kreinath 2004b; 2005; 2006; Kreinath *et al.* 2006; La Fontaine (ed.) 1972; Laughlin 1990; Lawson 1976; Lawson & McCauley 1990; Leach 1966; 1968; 1976; Lindgren 1997; Luckmann 1985; MacAloon (ed.) 1984; Marglin 1990; Munn 1973; Nagendra 1971; Ohnuki-Tierney 1987; Ortner 1975; 1978; Penner 1985; Rappaport 1968; 1971; 1974; 1979; 1980; 1992; Scheffler 1981; 1993; 1997; Severi 1993b; 2006; Sperber 1975; Staal 1979; 1989; Staiano 1979; Strathern & Stewart 1998; Strecker 1988; Tambiah 1981; 1985; Toren 1993; T.S. Turner 2006; V.W. Turner 1974b; 1974c; 1977; Verkuyl 1997; Von Ins 2001; Werlen 1984; Wheelock 1982; Wiedenmann 1989; 1991; Williams & Boyd 1993; Wulf & Zirfas (eds) 2003; Wuthnow 1987.

4.1 Agency (agn)

Ahearn 2001; Andresen (ed.) 2001; Barrett & Lawson 2001; Bauman & Briggs 1990; Bell 1992; Bourdieu 1975; Cheal 1988; Collins 1998; Crapanzano 2000; Drewal 1992; Droogers 2004; Girard 1987; Hoëm 1998; Hughes-Freeland 1998; Humphrey & Laidlaw 1994; Kapferer 1983; 1997; 2000; Kelly & Kaplan 1990; Laidlaw & Humphrey 2006; Lawson & McCauley 1990; McCauley & Lawson 2002; Sax 2006; Schechner 1981; Schieffelin 1985; 1996; Travers 1982; Wimmer & Schäfer 1998.

4.2 Complexity (and Redundancy) (cpl)

Alcorta & Sosis 2005; Anttonen 1992; Auffarth 1999; Braungart 1996; Burkert 1987; 1996; Caduff & Pfaff-Czarnecka (eds) 1999; Chwe 2001; Collins 1998; Douglas 1966; Drexler 1993; Galaty 1983; Gladigow 2004; 2006; Handelman 1990; 2006b; Houseman 2000; Jackson 1968; Kapferer 1983; 1986; Lang 1988; Leach 1966; 1968; 1976; Ohnuki-Tierney 1987; Platvoet 2006; Price 1988; Rao 2006; Rappaport 1992; Severi 1993b; 2002; P. Smith 1982; J.P. Sørensen 1993; Sperber 1975; Staal 1979; Stausberg 2003; Stolz 1997; Tambiah 1981; 1985; Thomas 1998; 2000; 2006; Wulf *et al.* (eds) 2001.

4.3 Deference (dfr)

Bloch 2006; Goffman 1967; James 1983.

4.4 Dynamics (dyn)

Ahlbäck (ed.) 1993; Alcorta & Sosis 2005; Anttonen 1992; Bateson 1974; Bauman & Briggs 1990; Bell 1990; 1992; 1993; Bird 1980; Blackburn 1988; Blanchard 1980; Bloch 1986; Bocock 1974; Bourdieu 1975; Brown 2003; Bruner (ed.) 1984; Burkert 1972; 1987; Cheal 1988; Crumrine 1970; 1983; Delattre 1978; Douglas 1966; 1970; Drewal 1992; Droogers 2004; Emigh 1996; Etzioni 2000; Fernandez 1986; 2006; Frankiel 2001; Geertz 1973; Gerholm 1988; Grainger 1974; Grimes 1988a; 2003; Hahn 1977; Handelman 2004; 2006a; 2006b; Handelman & Kapferer 1980; Harrison 1992; Harth 2006; Harth & Schenk (eds) 2004; Herdt (ed.) 1982; Honko 1975; 1979; Houseman 1993; James 1983; Jeserich 2006; Kapferer 1983; 1997; 2000; 2004; 2006a; 2006b; Kelly & Kaplan 1990; Kreinath 2004a; 2006; Kreinath *et al.* (eds) 2004; La Fontaine (ed.) 1972; Lorenz 1966; McCauley & Lawson 2002; Michaels 1999; 2000; Moore & Myerhoff 1977; Ohnuki-Tierney 1987; Ortner 1978; Rao 2006; Rao & Köpping 2000; Rappaport 1974; 1979; Rothenbuhler 1998; Schechner 1973; 1974; 1981; 1991; 1994; Schechner & Appel 1990; Scheffler 1993; Schieffelin 1985; 1996; 1998; Severi 1993b; J.Z. Smith 1987b; J.P. Sørensen 1993; Thomas 2000; 2006; Toren 1993; V.W. Turner 1969; 1985a; 1985b; Van Baaren 1983; Wallace 1966; Wiedenmann 1989; 1991; Wulf & Zirfas (eds) 2003; 2004; Wuthnow 1987.

4.5 Efficacy (eff)

Ahern 1979; Alcorta & Sosis 2005; J.C. Alexander 2004; Argyle 2002; Babcock 1978; Barrett & Lawson 2001; Beattie 1966; 1970; Bell 1990; 1992; 1993; 1998; Bird 1980; Blackburn 1988; Blasi 1985; Bloch 1974; 1987; Bourdieu 1975; 1982; Brown 2003; Cazeneuve 1971; Chwe 2001; Cole 2004; D'Aquili & Newberg 1999; Douglas 1966; 1970; Dow 1986; Dulaney & Fiske 1994; Elsbree 1982; Fernandez 2006; Finnegan 1969; Fiske & Haslam 1997; Galaty 1983; Girard 1987; Goffman 1974; Grimes 1988b; 1990; 2003; Handelman 1980; 1990; Hockings 1968; Holm 2003; Houseman 1992; 1993; 1998; 2002; 2004; Howe 2000; Humphrey & Laidlaw 1994; Innis 2004; Janowitz 2004; Jones 2000; Kapferer 1979; 1983; 2000; Keesing 1991; Kelly & Kaplan 1990; Kertzer 1988; Köpping 2003; Kreinath *et al.* (eds) 2004; Laughlin 1990; Laughlin *et al.* 1986; Lawson & McCauley 1990; Leach 1968; Lewis 1980; Marglin 1990; Matthews 1980; McCauley & Lawson 2002; Moore & Myerhoff 1977; Myerhoff 1990; Needham 1967; Ortner 1975; 1978; Pertierra 1987; Prattis 2001; Rao & Köpping 2000; Rappaport 1974;

1979; 1980; 1999; Ray 1973; Rothenbuhler 1998; Schechner 1974; 1981; 1988a; 1994; 2002; Scheff 1977; Schieffelin 1985; 1996; 1998; Severi 1993a; 1993b; 2002; 2006; Sharf 2005; J. Sørensen 2001; J.P. Sørensen 1993; 2003; 2006; Tambiah 1968; 1973; 1985; T.S. Turner 1977; 2006; V.W. Turner 1967; 1975; Wallace 1966; Wiedenmann 1991; Williams & Boyd 1993; Wulf & Zirfas (eds) 2003.

4.6 Embodiment

See emb under 3.8 Praxis.

4.7 Emotion (and Experience) (emo)

Alcorta & Sosis 2005; Andresen (ed.) 2001; Anttonen 1992; Argyle 2002; Baranowski 1998; Baudy 1998; Bell 1992; Bloch 1986; 1987; Bocock 1970; 1974; Boudewijnse 2006; Brandon 1975; Bruner (ed.) 1984; Burkert 1972; Cheal 1988; Cole 2004; Crapanzano 2000; Csikszentmihalyi & Bennett 1971; Csordas 1983; D'Aquili 1985; D'Aquili & Newberg 1999; Dissanayake 1979; Douglas 1966; 1970; Dow 1986; Dupré 1992; Erikson 1977; Fernandez 1972; 1977; 2006; Fischer-Lichte & Wulf (eds) 2001; Gebauer & Wulf 1998; Geertz 1966; 1973; Gerholm 1988; Goffman 1967; Greenfield 2005; Hahn 1977; Houseman 1992; 1998; 2000; 2002; Humphrey & Laidlaw 1994; Jackson 1968; Jeserich 2006; Jones 2000; Kapferer 1983; 1986; 2004; Kapferer (ed.) 1979; Keesing 1991; Kertzer 1988; Köpping & Rao 2003b; Laughlin 1990; Laughlin *et al.* 1986; Lévi-Strauss 1990; Lewis 1980; Luckmann 1985; Lüddeckens 2006; Marglin 1990; Matthews 1980; McCauley 2001; McCauley & Lawson 2002; Merkur 1991; Moore & Myerhoff 1977; Myerhoff 1990; Needham 1967; 1985; Ortner 1978; Peacock 1990; Rao 2006; Rappaport 1974; 1979; 1999; Reeves & Bylund 1992; Schechner 1970; 1981; 1982; 1991; 2002; Scheff 1977; Scheffler 1993; Schieffelin 1985; 1996; 1998; 2006; Schilbrack (ed.) 2004; Seeman 2004; Severi 1993a; 1993b; Shaughnessy (ed.) 1973; Smart 1972; J.Z. Smith 1980; Thomas 1998; V.W. Turner 1967; 1969; 1974a; 1974b; 1975; 1979; V.W. Turner & Bruner (eds) 1986; Whitehouse 2002; Winkelman 1986; Wulf & Zirfas (eds) 2003; 2004; Wuthnow 1987; Young-Laughlin & Laughlin 1988; Zuesse 1975.

4.8 Framing (frm)

Babcock 1978; Bauman 1975; Bauman & Briggs 1990; Bruner (ed.) 1984; Chambers 2004; Cheal 1988; Csikszentmihalyi & Bennett 1971; Gladigow 2006; Goethals 1997; Goffman 1974; Handelman 1977;

1979; 1980; 1981; 1990; 2004; 2006b; Handelman & Kapferer 1980; Houseman 1998; Hughes-Freeland 1998; Innis 2004; Jackson 1968; Kapferer 2006a; Keesing 1991; Köpping (ed.) 1997; 1998; Köpping & Rao 2003a; 2003b; Kreinath 2004a; 2004b; Kreinath *et al.* (eds) 2004; Leach 1976; Lewis 1980; MacAloon (ed.) 1984; Myerhoff 1990; Needham 1967; Ohnuki-Tierney 1987; Rao 2006; Rao & Köpping 2000; Roberts 1988; Schechner 1966; 1973; 1974; 1977; 1982; 1988b; 1991; Sharf 2005; Stausberg 2006a; Thomas 2006; T.S. Turner 2006; V.W. Turner 1977; 1984; Von Ins 2001; Wulf & Zirfas 2004.

4.9 Language (lan)

Ahearn 2001; Bauman & Briggs 1990; Fischer-Lichte & Wulf (eds) 2001; Gossen 1978; Grainger 1974; Klein (ed.) 1987; Kreinath 2005; Lawson 1976; Leach 1966; 1968; 1976; Lindgren 1997; Lüger 1983; Penner 1985; Schaller 1988; Scheffler 1997; Severi 1993b; 2002; 2006; Uhl & Boelderl (eds) 1999; Von Ins 2001; Werlen 1984; Wheelock 1982.

4.10 Media (med)

J.C. Alexander 2004; Barthelmes & De la Motte-Haber (eds) 1999; Blackburn 1988; Bloch 1974; 1986; Blondeau & Schipper (eds) 1990 / [1990] / 1995; Chwe 2001; Csaszi 2001; Dahm 2003; Fischer-Lichte & Wulf (eds) 2001; 2004; Goethals 1997; Goffman 1967; Grimes 1990; 2002; Handelman 1990; 1997; Hockings 1968; Hughes-Freeland 1998; Hughes-Freeland (ed.) 1998; 2006; Hughes-Freeland & Crain 1998; Hughes-Freeland & Crain (eds) 1998; Jackson 1968; Jones 2000; Kapferer 1983; 1986; Kreinath *et al.* (eds) 2004; Lang 1988; Leach 1976; Munn 1973; Platvoet 1995; Rothenbuhler 1998; Scheff 1977; Stolz 1997; Sullivan 1986; Thomas 1998; 2000; 2006; V.W. Turner 1974a; 1985a; Von Ins 2001; Winkelman 1986; Wulf & Zirfas (eds) 2003; Young-Laughlin & Laughlin 1988.

4.11 Participation (par)

Alcorta & Sosis 2005; J.C. Alexander 2004; Argyle 2002; Baumann 1992; Bell 1992; Bocock 1970; Bourdieu 1975; Cartry 1992; Chambers 2004; Chwe 2001; Crumrine 1983; Drewal 1992; Droogers 2004; Etzioni 2000; Fernandez 1986; Girard 1987; Goffman 1967; Grimes 1988b; 1990; Houseman 1998; 2000; 2004; Hughes-Freeland 1998; Innis 2004; Kapferer 1986; Kreinath *et al.* (eds) 2004; Lee 2005; McCauley & Lawson 2002; Rappaport 1974; 1978; 1979; 1980; 1992;

1999; Reeves & Bylund 1992; Schechner 1974; 1977; 1981; 1982; 1991; 2002; Schieffelin 1985; 1998; 2006; Severi 2002; Stausberg 2006a; Thomas 2000; 2006; Whitehouse 2002; Wimmer & Schäfer 1998; Zuesse 1975.

4.12 Reflexivity (rfl)

Bauman & Briggs 1990; Baumann 1992; Bell 1993; Bird 1995; Brown 2003; Bruner (ed.) 1984; Burkert 1972; Cartry 1992; Chambers 2004; Chwe 2001; Clothey 1998; Crumrine 1983; Csordas 1983; Drewal 1992; Fernandez 1986; Galaty 1983; Gerhardt 2004; Goffman 1967; Grimes 1988a; 1988b; 1990; Handelman 1981; 1990; 1996; 2004; Handelman & Kapferer 1980; Harth 2006; Hauschildt 1993; Hoëm 1998; Houseman 2002; Hughes-Freeland & Crain (eds) 1998; Jennings 1982; Jensen 1986; Jeserich 2006; Kapferer 1983; 1986; 2004; Köpping 1998; 2003; Köpping & Rao (eds) 2000; 2003a; Kreinath *et al.* (eds) 2004; Kreinath *et al.* 2006; Leertouwer 1973; Lewis 1980; MacAloon 1984; MacAloon (ed.) 1984; Ohnuki-Tierney 1987; Paul 1990; Platvoet 2004; Price 1988; Rao 2006; Rao & Köpping 2000; Rappaport 1974; 1978; 1980; Schechner 1974; 1977; 1982; 1988c; 1991; Severi 2002; J.Z. Smith 1998; H.-G. Soeffner 1992; Stausberg 2006a; Strecker 1988; Sullivan 1986; Thomas 1998; 2000; 2006; V.W. Turner 1977; 1979; 1982; 1984; 1985a; 1985b; V.W. Turner & E. Turner 1982; Whitehouse 2002; Wimmer & Schäfer 1998; Wulf & Zirfas 2004; Wuthnow 1987; Zuesse 1975.

4.13 Rhetorics (rht)

Blackburn 1988; Bourdieu 1975; Bruner (ed.) 1984; Cartry 1992; Csordas 1983; Dissanayake 1979; Fernandez 1972; 1974; 1977; 1986; 2006; Galaty 1983; Goffman 1967; Grimes 1990; Hymes 1975; Kertzer 1988; Kreinath *et al.* (eds) 2004; Lüger 1983; Schieffelin 1985; J.P. Sørensen 2003; 2006; Strecker 1988; 1998; T.S. Turner 2006; Werlen 1984; Wiedenmann 1989; 1991.

4.14 Transmission (tra)

Alcorta & Sosis 2005; Bloch 2006; Boyer 1994; Burkert 1972; Cheal 1988; Chwe 2001; Droogers 2004; Gladigow 2004; Greenfield 2005; Holm 2003; Houseman 1998; Humphrey & Laidlaw 1994; Kreinath *et al.* (eds) 2004; Lorenz 1966; Schechner & Appel 1990; Severi 1993a; Stausberg 2003; Stolz 1997; Thomas 2000; Whitehouse 2006.

4.15 Virtuality (vir)

Drewal 1992; Emigh 1996; Geertz 1966; Grimes 2002; Kapferer 1997; 2000; 2004; 2006b; Köpping & Rao 2003a; Ortner 1975; 1978; Tambiah 1981; Williams & Boyd 1993.

C. Relevant Subjects, Not Directly Covered in Volume I

In alphabetical order

Authenticity (aut)

J.C. Alexander 2004; Chwe 2001; Crumrine 1983; Douglas 1970; Goffman 1967; Grimes 1988b; Handelman 1990; Harrison 1992; Houseman 2002; Rao & Köpping 2000; Schechner 1982; 2002; J.Z. Smith 1998; V.W. Turner 1979; 1982; V.W. Turner & Bruner (eds) 1986.

Comparison (cpr)

Brandon 1975; Cohen 1979; Douglas 1966; 1970; Drexler 1993; Dulaney & Fiske 1994; Eibl-Eibesfeldt 1979; Fiske & Haslam 1997; Frankiel 2001; Goethals 1997; Handelman 2006a; Handelman & Kapferer 1980; Honko 1975; 1979; Jones 2000; Kreinath 2004b; Kreinath *et al.* (eds) 2004; Lang 1988; Leertouwer 1973; Lorenz 1966; McCauley & Lawson 2002; Needham 1985; Platvoet & Van der Toorn (eds) 1995; Roth 1995; Schechner 1988b; 1994; P. Smith 1982; Snoek 1987; J.P. Sørensen 2003; V.W. Turner 1974a; Wiedenmann 1991.

Dance (dnc)

Alcorta & Sosis 2005; Beattie 1966; Blackburn 1988; Bloch 1974; 1989; Chwe 2001; Kapferer 1983; Marglin 1990; Schechner 1970; 1974.

Ecology (ecl)

Dow 1986; Grimes 2003; Jensen 1986; Rappaport 1968; 1971; 1974; 1978; 1979; 1999; Schechner 1974; J.Z. Smith 1980; V.W. Turner 1969.

Economics (ecn)

Cohen 1979; Douglas 1966; Drewal 1992; Kapferer 1983; Rappaport 1968; P. Smith 1982; Wuthnow 1987.

Explanation (exp)
Alcorta & Sosis 2005; Argyle 2002; Baranowski 1998; Bloch 1992; Boyer 1994; Burkert 1972; Cazeneuve 1971; Cheal 1988; D'Aquili 1985; Dow 1986; Gerhardt 2004; Girard 1987; Goethals 1997; Grimes 1988b; Laidlaw & Humphrey 2006; Lawson & McCauley 1990; Leertouwer 1973; Lorenz 1966; Marshall 2002; Matthews 1980; McCauley & Lawson 2002; Merkur 1991; Needham 1985; Penner 1969; 1989; Platvoet & Van der Toorn (eds) 1995; Scheffler 1981; 1993; Segal 2000; Staal 1989; Tambiah 1973; 1985; Winkelman 1986.

Guesture (gst)
Bateson 1974; Baudy 1998; Blasi 1985; Bloch 1986; Chwe 2001; Doty 2000; Eibl-Eibesfeldt 1979; Emigh 1996; Fernandez 1972; Gebauer & Wulf 1998; Goffman 1967; Houseman & Severi 1994; Lévi-Strauss 1990; Lewis 1980; Rappaport 1999; Schechner 1982; 1991; Scheffler 1981; 1993; 1997; Smart 1972; H.-G. Soeffner 1988; Williams & Boyd 1993; Wulf *et al.* (eds) 2001; Wuthnow 1987; Zuesse 1975.

Habitus (hab)
Bourdieu 1982; Braungart 1996; Hollywood 2002; Kapferer 2006a; McCauley & Lawson 2002; Pertierra 1987; Schieffelin 1998; Wulf 2006; Wulf *et al.* (eds) 2001.

Identity (idn)
Argyle 2002; Bell 1990; Bird 1980; Blackburn 1988; Bocock 1974; Bourdieu 1982; Bruner (ed.) 1984; Cole 2004; Crapanzano 2000; Crumrine 1983; Davies 1997; Douglas 1970; Drewal 1992; Driver 1994; Emigh 1996; Erikson 1977; Fernandez 1986; Girard 1987; Goffman 1967; Grimes 1990; Handelman 1979; 1980; 1981; Harrison 1992; Hockings 1968; Hoëm 1998; Honko 1975; Houseman 1992; 1998; 2002; Houseman & Severi 1994; Hughes-Freeland & Crain 1998; Hughes-Freeland & Crain (eds) 1998; James 1983; Jeserich 2006; Kapferer 1979; 1983; Kapferer (ed.) 1979; Kelly & Kaplan 1990; Kertzer 1988; Lewis 1980; Moore & Myerhoff 1977; Paige & Paige 1981; Platvoet 1995; Platvoet & Van der Toorn (eds) 1995; Rappaport 1980; Schechner 1993; P. Smith 1982; Snoek 1995; Stausberg 2006a; Thomas 2000; Travers 1982; V.W. Turner & Bruner (eds) 1986; Wimmer & Schäfer 1998; Wulf & Zirfas (eds) 2003.

Intentionality (int)
Blasi 1985; Cheal 1988; Hahn 1977; Harth 2006; Houseman 2004; Humphrey & Laidlaw 1994; Kapferer 2006b; Laidlaw & Humphrey 2006; J. Sørensen 2005; Wuthnow 1987.

Music & Rhythm (mus)
Alcorta & Sosis 2005; Argyle 2002; Baranowski 1998; Barthelmes & De la Motte-Haber (eds) 1999; Bellah 2003; Cartry 1992; Innis 2004; Kapferer 1983; Leach 1976; Needham 1967; Severi 2006; Sharf 2005; Staal 1989; Stausberg 2003; Terrin 1999.

Power, violence, hierarchy (pow)
Alcorta & Sosis 2005; Bauman 1975; Bell 1990; 1992; 1993; Bloch 1974; 1986; 1987; 1989; 1992; 2006; Bourdieu 1975; Burkert 1972; 1996; Caduff & Pfaff-Czarnecka (eds) 1999; Cannadine & Price (eds) 1987; Chwe 2001; Cohen 1979; Cole 2004; Collins 1998; Comaroff & Comaroff 1993; Crumrine 1983; Dahm 2003; D'Aquili *et al.* (eds) 1979; Douglas 1966; 1970; Drewal 1992; Driver 1994; Emigh 1996; Erikson 1977; Geertz 1980; Gerhardt 2004; Girard 1987; Handelman 1997; Harrison 1992; Harth 2006; Herdt (ed.) 1982; Holdrege (ed.) 1990; Hollywood 2002; Houseman 1992; 1998; Howe 2000; Hughes-Freeland & Crain 1998; Jones 2000; Kapferer (ed.) 1979; 1983; 1997; 2000; Kelly & Kaplan 1990; Kertzer 1988; Leertouwer 1973; Lukes 1975; Moore & Myerhoff 1977; Myerhoff 1990; Ohnuki-Tierney 1987; Paige & Paige 1981; Pertierra 1987; Platvoet 1995; 2004; Rao 2006; Rappaport 1968; 1980; Sax 2006; Schechner 1973; 1987; Schieffelin 1996; Schilbrack (ed.) 2004; J.Z. Smith 1987a; Snoek 1995; Tambiah 1968; 1985; Thomas 2000; Toren 1993; Travers 1982; V.W. Turner 1974a; 1977; Wulf 2006; Wulf *et al.* (eds) 2001; Wulf & Zirfas (eds) 2003.

Reference, Denotation, Expression & Exemplification (ref)
Bateson 1974; Bloch 1987; Delattre 1978; Douglas 1966; Handelman 1977; Hollywood 2002; Houseman 1993; Innis 2004; Jeserich 2006; Lawson & McCauley 1990; Michaels 2006; Penner 1985; Rappaport 1971; Scheffler 1981; 1993; 1997; J.P. Sørensen 1993; Staal 1979; Williams & Boyd 1993.

Representation (rep)

Beattie 1966; 1970; Bloch 1986; 1992; Bourdieu 1975; Brandon 1975; Cartry 1992; Drewal 1992; Fernandez 1972; 1977; Finol 2003; Geertz 1966; Grimes 1988b; 1990; Handelman 1990; 1997; Kapferer 2004; 2006a; Kertzer 1988; Kreinath 2004b; Kreinath *et al.* (eds) 2004; Laughlin 1990; Lawson 1993; Lawson & McCauley 1990; Lewis 1980; McCauley & Lawson 2002; Moore & Myerhoff 1977; Myerhoff 1990; Rappaport 1971; 1992; Scheffler 1997; Schieffelin 1996; Sinding-Larsen 1984; J.Z. Smith 1980; Snoek 1995; Sperber 1975; Von Ins 2001.

Space (spc)

Ahlbäck (ed.) 1993; Anttonen 1992; Baudy 1998; Erikson 1977; Fernandez 1972; Finol 2003; Goethals 1997; Goffman 1974; Grimes 1999; Houseman 1998; Jones 2000; Kapferer 1983; Köpping & Rao 2003b; Kreinath 2004b; Sax 2006; Schechner 1966; 1970; 1991; 1993; 2002; Shaughnessy (ed.) 1973; J.Z. Smith 1980; 1987a; 1998; Terrin 1999; Thomas 1998; 2000; V.W. Turner 1974a; 1977; Williams & Boyd 1993; Zuesse 1975.

Symbol(ism) (sym)

Alcorta & Sosis 2005; Asad 1988; Babcock 1978; Beattie 1966; 1970; Bird 1980; 1995; Bloch 1974; 1987; 1989; Bocock 1974; Boudewijnse 2006; Boyer 1994; Brandon 1975; Bruner (ed.) 1984; Cohen 1979; Dahm 2003; Doty 2000; Douglas 1966; 1970; Dow 1986; Emigh 1996; Fernandez 1974; 1977; 1986; Finnegan 1969; Finol 2003; Fox 1980; Gebauer & Wulf 1998; Geertz 1966; 1973; 1980; Goethals 1997; Gossen 1978; Grainger 1974; Grimes 1982; Gusfield & Michalowicz 1984; Handelman 1990; Handelman & Kapferer 1980; Harris 1997; Henn 2003; Hockings 1968; Houseman 1993; 1998; Innis 2004; Janowitz 2004; Jensen 1986; Jones 2000; Kapferer 1983; 2004; Keesing 1991; Kertzer 1988; Köpping (ed.) 1997; Kreinath 2005; 2006; La Fontaine (ed.) 1972; Laidlaw & Humphrey 2006; Laughlin 1990; Laughlin *et al.* 1986; Lawson 1976; Lawson & McCauley 1990; Leach 1966; 1968; 1976; Lewis 1980; Luckmann 1985; MacAloon 1984; Merkur 1991; Moore & Myerhoff 1977; Munn 1973; Nagendra 1971; Needham 1985; Ohnuki-Tierney 1987; Ortner 1975; 1978; Paul 1990; Penner 1969; 1989; Pentikäinen 1979; Platvoet 1995; 2006; Prattis 2001; Rao 2006; Rappaport 1971; 1974; 1978; 1992; 1999; Roth 1995; Rothenbuhler 1998; Scheffler 1981; 1993; 1997; Schieffelin 1985; 1998; Schjødt 1986; Severi 1993a; 1993b; Sinding-Larsen 1984; J.Z. Smith 1980; 1998;

Sperber 1975; Staal 1979; Staiano 1979; Strathern & Stewart 1998; Strecker 1988; 1998; Sullivan 1986; Tambiah 1981; 1985; Thomas 1998; Toren 1993; V.W. Turner 1967; 1969; 1974a; 1974b; 1974c; 1975; 1977; 1982; 1985b; Uhl & Boelderl (eds) 1999; Wallace 1966; Wiedenmann 1991; Wuthnow 1987.

Time (tim)

Anttonen 1992; Baranowski 1998; Bellah 2003; Bloch 1986; 1987; Cheal 1988; Csikszentmihalyi & Bennett 1971; Drewal 1992; Dupré 1992; Finol 2003; Goethals 1997; Goffman 1974; Handelman 1990; 2004; Jackson 1968; Kapferer 1983; 1986; 1997; 2004; Kelly & Kaplan 1990; Köpping & Rao 2003b; Leach 1976; Rappaport 1974; 1992; 1999; Schechner 1966; 1970; 1991; 1993; 2002; Schechner & Appel 1990; Schieffelin 1996; 1998; 2006; J.Z. Smith 1980; 1987a; P. Smith 1982; Snoek 1987; Terrin 1999; Thomas 1998; 2000; V.W. Turner 1969; 1977; 1985a; Von Ins 2001; Whitehouse 2002; Williams & Boyd 1993; Zuesse 1975.

APPENDIX C

ABBREVIATIONS OF TITLES OF PERIODICALS, USED IN THE REFERENCES TO THE REVIEWS OF MONOGRAPHS AND EDITED VOLUMES (IN PARTS A, D & E)

Abbrev.	**Periodical**
AA	American Anthropologist. Journal of the American Anthropological Association
AALR	Anglo-American Law Review. A Quarterly Review
AAPSS	American Academy of Political and Social Science Annals
AAW	Anzeiger für die Altertumswissenschaft
AC	L'Antiquité classique
ActaSoc	Acta Sociologica. Scandinavian Review of Sociology
AE	American Ethnologist. A Journal of the American Ethnological Society
AES	Archives européennes de sociologie
Afr	Africa. Revista Española de Colonización
AFS	Asian Folklore Studies
AH	Anthropology and Humanism
AHR	The American Historical Review
AJP	American Journal of Philology
AJPH	Australian Journal of Politics and History
AJS	The American Journal of Sociology
Anthr	Anthropos
ANZJS	Australian and New Zealand Journal of Sociology
AQ	Anthropological Quarterly
ARG	Archiv für Religionsgeschichte
AS	African Studies. A Journal Devoted to the Study of African Anthropology, Government and Languages
ASR	American Sociological Review. Official Journal of the American Sociological Association
ASSR	Archives de sciences sociales des religions
ATJ	Asian Theatre Journal
BJA	The British Journal of Aesthetics
BJS	The British Journal of Sociology

BMC	Bulletin of the Menninger Clinic
BSOAS	Bulletin of the School of Oriental and African Studies
BTLV	Bijdragen tot de Taal-, Land- en Volkenkunde
CA	Current Anthropology. A World Journal of the Science of Man
CambAnth	Cambridge Anthropology. A Journal of the Department of Social Anthropology, Cambridge University
CanbAnth	Canberra Anthropology. The Asian Pacific Journal of Anthropology
CC	Christian Century. A Journal of Religion
CD	Cultural Dynamics. An International Journal for the Study of Processes and Temporability of Culture
CE	Communication Education
ChH	Church History. Studies in Christianity & Culture
CIS	Cahiers internationaux de sociologie
CJAS	Canadian Journal of African Studies
CJH	Canadian Journal of History
CJPS	Canadian Journal of Political Science / Revue canadienne de science politique
Com	Commonweal
CP	Contemporary Psychology. A Journal of Reviews
CR	The Classical Review
CS	Contemporary Sociology. A Journal of Reviews
CSR	Christian Scholar's Review
CSSH	Comparative Studies in Society and History. An International Quarterly
CTNS	CTNS Bulletin (of the Center of Theology and the Natural Sciences)
DA	Dialectical Anthropology. An Independent International Journal in the Critical Tradition Committed to the Transformation of our Society and the Humane Union of Theory and Practice
DS	Discourse Studies. An Interdisciplinary Journal for the Study of Text and Talk
EG	Études Germaniques. Allemagne, Autriche, Suisse, pays Scandinaves et Néerlandais. Revue trimestrielle de la société des études germaniques
EJC	European Journal of Communication
El	Elenchos

EQ	Evangelical Quarterly. A Theological Review, International in Scope and Outlook, in Defence of the Historic Christian Faith
ERGS	ETC: A Review of General Semantics
Eth	Ethics. An International Journal of Social, Political and Legal Philosophy
Ethn	Ethnos
Ethnoh	Ethnohistory. A I E C: American Indian Ethnohistorical Conference
GB	Grazer Beiträge. Zeitschrift für die Klassische Altertumswissenschaft
GM	Giornale di Metafisica
Gym	Gymnasium. Zeitschrift für Kultur der Antike und humanistische Bildung
HC	Human context / Le domain humain / Der Mensch und seine Welt
HER	Harvard Educational Review
HJ	The Heythrop Journal. A Quarterly Review of Philosophy and Theology
Homme	L'Homme. Revue française d'anthropologie
HR	History of Religions. An International Journal for Comparative Historical Studies
IA	International Affairs
IJCS	International Journal of Comparative Sociology
IJMES	International Journal of Middle East Studies
ISP	International Studies in Philosophy
JAAR	Journal of the American Academy of Religion
JAF	Journal of American Folklore. The Quarterly Journal of the American Folklore Society
JAfrH	The Journal of African History
JAH	Journal of Asian History
JAR	Journal of Anthropological Research
JAS	Journal of Asian Studies
JASO	Journal of the Anthropological Society of Oxford
JC	Journal of Communication. An Official Journal of the International Communication Association
JCR	Journal of Contemporary Religion
JDS	Journal of Developing Societies
JIES	The Journal of Indo-European Studies
JIH	Journal of Interdisciplinary History

JJRS	Japanese Journal of Religious Studies
JJS	The Jewish Journal of Sociology
JJSt	The Journal of Japanese Studies
JMAS	Journal of Modern African Studies. A Quarterly Survey of Politics, Economics & Related Topics in Contemporary Africa
JMC	Journal of Material Culture
JOP	The Journal of Politics
JPMS	Journal of Political and Military Sociology
JPNP	Journal de psychologie normale et pathologique
JPS	The Journal of the Polynesian Society. A Quarterly Study of the Native Peoples of the Pacific Area
JR	The Journal of Religion
JRA	Journal of Religion in Africa / Religion en Afrique
JRAI	Man. The Journal of the Royal Anthropological Institute of Great Britain and Ireland
JRAS	Journal of the Royal Asiatic Society of Great Britain and Ireland
JRomS	The Journal of Roman Studies
JRS	Journal of Ritual Studies
JSAm	Journal de la société des américanistes
JSAS	Journal of Southern African Studies
JSEAS	Journal of Southeast Asian Studies
JSH	Journal of Social History
JSSR	Journal for the Scientific Study of Religion. Official Journal of the Society for the Scientific Study of Religion
JTS	The Journal of Theological Studies
Kl	Klio. Beiträge zur Alten Geschichte
KZfSS	Kölner Zeitschrift für Soziologie und Sozialpsychologie
Lis	The Listener
LS	Language in Society
Man	Man. A Monthly Record of Anthropological Science
Mank	Mankind. Official Journal of the Anthropological Societies of Australia
MD	Modern Drama. A Journal Devoted to the Drama Since Ibsen
Mind	Mind. A Quarterly Review of Psychology and Philosophy
Month	Month. A Catholic Review
MTSR	Method and Theory in the Study of Religion. Journal of the North American Association for the Study of Religion

NB	New Blackfriars. A Monthly Review
NS	New Statesman
NTT	Nederlands Theologisch Tijdschrift
Numen	Numen. International Review for the History of Religions
NYRB	The New York Review of Books
Oc	Oceania. A Journal Devoted to the Study of the Native Peoples of Australia, New Guinea and the Islands of the Pacific Ocean
PA	Pacific Affairs. An International Review of Asia and the Pacific
Paid	Paideuma. Mitteilungen zur Kulturkunde
Per	Perspective. A Quarterly of Literature and the Arts
Periph	Peripherie. Zeitschrift für Politik und Ökonomie in der Dritten Welt
PoT	Poetics Today. International Journal for Theory and Analysis of Literature and Communication
PPR	Philosophy and Phenomenological Research. A Quarterly Journal
PSC	Philosophy and Social Criticism. An International, Interdisciplinary Quarterly Journal
PSQ	Presidential Studies Quarterly. Official Publication of the Center for the Study of the Presidency
PSS	Philosophy of the Social Sciences. An International Journal
PSt	Political Studies. The Journal of the Political Studies Association of the United Kingdom
RA	Reviews in Anthropology
Race	Race. The Journal of the Institute of Race Relations (London)
RAL	Research in African Literatures. Official Journal of the African Literature Committee of the African Studies Association of America, and the African Literature Seminar of the Modern Language Association
REG	Revue des études grecques. Publication de l'association pour l'encouragement des études grecques
Rel	Religion. A Journal of Religion and Religions
Reli	Religiologiques. Sciences Humaines et Religion
RFS	Revue française de sociologie
Rhet	Rhetorik. Ein internationales Jahrbuch

RHR	Revue de l'histoire des religions. Revue trimestrielle publiée avec le concours du Centre National de la Recherche Scientifique et du Centre National du Livre
RIS	Rassenga Italiana di Sociologia
RRR	Review of Religious Research. Official Journal of the Religious Research Association
RS	Recherches sociologiques
RSR	Religious Studies Review. A Quarterly Review of Publications in the Field of Religion and Related Disciplines
SA	Sociological Analysis. A Journal in the Sociology of Religion
SAs	South Asia. Journal of South Asian Studies
SAR	South Asia Research
SB	Social Biology
Sc	Science
SEA	Social and Economic Administration
Sel	Selma
Sem	Semiotica. Journal of the International Association for Semiotic Studies
SF	Social Forces. A Scientific Medium of Social Study and Interpretation
SHR	Southern Humanities Review
SJTh	The Scottish Journal of Theology
SMSR	Studi e Materiali di Storia delle Religioni
Soc	Sociologus. Zeitschrift für empirische Ethnosoziologie und Ethnopsychologie
SocAn	Social Analysis. Journal of Cultural and Social Practice
SocBul	Sociological Bulletin. Journal of the Indian Sociological Society
Sociol	Sociology
SocRel	Sociology of Religion. A Quarterly Review
SocTrav	Sociologie du travail. Revue publié avec le concours du Centre National de la Recherche Scientifique, CNRS
SoRA	Southern Review. An Australian Journal of Literary Studies (Adelaide)
SR	The Sociological Review
SSI	Information sur les sciences sociale / Social Science Information
SSoc	Science and Society. An Independent Journal of Marxism
SSR	Sociology and Social Research. An International Journal

StM	Studia Monastica. Commentarium ad rem monasticam historice investigandam
StudRel	Studies in Religion. Sciences religieuses
TA	Tidsskriftet antropologi
Tab	The Tablet
Theol	Theology. A Monthly Journal of Historic Christianity
ThLZ	Theologische Literaturzeitung. Monatsschrift für das gesamte Gebiet der Theologie und Religionswissenschaft
ThSt	Theological Studies
TLS	Times Literary Supplement
TTo	Theology Today. The Life of Man in the Light of God
TVT	Tijdschrift voor Theologie
Uomo	L'Uomo
USQR	Union Seminary Quarterly Review
VF	Verkündigung und Forschung
WF	Western Folklore
Wor	Worship. A Review Concerned with the Problems of Liturgical Renewal
WZM	Wege zum Menschen. Monatsschrift für Seelsorge und Beratung, heilendes und soziales Handeln
ZKTh	Zeitschrift für Katholische Theologie
ZPT	Zeitschrift für Padagogik und Theologie. Der evangelische Erzieher
ZRGG	Zeitschrift für Religions- und Geistesgeschichte / Journal of Religious and Intellectual History
Zygon	Zygon. Journal of Religion and Science

APPENDIX D

LIST OF AUTHORS WHOSE WORK IS DISCUSSED IN THE SECONDARY LITERATURE (PART B)

See also the reviews listed in the abstracts (Part A) for further discussion of the work of theoreticians.

Of an author, who's name is given in **bold**, at least one publication is included in the bibliography of primary literature above (Part A).

The titles are listed in chronological order.

Babcock, B.A.: Piette 1997
Bataille, G.: Olson 1994; Strenski 2003
Bateson, G.: Piette 1997
Bell, C.M.: Owen 1998
Bettelheim, B.: Brunotte 2003
Bloch, M.E.F.: Gellner 1999
Blüher, H.: Brunotte 2003
Bourdieu, P.: (Audehm in) Wulf, Göhlich & Zirfas (eds) 2001
Burkert, W.: Mack 1987; Segal 2000
Butler, J.: (Tervooren in) Wulf, Göhlich & Zirfas (eds) 2001
Douglas, M.: Isenberg & Owen 1977; Giobellina-Brumana & Gonzalez 1981; Fardon 1999
Durkheim, É.: Miller 1982; Camapny 1992; (Kippenberg in) Michaels (ed.) 1997; Warfield 2001; Strenski 2003
Eliade, M.: (Berner in) Michaels (ed.) 1997; Brunotte 2003
Erikson, E.H.: Capps 1979
Evans-Pritchard, E.E.: Förster 2004
Frazer, J.G.: Ackerman 1975; Ackerman 1987; Ackerman 1991; Calder III 1991; (Wißmann in) Michaels (ed.) 1997; Segal 2000
Freud, S.: Gay 1979; (Zinser in) Michaels (ed.) 1997
Gaster, T.: Grimes 1976
Geertz, C.: Carey 1975; Buswell III 1979; Gellner 1999
Girard, R.: Mack 1987; Thomas 1998
Gluckman, M.: Handelman 1976; Kapferer 1987; Tufis 2001
Goffman, E.: Dawe 1973; Miller 1982; Manning 1989; Hettlage & Lenz (eds) 1991; Piette 1997; (Bausch in) Wulf, Göhlich & Zirfas (eds) 2001
Grimes, R.L.: Frankiel 2001
Harrison, J.E.: Carpentier 1994; Brunotte 2001; Brunotte 2003;

Calder III 1991; Tybjerg 2001; Brunotte 2003
Hertz, R.: Neubert 2004
Hoens, D.E.: Platvoet 1983
Hubert, H. & Mauss, M.: Strenski 1997; Strenski 2003
Kohut, H.: Gay 1979
Lawson, E.Th. & R.N. McCauley: Levine 1998; Malley & Barrett 2003
Leach, E.R.: Tambiah 2002
Lévi, S.: Strenski 1996; Strenski 2003
Lévi-Strauss, C.: Giobellina-Brumana & Gonzalez 1981
Lévy-Bruhl, L.: Douglas 2003
Loisy, A.: Strenski 2003
Mannhardt, W.: Tybjerg 1993; Tybjerg 2001
MacAloon, J.: Piette 1997
Mauss, M.: (Mürmel in) Michaels (ed.) 1997; see also Hubert, H.
Mead, G.H.: (Jörrisen in) Wulf, Göhlich & Zirfas (eds) 2001
Nietzsche, F.: Gibson 1991
Pareto, V.: Héran 1994
Peirce, C.S.: Geerts 1990
Rappaport, R.A.: Strathern & Stewart 1999; Messer & Lambek (eds) 2001; Robbins 2001; Wiebe 2004
Réville, A.: Strenski 2003
Réville, J.: Strenski 2003
Robertson Smith, W.: Brunotte 2001; Calder III 1991; (Kippenberg in) Michaels (ed.) 1997; Strenski 2003
Schechner, R.: Piette 1997
Scheffler, I.: Matthews 1981
Schurtz, H.: Brunotte 2003
Smith, J.Z.: Mack 1987; Grimes 1999
Staal, F.: Price 1988; Cunningham & Strenski (eds) 1991; Verkuyl 1997
Tambiah, S.J.: Ghosh 1987
Tiele, C.P.: Platvoet 1983; Strenski 2003
Turner, V.W.: Collins 1976; Grimes 1976; Gay 1983; Segal 1983; Bynum 1984; Grimes 1985; Schechner 1988; Ashley (ed.) 1990; Boudewijnse 1990; Geerts 1990; Grimes 1990; Alexander 1991; Deflem 1991; Almeida 1992; Handelman 1993; Boudewijnse (ed.) 1994; (Bräunlein in) Michaels (ed.) 1997; Piette 1997; Kalocsai 2000; Tufis 2001; (Wagner-Willi in) Wulf, Göhlich & Zirfas (eds) 2001; Brunotte 2003; Förster 2003; Förster 2004
Tylor, E.B.: Strenski 2003
Van Baal, J.: Platvoet 1983
Van Beek, W.E.A.: Platvoet 1983
Van Gennep, A.: Belmont 1974; Zumwalt 1982; Stagl 1983; Renard 1986; Belier 1994; (Schomburg-Scheff in) Michaels (ed.) 1997; Tufis 2001; Hockey 2002; Calame 2003
Weber, M.: Nagendra 1970; Héran 1994
Xunzi: Campany 1992

APPENDIX E

ADDRESSES OF CONTRIBUTORS TO *THEORIZING RITUALS*

Editors:

Prof. Dr. Jens Kreinath
Department of Anthropology
216 Neff Hall
Wichita State University
1845 Fairmount St.
Wichita, KS 67260–0052
U.S.A.
Jens.Kreinath@wichita.edu

Prof. Dr. Jan A.M. Snoek
Institut für Religionswissenschaft
Universität Heidelberg
Akademiestr. 4–8
69117 Heidelberg
Germany
Jan.Snoek@zegk.uni-heidelberg.de

Prof. Dr. Michael Stausberg
Universitet i Bergen
IKRR
Øisteinsgate 3
5007 Bergen
Norway
Michael.Stausberg@krr.uib.no

Contributors:

Dr. Dorothea Baudy
Fürstenbergstrasse 49
78467 Konstanz
Germany
Dorothea.Baudy@access.unizh.ch

Prof. Dr. Catherine Bell
Religious Studies Department
Santa Clara University
500 El Camino Real
Santa Clara, CA 95053
U.S.A
cbell@scu.edu

Prof. Dr. Maurice Bloch
Department of Anthropology
London School of Economics
Houghton Street
London, WC2 2AE
U.K.
maurice.bloch@wanadoo.fr

H.B. Boudewijnse MA
Voormeulenweg 58
1402 TM Bussum
The Netherlands
boudewijnse@casema.nl

Prof. Dr. James W. Boyd
Department of Philosophy
Colorado State University
Fort Collins, CO 80523
U.S.A.
jwboyd@lamar.colostate.edu

Prof. Dr. James W. Fernandez
Department of Anthropology
University of Chicago
Chicago, IL 60637
U.S.A.
jwf1@uchicago.edu

Prof. Dr. Burkhard Gladigow
Eberhard Karls Universität
Tübingen
Abteilung für
Religionswissenschaft
Beim Kupferhammer 5
72070 Tübingen
Germany
b.gladigow@web.de

Prof. Dr. Ronald Grimes
Department of Religion &
Culture
Wilfrid Laurier University
Waterloo, Ontario, N2L 3C5
Canada
rgrimes@wlu.ca

Prof. Dr. Don Handelman
Department of Sociology &
Anthropology
The Hebrew University of
Jerusalem
Jerusalem 91905
Israel
mshand@mscc.huji.ac.il

Prof. Dr. Dietrich Harth
Synchron Publishers Heidelberg
Oppelnerstraße 49
69124 Heidelberg
Germany
harthdiet@aol.com

Prof. Dr. Michael Houseman
Ecole Pratique des Hautes
Etudes
Vème section
Centre d'études des mondes
africains
Site d'Ivry
UMR 8171
46, rue de Lille
75007 Paris
France
houseman@attglobal.net

Prof. Dr. Felicia Hughes-Freeland
Department of Sociology and
Anthropology
University of Wales Swansea
Singleton Park
Swansea, SA2 8PP
U.K.
F.Hughes-Freeland@swansea.
ac.uk

Prof. Dr. Caroline Humphrey
King's College
Cambridge, CB2 1ST
U.K.
ch10001@cam.ac.uk

Florian Jeserich
Am Schlagbaum 23
42489 Wülfrath
Germany
Premajesse@compuserve.de

Prof. Dr. Bruce Kapferer
Institutt for sosialantropologi
Fosswinckelsgt. 6
5007 Bergen
Norway
Bruce.Kapferer@sosantr.uib.no

Dr. James Laidlaw
King's College
Cambridge, CB2 1ST
U.K.
jal6@cam.ac.uk

Prof. Dr. E. Thomas Lawson
Department of Comparative Religion
2010 Moore Hall
Western Michigan University
1903 West Michigan Avenue
Kalamazoo, MI 49880
U.S.A.
lawson@wmich.edu

Prof. Dr. Dorothea Lüddeckens
Religionswissenschaftliches Seminar
Universität Zürich
Kirchgasse 9
8050 Zürich
Switzerland
lueddeckens@gmx.de

Prof. Dr. Axel Michaels
Südasien-Institut
Abt. Klassische Indologie
Im Neuenheimer Feld 330
69120 Heidelberg
Germany
Axel.Michaels@urz.uni-heidelberg.de

Prof. Dr. Rosalind Morris
Department of Anthropology
Columbia University
MC 5540
1200 Amsterdam Avenue
New York, NY 10027
U.S.A.
rcm24@columbia.edu

Dr. Jan G. Platvoet
Gildenring 52
3981 JG Bunnik
The Netherlands
jgplatvoet@hetnet.nl

Dr. Ursula Rao
Institut für Ethnologie
Universität Halle
06099 Halle
Germany
rao@ethnologie.uni-halle.de

Prof. William Sax, PhD
Head, Dept. of Anthropology
South Asia Institute
INF 330
69120 Heidelberg
Germany
William.Sax@urz.uni-heidelberg.de

Prof. Dr. Edward L. Schieffelin
Department of Anthropology
University College
Gower St.
London, WC1E 6BT
U.K.
e.schieffelin@ucl.ac.uk

Prof. Dr. Robert A. Segal
School of Divinity, History and Philosophy
University of Aberdeen
King's College
Aberdeen
AB24 3UB
Scotland
r.segal@abdn.ac.uk

Prof. Dr. Carlo Severi
EHESS
Laboratoire d'Anthropologie Sociale
Collège de France
52 rue du Cardinal Lemoine
75005 Paris
France
Carlo.Severi@ehess.fr

Prof. Dr. J. Podemann Sørensen
University of Copenhagen
TORS Carsten Niebuhr Department
Snorresgade 17–19
Copenhagen 2300
Denmark
podemann@hum.ku.dk

Prof. Dr. Dr. Günter Thomas (Th.M.)
Ruhr-Universität Bochum
Evangelisch-Theologische Fakultät
GA 8/155–157
44780 Bochum
Germany
guenter.thomas@rub.de

Prof. Dr. Terence Turner
Department of Anthropology
261 McGraw Hall
Cornell University
Ithaca, NY 14853
U.S.A.
tst3@cornell.edu

Prof. Dr. Harvey Whitehouse
School of Anthropology
University of Oxford
51–53 Banbury Road
Oxford, OX2 6PE
U.K.
h.whitehouse@qub.ac.uk

Prof. Dr. Ron Williams
Philosophy Department, 1781
Colorado State University
Ft. Collins, CO, 80523–178
U.S.A.
Ron.G.Williams@colostate.edu

Prof. Dr. Christoph Wulf
Interdisciplinary Centre of Historical Anthropology
Freie Universität
Arnimallee 11
14195 Berlin
Germany
chrwulf@zedat.fu-berlin.de

Contributers to the "Lexicographic Survey":

Prof. Dr. Jan Assmann
Ägyptologisches Institut
Universität Heidelberg
Marstallhof 4
69117 Heidelberg
Germany
Jan.Assmann@urz.uni-heidelberg.de

Prof. Dr. Angelos Chaniotis
All Souls College
Oxford, OX1 4AL
U.K.
angelos.chaniotis@all-souls.oxford.ac.uk

Prof. Dr. Armin Geertz
Department of the Study of Religion
Århus Universitet
Bygning 1442
Tåsingegade 3
8000 Århus C
Denmark
awg@teo.au.dk

Prof. Dr. Joachim Gentz
23/7 Sciennes Road
Edinburgh EH9 1NX
U.K.
jgentz@gwdg.de

Dr. Hans-Michael Haussig
Universität Potsdam
Institut für Religionswissenschaft
Am Neuen Palais 10
14469 Potsdam
Germany
haussig@rz.uni-potsdam.de

Dr. Nils P. Heeßel
Assyriologie
Hauptstr. 126
69117 Heidelberg
Germany
nils.heessel@ori.uni-heidelberg.de

Prof. Dr. Dr. Manfred Hutter
Abteilung für Religionswissenschaft
Institut für Orient- und Asienwissenschaften
Adenauerallee 4–6
53113 Bonn
Deutschland
mhutter@uni-bonn.de

Prof. Dr. K. Kollmar-Paulenz,
Institut für Religionswissenschaft,
Universität Bern
Vereinsweg 23
3012 Bern
Switzerland
karenina.kollmar-paulenz@relwi.unibe.ch

Prof. Dr. P.G. Kreyenbroek
Seminar für Iranistik
Weender Landstrasse 2
37073 Göttingen
Germany
gkreyen@gwdg.de

Dr. Robert Langer
Ruprecht-Karls-Universtität
Heidelberg
SFB 619: C7 (Islamwissenschaft)
Seminar für Sprachen und
Kulturen des Vorderen Orients
Sandgasse 7
69117 Heidelberg
Germany
robert.langer@ori.uni-
heidelberg.de

Prof. Dr. Axel Michaels
Südasien-Institut
Abt. Klassische Indologie
Im Neuenheimer Feld 330
69120 Heidelberg
Germany
Axel.Michaels@urz.uni-
heidelberg.de

Jordan Paper
2594 Beach Dr.
Victoria, BC
Canada, V8R 6K4
jpaper@yorku.ca

Kenn Pitawanakwat
171 Wickstead Ave.
North Bay, ON
Canada P1A 3G6

Prof. Dr. Inken Prohl
Institut für Religionswissenschaft
Akademiestrasse 4–8
69117 Heidelberg
Germany
inken.prohl@zegk.uni-
heidelberg.de

Prof. Dr. Håkan Rydving
Universitet i Bergen
IKRR
Øisteinsgate 3
5007 Bergen
Norway
hakan.rydving@krr.uib.no

Prof. Dr. Peter Schalk
Department of Theology
Box 511
75120 Uppsala
Sweden
peter.schalk@telia.com

Prof. Dr. Wolfgang Scharlipp
University of Copenhagen
TORS Carsten Niebuhr
Department
Snorresgade 17–19
Copenhagen 2300
Denmark
schar@hum.ku.dk

Dr. Olof Sundqvist
Eriksgatan 11a
752 18 Uppsala
Sweden
ost@hig.se